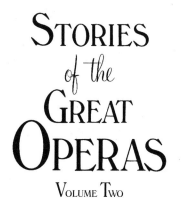

STORIES
of the
GREAT
OPERAS
VOLUME TWO

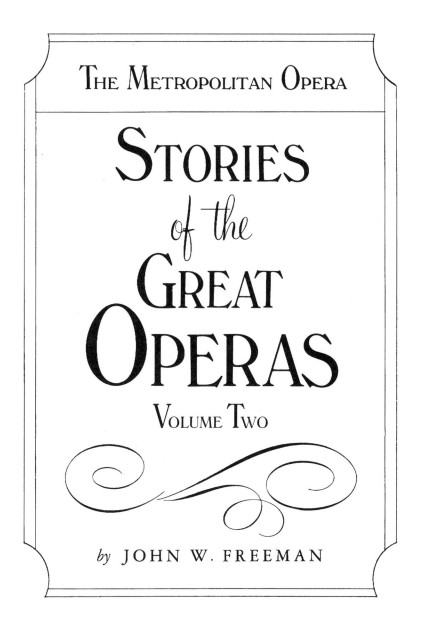

THE METROPOLITAN OPERA

STORIES
of the
GREAT
OPERAS

VOLUME TWO

by JOHN W. FREEMAN

THE METROPOLITAN OPERA GUILD

W·W·NORTON & COMPANY·NEW YORK·LONDON

Printed in the United States of America
First Edition

————————————————————————

For information about permission to reproduce selections from this book, write to Permissions,
W. W. Norton & Company, Inc., 500 Fifth Avenue, New York, NY 10110.

*The text of this book is composed in Garamond, with the display set in Windsor. Composition
and Manufacturing by the Maple-Vail Book Manufacturing Group. Book design by Antonina
Krass adapted by Jack Meserole. Cover illustration: Credit*

————————————————————————

Library of Congress Cataloging in Publication Data
Main entry under title:
The Metropolitan Opera stories of the great operas.
I. Operas—Stories, plots, etc.   I. Freeman, John W.
II. Metropolitan Opera (New York, N.Y.)   III. Title:
Stories of the great operas.
MT95.M49   1984   782.1'3   84-8030

ISBN 0-393-04051-8

W. W. Norton & Company, Inc., 500 Fifth Avenue, New York, N.Y. 10110 http://web.wwnorton.com

W. W. Norton & Company Ltd., 10 Coptic Street, London WC1A 1PU

1 2 3 4 5 6 7 8 9 0

This book is dedicated to the memory of
Harriet Gilpatric Patton
Managing Director, Metropolitan Opera Guild, 1959–68

Contents

CONTENTS

Contents by Opera Titles

CONTENTS BY OPERA TITLES

FOREWORD

BY BEVERLY SILLS

Like many other Americans of my generation, I became interested in opera at an early age. I began by listening to my mother's collection of Amelita Galli-Curci and Lily Pons records, and then was taken (at age eight) to hear Pons at a Met performance of *Lakmé.* It was at that moment that I decided to become an opera star. Not just an opera singer, but an opera star! I also decided I was going to look exactly like Lily Pons, despite the fact that at age eight I was already three inches taller and outweighed her by thirty pounds. (Incidentally, Lily and I became great friends, and a short while before she died she came to see me in a performance of *The Daughter of the Regiment.* She scolded me by saying that she had made her entrance on a white horse. I told her I would have done the same, except that we could not find a horse big enough.)

Soon after hearing Pons at the Met came the clincher: my mother gave me a book entitled *Operas Every Child Should Know.* This was a large yellow tome, and it quickly became the most well-thumbed volume I owned—I couldn't get enough of the stories of *Lohengrin, Rigoletto, Le Nozze di Figaro,* and *La Bohème.* (The book you're reading now, by the way, has several stories that every child *doesn't* need to know, but then I doubt if I would have gotten too far into *Die Soldaten* when I was eight.)

A dozen years ago, John W. Freeman published his first book of opera stories. *The Metropolitan Opera—Stories of the Great Operas* tells the plots of 150 operas: all the ones I adored as a child, and have continued to love into my adulthood. For the most part, the first book includes the works I performed as a singer, as well as many I oversaw in my days as general director of New York City Opera. Many, but not *all.* And that leads to one of the reasons I'm delighted that John has written a second volume covering 125 operas that are less familiar, but which one is still likely to see performed in opera houses around the world.

I suspect that anyone reading this book will already be familiar with what we call the standard repertory. This standard repertory changes with time; some operas have been popular since their premiere, and will always be performed, because audiences always want to hear them. But opera and recording companies know that many opera-lovers are also eager to discover works that are new to them: either operas that have been recently composed, or those from the past that are awaiting rediscovery. (It's very much like food: as much as I love pasta, I certainly wouldn't want to dine on it every night—especially if it's always prepared the same way!) Thanks to these more adventurous opera fans, the repertory has kept changing in the last forty years. I might add that operas also go in and out of fashion because of the availability and interests of singers.

Whatever the reasons, the repertory of works performed has widened in the latter part of this century, and that can only be to the good of opera. For more than thirty years I was associated with New York City Opera, a company that has always prided itself on presenting the more unusual fare. When I look down the table of contents for this book, I see quite a few operas that received their world or U.S. premiere at City Opera—*Lizzie Borden, The Tender Land, X, The Good Soldier Schweik, The Fiery Angel, Die Schweigsame Frau, The Crucible, I Quatro Rusteghi,* even one in which I created a role, *Six Characters in Search of an Author.* And we mounted productions of twenty-six other operas on the list. I'm very happy to see that the book also includes the work in which I made both my La Scala and Metropolitan Opera debuts, Rossini's *Le Siège de Corinthe.*

When I was general director of City Opera, we were pioneers in the practice of projecting supertitles, so that American audiences finally could know what all the singing was about. At that time I took quite a lot of heat from critics who thought I was encouraging audiences to come to opera performances without any preparation. Of course this is ridiculous—I'm a firm believer that the more you know a about a work of art, the more you will enjoy it. (That goes for *Hamlet* and Mahler's Eighth Symphony, as well as for *Parsifal.*) I think it is perfectly ridiculous to sit for three hours listening to music sung in a foreign language. Why pretend you know what is going on when you really don't? That's why we did the titles in the first place, and why I'm delighted that this book includes so many operas that are less well known, but that operagoers may have a chance to see in performance. Read any of the synopses in this book before attending, and I'm sure you'll get more out of the experience of seeing and hearing the work than if you had walked in cold—titles or no titles.

That covers the practical use of this book. I hope you will also find that opera stories make wonderful reading, even when you're not boning up for a performance. They may stretch credulity (like *I Lombardi*), or wreak havoc with historical fact (like *L'Africaine*), or be complicated enough to require several readings to determine who's on first at any give time (try *Tancredi*). But these stories are rarely dull, and reading them, it's easy to see how they inspired the great composers. Give them a chance—you may find yourself as captivated by these tales as I was by my *Operas Every Child Should Know.* (By the way, my second favorite book was called *Merry Murphy, the Irish Potato.*)

PREFACE

Opera by reputation is a reactionary, static art form. Still, since 1984, when our first volume of opera stories was published, many changes have reshaped the scene. The introduction of the compact disc has stretched the repertory of available opera recordings to include dozens, perhaps eventually hundreds, of titles previously known only by name, if at all. In the viewer's home, video formats have preserved and disseminated so many opera productions that it is now possible for home viewers to compare different ways of staging a work. In the theater, projected titles have knocked down the language barrier for audiences.

The impact of these changes has been to stretch our horizons in every direction at once. Within the recent past, it is cause for domestic pride that the first four entries in this volume are American; of these, the first two were written since the publication of the earlier volume. Looking farther back, Handel's 300th birth anniversary (1985) set in motion a wave of interest in baroque and early operas, matched by a generation of singers trained to perform them. Composers important during the early twentieth century, such as Schreker, Zemlinsky, and Janáček, have emerged from long shadows of neglect, while later names—Adams, Corigliano, Davis, Glass—have found their way into the limelight. Since the demise of the Soviet hegemony, a tide of Russian and Eastern European singers and repertory has surged forth.

Changes of fashion have also affected vocal categories, as the cast listings reflect. The terms "alto" and "contralto," once seen regularly on the cast page of scores and librettos, and hardly used nowadays: lower female voices are billed as "mezzo-soprano," a rubric that conceals many an aspiring soprano. If the specialty of the lower female voice has declined, another has been on the rise—that of the spinto, a soprano or tenor somewhere between lyric and dramatic. Meanwhile, the "coloratura soprano," or old-fashioned canary, seems to be a dated phenomenon, now that mezzos, tenors, baritones, and basses often prove adept at coloratura as well. The countertenor, heretofore little known outside the early-music movement and oratorio, has taken to the opera stage with the baroque revival.

The notion still holds true that the more things change, the more they stay the same. Producers and consumers of live, staged opera remain cautious, continuing to prefer what they know. In no other performing art is such endless repetition of the same repertory tolerated. From the management point of view, economic as well as artistic realities circumscribe the options. The difference now is that in the CD era, the more inquisitive opera-lover can make the acquaintance of a previously unimaginable wealth of works. (Within limits: a disc performance is only a pale replica of a live one, and many "pirate" discs preserve performances better forgotten.)

In choosing the contents for this book, several consultants made additions to, and subtractions from, the starting list of opera titles. Which way is the repertory heading? Beyond the theater repertory, relatively contained and slow to expand, there is now the recorded repertory to consider; but this book, optimistically, is weighted toward works one might hope to see onstage.

During the eighteenth, nineteenth, and early twentieth centuries, opera was a popular art form, spawning new titles in abundance. During the twentieth, the bill of fare of major theaters began to ossify, and one frequently hears the handy excuse that "If a work is no longer given, there's a good reason." The reason may be artistic, but all too often it is lack of curiosity, knowledge, or enterprise. In the repertory of the average theater, room cannot be found for more than a handful of operas that have stood the test of time.

Popular favor, while essential to a work's longevity, is not the only measure of its viability or artistic quality. Quite a few of the works in the current repertory are open to question, and those absent are not all certifiable duds. Historical annals testify to the existence of thousands of operas. Yet people have asked, "Where in the world could you find 125 more to put in your book?" Most of the 125 come from two categories: those for which there wasn't room last time, and those that have emerged in various theaters since then. (Mussorgsky's *Khovanshchina,* for instance, returned to the Metropolitan Opera repertory after nearly four decades' absence.) In accommodating the works eventually chosen, we had to pass over many suggested titles. Operettas and zarzuelas, except for a few that have made their nest in the opera house, were reluctantly omitted; they deserve a book of their own.

The aim here is to summarize plots more fully than the brief paragraphs sound in programs and record notes. A quick synopsis, though essential when the house lights are about to go down, has to skip a great deal of what is happening. (In centuries gone by, when house lights stayed up, audiences could consult their librettos during the performance.) This book has been prepared by combing through the texts and addressing some of the stickier questions.

Surprisingly often, for example, date and place of action are not specified, or are only hinted at. The same is true for stage directions, often not carried over from score to printed libretto. The dates of action of *Rinaldo* or *I Lombardi* can be approximated by boning up on the Crusades, but where plots are concerned, myth tends to take over from history. The Rinaldo of Handel's opera reappears as Renaud in Gluck's *Armide.* Roland, dimly based on a historical person of Charlemagne's reign, appears in Massenet's *Esclarmonde* and as Orlando in various Italian operas of the baroque period. (In *The Greek Myths,* Robert Graves gives variant versions of each myth.) When Gluck, following the conventions of opera seria, lets Iphigénie marry Achille in a happy ending, there is confusion in store for the House of Atreus in *Elektra*—where the action has been triggered by Iphigenia's death—or for the Achilles who dies a bachelor in Tippett's *King Priam.*

As in the earlier volume, the proper names of characters are given here as they appear in the language of the original libretto. Other designations—by rank, occupation, or description—are given in English. Names of historical or mythological characters as themselves, rather than as opera characters, are given in the usual English form.

Baroque opera presents its own problems. How to keep multiple plot strands clear when several of the characters (some of them cross-dressing) impersonate others all at once, or when they have similar-sounding names, such as Hébé and Phébé in *Castor et Pollux,* Garibaldo and Grimoaldo in *Rodelinda?* It may help to remember that singers did little acting during the baroque period; most of the entertainment onstage was supplied by dancers and scenic changes. Also helpful is the time-honored convention that when a person is in disguise, the other characters may be fooled by the disguise, though the audience is not.

There is one pitfall that every opera storyteller is helpless to avoid. A "creative" director/designer taking the driver's seat may steer characters, plot, time, and location right off the composer's and librettist's road map. When this happens, however, the original relationships and interaction among the characters are still at work. And luckily, rationality can be checked at the door of an opera house. History deals with what happened; opera deals with how people feel about it. Music creates its own emotional logic, just as Wagner creates his own time frame. In *Parsifal* he has Gurnemanz explain cryptically, "Here time becomes space"—a fair description of the illusion generated by music.

If the slow-moving world of opera has moved so much between the two installments of this book, 1984–96, we can assume it will keep moving. Technology has become the pacesetter. Consider again what CDs, video, and projected titles have opened up. Future works cannot succeed as retreads of the old, but since we are dealing with a retrospective, self-referencing art form, we can expect its future to be evolutionary—informed, that is, by the wealth of its past literature, now researchable as never before. Opera has seldom had an easy life, but reports of its death have been greatly exaggerated.

JOHN W. FREEMAN

ACKNOWLEDGMENTS: The author wishes to thank Paul Gruber, director of program development for the Metropolitan Opera Guild, and Michael Ochs, music editor at W. W. Norton and Company, for their support in bringing this project to fulfillment. Development of the list of operas included was undertaken with the aid of comments from David Hamilton and the following *Opera News* staff members: Jane L. Poole, Patrick J. Smith, and Marylis Sevilla-Gonzaga. Invaluable help in planning the book and checking the manuscript was provided by Elaine B. Kones, advertising director of *Opera News,* with proofreading assistance from Stephanie Wieder. Susan Kerschbaumer of the Metropolitan Opera Guild's Education Department contributed historical and literary insights relating to early operas and the Preface. Prof. Harlow Robinson, chairman, Department of Modern Languages, Northeastern University, Boston, advised on Russian operas and transliterated their quotations. Linguistic guidance for Czech operas came from Yveta Synek Graff and Prof. Miroslav Turek.

For rare librettos, other source materials, and information, further thanks to Alix Barthelmes (Opera Orchestra of New York), Jack Bloom (Baldi, Bloom & Whelan Advertising), Sarah Folger (Harmonia Mundi U.S.A.), John M. Gehl, Glendower Jones (Classical Vocal Reprints), Nimet Saba Habachy (WQXR, New York), Pekka Hako (Finnish Music Information Centre), Herbert Handt, Andy Karzas (WFMT, Chicago), May S. Kurka, Gary D. Lipton (Qualiton Imports), C. J. Luten, Roger Newhall, Mary Jane Phillips-Matz, Ellen Schantz (Atlantic Classics), Susan Schiffer (Sony Classical), Arthur R. Smith (OPERA America), Patrick J. Smith (editor, *Opera News*), Steven Smith (Koch International), Richard Traubner, Robert A. Tuggle (Metropolitan Opera Archives), and Steven White (San Francisco Opera).

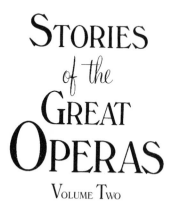

STORIES
of the
GREAT
OPERAS
VOLUME TWO

JOHN ADAMS
b. 1947

*T*he music of New Hampshire–born John Adams, though sometimes termed "minimalist" or "postmodern," defies categorization. Adams has the curiosity of an inventor and the courage of an innovator. He has also been willing to meet his audience halfway, since the idea of music as an abstract or intellectual exercise does not interest him. *Nixon in China,* though its production by Peter Sellars was sui generis, has proved to be a landmark, one of the most widely recognized and accepted recent American operas.

Adams and his librettist, Alice Goodman, discerned both the populist and the poetic possibilities in a new genre that has been dubbed "CNN opera." (Another example is Anthony Davis' *X: The Life and Times of Malcolm X.*) This makes mythology of recent events still within the audience's experience—poetically reinterpreting history that has affected the world at hand. Such works differ markedly from the mythological operas of the classic period, which were removed in time from their subject, however timely its underlying themes might be. During a Christian era in predominantly Catholic countries (Italy and France), no one believed in the divinity of Zeus, Diana, or Cupid, but they appeared, exercising their power over mere mortals, in one opera after another. Figures such as Richard Nixon and Malcolm X are too recent to have become such safe symbols: their significance is still alive, and the dust of controversy has not settled around them. It is media attention—including the zoom lens of opera—that has given them legendary, larger-than-life status.

After taking an M.A. at Harvard, where he also studied composition with Leon Kirchner, Adams moved to California. He was attracted to the work of

Steve Reich and Philip Glass, which, like his, was called minimalist—a style characterized, according to the critic Michael Steinberg, by "repetition, steady pulse and consonant harmony." (These are also traits of most classical and romantic composers, such as Haydn, Rossini, or Chopin, with their left-hand arpeggio figures.) The minimalist label has proved at once too limiting and too vague: it is used pejoratively to mean monotonous. Steinberg hastens to add, "Adams' music enters the ear easily, but it is not simple, certainly not simple-minded, and never predictable."

Alice Goodman researched her characters before writing verse that distilled something inner and telling about their private and public personas. Adams' vocal writing follows, and plays upon, the musical vernacular of American speech as expressed in popular song. His second opera, *The Death of Klinghoffer* (1991), takes a different tack, relying on oratorio structures to line up two opposed points of view and explore the depth of each. There is less overt drama, less interplay of character. His next stage work, *I Was Looking at the Ceiling and Then I Saw the Sky,* was characterized by Patrick J. Smith in a 1995 report in *Opera News* as "a politically correct multicultural stew, comprised of one part 1930s agitprop theater, one part old-fashioned revue and a larger part rock showbiz."

In an interview with Mark Swed published in the Fall 1995 *Schwann Opus,* Adams said, "I don't think there's any real reason why there couldn't be a great tradition of American opera. Our life is so full of all the imagery, themes and human predicaments that feed opera."

NIXON IN CHINA

THREE ACTS
MUSIC: John Adams
TEXT (English): Alice Goodman
WORLD PREMIERE: Houston Grand Opera, October 22, 1987

CHARACTERS

Ch'iang Ching, *wife of Mao Tse-tung* . . . . Soprano
Pat Nixon, *wife of Richard Nixon* . . . . Soprano
Nancy T'ang, *first secretary to Mao* . . . . Mezzo-Soprano
Second Secretary to Mao . . . . Mezzo-Soprano

Third Secretary to Mao	Mezzo-Soprano
Mao Tse-tung	Tenor
Chou En-lai	Baritone
Richard Nixon	Baritone
Henry Kissinger	Baritone

ACT I An airfield outside Beijing, morning of Monday, February 21, 1972.
Military contingents circle the field (chorus: *Soldiers of heaven hold the sky*)
before the official U.S. plane, *The Spirit of '76*, arrives. Premier Chou En-lai
and a few other officials go to meet it. President and Mrs. Nixon emerge and
exchange greetings with them. A band plays as the American party disem-
barks. Nixon is introduced to various officials and reflects on the significance
of his mission, the importance of having it succeed (*It's prime time in the U.S.A.
yesterday night*).

§ Nixon meets Chairman Mao Tse-tung in the latter's study, accompanied by
Chou and Henry Kissinger. After a photo opportunity and a few pleasantries,
the conversation turns to Mao's political philosophy (*We no longer need Confucius*), but he soon tires, and his guests discreetly withdraw.

§ Evening. The Nixons are fêted in the Great Hall of the People (Chou: *Ladies
and gentlemen, Comrades and friends*). Nixon returns Chou's toast, urging, "Let
us, in these five days, start a long march on new highways." Conviviality
reigns.

ACT II The second day. Pat Nixon, on a sightseeing day without the president, is presented with a glass elephant. She is shown the Great Wall, a clinic,
a pig farm, and a school. At the Summer Palace, she invokes the simple virtues
that can unite peoples (*This is prophetic!*), before going on to visit the Ming
Tombs.

§ That evening, at the Peking Opera, the Nixons are joined by Mme. Mao,
whose leadership in the Cultural Revolution has exerted a dominant influence
on the repertory. A ballet, *The Red Detachment of Women*, begins. A dancer
portrays Wu Ching-hua, a girl held prisoner on a tropical island plantation by
Lao Szu, a lascivious overseer, played by the same singer as Henry Kissinger.
Defying her captor, the girl escapes but is caught. As mercenaries start to
whip her to death, Pat Nixon impulsively interferes with the stage action to
protect her. Rescued, the girl joins comrades in the Red Detachment.

In another scene of the ballet, at the tyrant's mansion (Dance of the Mercenaries), his entertainment is infiltrated by revolutionaries disguised as a merchant and a group of hired entertainers. The girl and her new comrades have
come to liberate the village. Now it is Mme. Mao who interferes in the action,
firing a pistol and taking the stage herself (*I am the wife of Mao Tse-tung*),
backed up by enthusiastic revolutionaries.

ACT III   The last night in Beijing. A huge portrait of Mao dominates the background. All the participants are exhausted after so many receptions and events in so few days. In their respective bedrooms, the Nixons and the Maos recall earlier chapters in their lives that have led them to this time and place. Chou, in his closing reflection (*I am old and cannot sleep forever, like the young*), wonders about his own life: "How much of what we did was good? Everything seems to move beyond our remedy."

EUGEN D'ALBERT
1864–1932

*T*hough he was born in Scotland and died in Latvia, Eugen d'Albert was considered a German composer. He himself eventually took Swiss citizenship; his parents were German, the father's family being of Italian and French origin. Like Busoni and Wolf-Ferrari, the younger d'Albert showed his cosmopolitan heritage in his work. Like Smetana, he began as a concert pianist, encouraged by Liszt; and like Busoni, he remained a keyboard virtuoso throughout his career. (His piano pupils included Frederick Loewe, composer of *My Fair Lady,* who also studied with Busoni.)

Composition was rather a sideline with d'Albert, but he worked hard at it nevertheless, mastering an impressive technique. He studied with Arthur Sullivan and Hans Richter but is considered to have been largely self-taught. His love of the lyric stage is evident in his output of operas: *The New Grove Dictionary of Opera* lists twenty. Few of these enjoyed more than a brief success, but the seventh, *Tiefland,* influenced by the verismo style of Mascagni and Leoncavallo, has persisted in the repertory of European theaters. Though the characters are little more than stereotypes and the situations rigged by formula, the work builds its climactic scenes with unerring effect. The simplistic underlying symbolism of highland versus lowland—the high moral ground, the corruption of lowdown valley life—takes on graphic power. Here the irrational nature of opera as an art form transforms material that by itself seems banal and old-fashioned.

Aware of the visual magic implicit in this story, the actress/filmmaker Leni Riefenstahl—in technique and cinematic vision a German Orson Welles, but under a permanent cloud in the film industry for *Triumph of the Will,* her propaganda documentary for the Third Reich—returned to the mountains during World War II to make a film version of *Tiefland* in which music retreats into the background. A specialist in mountain photography, Riefenstahl captured in visual terms the mood of distance, longing, and spatial purity that d'Albert draws through music. In his opera, as in Alfredo Catalani's *La Wally,* one forgets the story and yields to a setting where passions resonate with magnitude, even though man's very existence is dwarfed by the towering landscape. Few other operas, apart from Wagner's *Ring* cycle, connect so much of the power of drama to that of nature itself.

TIEFLAND

(Lowland)

PROLOGUE AND TWO ACTS
MUSIC: Eugen d'Albert
TEXT (German): Rudolf Lothar (Rudolf Spitzer), based on Angel Guimerá's play *Terra Baixa*
WORLD PREMIERE: Prague, Neues Deutsches Theater, November 15, 1903
REVISED VERSION: Magdeburg, January 6, 1905
U.S. PREMIERE: New York, Metropolitan Opera, November 23, 1908

CHARACTERS

Marta, *employed by Sebastiano* . . . . Soprano
Pepa, *employed by Sebastiano* . . . . Soprano
Antonia, *employed by Sebastiano* . . . . Soprano
Nuri, *a young girl* . . . . Soprano
Rosalia, *employed by Sebastiano* . . . . Contralto
Pedro, *a shepherd* . . . . Tenor
Nando, *a shepherd* . . . . Tenor
Sebastiano, *a rich landowner* . . . . Baritone
Moruccio, *a miller* . . . . Baritone
Tommaso, *the village elder* . . . . Bass

The libretto places the action "partly on a mountain pasturage in the Pyrenees, partly in the Spanish Lowland of Catalonia at the foot of the Pyrenees." The period probably is that of the time of composition—late nineteenth and early twentieth century.

PROLOGUE   At Roccabruna, on a rocky slope high in the Pyrenees, early on a misty starlit morning, two shepherds, Nando and Pedro, greet each other. Pedro says that in his lonely work he goes for months at a time without seeing anyone *(Drei Monate sind's her).* He tells of a dream in which the Virgin Mary appeared, promising him a wife and happiness. He throws a stone at random to find from which direction his wife will come. It falls near Sebastiano, owner of the surrounding land, who approaches with Marta—one of his serfs, evidently his mistress as well—and the village elder, Tommaso. Sebastiano tells Marta he has decided she should marry Pedro. She refuses and runs off, but Sebastiano broaches the idea to Pedro, offering him a job as miller down in the valley. Pedro, smitten by his glimpse of Marta, is overwhelmed, the more so when he learns the wedding will take place the next day.

ACT I   At the mill in the valley, things are in disrepair, the miller having died recently. His assistant, Moruccio, sits sifting grain as three local gossips—Pepa, Antonia, and Rosalia—run in, excited by rumors of Marta's wedding. A young girl, Nuri, joins them and gives a rhapsodic description of the local landscape, all Sebastiano's property *(Er sagte mir),* before finally telling the others what they want to hear—news of the wedding. Innocently, Nuri goes on to mention that she once heard Sebastiano speak of Marta's belonging to him forever *(An einem Abend war's).* The three gossips exchange knowing remarks, interrupted by Marta, who brusquely dismisses them, then tells Nuri of her unhappiness before sending the girl away as well. Alone, Marta gives vent to her misery *(Sein bin ich, sein!):* to Sebastiano, she is just another piece of property.

To avoid her unwelcome bridegroom, she withdraws when peasant voices are heard approaching. Moruccio acquaints the naive, mountain-dwelling Tommaso with the facts *(Das ist bald getan):* when Marta came to this part of the country as a young girl, Sebastiano installed her stepfather as miller and took the girl as his mistress. Now Sebastiano wants to quell gossip by marrying Marta off, so he can find a wealthy wife. The old man refuses to believe this, but a fight is averted when villagers arrive with Pedro. Sebastiano too arrives and sends away the others, including a Priest, so he can have a word with Marta, who begs him to spare her this ordeal. He says he would never marry her to anyone she liked *(Ein andrer wäre dir wohl lieber!),* because she will always be his. The others return, having dressed Pedro in wedding finery. As most of the party leaves for the church, Sebastiano quietly tells Marta he will come to her that night: his signal will be a lantern. Then he stays behind at the request of Tommaso, who wants the truth about what he has heard. Sebastiano dismisses this as idle gossip, but Moruccio calls him a liar, saying he often has seen Sebastiano go to Marta's room at night. Sebastiano fires the millhand and orders him to leave town. Tommaso now believes Moruccio, and he is ashamed of his own unwitting part in the deception, but it is too late to stop the wedding.

After the ceremony, Pedro and Marta return to the mill. Seeing her unresponsive and dejected, he offers her a Taler (a valuable coin) he once received from Sebastiano after nearly losing his life to a wolf that stalked his herd *(Du meinst wohl gar)*. As he tells the story, she is moved by his sincerity, but in view of Sebastiano's impending visit, she says they will sleep in separate rooms. She struggles to reveal the truth about her past, only to be interrupted by the appearance of a lantern. Pedro suspects an intruder, but the lantern disappears. To avoid going to her room, Marta stays to sleep where she is; Pedro lies down near her.

ACT II   At dawn, Nuri appears, singing cheerfully *(Wer darf noch traurig sein)*. Pedro awakens, troubled by the growing realization that he must have a rival. When Marta curtly sends Nuri away, Pedro, with a touch of bitterness, flirts with the girl and says he will leave with her. Marta wants him to stay, but as she starts to follow him, she meets Tommaso, who has come in hopes of helping Pedro. The old man accuses Marta, but she softens his heart by telling how she came there at fourteen with her stepfather (her mother having died) and fell under the "protection" of Sebastiano *(Ich weiss nicht, wer mein Vater war)*. Though she married Pedro unwillingly, she now appreciates him more and more and wants to keep him as her husband. She will have to tell Pedro the truth; Tommaso prays for her success *(In seine Arme schliess dich Gott)* and leaves, just as Nuri returns with the three gossips. Pedro comes back and confronts them, demanding to know whatever it is that everyone else seems to know. His anger frightens them off.

Marta brings Pedro his supper, but he announces he is going back to his pastures. She asks him to stay, pleads for forgiveness, and confesses her past relationship with another man *(Mit ihm, den ich liebe!)*. Preferring death to desertion, she then pretends to have deceived him on purpose, urging him to kill her. He strikes at her with a knife, wounding her arm, and is horrified at what he has done. But she claims she really deserves to die *(Siehst du denn nicht, das mir das Leben zur Last?)*. As she falls half-fainting in his arms, he admits he loved her from the first *(Ich soll dich töten?)* and wants to take her back to the mountains. They prepare to go, but Sebastiano appears and orders Marta to dance, as she used to do for him *(Hüll in die Mantille dich fester ein)*, this time to entertain his prospective father-in-law, who is about to arrive. Annoyed by Pedro's resistance, he boxes his ear and calls villagers to take the shepherd away. As he is led off, Pedro at last realizes who his enemy is. Tommaso appears, having told the truth to Sebastiano's prospective father-in-law, who now forbids the wedding. As the old man leaves, Sebastiano tries to claim

Marta for himself, but she defies him. Pedro bursts in, challenging him to fight. Sebastiano says he has no knife, so Pedro throws away his own and offers to fight with bare hands. When Sebastiano tries to retrieve the knife, Pedro strangles him. The villagers rush in to see what has happened. Pedro, declaring them free of the wolf at last, heads back to the Highland with Marta.

DOMINICK ARGENTO
b. 1927

*B*orn in Pennsylvania to Sicilian immigrant parents, Argento showed
an early interest in music, but study was postponed by military service until he had reached the age of twenty. Then he enrolled at
the Peabody Conservatory, Baltimore, where he worked with Nicolas
Nabokov. He also studied with Hugo Weisgall, who was living in Baltimore.
A Fulbright grant and two Guggenheim fellowships took him several times
to Italy, where he eventually established a regular summer residence.

Working toward his master's degree at Peabody, he pursued a growing
interest in opera and composed his first essays in the form, meanwhile moving
on to the Eastman School in Rochester, New York, for further graduate studies
toward his Ph.D. Among Argento's teachers during this postgraduate period
were Henry Cowell (at Peabody), Howard Hanson, Alan Hovhaness, and Bernard Rogers (at Eastman). Once having completed his formal education, he
was invited in 1958 to join the faculty at the University of Minnesota and
moved to Minneapolis, where he made his permanent home.

Commissions in the Minneapolis area brought several stage works from
Argento's pen before his first widely recognized opera, *Postcard from Morocco*
(1971), which showed a gift for fantasy and characterization. A major commission from New York City Opera produced *Miss Havisham's Fire* (1979), based
on Dickens' *Great Expectations*. For the bicentenary of the University of Minnesota he wrote *The Voyage of Edgar Allan Poe,* later taken to Göteborg, Sweden,
as part of an exchange of productions. By this time, Argento had established
himself as a prolific opera composer whose output could be compared in quan-
tity and variety to that of Benjamin Britten.

In a more traditional vein, and turning toward Italy for inspiration, Argento wrote *Casanova's Homecoming* (1983) and *The Aspern Papers* (1988), providing his own librettos for both, as he had done for his monodrama *A Water Bird Talk* a decade earlier. He was not the first to adapt Henry James' *The Aspern Papers* as an opera—another American, Philip Hagemann, already had done so—but to Argento belongs the idea of making Aspern a composer rather than an author. From a literary viewpoint this may be a dubious switch, but it allowed Argento to indulge his love for music of the bel canto period without giving up his status as a modernist.

Though he uses serial techniques as part of his tonal arsenal, Argento has not tended to treat the voice as simply another instrument. In fact it is his loyalty to the vocal, lyrical nature of opera that has given him such a purchase on the attention of American opera audiences.

THE ASPERN PAPERS

THREE ACTS
MUSIC: Dominick Argento
TEXT (English): the composer, after Henry James' novella
WORLD PREMIERE: Dallas Civic Opera, Music Hall, November 19, 1988

CHARACTERS

Juliana Bordereau, *an opera singer* . . . . Soprano
Tina, *her niece* . . . . .Mezzo-Soprano
Sonia, *a young singer* .Mezzo-Soprano
Aspern, *a composer* . . . . Tenor
The Lodger, *a writer* . . . . Baritone
Barelli, *an impresario* . . . . Bass-Baritone

PROLOGUE I   *Quintet* A villa near the northern end of Lake Como, 1895. As the curtain rises on a dark stage, a voice is heard *(Snow and cypress, glacier and leaf),* its words contrasting a far-off time with the present. Juliana Bordereau, once a famous opera singer, now in her nineties, is discovered sitting in a wheelchair, describing events of 1835, which are reenacted simultaneously with her memory of them. Barelli, an impresario, made her career and became her lover. About the time when he discreetly took a younger mistress and protégée, Sonia, and installed her in a villa on the other side of the lake, he introduced Juliana to the composer Aspern. She was to star in his next work—and he to become her lover. Barelli, Sonia, the young Juliana, and Aspern are seen on the terrace admiring the view of the lake, paraphrasing Longfellow (Barcarole—quartet, Barelli: *"No sounds of wheel or hoofbeat break the silence of the summer night"*).

The Lodger. An early summer afternoon, 1895. A Lodger has appeared, ostensibly looking for a place to work at his writing. He is being shown around by Tina, Juliana's spinster niece. If he will pay 3,000 francs a month, Juliana says brusquely, he may have rooms. Though startled by so high a rent, he agrees. After Juliana has left, the Lodger questions Tina about her. She divulges little *(There isn't much to tell)*, prompting him to ask about the composer Aspern. When Tina discovers the Lodger has written about Aspern and is looking for more material, she becomes alarmed and leaves quickly.

The Quartet. On a late midsummer afternoon in 1835, the young Juliana in the music room goes over an aria from Aspern's work in progress, *Medea* (*"O! wretched fate!"*) while on the terrace a Painter, watched by Barelli, tries to work on a small oval portrait of Aspern. The composer, busy chatting with Barelli, will not hold a pose. Though Aspern has indicated a growing interest in Sonia—her role of Creusa in the new opera will be expanded—he seems happily engrossed in his relationship with Juliana, giving Barelli hope that inspiration will cause *Medea* to be completed soon.

The Portrait. On a late midsummer morning in 1895, the Lodger is writing to the person who told him about Juliana (*"My Dear Mrs. Prest"*), complaining that the two women have avoided him for a fortnight, so he cannot begin sounding them out. Juliana and Tina appear, thanking him for the flowers he has sent regularly. Juliana suggests, to Tina's embarrassment, that the Lodger take the niece for a ride in his boat. Then she probes the Lodger's motives by showing him the oval portrait of Aspern: how much would he suppose it to be worth? Though not admitting he recognizes it, he ill conceals his interest, and she is on the verge of accusing him of prying when Tina interrupts. After the old lady has retired, the Lodger voices his concern that the Aspern mementos be saved. Tina replies that Juliana loves them too much to destroy them.

Trio. Around noon on a late summer day in 1835, Aspern rehearses Sonia in music for *Medea* (*"O Sea-born Goddess"*) while Juliana, seated, coaches the younger singer. During Barelli's absence of several months, Juliana has befriended the girl, who has frequented the villa. When Juliana steps out, it becomes apparent that Aspern is more than musically involved with Sonia. He starts to embrace her, but she reminds him of how much Juliana has done for both of them. He replies that his affection for Juliana is different from the love he feels for Sonia (*Kind to* you? *How do you think* I *feel?*). Returning with coffee, Juliana overhears him plan to slip away late that night in the rowboat and join Sonia.

The Music Room. 1895. At midnight, the Lodger and Tina return from their excursion (Tina: *On the stroke of midnight!*). Tina has scarcely had a chance to offer help with his research when Olimpia, the maid, draws her away with urgency. Alone, the Lodger reflects on how Tina's loneliness has made her receptive to his needs *(What a yielding nature she has)*. Meanwhile, Tina is seen entering the long-unused music room, where she sees that the dust cover on the secretary has been disturbed. She emerges to tell the Lodger that Juliana was taken ill during their absence. Apparently in a state of excitement, Juliana removed the Aspern memorabilia from the music room. The old lady is now asleep in a downstairs room; Tina will sit up with her and watch. Alone, the Lodger enters the music room and starts to look around. He finds nothing but is startled by the appearance of the furious Juliana, who curses him as a scoundrel before collapsing in Tina's arms.

ACT II

PROLOGUE II   *The Lost Medea.* The Lodger relates what happened next *(It was the worst thing I have ever done)*: he left for a few weeks' absence after learning that Juliana survived her confrontation with him. As he speaks, Aspern, Juliana, Sonia, and Barelli are seen putting on the costumes of Jason, Medea, Creusa, and Creon. They mime the story of *Medea* while the Lodger, apart, reads Barelli's written synopsis *("Abandoned by her husband, Jason")*. When the story is over, they fade from view. The Lodger reflects on the fate of the work *(The score had been destroyed)*. Not accepting Juliana's official explanation—that Aspern, dissatisfied, burned it shortly before his death—the Lodger believes the old lady has kept it because destroying it "would be the same thing as murdering their own child," like Medea herself.

Flashback to 1835, evening of the day when young Juliana overheard Aspern arrange an assignation with Sonia. Aspern happily tells Juliana he has just finished *Medea*. He asks her to repeat with him that this, his best work, will immortalize their love, which inspired it (duet: *A hundred years from now*). Briefly carried away by the elation of the moment, she suggests champagne, but he says he will need a clear head to review the work once more that night. Juliana goes off to bed but first unties the rowboat from its mooring and pushes it out into the lake. When he finds the boat gone, Aspern swims out into the lake toward Sonia's villa.

The Proposal. 1895. The Lodger returns, to learn from the Gardener that the old lady has died. Tina greets him pleasantly and offers him the oval portrait of Aspern. There was a great deal of music, she says, but she is not at liberty to show it to him. If he were a member of the family. . . . Although Juliana had no use for the Lodger, she cared for Tina and wanted to see her happy. . . .

Gradually he realizes she is proposing marriage as a condition for access to the manuscripts. As soon as he indicates he could not accept, she rushes away. The Lodger resolves to leave the next day.

Solo. Midafternoon, early autumn 1835. In the aftermath of Aspern's death, Barelli wonders how it could have come about (*. . . out in the boat by himself to rethink the opera*). Juliana has told him the manuscript was burned; also that she is retiring from the stage. Stunned by his multiple loss, he bids her farewell. She closes up the music room and withdraws, cradling the manuscript as if it were a child.

The Score. The same, 1895. On his way out, the Lodger hears Tina singing and playing Aspern's Barcarole. Accompanying her is an apparition of the four figures—Aspern and Juliana, Barelli and Sonia—in their *Medea* costumes. Wondering if he can still save the coveted Aspern Papers, he enters the room. Tina seems transformed, looking young and beautiful to the Lodger, who decides he can pay the price after all (*How could she look at me with such mildness . . . ?*). His approach to Tina is dampened, however, by her statement that she burned the opera the night before. She no longer appears beautiful to him. After he has made his escape, she removes *Medea* from the secretary and sets fire to the first pages. The four costumed figures briefly reappear, then fade from sight as she continues to burn the manuscript.

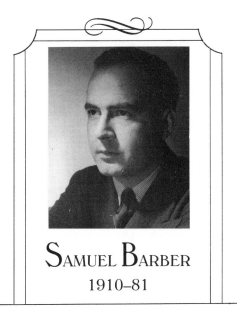

SAMUEL BARBER
1910–81

Generally considered a neoromantic, Samuel Barber was "postmodern" long before the term came to be used. Born into musical surroundings—his aunt and uncle were the contralto Louise Homer and her composer husband, Sidney—Barber showed talent from the age of seven and at fourteen was enrolled in the Curtis Institute of Music in Philadelphia. There he met another composition student, Gian Carlo Menotti, who became a lifelong friend; both studied with Rosario Scalero. Barber also trained his baritone voice under Emilio de Gogorza and studied piano. After a brief singing career, in the mid-1930s he spent two years at the American Academy in Rome. Soon thereafter, with recognition for his *First Essay for Orchestra* and *Adagio for Strings* (adapted from a string quartet), he concentrated on composition.

Barber went on to write in almost every genre, including numerous songs, but apart from one juvenile effort, he did not embrace the lyric stage until 1958, when his *Vanessa,* to a libretto by Menotti, was produced at the Metropolitan Opera. The next summer, a short chamber opera, *A Hand of Bridge,* was introduced at the Festival of Two Worlds In Spoleto, Italy. Though *Vanessa* won Barber a Pulitzer Prize, he felt the need for adjustments and offered a revision in 1964, duly mounted at the Met the following year.

For the opening of the new Metropolitan Opera House at Lincoln Center in 1966, Barber was commissioned to write *Antony and Cleopatra,* with a text adapted by Franco Zeffirelli from Shakespeare's play. Badly received by the press, tolerated with no great enthusiasm by the public, the work had only eight performances, limited to that first season. Zeffirelli's lavish production seemed to weigh down a basically lyrical work, whose love story took second place to a variety of other elements. Once again the composer resorted to revision, reducing the scenes devoted to Roman politics while adding music to build up the love scenes. The new version, staged by Menotti at the Juilliard American Opera Center in 1975, is the one produced since. It was recorded at the Spoleto Festival in 1983 and telecast from Lyric Opera of Chicago a decade later.

Barber's operas appeal to traditional-minded audiences, thanks to the composer's familiarity with the style and musical gestures of the standard repertory. Rather than simply emulating past examples, however, he built upon them, incorporating arias, duets, and ensembles into a flexible format. Setting words to music, he was guided by sheer love of the voice, backed by his training as a singer and experience in songwriting. While there is not a great deal of modernity in Barber's musical vocabulary, it is nevertheless unmistakably contemporary, especially in his expert use of the orchestra.

ANTONY AND CLEOPATRA

PROLOGUE AND THREE ACTS

MUSIC: Samuel Barber

TEXT (English): Franco Zeffirelli, based on William Shakespeare's play

WORLD PREMIERE: New York, Metropolitan Opera, September 16, 1966

REVISED EDITION

TEXT (English): Gian Carlo Menotti

WORLD PREMIERE: New York, Juilliard American Opera Center, February 6, 1975

CHARACTERS

Cleopatra, *Queen of Egypt* . . . . Soprano
Octavia, *Caesar's sister, Antony's second wife* . . . . Soprano
Charmian ⎱ *Cleopatra's attendants* . . . . ⎰ Mezzo-Soprano
Iras ⎰ . . . . ⎱ Alto
Octavius Caesar, *triumvir of Rome* . . . . Tenor
Mardian, *a eunuch* . . . . Tenor
A Messenger . . . . Tenor

Eros, *Antony's armor bearer*. . . . . Tenor or High Baritone
Thidias, *ambassador from Caesar* . . . . Tenor or High Baritone
Dolabella, *Caesar's friend* . . . . Baritone
Marc Antony, *triumvir of Rome* . . . . Bass
Enobarbus, *Antony's companion in arms*. . . . . Bass
A Soothsayer . . . . Bass
Alexas, *attendant on Cleopatra*. . . . . Bass

The historical events dramatized by Shakespeare in his play *Antony and Cleopatra* culminated in the death of the two principals in the year 30 B.C. Antony was fifty-three years old, Cleopatra thirty-nine, Caius Octavius (later Augustus) Caesar thirty-three. The action of the opera begins about 40 B.C. and transpires over a decade.

PROLOGUE   A Chorus representing various parts of the Roman Empire harshly criticizes Marc Antony's sybaritic lifestyle in Egypt and urges his return to Rome *(From Alexandria this is the news).*

ACT I   In Cleopatra's palace in Alexandria, Antony declares he must leave this luxurious life. Scarcely has he resolved to tell Cleopatra than she appears with her attendants, telling him to leave her if he must. Briefly they are alone together *(You and I must part)* before she watches him go.

§   In Rome, the Senate greets Antony like a returning hero. Octavius (later Augustus) Caesar, who neither likes nor particularly trusts him, soon gets into an argument with him about Antony's unresponsive behavior while in Egypt, but the Senators try to calm them. All take their seats except Agrippa, who suggests marriage between Antony and Augustus' widowed sister Octavia to patch things over. Antony, whose wife, Fulvia, has recently died, listens to the idea.

§   In her palace, Cleopatra whiles away the time of Antony's absence *(Give me some music).* Her dreamy mood changes abruptly when news arrives of Antony's marriage, and her attendants Charmian and Iras have to restrain her from attacking the Messenger. Calming down, Cleopatra questions the Messenger, who obliges with an unflattering description of Octavia.

§   At the close of a banquet in Rome, Octavius voices the hope that the wedding will mark a new era in his and Antony's relations. When Octavius and his sister have left, Antony sits moodily apart while Enobarbus tells fellow officers about the start of his friend's affair with Cleopatra *(When first she met Mark Antony).* As if in a vision, Cleopatra appears from a distance on her barge *(Where's my serpent of old Nile?).*

ACT II   On the floor of the Roman Senate, Octavius angrily relates that Antony, back in Egypt, has taken the throne alongside Cleopatra and made her ruler of several provinces. Open warfare now seems inevitable to restore Roman rule.

§ By a pool in Cleopatra's garden, a Soothsayer reads Charmian and Iras' palms. When Antony and Cleopatra wander in, the girls run off, but Enobarbus soon interrupts the lovers with news that Octavius has captured Toryne. Antony, suddenly serious, declares he will fight to restore his reputation. As he leaves, Cleopatra tells Enobarbus she intends to lead her own forces in the war.

§ Outside Antony's battle tent at night, Guards greet each other, then pause to harken to "ghostly music and visions," which one Guard says mean that Hercules, Antony's patron, is deserting him.

§ In the tent, Antony and Cleopatra lie embracing (duet: *Oh take, oh take those lips away*). Antony rouses himself and calls his shield bearer, Eros, to bring his armor. Cleopatra pushes Eros aside to help Antony dress.

§ The Egyptian forces draw up for battle at Actium (*On to our ships*) and depart. Sounds of strife are heard in the distance. Enobarbus enters with other Roman soldiers, having watched in horror as the Egyptian naval forces retreated to Alexandria at the height of the fray, followed by Antony himself. After they move on, Antony enters, despairing at the disgrace and disaster of the battle (*Hark! the land bids me tread no more upon it*).

§ In Cleopatra's palace, she tells Octavius' ambassador, Thidias, that she surrenders. Antony storms in, ordering Thidias whipped for his supposed insolence, then throwing Cleopatra to the floor in his rage at her betrayal. When he has left, she asks her attendants to take her to the monument, intending to feign suicide in order to win back his sympathy.

§ On a battlefield, Enobarbus, having deserted his chief, feels even guiltier when a soldier reports that Antony has sent all Enobarbus' belongings after him. Feeling there is nothing left for him but a disgraceful death, he upbraids himself (*O sov'reign mistress of true melancholy*) and wanders off.

Inside Antony's tent, Eros brings the report that Cleopatra is dead. Antony, determined to join her (*Where souls do couch on flow'rs*), reminds the youth of his oath to kill his master if asked. Rather than do so, Eros takes his own life. Antony then falls on his sword but, finding himself still alive, calls for someone to dispatch him: no Guard will do it. Alexas, Cleopatra's eunuch, arrives at the tent to fetch Antony to Cleopatra.

ACT III   Antony is brought to Cleopatra's monument (duet: *O sun, burn the great sphere thou movest in*). Kissing him as he dies, she praises his nobility. Octavius suddenly appears, treating her respectfully but warning her not to take her own life. He pauses to bid farewell to Antony's body (*The breaking of so great a thing),* lamenting that their fates were irreconcilable.

Inside the monument, Cleopatra learns from Dolabella, Octavius' emissary, that she is to be led to Rome in a triumphal procession. Thanking him for the warning, she asks her attendants what they think of that *(Nay, 'tis most certain. Saucy lictors will catch at us like strumpets).* Guards admit a Rustic bringing a basket of figs, among which are concealed several asps. She dismisses him and asks for her royal regalia *(Give me my robe, put on my crown).* Iras, having slipped her hand into the basket, dies of the poisonous snakebite. Cleopatra lets the snakes bite her as well, and her example is followed by Charmian. The Chorus marks her passing *(She looks like sleep. . . . No grave on earth shall clasp in it a pair so famous).*

JACK BEESON
b. 1921

*I*ndiana-born Jack Beeson chose an academic path into the world of music, studying at the Eastman School under Burrill Phillips, Bernard Rogers, and Howard Hanson, then working privately with Béla Bartók in New York and pursuing graduate studies at Columbia University, where service as a répétiteur with the opera workshop stimulated his affinity for the lyric stage. During graduate studies he also began a teaching career, lecturing at the Juilliard School, becoming a professor at Columbia and eventually chairman of the music department there from 1968 to 1972. Meanwhile, he earned numerous awards and study grants and worked with a variety of organizations involved in the furtherance of contemporary music.

In addition to chamber music and songs, he devoted himself largely to opera composition. In 1950 he wrote *Jonah,* an unpublished work that won special mention in an international competition sponsored by the Teatro alla Scala, Milan, the following year. Next came *Hello Out There,* a chamber opera based on a one-act play by William Saroyan, performed by the Columbia University Opera Workshop in 1953, during his years of teaching at Columbia. *Lizzie Borden* in 1965 ventured into a markedly different style—one of anguished atonality rather than folksy lyricism.

As in Marvin David Levy's *Mourning Becomes Electra,* there is no suspense as to the outcome in *Lizzie Borden.* Assuming Lizzie guilty of the murders, the authors devote their energies to probing her tormented psyche, showing how she was inwardly driven to the deed, which bears the inevitability of Greek tragedy.

In *My Heart's in the Highlands,* Beeson returned to the world of Saroyan and the medium of chamber opera. The work was produced for television over NET in 1970. Romantic comedy engaged his interest with *Captain Jinks of the Horse Marines,* staged in Kansas City in 1975. (This opera shares with Adolphe Adam's *Le Postillon de Lonjumeau* the distinction of having a title unrelated to the action: it is the name of a song quoted in passing.) Sheldon Harnick was the librettist for *Captain Jinks,* basing it on a once popular period play by Clyde Fitch. *Dr. Heidegger's Fountain of Youth,* Beeson's next opera was again written with Harnick, this time drawing on a story by Nathaniel Hawthorne devoted to the premise that age does not necessarily bring wisdom.

Beeson's style, while varied, adheres to standards of accessibility in both subject and musical style. As a result, his operas have been well received. *Lizzie Borden,* on the timely subject of domestic abuse, was chosen by Glimmerglass Opera at Cooperstown, New York, for its 1996 season.

LIZZIE BORDEN

THREE ACTS AND EPILOGUE
MUSIC: Jack Beeson
TEXT (English): Kenward Elmslie, based on Richard Plant's scenario
WORLD PREMIERE: New York City Opera, March 25, 1965

CHARACTERS

Elizabeth (Lizzie) Andrew Borden,
    Andrew's elder daughter. . . . . .Mezzo-Soprano
Margret Borden, *her younger sister* . . . . Soprano
Abigail Borden, *their stepmother* . . . . Soprano
Rev. Harrington . . . . Tenor
Capt. Jason MacFarlane. . . . . Baritone
Andrew Borden . . . . Bass-Baritone

The murder of Andrew Borden and his wife took place on August 4, 1892. Because of Borden's prominence and his daughter Lizzie's being accused of so brutal a murder, the case drew an unusual amount of publicity. Though Lizzie Borden (1860–1927) was tried and acquitted, many then and since continued to doubt her innocence. The libretto departs freely from the actual circumstances of the case, which also gave rise to stage, film, and television dramatizations and the ballet *Fall River Legend*.

ACT I   In the living room of the Borden house in Fall River, Massachusetts, Sunday-school children are rehearsing a hymn, coached by Andrew Borden's elder daughter, Lizzie, a spinster in her early thirties. Rev. Harrington speaks to her about the weakening situation of Old Harbor Church, which has been losing key parishioners and their financial support. He wishes he could approach Lizzie's father, the richest man in town, but Lizzie says it is no use: since the death of her mother, Andrew has turned away from the church, and the only way of reaching him would be through his new wife, Abigail.

When Andrew, a stern figure, enters the house, Rev. Harrington withdraws. As he studies his ledgers, Lizzie broaches the subject of needing a new gown in which to address a church missions meeting in the fall. He refuses money and rebukes her (*You are headstrong and vain, Elizabeth*). After she leaves, he reviews to himself the credo that has made him successful (*I worked hard, I worked long*). A wordless scene follows in which Lizzie and her younger sister, Margret, are joined at the noon meal by Andrew and his second wife, Abigail (Abbie), whose affected ways and influence over Andrew inspire envy and hatred from Lizzie.

§ In the girls' room that afternoon, Margret considers the view from their window (*In the garden the flowers wither and die*). Margret is apprehensive because her suitor, Capt. Jason MacFarlane, is expected that evening to speak to her father, and both girls are sure the men will quarrel (Lizzie: *Two years you've delayed*). After Lizzie leaves, Margret muses on the oppressive atmosphere and longs for the day when she will be free (*The house watches and spies*).

ACT II   After dinner that evening, Abbie sings a parlor song, accompanying herself at the harmonium (*Hirondelle. . . . Rossignol*). When Andrew appears, she tells him the harmonium is worn out and asks for a piano for their wedding anniversary, the next day. He balks at the expense, causing her to say she feels treated like a servant, which she was when she first came to the house—everything still revolves around Evangeline, Andrew's first wife (*To your daughters I'm still only the hired help*). To placate her, Andrew says he may buy the piano and will replace Evangeline's portrait, which commands the living room; he takes it down. When the girls join them. Abbie pretends interest in the tapestry Lizzie is working on, but Lizzie's lack of response prompts an outburst from Abbie (*Not another of your stony-faced evenings!*).

The quarrelsome atmosphere is disturbed by the doorbell: Rev. Harrington arrives with Capt. Jason MacFarlane and introduces him. Andrew speaks disparagingly of Jason's ship (*I've seen the likes of your crew*) and goes brusquely to lock up the house. While Abbie entertains Rev. Harrington and Lizzie returns to her needlework, Jason exchanges a few words with Margret (ensemble: *I longed to wander through a cool garden with you*). Jason proposes a toast to the end of summer, asking everyone to say what they would like to harvest in the fall. When Andrew returns, the parlor game doesn't interest him, and he rudely bids good-night to Rev. Harrington. Andrew is now aware that Jason has come to speak to him about Margret. She and Abbie withdraw upstairs. Though Andrew accuses Jason of being after Margret's money *(Money's never beside the point)*, he offers consent—if Jason will marry his elder daughter instead *(You have my consent to marry—Lizzie!)*. When Jason refuses, Andrew orders him to leave.

Andrew forbids Lizzie to see the preacher or the children's choir or to have anything more to do with Jason. He orders her to be loving toward Abbie, whose voice draws him upstairs. Lizzie, staying downstairs, sees her life stretching drearily ahead of her. She imagines Jason coming to the door, then addresses her mother's portrait, then goes to the tapestry she has been embroidering, with its images of Adam and Eve. Unhinged by her own anxiety and repressed anger, she cowers like a cornered animal.

ACT III The next morning, as Lizzie mends her mother's wedding dress in the garden, Andrew's voice is heard ordering Margret as well to avoid any contact with Jason. Abbie, mindful of their wedding anniversary, tries to calm him and tells Margret they will not be home for supper. Margret goes to Lizzie, who offers her the dress for her own wedding. When Andrew and Abbie have left, the daughters wonder if Jason will come back. Soon his voice is heard outside, asking Margret to come away with him *(I forced myself to wait)*. She lets him in the garden gate. While Lizzie sorts through an old trunk, Jason offers Margret souvenirs from the West Indies *(On those green islands)*. The couple leaves, unnoticed by Lizzie, who slips into a fantasy world where she, not Margret, is Jason's bride, as her father had suggested *(Margret, may I wear it?)*. She puts on her mother's wedding dress. Abbie, unexpectedly returning, looks out the window and notes Lizzie in the dress. She hints that on her way home she saw the couple make their escape *(A little bird tells me)*. She adds that she and Andrew would like the house to themselves—why doesn't Lizzie escape too *(A lady of advancing years)*? Lizzie retorts that just as Abbie waited for Evangeline to die so she could marry Andrew *(You waited for it!)*, so Lizzie will watch and wait. Each woman wants the house for her own. Furiously, Abbie tears at the wedding dress and storms out. Lizzie looks into the mirror with loathing and smashes it with her fist.

Later that afternoon, Lizzie sits as if in a trance *(Kill time. Kill time)* while Jason gathers Margret's belongings from the daughters' room. When he asks for the packet of his letters to Margret, Lizzie wants to keep them, fantasizing that they were really meant for her *(Keep my secret)*. Abbie appears from her room, urging Jason to leave before Andrew returns. Jason goes hastily, without the letters. Abbie retires to her room after caustically ordering Lizzie to set the supper table for two. Lizzie tears up the letters, grasps the scimitar from Abbie's decorative "Turkish corner," and runs upstairs. A terrible scream is heard from the master bedroom.

Andrew enters, calling for Abbie. In the growing darkness, he assumes the figure at the head of the stairs is she *(Why didn't you answer?)*. When he does recognize Lizzie, she has identified herself with Evangeline, whose wedding dress, bloodstained, she is still wearing. Saying they now have the house to themselves, she stays on the stairs, causing the alarmed Andrew to rush past her in search of Abbie. Then she follows him.

EPILOGUE   Years have passed. In the living room, where Evangeline's portrait again hangs, Lizzie has taken Andrew's place, poring over his ledgers *(Count the columns that add up to nothing)*. Though it is dusk, Rev. Harrington stops for a brief visit. With apologies he returns her contribution, which the Church has voted not to accept, in spite of her legal vindication. She is briefly interested to hear that he has had a letter from Margret, but then she resumes her cold façade and dismisses him. Meanwhile, voices outside are heard singing verses of a children's game that has gained currency *(Lizzie Borden took an ax, gave her mother forty whacks)*.

VINCENZO BELLINI
1801–35

Of the troika of masters of the so-called bel canto school of opera, Vincenzo Bellini was the youngest, born nine years after Rossini and four after Donizetti. He also had the shortest life, dying short of his thirty-fourth birthday. Although "bel canto" is a general term for the classical Italian school of singing, these are the composers who brought it into the Romantic movement with particular stylistic success. The characteristic of their writing for the voice is long melodic line with liberal ornamentation, designed to make maximum use not only of the singer's virtuosity but of his or her expressive powers. It is taken for granted that the singer has good coloratura technique and breath control, plus the ability to expand or contract the volume of a phrase or long-held note *(messa di voce)*.

In the late nineteenth century, when the emphasis began to shift toward less ornate "power singing" required by the large orchestras and theaters of grand opera, the bel canto operas began to fall into neglect. Only a few were performed with any frequency, and those only by high coloratura sopranos, the one class of voice that was still being trained with the required agility. Of Rossini's work little survived beyond *Il Barbiere di Siviglia*, of Donizetti's little beyond *Lucia di Lammermoor* and *L'Elisir d'Amore*, of Bellini's only an occasional revival of *Norma*.

After World War II, when a gradual revival of interest in virtuosic dramatic singing began, such singers as Leyla Gencer, Maria Callas, Renata Scotto, and Joan Sutherland emerged to carry the banner for the neglected operas of the early nineteenth century. There are no recordings by the great singers of the Rossini-Donizetti-Bellini period, so the performing style had to be reconstructed largely by conjecture, guided by practices traditionally handed down through the teaching and coaching professions. Audiences experienced little problem with the relatively unfamiliar idiom of the bel canto operas, however, and these increasingly resumed their place in the working repertory.

Bellini, of Sicilian birth, was noted particularly for the extreme length of his melodies and for their sad coloration, often called "elegiac." He had written two operas for Naples before his first big success, *Il Pirata,* was performed in Milan in 1827. This was followed by *La Straniera* and *Zaira,* neither as great a hit, but with *I Capuleti e i Montecchi, La Sonnambula,* and *Norma* he achieved an unbroken series of popular triumphs. These, as well as his subsequent *Beatrice di Tenda* and final *I Puritani,* were duly staged during the years following the bel canto revival of the 1950s. With dramatic coloratura sopranos and mezzo-sopranos leading the way, tenors, baritones, and even basses began to study and master coloratura technique, so the standards of performance rose steadily during that period until florid singing once again achieved the legitimacy it had lost a century earlier.

Bellini's music, with its poignancy and inflection, remains singular. The final scene of Richard Wagner's *Götterdämmerung* is clearly modeled, from a theatrical point of view, on the finale of *Norma.* More directly musical was the spell cast by Bellini on Chopin and Liszt, who knew him in Paris. In the long-spun *andante* movements that both keyboard virtuosos wrote for piano, one can almost hear a soprano voice lingering over the melodies of a Bellini heroine.

IL PIRATA

(The Pirate)

TWO ACTS

MUSIC: Vincenzo Bellini

TEXT (Italian): Felice Romani, based on Isidore J. S. Taylor's play *Bertram, ou le Pirate,* in turn based on R. C. Maturin's play *Bertram*

WORLD PREMIERE: Milan, La Scala, October 27, 1827

U.S. PREMIERE: New York, Richmond Hill Theater, December 5, 1832

CHARACTERS

Imogene, *Duchess of Caldora* . . . . Soprano
Adele, *her companion* . . . . Soprano

Il Pirata

Gualtiero, *former Count of Montaldo* . . . . Tenor
Itulbo, *Gualtiero's lieutenant.* . . . . Tenor
Ernesto, *Duke of Caldora* . . . . Baritone
Goffredo, *a hermit* . . . . Bass

A preface to the libretto explains that prior to the action, Imogene was in love with Gualtiero, Count of Montaldo, who was—along with her father—among the adherents of Manfredo, pretender to the Sicilian throne. It was a rival claimant, Charles of Anjou, who won out in 1266. Gualtiero, exiled, became a pirate, hoping eventually to rejoin his beloved Imogene, but she meanwhile was forced into marriage with another suitor, Ernesto, who had been on the winning side.

ACT I   Sicily, latter thirteenth century. Fortune has turned against the outlaw Gualtiero, whose pirate fleet has been defeated by the forces of Ernesto on behalf of King Charles. As the people of Caldora look anxiously to sea during a storm, Gualtiero and his crew are cast ashore. He is recognized by his old tutor, Goffredo, who now lives as a hermit. Gualtiero asks what has become of Imogene, whom he still loves *(Nel furor delle tempeste)*. Goffredo is loath to answer, but when the people say the local duchess—Imogene herself—is on her way to help the shipwreck victims, he urges Gualtiero not to let himself be discovered by his enemies.

Imogene arrives at the beach and greets the survivors. Questioning Gualtiero's friend Itulbo, she learns to her distress that the pirate captain may have been lost during the recent sea battle. Aside to her companion, Adele, Imogene confides a recent dream in which she imagined Gualtiero wounded and dying upon a beach; her husband accused her of causing the man's death and dragged her away *(Lo sognai ferito, esangue)*. Gualtiero, briefly stepping outside the hermit's hut, recognizes Imogene. When the sound of his voice stirs further memories of her lost love, her companions see how upset she is and lead her back to her nearby castle of Caldora.

§ That night, outside the castle, the shipwreck victims have been enjoying the duchess's hospitality *(Evviva! allegri!)*. Itulbo, afraid their identity will be discovered, wants them to quiet down, but they share more drinks before returning to the castle. Imogene emerges, having sent Adele to find the mysterious stranger whose voice she heard on the beach. Gualtiero approaches, unrecognized at first, and answers her solicitous questions about his misfortunes, which she compares to her own. When he reveals his identity and accuses her of betraying him, she replies that she had to marry Ernesto in order to save her old father from death in prison (duet: *Il genitor cadente*). They are interrupted by ladies-in-waiting who bring Imogene's child. Gualtiero seizes his enemy's son, threatening to do away with him. At the sight of Imogene's distress, he relents and gives the boy back to her, then hurries away.

Scarcely has Imogene breathed a sigh of relief when word comes that her husband has returned triumphant from the sea battle. His soldiers march in, singing of their exploits (*Più temuto, più splendido nome*). Ernesto joins them (*Sì, vincemmo*) and cannot understand why Imogene seems depressed at such a glorious moment. Her anxieties are justified when Ernesto sends for the leader of the shipwrecked crew to question him. Itulbo answers in Gualtiero's stead, saying they are from Liguria, "where all strangers are welcome." Ernesto notes that the Ligurians sheltered his enemy, Gualtiero, and provisioned the pirates, so he orders the crew held until he can find out more about them. Upon Imogene's intercession, however, he agrees to let them leave, if they will do so the next morning. Aside, Gualtiero threatens Imogene with dire consequences if she will not meet him one more time, while Ernesto wonders why he mistrusts these strangers (sextet, Gualtiero: *Parlarti ancor per poco*). Because Imogene is afraid to meet with him, Gualtiero starts to throw himself on Ernesto, but Itulbo and Goffredo restrain him. Imogene swoons, revives, and is led away, while Ernesto fears for her sanity; Gualtiero, recklessly longing for revenge, is dragged away by his retainers.

ACT II Imogene's ladies-in-waiting express concern for her as she rests in her chamber. When they have left, Adele tells her she may now go to meet Gualtiero, who has sworn not to leave without seeing her. Ernesto enters, however, challenging her indifference. She admits she still loves Gualtiero, "but as one loves a man dead and buried" (duet, Ernesto: *Tu m'apristi in cor ferita*). Then Ernesto receives a note saying Gualtiero lives and is present in the castle. Imogene warns of sure bloodshed, but Ernesto, furious, dashes from the chamber.

§ On the castle terrace toward daybreak, Gualtiero refuses to be persuaded by Itulbo that they should make their escape immediately, as Ernesto stipulated. Gualtiero wants to defy Ernesto, risking his own men's lives if necessary. Itulbo leaves as Imogene comes for a last rendezvous with Gualtiero, who delivers his ultimatum: either she flees with him, thereby punishing Ernesto with her loss, or Gualtiero stays and fights. Refusing to dishonor her marriage vows, no matter how unwelcome, she asks Gualtiero to forgive her and fly from Ernesto's wrath. As she bids him farewell, Ernesto draws near and sees their last embrace (trio, Gualtiero: *Cedo al destin orribile*), then bursts forth to challenge his rival. Both men are spoiling for a fight and ignore Imogene's pleas to kill her instead. They rush off. With Adele, who has come to comfort her, Imogene heads after the men, still hoping to stop them.

§ In the castle later that day, the duke's followers form a funeral procession and swear to avenge his death at the hand of Gualtiero (*Lasso! perir così*). To their surprise, Gualtiero dares to appear. He throws down his sword and says he is ready for their vengeance, but they reply he must first be condemned by a tribunal. Turning to Adele, he asks her to carry his last farewell to Imogene, in hopes that she will pray for him in death *(Tu vedrai la sventurata).* He leaves with the knights to face his fate. Imogene wanders in, distracted, imagining she has saved her son from assassins and brought him to his dying father. When the boy actually appears, she speaks consolingly to him *(Deh! tu, innocente)* until a trumpet sounds from the Council Chamber, announcing Gualtiero's condemnation. Realizing, despite her madness, that he is about to die, she pictures the scaffold *(Il palco funesto per lui s'innalzò)* and declares herself ready to die too, of grief.

I Capuleti e i Montecchi

(The Capulets and the Montagues)

TWO ACTS

MUSIC: Vincenzo Bellini

TEXT (Italian): Felice Romani, after his libretto for Nicola Vaccai's *Giulietta e Romeo* (1825), in turn based on Luigi Scevola's tragedy of the same name

WORLD PREMIERE: Venice, La Fenice, March 11, 1830

U.S. PREMIERE: New Orleans, St. Charles Theater, April 4, 1837

CHARACTERS

Giulietta, *Capellio's daughter* . . . . Soprano
Romeo, *scion of the Montecchi* . . . . .Mezzo-Soprano
Tebaldo, *betrothed to Giulietta* . . . . Tenor
Lorenzo, *doctor to the Capuleti* . . . . .Tenor or Bass
Capellio, *patriarch of the Capuleti* . . . . Bass

Felice Romani's libretto draws upon Matteo Bandello's ninth novella, source of Shakespeare's story for *Romeo and Juliet,* and also upon Giuseppe Foppa's libretto for Nicola Zingarelli's opera *Giulietta e Romeo* (1796), which is further indebted to Gerolamo della Corte's *Storie di Verona.* The setting is thirteenth-century Verona, during the feuds between the Ghibellines and Guelphs.

ACT I   In a hall in the castle of Capellio (Capulet), his followers, members of the Guelph faction, prepare to meet an onslaught by their hereditary enemies the Montecchi (Montagues), who are Ghibellines. Tebaldo (Tybalt) and Capellio say the attack will be led by Romeo, whom they know by reputation as the slayer of Capellio's son. Romeo has offered a truce, which Capellio angrily says he will reject, despite the intercession of his adviser, Lorenzo (Laurence). Tebaldo, who wants to marry Capellio's daughter, Giulietta, declares he will personally avenge his prospective father-in-law against Romeo *(È serbata a questo acciano)*. When Capellio decides the marriage should take place at once, Lorenzo warns that Giulietta is too ill with a fever. Tebaldo does not want to upset her, but Capellio insists on going ahead with the ceremony.

Romeo, unrecognized, enters as an envoy from the Montecchi seeking peace. He proposes that the two sides rule the city as equals and that Giulietta marry Romeo—who, he says, killed Capellio's son as a result of the fortunes of battle and wishes to atone by becoming a son to Capellio *(Se Romeo t'uccise un figlio)*. When the Capuleti refuse his terms, Romeo warns they must bear the blame for the bloodshed that will follow (ensemble: *Guerra a morte, guerra atroce!).*

§ In her chambers, Giulietta dreads her impending marriage and longs to be reunited with Romeo, with whom she is secretly in love *(O quante volte).* Lorenzo, who knows of her secret, comes to tell her that Romeo is in Verona. When the young man arrives by a secret door, Lorenzo leaves. Romeo pleads ardently with Giulietta to elope with him (duet: *Sì, fuggire: a noi non resta),* but her loyalty to her family is too strong. He threatens to confront Capellio, withdrawing only when she begs him to spare her further grief.

§ In a courtyard of the palace, the Capuleti set aside their militancy to cele-brate the wedding (chorus: *Lieta notte, aventurosa).* Romeo, disguised, infiltrates the party and tells Lorenzo his forces are ready to strike, rescuing Giulietta. Sounds of conflict are heard from outside. As the Capulets rush to arms, Giu-lietta appears, lamenting that she is the cause of more bloodshed *(Tace il fra-gor).* When Romeo finds her and tries once again to take her away, she still holds back. His henchmen arrive to reinforce him against new threats from Capellio and Tebaldo, who now realize who he is. While Giulietta and Lorenzo pray vainly for peace, the opposing forces prepare to have at each other outside (ensemble: *Soccorso, sostegno accordale, o cielo).*

ACT II   In the palace, Giulietta anxiously awaits news of the outcome of the conflict. Lorenzo comes to tell her Romeo is safe, rescued by his men; but while Romeo waits for reinforcements, Giulietta is to be taken to Tebaldo's castle by order of Capellio. Lorenzo offers Giulietta a potion to put her into a sleep so deep that people will believe her dead. Hearing her father approach, she takes the potion and starts to feel faint. When Capellio enters, she begs him to embrace and forgive her in death *(Deh! padre mio),* but he sends her to her chambers, telling her she must leave in the morning. Though he now doubts the wisdom of his own sternness, he cannot relent *(Qual turbamento io provo!)* and orders his retainers to keep watch on Lorenzo, who is to be confined to quarters.

§ At a deserted spot on the castle grounds, Romeo waits in vain for Lorenzo, who was to bring news of Giulietta. Instead, Romeo meets Tebaldo, who recognizes and challenges him (duet: *Un Nume avverso, un Fato*). As they are about to duel, sounds of a mourning procession intrude (chorus: *Pace alla tua bell'alma*). When they realize Giulietta has died, both men are so grief-stricken that they too long for death; but since they blame each other for the tragedy, neither will put the other out of his misery (duet: *Svena, ah! svena un disperato*).

§ Among the tombs of the Capulets, Romeo leads his followers to Giulietta's bier, where they leave him crying out to her to lead him to heaven *(Tu sola, O mia Giulietta)*. Overcome with grief, he takes poison—but at that moment, Giulietta starts to revive. She cannot understand why Lorenzo did not alert him about the sleeping potion. When she realizes he is dying, she wants to join him in death *(Ah! crudel! che mai facesti?),* but he tells her she must live to mourn him. The Montecchi, pursued by the Capuleti, return to find Romeo's body and Giulietta, dead of grief, by his side. Lorenzo and the Montecchi accuse Capellio of causing the lovers' death.

BEATRICE DI TENDA

TWO ACTS
MUSIC: Vincenzo Bellini
TEXT (Italian): Felice Romani, after Carlo Tedaldi-Fores' play
WORLD PREMIERE: Venice, La Fenice, March 16, 1833
U.S. PREMIERE: New Orleans, St. Charles Theater, March 5, 1842

CHARACTERS

Beatrice di Tenda, *Filippo's wife, widow of Facino Cane* . . . . Soprano
Agnese del Maino . . . . .Mezzo-Soprano
Orombello, *Lord of Ventimiglia* . . . . Tenor
Anichino, *Facino's former minister, Orombello's friend*. . . . . . . Tenor
Rizzardo del Maino, *Agnese's brother* . . . . Tenor
Filippo Maria Visconti, *Duke of Milan* . . . . Baritone

The Visconti, an eminent Ghibelline family, ruled the Duchy of Milan from the thirteenth century until 1447. Though Felice Romani's libretto appears to be pure fiction, its plot borrowed largely from his own successful *Anna Bolena* for Donizetti three years earlier, there was a historical Filippo Maria Visconti (1392–1447), whose rule marked the formal end of the dynasty, and whose namesake appears in the opera.

ACT I Courtiers of Filippo Visconti wonder why he is departing so early from the festivities at the castle of Binasco. Though his wife, Beatrice di Tenda, has conferred estates on him and given him his power, he admits he is tired of her and bored with the party, of which she is hostess. The Courtiers hint that their loyalty might weaken if he does nothing to free himself from this burden *(Se più soffri, se più taci)*. From a distance he hears the voice of Agnese del Maino, with whom he is infatuated, singing about love's basic importance to life *(Ah! non pensar che pieno)*. This inspires him, egged on by his retainers, to pour out his feelings for her *(Come t'adoro, e quanto)*.

§ In her apartments, Agnese sits waiting for Orombello, to whom she has sent an anonymous love letter. He arrives, thinking the letter to be from Beatrice, whom he himself loves. Embarrassed, he starts to excuse himself, but Agnese draws him on with insinuations about someone who loves him, despite a highly placed rival *(Nulla è un regno a core amante)*, so he assumes she knows his secret. But when he utters the name of Beatrice, Agnese's shock reveals his mistake. He pleads with her not to jeopardize Beatrice's life and reputation *(La sua vita e la sua fama)*; Agnese, thinking no farther than of her injured pride, dismisses him angrily.

§ In a shady grove, Beatrice rests with her attendants. Not only she but all her people, she says, must suffer at the hands of the ungrateful Filippo *(Ma la sola, ohimè! son io . . . ?)*. As she moves on, Filippo and his confidant Rizzardo del Maino (Agnese's brother) arrive, following her. Filippo sends Rizzardo to fetch her back, then accuses her of hatred and rancor toward him. She denies such feelings but admits her sorrow and jealousy *(Duolo d'un cor piagato)*. Next, producing papers purloined from her, he charges her with disloyalty and infidelity *(Qui di ribelli sudditti)*. She replies that her subjects' complaints about him are not unjustified. When she demands return of her papers, Filippo refuses and says she deserves to be sentenced to death. She trusts the world to see justice done.

§ In a remote part of the castle, near a statue of Beatrice's late first husband, Duke Facino, men-at-arms loyal to Beatrice discuss recent developments and comment that Filippo is overreaching himself *(L'amore o l'ira a tradirsi il porterà)*. After they have withdrawn, Beatrice appears, asking forgiveness of Facino's spirit for her foolishness in being misled by Filippo *(Deh! se mi amasti un giorno)*. Orombello overhears her and assures her of his own support; further, many of her subjects are willing to rebel against Filippo's tyranny, awaiting only her approval *(Della tua sventura)*. Beatrice is afraid that Orombello, rumored to be her lover, is the wrong person to lead an insurrection. He confesses that he does love her. He has fallen to his knees when Filippo surprises them, accompanied by Rizzardo, Agnese, and others of the court. Beatrice realizes that Filippo now has the perfect excuse for recriminations against her. Agnese exults in her revenge; Orombello laments that he has brought ruin upon Beatrice; and the courtiers dread what may happen next (ensemble: *Oh! vil rampogna!*). Filippo orders both Beatrice and Orombello imprisoned. When Beatrice asks if no one will rise to her aid (*Nè fra voi si trova*), the Courtiers reply that her innocence will defend her.

ACT II   A tribunal is set up in the castle. Men of the court tell the women that Orombello, after bearing as much torture as he could (*Dal tenebroso carcere*), broke down and confessed himself guilty, with Beatrice as his accomplice. Filippo enters, accompanied by Anichino, minister to Beatrice's previous husband and a friend to Orombello. Anichino tries to warn Filippo that the trial will set the populace against him (*E qual v'ha legge*), but Filippo is unafraid. Judges and Courtiers file in, with Rizzardo heading the tribunal. Agnese, conscience-stricken, cannot enjoy her triumph. Filippo addresses the Judges (*Giudici, al mio cospetto*), who call Beatrice to defend herself. Filippo accuses her of plotting against him and indulging in "obscene amours," which she hotly denies. Orombello, brought in as witness, denies his forced confession. Threatened with further torture, he asks only Beatrice's forgiveness (ensemble, Beatrice: *Al tuo fallo ammenda festi generosa*). Filippo, shaken, suggests a face-saving suspended sentence, and Anichino suggests releasing the prisoners, but the Judges will not hear of it, insisting on further torture for both. Though Beatrice warns Filippo that heaven will judge his infamy, he seconds the order to lead her and Orombello back to prison.

Agnese approaches Filippo and confesses her part in causing Beatrice to be condemned unjustly, but Filippo dismisses her, saying he alone is responsible. He wonders to himself whether his own certitude of Beatrice's guilt is justified (*Rimorso in lei?*). Anichino brings the death warrant—signed by the entire Council, though Beatrice did not confess even under torture. Filippo wants to remain firm but is assailed by doubt, recalling how Beatrice reached out to him in his unlucky days (*Qui m'accolse oppresso, errante*). But when news comes that rebel forces, loyal to Beatrice's first husband, are assembling to rescue her, Filippo signs the warrant. He rationalizes that the audacity of Beatrice and her followers has condemned her (*Non son io che la condanno*).

§   Beatrice's entourage, dressed in mourning, assembles outside her cell, where she is at prayer (chorus: *Ah! no, non sia la misera*). She emerges, proud of having survived torture without betraying her honor (*Nulla io dissi*), hoping that those who condemned her will themselves be condemned by the world. Agnese approaches and confesses her guilt, but Orombello's voice from his cell moves Beatrice to forgive her (trio, Orombello: *Angiol di pace all'anima*). As Rizzardo approaches with guards to lead Beatrice to the headsman's block, Agnese faints. Beatrice asks her friends to pray for the guilty Filippo, not for herself, and to assure Agnese of her forgiveness (*Ah! se un'urna è a me concessa*). "As one fleeing his chains I leave my sorrow on earth," she declares. All kneel as the guards lead her away.

HECTOR BERLIOZ
1803–69

ecause Berlioz's operas are seldom performed, one does not think of him as an opera composer. Yet so vivid was his imagination that the theater seems the only place for it. Having limited access to the stage, he invented a theater of the mind. One of his symphonic scores never meant for the stage, *La Damnation de Faust,* has found its way there despite his intentions. To be sure, the "dramatic symphony" *Roméo et Juliette* is too poetic and fanciful for the stage, but *La Damnation* contains enough dramatic narrative to submit to the transformation.

Because of the individuality of his ideas, Berlioz remained all his life an outsider to the Parisian musical establishment, though in his youth he did win a Prix de Rome. Influenced by German romanticism, notably Carl Maria von Weber, he was considered by his countrymen not to write very French-sounding music, and significantly he found greater appreciation in Germany. Yet he equally admired Gluck, Spontini, and Étienne-Nicolas Méhul, all of whose work adhered closely to the ideals of French *tragédie lyrique.* For his dramatic ideas Berlioz was greatly indebted to Shakespeare. There is a touch of *The Tempest* in the way he made use of the French convention of opera-ballet for the Royal Hunt and Storm in *Les Troyens,* and the Will-o'-the-wisps in *La Damnation de Faust* seem to have slipped in from another part of that same forest. He earlier used the ballet for dramatic purposes in the Roman Carnival of *Benvenuto Cellini.*

Cellini was the first of Berlioz's opera projects to survive and the first to reach the stage. It remains remarkable for its attempt to capture something of what the artistic life is really like. Though Cellini is romanticized, for Berlioz anything romantic was part of everyday artistic reality. His opera stands along-side Hindemith's *Mathis der Maler* and Pfitzner's *Palestrina* as one of few that penetrate the fog of fictional cliché to deal with what it feels like to forge a work of art. Symbolically, to create one masterpiece, Cellini throws into the furnace of his creativity everything he has achieved so far. Characteristically for a romantic (or mythological) hero, he will be reduced to nothing if he fails. But of course he does not fail, because he is a master: the sum total of his previous work saves him and becomes his crowning achievement. Even his enemies and critics have to admit it. Berlioz must have gloried in that moment, which seldom came in his own life.

La Damnation de Faust, an opera in spite of itself, treats scenes from Goethe's drama with uncommon insight. There is some of the composer's special plead-ing, too. When Méphistophélès leads Faust to hear drunken students execute an "Amen" fugue, he warns, "Listen well to this! We're going to see, dear doctor, bestiality in all its candor"—an editorial comment on what academics do to music. It is hard to know which to admire most in this score—the portrayal of Faust's conflict between idealism and abandon, Méphistophélès' own split between urbanity and savagery, Marguerite's rueful growth of aware-ness, or the light fantastic of the sprites, who seem "the stuff that dreams are made on." As the title indicates, Faust goes to hell; Berlioz believes all artists must.

Despite the grandeur of *Les Troyens,* it is Berlioz's last opera, *Béatrice et Bénédict,* that is his most touching and therefore his deepest. With Shake-speare by his side again, he could not fail. Academe comes under fire once more, here in the person of the pedant Somarone, but by this time the joke has lost its sting. It is to the on-again-off-again romance of the protagonists that Berlioz tunes his lyre, setting free a gallant valedictory to his theatrical muse.

BENVENUTO CELLINI

TWO ACTS
MUSIC: Hector Berlioz
TEXT (French): Léon de Wailly and August Barbier, after Cellini's autobiography
WORLD PREMIERE: Paris, Opéra, September 10, 1838

U.S. PREMIERE (concert performance): New York, Philharmonic Hall,
  March 22, 1965
U.S. STAGE PREMIERE: Boston, Orpheum Theater, May 3, 1975

CHARACTERS

Teresa, *Balducci's daughter* . . . . Soprano
Ascanio, *Cellini's apprentice* . . . . .Mezzo-Soprano
Benvenuto Cellini, *a goldsmith* . . . . Tenor
Francesco, *an artisan* . . . . Tenor
Fieramosca, *Sculptor to the Pope* . . . . Baritone
Pompeo, *a swordsman* . . . . Baritone
Pope Clement VII . . . . Bass
Cardinal Salviati . . . . Bass
Balducci, *papal treasurer* . . . . Bass
Bernardino, *an artisan* . . . . Bass

The historical Pope Clement VII was Giulio de' Medici, nephew of Lorenzo de' Medici and patron of Raphael and Michelangelo, as well as of Benvenuto Cellini.

ACT I   Rome, sometime during the period 1523–34. Carnival season. In his apartments, papal treasurer Balducci fumes that the Pope has called in a Florentine, Benvenuto Cellini, to discuss a sculpture commission that Balducci would rather see go to the official sculptor, Fieramosca, his prospective son-in-law. Revelers in the street annoy him, especially since Cellini—who courts his daughter, Teresa—is among them (ensemble: *C'est bien lui*), but Balducci must be off to the Vatican, where the Pope is waiting for him. Teresa bemoans her conflicting loyalties to suitor and family *(Se condamner à toujours feindre)*, only to be distraught further by Cellini's arrival, quickly followed by that of Fieramosca (trio: *O Teresa, vous que j'aime plus que ma vie*). From a hiding place, Fieramosca hears Cellini propose eloping with the girl the next evening; he swears to foil them. When Balducci returns, Cellini makes his escape, so Balducci finds instead the hiding Fieramosca, who cannot give a satisfactory explanation of his presence. Balducci calls neighbors, who threaten the intruder with a beating (ensemble: *Emmenons-le dans le jardin*), but Fieramosca gets away.

§ The next day, Cellini waits for Teresa at the Piazza Colonna *(La gloire était ma seule idole)*. Some of his friends and apprentices appear (metalworkers' song: *Si la terre aux beaux jours se couronne*), celebrating Mardi Gras. One apprentice, Ascanio, brings a bag of money but reminds Cellini that it represents a commission from Pope Clement to deliver a finished statue the next day. The consensus among Cellini's friends is that the papal treasurer, Balducci, has paid too little for the commission. Resolving to teach him a lesson, they hurry to a nearby street theater, leaving the coast clear for Fieramosca, who thinks that by disguising himself as a Capuchin monk he can abduct Teresa (*Ah! qui pourrait me résister?*).

Heading for the theater, Balducci enters with his daughter while Cellini and Ascanio prepare their own abduction plan. As crowds press in to see the play, the open-air stage is revealed, with a pantomime that makes fun of Balducci. Cellini and Ascanio, Fieramosca and his cohort Pompeo, all dressed as monks, make their way through the crowd as the commedia dell'arte continues, parodying Balducci's stinginess toward Cellini and favoritism toward Fieramosca.

In the audience, the real Balducci loses patience with the insult and attacks the stage, triggering pandemonium. The two pairs of "monks" approach Teresa, confusing her as to which is which. Cellini, sword in hand, challenges Fieramosca, who tries to get away, leaving Pompeo to be run through. Cellini is arrested for the murder (ensemble: *Assassiner un capucin!*), while Teresa protests in vain that he acted to save her from kidnapping. The sculptor is soon freed by his friends, who set upon the guards. In the ensuing turmoil, Fieramosca is seized instead as the fugitive "monk" who killed Pompeo.

ACT II   The following day, Ash Wednesday, Teresa goes to Cellini's studio, still believing he is under arrest. But he appears, breathless and disheveled, to tell of his adventure (*Ma dague en main*): he escaped the crowd by joining a group of friars dressed, like himself, in white. The lovers to plan to elope to Florence (duet: *Quand des sommets*), but Ascanio alerts them to the approach of Fieramosca with the irate Balducci, who accuses Cellini of kidnapping his daughter. Teresa gives herself up, but when Fieramosca timidly claims her as his fiancée, Cellini menaces him. At this moment the Pope appears. Though inclined to indulge Cellini, he registers annoyance that his commissioned statue is incomplete, declaring someone else will have to cast it. Cellini refuses indignantly and, when the pontiff orders him arrested, seizes a hammer and threatens to destroy the clay original. As a condition for finishing the work himself, he demands pardon for his faults, as well as Teresa's hand and the rest of the day to do the casting. The Pope declares Cellini will be hanged if the statue is not finished by nightfall (ensemble: *Ah! le démon me tient en laisse*). Feeling that Cellini has undone himself by his habitual recklessness, Teresa fears—while Balducci and Fieramosca rejoice—that nothing can save him.

§ At the entrance to a foundry improvised in the Coliseum, Ascanio makes light of his master's foibles (*Mais qu'ai-je donc?*). Cellini wanders in, briefly imagining a more peaceful life (*Sur les monts les plus sauvages*) before rousing his workmen to mix bronze for his statue, *Perseus with the Head of Medusa*. Fieramosca comes to demand satisfaction: he and Cellini must duel behind a nearby cloister. He leaves, followed by Cellini, who brushes past Teresa as she arrives. The girl still hopes to elope, but instead she sees Fieramosca, who used the duel as a ruse to get Cellini out of the foundry and now tries to stop the workmen by offering them more money. The sculptor quickly reappears and turns the tables on Fieramosca by forcing him to join the workers himself. As the men proceed into the foundry, Balducci arrives to retrieve his daughter but is restrained by the Pope, who calls upon Cellini to deliver the statue. The inner curtain opens to reveal the foundry (ensemble: *Quelle paleur sur son visage!*). As still more metal is needed, Cellini orders his earlier work gathered up and thrown into the crucible, which proceeds to blow its top with a bang. For a moment Cellini believes he is ruined, but the casting turns out to be complete. Even Balducci and Fieramosca join in admitting his triumph, as all hail the power of "metals, those underground flowers," and of the people who fashion them into works of art.

La Damnation de Faust

(The Damnation of Faust)

FOUR PARTS AND TWO EPILOGUES

MUSIC: Hector Berlioz

TEXT (French): by the composer and Almire Gandonnière, after Gérard de Nerval's version of Johann Wolfgang von Goethe's drama

WORLD PREMIERE (concert performance): Paris, Opéra Comique, December 6, 1846

STAGE PREMIERE: Monte Carlo Opéra, February 18, 1893

U.S. PREMIERE (concert performance): New York, Steinway Hall, February 12, 1880

METROPOLITAN OPERA PREMIERE (concert performance): February 2, 1896

METROPOLITAN STAGE PREMIERE: December 7, 1906

CHARACTERS

Marguerite . . . . Soprano
Faust. . . . . Tenor
Méphistophélès. . . . . Bass
Brander . . . . Bass

PART I Sixteenth-century Hungary. [To include his setting of the traditional Rákóczy March, Berlioz switched the opening scene from the Germany of the original legend.] Alone in the fields at sunrise, learned old Dr. Faust, with tired indifference, contemplates the springtime renewal of nature *(Le vieil hiver)*. A chorus of country people in the distance *(Les bergers laissent leurs troupeaux)* briefly stirs his nostalgia for simple happiness.

§ Elsewhere on the plain, Faust hears an approaching army. Indifferent to worldly glory, he envies the soldiers' enthusiasm for victory, then withdraws as they pass (Rákóczy March).

PART II In his study in northern Germany, Faust finds that wisdom, like the pleasures of the countryside, can no longer move him *(Sans regrets j'ai quitté les riantes campagnes)*. Tired of life, he is about to take poison when an Easter hymn outside *(Christ vient de ressusciter!)* revives memories of youthful piety: in hopes that religious inspiration may return and sustain him, he decides to live. Suddenly, Méphistophélès appears before him, ironically commenting on his apparent reconversion *(O pure émotion!)*. Though Faust at first views the demon with contempt, he is swayed by promises of gratification and worldly knowledge. The two disappear into the air.

§ In Auerbach's cellar tavern in Leipzig, Méphistophélès offers Faust the first pleasure—hearty companionship. Among students making merry *(Oh! qu'il fait bon quand le ciel tonne)*, a student, Brander, offers a song about a rat whose high life in a kitchen was ended by a dose of poison *(Certain rat, dans une cuisine)*. As the students offer up a fugal "Amen" for the creature, Méphistophélès remarks to Faust, "We're going to see bestiality in all its candor." Taking center stage himself, the devil renders a song about a flea who brought his relatives to infest a whole royal court *(Une puce gentille)*. Tiring of this jollity, Faust asks to be taken to someplace more peaceful.

§ In woods and meadows along the banks of the Elbe, Méphistophélès puts Faust into charmed sleep on a bed of flowers *(Voici des roses)*, where Sylphs join in serenading him (chorus: *Dors, heureux Faust*). Faust dreams of "Margarita" (Latin for Marguerite), soon to become his lover. Congratulated by Méphistophélès on their good work in charming Faust, the Sylphs dance around the sleeper and gradually vanish (ballet). Awakening, Faust apostrophizes the beautiful girl he has seen in his dream. Méphistophélès promises to lead him to her door, which means passing through a crowd of students and soldiers in the town (students' chorus: *Iam nox stellata*) as evening falls.

PART III In Marguerite's room, Faust hails the idea of meeting such an ideal, innocent young woman *(Merci, doux crépuscule!)*. Méphistophélès dashes in, telling Faust to conceal himself, as she soon will be there. Both men disappear. Marguerite enters and recalls a ballad about a King of Thule (a northern country of mythology) who always remained sadly faithful to his lost lover (Gothic song: *Autrefois un roi de Thulé*). Apart, Méphistophélès calls upon Will-o'-the-wisps, "spirits of inconstant flames," to enchant and deceive the girl. After they dance around him (Minuet of the Will-o'-the wisps), he offers a sarcastic serenade outside Marguerite's window, predicting her loss of innocence *(Devant la maison de celui qui t'adore)*. As the spirits vanish, he stands back to witness the seduction.

In the room, Faust steps forward, declaring his love *(Ange adoré, dont la céleste image)*. Marguerite, it seems, has been made to dream of Faust, just as he has dreamed of her (duet: *En songe je t'ai vu*). Meanwhile, however, neighbors—aware that a man is in Marguerite's room—gather outside the house. Méphistophélès bursts in, crying that the girl's reputation must be saved: already the neighbors are calling her mother to the scene *(Holà! mère Oppenheim)*. After a hasty farewell (trio, Faust: *Je connais donc enfin*), Faust and Méphistophélès escape through the garden.

PART IV   Time has passed. Loved and abandoned by Faust, Marguerite now finds herself in the same predicament as the bereaved King of Thule *(D'Amour l'ardente flamme)*. Soldiers and students are heard in the distance, reminding her of the night Faust first came to her house. She longs for him—but he does not return.

§ Amid forests and caves, Faust calls upon nature to relieve his world-weariness *(Nature immense)*. Méphistophélès appears and says Marguerite is in prison, having given her mother too much of a potion that was used to make the old woman sleep during Faust's amorous visits. As his price for leaving Marguerite to be saved by heavenly powers, Méphistophélès demands Faust's signature on a contract: he must sell his soul to the devil. Able to think only of the present moment, Faust signs, and the two are off on a pair of black horses.

§ On their wild ride, they pass country people praying by a wayside shrine, then enter a realm of hellish apparitions (Faust: *Nos chevaux frémissent*). As they fall into the abyss, demons and damned spirits hail Méphistophélès in their own mysterious language *(Ha! Irimiru Karabrao! Has! Has!)*, and Princes of Darkness welcome the newly damned Faust.

EPILOGUE ON EARTH   A voice reports that hell has fallen silent after Faust's arrival: "A mystery of horror is accomplished."

EPILOGUE IN HEAVEN   Seraphim announce Margarita, again calling her by her Latin name, and welcome her as an innocent soul misled by love (chorus of apotheosis: *Remonte au ciel, âme naïve)*.

BÉATRICE ET BÉNÉDICT

TWO ACTS

TEXT (French): the composer, after Shakespeare's *Much Ado About Nothing*

WORLD PREMIERE: Baden-Baden, Theater der Stadt, August 9, 1862

U.S. PREMIERE (concert performance): New York, Carnegie Hall, March 21, 1960

U.S. STAGE PREMIERE: Washington, D.C., Opera Society of Washington, June 3, 1964 (in English)

CHARACTERS

Héro, *Léonato's daughter* . . . . Soprano
Béatrice, *Léonato's niece*. . . . . .Mezzo-Soprano
Ursule, *Héro's companion* . . . . Contralto
Bénédict, *an officer* . . . . Tenor
Claudio, *an officer*. . . . . Baritone
Don Pedro, *a general*. . . . . Bass
Léonato, *governor of Messina* . . . . Bass
Somarone, *court music master* . . . . Bass

The Moorish occupation of Sicily took place in the ninth century A.D., prior to the Norman conquest of the island. The exact period of the action would be hard to ascertain, since further skirmishes between the Sicilians and the Moors likely took place. As late as 1492, the kingdom of Granada in Spain remained under Moorish rule.

ACT I On the grounds of Léonato, governor of Sicily, a crowd hails Don Pedro's victory over the Moors. Léonato arrives with his daughter, Héro, and his niece Béatrice. Héro is delighted that her beloved Claudio, Don Pedro's right-hand officer, is returning safely from the war. Béatrice inquires scornfully about Bénédict of Parma, who is also returning, and with whom she maintains a running battle of words. Soon after Héro contemplates the joy of meeting Claudio again (*Je vais le voir),* he arrives with Don Pedro and Bénédict. Béatrice promptly resumes her barbed banter with Bénédict (duet: *Comment le dédain pourrait-il mourir?*), which evidently both of them enjoy. After she leaves, Bénédict learns from Don Pedro that Claudio and Héro will be married. Bénédict assures the other two men that he himself would never be tempted to marry (trio: *Me marier? Dieu me pardonne!*): he swears he will die a bachelor. If he were to succumb, he adds, there should be an epitaph put on his house reading "Here you may see Bénédict the married man."

The music master, Somarone, arrives to rehearse an epithalamium (wedding ode) he has prepared (chorus: *"Mourez, tendres époux"*), but it doesn't go to his satisfaction, so he adds some embellishments and runs through it again, with commentary, for Don Pedro. As the musicians depart, Bénédict slips behind some bushes and overhears a dialogue staged for his benefit by Léonato and Don Pedro, in which they declare that Béatrice is really in love with Bénédict, though she hides the fact. This surprises the young man, who, once he is alone, vows to requite her love *(Ah! Je vais l'aimer)*. He leaves in a happy frame of mind.

Héro enters with her lady-in-waiting, Ursule, and they savor the joke that is being played on Bénédict, then comment on the beauty of the calm evening that has descended (nocturne duet: *Nuit paisible et sereine!*). Ursula picks roses and hands them to the pensive bride-to-be.

ACT II   Inside the governor's palace, with festivities in full swing, Somarone sings the praises of Sicilian wine *(Le vin de Syracuse,)* but, having consumed too much of it himself, cannot improvise a second verse. Apart, Béatrice is agitated, having heard from Héro and Ursula that Bénédict secretly loves her. She now recalls the anxiety she felt during his absence *(Il m'en souvient)* and admits to herself that she loves him in return. Accordingly, she bids farewell to her brittle frivolity. When Héro and Ursule join her, they are surprised at her changed mood as she wishes happiness for the engaged couple (trio, Héro: *Je vais d'un coeur aimant)*, though she insists marriage would not be a happy fate for herself. Alone again, she is touched to hear a distant wedding chorus *(Viens, de l'hyménée)* and startled by the arrival of Bénédict. They spar briefly but without their old conviction, each seeing signs of love in the other.

The wedding party arrives (march, ensemble: *Dieu qui guidas nos bras)*. When Léonato produces a second wedding contract, Don Pedro asks for whom it is meant. Bénédict and Béatrice call each other's bluff and agree, with pretended reluctance, to marry. The others produce a sign reading "Here you may see Bénédict the married man" as the couple agrees to a truce—though tomorrow they may renew their war of wits (scherzo duettino: *L'amour est un flambeau)*.

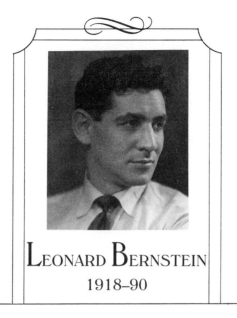

LEONARD BERNSTEIN
1918–90

The most famous American musician of his generation, Leonard Bernstein excelled equally as a pianist, conductor, and composer. If he was not a child prodigy, it is only because he was not immediately exposed to music: he discovered it for himself, after the age of ten. Though his parents frowned on the idea of a musical career, young Bernstein persisted through studies at Harvard, and later at the Curtis Institute. His teachers included Walter Piston in composition, Fritz Reiner and Serge Koussevitzky in conducting. In 1942 he was appointed Koussevitzky's assistant at Tanglewood, where he led the U.S. premiere of Britten's *Peter Grimes* in 1946. Meanwhile, in 1943, he was named assistant conductor to Artur Rodzinski with the New York Philharmonic. During November of that year, Bernstein made a much publicized (and broadcast) impromptu podium debut when guest conductor Bruno Walter suddenly was taken ill. In the period 1958–69, Bernstein would serve as the first American-born music director of the Philharmonic.

Success as a conductor on an international basis constantly challenged his time to work as a composer, but again Bernstein proved persistent. Grounded in popular as well as classical music, he provided the Broadway theater with hit shows—*Wonderful Town* (1953), *Candide* (1956), and *West Side Story* (1957). Like George Gershwin before him, he also aspired to write operas, but in this genre his only contributions were *Trouble in Tahiti* and its sequel, *A Quiet Place.* He made a name for himself as an opera conductor, leading *Medea* and *La Sonnambula,* both with Maria Callas, in productions directed by Luchino Visconti at La Scala in Milan in 1954–55. Later he conducted at the Vienna State

Opera and Metropolitan Opera and made several opera recordings, along with a vast number of symphonic recordings.

Candide, several times revised, started life as an elaborately produced Broadway show in which Lillian Hellman's book, freighted with social criticism aimed at political and religious intolerance, struggled with Bernstein's energetic, lighthearted score. In the course of reworking, Hellman's participation was ended and the playful satire of the score set free—though it proved a mistake, on the other hand, to stage the work too flippantly. The overture and several of the songs took on a life of their own.

Trouble in Tahiti, a chamber opera including elements of popular music, never exerted the appeal of *Candide* but continued to fascinate Bernstein because of its personal, quasi-autobiographical subtext: the composer had undergone psychoanalysis. In time he returned to amplify the story of Sam and Dinah—rather, of their family after Dinah's death—with the collaboration of Stephen Wadsworth, an emergent stage director, who was also a friend and contemporary of Bernstein's children.

The libretto of *A Quiet Place,* larded with 1970s Ivy League campus argot and made up largely of incomplete sentences, challenges the listener and the reader, but it was what Bernstein wanted. The opera contains some of his most personal, least exhibitionistic writing. Conceived as a private statement, it holds its own among the many legacies of a multifaceted genius.

CANDIDE

TWO ACTS

MUSIC: Leonard Bernstein

ORIGINAL VERSION

TEXT (English): Lillian Hellman, lyrics by the composer, Richard Wilbur, John Latouche, and Dorothy Parker, after Voltaire's novel

WORLD PREMIERE: Boston, Colonial Theater, October 29, 1956

SECOND VERSION

TEXT (English): Hugh Wheeler, lyrics by the composer, Wilbur, Stephen Sondheim, and Latouche

WORLD PREMIERE: Brooklyn, Academy of Music (Chelsea Theater), December 19, 1973

OPERA HOUSE VERSION

TEXT (English): Wheeler, lyrics by the composer, Wilbur, Sondheim, and Latouche

WORLD PREMIERE: New York City Opera, October 13, 1982

CANDIDE

CHARACTERS

Cunegonde	Soprano
Old Lady	Mezzo-Soprano
Candide	Tenor
Governor of Buenos Aires	Tenor
Dr. Pangloss	Baritone

ACT I In mid-eighteenth-century Westphalia, Candide—illegitimate nephew of the local Baron—is in love with Cunegonde, the Baron's daughter (*Life is happiness indeed*). Maximilian, the Baron's vain son, shares Candide's optimism; an ensemble develops between them, Cunegonde, and Paquette, the servant girl. These young people have been instructed in the art of happiness by Dr. Pangloss, their philosophical tutor, who reviews his lessons with them (*The best of all possible worlds*).

As Pangloss takes Paquette aside for private instruction in the art of love, Candide and Cunegonde confess their own love and dream of a life together (duet: *Oh, happy we*). Their happiness is short-lived: the Baron and his wife and son are outraged that a social inferior should court the girl. Thrown out, Candide wanders disconsolately, his only comfort Pangloss' idea of man's essential goodness (*It must be so*). He sleeps in a field and is rudely awakened by the Bulgar army, which presses him into service. When he tries to desert, he is given a thorough beating, barely recuperating when the Bulgars decide to wage war against the Abars (chorus: *Sieg heil, Westphalia!*). They attack the castle, leaving the Baron, his family, and entourage for dead. Candide laments the loss of his beloved (*Cunegonde, is it true?*).

§ Some time later, Candide gives alms to a decrepit old beggar who turns out to be Pangloss, somehow resurrected by the pain of the anatomist's scalpel in the mortuary. Despite his harrowing experience, Pangloss clings to optimism (*Dear boy, you will not hear me speak*). Even the syphilis that has disfigured him is a result of the fact that "Men worship Venus everywhere."

The two vagrants are offered work on a ship sailing to Lisbon. As they arrive, an earthquake erupts, killing 30,000 people, but Pangloss continues to argue that everything must be for the best in the best of all possible worlds. Amid a festive atmosphere (chorus: *What a day for an auto-da-fé!*), he and Candide are arrested as heretics. Pangloss insists he cannot be executed, because he is too sick to die: he traces the history of the syphilis that Paquette passed on to him. Unmoved, the Inquisitors find the two men guilty, and Pangloss is hanged. Candide, though flogged, clings to his belief in Pangloss' philosophy. As he begins his travels throughout the world, he reflects that if things don't work out for the best, the fault must lie within himself (*It must be me*).

§ Meanwhile, in Paris, Cunegonde has surfaced as an enterprising courtesan, whose clients include a wealthy Jew, Don Issachar, and the Cardinal Archbishop of the city. Though occasionally gnawed by remorse for her lost innocence, she consoles herself with finery *(Glitter and be gay).* Candide, arriving in the City of Light, cannot believe his eyes when he finds her alive (duet: *You were dead, you know).* They waltz happily until alerted by Cunegonde's companion, the Old Lady, that her two keepers are about to arrive. When they do, Cunegonde inadvertently stabs both of them fatally.

Collecting her jewels, she manages to escape to Cadiz with Candide and the Old Lady, who regales the pair with her harrowing, polyglot life story. During the narrative, thieves make off with Cunegonde's jewels, leaving the trio destitute. But the Old Lady, nothing daunted, proposes to sing for their supper *(I am so easily assimilated),* boasting that she can make her way anywhere. The Spaniards indeed take to her, but soon it becomes apparent that the French police are in pursuit, so Candide accepts a commission to fight for the Jesuits in South America, taking the others with him. As they embark, the Captain of the ship joins them in bidding farewell to the Old World and looking forward to the New (quartet: *Once again we must be gone).*

ACT II   The refugees arrive in Buenos Aires. Unknown to them, Maximilian and Paquette—miraculously resurrected from the massacre in Westphalia, and now both disguised as slave girls—arrive there at the same time. The local Governor has fallen in love with Maximilian but, discovering his error, redirects his attention toward Cunegonde. When she coyly insists on marriage, he turns his proposition into a proposal (duet: *Poets have said love is undying, my love).* Meanwhile, a Jesuit father has taken a fancy to Maximilian and leads "her" away, while the Old Lady convinces Candide that he is still trailed by the police and had better hide in the jungle. Smugly, Cunegonde and the Old Lady salute their invincible feminine attractions (duet: *We are women!).*

§ Struggling through the jungle with a half-caste guide, Cacambo, Candide encounters barbaric wonders and eventually finds a Jesuit encampment, where South America is hailed as a new Garden of Eden, a place of innocence restored. The Father and Mother Superior turn out to be Maximilian and Paquette. Candide reveals that Cunegonde too is still alive, but the reunion turns sour when he says he means to marry her: Maximilian still insists Candide is a socially unacceptable match. After inadvertently stabbing Maximilian to death, Candide again takes refuge in the jungle.

§ Three years have passed. Installed with the Governor in his palace, Cunegonde and the Old Lady are succumbing to boredom (trio: *Quiet).* Cunegonde complains that the Governor still has not made good his promise to marry her.

§ Candide and Cacambo, surviving precariously in the jungle, find a boat and follow a river to a cavern that leads them to Eldorado, the land of Pangloss' dreams. Candide tires of the ideal life there, because he misses Cunegonde and hopes to ransom her with golden sheep and jewels from Eldorado. Praising the beauty and hospitality of the place, he takes his leave *(Up a seashell mountain)*. As he and Cacambo climb the precipitous mountains surrounding Eldorado, they lose all but two of the golden sheep; Candide, afraid to risk returning to Buenos Aires, sends Cacambo with one sheep to ransom Cunegonde, whom he will meet in Venice.

§ Candide finds his way to Surinam, a Dutch colony, where he encounters Martin, a philosopher as pessimistic as Pangloss was optimistic. The human condition, Martin insists, is vicious and absurd *(Words words words)*. An unscrupulous Dutchman named Vanderdendur persuades Candide to give up his golden sheep for a ship, the *Santa Rosalia,* that will take him to Venice *(Bon voyage);* but the ship soon sinks, drowning Martin and Vanderdendur as well. Candide rescues the sheep and finds himself aboard a raft rowed by Pangloss, incredibly restored to life. Also on board are five deposed kings, who vow to reform their lives and live humbly if ever they reach land (barcarolle: *I do hereby make a motion*).

§ Arriving in Venice, the kings take to the gaming tables while Candide, still with his golden sheep, looks for Cunegonde. He finds Paquette there as the city's head demimondaine; Maximilian, again restored to life, as the corrupt chief of police; and Cunegonde and the Old Lady assisting at the casino. The Old Lady complains that her cleverness gets her nowhere, as all gambling profits go to the manager, Ragotski; he in turn complains that he loses his profits in bribes to the chief of police, who complains that some crook is blackmailing him (ensemble: *What's the use?*). Pangloss alone seems to have turned lucky, winning at roulette (ensemble: Venice Gavotte). Unmasking, Candide and Cunegonde recognize each other.

When Candide sees that his optimism and his idealization of Cunegonde have been only an illusion *(Is it this, the meaning of my life),* he retreats into morose, thoughtful silence. The group has just enough money to buy a small farm. There they endure their foibles and failings (chorus: *Life is neither good nor bad*). Candide finally breaks his silence, saying they all must put their illusions behind them, accepting themselves—and loving each other—as they are. He proposes marriage to Cunegonde (ensemble: *You've been a fool, and so have I*). When the group concludes that "We'll build our house, and chop our wood, and make our garden grow," Pangloss, the incurable optimist, again miraculously resurrected, finds this an ideal resolution.

A Quiet Place

THREE ACTS
MUSIC: Leonard Bernstein
TEXT (English): Stephen Wadsworth
WORLD PREMIERE: Houston Grand Opera, June 17, 1983
REVISED VERSION PREMIERE: Milan, La Scala, June 19, 1984

CHARACTERS

Dede, *Dinah and Sam's daughter* . . . . Soprano
Dinah, *Sam's wife* . . . . .Mezzo-Soprano
Susie, *Dinah's best friend* . . . . .Mezzo-Soprano
Mrs. Doc, wife of the family doctor . . . . .Mezzo-Soprano
François, *Dede's husband* . . . . Tenor
Old Sam . . . . Baritone
Young Sam . . . . Baritone
Junior, *Dinah and Sam's son* . . . . Baritone
Bill, *Dinah's brother* . . . . Baritone

ACT I   The action takes place in an unspecified suburban American town around the time of composition (1970s and early 1980s). With the stage in darkness, fragments of conversation are overheard, indicating that a woman (Dinah) has been killed in an automobile accident.

Dinah's older brother, Bill, and her best friend, Susie, arrive at the funeral parlor. Dinah's Analyst equivocates when Susie asks whether Dinah's death might have been partly self-willed. Doc, the family physician, confirms Bill's suspicion that Dinah had been drinking. Mrs. Doc says bluntly that Dinah drank because she was miserable. After some gossip about Dinah and Sam's children, the guests agree it was a difficult marriage (chorus: *Dinah and Sam. How did they ever stay together?*).

The couple's daughter, Dede, estranged from her father, arrives and tries to introduce her French Canadian husband, François, but Sam turns away. Dede is nervously effusive when greeted by Susie *(Have you got an hour or two?);* then she presents François, who has never met any of the family circle. When Doc tries to tell her about her mother's death, she doesn't want to hear. Sam has remained aloof from everyone—"As if he feels some guilt," Bill remarks. The guests cannot help noticing this *(Hard to say the right words);* growing uncomfortable, they would like the service to be over. Dede says that Junior, her brother, is on his way: he wanted to stop and look at the family house. Deciding not to wait for him, Bill gets the service started (Funeral Director: *This business of death, it is hard).* Doc, Mrs. Doc, and Dede read literary quotations (ensemble, Doc: *"Who can find a virtuous woman?").* The service is disrupted by the arrival of Junior, disheveled *(Hey, thanks for waiting);* adjusting to his intrusion, the others resume. The Funeral Director opens the coffin, and the guests prepare to leave (chorus: *Who are we to judge?).* When Sam is left alone with his family, he breaks his silence *(You're late. You shouldn't have come),* rambling on bitterly about the disappointments of his life, saddled with children he doesn't understand. None of them wants or knows how to approach him.

In a flashback to adolescent years, Dede, François, and Junior relive their distressing lack of contact with their fathers (trio: *Dear Daddy).*

Returning to the present, Junior slips into a psychotic episode and taunts Sam with an improvised song and striptease *(Hey, Big Daddy, you drivin' me batty).* They nearly come to blows but stop when they accidentally knock shut the coffin lid. Sam leaves, followed by the shaken Dede, followed by François. Junior makes an attempt to regain his composure and approaches his mother's coffin with tenderness.

ACT II   In the master bedroom, Sam reads Dinah's diary, which reveals her discontent. After a couple of days' entries, he looks up, reminiscing. As he does so, a dance-band Trio moves around him *(Mornin' sun kisses the windows. . . . Suburbia!).* As the Trio fades, Sam remembers Dinah and himself, in flashback, as a young couple bickering at the breakfast table *(How could you say the thing that you did . . . ?),* unsuccessful in their attempts to reconcile their respective malaise. Saying he can't go to Junior's school play because he has to win the handball tournament at his gym, Sam leaves for work.

Sam's flashback continues as he enters his office in one part of the stage and Dinah goes to her psychiatrist in another part. At work, Sam seems to deal more successfully with his life: the Trio reappears to congratulate him *(Oh, Sam, you're an angel).* In her psychiatrist's office, Dinah tells a dream in which a voice calls her to a quiet place of her own *(I was standing in a garden).* Meanwhile, Sam questions his secretary as to whether he ever made a pass at her, as Dinah has accused him of doing. Dinah ends her account of the dream with her sad awakening. On their way to lunch, Sam and Dinah accidentally meet on the street; each improvises an alibi so they will not have to have lunch together. Each on his own recalls that ten years ago, at the start of their marriage, things were different (duet: *Long ago, you were all strength and life and joy to me).* But they have never found their quiet place.

Later that night, the scene shows Sam in the master bedroom at one side, Junior's old bedroom at the other. As Sam peruses Dinah's diary, Dede enters and asks if she can help sort through her mother's things. At the same time, François enters Junior's room and tries to calm him. The two conversations progress simultaneously. Dede and Sam tentatively reach out to each other. Junior reminds François that the two of them used to be lovers, then progresses to claiming that he sexually molested Dede as a child (*But first I'd like to sing you a little song*), adding that since both children were adopted, the relationship wasn't really incestuous. Meanwhile, Dede has tried on one of Dinah's youthful dresses, reminding Sam of earlier times. Junior now declares that Sam had discovered him and Dede in bed together and went to get a gun (quartet, Sam: *My God!* Dede: *How do you like me?*); François, knowing Junior's instability, realizes he is indulging in psychotic fantasy. The sight of Dede as Dinah has reawakened Sam's kinder feelings. Junior regresses to childhood talk, trying to recall an early Christmas when there was a sense of family togetherness— but his parents fought, frightening him. Dede and Sam embrace in a rediscovery of warmth. Then she leaves Sam to his diary reading, and François, having given Junior a sedative, leaves his room.

Meeting Dede on the landing, François turns to her for stability (duet: *There is so much. Too much*). She suggests that they clear Dinah's overgrown garden the next day, restoring her "quiet place." As they leave the landing, Sam goes to Junior's room and thinks of kissing his sleeping son but cannot. (Chorale— chorus: *The path of truth is plain and safe*). The Trio returns and moves around Sam, lost in his memories (*trio: Skid a lit day*). As a young man, he appears in the gym, full of self-confidence (*There's a law about men*): in this fantasy, he used to see himself as a winner.

The mood of his recollected scene changes when Dinah comes out of the movie theater where, out of boredom, she has gone to see *Trouble in Tahiti* (*What a terrible, awful movie!*). She softens somewhat in repeating the song "Island Magic" from the film, a tune picked up by the Trio. Young Sam returns home from work, as disgruntled as Dinah (*There's a law that a man has to pay for what he gets*). To ironic commentary by the Trio (*Evenin' shadows*), he tries to talk with Dinah about their relationship, but soon both realize the futility and decide to go to a movie—*Trouble in Tahiti.*

After this flashback, Sam returns to Junior's room and kisses him as he lies sleeping.

ACT III Early the next day, Dede has been clearing Dinah's garden (*Morning! Good morning*). Junior arrives with a breakfast tray. They reenact childhood games and their parents' mealtime arguments. When François joins them, they reenact Dede's visit to Canada when she first met him (trio: *Happy twenty-first birthday*). Sam arrives and, seeing them play tag, joins the game, in the course of which he ends up embracing François and welcoming him to the family. Accompanied by Dinah's voice in the background, Sam reads aloud from her diary, ending with the lines: "We're only who we are, so who will accept and live . . . ?" The three young people discuss their plan to stay on for a few more days; Sam is receptive, suggesting they make the garden a joint project. Soon, however, they are arguing about who will sleep in which room. Junior throws the diary up in the air, and as the pages fall, each person gathers some of them. Regressively, Junior tries to find a place for himself in his family *(You see, Daddy, that death does bring some relief)*. Sam signals the reconciliation by saying, "The door is open," then embraces Junior. Taking François' hand, Dede approaches them and takes her father's hand also as the chorus adds "Amen."

Benjamin Britten
1913–76

*T*he premiere of *Peter Grimes* in London in June 1945 marked the emergence of Benjamin Britten as an opera composer. It also marked a turning point for English opera, which had yet to fulfill the promise held forth by Henry Purcell two and a half centuries earlier. During the early 1940s, Britten had manifested his ability as an instrumental writer, emerging as the most talented English composer of his generation. That he would prove also to be one of the major opera composers of the twentieth century came as a surprise, not least to himself.

In later years, when it was pointed out that all his operas were quite different, Britten replied that he hoped they were. He explored not only different subject matter but different genres, delving into children's opera, television opera, and a type he called "parables for church performance." Utterly professional in technique, he resembled Richard Strauss in being able to write down any sound he wanted to hear. To Aaron Copland he observed that the most important qualification for an opera composer is the ability to write whatever sort of music the stage situation may require. Yet for all the variety of his work, there is a point of view and thematic concern that remain constant. A conscientious objector during World War II, Britten was preoccupied with the struggle of good against evil in human nature. Recognizing the relative weakness of good—its vulnerability, its inability to defend itself—he sympathized with those he saw as victims. Furthermore, as a pacifist and a homosexual, he knew the meaning of social disapproval and the plight of the outsider.

With the insight and breadth of vision given to him as an artist, however, Britten was able to avoid limiting his concerns to the subjective and local. His operas convey a classical sense of the human condition. In *The Rape of Lucretia,* the subject is purity abused and violated. In *Gloriana,* his only venture into historical drama, he dealt with the conflict of love and ambition, and with the burden of power. *A Midsummer Night's Dream* conveys the fanciful nature of illusion, the ease with which misunderstanding can turn a playful situation serious. His last opera, *Death in Venice,* deals with the quandary of a successful artist whose secure hold on life disintegrates when he falls prey to an involuntary infatuation.

The broader theme of *Death in Venice* is that of the fatal pull between the Dionysian and the Apollonian—what happens when the force of instinct takes over from the rational, controlled intellect. Aschenbach in *Death in Venice* cannot survive this calamity, yet in his dying vision he clings to the Apollonian ideal, an image not only of art but of spiritual hope. One thinks of Britten in the same way. He was at his best portraying inhibited characters. Never comfortable with raw emotion, Britten could deal with it only through composure—that is, through composition. Polarity between the forces at work within his imagination is what keeps his music alive, interesting, and universally relevant.

THE RAPE OF LUCRETIA

TWO ACTS
MUSIC: Benjamin Britten
TEXT (English): Ronald Duncan, based on André Obey's play *Le Viol de Lucrèce*
WORLD PREMIERE: Glyndebourne Festival, July 12, 1946
U.S. PREMIERE: Chicago, Shubert Theater, June 1, 1947

CHARACTERS

Female Chorus . . . . Soprano
Lucia, *Lucretia's maid* . . . . Soprano
Lucretia, *wife of Collatinus* . . . . Mezzo-Soprano
Bianca, *Lucretia's old nurse* . . . . Mezzo-Soprano
Male Chorus . . . . Tenor
Tarquinius, *an Etruscan prince* . . . . Baritone
Junius, *a Roman general* . . . . Baritone
Collatinus, *a Roman general* . . . . Bass

A mixture of history and legend surrounds the Etruscan family of the Tarquins. At the end of the forty-four-year reign of Servius Tullius, he was murdered and his throne taken by his son-in-law Lucius Tarquinius Superbus (Tarquin the Proud). The son of this Tarquin was Sextus Tarquinius, whose rape of the virtuous noblewoman Lucretia triggered a rebellion that cost him his throne in 510 B.C., after which his relatives Tarquinius Collatinus and Lucius Junius Brutus (Lucretia's brother) became consuls. The opera has Collatinus and his wife, Lucretia, domiciled in Rome rather than in the countryside at Collatio, where they actually lived.

ACT I   The Male and Female Chorus (soloists) introduce the opera in dialogue by describing Sextus Tarquinius' arrogant, ruthless ways. They speak as historians, from the viewpoint of a later, Christian epoch. Tarquinius is seen drinking with his officers, including Junius and Collatinus, at their military encampment outside Rome. The night before, some of the officers visited the city unannounced to see if their wives were faithful; only Collatinus' wife, Lucretia, was found at home. Tarquinius and Junius argue and scuffle, but Collatinus separates them. After a toast to Lucretia, Junius complains that her virtue has made him look like a fool *(Lucretia! I'm sick of that name)*. Tarquinius, however, considers her a challenge.

Interlude: The Male Chorus describes Tarquinius' ride to Rome to test Lucretia's virtue.

§ At Collatinus' home, Lucretia is spinning with Lucia and Bianca, women of her household. She sorely misses her husband *(How cruel men are to teach us love)*. The hour growing late, all prepare to go to bed, but when a loud knocking is heard, the women have no choice but to accommodate Tarquinius' request for hospitality.

ACT II   The two Choruses discuss the Etruscans' success in ruling Rome, for which they were hated by the native Romans. As Lucretia lies asleep, Tarquinius approaches stealthily, savoring his conquest *(Within this frail crucible of light)*. He wakes her with a kiss, and when she realizes his intentions, she protests fervently, but he forces her to submit.

Interlude: The two Choruses decry the inability of virtue to defend itself against the strength of sin, alluding to Christ's suffering on the Cross for the sins of mankind.

As the new summer day begins, Lucia and Bianca cheerfully gather flowers. They remark on having heard Tarquinius leave early that morning. Lucretia emerges from her room, unsuccessful at concealing her distraught condition. She tells Lucia to send a messenger to Collatinus, asking him to return home at once *(Give him this orchid)*, then withdraws to her room. But Collatinus, warned by Junius that trouble might be afoot, has already come back, accompanied by Junius. Lucretia appears, wearing mourning, and tells how she was violated *(Then turn away, for I must tell)*. She stabs herself and dies in Collatinus' arms, crying, "Now I'll be forever chaste, with only death to ravish me." Junius declares this an outrage that will bring Etruscan rule to its end. The bystanders kneel by Lucretia's body.

Epilogue: The two Choruses again weigh the meaning of sin, saying it is not all there is in the world, since Christ died to redeem mankind.

GLORIANA

THREE ACTS
MUSIC: Benjamin Britten
TEXT (English): William Plomer, after Lytton Strachey's *Elizabeth and Essex*
WORLD PREMIERE: London, Covent Garden, June 8, 1953
U.S. PREMIERE (concert performance): Cincinnati, Music Hall, May 8, 1956
U.S. STAGE PREMIERE: New York, Metropolitan Opera (English National Opera), June 23, 1984

CHARACTERS

Queen Elizabeth I	Soprano
Penelope, Lady Rich, *Essex's sister*	Soprano
Frances, *Countess of Essex*	Mezzo-Soprano
Robert Devereux, *Earl of Essex*	Tenor
Charles Blount, Lord Mountjoy	Baritone
Sir Robert Cecil, *secretary of the council*	Baritone
Henry Cuffe, *a satellite of Essex*	Baritone
City Crier	Baritone
Sir Walter Raleigh, *captain of the guard*	Bass
Ballad Singer	Bass

ACT I Latter years of the reign of Queen Elizabeth I (c. 1600–03). During a jousting tournament, the Earl of Essex (Robert Devereux) is watching in irritation as Mountjoy, a rival for the queen's attention, wins a match, amid plaudits from the crowd. Essex takes his first opportunity to pick a fight with Mountjoy, who wounds him slightly on the arm as the queen appears, demanding to know what happened *(The Earl of Essex hangs his head)*. Arbitrating, she asks the opinion of Sir Walter Raleigh, who dismisses the hotheaded quarrel *(Both lords are younglings).* Elizabeth tells them to fight her enemies, not each other (ensemble: *Anger would be too strong).*

§ In a private apartment at Nonesuch Palace, the queen's residence, Elizabeth and Lord Cecil remark on the rashness of Essex. Declaring herself "wedded to the realm," Elizabeth says she wants no husband. Cecil counsels her to rule firmly *(O Princess, whom your people love),* and warns that Spain is threatening again to send an armada against England. When Essex pays a call on his cousin, the queen, Cecil withdraws. Essex offers a cheerful lute song *(Quick music's best),* then a more pensive one *(Happy were he),* and a certain intimacy of affection becomes apparent between them (duet: *O heretofore, though ringed with foes),* but Elizabeth stops him from a more overt declaration. Seeing Raleigh's shadow in an adjoining room, Essex complains that both Raleigh and Cecil oppose his claim to subdue and govern rebellious Ireland. Putting off a decision on this, she sends him away and resolves again to give priority to her duties as sovereign *(On rivalries 'tis safe for kings),* praying for God's guidance.

ACT II   At the Guildhall in Norwich, the queen accepts the homage of the local citizenry. As an allegorical masque is performed and danced, Essex, in the royal retinue, chafes at his enforced idleness and the queen's hesitation to appoint him to conquer Ireland.

§ In the garden of Essex House in the Strand, London, Mountjoy has a rendezvous with Lady Penelope Rich, Essex's married sister, with whom he is conducting a love affair (duet: *My rare one).* When they overhear Essex complaining to Lady Essex about Raleigh's influence and the queen's reluctance to authorize the Irish campaign, they step forward and beg Essex to curb his impatience: all of them should bide their time until the aging Elizabeth dies, so they can increase their own political power.

§ Courtiers are dancing at an evening party at the Palace of Whitehall in London. When the ladies withdraw to change clothes, Lady Essex, whose dress outshone the queen's, takes care to reappear in something plain. Elizabeth, however, shows her anger by entering in Lady Essex's fancy gown, which fits her badly; she humiliates Lady Essex for having the audacity to outdress the queen. Elizabeth then leaves to change back into her own clothes while Essex fumes at the insult, but when she returns, it is to inform him that she has decided to make him Lord Deputy in Ireland, where he is to defeat the rebel leader Tyrone. Raleigh and Cecil privately hope he has overreached himself and is riding for a fall, but the court is enthusiastic (chorus: *Victor of Cadiz, overcome Tyrone!)* as Elizabeth invites Essex to lead her in a final dance.

ACT III   An anteroom to the queen's dressing room at Nonesuch, early morning. Maids-of-honor discuss news from Ireland: after a summer of inconclusive skirmishing, matters are stalemated in a truce. Unexpected and unannounced,

Essex bursts in, saying he must see the queen at once. Though she is not yet fully dressed or made up, she dismisses her retainers, then accuses Essex of failing in his mission. He protests that enemies at home are a greater threat to both of them (duet: *O, put back the clock*). Sadly she realizes that advancing age has extinguished the romantic hopes she once had for their relationship. Dismissing him, she resumes her toilette. Presently, Cecil appears, warning that Ireland may form an alliance with France or Spain; Essex, furthermore, seems rebellious. Convinced now that Essex is a liability, Elizabeth declares he must be held in check and closely watched: "It is I who have to rule."

§ In a London street, older citizens and a blind Ballad Singer comment on the brashness of youths who rally to the cause of Essex, who is now openly defiant of Cecil and Raleigh, the queen's advisers, and hopes to supplant them. A City Crier reads a proclamation declaring Essex guilty of treason.

§ At Whitehall, Cecil warns his fellow councilors that Elizabeth may pardon Essex, whom they have condemned to death as a traitor. When the monarch enters, they tell her their unanimous verdict. Saying she will not yet sign his death warrant, she dismisses them and struggles with her conflicting emotions *(I grieve, yet dare not show my discontent)*. Raleigh interrupts her to usher in Mountjoy with Essex's wife and sister, who beg the queen to be merciful. Enraged by the boldness of Lady Rich's pleas, Elizabeth signs the warrant, and Raleigh leaves with it, followed by the others. Left alone, the queen enters a reverie in which figures of the court and of the royal succession appear and disappear. She addresses the audience *(I have ever used to set the last Judgement Day before mine eyes)* and, reconciled to her own death, gradually fades from view.

A MIDSUMMER NIGHT'S DREAM

THREE ACTS
MUSIC: Benjamin Britten
TEXT (English): the composer and Peter Pears, adapted from Shakespeare's play
WORLD PREMIERE: Aldeburgh Festival, June 11, 1960
U.S. PREMIERE: San Francisco Opera, October 10, 1961

CHARACTERS

Tytania, *Queen of the Fairies* . . . . Soprano
Helena, *in love with Demetrius*. . . . . Soprano

Hermia, *in love with Lysander* . . . . .Mezzo-Soprano
Hippolyta, *betrothed to Theseus* . . . . Contralto
Cobweb ⎫
Peaseblossom ⎬ *fairies* . . . .
Mustardseed ⎪
Moth ⎭
      ⎧Treble
      ⎪Treble
      ⎨Treble
      ⎩Treble
Oberon, *King of the Fairies* . . . . .Countertenor
Lysander, *in love with Hermia* . . . . Tenor
Flute, *a bellows-maker* . . . . Tenor
Snout, *a tinker* . . . . Tenor
Demetrius, *in love with Hermia* . . . . Baritone
Starveling, *a tailor* . . . . Baritone
Bottom, *a weaver* . . . . Bass-Baritone
Theseus, *Duke of Athens* . . . . Bass
Quince, *a carpenter* . . . . Bass
Snug, *a joiner* . . . . Bass
Puck . . . . Speaking Role

ACT I   In a wood in mythological Athens, Fairies enter, followed by Puck, then by Oberon and Tytania, who are in the midst of a marital falling-out. Oberon wants to keep an Indian boy as his page, but Tytania refuses to give the boy up and leaves angrily with her Fairy troupe. To torment her, Oberon tells Puck to fetch a rare flower whose juice, placed on a person's eyelids, cause instant infatuation with the first creature the person sees on awakening. When Puck has left on this errand, Oberon withdraws as two lovers, Lysander and Hermia, appear, bemoaning the fact that Hermia is bound by her father's wish (and therefore by Athenian law) to marry a certain Demetrius (duet: *I swear to thee*). No sooner have they wandered off than Demetrius himself comes in, pursued by Helena, who loves him unrequited; he tells her, none too politely, to stop bothering him. As they part, Oberon returns, declaring to himself that he will reverse these lovers' fixations. When Puck brings the flower, Oberon plans to place its drops on the eyelids of the sleeping Tytania (*I know a bank where the wild thyme blows*); he tells Puck to do the same to Demetrius, making sure that when Demetrius wakes it will be to the sight of Helena. Both depart on their missions. Into the wood steal six rustic artisans to prepare the play of Pyramus and Thisbe, directed by the carpenter Peter Quince, who has some trouble assigning roles to his doubtful colleagues. At length they agree on the casting and leave, planning to rehearse that evening. Lysander and Hermia reappear and lie down to sleep, but Puck, wandering in search of the Athenian youth described by Oberon, mistakes Lysander for Demetrius and places the drops on *his* eyelids (*Through the forest I have gone*).

No sooner has Puck left than Demetrius runs past, still trying to shake the attentions of Helena, who succumbs to fatigue and lies down. Seeing Lysander nearby, she wakes him, only to have him declare his love for her. She leaves in distress, but Lysander takes off after her, whereupon Hermia stirs alone from a nightmare *(Lysander, help me, what a dream was here)*. Distraught to find her lover gone, she starts off in search of him. Tytania now returns with her entourage (Fairies: *You spotted snakes*), who leave her alone to sleep. Oberon steals in and places the magic drops on her eyelids *(What thou seest when thou dost wake)*.

ACT II With Tytania still sleeping, the rustics return for their rehearsal. After discussing problems in the script, they are spied by Puck as they start to practice. Playing the part of a horse, Bottom the weaver puts on a donkey's-head mask; as his mates tease him by leaving him alone, he launches into a song to show he is not afraid *(The woosell cock, so black of hue)*. This wakes Tytania, who is immediately smitten with him and summons her Fairies to wait on him. Flattered by the attention, he plays along, at length falling asleep in Tytania's arms as darkness falls. Oberon and Puck look in, pleased at the success of their prank, but when Demetrius appears, following Hermia to protest innocence of her accusation that he has killed his rival, Lysander, Oberon and Puck realize the other drops went to the wrong Athenian youth. As Hermia storms out, Demetrius collapses in sleep, whereupon Oberon places drops on his lids—better late than never.

Oberon and Puck then stand aside to witness the infatuation of Lysander for Helena, who is still trying to escape him. Demetrius, waking, is suddenly smitten with her *(O Helen, goddess, nymph)*. Helena, feeling herself the victim of some sort of conspiracy, turns to Hermia—who has just arrived in search of Lysander—and accuses her of being part of it *(Injurious Hermia, most ungrateful maid)*. There follows a wild exchange among the four lovers, all misunderstanding each other and what has happened (ensemble: *What, can you do me greater harm than hate?*). Both women persist in their love for their respective men, who are now at cross purposes because of the potion. As they disperse, Oberon turns on Puck, accusing him of having caused this confusion and ordering him to remedy it by putting the drops in Lysander's eyes one more time. Oberon vanishes, and Puck—encountering Lysander, who is trying to find Demetrius in order to fight him—pretends to be Demetrius, playing hide-and-seek with Lysander until the exhausted youth falls asleep. Puck then plays a similar trick on Demetrius, whom he has found, who also falls asleep. Soon the exhausted Helena and then Hermia return. When they too fall asleep, Fairies surround the four lovers *(On the ground, sleep sound)*.

ACT III Early next morning, as Tytania, Bottom, and the two pairs of lovers lie asleep on the ground, Oberon and Puck return. Oberon releases Tytania from her spell, and the reconciled pair dance. They disappear before the lovers rise *(We are awake!)*, convinced that the previous night's events were just a bizarre dream. After they leave, Bottom stirs *(When my cue comes, call me)* and wanders off just before his colleagues arrive, glumly searching for him. When he comes back to find them, they make ready to take their play to the palace of Duke Theseus.

§ At the palace, Theseus is preparing to wed Hippolyta. The lovers appear before him, explaining as best they can the adventures of the night before. Lysander admits he and Hermia hoped to escape Athens and its law so they could marry; Demetrius admits he pursued them in anger, followed by the faithful Helena, because he was engaged to Hermia and wanted her for himself. Theseus, seeing them sorted out properly, says he will overrule Hermia's father and unite the lovers. Now the rustics offer their play *(If we offend, it is with our good will)*. After Quince pronounces the prologue *(Gentles, perhaps you wonder at this show)*, Snout the tinker says he will represent the wall through which Pyramus (Bottom) and Thisbe (Flute the bellows-maker) exchange their doomed vows, accompanied by comments from the audience. Snug the joiner plays a Lion; Starveling the tailor, carrying a lantern, represents the Moon. The play soon comes to its Romeo-and-Juliet ending, and when the guests leave—" 'Tis almost fairy time"—they are followed by the Fairies *(Now the hungry lion roars)*, Puck, Oberon, and Tytania, to hold sway for the rest of the night (ensemble: *Now until the break of day*). As they dance off, Puck is left alone to deliver a brief epilogue *(If we shadows have offended, / Think but this [and all is mended] / That you have but slumber'd here, / While these visions did appear)*.

DEATH IN VENICE

TWO ACTS
MUSIC Benjamin Britten
TEST (English): Myfanwy Piper, based on Thomas Mann's novella
WORLD PREMIERE: Aldeburgh Festival, June 16, 1973
U.S. PREMIERE: New York, Metropolitan Opera, October 18, 1974

CHARACTERS

The Voice of Apollo .Countertenor
Gustav von Aschenbach, *a novelist* . . . . Tenor
The Traveller, *who also appears as:* . . . . Bass-Baritone
   The Elderly Fop
   The Old Gondolier
   The Hotel Manager
   The Hotel Barber
   The Leader of the Players

The Voice of Dionysus
Tadzio, *a Polish adolescent* . . . . .Dance Role
The Polish Mother, *Tadzio's mother* . . . . .Dance Role
Jaschiu, *Tadzio's friend*. . . . . .Dance Role

Thomas Mann's short story *Tod in Venedig* was written in 1911 and takes place at that time, though opera productions may choose a later period.

ACT I *Munich.* The distinguished novelist Gustav von Aschenbach, at the threshold of old age, realizes he has run out of inspiration *(My mind beats on, and no words come).* Passing the entrance to a cemetery, he sees a strange Traveller, who will reappear to him as a tempter under various guises. The Traveller speaks of alluring foreign places *(Marvels unfold!).* Though sudden impulse is alien to him, Aschenbach decides he needs a trip south.

§ (On the boat to Venice) A group of Youths and an Elderly Fop, another version of the tempter figure, look forward to amorous adventures *(We'll meet in the Piazza).* Aschenbach is repelled.

Overture: Venice.

§ (The journey to the Lido) Aschenbach intends to take a gondola to the Riva degli Schiavoni, but he falls into the hands of an Old Gondolier—another incarnation of the tempter, this one with overtones of Charon, boatman of the River Styx—who takes him to the Lido instead. En route, Aschenbach throws coins to a boatload of boys and girls. When he reaches the Lido, he turns to pay but finds the Gondolier has disappeared. The hotel personnel explain: he was "A man without a license." Aschenbach notes the boat's resemblance to a coffin *(Mysterious gondola).*

§ *The first evening at the hotel.* He is greeted by the Hotel Manager, another version of the tempter. Alone in his room, Aschenbach reflects on the fundamentals of his art—"simplicity, beauty, form" *(So I am led back to Venice once again).* He watches a multinational group of tourist families prepare for supper in the hotel restaurant. Of particular notice is a Polish family, whose adolescent son, Tadzio, strikes Aschenbach as an embodiment of classical grace *(Surely the soul of Greece).* Aschenbach admits, "There is indeed in every artist's nature a wanton and treacherous proneness to side with beauty."

§ *On the beach.* Aschenbach feels the sirocco blowing in, overcoming him with an unhealthy torpor that prevents work; perhaps he should leave Venice. But his interest is revived by the Polish youth, who leads some children's games. Aschenbach figures out that "Tadzio" is a nickname for Tadeusz. He goes on to reflect that since the death of his wife and marriage of his only child, he has "grown reserved, self-sufficient . . . dependent not upon human relationships but upon work." His point of view starts to change: "How much better to live not words but beauty—to exist in it, and of it."

§ *The foiled departure.* He crosses by gondola to the main part of Venice, where his sense of oppression returns, reinforced by the bother of peddlers and beggars *(Enough, I must leave).* He goes back to his hotel and starts to check out but notices the wind has changed, and he feels regret at seeing the last of Tadzio, who passes him in the hall. Meanwhile, the Porter has dispatched Aschenbach's luggage on the wrong train; now he must wait until it can be retrieved. He senses himself vacillating *(I am become like one of my early heroes).* From his room he sees Tadzio playing on the beach and realizes that is why he is reluctant to leave.

§ *The Games of Apollo.* On the beach, Aschenbach watches the other Hotel Guests rejoice in the improved weather (chorus: *Beneath a dazzling sky).* The Voice of Apollo, which is also the voice of Aschenbach's other tempters, signals the start of the games *(He who loves beauty worships me).* Tadzio enacts the role of Apollo driving his sun chariot, then dances as the onlookers note, "Beauty is the only form of spirit that our eyes can see." The youths compete in a variety of athletic events—running, jumping, discus and javelin throwing, wrestling. As Tadzio wins every event, Aschenbach is moved to write again *(The boy, Tadzio, shall inspire me),* propelled by the insight that "When the mind bows low before beauty. . . . Then Eros is the word." He would like to speak to Tadzio and befriend him, but when he cannot bring himself to do so, he realizes that what he feels toward the boy is love.

ACT II   Some time later, holding a book, Aschenbach reflects on his failed attempt to sublimate his love for Tadzio into the beauty of the written word *(So, it has come to this).* "What I wrote was good. . . . But when it was done, I felt degraded—as if I had taken part in an orgy." Deciding simply to strike up a conversation with the boy—to reduce his idealization to a realistic basis— he had found himself again unable. "Who really understands the workings of the creative mind?"

§ *The Hotel Barber's shop, I.* More time has passed. Aschenbach is seated while the Hotel Barber, another incarnation of his tempter, shaves and trims him, chattering about the weather and the Hotel Guests *(Guardate, Signore!).* He mentions "the sickness" but, when Aschenbach questions him, dismisses it as nothing.

§ *The pursuit.* Crossing from the Lido to Venice, Aschenbach catches a whiff of disinfectant over the canal. Disembarking, he hears people reading from a public health notice: precautions should be taken against infection. From a German newspaper *(Let me see what my countrymen say)* he learns that while Venetian officials have denied rumors of cholera, it is advisable for German citizens to return home. Aschenbach ignores this and starts watching the Polish family closely to be sure they don't leave. His pursuit, noticed by Tadzio's Mother, becomes obsessive as he follows them to St. Mark's Cathedral, then in a gondola *(Ah, Tadzio, Eros, charmer)*. Back in his room, he tries to compose himself *(Gustav von Aschenbach, what is this path you have taken?)*, but rationalizes that for the heroes of classical Greece, "It was no shame . . . to be enthralled, rather . . . it brought them honor."

§ *The Strolling Players.* On the terrace after dinner, the Hotel Guests watch a small band of singers and acrobats *(The players are here)*. After a couple of songs, the Leader of the Players (another tempter figure) passes the hat and is questioned by Aschenbach about the rumors of a plague in Venice. The Leader scoffs at the idea *(Ha! That's a good one)*, then leads his troupe in a laughing song that seems to ridicule the audience. Aschenbach notes that he and Tadzio are the only ones not joining in the vulgar laughter.

§ *The travel bureau.* An English Clerk is confronted with a crowd of tourists who want to leave. Unable to cope with them all, he announces the office is closed. Aschenbach approaches him about the plague rumors, which the Clerk at first denies but then confirms in considerable detail *(In these last years, Asiatic cholera has spread)*: the city hospital is full, public morality is in decline, and a quarantine is likely.

§ *The Lady of the Pearls.* Aschenbach decides to warn Tadzio's Mother to escape with her family. When she draws near, however, he cannot and turns into his room *(So—I didn't speak! Once again I have failed to make everything decent and above board)*.

§ *The dream.* Aschenbach dreams of a dialogue between Apollo and Dionysus. Apollo speaks of reason, beauty, and form, Dionysus of giving in to instinct and impulse. Apollo will not stay to watch Dionysus' followers at their revels. Waking suddenly, Aschenbach exclaims that he has fallen from his ideals into a Dionysian state: "Let the Gods do what they will with me."

§ *The empty beach.* From a beach chair, Aschenbach watches Tadzio and a few friends, the only others there, play and run off.

§ *The Hotel Barber's shop, II.* The Barber touches up Aschenbach's graying hair and applies makeup to give him a more youthful appearance—like that of the Elderly Fop in Act I *(Yes! a very wise decision)*.

§ *The last visit to Venice.* With feigned cheerfulness, Aschenbach sets out by gondola for Venice, where he encounters the Polish family; for the first time, Tadzio shows recognition toward him. Aschenbach buys strawberries, only to find that like himself they are soft, musty, and overripe. Tired and ill, he sits down and reflects on Socrates' words: "Does beauty lead to wisdom, Phaedrus?

Yes, but through the senses. . . . And senses lead to passion. . . . And passion to the abyss."

§ *The departure.* The Hotel Manager worries about business as the Porter notes how many are leaving. When Aschenbach comes in and sees baggage in the lobby, he learns that the Polish family is about to go.

§ He walks dejectedly to the beach, where Tadzio and some other children are playing again. Jaschiu, another youth (Dionysus), gets the better of Tadzio (Apollo) for the first time and wrestles him to the ground. The feverish Aschenbach tries to intervene but is too weak to rise. Jaschiu lets go of Tadzio, who walks out to sea. Distant voices, then Aschenbach himself, call Tadzio's name. When Tadzio beckons to Aschenbach to follow him, Aschenbach slumps dead in his chair.

FERRUCCIO BUSONI
1866–1924

*B*usoni, a connoisseur's composer, is one of the most fascinating musical figures of his era. Like Wolf-Ferrari, he was of double nationality, having one German and one Italian parent. Drawn to the culture of both countries, he saw no need to make a choice. A cosmopolitan and an intellectual, he was also an impassioned pianist and pursued a career on the concert stage, meanwhile teaching and influencing a generation of pianists and composers, among them Jean Sibelius. Some of his keyboard transcriptions were written for his own use as a pianist, but his original compositions—unlike those of other virtuosos, such as Rachmaninoff—were not designed to further his public persona as a performer. Busoni wrote for himself, but only for his private self.

His aim in opera was to create a psychological atmosphere and deal with ideas rather than conventional dramatic action. His heart was not on his sleeve: it was in his head. Thus he stood at an opposite pole from the demonstrative verismo of his Italian contemporaries, and equally far from the overwrought expressionism of the Germans. His early opera *Der Brautwahl* was based on one of E. T. A. Hoffmann's fantastic tales. When World War I engulfed Europe, Busoni felt his heritage being threatened and divided. His short operas *Arlecchino* and *Turandot* reflect the irony and pain of this situation, though they are flecked with the fanciful light of commedia dell'arte. Both works were produced in 1917 in neutral Zurich, as Hindemith's *Mathis der Maler* would be twenty years later.

Busoni labored long and intermittently on his chef d'oeuvre, *Doktor Faust,* in which he summed up his artistic credo. Though his style threatens to be erudite and dry, drawing on the whole historic reservoir of European musical culture, he wrote knowingly for the voice and possessed a feeling for the stage. In these respects too his *Doktor Faust* is akin to *Mathis der Maler*. Both are dense, serious works, requiring and rewarding close attention. Both treat the nature and dilemma of creativity. Busoni's Faust, unlike Hindemith's Mathis, is not an artist; but he stands for the artist. He exemplifies curiosity, ego, audacity, individualism, and unconventionality. He longs to find meaning in experience, and he sees transcendent symbolism in things and events.

Busoni's *Turandot* is quite different from Puccini's subsequent version, the latter being largely romanticized via Schiller's adaptation of the Gozzi "fable." Puccini's work is lush, Busoni's lean. In common with Puccini's valedictory, however, *Doktor Faust* was left unfinished at the composer's death. To Busoni's pupil Philipp Jarnach fell the task of rounding out *Doktor Faust* with other Busoni music. Antony Beaumont in 1985 introduced a new version. Even if completed by Busoni, though, *Doktor Faust* would have left a question mark: such is the nature of this singular, searching work, a thinking man's opera.

TURANDOT

TWO ACTS
MUSIC: Ferruccio Busoni
TEXT (German): the composer, after Carlo Gozzi's play
WORLD PREMIERE: Zurich, Stadttheater, May 11, 1917
U.S. PREMIERE (concert performance): New York, Avery Fisher Hall
   (Little Orchestra Society), October 10, 1967
U.S. STAGE PREMIERE: Hartford, November 15, 1986

CHARACTERS

Turandot . . . . Soprano
The Queen Mother of Samarkand . . . . Soprano
Adelma, *Turandot's confidante* . . . . .Mezzo-Soprano
Kalaf, *a young, unknown prince* . . . . Tenor
Truffaldino, *chief eunuch* . . . . Tenor
Barak, *Kalaf's servant* . . . . Baritone
Emperor Altoum, *Turandot's father* . . . . Bass
Tartaglia ⎫ *Altoum's ministers* . . . . ⎧Bass
Pantalone⎭   ⎩Bass

ACT I China, legendary antiquity. At one of the gates of Peking, the foreign Prince Kalaf, whose wanderings have brought him here, greets the city *(Peking! Stadt der Wunder!)*. Unexpectedly he meets an old man, Barak, a former retainer of his, who now lives near the city gate in a humble cottage. When Kalaf says he means to see the emperor, Barak warns him that the court is under a pall cast by Princess Turandot, who is beautiful and intelligent but an implacable man-hater. Her spurned suitors, unable to answer her three riddles, have been beheaded, and their heads are arrayed on pikes along the city walls. Even now the Prince of Samarkand, the latest to fail, is on his way to the executioner. The doomed prince's mother appears with her retinue, bemoaning her son's fate and cursing Turandot *(O! Verweilt!)*. When she hurls into the gutter Turandot's portrait, which had so beguiled her son, Kalaf retrieves it and is himself smitten by its beauty, even though the freshly severed head of the Prince of Samarkand is borne past. Kalaf angrily vows to avenge the slain suitors and rushes through the gates, evading the guards, who sound an alarm and seize Barak.

§ In the palace throne room, Truffaldino, the chief eunuch, directs slaves in positioning furniture for the emperor's arrival *(Rechts zunächst der grosse Thron)*. If only these suitors were converted into eunuchs like himself, he reflects, they would not be so foolishly motivated to risk their lives. Emperor Altoum appears with his court, who hail him (chorus: *Segen auf sein Haupt*). His two ministers, Pantalone and Tartaglia, comment that back home in Italy everyone loves murder dramas, but here at court such matters are in poor taste. The Emperor prays to Confucius for guidance: if only a suitor could succeed in overcoming his daughter's stubbornness *(Konfutse, dir hab' ich geschworen)*. Resignedly he receives Kalaf, who announces himself as a fairy-tale prince. Offered a chance to reconsider his rash quest, Kalaf says he wants only "Death or Turandot," though the ministers warn him the riddles won't be easy (quartet: *Entweiche, entweich' der Gefahr*). A march ushers in Turandot, escorted by Truffaldino. She addresses Kalaf haughtily but is privately unsettled by the strange gentleness she senses in him; the court agrees that this suitor seems different from the others (chorus: *Ja, andren gleicht dieser nicht*). Turandot's attendant Adelma recognizes Kalaf, whom she idolized as a young girl and now privately hopes to win back.

Turandot reads the riddles. First: What creeps on the earth yet flies toward heaven, fumbles in darkness yet sheds light, follows the past yet looks to the future? *(Was kriecht am Boden)*. Kalaf correctly answers: the human intellect. Second: What is unstable but persistent . . . the less it's established, the less it's defied? *(Was ist beständig)*. Again Kalaf has the answer: custom. Third: What has endured through the ages and bursts forth in ever more glorious bloom? *(Was ist, das aus den Wurzeln der Zeiten)*. To throw him into confusion, Turandot removes her veil, dazzling him with her beauty; but Kalaf again is able to reply correctly: art. General rejoicing breaks out, but Turandot, having lost face, impulsively tries to stab herself; the dagger is snatched away from her. Kalaf, not wanting to force her against her will, generously offers to release her and leave if she can answer his own riddle: What is the family and name of the foreign prince? *(Wes Stamms und Namens ist der fremde Prinz)*.

ACT II Turandot is entertained in her apartments by dancers and singers as dawn approaches. Sending them away, she wonders what her true feelings are toward the prince: though love and hate contend within her, she is still inclined to defer to her pride *(Dass ich ihn liebe)*. Truffaldino comes with his report: he stole into Kalaf's room, administered a potion—and heard the young man utter only "Death or Turandot" *(Ich schlich geschickt)*. Annoyed at his failure to get the name, Turandot dismisses him. Her next visitor is the emperor. As his ministers root for him on the other side of the door, he tries to coax Turandot with news that the foreign prince is really a fine catch, of noble birth; but this doesn't work, and he leaves. Adelma now admits to Turandot that *she* knows the stranger's name (duet: *Adelma, meine Freundin)*: if Turandot will free her from servitude, she will reveal it. Turandot agrees, and Adelma whispers Kalaf's name in her ear. (Intermezzo.)

§ In the throne room, Turandot makes her entrance before the emperor to the strains of funeral music, meant to denote her downfall. But she does know Kalaf's name and tells it to him *(Noch nicht . . . Die Rache mir süsser zu gestalten)*. Distressed, he turns to leave, but she asks him to stay: he has softened her soul and awakened her heart. To the delight of all except Adelma and Truffaldino, the couple embraces, considering another riddle: What is the power that unites all humanity? *(Was ist's, das alle Menschen bindet)*. The answer is love. A Buddha statue is revealed, before which Turandot and Kalaf are wed.

DOKTOR FAUST

SIX SCENES
MUSIC: Ferruccio Busoni
TEXT (German): the composer, after the 16th-century puppet-plays, and Christopher Marlowe's *Dr. Faustus*
WORLD PREMIERE: Dresden, Sächsisches Staatstheater, May 21, 1925
U.S. PREMIERE (concert performance): New York, Carnegie Hall, December 1, 1964
U.S. STAGE PREMIERE: Reno, Nev., Pioneer Theater, January 25, 1974

DOKTOR FAUST

CHARACTERS

The Duchess of Parma . . . . Soprano
Mephistopheles, *in his various disguises:* . . . . Tenor
    A Man Dressed in Black
    A Monk
    A Herald
    A Chaplain
    A Courier
    A Night Watchman
The Duke of Parma . . . . Tenor
Dr. Faust . . . . Baritone
Wagner, *his assistant* . . . . Baritone
The Girl's Brother, *a soldier.* . . . . Baritone
The Master of Ceremonies . . . . Bass
The Poet . . . . Speaking Role

In a spoken prologue, the Poet tells the audience that "Plays of unreality require the help of music"—a statement of Busoni's belief in the poetic theater and his disavowal of realism. The Poet adds that what follows is an ancient play from the puppet theater.

OVERTURE   Easter Vesper and Nascent Spring (chorus: *Pax*).

PROLOGUE I   In Wittenberg, Germany, during the Middle Ages. Faust, Rector Magnificus of the university, is at work on an experiment in his laboratory one morning as his pupil Wagner enters to say Three Students from Cracow have appeared unannounced to give Faust a book on black magic, *Clavis Astartis Magica* (The Key to Astarte's Magic). Faust reflects that power at last will be his *(Faust, nun erfüllt sich dein Augenblick!)*. They enter, dressed in black, and say the book is his because he is the master. When he asks what he must give in return, they reply mysteriously, "Later"; as to whether he will see them again, "Perhaps." They go before he can question them further. When Wagner reappears and says he saw no one enter or leave, Faust realizes the visitors were supernatural.

PROLOGUE II   At midnight that night, Faust opens the book and follows its instructions, using his belt to form a circle on the floor, into which he steps and calls Lucifer, the fallen angel. A pale light dances around the room. In reply to unseen voices, Faust declares his Will: he wishes spirits at his command. But when six flames appear, he is unimpressed by the speed at which the first five say they can move, so he dismisses them. Only when the sixth voice—that of Mephistopheles—says, "I am as swift as the thoughts of man," does Faust ask the spirit to materialize and serve him. Faust asks for all his wishes to be granted, to have all knowledge and the power of genius *(Beschaffe mir für meines Lebens Rest)*. When Faust learns that after death he must be at

Mephistopheles' service, he at first refuses, but the devil reminds him that his creditors and foes are at the door: with Faust's consent, Mephistopheles causes them to drop dead. Then, as a chorus in the distance marks Easter morning with a Credo, Faust signs the pact in blood, wondering what has become of his Will. The shock of realizing he has forfeited his soul causes him to fall in a faint. Gloating, Mephistopheles tears the contract from his hand.

INTERMEZZO   In a romanesque chapel of the minster next door to Faust's house, the Soldier—brother of Gretchen, whom Faust has seduced and abandoned—kneels, praying that he may find and punish the offender (*Du, der du nicht allein der Gott der Milde*). Mephistopheles points him out to Faust, who wants him eliminated but doesn't want to do the job himself. So Mephistopheles, in the guise of a monk, offers to hear the Soldier's confession. Instigated by Mephistopheles, a military patrol bursts in and kills the Soldier, claiming it is he who murdered their captain. This death is now to be on Faust's conscience.

SCENE I   In the Ducal Park at Parma, Italy, a wedding ceremony is under way for the Duke and Duchess of Parma. The Master of Ceremonies announces a special guest, the illustrious magician Dr. Faust. The guests watch as Faust enters with his herald (Mephistopheles) and an impressive train (chorus: *Er naht, mit ihm das Wunderbare*). The Duchess finds him immediately alluring, but the Duke senses that "Hell has sent him here." Faust changes the daylight to night so he can perform his enchantments, of which the first, at the Duchess' request, is an apparition of King Solomon and Queen Balkis; their resemblance to Faust and the Duchess is apparent. Next come Samson and Delilah, followed by John the Baptist with Salome. When an Executioner (resembling the Duke) threatens the Baptist (who resembles Faust), the Duchess cries out that the Baptist must be saved. Aside, Faust asks the Duchess to come away with him; she wants to but is hesitant. The Duke orders the show ended and announces dinner, but Mephistopheles warns Faust to flee, as the food will be poisoned. The two will leave together. The Duchess wanders back in, declaring she will follow Faust (*Er ruft mich . . . zieht mich*), and leaves. Mephistopheles, in the guise of a court chaplain, comes back in with the Duke, advising him against sending pursuers after the lovers; instead, he should marry the sister of the Duke of Ferrara, who is threatening him with war. (Orchestral interlude: Sarabande.)

SCENE II   In a tavern in Wittenberg, some students drunkenly discuss Plato and metaphysics. They ask for words of wisdom from Faust, who declares, "Nothing is proven, and nothing is provable" (*Nichts ist bewiesen*). He cites Martin Luther, whereupon the Catholic and Protestant students start to argue (double chorus: *Te Deum laudamus / Ein' feste Burg*). When their religious quarrels subside, Faust reminisces about his affair with the Duchess. Mephistopheles, in the guise of a courier, appears to say she has died and sent a gift of remembrance—the body of an infant, which he throws at Faust's feet. Mephistopheles regales the students with the tale of Faust's seduction of the Duchess *(Gemach, ihr, den Boten)*—whom, as it develops, he abandoned. To show that the case is not so serious, he turns the child's body into a bundle of straw and sets fire to it: "I turn to ashes that which is dead . . . a fairer sight shall rise to comfort you." From the flames appears a vision of Helen of Troy. The students back away, and Mephistopheles leaves. Faust apostrophizes the vision *(Traum der Jugend)* and tries to embrace her, but she eludes him. In her place three vague, dark figures appear—the Three Students from Cracow, who tell Faust to return the magic book. He says he has destroyed it. They reply that he must die upon the stroke of twelve. As they disappear, Faust with relief welcomes the end of life *(Vorbei, endlich vorbei!)*.

SCENE III   On a snow-covered street in Wittenberg, outside the church, Mephistopheles appears as the Night Watchman to announce that it is eleven o'clock *(Ihr Männer und Frauen)*. Wagner, who has succeeded Faust as Rector and now lives in Faust's former house, next door, is escorted there by sycophantic students and bids them good-night *(Je nun, der Faust war mehr von einem Phantasten)*. As they leave the street, Faust wanders in alone and looks at his old home *(Das Haus ist mir bekannt)*. Voices in the church sing of judgment and salvation, and Faust hopes to perform one last good deed that might redeem him. He approaches a beggar woman carrying a child—only to see it is the Duchess, who hands him the child and says there is still time to complete his work before midnight *(Nimm das Kind)*. She vanishes. Imagining that he still might be saved, Faust turns to enter the church, but the Soldier (from the Intermezzo) appears before him, barring his way. "If only I could pray," Faust says—but he cannot remember the words *(O beten! Wo die Worte finden?)*. By the light of the Night Watchman's lamp, Faust sees the figure of the crucified Christ change into that of Helen of Troy, signifying his damnation.

Making a circle on the ground with his belt, he steps into it with the child's body and bequeaths to it his own Will, the primal force of life: "Above the law then shall I stand, at once embracing all the ages, and unite myself with mankind forever—I, Faust, one eternal Will!" With this he dies. As the Watchman calls out the midnight hour, a naked, half-grown youth, with a flowering branch in his right hand, appears from the spot where the child's body lay. The Watchman (Mephistopheles), seeing Faust on the ground, remarks, "Has this man met with some misfortune?"

The Poet speaks again to the audience, wondering if the alchemy of art can produce true gold: "The poet's travail is his sole reward. . . . So, rising on the shoulders of the past, the soul of man shall reach his heaven at last."

ALFREDO CATALANI
1854–93

A native of Lucca, the home city of Puccini (four years his junior), Alfredo Catalani came to suffer more and more from the success of Puccini, who he felt was unfairly promoted by the publisher Ricordi. Though he died before the years of Puccini's biggest success, Catalani grew increasingly embittered, discouraged, and suspicious as failing health impaired his own career. He died at thirty-nine, not so much forgotten as neglected by the public, which preferred the timelier, harder-hitting products of the up-and-coming verismo (realism) school, notably Mascagni's *Cavalleria Rusticana* (1890) and Leoncavallo's *Pagliacci* (1892).

The movement called *scapigliatura* (literally, "dishevelment"), referring to the young "Bohemians" who embraced verismo, held some appeal for Catalani at the outset, but his own instincts and temperament were those of an intense romantic. He cared neither for the blunt, prosaic language of the verismo librettos nor for the punchy musical style, akin to popular and folk music, that propelled them. Instead, like another largely forgotten contemporary of his, Antonio Smareglia, he preferred the accents of German romanticism, following in the path of Weber and Wagner, though with a pronounced Italian accent in melodic style. Wagnerism, like verismo, represented the utmost in modernity at the time, so Catalani and Smareglia's choice cannot be called reactionary, but neither man possessed the bold individuality to carry it forward.

Catalani's fourth opera, *Edmea,* was his first to succeed and introduced him to the man who would be his most faithful champion, Arturo Toscanini. While preparing for the premiere, Catalani arranged for the nineteen-year-old cellist, who had just returned from an impromptu conducting debut in South America with a touring opera company, to sight-read *Edmea* at the piano while Catalani himself remained concealed in an adjoining room. Impressed by Toscanini's comprehension of the score, the composer stepped forward and invited him to lead the premiere at the Teatro Carignano in Turin—Toscanini's professional debut as a conductor in Italy. A loyal friendship followed, but though Toscanini did his best to interest the public in Catalani's operas and even named two of his children (Walter and Wally) after characters in them, the mood of the time was not receptive.

In the fall of 1892, the year he led the premiere of Leoncavallo's *Pagliacci*, Toscanini undertook to introduce Catalani's final opera, *La Wally*, to the composer's hometown, Lucca. It was a labor of love: a year and a half later, in the torpor of a Milan summer, he would be the only friend beside Catalani's deathbed. The composer, who had endured an enervating love affair with the wife of a painter colleague, had lost not only his health but his will to live. A victim of tuberculosis, he also felt himself done in by changing times and tastes. Even so, times and tastes do not stop changing, and *La Wally* did not die with him. It has held a modest place in the repertory, chiefly in Italy, and the earlier *Loreley* is occasionally revived as well. The mournful tone of *La Wally* captures the mood of its bleak Alpine setting, and the heroine's determined spirit is reflected in her music. Beyond even Catalani's fevered imagining, Wally's "Ebben? Ne andrò lontana" one day would achieve currency as part of a film soundtrack *(The Diva)*.

LA WALLY

FOUR ACTS
MUSIC: Alfredo Catalani
TEXT (Italian): Luigi Illica, after Wilhelmine von Hillern's *Die Geyer-Wally*
WORLD PREMIERE: Milan, La Scala, January 20, 1892
U.S. PREMIERE: New York, Metropolitan Opera, January 6, 1909

CHARACTERS

Wally . . . . Soprano
Walter, *a strolling minstrel* . . . . Soprano

ALFREDO CATALANI

Afra, *innkeeper at Sölden* . . . . .Mezzo-Soprano
Giuseppe Hagenbach, *huntsman of Sölden* . . . . Tenor
Vincenzo Gellner, *Stromminger's steward* . . . . Baritone
Stromminger, *Wally's father*. . . . . Bass
An Old Soldier. . . . . Bass

ACT I In Hochstoff, an Alpine Swiss town, sometime during the nineteenth century, the citizens are celebrating the seventieth birthday of Stromminger, a wealthy landowner. Stromminger's steward, Vincenzo Gellner, shoots down a target in honor of his boss. Stromminger remarks that some fellow in the nearby village of Sölden is supposed to be a wonderful marksman. Gellner knows who is meant: Giuseppe Hagenbach. Young Walter, a ballad singer, comes looking for Stromminger's daughter, Wally, in hopes of performing a song with her. Since she isn't around, he sings it alone—a tribute to the edelweiss, a flower that once, according to legend, was a girl who got buried in an avalanche *(Un dì, verso il Murzoll)*. The song, it turns out, was written by Wally herself.

Huntsmen are heard drawing near *(Sù, cacciator, ritorna)*; they enter the square carrying the skin of a bear shot by Hagenbach. He tells how he struggled with the bear *(Su per l'erto sentier)*, but Stromminger calls him a braggart, adding that Stromminger once bested Hagenbach's father. Enraged and insulted, Hagenbach knocks the older man down. A brawl is averted when Wally enters and upbraids Hagenbach for attacking her father. Impressed by her boldness, Hagenbach subsides, and the crowd disperses. Stromminger, left alone with Gellner, nurses his grievances, to which Gellner adds another: Wally seems to be in love with Hagenbach. Knowing that Gellner himself loves Wally, Stromminger promises him his daughter's hand and calls her from the house. Leaving, he announces that the wedding should take place within the month.

Alone with Gellner, Wally asks him to give her up. Gellner, however, protests that his feelings are too strong for that *(T'amo ben io!)*. When Stromminger comes back, she reiterates her refusal to accept a man she doesn't love. She must give in by nightfall, he replies, or his house will be closed to her. The men leave Wally alone to decide she will leave this place and go far away among the snowy mountains *(Ebben? Ne andrò lontana)*. She tells Walter and some other passing villagers. Walter says he will go with her, and they start off, singing the edelweiss song together.

ACT II A year later, in Sölden, at a fair for the feast of Corpus Christi, villagers crowd the square. An Old Soldier teases Walter about his "boss," but Walter retorts that despite his newfound interest in pretty women, he and Wally are just friends. The Old Soldier notes that since Stromminger's recent death, Wally has become an heiress and a very attractive match, but the general opinion holds that she is too independent to get involved with anyone (ensemble: *Ai giovanotti piace lo scherzar*). A local custom is a Kissing Dance, but Wally, arriving on the scene, says it wouldn't be so easy to get a kiss from her: until now, she has been kissed only by the sun and the wind *(Finor non m'han baciata),* and when she does kiss someone, he will be hers. She looks meaningfully toward Hagenbach as the others file into church.

Sitting down at the Eagle Tavern with Gellner, who has avoided her since she took over the family property, Wally fires him as supervisor. He refuses the money she offers, declaring he loves her more than ever, though she repeats that she never can return his feeling (duet: *Non t'ho dimenticato!*). He upsets her by suggesting that Hagenbach may be about to marry Afra, the hostess at the tavern. Wally behaves rudely toward Afra when she reappears, throwing at her feet the purse of money refused by Gellner, but Hagenbach takes the money and gives it to the musicians to play a Ländler. With some of the young men, unknown to Wally, he lays a bet that he can get a kiss from her. Then he turns upside down an eagle feather in his hat, signifying by local custom that some promise or vow is no longer valid. Gellner notices this and warns Wally to watch out. Hagenbach invites Wally to dance. For a time, engaged in amorous talk, they seem oblivious to the others, and finally he kisses her— to general acclaim. Hagenbach snaps back to reality as the other young men remind him of his wager by dragging him off to celebrate. Wally, stunned to think she has been the victim of a mere game, is taunted by the other women. When Gellner starts to lead her away, she declares in cold fury, "I want him dead!"

ACT III   On the left, a street in Hochstoff showing the path that leads across a ravine and then up the mountain. On the right, the interior of the Stromminger house, with Wally's bedroom visible. Townspeople, including Wally and Walter, return wearily at evening from the festival at Sölden. Wally asks to be left alone in her room, where she tries to pray but cannot. Meanwhile, in the street, Gellner questions the drunken Old Soldier as to Hagenbach's whereabouts: he might be heading toward Hochstoff, though this late on so dark a night it would be unlikely. Wally sorts out her feelings, admitting to herself that she loves Hagenbach, does not want him dead, and will have to tell Gellner in the morning *(Nè mai avrò pace?).*

Hagenbach, however, does pass by, and the waiting Gellner knocks him off the footbridge into the ravine, then taps on Wally's window to tell her. She drags him outside to make him descend the ravine with her, but he is terrified and escapes. Hearing a groan from below, Wally rouses the villagers for help. Impatiently she heads alone into the ravine, reappearing with the unconscious man lashed to her body. After kissing him, Wally tells Afra to have him back—and to tell him, when he regains consciousness, that she returned the kiss he gave her.

ACT IV   Outside Wally's hut on the Murzoll mountainside, Walter begs her to come back down to the village for Christmas: snow will soon block the path. She refuses, giving the boy her pearl necklace—"my tears frozen by sorrow"—as a keepsake. He disappears down the path. As the snow sweeps around her, she sees her past life vanishing *(Eterne a me d'intorno piange la neve lacrime!)*. Walter's voice echoes in the distance with her edelweiss song. Identifying with the girl in the song, Wally imagines herself called by the "blessed maidens," but the voice outside is Hagenbach's: he has followed her there *(A te ne vengo come a un santo altar!)*. He tells how he conquered his pride and doubt to realize he truly loves her, affirming this even after she admits she ordered Gellner to kill him. Carried away by emotion, they imagine a life together at last *(Vieni, una placida vita),* but returning to reality, they see the blizzard mounting. Hagenbach scouts the path, only to call back that it has vanished under the snow. Then an avalanche rumbles, hurling Wally to the ground. Seeing that Hagenbach has been buried, Wally throws herself from the precipice formed by the snowslide, crying that she will join him in death.

EMMANUEL CHABRIER
1841–94

A leader in the movement of French Wagnerism known as Le Petit Bayreuth, Chabrier presents a paradox. On the one hand, he was an enthusiastic admirer of Wagner, with whom he shared a sense of harmonic adventure. Of Chabrier's ten operas, *Gwendoline* and the unfinished *Briséïs* (both undermined by an unskillful librettist, Catulle Mendès) show his Wagnerian bent. On the other hand, he was a thoroughly French individualist, a master of the opéra-comique style, who pulled Wagner's tail with his *Souvenirs de Munich* and Quadrille on themes from *Tristan und Isolde* for piano duet.

Though said to be largely self-taught in composition, Chabrier did study piano, violin, and theory with various teachers from about the age of ten. His father, who insisted the boy go into the legal profession, did not oppose his musical interests but simply refused to allow them as a career. At the age of twenty, Chabrier was graduated from law school and took a post in the Ministry of the Interior, composing energetically on the side. His first notable success came with an opéra comique, *L'Étoile* (1877), which had forty-eight performances at Offenbach's theater, the Bouffes Parisiens.

Three more light works followed, but in November 1880, having experienced an epiphany at his introduction to *Tristan und Isolde* in Munich, Chabrier resigned his government post and dedicated himself to a musical calling. *Gwendoline,* his first major serious opera, followed at Brussels in 1886 after he had written three more light works. Set in medieval England, *Gwendoline* uses the Wagnerian leitmotif in a free harmonic style that shows the progressive side of Chabrier's musical nature.

His crowning achievement, however, was another lighthearted comedy, *Le Roi Malgré Lui,* this time a full-length work with a rather involved, far-fetched plot. After three performances at the Opéra Comique in Paris, the theater was destroyed by fire, but the work had other productions, even in Munich and Leipzig. (Richard Wagner's widow, Cosima, little known for her sense of humor, is said to have hated it.)

Chabrier, though he must have enjoyed his gift for comedy, wanted equally to be accepted as a serious composer, and in this aim he encountered mostly frustration. His spiritual descendants—André Messager, Reynaldo Hahn, Claude Debussy, Francis Poulenc—chose instead to admire his essential Frenchness. Unlike the basically conservative Offenbach, who inspired them all, Chabrier was an adventurous, spirited soul whose freshness and originality blended with subtlety and sophistication to produce work that appealed even more to the connoisseur than to the general public. Above all, he possessed the elusive quality of wit.

LE ROI MALGRÉ LUI

(The King in Spite of Himself)

THREE ACTS

MUSIC: Emmanuel Chabrier

TEXT (French): Émile de Najac and Paul Burani, revised by Jean Richepin and the composer, after François Ancelot's comedy

WORLD PREMIERE: Paris, Opéra-Comique, May 18, 1887

U.S. PREMIERE (concert performance): Williamstown, Mass., Williams College, November 16, 1972

U.S. STAGE PREMIERE: New York, Juilliard American Opera Center, November 18, 1976 (in English)

CHARACTERS

Alexina, *Duchess of Fritelli* . . . . Soprano
Minka, *one of Count Laski's serfs.* . . . . Soprano
Count de Nangis, *a member of the King's suite* . . . . Tenor
Basile, *an innkeeper.* . . . . Tenor
Henri de Valois, *King of Poland* . . . . Baritone
Duke of Fritelli . . . . Baritone
Count Laski, *a Polish patriot* . . . . Bass

ACT I   A castle outside Cracow, 1574. Henri of Valois, Duke of Anjou, has been elected King of Poland. The day before his coronation, his homesick friends idle away their time (*À nous voir, nous gentilshommes*). The Count of Nangis, Henri's best friend, tells how he spent the past week looking around the city (*Huit jours! Mort de ma vie!*). He has recruited a motley group of soldiers (chorus: *Solides, fidèles*), who are led off for training. Nangis reveals that disgruntled Polish nobles, headed by Albert Laski, the Prince Palatine, support the Austrians rather than the French and are planning a coup. The French have named as chamberlain the Venetian-born Duke of Fritelli, not realizing he is married to Alexina, Laski's niece, and cannot be trusted. Fritelli, fussing over plans for the coronation, bursts into a mazurka describing the differences between the Poles and the French (*Le Polonais est triste et grave*). Nangis, it develops, also is involved with a local woman—Minka, a serf—but says she stays in Laski's service only to spy on the conspiracy. When Minka appears, Nangis rushes to her side (*Toi, mon enfant, c'est toi*). The idea of freedom to love is new to her (*Hélas! À l'esclavage*), but she agrees to meet Nangis that evening. Before she can tell him about the conspirators' doings, Henri wanders in, incognito, holding a letter from home (*Beau pays, pays du gai soleil*), so Nangis conceals the girl. Henri complains that as king he will be expected to marry an aging Polish princess, but his heart belongs to one Alexina Lowenska, whom he once met in Venice. Fritelli, reappearing, realizes the reference is to his own wife.

After Henri and Nangis have left, Alexina comes to tell Fritelli he must take her to a ball that her uncle, Laski, is giving that evening. The plan is to kidnap Henri and crown an Austrian archduke instead (*Ah! d'amour plus un mot*). For her safety, Fritelli hides her in his apartments. When Minka comes looking for Nangis, she meets Henri; unaware who he is, she confesses her love for Nangis (*Je l'aime de toute mon âme*) and mentions the plot. Henri, delighted at the idea of being thrown out of Poland, sends her away and calls Fritelli, whom he orders to take him, now posing as Nangis, to the plotters' ball. When the court reenters, Henri has the real Nangis arrested on a pretext, to keep him out of the way. Fritelli introduces Alexina; remembering their encounter in Venice, she and Henri recognize each other at once (trio: *Quelle surprise!*), though of course he is now called "Nangis." Minka sings outside— a cue to the real Nangis for their rendezvous. The trio ducks behind a curtain as soldiers file back in. When Fritelli lets himself be caught, Nangis slips away from the distracted guards.

ACT II   In the ballroom of Laski's palace, guests dance (Fête Polonaise) while the host gathers his conspirators, who object to Henri because he was chosen by the people rather than by themselves, the aristocracy. Henri is introduced as "Nangis," the king's former friend, now in disgrace and thirsting for revenge (ensemble: *Rien n'est aussi près de la haine*). Learning by chance that Alexina is Fritelli's wife, Henri reproaches Fritelli for not telling him; Fritelli says that love for his wife is his only reason for having pretended to conspire against the French. The two men take their conversation to another room as slave girls enter, joking with Minka about her luck in finding a noble lover (*Ah! quelle affaire*). She sings a Gypsy song (*Il est un vieux chant de Bohème*), at the end of which Nangis is heard responding outside. Before she can join him, Henri and Fritelli return. Thinking Fritelli has tricked him into an ambush, Minka tries to warn Henri, though she still doesn't know who he is; he replies that they have come to undermine the conspiracy by joining it. Fritelli locks Minka up for safekeeping, then leaves to find Laski.

Facing Alexina alone for the first time, Henri tries to explain why he left her so abruptly in Venice (barcarole duet: *Oui, je vous hais*). Fritelli brings Laski, who administers the conspirators' oath to Henri (ensemble: *Par l'Évangile et Notre-Dame*). Henri tells the others he will produce the king, and asks to be alone; then he finds Minka and persuades her to fetch Nangis (serenade, Minka: *Ah! Viens! Minka fidèle*). Conspirators return and capture Nangis, believing, despite his protests, that *he* is the king. When even Henri insists, Nangis says very well, he'll *be* the king (*Je suis le Roi!*). Improvising the role, he finally catches on to Henri's agenda: escape to France. When the conspirators decide the ruler must die (finale: *Avant une heure, il faut qu'il meure!*), Henri bravely admits *he* is the king—but no one will believe him. Lots are drawn, and "Nangis" is chosen, putting Henri in the awkward position of having to assassinate himself. He enters the adjoining room where the real Nangis is sequestered, only to find that Minka has let the prisoner escape. Henri still promises to free the Poles from their new ruler.

ACT III At an inn, amid preparations to celebrate the coronation. Fritelli tells the innkeeper that an Austrian archduke will take the throne instead of Henri. The latter, still posing as Nangis, appears and announces his departure for France. But Alexina arrives to say she told the archduke the conspiracy failed—so he returned to Austria! Fritelli, dreading the resumption of his wife's affair with Henri (*Je suis du pays des gondoles*), lies to Alexina that her old flame, having killed the king, is a broken man, in hiding. They resolve to find him and help him flee. Minka is looking for the real Nangis, since his departure (as "king") also has been arranged. The two women despair at the loss of their French lovers (nocturne: *O rêve éteint!*), but Alexina hopes to see hers again and goes to disguise herself as a maid to escort him to the frontier. Minka, close to suicide, is stayed by the arrival of Nangis, who declares that Love is the only real king (*Il n'est plus, hélas, celui que j'aime!*). They set off for the frontier to find Henri, who meanwhile shows up with the "maid" Alexina; Fritelli, not recognizing his wife, urges them to hurry off. When Minka and Nangis return with the royal retinue, explanations follow. The men's identities are cleared up, and Henri decides to stay and rule a "court of love." Sending Fritelli away as emissary to Paris, he can continue his romance with Alexina, and Nangis can marry Minka (finale: *La Garde fidèle*).

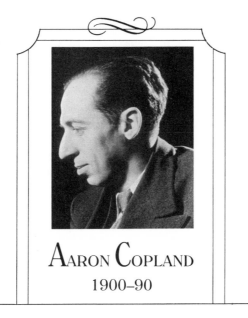

AARON COPLAND
1900–90

New York–born and partly Paris-trained, Aaron Copland spent his formative years during the 1920s, when, as he recalled, "Nobody was interested in opera—nobody, that is, who cared about 'new music.' We were all interested in ballet. Even in America, opera was for groundlings. Later, in just the same way, everybody wanted to write an opera."

Everybody, that is, except Aaron Copland, who approached opera with extreme caution, not to say reluctance. "To have the courage to cope with 'la forme fatale,' " he told *Opera News* in a 1963 interview, "you have to feel as if you were born to do that particular thing. The urge has to be so strong that you cannot wiggle out of facing those particular problems. If, because of some inner drive, little else in music attracts you, then you are an honest-to-God opera composer."

True to the outlook of his generation, Copland did some of his most distinguished work for the dance theater. His *Appalachian Spring, Billy the Kid,* and *Rodeo* became classics. He also wrote film scores, notably for *Our Town* and *The Red Pony,* and his popularity was such that almost any new work he composed would be taken up for performance—even an opera. Copland remained cautious: "I begin counting up the time of composition and cost of production—both great. Then, in two and a half hours, everybody decides whether it's any good or not. That's an awfully short time to judge the work of two years."

For this reason, also because of his populist social convictions, Copland's two operas were conceived outside the conventional format. *The Second Hurricane* (1936) is a "play opera" for high school performance. Of *The Tender Land* (1954) he explained, "I was trying to give young American singers material that they do not often get in the opera house . . . with a natural language that would not be too complex. . . . The result was closer to musical comedy than [to] grand opera. The music is very plain, with a colloquial flavor."

The artful simplicity that worked perfectly in *Appalachian Spring* did not work so readily in *The Tender Land,* and after the first performances by New York City Opera, Copland made adjustments to the score. Much of the problem lies with the *faux-naïf* libretto, too folksy to be believed. The characters and dialogue, like those in a 1940s movie, are stereotyped to the point of cliché, and their motivations, like those in the Elmer Rice–Kurt Weill *Street Scene,* are dramatically convenient rather than psychologically credible. A Midwestern farm girl might well leave home—but not on the eve of the most important day of her life so far, her high school graduation. Armed with nothing but a cardboard suitcase, she heads down a dusty road to nowhere.

Despite its lack of a real dramatic crux, *The Tender Land* is musically touching, sometimes deeply so. Copland in his down-home mode succeeds because his sympathies are genuine: this music speaks of the broad American landscape and those who live close to it. When Copland first wrote such music, during the Great Depression—the years of Carl Sandburg, James Agee, and Walker Evans—it had not been heard before. People listened, and they still do, because as American music it rings true.

THE TENDER LAND

THREE ACTS
MUSIC: Aaron Copland
TEXT (English): Horace Everett (Erik Johns)
WORLD PREMIERE: New York City Opera, April 1, 1954

CHARACTERS

Laurie . . . . Soprano
Ma Moss, *her mother* .Mezzo-Soprano
Mr. Splinters, *postman* . . . . Tenor
Martin, *a drifter* . . . . Tenor
Top, *a drifter* . . . . Baritone
Grandpa Moss . . . . Bass
Beth, *Laurie's sister* . . . . Spoken Role

ACT I On a Midwestern American farm in the mid-1930s, Ma Moss sits sewing on the front porch *(Two little bits of metal)* while her youngest child, Beth, plays with a doll named Daniel. The postman, Mr. Splinters, arrives with a package—a graduation dress from Chicago by mail order for Laurie, the older daughter, for her high school graduation the next day. Ma invites Splinters to the family graduation party that night. Conversation turns briefly to a report that two drifters, suspected of molesting a local girl, are being sought by the sheriff. Splinters leaves on his rounds, and Ma opens the package *(This is like the dress I never had)* before going inside to prepare for the party.

Laurie arrives home from school, reflecting on how quickly the time has passed since she left childhood *(Once I thought I'd never grow tall as this fence)*. She realizes she has reached a turning point in her life. When Ma comes back out, and they talk about the generation gap in understanding between Grandpa Moss (Laurie's father having died) and Laurie herself, Ma slaps the girl for her impertinence, then realizes she is no longer a child and apologizes. Ma reenters the house, and Laurie steps out of sight when she hears strangers approaching.

Top and Martin, two migrant workers, arrive in hopes of helping with the harvest. Top, apparently the more shiftless of the two, mentions having once been married and having been in jail. They discover Laurie and introduce themselves good-naturedly. Martin, seconded by Top, explains their wandering life *(We're from the big north)*. Grandpa Moss arrives at the house and sends Laurie away while he talks to the men. Though he wants to hire extra hands, he is leery of strangers; they hope to persuade him otherwise (Martin: *A stranger may seem strange, that's true*). He agrees, and they are invited to stay, which inspires them to some horseplay (interlude). When Ma comes out, she questions them, thinking of the drifters who have been reported. They sense her suspicion, but Top finds Laurie attractive and asks Martin to keep Grandpa occupied during the evening so he can spend some time with her. As if intoning a hymn, Martin, joined by the others, welcomes the opportunity to bring in the harvest (quintet: *The promise of living*).

ACT II That evening, a jovial atmosphere prevails around the table. After Grandpa proposes a toast to Laurie, she shares with the guests her thoughts about how quickly time passes *(Thank you, thank you all)*. Table and chairs are pushed back to make room for dancing (ensemble: *Stomp your foot upon the floor*), but Ma takes Mr. Splinters aside to explain her uneasiness about the two strangers; he agrees to go fetch the sheriff "for a few questions." Meanwhile, Top regales Grandpa with a tall story in the form of folk song *(Oh, I was goin' a-courtin')*, and there is more dancing.

It is now Martin who has taken an interest in Laurie; they go out on the porch together, and he tries to comfort her anxieties about graduation and the life ahead, saying he would like to settle down *(Quiet ... Tomorrow you'll be graduated).* By the time he has finished, he has proposed marriage to her. She admits she returns his feeling (duet: *I love you, I do).* Grandpa, after quite a lot of berry wine, stumbles out onto the porch and sees the couple; in a rage, he denounces the two newcomers. Ma comes out and tells Laurie these are the drifters who molested a local girl, but Mr. Splinters arrives to say the guilty ones have already been arrested in the next county. This does not mollify Grandpa, who tells Laurie if she shows such independence again, he'll curse the day she was born. The girl runs inside. Sobered by his own rashness, Grandpa still tells the young men they must leave the next day. The other guests say good-night.

ACT III   Later that night, Martin comes out of the shed and wanders in the yard *(Is there someone in there that's called Laurie?).* Laurie hears him and comes out of the house. He tries to explain that though he loves her, he must leave at dawn. She replies that she wants to come too *(Then take me with you!).* After she returns to the house, he has second thoughts *(Daybreak will come in such short time).* Top emerges from the shed and, from a practical point of view, talks him out of the quixotic idea of bringing Laurie along *(Hoppin' the freight, after it's late).* They take their bundles and leave.

Later, Laurie comes back with her satchel packed *(The sun is coming up),* only to find Martin gone. She bursts into tears, rejects Beth's sympathy, then gets hold of herself as Ma approaches. Abruptly she announces she is leaving home, even though today is her graduation day: "I'm ready for leaving like this harvest is ready to be gathered in." Ma no longer recognizes the child she thought she knew. As Laurie slowly walks away, Ma watches her go, no longer trying to stop her *(All thinking's done, and all plans laid),* and realizes that now it is Beth's turn to grow to womanhood. In the composer's words, "She looks to her younger daughter as the continuation of the family cycle that is the whole essence of their existence."

JOHN CORIGLIANO
b. 1938

The son of the concertmaster (1943–66) of the New York Philharmonic, the young Corigliano studied with Otto Luening at Columbia, then with Vittorio Giannini at the Manhattan School, and privately with Paul Creston. Work as music programmer for radio stations, associate producer of television music programs, and music director for a theater made him conversant with the media as a means of reaching large audiences. He went on to teach composition at several institutions of higher learning, meanwhile pursuing an active and successful career as composer.

Corigliano's writing for the opera stage shows his concern for its traditions. His first such work, *The Naked Carmen* (1971), was a mixed-media score overlaid on material from Bizet's *Carmen,* presented through the ears, as it were, of current rock and pop styles. As early as 1979, he became involved, together with his friend the poet/dramatist William M. Hoffman, in a commission from the Metropolitan Opera to write what the two proposed as *The Final Figaro,* later developing into a "grand opera buffa" called *A Figaro for Antonia.* The starting point was to be *La Mère Coupable,* the third of Beaumarchais' plays about Figaro and the Almavivas. The work was intended to mark the Met's hundredth-anniversary season in 1983–84, but the project proved unexpectedly arduous, and delays were frequent, with the premiere finally taking place in late 1991.

After studying *La Mère Coupable,* Corigliano and Hoffman found it usable only as a basis for a fantasy in which elements of the Mozart and Rossini settings of the other two plays also would figure. The resulting text is complicated, involving alternately—sometimes simultaneously—life in the

85

afterworld among the Ghosts of Versailles, a new opera offered up by Beaumarchais for Queen Marie Antoinette, and surrounding events in Revolutionary Paris.

The idea of ghosts at Versailles is more than a literary conceit. I recall walking at dusk one Bastille Day in the early 1950s in the gardens of Versailles (at that time only partially restored) and saying out loud, though no one else was there, "This place is haunted": from behind the rows of bushes, with fireworks softly going off in the distant sky, the breeze seemed to coax the whispers of conspiratorial lovers. In a book entitled *Hauntings,* published by Time-Life in 1989 in the series *Mysteries of the Unknown,* the editors describe "a rare type of haunting called retrocognition—a term based on the Latin for *backward knowing*—percipients say they experience past events and environments as if transported back in time." The case cited is that of two English schoolteachers, Anne Moberly and Eleanor Jourdain, who in 1911 recorded in a book called *An Adventure* their visit a decade earlier to Versailles.

Approaching the Petit Trianon, they had encountered "two grave-looking men in green coats and three-cornered hats . . . a cloaked man with a look of evil on his swarthy, pockmarked face" and "a handsome gentleman with long, dark curls under a wide-brimmed hat, wearing buckle shoes and a cloak." At the Petit Trianon they saw a woman sketching who resembled Marie Antoinette. The pair revisited France later to find more "dreamlike sensations and uncanny perceptions" at the Hameau, Marie Antoinette's reproduction of a peasant village, and Miss Jourdain noted down eleven bars of music heard from the Petit Trianon.

This is not the only food for thought in *The Ghosts of Versailles.* Writers do play fast and loose with history, especially when they write operas—as Corigliano and Hoffman have Beaumarchais doing. And figures of history often stage their own actions as melodramatically as any librettist.

THE GHOSTS OF VERSAILLES

TWO ACTS
MUSIC: John Corigliano
TEXT (English): William M. Hoffman
WORLD PREMIERE: New York, Metropolitan Opera, December 19, 1991

CHARACTERS

Marie Antoinette . . . . Soprano
Rosina, Countess Almaviva. . . . . Soprano
Florestine, *Count Almaviva's illegitimate daughter* . . . . Soprano
Susanna, *Figaro's wife* . . . . .Mezzo-Soprano
Cherubino, *former page of Almaviva* . . . . .Mezzo-Soprano
Samira, *an Egyptian singer* . . . . .Mezzo-Soprano
Woman with Hat .Mezzo-Soprano
Count Almaviva . . . . Tenor
Patrick Honoré Bégearss, *Almaviva's friend* . . . . Tenor
Léon, *Rosina's son by Cherubino* . . . . Tenor
Figaro, *Almaviva's servant* . . . . Baritone
Pierre-Augustin Caron de Beaumarchais . . . . Bass-Baritone
Suleyman Pasha, *the Turkish ambassador* . . . . Bass
Wilhelm, *Bégearss' servant* . . . . Speaking Role

ACT I   The present. In a vague world peopled by ghosts from the Ancien Régime, a Woman with Hat descends, seated in an armchair, singing verses from Beaumarchais' play *Le Mariage de Figaro* to a traditional tune. The ghosts of Louis XVI and a Marquis appear, playing cards; they and some elegantly dressed women note that Queen Marie Antoinette is being courted by Beaumarchais, a commoner. To relieve the prevailing boredom, a small theater is being set up for Beaumarchais to present his new opera. Marie Antoinette appears, rejecting the attentions of Beaumarchais, who serenades her *(All-powerful Queen of Beauty)*. She is haunted by her execution *(They are always with me),* though within her memories of the fatal day there is a peaceful, idyllic image of herself when happy *(Once there was a golden bird).*

Beaumarchais announces his opera—*A Figaro for Antonia* ("Antonia" is his and Louis' name for Marie Antoinette). It is set in 1793, at the start of the Reign of Terror, in the Almaviva mansion in Paris, where Figaro, who has been trying to shave a client, is being pursued by creditors. He succeeds in locking them out and reflects with self-satisfaction that everyone is jealous of his cleverness *(They wish they could kill me).* He recites details of his checkered career, which resembles that of Beaumarchais. His pursuers break through the locked door.

Beaumarchais closes the curtain. The ghosts are pleased, except for Marie Antoinette, who tells Beaumarchais his opera is painful because it is "so beautiful, so full of life." He offers to bring her back to life, using his powers as an artist: his talisman will be the Queen's diamond necklace. Using it, he unveils the small stage again, showing Count Almaviva, the Spanish ambassador to France, who has been given the necklace to sell to the English ambassador during a reception at the Turkish Embassy. Beaumarchais introduces his other characters: Rosina (Countess Almaviva), whose son Léon, fathered by the page Cherubino, is now grown and has fallen in love with Florestine, the count's illegitimate daughter by another woman. But Almaviva refuses to approve their marriage, insisting that Florestine marry his friend Bégearss.

Almaviva announces that sale of the necklace will enable the queen to escape to America. Figaro and his wife, Susanna, enter and make no headway in trying to persuade the count to allow Léon and Florestine to wed. When Almaviva angrily fires Figaro, the two servants wonder what they will do next. They hide when Bégearss arrives, beating his servant Wilhelm for being too stupid to remember where the necklace is supposed to be sold. Bégearss relishes his plot to betray Almaviva (by intercepting the sale of the necklace) and marry Florestine. Rhetorically he reminds his enemies that the worm—i.e., himself—is the king of beasts *(Oh, the lion may roar)*. Meanwhile, Wilhelm remembers that the Turkish embassy is where the necklace is to be sold.

Beaumarchais introduces his next scene, in which Bégearss fans the flames of Almaviva's anger against his wife, thereby ensuring that Florestine and Léon will not be allowed to marry. When the countess laments her dalliance with Cherubino, Beaumarchais moves the action back twenty years to the Almavivas' garden outside Seville. There the young countess is seduced by Cherubino (duet: *Come now, my darling, come with me)*. Beaumarchais takes advantage of the scene to move closer to Marie Antoinette, who no longer resists him. Louis interferes, threatening the playwright, but when they duel, it becomes apparent that ghosts, being immaterial, cannot be run through by a sword (quartet: *He will cut you into pieces)*. Gleefully the ghosts stab at each other.

Beaumarchais' opera resumes with the reception at the Turkish embassy, where an exhibition duel is staged for the entertainment of the guests. When the British Ambassador arrives, he and Almaviva converse, oblivious to the fact that they are the center of attention for everyone who knows about the necklace. A sneeze from the Pasha, their host, interrupts the sale, which is further delayed by announcement of a song by the Egyptian chanteuse Samira *(I am in a valley and you are in a valley)*. When she has finished, the two men try to resume their transaction, but Figaro, disguised as one of the dancing girls, lifts the necklace from Almaviva's pocket. Chasing the thief, Almaviva unmasks him, and a general chase begins. Figaro evades his pursuers when a group of musicians files in. Cornered, he escapes by leaping from a balcony.

ACT II When Beaumarchais' opera resumes on the small stage, the ghostly audience returns to its seats, still bantering. Marie Antoinette warns that in tampering with history, Beaumarchais may lose his immortality: "If you change the past, you may be caught here forever." Onstage, at the Almaviva residence, the count nervously awaits Figaro's return so he can get the necklace back. But when Figaro does appear, he decides the "spoiled, arrogant, decadent" queen doesn't deserve to be rescued, so he will use the necklace to save the Almavivas instead. Almaviva is furious with him; in the audience, so is Beaumarchais, because Figaro is departing from the script. Beaumarchais rings down the curtain and tries to explain to the disillusioned Marie Antoinette (*Figaro was supposed to return the necklace*). He envisions a new future for her— "History as it should have been." Seeing her unconvinced, he enters the world of the small stage, determined to force Figaro's obedience.

The stalled action of Beaumarchais' opera resumes with the Almaviva household in turmoil: Figaro has made off with the necklace again. Susanna and the Countess console each other over the marital love that "thieving time" has taken from them (duet: *As summer brings a wistful breeze*). Beaumarchais, as a ghost, approaches Figaro when he sneaks back in and tries to scare him into returning the necklace. When this fails, he leads Figaro away . . .

. . . to meet the queen face to face. Figaro calls her an "evil spirit" and a "monster," so she asks Beaumarchais to prove her innocence. The playwright conjures up the scene of her trial by the Revolutionary Tribunal, October 14– 15, 1793, himself enacting the role of the presiding judge. With dignified simplicity, Marie Antoinette replies to the accusations, but the bloodthirsty crowd wants her head (women's chorus: *A-chop, chop, chop*). When Figaro sees her summarily condemned, he changes his mind and pledges to save her. The scene dissolves to a Paris street, where Bégearss agitates the crowd, comparing the aristocrats to rats who spread plague (*Women of Paris! Listen to their little feet!*).

§ At a gathering of surviving aristocrats in Paris, witnessed by some of the ghosts, Almaviva welcomes his guests soberly (*Friends, welcome. For one last time we come together*). Léon and Florestine recall the early days of their romance, while Almaviva and his wife each remember the indiscretions that led to the young people's birth (quartet: *Remember the chestnut trees. . . ?*). The doors burst open to reveal Bégearss, leading soldiers to arrest the guests. He demands the necklace, which Figaro steps forward and hands to him. He also demands to marry Florestine, threatening to have the family put to death. When Beaumarchais tries to use his poetic license to have the Almavivas released, he finds he cannot: as Marie Antoinette predicted, he has lost his immortality and the powers that go with it. Bégearss orders everyone taken to prison, but Susanna creates a diversion by accusing Wilhelm (Bégearss' servant) of having made her pregnant; this enables Figaro and Beaumarchais to escape. As the ghosts are left behind, Marie Antoinette is touched to realize that Beaumarchais has acted out of love for her.

§ Night in the Conciergerie prison, where condemned aristocrats fantasize they are back in their world of intrigue and gossip. The Almavivas and Susanna are hauled in. At last there is reconciliation among them, with Almaviva admitting his prideful errors (quintet: *O God of love, O Lord of light*). After a *Miserere* at the cell of Marie Antoinette, she bids everyone farewell.

Two sinister figures enter and turn out to be Figaro and Beaumarchais; Figaro has secured the key to let them all out except the queen, whose key is in Wilhem's care. To lure Wilhelm back, the countess cries for help, saying she feels faint. He appears and succumbs to the women's blandishments; Susanna knocks him out with his rifle butt and steals his keys. When Bégearss reappears on the stairs leading to the queen's cell, Figaro denounces him as an enemy of the Revolution for having the queen's necklace. Guards find it in Bégearss' pocket and haul him off to the guillotine. Figaro, who has recovered the necklace during the scuffle, escapes with guards in pursuit. Alone, Beaumarchais frees Marie Antoinette, but though she confesses her love for him, she will not leave, having resolved to go through with her destiny *(She must stay and ride the cart)*.

§   In the Place de la Révolution on October 16, 1793, citizens gather to watch the queen's execution and the ascent of a Montgolfier balloon. She is led to the block as the crowd breaks into the *Marseillaise.* Meanwhile, the Almaviva household steals into the balloon and takes off for home. The vision fades, and the ghosts are seen at the Almaviva villa in Spain. United for eternity with "Antonia," Beaumarchais puts the necklace around her neck and kisses her hand.

ANTHONY DAVIS
b. 1951

New Jersey–born Anthony Davis was graduated from Yale University and attracted musical attention as leader of Episteme, an improvisational performing group. At the American Music Theater Festival in Philadelphia he developed his first opera venture, *X: The Life and Times of Malcolm X,* which was given its premiere at New York City Opera in 1986. Working from a story by the composer's brother Christopher, his cousin Thulani fashioned the libretto in the manner of a documentary film, with vivid episodes dramatizing key moments in Malcolm's life.

Together with John Adams' *Nixon in China* and Ezra Laderman's *Marilyn* (1993), *X* represents a new avenue of musical theater based on what might be termed "recent biography." (In Adams' case, several of the principals were still living when the work was written; none registered a response to it.) This would appear a risky sort of enterprise: not enough time may have elapsed for artistic perspective to be achieved. In the case of Nixon's visit to China, however, the episode had acquired a sort of legendary status, and the same can be said for the eventful, controversial life of Malcolm X. With *Marilyn,* it was more a case of abstracting a pop icon—a procedure followed in Dominick Argento's opera *The Dream of Valentino* (1994). One of the most interesting works in this recent genre, *H. H. Ulisse* (1984) by Jean Prodromidès, freely and imaginatively relates the life of the eccentric millionaire entrepreneur Howard Hughes to the myth of Ulysses as told by Homer.

The distinction of *X* lies in both its immediacy and its deliberate eclecticism. To convey the feel of Malcolm's era, Davis makes creative use of every type of music available. Though his underlying plan of construction is related to traditional opera, he introduces African-American hymns and spirituals, various types of popular music, and the vocabulary of contemporary concert music, with its atonality and rhythmic complexity. In this respect, X may be said to continue along the path initiated by Scott Joplin in *Treemonisha* and George Gershwin in *Porgy and Bess.* It was none other than Antonín Dvořák, during his teaching period in America, who declared African-American music to be one of the prime sources for an indigenous American style.

Having proved with X that "art" music need not be segregated from popular forms, Davis moved on in his next opera, *Double Moon* (1989), to address a quieter, more elusive theme, Deborah Atherton's science-fiction libretto set on another planet.

X: THE LIFE AND TIMES OF MALCOLM X

THREE ACTS
MUSIC: Anthony Davis
TEXT (English): Thulani Davis, based on a story by Christopher Davis
WORLD PREMIERE: Philadelphia, Walnut Street Theater (American Music Theater Festival), October 9, 1985
REVISED VERSION: New York City Opera, September 28, 1986

CHARACTERS

Louise Little, *Malcolm's mother* . . . . Soprano
Betty, *Malcolm's wife* . . . . Soprano
Social Worker . . . . Soprano
Ella, *Malcolm's older sister* . . . . .Mezzo-Soprano
Street, *a hustler* . . . . Tenor
Elijah Muhammad, *leader of the Nation of Islam* . . . . Tenor
Malcolm. . . . . Baritone
Reginald, *his brother* . . . . Bass-Baritone
A Preacher . . . . Bass

ACT I Lansing, Michigan, 1931. At the home of Rev. Earl Little and his wife, Louise, an evening meeting of the local chapter of Marcus Garvey's Universal Improvement Association is under way, but Rev. Little, who is supposed to lead it, has not arrived yet. The group talks of the possibility of returning to Africa, as Garvey has proposed (chorus: *Takin' the Black Star home!*). Louise, anxious about her husband's absence, recalls how the Ku Klux Klan staged an attack at the time when her son Malcolm was born *(The air seems thin and fragile);* when her daughter Yvonne was born, the Klan burned their house to the ground. A Policeman comes to the door and reports that a man was run down by a streetcar. The men in the group learn that Rev. Little is the one killed; a mob of whites attacked him and pushed him in front of the streetcar *(These devils hunt us down).* Louise collapses into a catatonic state. As neighbors wonder what to do about the children, a white Social Worker arrives *(What is going on here?)* and declares that the children must be made wards of the state. Malcolm tries to stay behind and rouse his mother, who does not respond *(Momma, help me).* He is led away by his older sister Ella . . .

§ . . . who takes him to live with her in the Roxbury section of Boston *(Come with me, child).* About 1940, as he looks around the neighborhood, a man called Street advises him to become a hustler, living by his wits, avoiding exploitation by whites *(Play the game).* Malcolm catches on quickly, coached by Street, and soon they are arrested for pulling off a burglary.

§ Malcolm sits handcuffed in prison *(I would not tell you what I know).* The truth of his life story, he says, is not what his jailers want to hear: his father killed, his mother driven to insanity, he himself left no choice but a career of opportunism. He has come to recognize the evil that whites represent to him.

ACT II During the period 1946–48, Malcolm continues to brood angrily in jail, shunned by the other prisoners (chorus: *In the devil's grip).* He is visited by his brother Reginald, who claims his life has been turned around by "a man who showed me the truth." Malcolm is skeptical *(You talk in riddles).* Reginald speaks of black people as a nation, and of a prophet named Elijah, a God named Allah. From the background, Elijah's voice speaks to Malcolm.

§ Malcolm leaves prison in 1952, having studied the Koran and black history during his remaining time there. He meets Elijah, who tells him to take the name X "for what was lost . . . until God returns to speak a name that will be yours," and who instructs him in prayer according to the style of the Nation of Islam. Elijah tells him that only through awareness of their history can blacks regain their identity and freedom *(We have been blind):* it is time for Malcolm to spread Allah's word.

§ In 1954–63, the period of the American civil rights movement, Malcolm appears at 125th Street and Seventh Avenue in Harlem, where various speakers are addressing the crowd. A Woman Preacher tries to promote the idea of returning to African dress and customs *(We are an African people);* a Garvey Speaker has a few words. Then Malcolm takes over, saying it is time for blacks to wake up to Allah and to the history of their bondage *(Yes, we had it once).* He predicts the fall of the existing social order.

§ More rallies follow. Elijah appears and encourages Malcolm *(My son, I hear you speak).* Gradually, the number of Muslims—recognized by their style of dress—increases in the crowds. Malcolm spells out the objectives of the movement *(We want freedom, justice, equality).* In front of a mosque, Elijah and others join in restating these objectives *(We are a nation trapped inside a nation).* At one of the meetings, news arrives that President Kennedy has been shot. Asked by a reporter for his comment, Malcolm replies, "America's climate of hate is coming back on itself . . . a case of the chickens coming home to roost." Elijah, aware that the remark will be misinterpreted, is angry at Malcolm for making more enemies for the Nation of Islam *(Now Malcolm disobeys the Messenger!).*

ACT III   Not long afterward, Elijah censures Malcolm for his "loose tongue" and wonders aloud if his disciple has grown too powerful. As punishment, he orders Malcolm not to teach or speak in public.

§ Rebuked and silenced by Elijah, Malcolm begins to doubt his chief's infallibility and feels the need to renew his own faith by making the pilgrimage to Mecca. His wife, Betty, supports him in his search for inner truth *(When a man believes).* After embracing her and their daughters, he leaves *(Allah made me and left me here).*

§ At Mecca, Malcolm, not having learned the orthodox prayer ritual, is at first puzzled among the faithful as they invoke Allah. After an interlude of silent prayer and contemplation, he declares himself as one reborn *(My name is Shabazz)* and teaches himself to bow like the others.

§ 1964–65: Malcolm returns to a Harlem that has been newly stirred to turbulence by an incident in which a policemen shot a black youth. Telling reporters again that "A violent land breeds violent men," he refuses to take personal blame for the movement that has grown up. Meeting with his followers, Malcolm tells them that during his trip to Africa he has seen the beginning of the end of colonialism. He intends to begin the American crusade by presenting the denial of human rights before the United Nations. But Elijah and his personal army, the Fruit of Islam, accuse Malcolm of inciting disaster for their cause *(The Nation is a house of cards).*

§ A bomb has demolished Malcolm's home. Warned of threats against his life, he says his death will not stop the movement *(They can call me names)* and adds that having been set free by Allah, he considers himself a man of peace.

§ February 21, 1965: a meeting of the Organization of Afro-American Unity at the Audubon Ballroom in Harlem. As a speaker addresses the crowd, Malcolm makes his way toward the podium. He begins his speech with an Islamic blessing *(As-Salaam-Alaikum),* then falls as three men in the first rows rise and shoot him down.

Frederick Delius
1862–1934

*D*elius is remembered as a cosmopolitan composer. Born in England of German descent, he died in France. In between, he had lived in Florida as a young man and later in Norway, where he was friendly with Edvard Grieg and Christian Sinding. As an opera composer he took Wagner as his point of departure, but in his orchestral writing he worked close to the aesthetics of the so-called impressionists in France, notably Claude Debussy.

Delius regarded formal musical structure and thematic development with disgust, preferring a rhapsodic approach in which mood and color are paramount. He did make considerable use of the Wagnerian leitmotif system in his second opera, *The Magic Fountain,* dealing with Ponce de León's search for the fountain of youth, which led to the Spanish discovery of Florida. Delius' first opera, *Irmelin,* more typically relied on his gift for creating a fairy-tale atmosphere. Neither of these works was performed in his lifetime. The first of his operas that he heard was *Koanga* (1904), on a slave story; both it and *A Village Romeo and Juliet* (1907) were staged first in Germany, translated by the composer's wife, Jelka.

A Village Romeo and Juliet epitomizes Delius' gifts as a magician for the lyric stage. The sensuous delicacy and poetic nostalgia, the sense of dreamed happiness and loss, the element of Bohemian escapism and traduced innocence, all lead the listener into a world of glowing fantasy. In his remaining two operas, however, he tried something different. With *Margot la Rouge* (1902) he aimed, as Massenet did in *La Navarraise,* to write a verismo shocker in the fashionable vein of Mascagni's *Cavalleria Rusticana* and Leoncavallo's *Pagliacci.*

Realism was not Delius' strong suit, and he could not match his competitors' skill at portraying stark drama in music. With *Fennimore and Gerda* (performed in Germany in 1919) he turned to psychological portraiture, and in this he was more successful; but the tragic and happy elements of the original Scandinavian story make odd bedfellows in Delius' score, and he never achieves reconciliation or catharsis, only escape.

It is a revealing facet of the composer's artistic personality that he wanted so strongly to write operas, despite his lack of success with them. The dramatic movement in Delius' music is an inner movement, and the narrative element—like that in Jean Sibelius' tone poems—appeals vividly to the imagination without calling for, or serving the needs of, a specific text. The stage is too matter-of-fact, too much flesh and blood, for the kind and level of fantasy that Delius' tonal imagination was best in creating. In *A Village Romeo and Juliet,* however, he did achieve that rare equipoise where reality and dream blend into and transfigure each other.

A VILLAGE ROMEO AND JULIET

SIX SCENES

MUSIC: Frederick Delius

TEXT (English): the composer, based on Gottfried Keller's story *Romeo und Julia auf dem Dorfe*

WORLD PREMIERE: Berlin, Komische Oper, February 21, 1907 (in German)

U.S. PREMIERE: Washington, D.C., Opera Society of Washington, April 26, 1972

CHARACTERS

Sali, *Manz's son (as a child)* . . . . Soprano
Vreli (Vrenchen), *Marti's daughter* . . . . Soprano
Sali, *Manz's son (as a man)* . . . . Tenor
Manz, *a rich farmer*. . . . . Baritone
Marti, *a rich farmer* . . . . Baritone
The Dark Fiddler, *rightful heir to the wood* . . . . Baritone

(Libretto quotations are based on Tom Hammond's revised version for Sadler's Wells.)

A VILLAGE ROMEO AND JULIET

SCENE I Seldwyla, Switzerland, mid-nineteenth century. Between the farms of Manz and Marti lies a strip of unclaimed, overgrown land. As Manz works his plow, Marti does the same, each encroaching slightly on the unused plot. Their children, Sali (Manz's son) and Vrenchen (Marti's daughter), bring the fathers' lunch and spread it out in the shade, then go to the woods to play. They soon return as their fathers sit eating. A stranger, the Dark Fiddler *(O wild lonely singer)*, appears, playing his violin. Marti and Manz recognize him as the town trumpeter's grandson: though heir to the unclaimed land, he has no legal claim, being a vagabond of illegitimate birth. He tells the children to play on the land *(Listen, my children, you need have no fear)* but warns them to beware when it has been devoured by the plow. No sooner has he left than Manz and Marti fall to accusing each other of encroaching on the plot. In their rage they separate the children, forbidding them to play or speak together.

SCENE II Six years have passed. Marti's house and farm have fallen into disrepair: bitterness and litigation have brought ruin to both farmers. Sali comes in search of Vrenchen for the first time since the feud began. She is overjoyed but, fearing her father's return from town, says she will meet Sali later in the patch of woodland.

SCENE III The two young people, meeting at their old playground, are greeted once more by the Dark Fiddler *(You here? I'm not surprised)*, who says that since they are all reduced to beggars now, they may as well see the world together. Having made the suggestion, he leaves them to wonder about his intentions and to recall their earlier life (duet: *In childhood's happy days*), but they are soon interrupted again—this time by Marti, looking for his daughter. Angrily he starts to drag her home. Sali, trying to stop him, strikes and knocks him unconscious: Vrenchen fears he has killed him.

SCENE IV Vrenchen, about to lose the family property, sits mournfully at evening when Sali appears. They embrace (duet: *O Sali, I should have died if you had not come*), and she tells how she took her now demented father to the old people's home in Seldwyla. After agreeing to go away together, they fall into exhausted sleep. In their dreams they imagine their wedding. When they wake, they decide to go to the fair at Berghald.

SCENE V At the fair, peasants and vendors mingle in a festive crowd. Sali and Vrenchen, noticed and recognized by some of the townspeople, feel uncomfortable, so Sali suggests going to a place called the Paradise Garden, where no one will know them and they can dance all night.

Interlude: The Walk to the Paradise Garden

SCENE VI Outside the Paradise Garden, at an inn, the Dark Fiddler regales a group of vagabonds with his story of the disputed land *(So must I tell you how the strife began?)*, finishing as Sali and Vrenchen arrive. He invites them to come to the mountains with him and his friends (ensemble: *Vagabonds and comrades! We are free as air*), but when the troupe retires inside the inn, Sali and Vrenchen realize that the Bohemian life, with its easy virtue, is not for them. Moonlight floods and transforms the place, which Vrenchen recognizes as the Garden of Paradise. As Bargemen are heard singing on the river, the lovers decide to die together, choosing a boat filled with hay as their marriage bed. The Dark Fiddler emerges on the veranda of the inn, playing his violin, as Sali casts away from shore and pulls the plug from the bottom of the boat. Slowly the boat drifts downstream, bearing the embraced lovers, until it is seen sinking in the distance.

PAUL DUKAS
1865–1935

A man of broad culture, Dukas, like most French composers of his generation, felt the heavy importance of Wagner; but he was able to find his own way, and in fact his *Ariane et Barbe-Bleue* is said to have influenced Richard Strauss in writing the "silver rose" music for *Der Rosenkavalier.* Active as a critic, Dukas was familiar with older music as well as the new. He worked on the complete edition of Rameau's works, starting in 1895, at a time when such repertory was little known or dismissed as a curiosity.

Ariane et Barbe-Bleue, though based on a play by Maurice Maeterlinck, who also wrote the original *Pelléas et Mélisande,* is a more structured and traditional opera than Debussy's *Pelléas.* Much has been made of the fact that *Ariane* "explains" who Mélisande was and where she came from: she fled Bluebeard's harem and was found, wandering in the woods, by Golaud. In fact, however, Mélisande is a bit player in *Ariane,* whose text reveals next to nothing about her. It was not Maeterlinck's way to give out specifics. His Symbolist style supplied the libretto for one other opera, *L'Oiseau Bleu* (1919) by Albert Wolff. During the vogue for Maeterlinck's dramas, which started to fade when faced with the harsh realities of World War I, all three of the lyric works he inspired were staged by the Metropolitan Opera. Debussy's was the only certifiable survivor, but interest in Dukas' score did reappear late in the century.

The main problem with *Ariane et Barbe-Bleue,* as Darius Milhaud pointed out, is its lack of action: "There are those doors on the stage, and the doors are opened, and that's all." Much the same could be said about Béla Bartók's *Duke Bluebeard's Castle,* but in both Dukas' and Bartók's scores, musical color and intensity, not stage action, are what engage the listener. *Ariane* was the only opera that Dukas managed to complete. He planned others and started work on some, but in later life—like Sibelius after him—he turned self-critical and destroyed many of his manuscripts, both complete and unfinished. Dukas today is remembered chiefly for his tone poem *L'Apprenti Sorcier* (The Sorcerer's Apprentice), given fame by Mickey Mouse in Walt Disney's 1940 film *Fantasia;* this orchestral scherzo was originally meant to be part of Dukas' Symphony in C, which—like the rest of his output—is rarely heard.

ARIANE ET BARBE-BLEUE

(Ariadne and Bluebeard)

THREE ACTS
MUSIC: Paul Dukas
TEXT (French): Maurice Maeterlinck, after Charles Perrault
WORLD PREMIERE: Paris, Opéra Comique, May 10, 1907
U.S. PREMIERE: New York, Metropolitan Opera, March 29, 1911

CHARACTERS

Ariane		Soprano
Ygraine	*first four wives of Barbe-Bleue*	Soprano
Mélisande	*first four wives of Barbe-Bleue*	Soprano
Bellangère	*first four wives of Barbe-Bleue*	Soprano
Sélysette	*first four wives of Barbe-Bleue*	Mezzo-Soprano
The Nurse		Contralto
Barbe-Bleue		Bass
Alladine, *fifth wife of Barbe-Bleue*		Acting Role

The unspecified time and mythical place (Orlamonde), like those of Debussy's *Pelléas et Mélisande,* suggest Europe during the Middle Ages.

ACT I Voices of a peasant mob are heard outside Bluebeard's castle, variously calling for his death and accusing him of murdering his five wives, also warning an approaching woman, Ariane, not to enter. She and her Nurse do enter the castle. The Nurse, frightened by the rumors and cries, would like to escape, but Ariane is confident of her ability to deal with Bluebeard, saying his previous wives aren't dead, only "lost because they hesitated" (*Elles ne sont pas mortes*). Bluebeard has given her seven keys—six silver and one gold—to unlock the bridal jewels. She discards the first six, which are permitted, and concentrates on finding the forbidden door belonging to the golden seventh key. The Nurse, however, is curious about the permitted doors and starts to open them. First comes a chamber full of amethysts that tumble out, followed by others filled with sapphires, pearls, emeralds, rubies, and diamonds. Ariane shows only passing interest in the jewels until the fifth door, at which she adorns herself with diamonds, because to her they represent light and clarity (*O mes clairs diamants!*). The seventh door is revealed, and as the Nurse retreats in fear, Ariane unlocks and enters it alone. From inside, the voices of the previous wives are heard (ensemble: *Les cinq filles d'Orlamonde*). Their song grows stronger as Ariane follows it toward its source. Suddenly Bluebeard appears in the hall. He tells Ariane he can still forgive her if she will stop trying to find out his secrets, but she replies she can forgive *him* only if she knows everything. As he starts trying to drag her away, the Nurse admits the angry mob of peasants. Sending them away, Ariane says she has not been harmed.

ACT II   Ariane carries a lamp down the stairs into a dark underground vault. She tells the Nurse that Bluebeard, having given in to her demand to know what is down there, will let them out again; but, she adds, it is better to be set free by one's own hand. As the Nurse hangs back, Ariane explores the vault and finds the previous five wives, whom she greets affectionately and reassuringly (*Ah! Je vous ai trouvées!*). They are fearful, startled by the light she has brought. Ariane learns their names—Sélysette, Ygraine, Mélisande, Bellangère, Alladine—and is surprised that they do not seem glad to be rescued (*Mais toi-même, tu ne ris pas encore!*). Why have they accepted their fate so submissively? As she asks, dripping water puts out her lamp and she becomes aware of a soft glow that illuminates the cavern. Though the others warn her against trying to find a way out, she manages to open an interior shutter, then finds a window and smashes its panes, unleashing a flood of sunlight (*Voilà, celle-ci encore*). Only then do the others overcome their fear and climb up to join her in looking out toward the sea. Ariane discovers stone steps leading down the cliffside (*Oui, embrassez-vous*) and urges the others to follow her.

ACT III   Back in the main hall of the castle, with the gems still spilling out of their doorways, the wives are adorning themselves. Sélysette says that if they had escaped, they would have missed the castle (*Nous n'avons pu sortir du château enchanté*); besides, it is safe, with Bluebeard no longer there. Ariane has no idea where he might have gone but suspects he will return, perhaps with reinforcements. The peasants, however, seem to be keeping watch outside on the wives' behalf. Mélisande has hidden her long golden hair, which Ariane urges her to uncover. Ariane also helps the others to show their natural beauty, handing them jewels, giving advice and encouragement. The disheveled Nurse hurries in to report that Bluebeard is on his way back, and the peasants are waiting in ambush. From the windows, the wives watch the ensuing conflict. Some of Bluebeard's retainers desert him, and as he too tries to flee, the peasants capture him and tie him up. When it looks as if they might throw him in a ditch, the wives cry out not to kill him. Retainers from the castle rescue him, and the mob brings him to the door.

While the wives cower in dread, Ariane opens the door. The peasants deposit Bluebeard inside, and Ariane dismisses them with thanks. The women come forward and start ministering to the wounded Bluebeard, who revives as Ariane cuts him free of his bonds. He rises to a sitting position, somewhat dazed. Ariane bids him farewell and tells the other women she will not be back: aren't they coming with her? *(Vois, la porte est ouverte et la campagne est bleue).* Apparently they are not. As Ariane leaves with the Nurse, the five women look at one another in silence, then at Bluebeard, who slowly raises his head.

MANUEL DE FALLA
1876–1946

*B*orn in Cádiz, a seaport city in Andalusia, Falla moved to Madrid with his family in 1897, when he was twenty-one. He tried his hand at composing *zarzuelas*—popular Spanish musical plays—and came under the helpful influence of a teacher, Felipe Pedrell, who made him aware of current musical developments abroad. When a competition was announced in 1904 for a one-act opera, he wrote *La Vida Breve* and won, only to discover that the work would not be produced. He eventually made his way in 1907 to Paris, considered the center of European musical life at the time. There he eked out a difficult existence with accompanying and teaching but was sustained by the friendship of eminent musicians, including Debussy. *La Vida Breve* was finally accepted for production in Nice and later at the Opéra Comique in Paris, just before the outbreak of World War I prompted Falla's return to Madrid.

In truth, *La Vida Breve*—quite unlike Mascagni's *Cavalleria Rusticana,* which had sparked the vogue for one-act operas—has little dramatic action. All attention is focused on the heartbreak of the central character, Salud, a young Gypsy woman betrayed by her spineless lover. The Spanish coloration and impassioned but elegant flavor of the music are attractive, and on a well-chosen double bill, with a strong singer as Salud, the work makes its effect. Of pithier stuff were the ballets that followed: *El Amor Brujo,* with contralto soloist (1916), and *El Sombrero de Tres Picos* (1919). The Ritual Fire Dance from *El Amor Brujo,* though a relative trifle, has become Falla's best-known composition, closely followed by his incomparable set of *Seven Spanish Folk Songs.*

After moving to Granada, Falla turned again to opera with *El Retablo de Maese Pedro* (1922), a chamber work for the puppet stage, based on an episode from Cervantes' *Don Quixote*. As early as 1926, Falla began the largest of his projects, the scenic cantata *Atlántida,* but he was destined never to finish it. After the Spanish Civil War, he moved to Argentina, where he continued to work on *Atlántida* until his death, just before his seventieth birthday. Completion of the score was entrusted to the conductor Ernesto Halffter, who turned out three successive versions; principal revisions involved cuts, as *Atlántida* proved long, unwieldy, and—again—undramatic. Nevertheless, though Falla had not wanted it staged, it was produced at La Scala in 1962, subsequently in Berlin and Buenos Aires.

Like his friend Maurice Ravel, Falla was anything but prolific. His music is characterized by fastidious taste and craftsmanship, as well as a certain patrician understatement, even when the material is animated and colorful. He made liberal use of Spanish modal and melodic styles but was equally attentive to the vocabulary of internationalism, thereby escaping the restrictive category of a regional or national composer.

LA VIDA BREVE

(The Short Life)

TWO ACTS
MUSIC: Manuel de Falla
TEXT (Spanish): Carlos Fernández Shaw
WORLD PREMIERE: Nice, Municipal Casino, April 1, 1913 (in French)
U.S. PREMIERE: New York, Metropolitan Opera, March 6, 1926

CHARACTERS

Salud, *a young Gypsy woman* . . . . Soprano
Her Grandmother . . . . Mezzo-Soprano
Carmela, *a young woman* . . . . Mezzo-Soprano
Paco, *Salud's suitor* . . . . Tenor
Manuel, *Carmela's brother* . . . . Baritone
Uncle Sarvaor. . . . . Bass

ACT I   Courtyard of a Gypsy house in the Albaicin (Falconer's Quarter) of Granada, adjoining a forge, 1913. Workmen toil as the Grandmother of Salud, a young Gypsy woman, sings about her pet bird—which, like Salud's love for a man of higher social station, has little hope of surviving its pangs. When Salud appears, however, the Grandmother tries to cheer her up, saying her beloved Paco surely will come to see her. Salud is not convinced, lamenting that only people who can laugh and enjoy life are able to go on living *(Vivan los que rien!);* those who weep and feel deeply are doomed to die. Allaying her fears, Paco arrives and reassures her of his unfailing love (duet: *Por ti yo desprecio las galas del mundo).* As they stand apart, oblivious, Salud's Uncle Sarvaor comes in and tells his sister, the Grandmother, that he has learned of Paco's imminent wedding to a girl of his own class. Sarvaor wants to kill the deceiver but is led away by the Grandmother.

§ Outside the house, with a view of Granada in the distance, Salud and Paco take leave of each other while the Grandmother restrains Sarvaor.

ACT II   In an alley of the city, Salud looks through the windows of a gaily lit house to see Paco with Carmela, the other woman *(Allí está! Riyendo!).* She wants to confront him but is deterred by the arrival of her Grandmother and Sarvaor, who try to console her. She sings near one of the windows *(Malhaya la jembra pobre),* and Paco, catching the sound of her voice, is disturbed. Sarvaor says he will take Salud into the house.

§ Inside, with festivities under way, Carmela's brother, Manuel, toasts the couple *(Feliz me siento).* Paco is shocked to see Salud brought in by Sarvaor, who tells the guests, "We will dance for you, we will sing for you." Unable to contain herself, Salud denounces Paco *(Me perdió! Me engañó),* who denies knowing her. The shock of his denial finishes her off, and she falls to the floor dead as the guests look on in horror. The Grandmother, entering "like a madwoman," curses Paco as a Judas as the curtain falls.

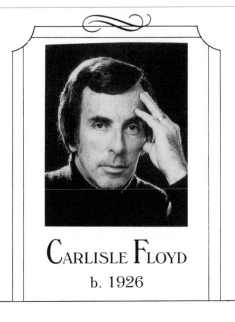

CARLISLE FLOYD
b. 1926

*S*econd only to Gian Carlo Menotti in frequency of performance as a contemporary composer on the American stage, Carlisle Floyd has made his mark by following the precepts of verismo. Writing his own librettos, he has avoided difficult or overly poetic texts, favoring directness of characterization and story line. Musically guided by the work of his teacher Ernst Bacon, he has adopted only as much complexity and modernism as his audience can readily accept. This may appear a prescription for blandness, but Floyd's gift for melodrama has been a distinguishing and saving grace. It also has made life easier for singers and stage directors, with the result that his works, more than most, have appealed to theaters cautious about mounting novelties.

A native of South Carolina, Floyd studied there, then at Syracuse University in New York State, where composition began to attract him. He had been pursuing a career as a pianist, but when his first two operas were produced—*Slow Dusk* in 1949 at Syracuse, *The Fugitives* in 1951 at Florida State University (Tallahassee), where he had begun teaching piano—a shift in emphasis took place. It was his third opera, *Susannah* (1955), that made and has sustained his reputation. Picked up by New York City Opera and other theaters, it soon joined those few twentieth-century American operas that have achieved repertory status. Floyd was now in demand as an opera composer, and his next works followed at fairly regular intervals: *Wuthering Heights* (1958), *The Passion of Jonathan Wade* (1962, later completely revised), *The Sojourner and Mollie Sinclair* (1963), *Markheim* (1966), *Of Mice and Men* (1970), *Flower and Hawk* (1972), *Bilby's Doll* (1976), and *Willie Stark* (1981).

Of Mice and Men, based on a John Steinbeck story well known in its film version, is somewhat freer and more contemporary in musical vocabulary than Floyd's earlier works—a trend that has continued through his subsequent ones. In the elemental simplicity of its character types, it invites comparison with Copland's *The Tender Land,* but Floyd's instinct for drama is stronger. As historical Americana, this and most of Floyd's other operas lie closer to such a work as Robert Ward's *The Crucible,* addressing issues as well as folkloric archetypes, and Floyd's sense of musical portraiture has served him well. It also has served singing actors who have created his roles onstage—Phyllis Curtin and Norman Treigle *(Susannah),* Theodor Uppman *(Jonathan Wade).*

Gentlemanly and unassuming, Floyd has pursued his career with a mixture of enthusiasm and modesty. Intensely self-critical, he has been given to wholesale rewriting—not for musical reasons alone, but because of the need to satisfy his stage instincts. This trait holds the key to his durable success.

OF MICE AND MEN

THREE ACTS
MUSIC: Carlisle Floyd
TEXT (English): the composer, based on John Steinbeck's novel and play
WORLD PREMIERE: Seattle Opera, January 22, 1970

CHARACTERS

Curley's Wife . . . . Soprano
Lennie Small, *a migrant farm worker* . . . . Tenor
Curley, *a ranch owner.* . . . . Tenor
Carlson, *a ranch hand* . . . . Tenor
Ballad Singer . . . . Tenor
Slim, *a ranch hand* . . . . Baritone
George Milton, *Lennie's friend* . . . . Bass-Baritone
Candy, *an old ranch hand* . . . . Bass

John Steinbeck's novel about American migrant workers during the Great Depression, published in 1937, was later made into a play and a film.

ACT I At night, somewhere in ranch country, two fugitives, George and Lennie, seek shelter in the woods as police cars shine searchlights in the background. When the men realize they are safe, George berates Lennie for getting them in trouble again. The big, burly but gentle Lennie, who is mentally retarded, alarmed a girl earlier that day by stroking her dress because he liked the soft fabric, causing her to cry attempted rape. George considers aloud how much easier things would be without Lennie (*My life would be so simple by myself*), but when Lennie offers to go off on his own, George won't allow it: he has promised Lennie's aunt to look after him. In his pocket, Lennie has been carrying a dead mouse (*It was somethin' I could stroke*), but George throws it away. When they get their own farm, he says, Lennie can have animals to take care of (*One day soon we'll save up enough*). Lennie falls asleep, leaving George with his thoughts.

§ The following evening, at the bunkhouse of a ranch, Curley, the young owner, complains to Candy, an old hand, that the new men he has signed up haven't appeared yet. Curley's Wife saunters in, bored (*I want to go into town tonight*). He is in no mood for her, and after glaring at each other, both leave in different directions. George and Lennie arrive and meet the other hands, who enter the bunkhouse. Curley's Wife comes to the doorway, feeling unwanted by her husband of two weeks, trying to get the attention of the other men, who consider her a tart and barely tolerate her. After she has wandered out again, a discussion starts as to whether Candy's ancient dog should be put out of his misery (Slim: *Your dog ain't no good to you no more*). Candy resists, but the majority prevails, and Carlson leads the dog outside. An atmosphere of strained silence prevails as a Ballad Singer is heard outside (*Movin' on . . . always movin' on*), followed by a shot. The Ballad Singer comes inside; Carlson returns from his mission, facing the group's silent reproach. Lennie asks George if he can have one of the puppies recently delivered by Slim's dog (duet: *It's a hard thing to see / It's what I want most in the world*), and the Ballad Singer ends his interrupted song.

ACT II   Several days later, George and Slim are playing checkers at the bunkhouse while others pitch horseshoes outside. Noticing that George is reading real-estate ads in the paper, Slim observes that the dream of settling down remains only an illusion for most (*Ev'ry ranch hand I ever knew*), but George declares his intention of achieving it (*I ain't gonna buck grain the rest of my life*). He calls Lennie to show him an ad for a farm they might be able to afford. Slim acts as though he's heard it all before and leaves. Candy, who has been asleep, joins the discussion between George and Lennie, offering to go in with them on the farm (trio, George: *Just to think of ownin' a place of your own*). At the excited sound of their voices, Curley's Wife enters, under her usual pretext of looking for Curley. The men try to send her away, not wanting to get in trouble with Curley, who soon arrives and picks a fight—first with George, then with Lennie, whose nervous laughter he interprets as scornful. Lennie tries to duck the blows from Curley's riding crop but finally grabs Curley's hand in a bone-crushing grip. Injured, Curley reels back. Slim asks him not to fire anyone; in return, the men will say nothing about his assault on Lennie. Curley agrees. He and the others blame Curley's Wife as the troublemaker, but before running off in tears, she retorts that Curley's overbearing manner is the real problem (*You never learned to leave folks alone*). After Curley too has left, George tends to Lennie's injuries and then, at Candy and Lennie's request, rereads the ad for the farm.

ACT III   Inside the barn the following afternoon, Lennie sorrowfully talks to his puppy, which has died. Climbing up to the hayloft, he accidentally knocks down an empty sack, startling Curley's Wife, who has just entered with a suitcase. She and Lennie fall into conversation, talking on parallel tracks about where they would like to go: Lennie to the farm, Curley's Wife to fame as a movie star in Hollywood (duet: *Our farm's got a small house*). When Lennie talks about his love for "soft things I can pet," Curley's Wife lets him stroke her hair to see how soft it is. After a few moments, concerned that he will mess her hairdo, she tells him to stop; when he doesn't, she raises her voice. Fearful of being discovered talking to her, which George has told him not to do, Lennie clamps his hand over her mouth, and when she struggles, he inadvertently strangles her. She falls limp. Confused and frightened, Lennie leaves. Candy, who has been watching the other hands pitch horseshoes, wanders into the barn and sees the body. In a hasty conference with George and Slim, it is agreed that George will have to take care of Lennie before Curley and Carlson find out about the woman's death and go after him.

§ A half-hour later, in the same clearing in the woods as Act I, it has grown dark as Lennie stumbles in, reproaching himself bitterly (*Oh, I feel cold inside*). George finds him, and they briefly recapitulate their exchange in Act I about George's having an easier time by himself and Lennie's striking out alone. Voices in the distance indicate that Curley and his men are searching the woods. George tells Lennie the men are looking for a runaway colt, then asks him to look across the river and visualize the home of their dreams (*One day soon we'll have us a farm*). As Lennie happily describes the place, George pulls out Carlson's pistol and shoots him in the back of the head. Lennie staggers back, holding on to George, then falls with arm outstretched, as if reaching toward his vision. George closes the ad for the farm in Lennie's hand, then sits by the body as the posse arrives. He doesn't acknowledge the men's presence. Curley and Carlson shrug and lead the others off, except for Slim, who stands by George, and the Ballad Singer, who sounds a few strains on his way out.

VITTORIO GIANNINI
1903–66

*L*ike Gian Carlo Menotti and Dominick Argento, Vittorio Giannini was able to graft his own Italian heritage onto his American roots, writing operas in which the lyrical and vocal elements receive their due. The Gianninis of Philadelphia were a musical family, with a singer father and violinist mother. One daughter, Dusolina, became an international opera star; the other, Eufemia (Mme Gregory), a singer and noted voice teacher. Young Vittorio studied at the Milan Conservatory, later at the Juilliard School in New York. The receipt of three Rome Prize fellowships in a row enabled him to return in 1932 to Europe, where his first opera, *Lucedia,* was given in Munich two years later.

Dusolina, who sang frequently in Germany, was influential in securing this premiere, and when Giannini's opera *The Scarlet Letter* was performed in Hamburg in 1938, she created the role of Hester Prynne, Meanwhile, Giannini had written his first radio opera, *Flora,* and was to continue in that new genre with *Beauty and the Beast* in 1938 and *Blennerhasset* in 1939. In all, he composed a dozen operas, some of them unperformed. By far the most successful was *The Taming of the Shrew,* a fast-paced but lyrically juicy comedy in the tradition of Ermanno Wolf-Ferrari. This work had a concert premiere in Cincinnati in 1953 and was televised by the NBC Opera Company the following year, introducing it to a substantial audience. Stage productions in New York, Chicago, and Kansas City (Missouri) followed.

One of Giannini's opera projects that did not see the light of day was *Casanova,* a subject later used by Argento. The next Giannini production after *The Taming of the Shrew* was *The Harvest,* seen in Chicago in 1961; a veristic melodrama, it proved a disappointing follow-up to its witty predecessor. Undaunted, the composer went on to write *Rehearsal Call* (Juilliard American Opera Center, 1962) and *The Servant of Two Masters* (New York City Opera, 1967), a Goldoni-based comedy more in the spirit of *The Taming of the Shrew.* In an era little attuned to his brand of conservatism, Giannini kept alive one of the most ingratiating veins of the romantic tradition.

THE TAMING OF THE SHREW

THREE ACTS
MUSIC: Vittorio Giannini
TEXT (English): Dorothy Fee, based on Shakespeare's play
WORLD PREMIERE (semistaged concert performance): Cincinnati, Music Hall, January 31, 1953
U.S. STAGE PREMIERE: Chicago, Lyric Theatre, November 3, 1954

CHARACTERS

Bianca, *Baptista's younger daughter* . . . . Soprano
Katharina, *her older sister* . . . . Soprano
Lucentio (Cambio), *suitor to Bianca* . . . . Tenor
Gremio, *suitor to Bianca*. Tenor
Grumio, *Petruchio's servant* . . . . Tenor
Petruchio, suitor to Katharina. . . . . Baritone
Hortensio (Licio), *suitor to Bianca* . . . . Baritone
Tranio } *servants of Lucentio.* . . . . { Baritone
Biondello }   Bass
Baptista, *a wealthy gentleman* . . . . Bass

ACT I A square in Padua, with facing houses of Baptista Minola, a wealthy gentleman, and Hortensio, a suitor to Baptista's younger daughter, Bianca. A young man from Pisa, Lucentio, enters with his servant, Tranio, in search of a place to stay. Baptista walks into the square, explaining to Hortensio and Gremio—another of Bianca's suitors—that he will not give his younger daughter's hand until his older daughter, Katharina (Kate), is married. Neither youth fancies Katharina, who shows herself at once to be a spitfire. As Baptista and his daughters enter their house, the suitors agree, despite their rivalry, to unite in finding Katharina a husband. They leave. Lucentio, smitten by the sight of Bianca, plots how he can gain admittance to Baptista's house. He and Tranio switch clothing, to the perplexity of another servant of Lucentio's, Biondello, who learns that Tranio will play the role of Lucentio as a student at the university, while Lucentio himself, under an alias, will become Bianca's tutor (trio, Lucentio: *Now when in somber habit forth I go*). They exit laughing.

Petruchio enters from the other side with his servant, Grumio, and knocks at the door of his friend Hortensio. His father having died and left him a comfortable fortune, Petruchio means to live in Padua and find a wife. Hortensio tries to interest him in Katharina—whose father, it turns out, was a friend of Petruchio's father. Hortensio asks Petruchio to take him along disguised as a music master, so he can gain access to Bianca. Gremio reappears, believing that in the disguised Lucentio he has found a tutor who will plead his case with Bianca. Petruchio, who welcomes the challenge of taming the shrewish Katharina (*Will I live? Think you a little din can daunt mine ears?*), presents himself at Baptista's house as a gentleman of Verona, then introduces the disguised Hortensio as "Licio," a musician. Gremio presents Lucentio as "Cambio," a scholar of Latin. Tranio, now posing as his own master, asks Baptista to receive him as a suitor to Bianca.

Petruchio, not one to mince words, asks Baptista what Katharina's dowry would be. Gremio and Tranio, equally interested in Bianca's dowry, learn that Baptista expects the winning suitor to prove himself by offering *her* the most, so they vie with each other (Gremio: *My house within the city*). A commotion in the house: Katharina, yelling at Hortensio, sends him out with a broken lute. Petruchio finds this show of temper stimulating (*I will woo her with some spirit when she comes*). Katharina emerges and meets Petruchio, sparring verbally with him from the first. Unfazed, Petruchio declares he will wed her next Sunday; she swears she will see him hanged first.

ACT II   In the garden of Baptista's house the following Saturday, Lucentio and Hortensio quarrel as to which will be first to give Bianca her lesson. While Hortensio tunes his lute, Lucentio gives the girl a Latin text with a concealed meaning: that he is actually not a pedagogue but a nobleman seeking her hand. Hortensio catches on to this and interrupts. After the Latin reading, Hortensio offers a silly musical anagram, which merely irritates Bianca. Petruchio and Grumio enter, wearing ragged old clothes, and Petruchio calls for Katharina, whom he embraces despite her resistance. She surmises that he has put on the disreputable outfit to humiliate her. When the men have left, Katharina tries to find out which suitor Bianca prefers. When Bianca will not say, Katharina slaps her. Baptista intervenes, scolding Katharina for her roughness, but Katharina retorts that she is being sacrificed to an unwanted marriage so that Bianca can wed. As dusk descends, Lucentio comes from the house, and it is apparent that he is Bianca's choice (duet, Lucentio: *Being your slave, what should I do . . . ?*). He tells his true identity and asks her to marry him secretly, but she does not want to anger her father. They exchange kisses and part.

§ The following morning in the garden, Lucentio draws Bianca into concealment as Katharina can be heard inside the house, reviling the servants. Hortensio strolls in and discovers the young lovers, then tells Tranio they have both been duped. Baptista escorts Katharina in her wedding dress, but Petruchio is late; Katharina, feeling herself made a fool of, bursts into tears (*No shame but mine*). Baptista receives a note from Petruchio, saying he has been detained and will meet them at church at noon; if Katharina is a moment late, the marriage is off. Insulted, Baptista wants to call it off himself, but Lucentio reminds him he has given his word. As the steeple bell strikes noon, Baptista drags Katharina across the square to church.

ACT III In Petruchio's house, a few days later, his servant Curtis is helping Grumio set the table. Grumio recalls how Katharina fell off her horse on the way back from the wedding (*Tell thou the tale*), and how Petruchio spent the night lecturing her and complaining about everything. "By this reckoning," declares Curtis, "he is more shrew than she," but Grumio sees that Petruchio has been trying to show her "how unjust and childish is a wilful spirit." Petruchio arrives, berating a servant, and hails Katharina to the table. A Tailor interrupts, offering a ladies' cap, about which Petruchio stages an unreasonable scene, throwing the Tailor out. Then he complains about the food and refuses it, though Katharina is starved. When Petruchio has stormed off to the kitchen, she complains alone about her plight (*Did he marry me to famish me?*) until Bianca unexpectedly arrives, asking for refuge for herself and Lucentio: they have eloped. Katharina conceals them as Petruchio returns, bringing another unexpected visitor—Vincentio, Lucentio's father. Petruchio, who already knows of the elopement, breaks the news to Vincentio just as further intruders arrive: Baptista with Tranio (Lucentio's servant, who has been posing as his master), Biondello and a Pedant made up to look like Vincentio. Allegedly this false "Vincentio" has come to give consent to his "son's" marriage to Bianca. Confronted by the real Vincentio, they try to bluff, and Vincentio becomes convinced that Tranio has murdered the real Lucentio in order to impersonate him (ensemble: *Where is my son, mine only son?*).

The young lovers emerge from hiding and, after apologies and unscrambling of identities, get their fathers' blessing. Petruchio bids them all welcome for a night's rest, saying they will celebrate tomorrow. Alone with Katharina, he finds her so worn out that she will agree with anything, just for the sake of peace (duet, Petruchio: *How bright and goodly shines the midday sun!*). Seeing her tears, he turns gentle, saying "Thou hadst but one fault—a wilful spirit. Since this is gone, there is no blemish left. I love thee, Katharina!" As they embrace, she declares that henceforth, "Taming my wild heart," she will requite his love (both: *Touch but my lips with those fair lips of thine*).

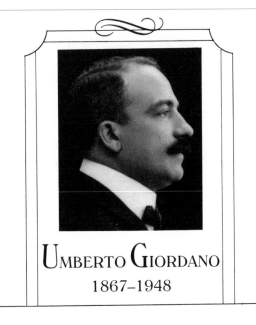

UMBERTO GIORDANO
1867–1948

*B*orn the same year as Arturo Toscanini, Giordano belonged to a generation of Italian musicians that came to maturity during the twilight of Giuseppe Verdi's career. As the turn of the century approached, while some emergent composers—notably Alfredo Catalani and Alberto Franchetti—strove to continue along the trodden paths of romanticism, a handful of others—Puccini, Leoncavallo, Mascagni, and Giordano—felt the need for something fresh. They enlisted under the banner of verismo (realism), which meant bringing opera up to date, using timely subjects with believable characters.

The two most enduring verismo operas, Leoncavallo's *Pagliacci* and Mascagni's *Cavalleria Rusticana,* in fact live up to veristic principles, but many other works by these composers do not. Puccini, who did not limit himself to veristic precepts, set contemporary subjects in *Madama Butterfly* and *Il Tabarro,* but most of his operas take place in remote places and times. What verismo really meant was a new, more immediate kind of theatricality. Along with lifelike staging and acting, the style of singing became more freely emotional, closer to popular song.

Giordano, the son of a pharmacist, was a native of Foggia, in the area of Naples. Like Leoncavallo, he was a southerner who made good in the more industrialized North. His rags-to-riches story began when his opera *Marina* gained sixth and last place in the competition sponsored by the publisher Edordo Sonzogno in 1888, of which *Cavalleria Rusticana* was the winner. Considering the total number of competitors (seventy-three), this was a lucky showing for a twenty-one-year-old beginner. Giordano's next opera, *Mala Vita,* was such a good example of verismo, portraying working-class life in Naples, that it shocked and offended the citizens of that city.

His two most lasting successes were *Andrea Chénier* (1896) and *Fedora* (1898), the first a costume drama set in the French Revolution, the second nominally a modern subject (even a bicycle is introduced onstage). Of his later works, *Madame Sans-Gêne* (1915) and *La Cena delle Beffe* (1924) enjoyed the best reception; both, like *Fedora,* were based on popular plays, vehicles for Sarah Bernhardt. The playwright Victorien Sardou, originator of *Fedora,* was famous for "the well-made play," but in this case his work does not bear close scrutiny. Fedora herself is an impulsive scatterbrain who acts first and thinks about it afterward, if at all. She embodies Sardou's patronizing belief that "Women in love are all the same woman"—a doctrine that enabled him to build a plot entirely on effects. The protagonist of *Fedora* is therefore hard for the composer or singer to portray in musical depth, but there is plenty of room for passion and angst, the staples of verismo. Giordano's timing and taut dialogue take up the slack, making a viable opera of such thin, contrived material.

Both Giordano and Puccini benefited from the generosity of Alberto Franchetti, a colleague of the verists if not a member of their group. It was Franchetti who disclaimed the text of *Andrea Chénier* so that Giordano would have a chance to set it, and he did the same with *Tosca* for Puccini. Franchetti's own works have lain rarely disturbed, but the two librettos he gave away produced operas that are still considered gripping musical theater.

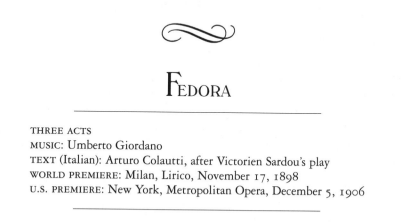

FEDORA

THREE ACTS
MUSIC: Umberto Giordano
TEXT (Italian): Arturo Colautti, after Victorien Sardou's play
WORLD PREMIERE: Milan, Lirico, November 17, 1898
U.S. PREMIERE: New York, Metropolitan Opera, December 5, 1906

CHARACTERS

Princess Fedora Romazov. .Soprano
Countess Olga Sukarev, *a Russian émigré in Paris* . . . . . . .Soprano
Count Loris Ipanov . . . . Tenor

UMBERTO GIORDANO

Baron Rouvel.	Tenor
De Siriex, *a French diplomat*.	Baritone
Cirillo, *a coachman*	Baritone
Lorek, *a surgeon*.	Baritone
Dr. Borov, *friend of Loris*	Baritone
Gretch, *a secret police officer*	Bass
Boleslao Lazinski, *a Polish pianist*	Mime Role

The action is contemporaneous with the first appearance of Sardou's play (1882).

ACT I   St. Petersburg, in the house of Count Vladimir Andreyevich, a captain of the guard and son of Yariskin, the chief of secret police. On a winter night, members of the staff while away the time. Vladimir will be late: this is his last night of freedom before marrying Princess Fedora Romazov. The servants count on her wealth to save the fortunes of their master, whom they describe as a wastrel. An unexpected ring of the doorbell scatters all except Désiré, the valet, and Dimitri, the footman, who admits Princess Fedora, looking for her fiancé. Taking a framed photo of him from the table, Fedora addresses it affectionately *(O grandi occhi lucenti di fede!)*. In the background, Grech (a police officer) and De Siriex (a French diplomat) carry the wounded Vladimir in from his sleigh. A surgeon, Lorek, soon follows, and when he sends for a priest as well as medicine, Fedora realizes the injury is serious.

Grech questions the servants, one of whom, Cirillo (Kiril), tells of driving Vladimir to the Shooting Club, where after a while he heard two shots and saw a man run out—too fast to get a look at him. De Siriex, who was passing by, says he accompanied Cirillo to follow a trail in the snow, which led to a nearby cabin. There Vladimir lay, bleeding, with his own revolver by his side, from which one shot had been fired. Because Vladimir, as the son of the police chief, had received threats on his life, Grech assumes this was the work of a Nihilist (revolutionary). Further details emerge: the cabin had been rented by an old woman. Vladimir had placed a letter from an old woman in his writing desk, and the letter had been removed by an uninvited visitor. Fedora, impatient with the police for their inaction, declares they are no match for their bold opponents *(Son gente risoluta, quei tenebrosi)*. By the bejeweled Byzantine cross she wears, she swears she will not rest until Vladimir has been avenged. Michele, the porter, is brought in and identifies the uninvited visitor as Loris Ipanov, who lives across the street. Grech hurries there with his men and searches the house. As he returns to report the suspect has fled, Fedora learns from the doctor that Vladimir is dead. She cries out and faints.

ACT II   Some time later, during a reception at Fedora's house in Paris, a flighty acquaintance, Countess Olga Sukarev, introduces her protégé, the Polish pianist Boleslao Lazinski. Fedora spots De Siriex among the arrivals and introduces him to . . . Loris Ipanov, the very man wanted for her fiancé's murder. Apart, one Dr. Borov warns Loris that this is not a safe place for him, but Loris explains he is in love with Fedora. Meanwhile, Fedora tells De Siriex that she has tracked Loris down and hopes he will confess his crime to her, though she admits she has gotten to like him. Banter continues among the guests, and Olga, pretending offense at being called a "cossack" by De Siriex (who is annoyed by her attentions to Lazinski), draws from the French diplomat a tribute to the prototypical Russian woman as passionate, gentle, fierce, and mysterious *(La donna russa)*. Fedora acts evasive with Loris, who tells her she must admit she returns his love *(Amor ti vieta di non amar)*. Borov is about to return to Russia; Fedora says she is going there herself the next day. When Loris regrets he cannot accompany her, she says she will try to help secure his pardon, if only he will tell her what the charges are. While Lazinski plays the piano for the guests, Loris explains he has been accused of laying a trap for Vladimir; though he insists he is no assassin, he knows Vladimir's father, the police chief, would never believe him. Drawing him out further, Fedora cannot conceal her horror when he says he did kill Vladimir—as "punishment." Loris leaves to fetch proof of his justification.

Lazinski has finished playing, to general applause. The party breaks up quickly when De Siriex reads a dispatch saying the Nihilists have made an attempt on the life of the czar. Fedora, who still believes Loris to be one of the conspirators, starts to write a letter detailing his confession. She talks with Grech, whose agents are nearby in readiness and have been following Loris' every move. Today, Grech says, Loris received a letter from his brother Valerian in Russia—another revolutionary, Fedora supposes. Telling Grech she has heard Loris' confession from his own lips, she gives the agent her letter to deliver to the Russian authorities—along with Loris, who is to be abducted to a Russian ship when he leaves her house.

When Grech has gone, Loris returns, facing Fedora's accusation that he was involved with the Nihilists, who today tried to assassinate the czar. He denies it, saying he shot Vladimir because of a woman. Loris' old mother had engaged a certain Wanda to read to her *(Mia madre, la mia vecchia madre)*; Loris fell in love with the girl and married her, against his mother's wishes, with Vladimir as one of the witnesses. Soon after, Loris discovered that Vladimir was writing secretly to Wanda and arranging meetings with her. As proof, Loris shows Fedora a packet of letters; reading them, she discovers that Vladimir was marrying her only for money and intended to continue the affair with Wanda. Loris describes how he confronted the couple at the rented cabin and threw Wanda to the floor, whereupon Vladimir fired at him and wounded him. Loris fired back and killed him with a single shot. Wanda escaped but has since fallen ill and died. Fedora, whose sympathies have just changed sides, falsely declares she has no idea who has been spying on Loris and following him. Loris weeps—not for himself, he says, but for his mother, whom he will not see again *(Vedi, io piango)*. Fedora says she will cancel her trip to Russia the next day so as to stay and protect him. A whistle tells her that Grech is ready to spring the trap. Fedora, without admitting her own part in it, tells Loris he will be walking into an ambush if he leaves. On the strength of his protestations of love, she persuades him to stay.

ACT III   In Switzerland, at Fedora's villa in the Bernese Oberland, the following May. Peasant Girls are heard singing about the arrival of spring *(Dice la capinera: "Vien primavera!")*. Fedora and Loris have been gathering flowers. Loris praises her as a "human flower"*(Te sola io guardo, o umano fior)*. Olga, capriciously dressed in mourning to suit her mood, enters and complains that she is bored with nature *(Sempre lo stesso verde)*. When a bell announces a visitor, Loris leaves while Fedora and Olga welcome De Siriex, who chanced to find the place while on vacation nearby; he has arrived by bicycle. In the chatter that follows, Olga reveals that the jealous Lazinski has broken up with her. Knowing her appetite for intrigue, De Siriex jokes that perhaps Lazinski was a secret agent, sent to spy on her *(Fatevi cor, Contessa!)*. She accepts his invitation for a bicycle ride and goes to get ready, whereupon he turns to Fedora on more serious matters. Yariskin, chief of the czar's secret police *(Lui! . . . cadde per l'empia sua crudeltà)*, arrested Loris' brother, Valerian, as a Nihilist plotter, and the young man died in prison. Receiving the news, his mother died on the spot. Fedora blurts out that she is to blame for both deaths. She has no time to explain before Olga returns, and the two cyclists leave for their excursion.

A Peasant Boy sings a sad song in the background, accompanying himself on a concertina, as Fedora succumbs to depression. She prays for Loris to be saved from the consequences of her reckless denunciation *(Dio di giustizia, che col santo ciglio)*. Loris returns and opens a message that has just arrived from Borov, who is on his way there. It says Loris has been pardoned; now he can go back to Russia and see his mother and brother. But another, slightly later message from Borov tells a different story: a letter from an unknown Russian woman in Paris betrayed Loris' confession to Yariskin, who ordered Valerian's arrest *("Jariskin recò al Imperatore la prova trionfal del tuo delitto")*. Learning of the death of his brother and mother, Loris curses himself—but also the spy who has been plaguing him. He vows to find her. Fedora pleads: suppose the poor woman had been blindly in love with Vladimir *(Forse con te li piange)?* Hearing that Borov has just arrived, Fedora fears he will tell Loris the truth about her. To end her own life, she pours poison from her Byzantine cross into a cup of tea. It finally dawns on Loris that the repentant Fedora must be the one who denounced him and incriminated his brother. He turns on her furiously, and she takes the poison, then collapses, murmuring that she hopes he will forgive her when she is dead *(Troppo tardi! Tutto tramonta, tutto dilegua)*. She refuses an antidote offered by Borov. Loris forgives and embraces her as she dies.

PHILIP GLASS
b. 1937

*T*here are two basic ways to pursue musical composition. One is to work within the traditions of the past and try to carry their development forward. (This would include serial music, whose principles have joined the flow of tradition during the course of the twentieth century.) The other is to try to write, as Elliott Carter has put it, "music that I haven't heard before"—making a distinct break with the past. Part of the remarkable achievement of Philip Glass has been to pursue both ways at once.

After thorough studies at the Peabody Conservatory, University of Chicago, Juilliard School, and Aspen Music School, under such teachers as William Bergsma, Vincent Persichetti, and Darius Milhaud, Glass had the qualifications of a mainstream composer. He disavowed his early work, however, and moved to Paris in 1964 to study further with Nadia Boulanger, the legendary teacher of several generations of American composers. His change of direction while in Paris began with the music of India, when he was hired to transcribe the sitar playing of Ravi Shankar for a film score.

At this point Glass, like Colin McPhee and Olivier Messiaen before him, became fascinated with the freely complex rhythmic structure of non-Western music. He visited India early in 1967 and worked with Ravi Shankar in New York after his return. The following year, he formed the Philip Glass Ensemble, which became the instrument through which he pursued his revaluation of the materials from which music is made.

Glass moved toward opera by way of the theater, writing incidental music for avant-garde productions. He joined forces with the stage director Robert Wilson to create *Einstein on the Beach,* first performed in Europe in 1976, then at the rented Metropolitan Opera House, twice filled with devotees who by that time had been attracted to Glass' music. *Einstein* proved to be the first of a trilogy about figures who have changed the course of history. Involving a great deal of dance and pantomime but relatively little "operatic" singing, *Einstein* is more "happening" than opera. Glass found himself more and more drawn into vocal writing, however, and with *Satyagraha* he created a rich choral tapestry. The third work of the trilogy, *Akhnaten,* is of a more spare and ascetic texture, as befits its subject.

Glass now devoted himself to a series of works variously characterized as music theater, chamber opera, and music drama, each carrying forward his exploration of the medium. At length he was invited to write for the traditional opera house, with its classical orchestra. *The Making of the Representative for Planet 8,* to a Doris Lessing text, was introduced by Houston Grand Opera in 1988. *The Voyage,* commissioned for the Met, was produced there in 1992. Conservative opera audiences and musicians now faced a kind of work to which few had any previous exposure, since Glass' success until then had been largely a cult phenomenon.

Like Wagner, Glass requires the audience to adopt a different time frame, one in which time is spun out and distended. Wagner used fragmentary motifs developed and built into large structures; Glass uses rhythmic patterns, which he develops gradually and incrementally through the introduction of small changes in harmony and meter. Because of the requirements of voice and text, Glass has had to search out his way of adding melody. The term "minimalism," often applied to work of this genre, is limiting and misleading. It fails to take into account, for example, the fact that most music already familiar, from the medieval to the baroque to our own day, is built on similar principles of repeated figurations. It is part of the alchemy of Glass' technique that he is able to make basic materials seem new and different, because his way of using them is new and different.

SATYAGRAHA

THREE ACTS
MUSIC: Philip Glass
TEXT (Sanskrit): the composer and Constance DeJong, adapted by DeJong from the *Bhagavadgita*
WORLD PREMIERE: Rotterdam, Stadsschouwburg, September 5, 1980
U.S. PREMIERE: Lewiston, New York, Artpark, July 29, 1981

CHARACTERS

Miss Schlesen, *Gandhi's secretary* . . . . Soprano
Mrs. Naidoo, *co-worker of Gandhi* . . . . Soprano
Kasturbai, *Gandhi's wife*. . . . . Alto
Mrs. Alexander, *European friend of Gandhi* . . . . Alto
Mohandas K. Gandhi . . . . Tenor
Mr. Kallenbach, *European co-worker of Gandhi* . . . . Baritone
Prince Arjuna, *mythological character* . . . . Baritone
Lord Krishna, *mythological deity* . . . . Bass
Parsi Rustomji, *co-worker of Gandhi* . . . . Bass

In the words of Robert T. Jones, in his introductory notes to the Sony recording of *Satyagraha*, "The figure of Mohandas K. Gandhi shines so compellingly through the history of the twentieth century that one is apt to lose sight of the real subject of Philip Glass' opera: Satyagraha, the philosophy of nonviolent resistance that Gandhi made into such a formidable political weapon. . . . Glass and Constance DeJong . . . begin their action in mythology, then move freely back and forth in time during Gandhi's formative South African years (1893–1914). Looming above the action . . . are three figures crucially linked to the Satyagraha philosophy: the Russian novelist Leo Tolstoy, Martin Luther King Jr. and the Indian mystic and Nobel Prize–winning poet Rabindranath Tagore."

ACT I (TOLSTOY) *The Kuru Field of Justice.* Tolstoy is at his desk throughout Act I. On a mythological battlefield, two armies face each other, headed by Prince Arjuna and Duryodhana. Lord Krishna stands downstage in the area separating the armies, which are seen in silhouette. As the lights come up, the soldiers are revealed to be a twentieth-century Indian and European army. Gandhi walks downstage between them, drawing a parallel between the mythic confrontation and the present one *(yo-tsyu-ma-na),* then joining with the mythic Arjuna to describe how the conflict came to pass. "Sure is death to all that's born, sure is birth to all that dies. . . . But if you will not wage this war . . . you will bring evil on yourself" *(u-thu chat twun e-mum dhar-myum).*

§ *Tolstoy Farm (1910).* Gandhi has founded a commune where the Satyagrahi—Indian immigrant workers pledged to resist the Europeans' racial discrimination—are starting to build their settlement. Weighing the ideas of contemplation and action, Gandhi states his view that work is preferable to idleness, providing one's motives are freed from the taint of desire *(yus-yu sarva su-ma-rum-bha).* His wife Kasturbai, assistants, and co-workers agree that in this way, theory and practice become one and the same thing (ensemble: *yud-ri-cha-la-bhu-sum-tŭsh-to).*

§ *The Vow (1906).* The Indian community in South Africa has taken a vow to resist peacefully, unto death, the British government's act requiring them to re-register, carry permits, and submit to arbitrary searches. Gandhi's secretary, Miss Schlesen, assists Parsi Rustomji, an Indian co-worker, in drawing together a crowd, which Rustomji addresses. He says that if one does right things for no ulterior reason or personal gain, only because they are right, then one is following the good path: "You sustain the gods, and the gods sustain you in return" *(dā-van bha-vu-yu-ta nā-nu)*. The people agree that one has to take the bitter with the sweet in performing the tasks of life.

ACT II (TAGORE)   *Confrontation and Rescue (1896)*. Returning from a sojourn in India with the intention of introducing more Indian workers into South Africa, Gandhi has drawn an angry crowd of Europeans, who harass him as he moves through one of their communities under a stormy sky, protected by Mrs. Alexander, a European supporter, who walks by his side, shielding him under her umbrella. As men in the crowd proclaim their self-interested motives *(i-dum u-dyu mu-ya lub-dhum)*, Mrs. Alexander declares them corrupted by desire, hypocrisy, and false conceptions *(ka-mum ash-re-tyu dush-poo-rum)*.

§ *Indian Opinion (1906)* —the title of a newspaper published by Indians in South Africa to strengthen the resistance movement. Late afternoon: workers on the commune are busy preparing the latest edition for the press. Gandhi's wife and colleagues restate the importance of working for a cause rather than for one's own gratification (ensemble: *tus-mad u-suk-tuh*). Such is the way the saints attained success. By setting a good example, one inspires and leads others.

§ *Protest (1908)*. When some leaders of the resistance movement were sentenced to jail for disobeying an order to leave South Africa, others got themselves arrested on various pretexts so they could overcrowd the jail. The government offered to make registration voluntary for the Indian aliens, who, on learning that the registration bill was enacted nevertheless, have gathered for a prayer meeting and to burn their registration cards. Gandhi preaches about the importance of bearing no hate toward anyone *(Sre Bhu-gu-van oo-va-chu)*. The person pleasing to God is the same to everyone, whether friend or foe, is indifferent to praise or blame and to worldy distractions. The chorus repeats the words of Scene 1: "Hold pleasure and pain, profit and loss, victory and defeat, to be the same, then brace yourself for the fight, so you will bring no evil on yourself" *(sŭ-khu-dŭk-khā su-mā krit-va)*.

ACT III (KING)   *Newcastle March (1913)*. When the South African government went back on its pledge to repeal two discriminatory laws—the Three Pound Tax and the Black Act, affecting Indian immigrant workers—the Satyagraha movement, led by Gandhi, exerted strong, nonviolent, organized pressure for repeal.

§ At evening, on the mythological battlefield on the South African plain (now the commune of the Satyagrahi), Gandhi's wife and his aide Mrs. Naidoo praise again the "integrated" person "whose soul views the selfsame way . . . friends, comrades, enemies, those who are indifferent *(nã-nu-vij-nã-nu-trip-tat-ma)*. Joined by Gandhi and his other aides, Miss Schlesen, Kallenbach, and Rustomji, they state, "This is the fixed, still state which sustains even at the time of death the athletes of the spirit" (sextet: *yu-tru ka-lã tv u-nav-ri tim chai-vu*). They go on to explain the soul's return to Brahma, perhaps to be reborn, as the Lord Brahma was reborn many times: "For whenever the law of righteousness withers away . . . then do I generate myself on earth . . . setting virtue on her seat again" *(pu-rit-na-ra-yu sa-doo-nam)*.

"South Africa had been the testing ground for Satyagraha, and in the next thirty-four years, Gandhi was to show that it was a tool of international scope" [from the concluding note of the libretto].

AKHNATEN

PROLOGUE, THREE ACTS AND EPILOGUE
MUSIC: Philip Glass
TEXT (English, Egyptian, Akkadian, and Hebrew): the composer in association with Shalom Goldman, Robert Israel, and Richard Riddell; vocal text drawn from original sources by Shalom Goldman
WORLD PREMIERE: Stuttgart, Kleines Haus, March 24, 1984
U.S. PREMIERE: Houston Grand Opera, October 12, 1984

CHARACTERS

Queen Tye, *Akhnaten's mother*. . . . . Soprano
Nefertiti, *Akhnaten's wife* . . . . Alto
Akhnaten, *King of Egypt*. . . . . .Countertenor
High Priest of Amon . . . . Tenor
Horemhab, *general, future pharaoh* . . . . Baritone
Aye, *Nefertiti's father*. . . . . Bass
The Scribe . . . . Speaker

Except for Akhnaten's Hymn to the Aten in Act II and the tourist guide's words near the end, to be delivered in the language of the audience, the opera is sung in three ancient Near Eastern languages—Egyptian, Akkadian, and Biblical Hebrew.

ACT I *Year 1 of Akhnaten's Reign—Thebes.* Ancient Egypt (c. 1375 B.C.). After the Scribe recites the funeral litany for Amenhotep III, the cortège enters (chorus: *Ankh ankh, en mitak*), wishing eternal life for the deceased pharaoh. The headless figure of Amenhotep, holding his head in his hands, follows as a small chorus bids him farewell on his journey to the underworld *(Ya inen makhent en Ra)*. The people of Thebes and Aye, the late ruler's adviser, join in a final salute.

Akhnaten, Amenhotep's son, is prepared for his coronation. Three officials—the High Priest of Amon, General Horemhab, and Aye—are joined by a large chorus in hailing Akhnaten as he receives the double crown of Upper and Lower Egypt *(Ye-nedj hrak yemi em hetepu)*. The Scribe recites the list of Akhnaten's titles. Akhnaten, his wife Nefertiti (daughter of Aye), and Queen Tye, his mother, approach the Window of Appearances and sing through it a hymn of acceptance and resolve that announces, in spirit, a new era *(Tut wu-a yeri enti)*. Akhnaten is left standing alone to watch the distant cortège float on barques across a mythical river to the Land of the Dead.

ACT II *Years 5 to 15—Thebes and Akhnaten.* Before a temple of Amon, the god's priests, led by the High Priest, sing a hymn in his praise *(Amen men khet nebet)*. Akhnaten and Queen Tye with a group of their supporters appear and attack the temple, pulling off its roof to admit the light of the Aten, the new abstract concept of a single god that they have chosen to replace Amon, symbol of the old order.

The Scribe recites a love poem as if directed toward the god *(Sesenet neftu nedjem)*. Akhnaten and Nefertiti repeat the verse, this time as a pledge to each other.

The City—Dance. The Scribe recites the inscriptions found on boundary markers for the new city called Akhetaten (The Horizon of the Aten), decreed by Akhnaten to be built on this exact spot and no other. The pharaoh and his entourage dance to inaugurate and celebrate the city. Then Akhnaten is left alone to recite his own Hymn to the Aten *(Thou dost appear beautiful on the horizon of heaven)*, expressing his personal inspiration for the religious and social reforms he intends to effect. Akhnaten's was the first known vision of an abstract monotheism. After he leaves the scene, distant voices intone Psalm 104 from the Hebrew Bible, reflecting the later fulfillment of Akhnaten's concept *(Ma rab-bu ma-a-se-kha ha-shem)*.

ACT III *Year 17 and the Present—Akhetaten.* On a divided stage, Akhnaten and his family are seen in the palace while outside are gathered the people, the Scribe, the outlawed Priests of Amon, and the military. The royal family, oblivious to those outside, sings a wordless song. The Scribe reads four messages from outlying provinces that have been sent to Akhnaten and ignored, begging for help to withstand invaders. Akhnaten and his two eldest daughters remain isolated inside, communing only with each other.

General Horemhab, Aye, and the High Priest of Amon step before the crowd to incite it further. Soon the palace is surrounded. Crying that the king must care for his land and people, the rebels break in and carry off the ruling family (chorus: *Lim-lik-mi sha-ri a-na na-ti-shu*).

Reciting an inscription from the tomb of Aye, the Scribe announces the end of Akhnaten's rule: Amon's sun has risen again. The Scribe goes on to tell that a successor has reestablished the rule of justice and restored Amon's temples. Groups of modern tourists appear, looking at the ruins of Akhetaten. The Scribe, appearing now as a twentieth-century tour guide, reads from books describing the present-day site *(To reach Tel-el-Amarna . . .),* where little is left.

EPILOGUE   The tourists have left the scene empty. Akhnaten and other ghosts of the principal characters move among the ruins. With Nefertiti and Tye, he sings wordlessly. Seeing Amenhotep's funeral cortège in the background, they form a cortège of their own and follow toward the heavenly land of Ra.

THE VOYAGE

PROLOGUE, THREE ACTS, AND EPILOGUE
MUSIC: Philip Glass
TEXT (English and Latin): David Henry Hwang
WORLD PREMIERE: New York, Metropolitan Opera, October 12, 1992

CHARACTERS

Commander . . . . Soprano
Ship's Doctor / Space Twin #1 . . . . Soprano
Isabella . . . . Mezzo-Soprano
Earth Twin #1 . . . . Mezzo-Soprano
The Scientist / First Mate. . . . . Tenor
Columbus. . . . . Bass-Baritone
Second Mate / Space Twin #2 . . . . Bass
Earth Twin #2 . . . . Bass

PROLOGUE

The Chorus is heard singing wordless music of the spheres. Descending from the heavens in a wheelchair, the crippled Scientist (through a computerized voice box) wonders at the eternal human quest for exploration, bounded only by our own physical limitations. One goal, perhaps, is the feeling of having transcended all boundaries. In the background, the Chorus poses questions that fascinate the curious mind (*Will time run backwards? . . . What is the mind of God?*).

ACT I   About the time of the end of the Earth's Ice Age (c. 50,000 B.C.), a spaceship hurtles out of control toward our solar system. On board, the Commander and her crew, expecting to be killed, voice their individual regrets and recollections, but a glimmer of hope flashes on the First Mate's computer screen: they are approaching a habitable planet. The ship crash-lands without killing them, and the Commander descends, after asking the First Mate for a computerized last look at their home planet, which is seen and heard emitting blinks accompanied by chordal bleeps. The Commander tells everyone to take one of the spaceship's glowing directional crystals, any pair of which, when rejoined, may one day point the way home.

The crew members visualize their fantasies of the world each would like to inhabit. The Second Mate sees a world ruled by machines—Europe during the Industrial Revolution, where the skies are turned black with factory smoke. The Ship's Doctor, whose secret ambition is to tell stories to eager listeners, sees herself in India, surrounded by children. The First Mate, whose only ambition is to continue the voyage, wherever it might lead, features himself spiritually transported to a mountaintop in Tibet. The Commander, whose dream is to escape humdrum reality, resolves to walk into whatever this new planet offers (*What will they want from me?*). She steps into the midst of a group of natives, who find her bizarre but whose curiosity is the mirror of her own (*What will she want from us?*).

ACT II   In the Spanish court at Granada in 1492, the Chorus salutes Columbus, about to embark for the New World, while Queen Isabella quotes Scripture relating to sea voyages. This turns out to be a recollection of . . .

   . . . Columbus at sea on October 11, 1492, thirty-two days out, with the men grumbling, nothing on the horizon. A vision of Isabella appears with inspiring words (ensemble: *Empowered by God*), while the First and Second Mates give orders to the crew in Spanish, then offer a prayer to the Virgin in Latin. When a bird is heard singing, they all know that land cannot be far off.

ACT III   The year 2092, 600th anniversary of Columbus' voyage. On a stage divided in two parts, Space Twins man a satellite station, while on the ground a pair of Earth Twins, archaeologists, meet after their separate researches, each with a discovery—one of the glowing crystals first seen in Act I. Still searching for signs of life somewhere out in the universe, the Space Twins continue to record and order what they see. Meanwhile, the Earth Twins compare the signal-emitting crystals they have found while digging on opposite sides of the globe. When the crystals are rejoined, their combined frequencies indicate on the Space Twins' computer map the spot in the cosmos from which the original visitors came (ensemble: *Sector 15, Vector 320, Quadrant 1479*).

At a spaceport several years later, an expedition is being readied to seek out the newly discovered planet from which other life once came to earth. The Commander points out that the voyage will take years *(Through the ages, all we have sought to know)*. Dignitaries gather to see the spaceship off.

Inside the ship, via telephone, the Commander and crew members bid their individual farewells to earthbound loved ones (ensemble: *I always imagined. . . .*). The space travelers fade away, revealing . . .

EPILOGUE . . . Columbus on his deathbed, 1506. Isabella again appears to him, excusing the expediency whereby she failed to keep her grandiloquent promises *(I gave you next best—the Spanish Inquisition)*, offering herself to him as a woman instead. Beyond the reach of such an appeal, Columbus asks himself eternal questions: What is man looking for? *(Is it foolish to seek the mind of God?)*. As his mind drifts farther away, she bids him good-bye. Columbus concludes, "Finally we take the voyage when the voyage takes us," and his bed is transported to the stars.

MIKHAIL GLINKA
1804–57

Considered the father of Russian opera, Mikhail Ivanovich Glinka actually worked in a milieu where numerous other composers, either native or residents from abroad, had composed operas to Russian texts. It fell to Glinka to create a national style by writing music that had roots in Russian soil. This he did by writing operas with peasant characters: it was considered culturally appropriate to associate peasants with folk music. Growing up on his family's estate near Smolensk, Glinka had absorbed a wealth of indigenous song and dance from the local peasantry. Largely self-taught in composition, he naturally used this sort of melodic and rhythmic material, being under no pressure from teachers or colleagues to embrace an international style.

When Glinka went to Italy in 1829 for a three-year stay, it was to learn about opera. Using techniques and forms similar to those of Donizetti and early Verdi, Glinka proceeded to adapt them to Russian-flavored music. History fueled his first opera, *A Life for the Czar,* and folklore his second, *Ruslan and Lyudmila.* Both have remained in the repertory in his native land and have been produced occasionally abroad. During the Soviet period, *A Life for the Czar* was considered too monarchist and was sanitized into *Ivan Susanin* (Glinka's original title), with textual adjustments emphasizing the heroism and patriotism of its protagonist rather than his loyalty to the sovereign.

A Life for the Czar is remarkable not for its indebtedness to foreign models but for its boldness in adapting these to a new nationalistic style. Glinka began the work in 1835, shortly after his return from Italy. Though the subject had been suggested by the poet Vasili Zhukovsky, a tutor to the Czarevich Alexander, Zhukovsky himself wrote only the epilogue and turned the bulk of the work over to another member of the court circle, Baron Rosen, who oddly enough was a German but tackled the jingoistic subject with gusto. Two other writers made smaller contributions to the final text.

The first act was tried out in private rehearsals at the palace of Prince Yusupov, where it was heard by Alexander Mikhailovich Gedeonov, director of the Imperial Theaters in both Moscow and St. Petersburg. With the support of the Venetian conductor Catterino Cavos, who had written an opera to the same subject two decades earlier, *A Life for the Czar* was accepted for performance in St. Petersburg. Produced after several delays, it was received generally well, though some turned up their noses at the use of commonplace musical material: one critic faulted the insertion of a coachman's song in Susanin's first solo. In fact, little actual folk music appears in the score; Glinka, having absorbed the style, invented his own folklike themes.

Czar Nicholas I, present at the premiere, congratulated the composer, who dedicated the score to him. By means of his assured, cosmopolitan technique, Glinka had made folk music acceptable in intellectual circles and laid the groundwork for Mussorgsky, Tchaikovsky, and Rimsky-Korsakov, all of whom revered him.

A LIFE FOR THE CZAR

(*Zhizn' za Tsarya*)

FOUR ACTS AND EPILOGUE
MUSIC: Mikhail Glinka
TEXT (Russian): Yegor Fyodorovich Rozen, Vladimir Sollogrub, Nestor Vasil'yevich Kukol'nik, and Vasili Andreyevich Zhukovsky
WORLD PREMIERE: St. Petersburg, Bolshoi, December 9, 1836
U.S. PREMIERE (concert performance): New York, Steinway Hall, November 14, 1871
U.S. STAGE PREMIERE: San Francisco Opera, December 12, 1936
REVISED VERSION
Ivan Susanin; new libretto by Sergei Gorodetsky
PREMIERE: Moscow, Bolshoi, February 21, 1939

MIKHAIL GLINKA

CHARACTERS

Antonida, *Susanin's daughter* . . . . Soprano
Vanya, *an orphan boy adopted by Susanin* . . . . Contralto
Sobinin, *Antonida's bridegroom* . . . . Tenor
A Polish commander . . . . Baritone
Ivan Susanin, *a peasant* . . . . Bass

The action takes place in the spring of 1613. After the General Assembly
elected the cossacks' candidate, Mikhail Fyodorovich Romanov (first of the
Romanov dynasty), to the Russian throne in February, the Poles invaded,
installing their own Prince Vladislav as czar. The new Russian czar-elect
escaped to a monastery at Kostromsk.

ACT I In the village of Domnin, peasants rejoice in the first signs of spring.
Though the country is torn by warfare, the people take assurance from the
report that Mikhail, the czar-elect, is safe. A local girl, Antonida, awaits the
imminent return of her fiancé, Bogdan Sobinin, from the war *(V pole chistoe)*.
Her father, Ivan Susanin, declares there can be no wedding until conditions
are more settled: Sigismund, the Polish king, has taken Moscow. Sobinin's
return by boat rouses enthusiastic greetings from the populace. He brings
news that Russian forces under Prince Pozharsky have driven the invaders
from the capital. Sobinin is distressed by the postponement of the wedding
(trio: *Ne tomi rodimyi!*), but Antonida and Susanin reassure him of their intentions. Because of the many rumors that have circulated, the people are still
uncertain as to the fate of their czar, but they long to have him on the throne
(chorus: *Slava Bogu i Tsariu!*).

ACT II In a ballroom in a Polish-occupied part of Russia, Polish nobles and
officers dance a Polonaise, confident that their forces have secured victory *(Bog
voini, posle bitv)*. There is more dancing (Cracovienne, Pas de Quatre, Mazurka),
during the last part of which a Messenger arrives with news that Prince Vladislav, placed on the throne by the Poles, has been deposed and Moscow retaken
by the Russians. Since Mikhail Romanov, the young Russian czar-elect, is still
in refuge at the monastery of Kostromsk, unaware as yet of this turn of events,
the soldiers propose to find and capture him *(Moguchestvo Polskoe vsë odoleet!)*.
As they leave, the other guests cheer them on.

ACT III In Susanin's hut, young Vanya, an orphan whom he has adopted,
sings about a homeless bird taken in by a kind nightingale *(Kak mat' ubili)*.
Susanin enters unnoticed and overhears the boy, then tells him that Mikhail
will reign as czar (duet: *Da, moi ptenchik podrostët*). Peasants enter, having finished their work in the forest and looking forward to Antonida's engagement
party later that day *(My na rabotu v les)*. When they have left, Antonida and

her fiancé join her father and Vanya in looking forward to the festivities (quartet: *Radost'! V zamenu dlia nas goria!*).

The celebratory mood is broken by the arrival of Polish soldiers. Susanin offers them hospitality, but they come straight to the point: he must show them the way to the czar. Annoyed by his resistance, they discuss among themselves how to deal with him while Susanin, aside, tells Vanya he will lead them astray in the forest, giving Vanya time to ride to the monastery and give warning. Vanya leaves at once. The soldiers tell Susanin he will die unless he does as they ask. He pretends to accept their offer of money. Antonida pleads with him not to go, but he tells her he has no choice but to obey, adding that she should go ahead with her wedding in his absence *(Veliat idti, povinovat'sia nado)*. The Poles pull her away from her father and depart with him.

Antonida's friends return and think her tears have to do with getting married and leaving home, but she tells them the Poles have taken her father and will surely torture him *(Ne ô tom skorbliu podruzhenki)*. Sobinin appears with a group of men from the village, who resolve to follow the Poles and attack them *(Vragi naleteli)*, while Antonida's girlfriends urge her to be courageous.

ACT IV   In the forest at night, Sobinin offers his men words of encouragement to continue on their mission *(Bratsy, v nevedomoi glushi)*.

§ Meanwhile, Vanya has made his way to the monastery, where at first his knocks go unanswered. Anxiously he prays to God to save the czar *(Ty ne plach', sirotinushka!)*, and at length some retainers come out to see what the boy wants. He tells them the enemy is approaching: the czar must leave at once. Hearing Vanya's story, they act quickly. He will show them the shortest way out.

§ Deep in the forest, the Poles suspect Susanin of misleading them. Tired and cold, beset by a storm, they are obliged to make camp for the rest of the night. As they sleep, Susanin, aware that his death is near, prays for strength to face it *(Chuiut pravdu!)*. He hopes Antonida will have a happy life and look after Vanya. No sooner has he lain down to rest than the Poles rouse themselves and discuss what to do with him. They wake Susanin and accuse him of playing them false. Proudly he admits having led them to a remote place in order to save the czar *(Tuda zavël ia vas)*. Frustrated and infuriated, the Poles fall upon Susanin and beat him to death. Too late, Sobinin and his men arrive and attack the Poles.

EPILOGUE   In Moscow's Red Square, the people hail their czar *(Slavsia nash russkii tsar')*, who is about to arrive. Soldiers and an Officer assure Antonida and Vanya that the czar and the people know of Susanin's heroism and will honor his memory.

CHRISTOPH
WILLIBALD VON
GLUCK
1714–87

he son of a forester on a private estate, Gluck received some musical education from Catholic schools in his home area, the Upper Palatinate, before running away from home as a teenager and going to Prague, where he heard Italian opera. Talent and ambition soon drew him on to Vienna, where he served as a household musician to Prince Lobkowitz, son of his father's employer. Of decisive importance was a trip to Italy, sponsored by another noble patron. There he wrote a series of Italian operas under the supervision of his teacher, Giovanni Battista Sammartini, and saw them produced during the period 1742–45. Having this basis for a growing reputation, he headed back north, traveling to England and through various parts of Europe before returning to Vienna in 1748. An opera commission from Empress Maria Theresa, and an advantageous marriage to the daughter of a well-to-do merchant, consolidated his career. In 1754 he was appointed court composer.

Having written operas up to that time in the prevailing elaborate Italian style, Gluck felt the need for reform along the lines of the French musical theater, in which text settings were simpler and more direct, with emotional expression taking precedence over vocal display. As an argument for a new simplicity, Gluck wrote *Orfeo ed Euridice,* given in Vienna in 1762. This was followed by *Alceste* in 1767 and *Paride ed Elena* (Paris and Helen) in 1770, but none of the three started the trend for which Gluck was hoping. Feeling his ideas would be understood better in Paris, he moved there in 1773 and produced *Iphigénie en Aulide* with the support of Queen Marie Antoinette.

Gluck found the Parisian musical public embroiled in controversy about the merits of traditional Italian opera versus the *tragédie lyrique* of Lully and Rameau. Gluck's relatively modern ideas—recitative with full orchestral accompaniment, a sparing use of set pieces—merely added fuel to the fire. Now Niccolò Piccinni, a distinguished composer of the Neapolitan school, was set up in Paris as a rival to Gluck. Piccinni's faction contributed to the failure of Gluck's *Alceste* in 1776—the year of American independence—but Gluck regained ground the following year with *Armide.* At length the directors of the Paris Opera invited both Gluck and Piccinni to set the same text, *Iphigénie en Tauride.* Gluck's version, presented first, was the successful one.

With the perspective of time, one sees that Gluck absorbed very well the concepts of fluent dialogue and a plastic flow of scenes evident in Rameau. Unlike Handel—with whom he shared an irascible temperament, but who disliked Gluck's work—Gluck placed relatively little store by the virtues of diligent counterpoint and worked-out musical forms, such as the fugue. Like Handel, however, he excelled at instrumental coloration, setting the mood of scenes and portraying his characters with distinct kinds of music. Familiar with vocal display, he realized its emptiness from a dramatic viewpoint, using a singer's virtuosity only where it could make an expressive point. A fitting tribute to his art came from Friedrich Melchior Grimm after the premiere of *Iphigénie en Tauride:* "I don't know whether what we heard is melody. Perhaps it's something even better. I forget the opera and find myself in a Greek tragedy." When Richard Wagner invoked Greek tragedy as his own ideal of theater, Gluck was the model he chose.

IPHIGÉNIE EN AULIDE

(Iphigenia in Aulis)

THREE ACTS
MUSIC: Christoph Willibald von Gluck
TEXT (French): Marie François Louis Gand Bailli du Roullet, also called Le Blanc, after Jean Racine's tragedy
WORLD PREMIERE: Paris, Opéra, April 19, 1774
U. S. PREMIERE: Philadelphia, Academy of Music, February 22, 1935

CHARACTERS

Iphigénie, *Agamemnon's daughter*	Soprano
Clytemnestre, *her mother*.	Soprano
Achille, *a Greek hero*	Tenor
Agamemnon, *King of Mycenae*	Bass-Baritone
Patrocle, *Greek chieftain, Achille's friend*	Bass
Calchas, *the High Priest*	Bass
Arcas, *captain of Agamemnon's guards*	Bass

ACT I During the Trojan War, Greek soldiers on their way to battle are becalmed at Aulis, a small Greek port in Boeotia. Their king, Agamemnon, declares his refusal to sacrifice his daughter Iphigénie, the price demanded by the goddess Diane (Diana) for restoring the winds. Though he prays for the goddess' understanding of a father's heart, he fears that once Iphigénie lands there she will fall victim to the implacable priest Calchas. When the Greeks call upon Calchas to interpret Diane's command, the priest, though reluctant to obey it, promises the people that a sacrifice will take place. He advises Agamemnon to submit to divine will, but the King cannot bring himself to do so *(Peuvent-ils ordonner)*; he has tried to spare Iphigénie by preventing her from coming there. Nevertheless, she arrives, accompanied by her mother, Queen Clytemnestre (Clytemnestra), and welcomed by the Greeks, who do not yet know she is the intended victim. Clytemnestre confides to the girl that Agamemnon wants her taken to Argos, ostensibly to separate her from her suitor, Achille (Achilles), who has proved faithless. No sooner has Iphigénie reviled his name, however *(Hélas! mon coeur sensible et tendre)*, than he appears and denies the accusation *(Cruelle, non jamais votre insensible coeur)*. At length she is convinced, and they decide to marry that same day.

ACT II Clytemnestre announces that the ceremony is being prepared with Agamemnon's blessing. Achille introduces Iphigénie to his friend Patrocle (Patrocles), and the Greeks celebrate with song and dance. But when the couple is about to leave for the temple, Arcas warns them not to go, telling Clytemnestre that Agamemnon means to sacrifice the girl: she is the victim specified by the goddess Diane. The crowd, seeing the young pair as their future rulers, swears to prevent the sacrifice, and Clytemnestre begs Achille to save Iphigénie *(Par un père cruel)*. He says he will confront Agamemnon, though Iphigénie begs him to remember that the man is her father (trio: *C'est mon père, seigneur*). When the women withdraw, Achille sends Patrocle to reassure Iphigénie that he will treat Agamemnon with respect. But at the King's arrival, his imperious manner quickly causes Achille to flare up in defiance. After the young warrior has left, raging, Agamemnon confronts his own inner conflict: he must do his royal duty, yet he hates what it imposes on him *(Allez! O toi, l'objet le plus aimable)*.

ACT III   The crowd has changed its mood and now insists on the sacrifice. Iphigénie, resigned to her fate, tells Arcas not to risk his own life in her defense. When Achille arrives, she tries to tell him the same thing (*Il faut de mon destin*), but he will not hear of it. He insists on taking her away, but she refuses the dishonor of escaping her fate, and he leaves declaring he will let himself be sacrificed first. Clytemnestre comes to bid her daughter an anguished farewell. Iphigénie goes off, and Clytemnestre frantically vows to die with her (*Ma fille! Je la vois*).

§   At a seaside altar, Iphigénie kneels praying to the gods while Calchas prepares to strike her with the sacrificial blade. Achille rushes in with his Thessalian followers, determined to rescue her, and bloodshed is prevented only when Diane herself appears, announcing that the gods, moved by Iphigénie's obedience and Clytemnestre's devotion, have relented in their demands: the girl will be spared and the becalmed winds restored. The news is greeted with gratitude and rejoicing (ensemble: *Mon coeur ne saurait contenir*) as the Greek soldiers embark for Troy.

[Note: in classical legend, Iphigenia was sacrificed, enabling the Greeks to fight and win the Trojan War, with the result that Clytemnestra exacted vengeance by conspiring to murder Agamemnon, setting in motion the events depicted in Strauss' *Elektra*. The constraints of opera seria, however, imposed on Gluck the convention of a conciliatory ending.]

ALCESTE

(Alcestis)

THREE ACTS
MUSIC: Christoph Willibald von Gluck
TEXT (Italian): Raniero de Calzabigi, after Euripides' play
WORLD PREMIERE: Vienna, Burgtheater, December 26, 1767
REVISED VERSION
TEXT (French): Calzabigi libretto translated and adapted by Marie
    François Louis Gand Bailli du Roullet, also called Le Blanc
WORLD PREMIERE: Paris, Académie Royale de Musique, April 23,
    1776
U.S. PREMIERE: Wellesley College, Mass., March 11, 1938
METROPOLITAN PREMIERE: January 24, 1941

CHARACTERS

Alceste, *Queen of Thessaly*	Soprano
Admète, *her husband*	Tenor
Évandre, *leader of the Pherae people*	Tenor
Apollo, *protector of the house of Admetus*	Baritone
High Priest of Apollo	Bass
Hercule	Bass
Voice of the Oracle	Bass
Thanatos, *an infernal deity*	Bass
A Herald	Bass

ACT I   Legendary Greek antiquity. Admète (King Admetus) lies at death's door. His queen, Alceste (Alcestis), enters with her children as the populace laments. She prays to the gods for mercy (*Grands Dieux, du destin qui m'accable*), then proceeds into the temple to make offerings.

§ Inside the temple, the High Priest and chorus appeal to Apollo to spare the king. But after the offerings are set forth, the Oracle announces that Admète must die unless someone else will die for him. Alone, Alceste realizes she must give up her own life for her husband, but because of the great love she bears him, it is not really a sacrifice (*Non, ce n'est point un sacrifice*). The High Priest comes to tell her that the gods have accepted her offer. Declaring it is easy to die for one's love, she adds that she will not ask the gods for pity (*Divinités du Styx*).

ACT II   The mood of the people has changed to one of rejoicing: Admète has been restored to health. The king enters, acclaimed by his subjects, but is grieved to learn that someone else must die in his place. He does not yet know it is Alceste, who joins him (duet: *Cher époux! O moment fortuné!*). As the people sing her praises, she struggles privately not to show her sorrow (*O Dieux! Soutenez mon courage!*). Admète innocently tries to cheer her (*Bannis la crainte*), wondering why she is in tears. Even when Alceste declares that she will love him unto death (*Je n'ai jamais chéri la vie*), he does not understand. But when he questions her as to who the victim will be, she admits it is herself. Admète accuses her of willingness to leave him: just as she cannot live without him, he cannot live without her (*Barbare! Non, sans toi je ne puis vivre*). Still she persists in her decision (*Ah, malgré moi*).

ACT III   Outside the palace, Évandre, one of the king's deputies, tells the people that the hour of Alceste's death is at hand. Unexpectedly the Greek hero Hercule (Hercules) appears, having completed his legendary labors. Learning of the queen's plight, he vows to save her from Hades (*C'est en vain que l'enfer*).

Alceste, about to meet death, approaches the gates of the underworld, repeating that she asks no mercy of the gods (*Ah, divinités implacables*). When

Admète appears, she bids him farewell (*Vis pour garder le souvenir d'une épouse*), but he pleads heatedly with her not to leave him (*Alceste, aux noms des Dieux*). Admète now addresses the gods of Hades, asking them to take his life, as originally ordained, but Alceste tries to dissuade him (duet: *Aux cris de la douleur*). Thanatos, god of death, says they must choose which of them will die (*Caron t'appelle*). Alceste declares herself the one and starts to enter Hades, while Admète tries to stop her or else go with her. At this point Hercule appears, and the spirits of the underworld retreat from his invincible strength. Apollo descends to acknowledge Hercule's victory over Alceste's death, and to wish long life to the royal pair.

As Apollo rises back toward the heavens, Hercule, Alceste, and Admète give thanks to him (trio: *Reçois, Dieu bienfaisant*), and the people rejoice.

ARMIDE

FIVE ACTS
MUSIC: Christoph Willibald von Gluck
TEXT (French): Philippe Quinault, after Torquato Tasso's poem *Gerusalemme Liberata*
WORLD PREMIERE: Paris, Opéra, September 23, 1777
U.S. PREMIERE: New York, Metropolitan Opera, November 14, 1910

CHARACTERS

Armide, *a sorceress, Princess of Damascus* . . . . Soprano
Phénice ⎱ *Armide's confidantes* . . . . ⎰Soprano
Sidonie ⎰ . . . . ⎱Soprano
A Demon, *in the form of Lucinde, the Danish knight's beloved* . . Soprano
A Demon, *in the form of Mélisse, Ubalde's beloved* . . . . Soprano
La Haine (Hatred) . . . . Alto
Renaud, *a Crusader hero* . . . . Tenor
The Danish Knight . . . . Tenor
Artémidore, *an officer in the Crusaders' army*. . . . . Tenor
Hidraot, *a magician, King of Damascus, Armide's uncle* . . . . Baritone
Ubalde, *a Crusader*. . . . . Baritone

This opera uses a modified version of the libretto set by Lully almost a century earlier. The action takes place around the time of the early Crusades, which began at the end of the eleventh century; but the literary treatment is mythological rather than pseudo-historical. During the period of the Crusades, the Holy Land and Turkey were scenes of recurrent struggle between European (Christian) and Middle Eastern (Islamic) forces.

ACT I   In a public square in Damascus, dominated by a triumphal arch, the sorceress Armide (Armida) laments her inability to subdue with her charms the most hated Crusade leader, Renaud (Rinaldo). In a dream, she has imagined that at the moment of conquering Renaud she was stricken powerless by love for him *(Les Enfers ont prédit cent fois)*. Her uncle, the master magician Hidraot, enters and tells her he would like to see her find a husband. She replies that only someone capable of defeating Renaud would be worthy of her love. Aronte, one of Armide's lieutenants, comes to report that Renaud has succeeded in rescuing the prisoners taken after the most recent military engagement. All Armide's court join in swearing to avenge his audacity.

ACT II   On a lonely plain, Artémidore, an officer in the army of Godefroi (Godfrey of Bouillon), thanks Renaud for rescuing him from capture by the Saracens. He pleads with Renaud, who has had a falling out with Godefroi, not to abandon the Crusaders' cause. Renaud replies that he prefers the freer life of a knight errant, whereupon Artémidore warns him to avoid the enchantments of Armide. After the two men withdraw, Hidraot comes to the spot with Armide and calls forth evil spirits to bring Renaud there *(Esprits de haine et de rage)*. Under his spell, the desert spot is transformed into a riverbank. Renaud is seen approaching their trap, so the two sorcerers leave. Admiring the natural beauty of the spot *(Les plus aimables fleurs)*, Renaud lies down to rest. As he sleeps, a Naiad, nymphs, and shepherdesses—all demons in disguise—weave enchantment over him and garland him with flowers. Armed with a dagger, Armide steals in, bent on killing her enemy, but the sight of him moves her to thoughts of a more tender conquest. She changes the demons into zephyrs that bear her and Renaud away.

ACT III   Alone in a desert place, Armide reflects on the danger of being taken captive by love for the foe she wanted to conquer *(Ah! si la liberté)*. Her attendants Phénice and Sidonie assure her she has enslaved the knight with her charms, but she realizes the danger of being disarmed by her conflicting emotions *(Hélas! que son amour est différent du mien!)*. Alone, she invokes Hatred *(Venez, Haine implacable!)*, who appears from the underworld with her followers. When the forces of Hatred perform a ritual to exorcise Love from her heart, however, Armide changes her mind. Rebuffed, Hatred warns her that she will lose Renaud to his pursuit of duty and glory. Shaken, Armide appeals to Love to calm her fears *(O Ciel! quelle horrible menace!)*.

ACT IV   In a desert wilderness, Ubalde and a Danish Knight, sent by the other Crusaders in search of Renaud, clear the way of guardian monsters conjured up by Armide. They spy the enchanted island palace where Armide holds Renaud in thrall.

§ On the island, demons dance as Ubalde and the Danish Knight draw near. A demon disguised as the Danish Knight's sweetheart, Lucinde, beckons to him (duet: *Jouissons du bonheur suprème*), but Ubalde warns him of the illusion. Another demon, in the form of Ubalde's beloved, Mélisse, nearly vanquishes *his* resolve; now it is the Danish Knight's turn to undeceive his friend. Using a golden scepter, the two men banish the visions (duet: *Fuyons les douceurs dangereuses*).

ACT V   At Armide's enchanted palace, Renaud, under her spell, fears she will leave him, but she more realistically fears it is he who will leave her *(Un noir pressentiment me trouble)*: his first love is knightly glory. Nevertheless, they pledge mutual love *(Non, je perdrais plutôt le jour)*, and spirits of pleasure dance around them. Ubalde and the Danish Knight find their way in and, during Armide's absence, show Renaud a diamond buckler to remind him of his military calling. Brought back to reality, Renaud rejects the trappings of idle romance and takes up his sword and shield. As he makes to leave with his friends, Armide returns and follows him, pleading in vain with him to stay, even offering to go with him. He is resolute, though he gallantly pledges to remember her with love. She retorts that he cannot really have loved her *(Ingrat! sans toi je ne puis vivre!)*. She swoons as the Crusaders depart, then, reviving, declares she surely will die. In near-delirium *(Le perfide Renaud me fuit)* she orders the demons to destroy the palace, and they take her away in a winged chariot.

IPHIGÉNIE EN TAURIDE

(Iphigénie in Tauris)

FOUR ACTS
MUSIC: Christoph Willibald von Gluck
TEXT (French): Nicolas-François Guillard, based on Guymond de la
    Touche's play, after Euripides' drama
WORLD PREMIERE: Paris, Opéra, May 18, 1779
SECOND VERSION
TEXT (German): Johann Baptist von Alxinger, based on the Guillard
    libretto
PREMIERE: Vienna, Burgtheater, October 23, 1781
U.S. PREMIERE: New York, Metropolitan Opera, November 25, 1916
    (in German)

CHARACTERS

Iphigénie, *High Priestess of Diane*. . . . . Soprano
Diane, *goddess of the hunt* . . . . Soprano
Pylade, *King of Phocis, Oreste's friend* . . . . Tenor
Oreste, *King of Argos and Mycenae, Iphigénie's brother* . . . . . Baritone
Thoas, *King of Scythia* . . . . Bass

Five years after the end of the Trojan War, Iphigénie (Iphigenia), rescued from a sacrificial death in Aulis, has been taken away with other Greeks to refuge in Scythia (today southern Russia), where she lives among the Taurians as a priestess of the goddess Diane (Diana).

ACT I   As a storm arises at sea, Iphigénie and other Greek priestesses pray in the temple of Diane for calm. When the storm abates, Iphigénie is seized by a vision of her family's palace in Argos: her father, Agamemnon, has died at the hands of her mother, Clytemnestre (Clytemnestra), while Iphigénie finds herself forced against her will to kill her own brother, Oreste (Orestes). She beseeches the goddess to end her exile and reunite her with her brother *(Ô toi qui prolongeas mes jours)*. Thoas, the Scythian ruler, enters with a crowd of his subjects; he has learned from the Oracle that his life is in danger unless a stranger is sacrificed *(De noirs pressentiments)*, and he wants Iphigénie to perform the sacrifice. The crowd announces that victims—two young Greeks—have been cast ashore by the recent storm. As preliminary ceremonies begin, the two young men, Oreste (traveling incognito) and his friend Pylade (Pylades), are brought in. Refusing to reveal the purpose that brought them to these shores, they are led off to prison.

ACT II   In their prison cell, Oreste laments that he is the cause of Pylade's death *(Dieux qui me poursuivez)*. Pylade replies that he is content to die in Oreste's company *(Unis dès la plus tendre enfance)*. Hardly has he voiced these sentiments, however, than guards arrive to take him away. At first driven to distraction by this turn of events, Oreste feels suddenly calm *(Le calme rentre dans mon coeur!)*, only to be surrounded by the Furies, who demand vengeance for his having killed his mother. They vanish when Iphigénie appears. Questioning the stranger, whom she does not recognize, she learns that her vision of Agamemnon's death was true; further, that Oreste avenged the murder by killing Clytemnestre. Dismissing the prisoner, Iphigénie laments with her fellow priestesses that her homeland and its rulers have been destroyed *(Ô malheureuse Iphigénie!)*. Assuming that Oreste is dead too, she prays for him *(Ô mon frère)*.

ACT III   In her quarters, Iphigénie, reminded of her lost brother by something about the Greek prisoner, determines to spare his life *(D'une image, hélas! trop chérie)*. He and Pylade are brought in, happy to be rejoined, startled to learn that the priestess chosen to sacrifice them is herself a Greek. She cannot avoid executing one of them but may be able to spare the other (trio: *Je pourrais du tyran*). Charging Oreste with carrying a message back to Argos, she chooses him to be spared. Left alone together, the two friends find it unbearable that either of them should live at the cost of the other's life (duet: *Et tu prétends encore que tu m'aimes*). Pylade implores Oreste to accept his sacrifice *(Ah! mon ami, j'implore ta pitié!)*, but when Iphigénie returns for the victim, Oreste offers himself instead. He threatens to kill himself if refused, so Iphigénie gives in, and as he is led away, she turns to Pylade with the message she wants delivered to her sister Electre (Electra) in Argos. Pylade now wonders who she is, but Iphigénie will divulge no more. She leaves Pylade, who swears to save Oreste or die in the attempt.

ACT IV   In the temple, Iphigénie again prays to Diane, saying something deep in her heart makes her unable to sacrifice the young Greek *(Je t'implore et je tremble)*; but receiving no sign from the goddess, she steels herself to do her duty. Oreste, welcoming an end to his torment, urges her to strike. While the priestesses prepare him for the ceremony and hand her the knife, Oreste, facing death, invokes the memory of his sister Iphigénie, who he believes died in Aulis. Now she and the other Greek priestesses realize who he is: her brother, their king. Their tearful recognition is disturbed by news that Thoas is on his way there, furious over his discovery of Pylade's escape. Bursting into the temple, Thoas ignores Iphigénie's explanation that she cannot sacrifice her own brother, and he is about to dispatch the victim himself when Pylade arrives with a band of Greek men and kills Thoas instead. Greeks and Scythians face off in combat, but Diane descends in a cloud, ordering the Scythians to obey her laws, while Oreste and Iphigénie are to return to Greece. Oreste tells Pylade that Iphigénie is his sister *(Dans cet objet touchant)*, amid rejoicing among the exiled Greeks.

FROMENTAL HALÉVY
1799–1862

*H*alévy was one of the principal composers of French grand opera, a genre that proved more important for its influence than for its staying power. Without the preeminence of Paris in the mid-nineteenth-century music world, and without the productions of Daniel-François Auber, Giacomo Meyerbeer, and Halévy at the Opéra, Verdi's *Aida*—which has far outlasted them all—would not have come into being, and neither would some of the more grandiose music dramas of Wagner. A form built primarily on theatrical effect, however, with music seen as a secondary feature, was hardly the vehicle to which a composer could entrust his aspirations. At best it offered a good way of making a living.

Auber and Meyerbeer were sometimes guilty of settling for triviality, but Halévy took his work seriously. A prize pupil of Luigi Cherubini, he had been groomed with a deep respect for the classics. He composed prolifically for the stage—some forty operas of both the grand and *comique* genres, as well as ballets—and found time as well for careers as a singing coach, administrator, and composition teacher. He was approaching the age of thirty-five before he attempted his first grand opera, *La Juive,* which became his greatest success during his lifetime and the one work by which posterity has remembered him. Even Wagner, who had turned against Meyerbeer, admired *La Juive,* and Berlioz, who grew tired of it, found kind words for Halévy as a craftsman.

La Juive was Halévy's first setting of a text by Eugène Scribe, whose atelier specialized in producing period epics, somewhat comparable to the Errol Flynn and Victor Mature movies of the 1940s. Because of the composer's gift for matching music to a historical milieu, and for working up a stirring chorus at a climactic moment, his score brought out the best in Scribe's libretto without overexposing its contrivances. The result is a theatrically powerful work, aided in its first production by the star tenor Gilbert Duprez as Éléazar. It was an arresting idea to turn a character part into the central role, and in the twentieth century such illustrious tenors as Enrico Caruso, Giovanni Martinelli, and Richard Tucker continued to make the most of it.

Halévy, a resourceful, skilled orchestrator, lacked the kind of musical imagination needed to carry his innovations over into other aspects of his writing. Because his operas broke little new ground, they were considered safe by the public. There was nothing in his makeup to suggest the restless imagination or feverish poetics of a Berlioz, or the melodic freshness of a Bizet (his own son-in-law). As an exemplar of his time, however, he stands in relief to its superficiality as a figure of dignity, humanity, and substance. Several of his other operas are probably as worthy of occasional revival as *La Juive,* which remains a crowd-pleaser and a thoughtful look at history.

LA JUIVE

(The Jewess)

FIVE ACTS
MUSIC: Fromental Halévy
TEXT: Eugène Scribe
WORLD PREMIERE: Paris, Opéra, February 23, 1835
U.S. PREMIERE: New Orleans, February 13, 1844
METROPOLITAN PREMIERE: January 16, 1885 (in German)

CHARACTERS

Rachel, *Éléazar's daughter* . . . . Soprano
Princess Eudoxie, *the emperor's niece.* . . . . Soprano
Eléazar, *a Jewish goldsmith.* . . . . Tenor
Léopold, *prince of the Empire.* . . . . Tenor
Ruggiero, *the city provost* . . . . Baritone
Albert, *sergeant in the emperor's army* . . . . Baritone
Cardinal de Brogni, *president of the Council of Constance* . . . . . . Bass

The action takes place at Constance (Konstanz) in southwestern Germany in 1414, at the time of the Council of Constance, during which Jan Hus was condemned to die at the stake as a heretic (see Janáček's *The Excursions of Mr. Brouček*).

ACT I   A public square. In church, the congregation sings a *Te Deum* in honor of victory over the rebel Hussites. In the street, citizens complain that despite their religious holiday, Éléazar the jeweler has not stopped working in his shop next door. Prince Léopold, though engaged to Princess Eudoxie, is in love with Éléazar's daughter, Rachel, and to court her has disguised himself as "Samuel," a young Jewish painter. He is recognized by Albert, an officer of the imperial guard, but begs for anonymity—even though his uncle, Emperor Sigismund, is coming to town for the trial of Jan Hus, whose supporters have been defeated by troops under Léopold. Ruggiero, a city official, reads a proclamation declaring the day a holiday; since Éléazar is still at work, Ruggiero accuses him of blasphemy. Éléazar and Rachel are about to be hauled off for execution when Cardinal de Brogni, head of the Council of Constance, appears and questions Éléazar. The two recognize each other from years before, when Brogni was not yet a cleric but had a wife and daughter, whom he later lost; Éléazar remembers him as the harsh magistrate who banished him from Rome. Though Brogni now saves him with a public pardon, Éléazar remains bitter (ensemble, Brogni: *Si la rigueur et la vengeance*).

With the crowd gone, Léopold serenades Rachel outside her window *(Loin de son amie)*. She appears and invites him to her father's house for a Seder that evening. He leaves as the citizens return, awaiting the imperial procession. Seeing that Éléazar and Rachel have been pushed aside and have taken refuge on the steps of the church, Ruggiero again accuses them of blasphemy, and the crowd is ready to throw them in Lake Constance. Léopold reappears and, with Albert's aid, stops the crowd; Rachel skeptically wonders how a Jewish painter was able to do this (ensemble, Léopold: *Que toujours elle ignore*).

ACT II   That evening in his house, Éléazar inaugurates Passover *(O Dieu de nos pères)* with other members of the Jewish community and the disguised Léopold. When knocking is heard at the door, religious trappings are hastily concealed and the visitors withdraw, except for Léopold, who remains off to one side, pretending to paint. Éléazar is surprised to find that his visitor is Princess Eudoxie. She inquires about a jeweled chain once worn by Emperor Constantine, which she wants to give to her fiancé, Prince Léopold (trio: *(Tu possède, dit-on, un joyau magnifique)*. Apart, Léopold is torn by remorse. Éléazar, looking forward to handsome payment, promises to deliver the chain the next day. As he escorts Eudoxie out, Léopold takes hurried leave of Rachel, promising to return.

Later that evening, Rachel anxiously awaits Léopold *(Il va venir)*. When he appears, he confesses that he deceived her: he is a Christian (duet, Rachel: *Lorsqu'à toi je me suis donnée*). Despite misgivings, she is persuaded to elope with him, but Éléazar returns and surprises the couple (trio: *Je vois son front coupable*). When he too learns that Léopold is an imposter, he attacks him, but Rachel pleads so eloquently *(Pour lui, pour moi, mon père)* that he desists. Léopold, however, feels such guilt that he cannot accept Rachel's hand and cries that he is accursed—an emotion seconded by Éléazar (trio: *Chrétien sacrilège*).

ACT III In Eudoxie's rooms, the princess receives an unexpected visit from Rachel (duet: *Qui t'amène?*). Ignorant of Eudoxie's relationship with Léopold, the girl asks to be taken under her protection as a servant; Eudoxie agrees and is about to dismiss her when Léopold enters. As he hides his shock at seeing Rachel, who doesn't recognize him, Eudoxie greets him as her fiancé (boléro: *Mon doux seigneur et maître*). Trumpets announce a celebration.

§ In an elaborate garden, nobles and officials watch a pantomime and dancing (ballet). Eudoxie and the guests hail Léopold as conqueror of the heretics. Éléazar arrives with the jeweled chain. Rachel now recognizes Léopold as the supposed Samuel and cries out that he is unworthy to receive such a tribute. In fact, she declares, he deserves to die for the crime of being involved with a Jewish girl; and the girl, as his accomplice, deserves to die with him (sextet, Léopold: *Je frissonne et succombe*). Since Léopold does not deny the accusation, Brogni is obliged by his duties of office to pronounce a curse on him and the two Jews for their offense against temporal and religious law (ensemble: *Anathème!*).

ACT IV In a hall leading to the Council Chamber, Eudoxie has Rachel brought in and pleads with her to save Léopold by saying her charge was a lie (duet: *Ah! que ma voix plaintive*). Brogni next speaks with her: will she recant, to save herself as well as her lover? She refuses, saying she wishes to die, and is led away. Brogni sends for Éléazar and tells him that only by renouncing his faith can he save himself and Rachel from condemnation by the Council (duet: *Ta fille en ce moment*). Éléazar indignantly refuses. To torment Brogni, he reminds him of the day the Neapolitans entered Rome, when Brogni saw his wife and infant daughter die in his burned, pillaged house. But the child did *not* die, says Éléazar: she was rescued by a Jew whom he knows. Though Brogni begs for more information, Éléazar says he wants the revenge of dying without revealing it (duet: *Oui, ce feu qui brille*). Brogni, beside himself, rushes out, and Éléazar confronts his own dilemma: for revenge on Brogni, he must sacrifice the innocent girl (*Rachel, quand du Seigneur*). As the crowd is heard outside calling for death, he imagines God's light guiding him and Rachel to martyrdom (*Dieu m'éclaire, fille chère*).

ACT V In a pavilion overlooking the city, Éléazar and Rachel are brought for execution. When Éléazar demands to know why Léopold is not there, Rachel admits she has exonerated him by claiming her accusation was false. As she asks his forgiveness (ensemble: *Je vais quitter la terre*) and Brogni begs again for his secret, Éléazar struggles with the belief that Rachel is better off in heaven than in the hands of these hateful infidels. At last, however, he tells her she can save herself if she will accept Christianity. She refuses. Brogni pleads once more: is his own daughter really alive? "There she is!" replies Éléazar, as Rachel is thrown into the flames, just before he himself goes to his death.

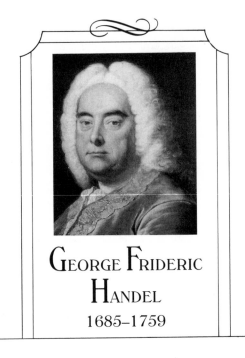

GEORGE FRIDERIC HANDEL
1685–1759

The tricentennial in 1985 of Handel's birth spurred an already ongoing revival of interest in his operas. Once the rage of London, they had fallen out of fashion there even during his lifetime, and in later centuries, because of their prolix, mannered plots and old-style vocal virtuosity, they were considered either unperformable or not worth the effort. As recently as the 1950s, performances that did take place often suffered from a pious, conscientious style that smacked of scholarship rather than the theater. The resurgence of interest in romantic eighteenth-century bel canto (Rossini, Bellini, Donizetti) proved more helpful, as singers started to equip themselves with coloratura agility and a feeling for its expressive use. Toward the end of the twentieth century, Handel singing has reached its highest level since the composer's day, and audiences have responded in kind.

A major difficulty in reviving Handel remains the casting of roles he wrote for castrated male sopranos and altos. *Faute de mieux,* these have to be entrusted to female singers, males at a lower octave, or countertenors. Each choice presents problems: female singers sometimes lack power and seem unconvincing in male roles; men at a lower octave are not performing in the register the composer wanted; countertenors often lack not only power but the ability to vary between loud and soft. Through trial and error, casting by the attributes of a given performer in each case, these problems can be solved. Perhaps the most promising development has been the appearance of a more sanguine breed of countertenor, capable of rendering dramatic accents with ringing conviction.

Handel was the major opera producer of his time. Inspired in that direction as a young man by the example of Reinhard Keiser, a decade his senior and chief of the Hamburg Opera, Handel wrote several Italian operas while still in Germany, then mastered the form in Italy. Starting in late 1706, he concentrated on liturgical music in Rome, where opera was not allowed; but soon he was writing operas for Florence, Naples, and Venice, where he was hailed as *il caro Sassone* (the dear Saxon). By 1710, Handel had returned to Germany and visited London, where *Rinaldo* (1711), stitched together with parts of previous scores, brought quick celebrity. Capitalizing on the rage for Italian opera there, he returned in 1712, taking up residence and becoming in effect an English composer.

He continued turning out operas in Italian, carried on a rivalry with Giovanni Bononcini, and endured the ups and downs of theater management. He also experimented with pasticcios, masques, pastorales, and eventually oratorios. After the decline of Italian opera as an entertainment in London, he turned his full attention to English oratorios (some of them stageworthy, for example, *Samson*) and held the interest of the public. In both opera and oratorio, Handel's secret of success was his innate *musical* dramatic sense (staging was not realistic in those days, and acting was minimal). He possessed the imagination and adaptability to modify the opera-seria format, so that his operas, far from all sounding similar, each took on its own coloration. This is reflected not only in his writing for voice but in the orchestration, which can set the stage as vividly as any scenery.

During the Victorian era, Handel became embalmed. His oratorios were performed by gigantic choruses. Even a whimsically ironic piece like "Ombra mai fu" from *Serse,* institutionalized as "Handel's Largo," was played at funereal tempo on stately occasions. As the centenary of the Edwardian era approaches, however, Handel's music is seen once again to be pleasurable. Though such works as *Alcina* and *Serse* are convoluted and artificial in plot, their musical elegance—given capable singers and imaginative staging—is no longer in doubt.

RINALDO

THREE ACTS
MUSIC: George Frideric Handel
TEXT (Italian): Giacomo Rossi, after a scenario by Aaron Hill based
   on Torquato Tasso's *Gerusalemme Liberata*

148

GEORGE FRIDERIC HANDEL

WORLD PREMIERE: London, Queen's Theatre, February 24, 1711
U.S. PREMIERE: Houston Grand Opera, October 16, 1975
METROPOLITAN PREMIERE: January 19, 1984

CHARACTERS

Armida, *enchantress, Queen of Damascus* . . . . Soprano
Almirena, *Goffredo's daughter, betrothed to Rinaldo* . . . . Soprano
Eustazio, *Goffredo's brother*. . . . . .Mezzo-Soprano
Rinaldo, *Crusader hero*. . . . . .Mezzo-Soprano
Goffredo, *Crusader general*. . . . . Tenor
Argante, *King of Jerusalem, in love with Armida*. . . . . Bass
A Christian Magician. . . . . Bass

During and since Handel's lifetime, *Rinaldo,* one of the most successful of his operas, has been performed in a variety of versions. The story below follows the Metropolitan Opera reconstruction of 1984.

ACT I   In A.D. 1099, at the siege of Jerusalem during the First Crusade, Goffredo (Godfrey of Bouillon), leader of the Crusaders, greets the knight Rinaldo (Renaud), who hopes to marry Goffredo's daughter, Almirena, as soon as victory is achieved. Almirena says she will delay her own happiness until the outcome *(Bel piacere è godere)*. Rinaldo replies that he too feels the pangs of love *(Ogni indugio d'un amante)*. A Herald announces Argante, King of Jerusalem, who rides in on a chariot. Though he thinks he hears threatening omens *(Sibilar gli angui d'Aletto),* he is unafraid and asks for three days' truce, which Goffredo grants. Alone, Argante reveals that his lover, the sorceress Armida, will use the time to fathom the enemy's secrets.

§   By a desolate rock near Armida's castle, Argante seeks her out to ask what she has learned from her occult sources. If Rinaldo is distracted from the fight, she says, the enemy will be weakened. She can accomplish this by sorcery *(Molto veglio, molto spero)*.

§   In her garden, Almirena asks the birds and breezes where her lover is *(Augelletti, che cantate)*. Rinaldo appears, and they pledge their love (duet: *Scherzano sul tuo volto)*, but Armida sweeps in with her helpers and abducts Almirena. To Goffredo, who arrives with his brother Eustazio and asks what happened, the dazed Rinaldo tries to explain *(Cor' ingrato, ti rammembri)*. Goffredo says they must hasten to a wise hermit for advice. Rinaldo asks the winds to speed his way *(Venti, turbini, prestate)*.

ACT II   At the shore, where a boat lies anchored and Mermaids sport in the water, Goffredo tells Rinaldo they will soon be able to find Almirena. One of the Mermaids invites them to board the vessel, which will take them to the lonely beach where Almirena languishes *(Il vostro maggio de' bei verdi anni)*. Goffredo, sensing a trap, tries to stop him, but Rinaldo swears that even if he has to brave the underworld, he will rescue Almirena *(Il Tricerbero humilato)*. He goes on board and is ferried out of sight.

§ At Armida's enchanted palace, Almirena begs the sympathetic Argante for her freedom, only to find that he has fallen in love with her. She weeps for her cruel fate *(Lascia ch'io pianga)*. Argante, touched, vows to take her away from Armida *(Basta che sol tu chieda)*, but Armida bursts upon the pair, cursing his treachery. Her attendant spirits capture Argante and lead him off, while Almirena is locked in a cage. Armida orders Rinaldo brought to her, so she can sacrifice him to her anger, but the sight of him inspires her with love instead. He resists her pleas and calls her a cruel tyrant (duet: *Fermati! No, crudel!*). By magic, Armida transforms herself into the likeness of Almirena. Rinaldo embraces her, but when she vanishes, he realizes he has been tricked and wonders desperately what has become of the real Almirena *(Cara sposa, amante cara)*.

ACT III   At the foot of the mountain capped by Armida's castle is the cave of a hermit, the Christian Magician. Goffredo finds it and calls him forth *(Tu, a cui vien concesso)*. Appearing astride a fire-breathing dragon, the Magician gives him a wand to subdue Armida's guardian monsters. Goffredo sets out on his quest.

§ Meanwhile, Rinaldo is seen fighting his own way past some of these monsters. At her palace, Armida reconciles with Argante, each confessing a momentary error in having loved someone else (duet: *Dunque mi sia concesso*). Almirena is brought and put back in her cage, where Armida declares she will bleed to death. Rinaldo bursts in, threatening Armida *(O infedel al mio desio)*. Goffredo appears, using the magic wand to make Armida and her castle vanish. Goffredo and Rinaldo are reunited with Almirena. The lovers are overjoyed (duet: *Alma mia! Dolce ristoro!*). When Goffredo exhorts Rinaldo to take his valor to the battlefield, the young knight pledges to conquer or die *(Mio cor, che mi sai dir?)*.

§ At the gates of Jerusalem, Rinaldo hails the sound of the trumpet calling his forces to glory *(Or la tromba in suon festante)*. Argante, defeated, is brought in fetters; acknowledging the superior magic of the enemy's faith, he and Armida console each other, and Armida penitently breaks the wand signifying her own power. Seeing this, Goffredo magnanimously frees her and Argante. All join in hailing virtue, the only true vanquishing power *(Vinto è sol della virtù)*.

RODELINDA

THREE ACTS
MUSIC: George Frideric Handel
TEXT (Italian): Nicola Francesco Haym, adapted from Antonio Salvi's
    libretto, after Pierre Corneille's play *Pertharite, Roi des Lombards*
WORLD PREMIERE: London, Haymarket Theater, February 13, 1725
U.S. PREMIERE: Northampton, Mass., Smith College, May 9, 1931
    (in English)

CHARACTERS

Rodelinda, *Queen of Lombardy, Bertarido's wife* . . . . Soprano
Bertarido, *King of Lombardy* . . . . Alto
Eduige, *Bertarido's sister* . . . . Alto
Unulfo, *a young nobleman* . . . . Alto
Grimoaldo, *usurper of Bertarido's throne* . . . . Tenor
Garibaldo, *Duke of Turin, Grimoaldo's friend* . . . . Bass

The action takes place in Lombardy, probably during the eleventh century, when the region, after a long period as part of Charlemagne's empire, began to experience a decentralization of political power. King Bertarido has been driven from the throne of Milan by Duke Grimoaldo with the help of Garibaldo, treacherous Duke of Turin. Queen Rodelinda believes her husband dead, unaware that he is hiding in the crypt of the Lombard kings, waiting for a chance to rescue her and their young son, Flavio.

ACT I   At the royal palace, mourning the loss of Bertarido, Rodelinda believes herself widowed but feels she must go on with life for the sake of their son *(Ho perduto il caro sposo)*. The usurper Grimoaldo enters and boldly pleads his love for her: if she will marry him, she can remain queen and have a king beside her once more. Indignantly she refuses *(L'empio rigor del fato)* and withdraws. Grimoaldo is advised by his henchman, Garibaldo, to break with Eduige, Bertarido's ambitious sister, who pursues him in the belief that she herself can share the throne with him.

Eduige appears, and Grimoaldo reminds her that when he courted her, she refused him; now that he has seized power, she is the one who wants the marriage, and it is his turn to refuse *(Io già t'amai, ritrosa)*. When he has left, Eduige calls on Garibaldo for help in humbling her erstwhile suitor *(Lo farò, dirò)*. Garibaldo, alone, states his own ambitions for the throne: by helping Eduige and feigning love for her, he hopes to edge closer to power *(Di Cupido impiego)*.

§ At the burial place of the Lombard kings in a cypress grove, Bertarido, disguised as a Hungarian, voices the sorrow of separation from Rodelinda *(Dove sei? amato bene!)*. He is sought out by Unulfo, who has become counselor to the usurper while remaining secretly loyal to Bertarido. In order to ensure the safety of Bertarido's refuge, Unulfo has not told the queen her husband is still alive: her sorrow will make the deception more credible. Unulfo persuades Bertarido that he must not let her see him. The two men conceal themselves as Rodelinda pays her respects to her husband's urn.

The scheming Garibaldo draws near and confronts Rodelinda with an ultimatum: either accept Grimoaldo's offer of marriage, ensuring her son's eventual place on the throne, or else accept death for herself and the boy. Having no choice, Rodelinda says she will submit to the marriage, but she swears Garibaldo will pay with his own life *(Morrai, sì, l'empia tua testa)*. When she has left, Grimoaldo steps forward and reassures his henchman that he will not let Rodelinda make good such a threat *(Se per te giungo a godere)*.

With both men gone, Bertarido emerges from hiding, distraught by his wife's capitulation. He means to punish her by waiting until after her remarriage to reveal that he is still alive *(Confusa si miri l'infida consorte)*.

Act II At the palace, Garibaldo persuades Eduige to be his if he will avenge her slight by Grimoaldo. He senses, however, that love for Grimoaldo still rules her heart. After he has left, she offers to help Rodelinda against Grimoaldo *(De' miei scherni per far le vendette)*. She leaves, and when Grimoaldo appears, Rodelinda asks, as a condition of marriage, that the treacherous Garibaldo be put to death. Grimoaldo says he will comply. Next she challenges him to put her son to death as well, saying she could not at the same time be mother to a legitimate ruler and wife to a usurper *(Spietati, io vi giurai)*. When she has left, Garibaldo urges him to accept her challenge and condemn the child; against his own conscience, Grimoaldo is tempted to comply *(Prigioniera ho l'alma in pena)*.

When Unulfo asks Garibaldo why he gave Grimoaldo such cruel advice, Garibaldo replies that a tyrant has to behave like one *(Tirannia gli diede il regno)*. Then he leaves Unulfo to realize that Garibaldo will betray his new king as readily as he did the old. But Unulfo hopes Bertarido will be heartened by the fierceness of Rodelinda's loyalty *(Fra tempeste funeste a quest'alma)*.

§ In "a remote place," Bertarido finds in the murmur of streams and springs, the echoes of caverns and hills, a reflection of his tears *(Con rauco mormorio al pianto mio).* He is recognized by the wandering Eduige, who is surprised to find her brother alive. As they converse, Unulfo comes and assures Bertarido that contrary to his belief, Rodelinda has been true. Saying his kingdom no longer matters, Bertarido looks forward only to reunion with his wife *(Scacciata dal suo nido).*

§ In Rodelinda's apartments, she is both overjoyed and fearful to learn that Bertarido is alive *(Ritorna, oh caro e dolce mio tesoro!).* He appears, apologizes for having doubted her, and they embrace. Grimoaldo, bursting in, fails to recognize Bertarido and accuses Rodelinda of faithlessness both to her late husband and to himself. To protect Bertarido, Rodelinda declares he is an imposter. Grimoaldo orders him arrested, saying he is doomed, whether or not he is really Bertarido *(Tuo drudo è mio rivale);* allowing the pair a last farewell, he leaves. Rodelinda bemoans the fact that her husband's return has caused her as much grief as his absence, but Bertarido is simply happy to see her (duet: *Io t'abbraccio, e più che morte.*)

ACT III In the palace, Eduige gives Unulfo a key to help the prisoner escape. Unulfo is delighted *(Un zeffiro spirò che serenò quest'alma).* To atone for her earlier ambitions, Eduige wants only to save the royal couple and their child *(Quando più fiera tempesta freme).* Garibaldo, however, tries to convince Grimoaldo that the supposed Bertarido should die: "Either kill the wretch or lose a kingdom." Grimoaldo is unwilling, since he would further alienate Rodelinda and deepen his own guilt *(Tra sospetti, affetti e timori).*

In a dungeon, Bertarido wonders whether it was love or fate that brought about his undoing *(Chi di voi fu più infedele).* A sword, thrown to him in the darkness by Eduige, lands at his feet. Seizing it, he attacks the first intruder who enters his cell, but this turns out to be his faithful Unulfo. Not severely hurt, Unulfo is able to guide Bertarido out into a secret passage. Meanwhile, Eduige fetches a lantern and comes to the cell with Rodelinda and the child Flavio; they find only Bertarido's bloodstained cloak. Fearing her husband dead, Rodelinda pours out her grief *(Se'l mio duol non è si forte).*

Emerging in a garden, Unulfo sets out to look for Rodelinda and the child. Bertarido savors the idea of regaining his rightful power *(Se fiera belva ha cinto).* He conceals himself as Grimoaldo enters. Longing for a moment's rest from his guilty and conflicting emotions, Grimoaldo confesses remorse for his misdeeds *(Pastorello d'un povero armento).* As he lies dozing, Garibaldo creeps up, steals his sword, and means to dispatch him. At this, Bertarido steps out of hiding and kills Garibaldo.

Rodelinda arrives, brought by Unulfo. Grimoaldo, owing his life to Bertarido, hails him as King of Milan. As for himself, he will marry Eduige and rule in Pavia. Rodelinda at last can feel the joy of reunion with her husband *(Mio caro bene! non ho più affanni).* Both couples and Unulfo hail the end of darkness and the rewards of virtue (quintet: *Dopo la notte oscura).*

ALCINA

THREE ACTS
MUSIC: George Frideric Handel
TEXT (Italian): anon., adapted from Antonio Fanzaglia's libretto for
    Carlo Broschi's opera *L'Isola d'Alcina* (1728), after Lodovico Ari-
    osto's *Orlando Furioso*
WORLD PREMIERE: London, Covent Garden, April 16, 1735
U.S. PREMIERE: Dallas Civic Opera, November 19, 1960

CHARACTERS

Alcina, *a sorceress* . . . . Soprano
Ruggiero, *a knight* . . . . Soprano
Morgana, *Alcina's sister* . . . . Soprano
Oberto, *a young nobleman* . . . . Soprano
Bradamante, *betrothed to Ruggiero* . . . . Alto
Oronte, *commander of Alcina's troops* . . . . Tenor
Melisso, *Bradamante's guardian* . . . . Bass

ACT I   In the mythical past (possibly in the Near East around the eleventh
century, when the Crusades began), on a desert island, two figures—Bradamante, disguised as her brother Ricciardo, and Melisso, also in soldier's garb—
meet Morgana, who tells them they are in the realm of the sorceress Alcina,
which they had been trying to find. Morgana, Alcina's sister, feels attracted to
"Ricciardo" *(O s'apre al riso).* She leads the two to Alcina's court.

§ There Bradamante recognizes Ruggiero, the lover who had abandoned her.
Alcina is adored by Ruggiero, whom she has ensnared with spells; she tells
Ruggiero of her love for him *(Di, cor mio, quanto t'amai).*
    Oberto, a young nobleman, asks the newcomers if they have any news of
his father, Astolfo. Father and son were shipwrecked there and kindly received
by Alcina, but Astolfo has disappeared—probably transformed into a wild
beast, like Alcina's other lovers. Oberto laments his loss *(Chi mi rende il genitor)*
and departs.
    Bradamante approaches Ruggiero, asking if he recognizes her; he says she
resembles his friend Ricciardo. Accused of abandoning Ricciardo's sister, Rug-

giero denies having loved anyone but Alcina, saying he now serves only Cupid
(*Sieguo Cupido*).

Oronte, commander of Alcina's troops, believes that the supposed Ricciardo
is his rival for Morgana's affections and challenges him, but Morgana enters
and offers protection. Bradamante blames the confrontation on jealousy, saying
she too knows its pangs (*È gelosia, forza è d'amore*). When she and Melisso have
left, Oronte confronts Morgana, who will not commit herself to him.

§ Outside Alcina's apartments, Oronte tries to warn Ruggiero that Alcina
turns her cast-off lovers into beasts (*Semplicetto! a donna credi?*). He even pretends that Alcina loves Ricciardo, causing Ruggiero to accuse Alcina when she
returns. When Bradamante as Ricciardo appears, plying Alcina with flattery,
Ruggiero feels this suspicion confirmed. Alcina again protests her love for him
(*Sì; son quella!*), but Ruggiero believes the disguised girl to be a man—and in
love with Alcina (*La bocca vaga*).

Morgana reappears, wanting to save Ricciardo from being turned into a
beast to appease Ruggiero's jealousy. Thinking fast, Bradamante tells Morgana
to reassure Alcina that Ricciardo is no rival but loves only Morgana. This has
the desired effect on the infatuated Morgana (*Tornami a vagheggiar*).

ACT II   In Alcina's palace, Ruggiero longs to see the enchantress again (*Col
celarvi a chi v'ama*) but is disturbed by Melisso, now disguised as Ruggiero's
old tutor. To disillusion Ruggiero about Alcina's magic kingdom, Melisso
gives him a charmed ring that enables him to see the palace as a mere waste-
land. To get Ruggiero away, Melisso tells him to put his armor back on and
pretend to Alcina that he wants to go hunting (*Pensa a chi geme*).

Bradamante reveals to Ruggiero that she is not Ricciardo but Bradamante.
When Ruggiero, suspecting sorcery, refuses to believe it, Bradamante wants
to avenge this rejection (*Vorrei vendicarmi*). Alone, Ruggiero wonders if he is
being deceived (*Mi lusinga il dolce affetto*).

Meanwhile, Alcina resolves to prove her love to Ruggiero by turning Ricciardo into a beast. Morgana enters to stop her; so does Ruggiero, assuring
Alcina he no longer fears Ricciardo as a rival. Morgana, however, still believes
Ricciardo is a man—and in love with her (*Ama, sospira*). When Ruggiero
leaves to go hunting, he pretends to pledge his love anew to Alcina (*Mio bel
tesoro*). Oberto appears, still trying to find his father (*Tra speme e timore*).

Warned that Ruggiero means to flee, Alcina resolves he shall not escape
unpunished (*Ah! mio cor! schernito sei!*). Even when Oronte tells Morgana that
Ricciardo too is scheming to escape, Morgana repeats her disavowal of Oronte's
own love, leaving him to lament its hold on him (*E un folle, è un vil affetto*).

Bradamante tells Oberto that when Alcina's spells are broken, he will see
his lost father again. Ruggiero, repentant, embraces Bradamante and looks
forward to the dissolution of this enchanted empire (*Verdi prati, selve amene*).

§ In her laboratory, Alcina calls upon spirits to help her keep Ruggiero, but they no longer respond *(Ombre pallide)*. Only after she leaves do they come forth and dance.

ACT III   In the entrance hall of the palace, Oronte gives Morgana a taste of her own medicine, claiming he has decided not to commit himself, though now she swears she loves him *(Credete al mio dolore)*. Alone, Oronte admits he loves her too *(Un momento di contento)*. After Alcina has learned from Ruggiero that his heart belongs to Bradamante, love vies with vengeance in Alcina's bosom *(Ma quando tornerai)*.

§ Melisso and Bradamante join Ruggiero to plan their escape. Ruggiero declares that love can prevail even in the heart of a wild beast *(Stà nell'Ircana pietrosa tana)*. Bradamante vows not to leave until she has rescued Alcina's every victim *(All'alma fedel)*.

§ Oronte tells Alcina her army and defenses are broken, while Ruggiero now threatens the island with his forces. She realizes all is lost *(Mi restano le lagrime)*.

§ An urn containing the power of Alcina's magic stands before her palace, where unseen voices herald the freedom that awaits those formerly under her spell (chorus: *Sin per le vie del sole)*. When Oberto comes, still looking for his father, Alcina hands him a dagger, telling him to use it to kill an approaching lion. From the animal's friendly manner, however, Oberto senses it is his father *(Barbara! Io ben lo so)*.

Alcina tries flattery and false humility on Ruggiero and Bradamante, but when they spurn her, she curses them. Ruggiero gives Oronte back his sword, saying it is time to smash the magic urn. Alcina rushes to stop him, and when Bradamante approaches the urn, Morgana stops her as well. But Melisso and Oberto join the others in urging Ruggiero to shatter the urn, which he does.

The palace disappears into the sea, visible through a vast underground cave, where Alcina's victims are turned back into men—among them Astolfo, who embraces his son Oberto. Amid dancing, the rescued men sing the praises of their regained liberty *(Dall'orror di notte cieca)*.

SERSE

(Xerxes)

THREE ACTS
MUSIC: George Frideric Handel

TEXT (Italian): anonymous revision of Silvio Stampiglia's libretto
   Xerse, based on Nicolò Minato's *Xerse*
WORLD PREMIERE: London, King's Theater, April 15, 1738
U.S. PREMIERE: Northampton, Mass., Smith College, May 12, 1928
   (in English)

CHARACTERS

Romilda, *Ariodate's daughter* . . . . Soprano
Atalanta, *her sister* . . . . Soprano
Serse, *King of Persia* . . . . .Mezzo-Soprano
Arsamene, *his brother* . . . . .Mezzo-Soprano
Amastre, *heiress to the kingdom of Tagor* . . . . Alto
Ariodate, *a prince, vassal to Serse* . . . . Bass
Elviro, *Arsamene's servant* . . . . Bass

Xerxes I, ruler of Persia from 486 to 465 B.C., known in the Bible as Ahasuerus
and in Old Persian as Khshayarsha, is famous in history for his victory over
the Greeks at Thermopylae in 480 B.C. during the Persian Wars.

ACT I   Serse (Xerxes) is sitting under a plane tree, thankful for its shade
(Ombra mai fu). His brother Arsamene (Arsamenes) comes looking for his
beloved, Romilda, whose voice is heard nearby in song. Serse has taken a fancy
to Romilda as his queen, but Arsamene discourages him, saying she is not
born to royalty. Nevertheless, Serse leaves to declare his love *(Io le dirò che
l'amo).* Romilda appears and is warned by Arsamene of Serse's intention. The
girl's sister, Atalanta, hopes that she herself might win Arsamene *(Sì, mio ben,
io per te vivo sol).* Serse returns and offers to share his throne with Romilda;
knowing she is reluctant because of her love for Arsamene, he banishes his
brother, who realizes he must comply *(Meglio in voi col mio partire).* Serse continues to court Romilda *(Di tacere e di schernirmi),* but when he leaves, she
restates her devotion to Arsamene *(Nè men coll'ombre d'infedeltà).*

§ In a courtyard, Amastre, earlier betrothed to Serse, appears disguised as a
soldier. She steps aside as Ariodate, Serse's general (father of Romilda and
Atalanta), returns from the wars with victorious troops (chorus: *Già la tromba).*
Serse appears and tells him somewhat cryptically that Romilda is to wed "a
royal spouse of Serse's lineage." After the soldiers march off, Serse admits his
own ambitions in love; overhearing, Amastre mistakenly hopes these refer to
her. Serse, however, continues to dote on Romilda *(Più che penso alla fiamma del
Core).*

§ Arsamene, exiled from court, gives a letter for Romilda to his servant,
Elviro, to deliver (Elviro: *Signor, lasciate fare a me).* Arsamene wonders which
emotion is stronger in his heart—grief or hope *(Non so se sia la speme).*

§ Amastre, hurt by Serse's rejection, wants revenge *(Saprà delle mie offese).*

§ Atalanta suggests to Romilda that Arsamene is not reliable—that marriage to Serse would be wiser. Sensing that Alalanta too loves Arsamene, Romilda accuses her of betrayal *(Se l'Idol mio rapir mi vuoi).* But Atalanta, left alone, is still resolved to win Arsamene *(Un cenno leggiadretto).*

ACT II   In a city square, Elviro, disguised as a vendor, sets up a flower stall *(Ah, chi voler fiora).* Amastre learns from the servant that her erstwhile fiancé, Serse, desires Romilda. Saddened by this confirmation of her fears, Amastre leaves as Atalanta approaches. Atalanta gets the letter away from Elviro, then tells him that Romilda no longer loves Arsamene. Seeing Serse approach, Atalanta lets him read Arsamene's love letter *("Allorchè nell'Ibero ascoso è il sole"),* which she claims was addressed to her. She even asks royal approval for her marriage to Arsamene, which Serse gladly grants. But, she warns, Arsamene will pretend he doesn't love her *(Dirà che non mi amò).*

Serse shows Arsamene's love letter to Romilda, who believes the lie that it was meant for Atalanta but persists in her love for Arsamene. Serse in turn cannot stop loving Romilda *(Se bramate d'amar chi vi sdegna).* Alone, she feels jealousy poisoning her heart *(È gelosia, quella tiranna).*

§ Amastre, in despair *(Anima infida),* wanders off as Arsamene comes to Elviro for news of Romilda, only to hear that Romilda now loves the king. Arsamene is thunderstruck *(Quella che tutta fe):* will the gods tolerate such treachery?

§ By the shore, Serse prepares to see Ariodate off on another military campaign. Arsamene appears, distraught. Serse offers to unite him with his beloved—meaning Atalanta. Arsamene, however, vows to win Romilda in whatever way he can *(Sì, la voglio, e l'otterò!).* When Atalanta arrives, Serse tells her that Arsamene has denied any love for her, but she insists he is only pretending *(Voi mi dite che non l'ami).* Alone, Serse ponders the uncertainty of love *(Il core spera e teme).* Elviro decides to get some wine instead of continuing the search for his master *(Del mio caro Bacco amabile).*

Serse falls into conversation with Amastre, still in her disguise as a soldier, and both complain of unsuccessful love. When Serse tries once more to woo the reluctant Romilda, Amastre steps forward and calls Serse a deceiver. Angrily, Serse orders this "man" arrested. Though Romilda believes her lover faithless, she still loves him *(Che cede al furore).*

ACT III   In a gallery, Romilda confronts Arsamene with his supposed betrayal. Atalanta, fearing her own duplicity will be discovered, concocts a tale about having pretended to be Arsamene's lover in order to protect Romilda from the king's wrath *(No, se tu mi sprezzi).* Arsamene and Romilda are reconciled, but when Serse approaches, Romilda says that if her father wants it, she will obey the king's wishes. Serse is overjoyed *(Per rendermi beato),* but Romilda confides to Arsamene that she will die if she has to wed Serse. She leaves Arsamene to lament the sorrows of love *(Amor, tiranno amor).*

§ In a grove, Serse tells Romilda's father, Ariodate, that he is ready to make good his promise of a royal spouse for Romilda and invites him to meet the bridegroom, whom Ariodate supposes to be Arsamene *(Del Ciel d'amore)*.

Romilda faces Serse with renewed determination to stick to her true love, even confessing that she and Arsamene have exchanged a kiss of betrothal. Serse responds by sending guards with orders to kill Arsamene.

§ Romilda meets the "soldier" Amastre and asks him to warn Arsamene of the death sentence. In return, Amastre asks Romilda to give Serse a note, though she fears her love is wasted on a traitor *(Cagio son io del mio dolore)*.

§ Arsamene, having heard he is condemned, suspects Romilda of trying to get him out of the way (duet: *Romilda infida)*.

§ In a temple, priests hail Jupiter's power *(Ciò che Giove destinò)*, and Ariodate greets Arsamene as Romilda's presumed bridegroom. With disbelief, Arsamene hears that Serse has ordered the wedding. The couple exchanges vows.

§ Hearing from Ariodate that the two are married, Serse is furious: his intentions were misunderstood. A love letter is delivered to him, but when Ariodate reveals that Amastre wrote it, Serse curses those who have conspired against his wishes *(Crude furie degli orridi abissi)*.

Serse angrily faces the newlyweds, who insist they were acting according to his wish. Amastre snatches the king's sword away—only to reveal her identity as his spurned fiancée. Impressed by her fidelity, Serse declares that he himself deserves death. With her forgiveness, he embraces her, begs the others' pardon, and wishes them happiness. As Romilda again pledges her love to Arsamene *(Caro voi siete all'Alma)*, all hail the restoration of peace and joy.

SAMSON

ORATORIO IN THREE ACTS
MUSIC: George Frideric Handel
TEXT (English): Newburgh Hamilton, from John Milton's *Samson Agonistes*
WORLD PREMIERE: London, Covent Garden, February 18, 1743
U.S. STAGE PREMIERE: Dallas Civic Opera, November 5, 1976
METROPOLITAN PREMIERE: February 3, 1986

SAMSON

CHARACTERS

Dalila, *Samson's Philistine wife* . . . . Soprano
Israelite Woman . . . . Soprano
Micah, *Samson's friend* . . . . .Mezzo-Soprano
Samson, *an Israelite hero* . . . . Tenor
Manoah, *Samson's father* . . . . Bass
Harapha, *a Philistine hero* . . . . Bass

The Philistines, who may have come from Crete, controlled coastal areas and were a threat in land struggles during the period of the Judges, c. 1200–1070 B.C., "a lawless time between Israel's invasion of Canaan and the first kings" (*The Lion Encyclopedia of the Bible*). The Philistines eventually were subdued by young David, who killed their hero Goliath with a single stone from a sling-shot. Samson, one of the Judges or champions of the Israelites, had succeeded earlier against the Philistines, wielding the jawbone of an ass; but his downfall was brought about by involvement with the Philistine woman Dalila (Delilah), who discovered that the secret of his strength lay in his long hair, and schemed to have it shorn off. Handel's oratorio version, based on Milton's *Samson Agonistes*, has been staged frequently.

ACT I   On a feast day in Gaza for the god Dagon, Philistines celebrate *(Awake the trumpet's lofty sound!)*. The blinded Samson, relieved for a day from his menial labors as a prisoner, laments his cruel destiny *(Torments, alas! are not confin'd)*. Accompanied by other Israelites, Micah, a woman friend of Samson's, commiserates with him *(Oh mirror of our fickle state!)*. Samson recalls how his strength lay in his hair; now, in his blindness *(Total eclipse!)*, he cannot take courage or comfort at the sight of daylight (chorus: *Oh first created beam!*). Micah speculates that marriage outside the tribe lies at the root of Samson's betrayal by his wife, Dalila. Samson agrees, then receives a visit from his father, Manoah, who is followed by an Israelite Man in bemoaning the hero's fate *(God of our fathers, what is man?* [Aria sometimes assigned to Micah]). Manoah recalls Samson's days of prowess *(Thy glorious deeds)*. When he describes the reveling Philistines, Samson begins to think of revenge on them *(Why does the God of Israel sleep?)*. The Israelites do not doubt the power of their God to vanquish Dagon *(Then shall they know)*. Manoah urges his son not to give up hope—he may yet be ransomed—but Samson is so dispirited that only death seems to await him. Micah sees Samson's glory restored after death *(Joys that are pure)*, a sentiment echoed by the other Israelites *(Then round about the starry throne)*.

ACT II   Manoah again urges Samson not to abandon hope, but Samson cannot forgive his own weakness in yielding to a woman's blandishments. Manoah suggests that perhaps God had a purpose in this, which is not yet clear to them (*Just are the ways of God to man*). Micah and her fellow Israelites call upon Jehovah to take pity on Samson (*Return, oh God of hosts!*). Dalila, weeping, comes in hopes of Samson's forgiveness (*With plaintive notes and am'rous moan*), comparing herself to a turtledove in search of its mate, but Samson remains adamant (*Your charms to ruin led the way*). Joined by a Virgin from her entourage, Dalila again implores Samson's pity (*My faith and truth, oh Samson, prove*), with other Virgins reiterating her plea. She tries a more sensuous appeal (*To fleeting pleasures make your court*), but he tells her to flee his wrath; her own anger aroused, she admits she saved her people by betraying him (duet: *Traitor to love!*). Having lost her gamble to win him over, she leaves. Micah deplores the vanity that often undermines members of her sex (*It is not virtue, valour, wit*), and the Israelites say a wife should not be false to her husband (*To man God's universal law*).

The giant Harapha arrives with other Philistines and taunts Samson, saying he could defeat him easily but would not fight a blind man (*Honour and arms scorn such a foe*). Samson dares Harapha to combat anyway (*My strength is from the living God*). Micah challenges the Philistines to prove Dagon's power over Samson's strength. The Israelites call upon the Almighty (*Hear, Jacob's God, Jehovah, hear!*), and the Philistines reply with a call to Dagon's festival (*To song and dance we give the day*). Then both groups join in invoking their respective deities (*Fix'd in his everlasting seat*).

ACT III   Harapha comes to Samson again, this time calling on him to prove his strength at the festival. When Samson replies that his religion forbids taking part in pagan rites, Harapha warns him to obey the summons (*Presuming slave, to move their wrath!*). With Harapha gone, Samson tells Micah he feels his strength returning as his hair has grown back, but it should not be prostituted to idols. After the Israelites have called upon God to empower Samson to save them (*With thunder arm'd, great God, arise!*), Samson changes his mind and tells the returning Harapha he will go. He prays for strength to uphold God's glory (*Thus when the sun*), urged on by Micah (*The Holy One of Israel be thy guide*) and the Israelites (*To fame immortal go*).

As Philistines are heard voicing their confidence (*Great Dagon has subdued our foe*), Micah, Manoah, and the Israelites wonder how Samson is faring at the festival. Manoah wishes he could ransom and save his son (*How willing my paternal love*). A "symphony of horror and confusion" sounds, with distant cries of Philistines (*Hear us, our God!*) as Samson with a superhuman effort pulls down their temple. A Messenger runs in with news of the mighty deed done by Samson, dead in the rubble with his foes. Micah (*Ye sons of Israel, now lament*) and the Israelites (*Weep, Israel*) grieve, and Samson's body is borne in (funeral march and chorus: *Glorious hero*). Manoah declares that while the Philistines lie in ruin, Samson has gained eternal fame. An Israelite Woman jubilantly hails his achievement (*Let the bright Seraphim*), echoed by all the Israelites (*Let their celestial concerts all unite*).

SEMELE

THREE ACTS
MUSIC: George Frideric Handel
TEXT (English): after William Congreve's libretto for an opera by
   John Eccles, based on Ovid's *Metamorphoses*
WORLD PREMIERE (concert performance): London, Covent Garden,
   February 10, 1744
U.S. STAGE PREMIERE: Evanston, Ill., Northwestern University, January 1959

CHARACTERS

Semele, *Cadmus' daughter* . . . . Soprano
Iris, *Juno's messenger*. . . . . Soprano
Ino, *Semele's sister* . . . . Alto
Juno, *Jupiter's wife* . . . . Alto
Athamas, *Prince of Boeotia* . . . . .Countertenor
Jupiter, *king of the gods* . . . . Tenor
Apollo, *god of the sun*. . . . . Tenor
Cadmus, *King of Thebes* . . . . Bass
Somnus, *god of sleep* . . . . Bass

Though the story of Semele originates in Greek legend, it is familiar through Ovid's *Metamorphoses,* Book III, in which some of the names were Latinized. Zeus is known as Jupiter (colloquially as Jove), Hera as Juno; but Apollo remains the same in both versions.

ACT I Thebes, classical antiquity. In Juno's temple, a sacrifice has just been made to the goddess. Semele, daughter of Cadmus, King of Thebes, is to be married to the Boeotian prince Athamas. Aside, however, the girl admits to misgivings: she is pleased by Jupiter's love for her and fears his vengeance should she refuse (*O Jove! in pity teach me which to choose*). Her sister Ino, who secretly loves Athamas, is unhappy about the marriage but cannot bring herself to say why (quartet, Cadmus: *Why dost thou thus untimely grieve?*). When thunder is heard and the fire at the altar goes out, Jupiter's disapproval is apparent (chorus: *Avert these omens*); Juno's wish for the union causes the flame to burn again, but once more Jupiter rains upon it and puts it out. With

Athamas calling on Juno for help and Semele covertly pledging herself to Jupiter, the altar itself disappears with a clap of thunder, and the priests tell those present to flee Jupiter's wrath *(Cease your vows, 'tis impious to proceed).*

Trying to console Athamas, Ino finds courage to confess her own love for him. Cadmus joins them and offers his sympathies to the disappointed groom *(Wing'd with our fears).* Priests and Augurs (soothsayers) offer solemn greetings to Cadmus, but . . .

. . . Semele already has been transported *(Endless pleasure, endless love)* to join Jupiter.

ACT II   In a countryside setting, the irate Juno calls upon supernatural powers to help destroy Semele *(Awake, Saturnia, from thy lethargy!).* The goddess' sister Iris warns that Semele is kept safe in a secret palace *(With adamant the gates are barr'd).* Juno replies that she will ask Somnus, god of sleep, to disable the dragons guarding the stronghold *(Hence, Iris, hence away!).*

§ In her room at Jupiter's palace, Semele rises from bed and longs for his return *(Oh sleep, why dost thou leave me?).* He promptly appears and reassures her of his love *(Lay your doubts and fears aside).* But when she seems to be wishing for immortality, he diverts her "dangerous ambition" by sending for her sister Ino. Before leaving, he conjures up an Arcadian scene of nymphs and swains to keep her amused *(Where'er you walk).* Semele is cheered to see Ino, who thrills at the scenery and "rural sports" they behold *(But hark! the heav'nly sphere turns round).*

ACT III   Juno and Iris find Somnus asleep in his cave. He is loath to wake until Juno mentions his beloved Pasithea, for whom he longs *(More sweet is that name).* In exchange for her promise of a reunion with Pasithea, Juno tells him, he must cause Jupiter to dream of Semele with such desire that on waking he will grant anything the girl asks. In addition, Juno needs to borrow Somnus' wand, so she can put Ino to sleep and appear to Semele in Ino's form.

§ In her room at the palace, Semele has troubled thoughts in her sleep. In the form of Ino, Juno slips into the room. Pretending astonishment at Semele's almost divine appearance in a magic mirror *(Behold in this mirror),* Juno arouses the girl's vanity (Semele: *Myself I shall adore.*) Then she counsels Semele to withhold her favors from Jupiter until he agrees to appear to her not in human shape but in godlike form as the "mighty thunderer" *(Conjure him by his oath).* With irony, Juno adds, "You shall partake then of immortality / And thenceforth leave this mortal state." Assured of Semele's doom, Juno leaves. When Jupiter enters, amorously aroused by his dream, Semele avoids his embrace, making him swear to grant whatever she wants. Rashly he agrees, whereupon she demands that he appear to her in godly form *(No, I'll take no less).* After she leaves the room, Jupiter reflects on his dilemma: if he grants her request, she will die *('Tis past recall).*

SEMELE

§ Juno, alone, gloats on her coming revenge *(Above measure is the pleasure)*.

§ Semele lies waiting for Jupiter. As he descends in the form of a storm cloud, she realizes she cannot withstand the burning heat of his lightning *(Ah me! too late I now repent)*. She dies; the cloud bursts, and the palace disappears.

§ Back at the Temple of Juno, the others express awe at what has transpired (chorus: *Oh terror and astonishment!*). Ino, who had dreamed of the catastrophe while Juno locked her in sleep, now recognizes with Athamas that Jupiter wants them to marry.

§ Apollo descends in a bright cloud upon Mt. Cithæron and declares that "From Semele's ashes a phoenix shall rise"—Bacchus, a god "more mighty than love." The chorus hails his prophecy *(Happy shall we be)*.

HANS WERNER HENZE
b. 1926

*T*he most frequently performed German opera composer of the post–
World War II period, Henze owes much of his artistic motivation
to his hatred of the elements in German society that led to the war.
This meant rejection of the values of his own family and a search
for a broader sense of the artist's use to humanity. Eventually an expatriate,
making his home in Italy, he has pursued an eclectic, international aesthetic
outlook. The distinguishing mark of his work is its sheer skill, whether in
marshaling large forms and resources (as in *The Bassarids*) or in devising tex-
tures of chamber-music delicacy. As he matured, Henze committed himself to
Marxism, but though his writing is accessible to any audience that has heard
much twentieth-century music, it is without trace of conscious simplicity or
"socialist realism."

Henze also has been drawn to dramatic experimentation, which he notes
was not in the purview of opera prior to Wagner's time. In the spoken drama—
that of Friedrich Lenz, Georg Büchner, or Heinrich von Kleist, for example—
there did exist an avant-garde during the nineteenth century, whereas in the
operas of Rossini, Bellini, and Donizetti there did not. Henze's socialist convictions therefore had to work somewhat at odds with his determination not
to write mere mass entertainment. His first major success, *Boulevard Solitude*
(1952), is a modernization of the Manon Lescaut story, portraying social alienation and exploitation. For his largest-scale opera yet in 1956 he produced
König Hirsch (King Stag), after one of Carlo Gozzi's fable plays. And in *Der*

Prinz von Homburg, he and Ingeborg Bachmann (later his librettist for *Der Junge Lord*) adapted one of Kleist's dramas, treating the dilemma of a sensitive dreamer caught up by military and political obligation, a feeling man whose conscience and duty are in conflict.

Bachmann, a prominent German writer, softened and humanized Henze's penchant for satire in *Der Junge Lord,* an assault on petit bourgeois, small-town provincial life. Again in *The English Cat* (1983), after Balzac, Henze was able to humanize his point beyond caricature and diatribe by playing on the interest of his characters. Meanwhile, in *Elegy for Young Lovers* (1961) and *The Bassarids* (1966), both to English librettos by W. H. Auden and Chester Kallman, Henze treated humanity more harshly and distantly. *Elegy* caricatures the artist as a *monstre sacré* who thinks only of his own work, regardless of its effect on the lives of others. In *The Bassarids,* Henze constructed his most massive score, a symphonic opera-oratorio on a mythological subject out of Euripides. Unlike Karol Szymanowski's *King Roger,* based on the same tale (or Britten's *Death in Venice,* which makes reference to it), Henze's version shows no mercy, recognizing that the Dionysian force, being an absolute, is stronger than any resistance that can be offered to it, and does not require acquiescence or understanding. Here, more than in many a romanticized adaptation of myth, Henze makes one feel the sweep of destiny that gripped and awed the classical authors.

A not dissimilar sense of power beyond man's reach recurs in *Das Verratene Meer* (The Sea Betrayed, 1990), after Yukio Mishima's novel. Measured against the fanciful elements and recurrent whimsy of some of his other stage works, this elemental strain carries to an extreme edge the uncommonly wide range of sensibility and stylistic variety apparent in Henze's writing. He and Benjamin Britten rank as the most sheerly versatile opera composers of the latter twentieth century.

DER JUNGE LORD

(The Young Lord)

TWO ACTS
MUSIC: Hans Werner Henze
TEXT (German): Ingeborg Bachmann, after a fable from Wilhelm
   Hauff's *Der Scheik von Alexandria und Seine Sklaven*
WORLD PREMIERE: Berlin, Deutsche Oper, April 7, 1965

U.S. PREMIERE: San Diego Civic Opera, February 17, 1967 (in English)

CHARACTERS

Frau Hasentreffer . . . . Soprano
Luise, *the Baroness' ward* . . . . Soprano
Ida, *The Baroness' companion* . . . . Soprano
Baroness Grünwiesel . . . . Mezzo-Soprano
Frau von Hufnagel . . . . Mezzo-Soprano
Lord Barrat, *Sir Edgar's nephew* . . . . Tenor
Wilhelm, *a student* . . . . Tenor
La Rocca, *an impresario* . . . . Tenor
Prof. von Mucker . . . . Tenor
Councilor Hasentreffer . . . . Baritone
Councilor Scharf . . . . Baritone
The Mayor . . . . Bass-Baritone
Sir Edgar . . . . Speaking Role
His Secretary . . . . Speaking Role

ACT I   In Hülsdorf-Gotha, a fictional town in the German provinces, on a summer weekend in 1830, most of the populace—including several dignitaries—promenades with ill-concealed expectation and curiosity. An English milord, Sir Edgar, is expected, but he is behind schedule. The Mayor practices his speech of welcome for the visitor, who, it develops, has bought a neglected, unoccupied mansion on the main square. He is expected to renovate the building, helping the local economy. Luise, ward of Baroness Grünwiesel, confides to her companion, Ida, that she really likes the student, Wilhelm, who has seemed to be attracted to her (trio, Luise: *Aber ich habe doch bloss das viele Geld*). The Schoolmaster rehearses his pupils in a welcoming chorus *(Zu uns kommt ein Edelmann),* but they are drowned out by the garrison band.

A carriage draws up, from which several oddly assorted domestic animals emerge. A second carriage brings servants and luggage. A third carriage produces a Secretary (at first taken to be Sir Edgar), and finally Sir Edgar himself, who politely accepts the folderol of the locals but does not utter a word. Speaking for him, his Secretary declines invitations to all honorary festivities, explaining that His Lordship is tired from the long journey. A sudden rain shower dampens everyone's mood.

§ In the drawing room of Baroness Grünwiesel, doyenne of local society, female visitors clap politely after Luise plays a piano piece. The Baroness declares it is time to find a suitable husband for this well-turned-out young lady *(Diese artige kleine Schelm).* Even Sir Edgar is mentioned as a candidate— and he has been invited for tea. Led by Frau von Hufnagel, the ladies declare that their manners are quite cosmopolitan *(Wir sind auf dem Laufenden)*. Their hopes are dashed when Jeremy, Sir Edgar's Moorish servant, brings a note declining the invitation of the Baroness, who promptly swoons. Pulling herself together, she denounces this eccentric foreigner who dares offend her *(Dieser Mensch täuscht sich)*. The others back her up as she threatens a social boycott: only Luise and Ida protest.

§ In the town square, a Neapolitan impresario, Amintore La Rocca, leads his modest troupe to the finale of its traveling circus act and delivers a brief epilogue *(Hochverehrtes Publikum!)*. Sir Edgar makes an unexpected appearance, sitting in a chair outside his house. He is on cordial terms with the local children but politely declines handshakes extended by the quartet of chief dignitaries. When La Rocca passes the hat, only Sir Edgar pays the performers, who show their gratitude by repeating their act for him. Aside, Luise and Wilhelm exchange a few words, agreeing to meet later behind the Englishman's house. The town fathers declare the performers have no license, but Sir Edgar indicates through his Secretary *(Genug, meine Herren)* that he will pay for it. Frustrated, the officials grumble while parents order their children not to like Sir Edgar. After Sir Edgar motions the performers to enter his house, the townspeople vent their rage *(Wir sind ihm nicht gut genug)*.

ACT II   It is winter. As Jeremy approaches Sir Edgar's house, laden with packages, children pelt him with snowballs and taunt him *(Hu, der böse Mohr)*. An approaching Lamplighter is alarmed to hear wild cries emanating from the house. He decides to go to the inn for help and some schnapps *(Leibhaftiger! Geister sind's nicht)*. Luise and Wilhelm, by now in the habit of meeting there, arrive and declare their love (duet: *Warum ich dich liebe?*), but because of the cold, they move on, making way for the Lamplighter, town fathers, and others. When the Mayor knocks to inquire what screams have been heard, the Secretary explains that Sir Edgar's nephew, Lord Barrat, recently arrived from London and has been struggling with German lessons. Soon, the Secretary assures them, Lord Barrat will be able to make his social debut *(Wenn es die Fortschritte Seiner Lordschaft erlauben)*.

§ The time has arrived for a reception at Sir Edgar's house. Begonia, the Creole cook, goes over her Jamaican recipe for gingerbread nuts *(Man nimmt halbes Pfund goldenen Sirup)* while the Secretary directs other servants in arranging the room. Guests start to appear, dying of curiosity. Sir Edgar makes his entrance with the dapper Lord Barrat. Though the youth's conversation consists only of a few blunt phrases, he enchants most of the guests with what they take to be his eccentric English manners—putting his feet on the table, and so forth. Wilhelm, however, is annoyed by Lord Barrat's rudeness and evident attraction for Luise. Finally he loses patience and pronounces Barrat insufferable. Barrat pays no attention and is discreetly led away, but Luise bursts into tears and swoons. The Baroness orders Wilhelm away, as the other ladies swoon too.

§ In the grand ballroom of the Town Casino, Luise confronts her confused feelings: Barrat has swept her off her feet. He enters and gives her a rose, then takes it back, scratching her hand with its thorns. Entranced, she listens as he recites a few lines he has learned by rote from German classics (*Ein bedeutend ernst Geschick waltet übers Leben*). Wilhelm, seeing them from the doorway, wonders desperately what to do. The Baroness waves him aside, beaming upon the lovers—whose engagement, it is hinted, may be announced at dinner (guests: *Und im guten Geist der Stunde*).

Dancing begins, but Barrat's behavior becomes wild and unpredictable. The young men of the town imitate his bizarre actions—grimacing, prancing about, creating more and more disorder, throwing decorum to the winds. When he grabs a trumpet from a musician, blasts on it, and then hits the musician over the head with it, some start to think he is going too far. Then he begins a frenzied dance with Luise, putting out the candles as he passes them. No longer able to keep up with him, the girl starts to panic. As his unruly antics reach a crescendo, Sir Edgar approaches him, trainer's whip in hand, and Barrat rips off his costume, showing himself to be the trained ape from La Rocca's circus. Stunned silence. Luise, shaken, embraces Wilhelm as the other guests gasp in horror at the exposure of their folly.

THE BASSARIDS

FOUR MOVEMENTS
MUSIC: Hans Werner Henze
TEXT (English): W. H. Auden and Chester Kallman, after Euripides' *The Bacchae*
WORLD PREMIERE: Salzburg, August 6, 1966
U.S. PREMIERE: Sante Fe Opera, August 7, 1968

CHARACTERS

Autonoe, *Agave's sister* . . . . Soprano
Agave, *Cadmus' daughter and Pentheus' mother* . . . . . .Mezzo-Soprano
Beroe, *an old slave, once nurse to Semele* . . . . .Mezzo-Soprano
Dionysus (also Voice and Stranger) . . . . Tenor

Tiresias, *an old blind poet* . . . . Tenor
Pentheus, *King of Thebes*. Baritone
Captain of the Palace Guard . . . . Baritone
Cadmus, *his grandfather, founder of Thebes* . . . . Bass

FIRST MOVEMENT   Thebes, chief city of Boeotia in ancient Greece, sometime prior to 1000 B.C. In the courtyard of the royal palace, citizens sing their welcome to Pentheus, new ruler of the city; its founder, Cadmus (Pentheus' grandfather), has abdicated in his favor *(Pentheus is now our lord)*. Pentheus, however, is not present, having chosen to spend his first days fasting in a retreat. When news is heard of the god Dionysus' arrival in Boeotia, the crowd leaves in a celebratory mood. The aged Cadmus appears with one of his daughters, Agave (Pentheus' mother), Beroe (Pentheus' old nurse), and the blind seer Tiresias. Both Tiresias and Agave are inclined to go to Mt. Cythæron and join in the worship of Dionysus, but Cadmus is doubtful. Tiresias impatiently leaves. The Bassarids, priests and priestesses of the cult of Dionysus, are heard in the distance *(Long have we waited)*, welcoming the god back to the tomb of his mother, Semele (another of Cadmus' daughters), who gave birth to him as a result of her seduction by Zeus. The Captain of the Palace Guard reads a proclamation from Pentheus forbidding anyone to believe the legend of Dionysus' divine birth. Pentheus himself appears and throws his cloak over the flame on the altar before Semele's tomb, extinguishing it. He angrily reenters the palace when he learns that Dionysus has drawn the people away. Agave starts to speak approvingly of her son's resolve *(He is a King, no Son but a father)*. She is soon distracted, however, by the offstage voice of Dionysus *(How fair is wild Cythæron)*, and with her sister Autonoe she almost involuntarily dances off.

SECOND MOVEMENT   When Pentheus reemerges from the palace, Cadmus warns him against rash action, but Pentheus replies that Dionysus is a false god and orders the Captain to mobilize his guard for a raid on the worshippers. As the Bassarids are heard warning of the attack *(Strange feet startle the road from Thebes)*, Pentheus declares to Beroe the falseness of Dionysus' allure *(Faithful Beroe! To you alone)*. The old woman, a surviving adherent of the ancient Greek cult of the Great Mother, mutters prayers for Pentheus' safety. As the Bassarids warn their followers to lie low by day and celebrate at night, Pentheus tells Beroe he has resolved to "live sober and chaste till the day I die."

The guards return with prisoners they have taken, including Agave, Autonoe, Tiresias, a Stranger, and a few others; most of the followers hid from the raiders. In the distance, the Bassarids call for Dionysus to avenge himself on Pentheus. The Captain takes some of the prisoners to be tortured while Pentheus questions Agave, who in vague terms describes an idyllic scene at

Mt. Cythæron *(On a forest footpath, round a far bend)*, saying nothing of Diony-sus. Beroe keeps trying to tell Pentheus that she recognizes the Stranger as Dionysus, but he pays no attention, instead ordering his mother and aunt confined to quarters. Then he questions the Stranger, who answers with inso-lent evasions and claims to be a Lydian named Acœtes, overtaken on his jour-ney home by a visitation from Dionysus *(I found a child asleep)*.

THIRD MOVEMENT   Losing patience with the Stranger, Pentheus orders him taken off for torture. An earthquake strikes; Pentheus' cloak floats away from Semele's tomb, and the altar flame burns again. The prisoners escape to Cythæron, and the Stranger reappears before Pentheus, warning that Dionysus' followers are strong enough to defeat the guardsmen. To questions about the Dionysian rites, the Stranger replies they will take place that night, then offers to give Pentheus further insight by showing him in a mirror . . .

. . . *The Judgment of Calliope* (intermezzo). In the mirror Pentheus sees his own repressed erotic fantasies, as laughter rings out from the Bassarids. Agave and Autonoe appear in deerskins as Aphrodite and Persephone, playing love games with the Captain, who is garbed as Adonis.

As twilight starts to fall, Pentheus, shocked by the vision, determines to go to the revels and see if such things are true *(Could I have only seen the raw deed)*. To avoid detection and mortal danger, the Stranger tells him, he must disguise himself as a woman. When Pentheus goes to do so, Beroe appears before Dio-nysus and begs mercy for the king, but Dionysus cannot forgive her for having lent her shape to Hera (Juno) when the goddess disguised herself as Beroe in order to deceive and destroy Semele. The old nurse leaves in despair as Pen-theus returns, dressed in one of his mother's gowns. Pentheus and the Stranger leave for Cythæron. In the empty city, Beroe and Cadmus fear that Pentheus is going to his death (Cadmus: *Fall night, fall Thebes, fall oblivion.*)

The Bassarids hail the beginning of their revels *(Now night opens wide all day locks)*. As a torchlight procession passes, Pentheus is seen crouching in the forest at Cythæron *(Waiting. For what?)*, then disappears from view. The voice of Dionysus is heard, warning that a trespasser has come to spy on the rituals and must be hunted down. Led by the ritually crazed Agave, the Maenads (female worshippers) find Pentheus, who cries out his name as they fall upon him and tear him apart with their bare hands.

FOURTH MOVEMENT   By the first light of dawn, Cadmus and Beroe wait outside the palace. Led by Agave, the Maenads approach, crying that the tro-phy of their hunt is a young lion. Followed by the Bacchants (male worship-pers), they enter the square (Maenads: *The God gave women the strength of Gods*), Agave bearing the head that she believes is a lion's. When Cadmus brings her to her senses, she begs the Captain of the guard to kill her; Beroe places the head with the other remains of Pentheus, which the guards have collected and brought back on a bier. Cadmus recognizes the end of his royal dynasty (ensemble: *Night and again the night*), while Autonoe puts the blame on her sister, Tiresias faults Pentheus for not heeding him, and the Bassarids claim ignorance of the murder.

The Stranger appears at Semele's tomb and reveals he is Dionysus. He banishes the survivors of the royal family, "each in a different direction," and orders the palace torched. He has achieved vengeance and vindicated his mother. He calls on Persephone, "Queen of the sunless realm," to release Semele from the underworld *(Rise, mother, rise from the dead)*. Renamed Thyone, she will share immortality with him as a goddess. After Dionysus has gone, fertility icons of himself and Thyone appear amid the remains of the palace. Tiresias, always among the first to embrace a new cult, reappears, kneeling before the statues with the other worshippers as vines descend, wreathing the columns and shrouding the ruins.

LEOŠ JANÁČEK
1854–1928

A relative latecomer to the international stage, Leoš Janáček had to wait until a quarter century after his death for his operas to achieve recognition. An indirect cause of their eventual vindication was the Communist takeover of Czechoslovakia in 1948, driving into exile such eminent musicians as the conductor Rafael Kubelik, who proceeded to lead Janáček performances in London. Another factor was the increase of recording activity in Czechoslovakia, so that Janáček's works became available on disc for the first time. Further, the U.S.-born Australian conductor Charles Mackerras went to Prague in 1947 to study with Václav Talich, returning to England as an exponent of Janáček performing style.

Janáček's operas were a treasure waiting to be discovered, and during the postwar period the climate of taste gradually changed in a direction more favorable to his quirky, individualistic style. Like Béla Bartók, Janáček was a nationalist, steeped in the folk-music roots of his own culture. But both men reached beyond their own borders—in Bartók's case because he emigrated to America, in Janáček's because of his curiosity and tough but compassionate nature.

Born in Hukvaldy (Hochwald) in Moravia, Janáček never stretched his career much past the Moravian capital, Brno, where he exerted influence as a teacher. Success in the more cosmopolitan city of Prague, however, was slow in coming. A late bloomer, he wrote most of his operas between the age of fifty and his death at seventy-four. His idiosyncratic vocal writing was built on a study of natural sounds and people's speech habits, which the composer recorded in his notebook. Like Mussorgsky, therefore, he wrote music closely allied to his language, even his local dialect. His instrumentation was lean and pointed, using—in comparison with Richard Strauss and others of his period—a modest classical orchestra, but often pushing it to its limits with difficult, intricate rhythms.

His first successful opera, *Jenůfa* (1904), is now an established part of the world repertory, closely followed by *Káťa Kabanová*. Among his later works, *The Excursions of Mr. Brouček* is one of the most curious. Divided in two dissimilar parts, it finds the composer rather out of his depth in depicting the world of aesthetic poseurs, of which he understood little, but resoundingly back in his element with the depiction of Czech history. The last of his operas, *From the House of the Dead,* was left incomplete at his death. First edited by two of his pupils, who conventionalized his sonorities, it recently has reappeared in versions closer to his sketches, a bolder and starker work.

Janáček remained free from associations of decadence, expressionism, or weltschmerz in his style, comfortably wedding nostalgic romanticism and warmth with the more adventurous forays of modernism. Judged a rough-edged maverick by his contemporaries, he turned out to be ahead of his time. He did not write operas for an existing market; he wrote them because he wanted to, and because the subjects inspired music in his imagination. It has taken time for his message to get through.

THE EXCURSIONS OF MR. BROUČEK

(*Výlety Páně Broučkovy*)

TWO PARTS
MUSIC: Leoš Janáček
TEXT (Czech): the composer, František Gellner, Viktor Dyk, F. S. Procházka, and others, after Svatopluk Čech's novel
WORLD PREMIERE: Prague, National Theater, April 23, 1920
U.S. PREMIERE: San Francisco, San Francisco Opera Ensemble, January 23, 1981 (in English)

CHARACTERS

Málinka/Etherea/Kunka. . . . . .Soprano
Potboy *at the inn* . . . . .Soprano
Kedruta . . . . .Alto

Matej Brouček, *a landlord*	Tenor
Mazal/Blankytný/Petřík, *a painter*	Tenor
Duhoslav/Vojta, *a painter*	Tenor
Harfoboj/Poet/Composer	Tenor
Míroslav, *a goldsmith*	Tenor
Oblačny/Vacek	Baritone
Apparition of Svatopluk Čech	Baritone
Sexton/Lunobor/Domšík	Bass-Baritone
Würfl/Čaroskvoucí/Town Councilor	Bass

Part I parodies the Aesthetic movement, of which Oscar Wilde was a prominent exponent; it was also parodied in Gilbert and Sullivan's *Patience* and had its counterpart in Central Europe.

Jan Hus (John Huss), the Czech religious reformer, referred to in Part II, was excommunicated in 1412 and burned at the stake in 1415 after being condemned by the Council of Constance for his supposedly heretical views. His followers, the Hussites, were outraged that a safe-conduct given Hus by Emperor Sigismund had been violated.

PART I

ACT I Prague, latter nineteenth century (Čech's novel was published in 1888). On one side of Vikárka Street stands St. Vitus' Cathedral and the home of its Sexton; on the other, the Vikárka Tavern, from which the Sexton's daughter, Málinka, exits angrily, arguing with her boyfriend, the painter Mazal. To spite him, she threatens to marry the middle-aged burgher Matej Brouček. Her father appears and makes plain his disapproval of Mazal as a suitor. When Brouček stumbles out of the tavern, Mazal jokingly asks him if he has fallen from the moon; but Brouček, who is Mazal's landlord, says he will throw the young man out for not paying his rent. Alarmed by their argument, Málinka fears no man will want her, but when Brouček assures her of her attractiveness, he in turn is alarmed by the Sexton, who seems to want Brouček to marry her. Brouček says he would do so—on the moon. In the pub, young artists are heard carousing in praise of love and beer (*Láska, čarovný květ*). Brouček heads home, and the Sexton takes Málinka into their house. Mazal reappears in the street, softly calling to Málinka at her window.

§ The scene dissolves to the steps of the Old Castle, where Mazal and Málinka have walked; after a few affectionate exchanges, they move on. Brouček, inebriated, climbs on the wall and addresses the full moon admiringly (*Nevypadáš tak zle*), ignoring the Potboy from the pub, who has been trying to catch up with him with sausages that Brouček forgot to take home. The Potboy is afraid harm has befallen Brouček, who sails off into the sky toward . . .

§ . . . the moon, arriving on which he lies unconscious. Blankytný (Azurean) appears and dismounts from his winged horse, Pegasus, wondering aloud in song what this strange creature may be. His song rouses Brouček, who notes the bard's resemblance to Mazal. Blankytný scorns this gross earthling, who mocks the sacredness of love *(Ty neznáš toho svatého žáru!).* Lunobor (Lunigrove) wanders in, "resembling a bundle of white hair and whiskers from which a hand stretches out, holding a long stick, at the end of which a large green net for Etherea is fixed." Etherea, the object of their attention, steps from her nearby castle, accompanied by handmaidens, and sings a dreamy song full of "poetic" imagery *(Své písně přináším vám);* Brouček thinks he recognizes her as Málinka. Enamored of Brouček, she leads him away on Pegasus while Blankytný fumes in jealous despair and Lunobor reads nonsense aloud from a book *(Přečtu mu tři kapitoly).*

ACT II In the lunar Temple of Arts, Čaroskvoucí (Wonderglitter) condescendingly encourages the work of various groups of musicians, painters, sculptors, and writers. When Etherea arrives with Brouček, they fall back in consternation, but Čaroskvoucí welcomes him as an "enlightened man." This reassures the artists, who swarm around Brouček. A Child Prodigy offers him a song about the moon *(Vzbuď se a poslyš!),* Etherea renews her attempts to seduce him *(Již prchám jako vánkem),* and Oblačný (Cloudy) urges him to think exalted thoughts *(Na modrém nebi zlaté slunce plane).* Dozing off during this last, Brouček mumbles in his sleep about beer and sausages; the artists take his words for inspired utterances, but when he wakes, they decide his grossness is repulsive, because he has referred to part of his body—his nose.

In the studio, Duhoslav (Rainbowglory) takes offense when Brouček would rather eat than admire Duhoslav's latest painting. This time the artists are disgusted by the fact that earthlings eat the flesh of other creatures. Čaroskvoucí takes Brouček to task for this *(Vy tedy bez lítosti vraždíte),* but when Etherea flies in, declaring her love for Brouček, he loses patience and blows on her, causing her to collapse, dead. Then he heads for Pegasus, who carries him away. The musicians, led by Harfoboj (Harper), offer an ode in Etherea's memory *(Požehnáni tvoji rtové),* and the scene dissolves back to . . .

§ . . . Prague, where Mazal and Málinka, returning from their walk, learn from the Potboy that Brouček has been found lying on the street and carried home.

PART II

ACT I The underground treasure chamber of King Václav (Wenceslas) IV. Voices in the tavern above argue about the existence of underground passages in the area. Bid good-night by the tavern keeper, Brouček tumbles into the vault. Frightened and disoriented, he finds a way out. After he has left, an apparition of the poet Svatopluk Čech (author of the original

Excursions of Mr. Brouček) recites an exhortation to the Czech people to live up to their glorious history *(Ó, slunce velkého dne);* the apparition vanishes, and Brouček is discovered in the Old Town Square of Prague. In the dark he tries to get his bearings and runs into a Town Councilor, who suspects him of being a spy for the enemy Emperor Sigismund. Brouček discovers he is in the year 1420. As townspeople gather, calling for his arrest, he faints from shock in front of the house of a patriot, Domšík, who comes out and asks who he is. Reviving, Brouček improvises an explanation: he is a loyal Czech, recently returned from Turkey. Armed men appear, readying for battle (chorus: *Začíná se den Páně!*).

§ The next morning in Domšík's house, overlooking the square. Brouček wakes and appraises the situation: he isn't about to risk his life for the Hussites, much as he admires their courage from a safe historical perspective *(Kdybych zde neseděl).* Domšík looks in and tells him to change his outlandish clothes for something appropriate. Kedruta, daughter of the house, shows in three friends of Domšík, who welcome Brouček as one of them. Kunka reports that a fiery sermon at the church next door has stirred the men of Prague to arms *(Aj, kázáni Rokycanovo).* A toast is drunk, and Míroslav the goldsmith proclaims the Hussite cause *(Žel, že jméno české potupeno!).* Brouček tries to explain diplomatically why he doesn't feel like fighting, but the others take up arms and rush out as sounds of conflict are heard in the distance. Kunka stays behind with Kedruta, praying for victory. Brouček slips back into his own clothes.

§ In the square at sunset, the people celebrate victory over Sigismund. Trying to escape from Domšík's house, Brouček gets no farther than the portico, where he tries to hide but is discovered. Hastily he concocts a story about his bravery in battle *(Možná, že jsem utrpěl).* Petřík (Peter), who actually fought, calls this a lie and tells how Brouček tried to surrender to the Germans *(Šel v našem šiku).* The townspeople indignantly put Brouček in a barrel and set it on fire.

§ In the courtyard at the Vikárka Tavern, safely back in the present, Brouček is discovered having spent the night in a barrel. Würfl, the proprietor, hears his unlikely mutterings about the liberation of Prague and helps him back indoors.

THE CUNNING LITTLE VIXEN

Přihody Lišky Bystroušky

THREE ACTS
MUSIC: Leoš Janáček
TEXT (Czech): the composer, after Rudolf Těsnohlidek's verses for drawings by Stanislav Lolek
WORLD PREMIERE: Brno, National Theater, November 6, 1924
U.S. PREMIERE: New York, Hunter College Playhouse (Mannes College), May 7, 1965 (in English)

CHARACTERS

Animals:
Bystrouška (Sharp-ears), *a vixen* . . . . Soprano
Zlatohřbítek (Golden-mane), *a male fox* . . . . Soprano
Kohout, *a rooster* . . . . Soprano
Chocholka, *a hen* . . . . Soprano
Lapák, *a dog* . . . . Mezzo-Soprano
Various forest animals . . . . Soprano, Alto, Tenor, Bass
Humans:
The Innkeeper's Wife . . . . Soprano
The Gamekeeper's Wife . . . . Contralto
Pásek, *the Innkeeper* . . . . Tenor
The Schoolmaster . . . . Tenor
The Gamekeeper . . . . Bass-Baritone
Harašta, *a poacher* . . . . Bass

ACT I   The action takes place in rural Czechoslovakia at no specified time and place, but probably in the mid-1920s, when Janáček composed the work. In a dark gulley in the woods, the Gamekeeper wonders if a storm may be on its way. He dozes off under a bush while a Cricket, a Grasshopper, and a Mosquito dance around him, mildly threatened by a Frog. Bystrouška (Sharp-ears), a young vixen, investigates the Frog, who jumps away, landing on the Gamekeeper's nose. He wakes, sees the vixen, and catches her.

§ The Gamekeeper has brought the vixen home to his farmyard. Lapák, the family dog, seems melancholy, but Bystrouška chatters on to him excitedly about her discoveries in the forest, where everything is still new to her (*Já taky nemám zkušenosti v milování*). When two of the Gamekeeper's children come and tease Bystrouška, she gets annoyed and tries to escape, so he ties her up. She soon notices the barnyard fowl and preaches to the hens, trying to convince them to rebel against the tyranny of the rooster. The rooster realizes this is a trick, but the hens are too stupid and fly into a panic instead, whereupon Bystrouška kills them all. Threatened with punishment by the irate Gamekeeper and his wife, she succeeds in breaking away.

ACT II   Back in the forest, Bystrouška baits the crotchety old Badger, to the amusement of the other animals, and finally drives him out of his lair by spraying it with urine, so she herself can move in.

§ At the village inn, the Gamekeeper and Schoolmaster are playing cards when the local Priest joins them, though he has nothing to contribute to their idle talk. The Gamekeeper teases the Schoolmaster about having a girlfriend (*Ty pot'óchlenče*). When the teacher retorts that he heard the Gamekeeper caught a vixen, he learns the story of her escape. As the hour grows late, the Gamekeeper and Schoolmaster none too steadily head for home.

§ Stumbling through the woods, the Schoolmaster has trouble keeping to the path (*Bud'to mám těžiště pohyblivé*) and eventually falls. As he sits on the ground, he catches a glimpse of Bystrouška and thinks, in his befuddlement, that it is the Gypsy girl Terynka, whom he loves. Teased by the hidden vixen, he lunges to embrace his sweetheart and leaps over a fence. The Priest comes along the same path, pauses to rest, and recalls his youth, when he too was interested in girls (*Já mladým studentem*). His reverie is disrupted by the Gamekeeper, who has spotted the vixen and is chasing her. The Schoolmaster rises from where he landed behind the fence; he and the Priest decide to get moving, while the Gamekeeper in the distance fires a shot.

On a moonlit summer night, Bystrouška lies outside her lair. A handsome male fox, Zlatohřbítek (Golden-mane), appears and offers to be her escort. To impress him, Bystrouška rattles on about her adventures with the Gamekeeper (*Vyrostla jsem tam*). Promising to visit again, he runs off, leaving her to wonder aloud if she is really so attractive. He reappears, bearing the gift of a rabbit, and begins to talk of romance, kissing her and proposing that they mate (*Nejsu lhář, nejsu lišák ulhané*. With little resistance she invites him into her den, while an Owl and Jay cluck at their brazen behavior. Bystrouška quickly reemerges, crying that the seducer will have to marry her. The Woodpecker performs a brief wedding ceremony, and the denizens of the forest dance happily.

ACT III   An autumn day at the edge of a clearing. Harašta, a poacher, comes along the path, singing a ballad (*"Déž sem vandroval"*), and is about to pick up a dead hare when the Gamekeeper accosts him. Feigning innocence, Harašta talks about how he shortly will marry Terynka. Guessing that the hare was killed by Bystrouška, the Gamekeeper sets a trap for her, and the two men withdraw. Bystrouška's cubs run in, followed by their parents, but suspect the trap. When Harašta is heard singing again, Bystrouška stays behind to tease the poacher by pretending she is lame. When he chases her and stumbles, she and her brood go for the chickens he has been carrying in his basket, but he fires his gun at them, fatally wounding Bystrouška.

§ On a green behind the inn, the Gamekeeper and his wife drink beer with the glum Schoolmaster, who is losing his beloved Terynka to the poacher this very day. Remarking that he's not getting any younger, the Gamekeeper leaves for a walk through the forest on his way home.

§ In the setting of Act I, the Gamekeeper, stopping to rest, recalls his courtship and early married days in this same woodland *(Neřikal jsem to?)*. He dozes off, and the animals of the forest appear. The Gamekeeper wakes and notices that Bystrouška is not among them, but he spots one of her cubs—the very image of its mother—and tries to catch it. Instead, he catches a Frog, which croaks that "Grandpa told me all about you." Bemused and contented, the Gamekeeper lets his gun slip to the ground.

FROM THE HOUSE OF THE DEAD
(Z Mrtvého Domu)

THREE ACTS
MUSIC: Leoš Janáček
TEXT (Czech): the composer, based on Dostoevsky's novel
WORLD PREMIERE: Brno, National Theater, April 12, 1930
U.S. PREMIERE: NET Television, December 3, 1969

CHARACTERS

Aljeja, *a young Tatar* . . . . .Soprano (or Tenor)
Filka Morozov, *in prison under the name Luka Kuzmič* . . . . . . Tenor
A Tall Prisoner . . . . Tenor
An Old Prisoner . . . . Tenor
Skuratov . . . . Tenor
Šapkin . . . . Tenor
Čerevin . . . . Tenor

LEOŠ JANÁČEK

A Guard. . . . . Tenor
A Short Prisoner . . . . Baritone
The Commandant . . . . Baritone
Šiškov . . . . Baritone
Alexandr Petrovič Gorjančikov, *a political prisoner* . . . . Bass

ACT I   Siberia, mid-nineteenth century. In the courtyard of a penal colony by
the River Irtish, prisoners are washing themselves by the early morning light.
Amid arguing and joking, there is news that an aristocratic prisoner is joining
them. The Commandant arrives leading Gorjančikov, still wearing city
clothes. When Gorjančikov says he is a political offender, the Commandant
orders him thrashed for his insolence, and he is led off. The Tall Prisoner holds
an injured eagle that has landed at the camp; to the men it represents freedom,
if it heals its broken wing and returns to rule the forest. As the prisoners get
ready for work detail, they recall their homes, which they don't expect to see
again (chorus: *Neuvidí oko již těch krajů*). Skuratov tries a few lines of a folk
song, mixing in bits about his life before he was arrested *(Našli se takoví)*.
Luka, a Ukrainian, launches into a narrative about how he stabbed a bullying
local governor *(Takový směšný byl)*. As he finishes, Gorjančikov, weak from his
beating, is pushed back into the enclosure.

ACT II   A year later, toward the end of the day, prisoners are working by the
riverbank. Gorjančikov tells Aljeja, a youth from Daghestan, that he would
like to teach him to read and write. Work ends as the Commandant ushers in
some civilian visitors, including a Priest, who blesses the river and the evening
meal. Skuratov, in an expansive mood, tells the story of how, as a soldier, he
fell in love with a German girl in the town of Yuryev, but her family wanted
her to marry a well-to-do older relative *(Poslouchejte! Poslali mne v Jurjev)*; Skuratov ended up shooting the bridegroom.

   From an improvised stage, an entertainment, acted by prisoners, is
announced: the opera *Kedril and Don Juan.* In this crude commedia dell'arte
scene, Don Juan, on the last evening of his life, summons the powers of hell,
then duels with and kills a knight who comes to Donna Elvira's defense. Next
he flirts with a Priest's Wife and is dragged away by devils. This is followed
by a pantomime, *The Fair Miller's Wife,* in which the heroine tries to conceal
various would-be lovers, including Don Juan, from each other and from her
jealous husband.

   As the show draws to a close, the Young Prisoner walks off with a local
prostitute. The Short Prisoner, annoyed that Gorjančikov seems to be putting
on airs by drinking tea with Aljeja, knocks over their teapot and punches
Aljeja. Guards restore order and herd the prisoners off.

ACT III   In the prison infirmary, the feverish Aljeja talks about miracles performed by Jesus *(To, když praví)* and proudly notes that he has learned to write.

On a nearby bunk, Luka lies dying. Šapkin relates how, as a vagrant, he was arrested for an attempted burglary *(I správník. Pro tuláctví).* Skuratov, delirious, starts to say he shot the German girl as well as her bridegroom. Other prisoners subdue him, and after most of them have quieted down, Šiškov tells his own story to Čerevin *(Statek velký, dělníků plno).* It concerns a rich farmer whose daughter, Akulka, supposedly had been seduced by one Filka Morozov, who signed up for the army and refused to marry her. With the girl's reputation ruined, her family wanted to marry her off. Šiškov himself married her, only to find that she was a virgin. He tried to get revenge on Filka but ended up killing Akulka herself, because she confessed she had always loved Filka. As he ends his story, Luka dies—and Šiškov recognizes him in death as the same Filka Morozov. "He was born of a mother, too," remarks the Old Prisoner philosophically. Gorjančikov's name is called by the guards, who lead him out: he is to be released.

§ In the courtyard, the Commandant, somewhat drunk, apologizes to Gorjančikov, so as to stay in his good graces, but reasserts his authority with the others. A Blacksmith removes Gorjančikov's fetters as the Commandant gives him his release papers. Aljeja, coming from the infirmary, bids a tearful farewell to Gorjančikov, who has been like a father to him. The prisoners release the eagle, whose wing has healed; as it takes off toward the forest, they briefly salute its freedom *(Svoboda, svobodička!)* while a Guard prepares to march them off to work.

Joonas Kokkonen
b. 1921

$\mathcal{S}$candinavian music is underrepresented in the rest of the world. The exception has been Jean Sibelius, whose symphonies and tone poems enjoy international repertory status. For other composers in Finland, however, the eminence of Sibelius has been a mixed blessing. It is hard to ignore the importance of so major a figure; to fall under his influence would be to lose one's identity, yet to disown it would be to cut off one's heritage.

"I have not a Sibelius complex!" Joonas Kokkonen has asserted—with a smile. Though he made his home near Sibelius' house in Järvenpää, outside Helsinki, he chose his own path musically. Neither a modernist of any particular school nor a conservative, Kokkonen stands aloof from fads and writes what he likes. Because he has always written with skill and individuality, and because he has taught several of the younger generation of composers, he has become the elder statesman of Finnish music, a post created by Sibelius.

Opera has more of a history in Finland than the outsider would suspect. Even before the nation won its independence in 1919, there was a strong cultural sense, exemplified around the turn of the century by the movement called National Romanticism. Sibelius was its chief avatar, but he wrote only one opera—a short one, *Jungfrurn i Tornet,* to a Swedish text—and it ranks only as a curiosity among his works. Sibelius' coloristic sense and narrative instinct found their ideal outlet in the tone poem, a form pioneered by Franz Liszt. Given Finland's limited producing facilities at the time, Sibelius did not follow Richard Strauss' lead and move his tone poems onto the stage.

Finnish opera received a modest boost in 1912 when the soprano Aino

182

Ackté tentatively organized a summer festival at Olavinlinna (Olaf's Castle) at Savonlinna. Several Finnish operas were produced, but only in 1975 did the premiere of Aulis Sallinen's *Ratsumies* (The Horseman) at Savonlinna launch an unforeseen opera boom. Two summers later, Kokkonen's *Viimeiset Kiusaukset* (The Last Temptations) appeared, with Martti Talvela—at that time the festival's director—in the leading role, which he had created for the 1975 premiere at the National Opera in Helsinki. (By the spring of 1980, the work had had a continuous run of 150 performances at the Alexander Theater in Helsinki.)

Lauri Kokkonen, the composer's playwright cousin, wrote the drama on which *The Last Temptations* is based. Like *The Horseman,* it draws on Finnish frontier history. This soon brought forth the pejorative term "fur-hat opera," coined by younger composers who did not want to be limited to nationalistic subjects: the world stage already beckoned. It is true that these two operas, together with Sallinen's subsequent *Punainen Viiva* (The Red Line), covered the frontier milieu so well that it would have been futile to go on emulating them. More recent Finnish operas have drawn their subjects from farther afield.

There is reason to be glad, however, that Kokkonen started out so close to home. In Paavo Ruotsalainen, the fundamentalist preacher of *The Last Temptations,* he created one of the strongest figures in twentieth-century opera. With his rough-hewn backwoods individualism, Paavo readily translates into many another culture, notably that of another young frontier nation, the United States. The final scene of *The Last Temptations* conveys a rare sense of catharsis and exaltation. In his only opera, which ranks as a national classic, Kokkonen forged a testimonial to the life and times of a real, wholly believable figure.

THE LAST TEMPTATIONS

(Viimeiset Kiusaukset)

TWO ACTS
MUSIC: Joonas Kokkonen
TEXT (Finnish): Lauri Kokkonen
WORLD PREMIERE: Helsinki, Finnish National Opera, September 2, 1975
U.S. PREMIERE: New York, Metropolitan Opera House (Finnish National Opera), April 26, 1983

JOONAS KOKKONEN

CHARACTERS

Riitta, *Paavo's first wife* . . . . Soprano
Juhana, *Paavo and Riitta's son.* . . . . Tenor
Jaakko Högman, *a blacksmith* . . . . Baritone
Paavo Ruotsalainen, *a farmer turned preacher* . . . . Bass
Anna Loviisa, *Paavo's second wife* . . . . Speaking Role
Albertiina, *a servant* . . . . Speaking Role
Three Women . . . . .Soprano, Mezzo-Soprano, Alto
Three Men . . . . Tenor, Baritone, Bass

The original play was inspired by the life of Paavo Ruotsalainen (1777–1852), a backwoods preacher who became one of the most influential evangelists of his day, spreading revivalism through rural Finland. He came into conflict with other religious leaders and with civil authorities, partly because of his stubborn individualism, partly because of the social protest inherent in the revivalist movement. He has been called "a real Luther" in a Lutheran country. The other principals in the cast are also actual historical figures.

ACT I   In his island cabin on a winter's night, Paavo lies on his deathbed, calling for his first wife, Riitta, who has been dead for twenty years. Albertiina, the housekeeper, goes to fetch Anna Loviisa, Paavo's second wife, but he doesn't recognize her. She tells Albertiina how she came to look after Riitta during her final illness, and afterward married Paavo. When the two women sing a revival hymn *("Jos sallit Isä vanhaksi"),* Paavo regains his presence of mind and tells them to leave him: "One must approach the gate of heaven alone." In the darkness, he feverishly begins to recall episodes of his life. . . .

§ At a country dance, Paavo appears as a young man courting Riitta. Despite warnings from the tempters—three men, three women, who test Paavo throughout the opera—that the marriage will bring thirty-three years of hardship, she accepts him.

§ In the smithy, Riitta accuses the blacksmith Jaakko Högman of having set Paavo on the course of wandering evangelism that made life so hard for his family *(Paavo juoksi seuramatkoillaan).* Högman replies that Paavo needed to be strengthened by inner knowledge of Jesus. Only Jesus, he adds, can open the gate of heaven for them; Paavo admits he is too weak to open it himself.

§ At the site of their homestead by the lakeshore, where they have brought their firstborn, Paavo declares he will build a house. But when he sees the gate to the pasture, he is afraid, thinking it is the unapproachable gate of heaven. The tempters and a gradually materializing crowd of villagers discuss the hardships the family found there, including an unseasonable frost. Paavo and Riitta grab leather reins to swing over the wheatfield to keep the frost from settling in, but their efforts are futile, and they accidentally trample on the baby.

§ About twenty years later, their son Juhana mends his father's knapsack and talks of leaving home to find his own life *(Kasvatan komean orhin)*. Riitta dreads the thought of life there without him.

Riitta has hidden the knapsack, symbol of Paavo's wandering, in hopes of persuading him that charity begins at home *(Missä on se korkea pirtti)*, but he finds it. They quarrel as he insists not only on leaving but on taking the last loaf of bread in the household, stuffing it into the knapsack. In her rage, Riitta hurls an ax at Paavo; it misses and falls to the floor. Paavo is left standing alone in his recollection of the episode, blaming himself for his callousness toward Riitta, for failing to reach enough people with his preaching, for being unable to open the gate that faces him *(En saa ovea auki)*.

In the aftermath of their quarrel, Riitta is visited by village women as Paavo sits in silence. The women have come to tell her that Juhana has been killed while on an errand to the mill. Riitta and Paavo are too stunned to register grief.

§ Some years later, with spring snow outside, Riitta lies on her deathbed, recalling to Paavo their life on the island *(Katso korkeita puita)*. She says she sees the gate of heaven open. As Paavo reads a psalm, Juhana appears in spirit and takes up the verse: "Praise the Lord, O my soul" *("Kiitä Herraa, minun sieluni")*. Riitta moves with Juhana toward the gate, leaving Paavo alone.

ACT II   In a courthouse yard, the three male tempters decide to test Paavo to see if he deserves to be remembered after death. He appears, calling the people together to preach to them *(Kirkonkelloja soitetaan)*. He was once charged with heretical opinions and had to defend them on this spot. The tempters torment him by misconstruing his past statements. Dressed in secular clothes that Paavo has scorned as worldly, the three woman tempters call for a polka with which to stamp on his prayers and piety *(Tansikaa virret pihan hiekkaan)*, saying this will be his memorial. He falls to his knees praying for salvation as a revivalist congregation, seemingly in answer, intones an encouraging hymn *(Sä suuriakin suruja)*.

Riitta comes to call Paavo to their island. He states again his need to preach a Christianity of faith rather than reason *(Minun on vielä ennen kuolemaani)*. He has been invited to address a graduation ceremony in Helsinki and feels he must go there.

§ Before the Cathedral of St. Nicholas in the capital, the three men pretend they don't know Paavo when he arrives, looking for his place on the dais. A common countryman cannot go there, they say. Questioning him about the books he has read, tracts of simple faith, they sneer at his lack of scholarship. Nevertheless, when dignitaries file in, he hears his favorite hymn being played and starts an address *(Ystävät, nöyrtykää)*—only to be shunned by the crowd. Giving up the attempt, he realizes the vanity and futility of his quest for recognition.

§ Riitta again calls Paavo to the island, but he feels unworthy to join her. Then he hears the blacksmith quoting from a religious text: "All temptations are caused by self-righteousness and a sense of one's own goodness" *("Kaikki kiusaukset johtuvat")*. Paavo and Riitta respond with other quotations, and Juhana recites part of the Lord's Prayer.

§ The scene returns to that of the beginning of Act I. Anna Loviisa and Albertiina, finding Paavo delirious on his deathbed, call two of his daughters and their husbands, plus a hired man and woman servant, to help calm him. Coming to his senses, Paavo realizes he has been hallucinating scenes from his past. The tempters were these six members of his household who just arrived: "Satan has sifted me tonight." He checks that his will is in order and tells them, "Upon my grave you must plant the prickliest tree, because I have been the prickliest of men." At his request, Albertiina reads from the book once given him by the blacksmith *("Sinä, joka olet nähnyt")*. Paavo starts his favorite hymn *("Sinuhun turvaan, Jumala")*; as others of his family enter and take up the strain, he stops singing and listens. From the distance, Riitta calls him once more to the island. At last he feels fit to approach the gate of heaven.

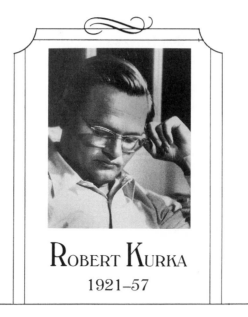

Robert Kurka
1921–57

A Creative Arts Award to Robert Kurka in 1957 from Brandeis University cited him as "a composer on the threshold of a career of real distinction." Leukemia ended his life soon afterward. Like Béla Bartók in similar circumstances, he struggled to get his last work ready during his illness. He had written all of *The Good Soldier Schweik*—already scheduled for performance by New York City Opera—and he was able to orchestrate up to the final scene, thereafter indicating his intentions on the manuscript; a colleague, Hershy Kay, filled out the remaining pages of score. The opera had its posthumous premiere a few months later, as part of an all-American spring season sponsored by the Ford Foundation's Program in Humanities and the Arts.

Born in Cicero, Illinois, Kurka was the son of a Czech father, who had emigrated to the United States by way of Vienna, and a mother born in Chicago to Czech parents. He grew up familiar with the Czech and German languages, also acquiring Russian and—through military service—Japanese. His instrument was the violin, though he briefly took on the tuba with the thought of playing it in an army band. While in uniform, he formed a string quartet with members of the Nippon Philharmonic in Tokyo, trying out some of his own music. Later, studying for his M.A. in composition at Columbia, he played in the student orchestra, which took part in some opera performances.

Opera, however, was not a special enthusiasm of his. He came to it through his interest in Jaroslav Hašek's novel *The Good Soldier Schweik* (1920–23), written, like the original of Janáček's *The Cunning Little Vixen,* in the style of a newspaper series. Having no operatic preconceptions, Kurka was free to invent a musical format that would fit Hašek's anecdotal approach. Kurka's solution, not unlike Berg's in *Wozzeck,* was a set of instrumentally conceived, closed musical forms. In fact, it was as a suite for band that his music for *Schweik* first appeared. The opera, rather than building to a single story-line climax, makes its points through a series of vignettes.

Because of the World War I milieu of Hašek's story, Kurka had the idea of scoring his work for a small "German band" of sixteen wind instruments plus percussion. Jaunty, motoric rhythms and march tunes keep pace with the author's satiric humor. Parallels have been drawn to the cabaret-based theater of Bertolt Brecht and Kurt Weill, but in *Schweik,* Brecht's "alienation effect" is absent, and the underlying seriousness is left for the audience to recognize.

Save for those of Philip Glass, few American operas since Virgil Thomson's have gathered such a cult following. Irving Kolodin wrote of "*Schweik*'s combination of revue, burlesque, opéra comique and 'musical.' " This very source of the work's appeal, oddly, had the effect of limiting its acceptance by opera houses: neither structured nor orchestrated in the conventional manner, it seemed to fall between Broadway and opera. Nevertheless, in 1981 Martin L. Sokol noted in *The New York City Opera: An American Adventure* that "*Schweik* has prospered . . . and has now had close to 100 different productions throughout the world, in more than a dozen languages."

Robert Kurka died short of his thirty-sixth birthday, leaving string quartets, concertos, and two symphonies. It was *Schweik,* however, that brought together all the aspects of his talent. Martin Bernheimer in the *Los Angeles Times* called it "a wonderful little opera—tough, bright, brittle, funny, poignant and accessible."

THE GOOD SOLDIER SCHWEIK

TWO ACTS
MUSIC: Robert Kurka
TEXT (English): Lewis Allen (Abel Meeropol), based on Jaroslav
   Hašek's novel
WORLD PREMIERE: New York City Opera, April 23, 1958

CHARACTERS

Katy Wendler . . . . Soprano
Mrs. Müller, *Schweik's housekeeper* . . . . Soprano

189

THE GOOD SOLDIER SCHWEIK

Mme. Kakonyi	Soprano
Baroness von Botzenheim	Mezzo-Soprano
Josef Schweik	Tenor
Sgt. Vanek	Tenor
Army Chaplain	Tenor
Bretschneider, *plainclothes policeman*	Tenor
Three Army Psychiatrists	Tenor, Baritone, Bass
Lt. Henry Lukash	Baritone
Palivec, *landlord of the Flagon*	Baritone
Police Officer	Baritone
Army Doctor	Baritone
Col. Klaus von Zillergut	Bass
Gen. von Schwarzburg	Bass
A Gentleman of the Kingdom of Bohemia	Speaking Role

ACT I   Prague, June 28, 1914. A Gentleman of the (pre–World War I) Kingdom of Bohemia, acting as prologue, describes Josef Schweik, who makes his living by forging pedigrees for dogs he finds on the street. A Newsboy passes, announcing the assassination of Archduke Ferdinand at Sarajevo.

§ In Schweik's apartment, he and his housekeeper, Mrs. Müller, discuss the news as he sits rubbing linament on his legs. He leaves for the tavern.

§ At the Flagon, a plainclothes policeman, Bretschneider, hears Palivec, the proprietor, admit he took down the emperor's portrait because it had flyspecks on it. Bretschneider arrests him for disrespect, taking Schweik along too for having discussed politics.

§ At police headquarters, Schweik is charged with supposed offenses. He is chatty and cooperative, but the Officer is not amused by his plea of feeble-mindedness (*I was let out from the army . . . as a chronic case*) and tells him he will be arraigned next morning.

§ In a prison cell, Schweik is thrown in with Palivec and others, who bemoan their lot (refrain: *I'm innocent*). Schweik tries to cheer them up (*We're all in a hell of a mess*) by saying the police are only trying to make a show of doing their job. Guards take him for interrogation.

§ Elsewhere at headquarters, three Psychiatrists argue about their different theories (*The Ego and the Id*) before Schweik is brought in. They ask him questions, to which he gives garrulous, irrelevant answers, convincing them he is a hopeless idiot.

§ Sent to an asylum for evaluation, Schweik sings happily of the carefree life there (*I never felt so good before*) and dances with the other patients until two Doctors appear. As they confer, he reflects to himself, seriously this time, about what war means *(Who will go to the war when it comes)*. The Doctors decide he has been faking in order to avoid military service, so he is discharged.

§ In the street, Mrs. Müller pushes Schweik in a wheelchair to join the army. Wearing his old uniform, he brandishes a pair of crutches, crying, "To Belgrade!"

ACT II   In a field infirmary near the frontier, Schweik and other malingerers complain of boredom (refrain: *Hey diddle diddle*). An army Doctor comes to "diagnose" the patients: for Schweik, who pleads rheumatism, he orders three enemas a day, then holds forth about the patients' sorry excuses *(In trying to evade the military draft)*. Baroness von Botzenheim, a dowager do-gooder, brings a basket of provisions and gifts, praising Schweik's courage *(Brave soldier, cripple' soldier)*. As soon as the Baroness leaves, the Doctor orders the men up and out.

§ In the guardhouse, Schweik and the others again bemoan their lot *(Oh, the army, it's a hell of a life)*. A Sergeant appears and orders them to attend chapel.

§ From his pulpit, a half-drunk Chaplain hectors the men about their desultory response *(Pray, damn it all!)*. When Schweik alone seems moved by the sermon, the Chaplain decides to take this man as his orderly.

§ Some time later in the camp, the Chaplain loses at cards to the dashing Lt. Lukash. He also loses his orderly, Schweik—the last thing he had to wager.

§ Schweik, now Lukash's orderly, reports that the cat ate the canary and ran away; to take its place, he has brought a dog, Max. He also reports that a young woman, Katy, has moved in; to help the situation, he has sent for her husband. Katy appears, embracing the lieutenant, but he tells her she cannot stay. Schweik brings the dog, which frightens her into clinging to Lukash even more tightly. Col. Klaus von Zillergut storms in to declare that the dog was stolen from *him*. The confrontation is joined by Katy's meek husband, Wendler, who has come to take her home. As the colonel fumes at Lukash (ensemble: *It's conduct unbecoming an officer*), the Wendlers sort out their differences, Schweik repeats his inane explanations, and the dog barks. Raging, the colonel orders Lukash to the front the next morning.

§ Aboard the Prague–Budejovice express, Lukash berates Schweik for letting his luggage get lost. Mistaking a bald passenger for a man he used to know, Schweik enrages the man, who pushes Schweik out of the compartment and introduces himself to Lukash as Gen. von Schwarzburg, on special inspection duty *(I see that you allow your orderly to fraternize with you)*. He dismisses Lukash, who finds Schweik and tells him to keep his distance. Saluting, Schweik accidentally trips the emergency-brake signal, stopping the train sharply. For this he is arrested.

§ A few days later, in a café in Budejovice, Lukash writes a mash note to Mme. Kakonyi, a married woman who caught his eye at the theater the night before. When Schweik returns from police detention, Lukash sends him to deliver the note.

§ On his way, Schweik runs into an old pal, Voditchka. They detour to the tavern.

§ In the tavern, patrons try to convince themselves they are "in carefree land." Finally remembering the letter, Schweik and Voditchka stumble out to deliver it.

§ Finding the address, they knock until a man appears. Though Schweik insists on delivering the letter to Mme. Kakonyi in person, her husband grabs it; he and Schweik scuffle. As the frightened wife appears, Voditchka punches Kakonyi. Police arrive to catch Schweik chewing and swallowing the letter.

§ In a dugout near the front, Lukash resignedly makes peace with Schweik before sending him and Sgt. Vanek off on patrol.

§ Amid devastation at the front, a gaggle of wounded men wanders by *(Wait for the ragged soldiers)*. Schweik and Vanek disagree about their directions and part company. Schweik decides to go for a walk *(I'll take a quiet road)*, leaving his gun.

§ The Gentleman of the prologue returns, saying that whatever has become of Schweik, he's always sure to be found somewhere.

ÉDOUARD LALO
1823–92

*T*he rising tide of French Wagnerism, which lasted from the mid-
nineteenth century until World War I, swept up several interesting
composers. Two of them—Ernest Chausson and Claude Debussy—
completed only one opera apiece. Édouard Lalo wrote two operas,
Albéric Magnard three, César Franck four, Ernest Reyer five. While it was
Wagner who led the way toward medieval or legendary subjects, through-
composed musical forms and chromatic harmonies, French composers found
their own personal, nationally flavored means of treating such material. One
of them, Camille Saint-Saëns, though influenced by Liszt in his tone poems
and keyboard writing, consciously resisted Wagnerism in his stage works.
Georges Bizet likewise avoided the pitfalls, though Don José's last lines in
Carmen would not have been written without *Tristan und Isolde*. Debussy's
involvement with Wagner amounted to a love-hate relationship: in some
respects their work is aesthetically opposite, yet *Pelléas et Mélisande* as a whole
hardly would have been conceived without *Tristan*, the most influential musical work of its epoch.

Le Roi d'Ys, a sort of French *Lohengrin,* was considered a disaster by its cast
right up through final rehearsal. To Lalo's surprise, the opening-night audience
called for several encores and cheered him to the rafters. *Le Roi d'Ys* has
remained in repertory in France, though its fortunes never prospered abroad,
except for the overture. The story came to the composer through his marriage
in 1865 to a singer, Julie de Maligny: while visiting her family's native countryside of Brittany and the Vendée, he learned of the legendary city of Ys. The
strong characters of Margared and Karnac, the Ortrud and Telramund of the

piece, provide classic opportunities for a dramatic mezzo-soprano and lyric-dramatic baritone of the French type, while Rozenn and Mylio offer equally typical music for a French-style lyric soprano and tenor.

Lalo, distantly of Spanish descent, is remembered as the father of Pierre Lalo, an influential music critic, and as the composer of the *Symphonie Espagnole* for violin and orchestra, created for the virtuoso Pablo de Sarasate. Other works that have kept Lalo's reputation alive are a Cello Concerto and the ballet *Namouna,* from which Serge Lifar derived his shorter dance piece *Suite en Blanc.* Less familiar today are the composer's attractive chamber music and lyrical songs, some written with his wife's contralto voice in mind.

LE ROI D'YS

(The King of Ys)

THREE ACTS
MUSIC: Édouard Lalo
TEXT (French): Édouard Blau, based on a Breton legend
WORLD PREMIERE: Paris, Opéra Comique, May 7, 1888
U.S. PREMIERE: New Orleans, French Opera House, January 23, 1890
METROPOLITAN PREMIERE: February 29, 1924

CHARACTERS

Princess Rozenn	} *the king's daughters* . . . . {	Soprano
Princess Margared		Mezzo-Soprano
Mylio, *a soldier*		Tenor
Prince Karnac, *an enemy leader*		Baritone
Jahel, *the grand chamberlain*		Baritone
The King of Ys		Bass
Apparition of St. Corentin		Bass

The modern French province of Brittany originally had its own Celtic language, accounting for the unusual names of the characters in *Le Roi d'Ys.* The action takes place in the legendary Breton city of Ys sometime during the Middle Ages.

ACT I   At Christmastime, the population of Ys has something extra to celebrate: peace will be restored by the wedding of Princess Margared to the enemy Prince Karnac (chorus: *Noël! C'est l'aurore bénie*). Margared's sister, Rozenn, detects her unhappiness, which Margared at first denies (duet: *En silence pourquoi souffrir?*) but soon confesses. She says she loves another, who went off to war with the two girls' childhood friend Mylio; neither man is thought to have survived. Bridesmaids crowd around Margared to prepare her for the wedding (chorus: *Venez, l'heure presse!*). Alone, Rozenn longs for the return of Mylio, whom she loves *(Par une chaîne trop forte),* and as if by a miracle, he appears before her. Though rumored dead, he was a captive (duet: *Si le ciel est plein de flammes*). The lovers must part for now and go their separate ways.

Karnac arrives, and the King greets him *(Dans un rival je trouve un fils!).* As the King is feeling his age, he is glad Karnac and Margared will be able to succeed him. Margared learns that Mylio has returned; though she still does not admit it, he is the one she loves. Knowing him to be alive, she cannot accept marriage to Karnac and makes a public refusal, to the horror of her own people and the indignation of Karnac and his men. When Karnac throws down his gauntlet before the King, declaring a renewal of war, Mylio picks it up, and the two warriors defy each other (ensemble: *O criminelle démence!*).

ACT II   From a room in the palace, Margared looks out at the countryside where Karnac is mobilizing for the attack. Ruefully she faces the fact that it is her sister, not herself, whom Mylio loves *(Lorsque je t'ai vu soudain reparaître).* She steps into hiding as the King arrives with Mylio and Rozenn. When the King tells Mylio it is time for battle, Mylio declares his confidence in victory under the protection of St. Corentin, patron saint of Brittany *(Oui, je le sens, je l'atteste).* Margared is in despair, while the others count on heaven for help (quartet: *Le ciel saura bénir nos armes*). Margared hears that Mylio and Rozenn will marry. After the men leave, she steps out to confront Rozenn, who now realizes her sister too loves Mylio. Spitefully, Margared hopes Karnac will win. Rozenn begs her to conquer her heartbreak for the good of the country *(Que la justice fasse taire),* but Margared, thinking only of revenge, wishes both lovers dead.

§ By a chapel outside the city, Mylio and his soldiers give thanks to St. Corentin for their victory. After they leave, Karnac stumbles in, bemoaning his defeat, calling the powers of hell to his aid. Margared appears, crying, "Hell hears you!"—she who could not share his love now shares his hatred (duet: *L'enfer t'écoute!*). A floodgate, she says, controls the fate of the city. She lacks the strength to open it alone; with his help, the ocean can be unleashed to inundate Ys. But when she taunts St. Corentin to save the city with a miracle, a ghostly vision of the saint appears, pronouncing a curse on them *(Malheur sur vous!).* Repentance is their only hope.

ACT III Outside Rozenn's chamber at the palace, Jahel, the King's grand chamberlain, tells a group of young lords that according to custom, they must petition the bride's attendants for permission to call for her. The girls go through the motions of refusing until Mylio appears and addresses his own serenade to the sequestered Rozenn (aubade: *Vainement, ma bien-aimée*). Finally the bride comes out and declares herself willing to marry *(Pourquoi lutter de la sorte)*, joining hands with Mylio as the procession moves into the adjacent chapel. Karnac enters and demands that Margared keep her promise, provoking her with a description of the newlyweds' happiness (duet: *Vois ton amant joyeux et beau*). Margared hurries away with Karnac to the floodgate before the wedding party returns.

Mylio and Rozenn sing of their happiness (duet: *À l'autel j'allais rayonnant*). He leaves her with the King when the latter comes looking for her. Father and daughter are overheard by Margared, who is remorseful when she realizes they still love her (trio: *Que dans l'asile choisi*). Shouts are heard in the background, and Margared, spied by the King, warns that death is approaching. Mylio comes to say he has killed Karnac, who opened the floodgate. As all flee to seek safety, the King drags along Margared, though she meant to stay behind and drown.

§ Those who have escaped the rising waters gather on top of a hill, praying for divine assistance (chorus: *O Puissance infinie!*). Margared declares that the sacrifice of a guilty person will stem the tide, adding that she herself is the one; the crowd cries for her death, but the King reminds them that only God should judge her. She leaps into the waves, crying to God to save the people and forgive her crime. As the sky lightens and the waters subside, the people give thanks.

JEAN-BAPTISTE LULLY
1632–87

$\mathcal{F}$lorentine-born Giovanni Battista Lulli, son of a miller, was taken to the French court at the age of fourteen as a domestic in the household of Mlle. de Montpensier, a cousin of King Louis XIV. In Paris, the youth became acquainted with the city's cultural life and began to acquire a reputation as a violinist, singer, and dancer. His employment by Louis as a court composer of instrumental music began in 1653, when Lulli was not yet twenty-one. Eight years later, he took out French citizenship, and not long afterward he was appointed overseer of the king's personal musical staff.

Though Jean-Baptiste Lully, as he was now known in France, composed ballets with spoken dialogue, he was dubious about the suitability of the vernacular for opera. The French loved their language too much to tolerate its being twisted and turned by vocal display. Lully remained little interested in opera until after the formation of the Académie d'Opéra in 1669. From that point on, he saw French opera as the wave of the future. Always a shrewd maneuverer, he gained control of the institution three years later, when it became known officially as the Académie Royale de Musique, colloquially as the Opéra. Its function was to supply operas for the court at Versailles, but performances also were given in Paris and were open to the public. Interest in this art form was widespread and partisanship intense.

Over a period of twelve years, in collaboration with the playwright Philippe Quinault, Lully dominated the opera stage in Paris, producing a series of *tragédies en musique* whose prologues glorified the reign of Louis XIV. The king himself took an interest in the choice of subject matter from classic literature. In keeping with current taste, ballet interludes played an important part.

Throughout his career, Lully was the center of controversies and power plays, but it was not until sixty-five years after his death that the so-called *Querelle des Bouffons* erupted—a public feud between partisans of French tragedy and those of Italian-style opera buffa. As a result of this dispute, a schism developed from which emerged the form known as *opéra comique,* with spoken dialogue, while the *tragédie lyrique,* dismissed as old-fashioned by its detractors, continued to rule the classical stage. Lully had founded it upon an astute amalgam of French dance forms and Italian vocal style, developing a successful type of *récitatif* for musical declamation of the French language. The influence of his style persists, via Debussy and Poulenc, to the present day in French musical prosody.

Lully's death at fifty-four resulted from gangrene infection caused by injury to his foot while he beat time with a staff during a concert—a rare example of the possibly fatal occupational hazards of conducting.

ATYS

PROLOGUE AND FIVE ACTS
MUSIC: Jean-Baptiste Lully
TEXT (French): Philippe Quinault, based on Ovid's *Fasti*
WORLD PREMIERE: St. Germain-en-Laye, court, January 10, 1676
U.S. PREMIERE: New York, Brooklyn Academy of Music (Les Arts Florissants), May 17, 1989

CHARACTERS

PROLOGUE
Flore, *a goddess* . . . . Soprano
Melpomène, *the tragic muse* . . . . Soprano
Iris, *a goddess* . . . . Soprano
Le Temps, *god of time* . . . . Baritone

TRAGEDY
Sangaride, *nymph, daughter of the River Sangarius* . . . . Soprano
Cybèle, *a goddess* . . . . Soprano

Doris, *nymph, Idas' sister*. . . . . Soprano

Mélisse, *confidante and priestess of Cybèle* . . . . Soprano

Atys (Attis), *relative of Sangaride*. . . . . .Countertenor

Le Sommeil, *god of sleep* . . . . .Countertenor

Célénus, *King of Phrygia, son of Neptune* . . . . Baritone

Idas, *Doris' brother, friend of Atys* . . . . Bass

PROLOGUE   In the palace of Time, the god praises the glory and wisdom of Louis XIV. Flore, goddess of spring, wishes to honor the king but arrives too late: he is leaving in March for foreign wars. Melpomène, muse of tragedy, brings her followers to offer the king instead the story of Atys.

ACT I   Legendary Asia Minor (now Turkey). On a mountainside in Phrygia consecrated to the goddess Cybèle, Atys—a young man befriended by King Célénus—announces Cybèle's arrival. Atys' friend Idas teases him about his feigned indifference to love. The youth admits he is actually susceptible to love's power, but he denies this when the river nymph Sangaride comes to usher in Cybèle's arrival. Sangaride, engaged to Célénus, confides to her friend Doris that her heart really belongs to Atys (*J'aime Atys en secret*). It is not long, however, before Atys confesses to Sangaride that he secretly loves her; he is surprised to learn that she returns his affection. They wish they could marry (duet: *Si l'Hymen unissoit mon destin et le vôtre*) but realize that duty and circumstance forbid this. Cybèle arrives with ceremony and invites everyone to her temple, where she will name her choice for high priest.

ACT II   In the temple, Célénus reveals to Atys his fear that Sangaride may love someone else, but Atys, concealing his own feelings, offers reassurance before leaving to further the wedding arrangements. Cybèle arrives and tells Célénus she has chosen Atys to be her high priest. To her attendant Mélisse, she confesses that she loves Atys and intends to let him know by means of a dream (*Fai venir le Sommeil*). Atys is brought back and invested with his new office.

ACT III   In Atys' palace as high priest, he laments the loss of Sangaride. Idas and his sister Doris come to inform him that Sangaride is equally unhappy and hopes to enlist the aid of the goddess Cybèle. Atys still cannot imagine betraying his sovereign, Célénus. Sending Idas and Doris to bring Sangaride, Atys hopes for the best (*Nous pouvons nous flater de l'espoir le plus doux*) but soon succumbs to sleep, in which he is visited by good and bad dreams. The former acquaint him with Cybèle's love for him; the latter warn of his fate should he refuse her. He wakes with a start to find Cybèle there. She tries to coax a favorable response from him but is interrupted by Sangaride, who implores help in avoiding an unwanted marriage. The goddess agrees and sends her off, but to Mélisse she reveals her suspicion that Atys may love Sangaride rather than herself. Dispatching Mélisse to help Atys perform his duties, she ponders her own distress *(Espoir si cher et doux).*

ACT IV   In the palace of the River Sangarius, Idas and Doris try to console Sangaride, who fears that Atys really loves Cybèle *(Hélas! j'aime un Perfide).* When Célénus comes to take Sangaride to their wedding, she says she will obey her father's wishes. Atys arrives and is shocked to sense that his beloved has turned against him. After Célénus leaves, the nymph accuses Atys of duplicity, but he convinces her of his unchanged love (duet: *Aimons en secret*).

   The god of the River Sangarius invites other river divinities to celebrate the wedding of his daughter Sangaride. But Atys arrives and, acting as high priest, announces that Cybèle forbids the wedding, claiming Sangaride for her own service. Despite Célénus' anger, Atys takes Sangaride away.

ACT V   In "delightful gardens," Célénus accuses Cybèle of robbing him of his happiness, but she replies they both have been betrayed by Atys and soon will be avenged *(J'amois Atys, l'amour a fait mon injustice).* Together they confront the lovers, who plead unsuccessfully for mercy. Summoned by Cybèle, Alecton appears from hell and strikes Atys with madness. In his delusion he mistakes Sangaride for a monster and kills her. So that he can realize what he has done, Cybèle restores his sanity. His grief starts to soften the goddess' heart, but after following Sangaride's body from the scene, he is brought back in, having stabbed himself. To save him in an eternal form, Cybèle transforms the dying youth into a pine tree. She calls Wood Nymphs and Corybantes to join her in lamenting Atys' death and consecrating the pine tree to evergreen life.

PIETRO MASCAGNI
1863–1945

*C*hance thrust Pietro Mascagni into the international limelight at the age of twenty-six. As the composer of *Cavalleria Rusticana,* which won a prize offered by the publishing house of Edoardo Sonzogno in 1890, Mascagni became the unwitting leader of the new movement known as verismo, or realism, and an exemplar of independence from the influence of Wagner. Everything about *Cavalleria Rusticana* was the opposite of what Wagner represented: it was short and to the point, innocent of philosophy, couched in an unvarnished musical vocabulary close to folklore. As one juror remarked, "This is the sort of music the public likes."

A number of composers have suffered the fate of being remembered for just one work. Consider Fromental Halévy, who wrote *La Juive* and—as far as the world is concerned—nothing else. Worst of all, however, is to remembered only for one's *first* success, as happened to Mascagni. No matter how hard he tried to live it down, to write something different, he was always pointed out as the composer of *Cavalleria Rusticana.* Later in life, when he conducted performances of it, he was accused of pacing it too slowly—of no longer knowing the work that the public had taken to its bosom over the years.

At first, the influence of Mascagni's flash success spread far and wide. There was a vogue for short operas; even Nikolai Rimsky-Korsakov, Richard Strauss, Sergei Rachmaninov, Arnold Schoenberg, and Manuel de Falla wrote them. Within Italy, Mascagni and his colleagues tried applying the verismo principles to other, longer works. Intrinsically, however, verismo turned out to have a short fuse. Its foundations had been laid back in 1876 with *La Gioconda* by Amilcare Ponchielli, with whom Mascagni studied at the Milan Conservatory.

After the turn of the century, the influence of verismo continued to be felt, but composers were increasingly hard-put to find new ways of developing it. Most took what they needed—a welcome immediacy of expression—and moved on to broader pastures.

Mascagni strove to transcend his image as a one-opera composer by trying rustic *comédie larmoyante,* sentimental commedia dell'arte, operetta, and poetic drama. His most successful foray into the last of these genres was *Iris,* produced only eight years after *Cavalleria Rusticana.* Anticipating a vogue for Oriental subjects that would sire several operas by French and Italian composers, he used *Iis* to explore colorful orchestration. Veristic melodrama still rears its head in Act II when Iris is confronted by her blind father, but most of the work is taken up with exotic fantasy and literary conceits. The arty libretto contains lengthy preambles, and symbolism plays an important role. Crude almost beyond belief, however, is the naming of two principal characters—Osaka and Kyoto—after cities.

Mascagni, who lived to be nearly eighty-two, kept his fame for what turned into more and more of a dated success with *Cavalleria Rusticana.* By the end of his life, he was little more than a relic of Italy's glorious operatic past. Because he had supported fascism and curried favor with Mussolini, he was even in disrepute. By surviving his colleagues Ruggero Leoncavallo and Giacomo Puccini, however, he had kept one big advantage over them: the stipend paid to theaters by the Italian government for producing the works of living composers.

IRIS

THREE ACTS
MUSIC: Pietro Mascagni
TEXT (Italian): Luigi Illica
WORLD PREMIERE: Rome, Costanzi, November 22, 1898
U.S. PREMIERE: Philadelphia, Academy of Music, October 14, 1902
METROPOLITAN PREMIERE: December 6, 1907

CHARACTERS

Iris, *a young girl* . . . . Soprano
Dhia, *heroine of a puppet play* . . . . Soprano
Osaka, *a rich young man* . . . . Tenor

Two Ragpickers . . . . Tenors
Kyoto, *owner of a geisha house* . . . . Baritone
The Blind Man (Il Cieco), *Iris' father* . . . . Bass
The Sun . . . . Chorus

The action takes place in Japan at an unspecified time in the past.

ACT I   An invisible chorus announces that the Sun is about to rise and ani-
mate the world *(Son Io! Son Io la Vita!)*. Iris, a young girl, awakens, telling of
a sad, frightening dream, from which the rising Sun has rescued her. The voice
of her father, the Blind Man, is heard calling. Meanwhile, two men, Osaka
and Kyoto, observe her furtively. Osaka wants her kidnapped but not harmed;
Kyoto, a procurer, is glad to oblige, proposing a ruse whereby a puppet show
will ensnare the girl. Iris leads her father into the sunlight, where he prays
silently. Women take their laundry to the river *(Al rio!)*, while Iris and her
father reflect on the grandeur of nature *(In pure stile)*. Osaka and Kyoto, disguised as strolling players, arrive with a troupe of performers to set up a
puppet theater. In their play, Dhia, a pathetic orphan girl whose tyrannical
father threatens to sell her to an old merchant, is saved by Jor (played by
Osaka: *Apri la tua finestra*), son of the Sun. While Iris marvels at the story,
some of the troupe surround and abduct her. Ordering the theater dismantled,
the two men leave a note and a purse full of money for the Blind Man and
depart. When the father begins to realize Iris has disappeared, some passing
Peddlers try to help him, suggesting the girl has gone to the Yoshiwara—the
pleasure district of the city. He insists on being led there.

ACT II   Captive in a luxurious house of amusement, Iris sleeps, surrounded
by geishas and Kyoto, who welcomes Osaka but tells him not to wake the
girl—who, he says, must be wooed with lavish presents. Left alone, she pieces
together the events that must have brought her to this strange place *(Ognora
sogni)*. When Osaka enters with gifts and starts to flatter her, she recognizes
his voice as that of Jor in the puppet show. Puzzled and embarrassed by his
seductive words, she recalls a picture she once saw in a temple *(Un di—ero
piccina)*, showing a poor girl devoured by a monster called Pleasure. Osaka still
tries to seduce Iris, but her insistence on going home starts to annoy him.
When Kyoto returns, Osaka takes his leave, saying Kyoto can do what he
wants with the girl, so Kyoto decides to dress her up and put her on public
display *(Colle piccine gran maestra e natura)*. To overcome her resistance, he scares
her by showing her a dark chute behind a concealed panel. Then he distracts
her with a puppet. Happy at recognizing the puppet that represented Jor, Iris
recalls his serenade *(Apri la tua finestra!)* while women clothe her in finery.
Then at Kyoto's command they open the screens to show Iris on a balcony to
crowds in the street (chorus: *Oh, meraviglia delle meraviglie!)*. Osaka too sees her,
and his desire is revived *(Iris, son io!)*, but Kyoto restrains him. Meanwhile, the

old Blind Man is led in. Iris calls out to him imploringly, but he hurls mud and curses at her for having degraded herself. In horror, Iris throws herself down the dark chute.

ACT III   That night, Ragpickers come to scavenge amid the refuse in a sewer of the city. One of them addresses a forlorn song to the Moon *(Ad ora bruna e tarda)*. Another picks up a large rock, believing it might be a treasure chest. A glimmer of light reveals some rich garments, and they find Iris' body, but when she shows signs of life, they are frightened away. In delirium the girl visualizes Osaka telling her that her desirability caused her downfall *(Ognun pel suo cammino)*, then Kyoto saying that crime has led him to ruin *(Rubai; fui bastonato)*, finally her father wondering who will care for him now *(Ohimè, chi allumerà nell'inverno il mio foco)*. Iris realizes she has lost everything of meaning to her and is totally abandoned *(Il picciol mondo della mia casetta)*. When the Sun starts to rise, she feels its rays trying to revive her, but death overtakes her as choral voices once again intone the Sun's hymn *(Ancor! Son Io, la Vita!)*. Flowers burst with bloom around her body as sunlight bathes it.

JULES MASSENET
1842–1912

$\mathcal{T}$ he fortunes of Jules Massenet have risen and fallen with those of French opera in general. Not only has the French repertory exercised an indifferent hold on the world's opera houses, but in France itself there has seemed to be little concern about keeping the country's lyric heritage in the style to which it should be accustomed. Except for the perennial *Carmen* and *Faust,* with an occasional *Manon* or *Louise,* French opera worldwide has seemed to be in eclipse since the period before World War II. Cycles of taste being what they are, however, this rich body of work may be waiting only for a revival of stylish performance such as that bestowed on the Italian bel canto repertory, with its attendant resurgence of a singing technique long considered outmoded, even lost.

Like Charles Gounod before him, Massenet has often been accused of pandering to the public's sweet tooth, lacing his brand of sentiment with touches of religiosity and larger helpings of implicit eroticism. Successful in its day, the formula still holds persuasive potential. Much of its secret lies in the composer's thoroughgoing professionalism. Like most French composers, he set the language expertly, letting the words make their full effect, slipping from recitative to arioso as gracefully as a lover taking his sweetheart's hand. A connoisseur of voices, he cultivated types of singer long specially identified with France—the flexible soprano with a soaring high register but also a throaty lower range, the velvety, not too heavy mezzo-soprano, the coaxing lyric tenor, the high, mellifluous baritone, the richly melodic bass. Accused of Wagnerism, he made generous use of the orchestra. Though Massenet's gifts, like Gounod's, lay in a style more personal than the panoply of grand opera, he could set up a big, throbbing ensemble in the Meyerbeer tradition when required. In short, he understood the stage and knew his craft—as well as his audience, with its Belle Époque preferences.

Hérodiade, a pseudo-Biblical epic, bears favorable comparison with some of Hollywood's exercises in the genre. It shortly preceded his masterpiece, *Manon* (1884), and the underrated *Le Cid,* which treats Pierre Corneille's classic tragedy with marked respect. *Esclarmonde,* which followed, was a vehicle for the American soprano Sibyl Sanderson, with whom the composer was infatuated; aside from her personal charms, she possessed a voice of remarkable extension, up to the much publicized "sol Eiffel" (G above high C). The prolix plot of *Chérubin* rivals that of Beaumarchais' comedies, while *Don Quichotte,* conceived for the talents of Feodor Chaliapin, taps a vein of poignancy and reflection befitting the composer's advancing years (he was sixty-eight). With Massenet's death, an era in French opera ended. That his works possess a charm beyond that of confectionery is something each generation can rediscover in its own way—provided it learns to address the style. Without the caressing, lightly sensual touch of idiomatic French singing, Massenet's music will not yield its perfume.

HÉRODIADE

FOUR ACTS
MUSIC: Jules Massenet
TEXT (French): Paul Milliet and Henri Grémont (Georges Hartmann), after Gustave Flaubert's story
WORLD PREMIERE: Brussels, Monnaie, December 19, 1881
U.S. PREMIERE: New Orleans, French Opera House, February 13, 1892

CHARACTERS

Salomé. . . . . .Soprano
Hérodiade, *her mother* . . . . .Mezzo-Soprano
Jean (John the Baptist) . . . . Tenor
Hérode, *Tetrarch of Judea* . . . . Baritone
Vitellius, *Roman proconsul* . . . . Baritone
The High Priest . . . . Baritone
Phanuel, *Chaldean astrologer* . . . . Bass

ACT I   Sometime during the third decade A.D. in Jerusalem, as day dawns, nomad chiefs and caravan merchants wake outside the palace walls *(Voici que le jour se lève)*. When quarrels spring up among the various tribes, Phanuel, a Chaldean, tries to calm them *(Encore une dispute!)*. Salomé comes from the palace and seeks him out, saying she does not know who her mother was, though she still hopes to find her; she also wants to find Jean (John the Baptist), who has shown kindness to her *(Il est doux, il est bon)*. When she has gone, Hérode (Herod Antipas) enters abruptly, looking for her and singing of his infatuation with the girl *(Salomé! ah! reviens! je te veux!)*. Instead he is met by his overbearing wife, Hérodiade (Herodias), who demands vengeance against Jean, who has insulted and reviled her *(Hérode! Ne me refuse pas)*. Though she demands the prophet's head, Hérode, mindful of the man's popularity (and his own) among the Jews, refuses; she swears to achieve her aim nevertheless. At this, Jean himself appears, denouncing her again before Hérode escorts her away. Salomé finds Jean and declares her love (duet: *Ce que je veux*), which he deflects by urging her to keep her feelings for him on a spiritual plane.

ACT II   Afternoon. Hérode is resting in his chamber, attended by slave girls, but soon wakes, obsessed with Salomé, of whom dancers remind him (Babylonian dance). A Babylonian slave girl offers wine that will help him visualize the one he loves (Hérode: *Vision fugitive*). He drinks it, only to succumb to passionate longing. The astrologer Phanuel enters, counseling Hérode about unrest among the Jews, who have been led by Jean to expect the Messiah. Hérode, confident of the people's support, dismisses the importance of prophets, but Phanuel cautions him about the strength and appeal of their religious conviction.

§   In the square before his palace, Hérode calls on the people to throw off the Roman yoke. They make a show of response, only to give way to fear and uncertainty when the Roman proconsul Vitellius approaches with troops. Hérodiade, counting on Vitellius' help in disposing of Jean (ensemble: *Vous qui tenez conseil sur les places publiques*), jealously notes how Salomé is favored by Hérode, while Vitellius is impressed by Jean's influence over his Canaanite followers.

ACT III   Phanuel, at his house overlooking the city, wonders what sort of man Jean must be *(Astres étincelantes que l'infini promène)*. Hérodiade seeks Phanuel out to plot astrological revenge on her rival, but Phanuel—knowing what neither woman knows, that Hérodiade is actually Salomé's mother—tries to dissuade her. He points out Salomé entering the Temple and says she is the lost daughter for whom Hérodiade has been longing. But in her fury Hérodiade repudiates the girl, declaring her daughter dead—she has no more child.

§   With faltering steps, Salomé enters the Temple, where Jean is now imprisoned: he is considered dangerous by both the Pharisees and the Romans.

Recalling the happiness of her early acquaintance with him *(Charme des jours passés)*, Salomé wishes, if he must die, that she may die with him. Hérode approaches, smarting under the Romans' display of power but vowing to save Jean, who can rally the Jews against them. Finding Salomé, he renews his protestations *(Salomé! Demande au prisonnier qui revoit la lumière)*. Indignant, she reveals she loves someone else. Hérode declares he will find out who it is and put them both to death.

The public fills the Temple, and the High Priest unveils the Holy of Holies amid ceremony (sacred dance). Vitellius asks the people to honor Rome, while the Priests ask Hérode for judgment against Jean. Hérode, not yet realizing that Jean is Salomé's beloved, plans to spare him if he will be politically useful. Vitellius too is in favor of treating him mercifully (ensemble: *Voilà donc ce mortel qui soulève le monde!*). But when Salomé runs forward, asking to die with Jean, Hérode condemns them both *(Prêtres, vous disiez vrai!)*. They are arrested, amid the crowd's amazement at the strength of their faith.

ACT IV In a dungeon beneath the Temple, Jean faces his destiny with confidence in eternal life *(Adieu donc, vains objets qui nous charment sur terre)*. Salomé appears; overjoyed to see her, he fears for her life, but she repeats her wish to die with him (duet, Jean: *Que je puis respirer . . . Il est beau de mourir en s'aimant*). The High Priest comes to lead Jean to execution, telling Salomé that because of her youth, Hérode has spared her. Slaves drag her away as Jean goes with the guards.

§ At Vitellius' palace, Romans celebrate their ascendancy *(Romains! nous sommes Romains!)*. Dancers entertain the guests (ballet). Salomé rushes in, breaking away from the slaves who brought her, and implores both Hérode and Hérodiade to save the prophet (duet, ensemble—Salomé: *Qu'il vive! sois clément et doux!*). Hérodiade, struggling with the knowledge that Salomé is her daughter, dares not expose herself to a mother's vulnerable feelings, but she is on the point of yielding when the Executioner enters with dripping sword, and all realize Jean is dead. Salomé, blaming Hérodiade, throws herself on the woman with a dagger, but Hérodiade stops her by blurting out, "Je suis ta mère!" (I am your mother). At this, Salomé stabs herself instead.

LE CID

FOUR ACTS
MUSIC: Jules Massenet

TEXT (French): Adolphe d'Ennery, Louis Gallet, and Édouard Blau,
    based on Pierre Corneille's drama
WORLD PREMIERE: Paris, Opéra, November 30, 1885
U.S. PREMIERE: New Orleans, French Opera House, February 23,
    1890
METROPOLITAN PREMIERE: February 12, 1897

CHARACTERS

Chimène . . . . Soprano
The Infanta, *the King's daughter*. . . . . Soprano
Don Rodrigue, *military hero known as Le Cid*. . . . . Tenor
The King. . . . . Baritone
St. Jacques *(vision of St. James)* . . . . Baritone
Don Diègue, *Rodrigue's father*. . . . . Bass
Count of Gormas, *Chimène's father* . . . . Bass

El Cid was the name given in history to Rodrigo Díaz de Bivar (1026–99), subject of the fictional play (1637) by Pierre Corneille, on which Massenet's opera is based.

ACT I   Spain, mid-eleventh century. In the house of Count de Gormas in Burgos, he and noble friends discuss two royal appointments: that of young Don Rodrigue, who is to be knighted, and that of a guardian for the Infanta (the King's daughter), to be announced. Gormas' daughter, Chimène, enters, overjoyed at Rodrigue's knighthood. Her father, seeing that she loves the young man, gives his approval. The Infanta herself appears, confessing that she too loves Rodrigue. He is not of royal blood and never could marry her, so she assures Chimène they are not rivals.

§ In a gallery connecting the palace to the cathedral, the King tells his people that the Moorish invaders have been beaten back, thanks to the military leadership of Rodrigue, whom he presents with the sword of St. James. Rodrigue pledges by the weapon to defend his country and the cause of justice (*Ô noble lame étincelante*), at the same time looking with love toward Chimène. Next the King names Rodrigue's old father, Don Diègue, as royal guardian—an appointment that infuriates Gormas, who feels entitled to it himself. Diègue tries to treat Gormas amicably as his prospective co-father-in-law, but Gormas provokes him with rude remarks and slaps him, causing Diègue to draw his sword. Gormas disarms the old man, who smarts under the humiliation (*Ô rage, ô désespoir, ô vieillesse ennemie!*). When Rodrigue emerges from the church, Diègue charges him with avenging the family honor. Rodrigue is torn, but he cannot escape his sense of duty.

ACT II   At night on the streets of Burgos, outside Gormas' palace, Rodrigue steels his resolve to proceed with his hated task *(Percé jusqu'au fond du coeur)*, then approaches the door, where Gormas appears. Gormas tries to dissuade him, but Rodrigue attacks and runs him through. Among those drawn by the commotion, Diègue thanks his son for avenging him, but the youth realizes that in doing so he has lost his heart's desire *(Quand vous revient l'honneur ravi)*. Chimène, weeping, demands to know who murdered her father. When she sees Rodrigue violently upset, she knows it was he.

§ In the city's main square, outside the royal palace, a crowd has gathered to watch a troupe of dancers (ballet). The King appears, and Chimène rushes to him, demanding justice: Rodrigue must be punished *(Sire! Je l'ai juré! Ni pitié! Ni pardon!)*. Diègue gives his account of the events *(Qu'on est digne d'envie)*, asking that his own life be forfeit so long as he dies with his honor avenged. Before the King can pass judgment, a Moorish envoy arrives, announcing that his leader, Boabdil, has come back with an army and challenges the Spaniards to battle. The King fears he has lost his ablest officer, Rodrigue, but the latter promises that if allowed to lead the Spanish forces, he will return to face whatever punishment the King decides (ensemble: *C'est la cause de Dieu*).

ACT III   In her room at night, Chimène weeps for her lost hopes *(Pleurez, mes yeux!)*. She is startled by Rodrigue, who wants to see her for one last farewell. Despite her obligation to hate him, she confesses she cannot *(Je ne puis! Hélas!)*. When he says he may die in battle, she says he must live to save the Spanish cause and vindicate himself *(Tu vas mourir!)*. Inspired by her love (duet: *Pour celui que j'aimais*), he vows to bring victory.

§ At their encampment near the sea, Rodrigue's forces relax and drink at evening, but he tells them they face a serious threat. If some wish to desert, they should do so now. Those remaining he urges to rest.

§ In his tent, Rodrigue privately fears that his hopes for personal happiness are doomed. Praying, he places his trust in God *(Ô souverain, ô juge, ô père)*. A vision of St. James appears, saying the Christian cause will defeat the infidels.

§ At dawn in the camp, Rodrigue rouses his soldiers and leads them forward, drawing the sword given him by the King (reprise: *Ô noble lame étincelante*).

ACT IV   In the royal palace in Granada, Diègue laments rumors, brought by deserters, of his son's death in battle *(Ainsi mon fils est mort!)*. Chimène and the Infanta, likewise sorrowful, join him, but the King comes to tell them Rodrigue is alive and victorious.

§ In a courtyard of the palace, Rodrigue returns, acknowledged by the vanquished Moorish leaders as Le Cid (in Arabic, *El Seid*, The Leader). When the

King asks what reward he wants, Rodrigue replies that it may cost him his life: Chimène is still obligated to exact justice for her father's death. She cannot bring herself to do so, whereupon he offers to kill himself with the sword the King gave him. But Chimène, asking forgiveness of her father's spirit, also forgives Rodrigue, and the lovers are united among general rejoicing (duet: *Serment d'amour, promesse éternelle*).

ESCLARMONDE

PROLOGUE, FOUR ACTS, AND EPILOGUE
MUSIC: Jules Massenet
TEXT (French): Alfred Blau and Louis de Gramont
WORLD PREMIERE: Paris, Opéra Comique, May 15, 1889
U.S. PREMIERE: New Orleans, French Opera House, February 10, 1893
METROPOLITAN PREMIERE: November 19, 1976

CHARACTERS

Esclarmonde, *the emperor's daughter* . . . . Soprano
Parséis, *her sister* . . . . .Mezzo-Soprano
Roland, *Count of Blois* . . . . Tenor
Énéas, *a Byzantine knight* . . . . Tenor
Bishop of Blois . . . . Baritone
Phorcas, *Emperor of Byzantium* . . . . Bass
Cléomer, *King of France* . . . . Bass

PROLOGUE   The Basilica at Byzantium (Constantinople), mid-eighth century A.D. From his throne, Emperor Phorcas announces his abdication in favor of his daughter Esclarmonde—like himself, an adept at the occult arts. She is to remain veiled until she reaches the age of twenty, when a tournament will decide who wins her hand. The doors of the iconostasis open to reveal Esclarmonde seated with her sister Parséis.

ACT I   Terrace of the empress' palace. Lamenting her enforced isolation, Esclarmonde tells Parséis of her love for the legendary French hero Roland, whom she once saw from a distance *(Le chevalier Roland, comte de Blois!)*. The knight Énéas, fiancé of Parséis, comes to report that on his recent voyage he was defeated in combat only once—by Roland, who then offered him friendship (*Il m'a tendu la main*) but remained in the court of Cléomer, whose daughter he is to wed. This news violently upsets Esclarmonde, who dismisses Énéas and swears she will use magic powers to win Roland's love. Calling on spirits (*Esprits de l'air!*), she conjures up visions of Roland hunting, then leaving Cléomer's kingdom to board a ship. Esclarmonde summons a magic chariot to take her to an enchanted island.

ACT II   On the island, the perplexed Roland wonders where he has been led, then falls asleep. Esclarmonde approaches and wakes him with a kiss (Roland: *Quelle forme vers moi se penchait . . . ?*), telling him she loves him and will be his wife if he will accept her without knowing her identity or seeing her face. Bewildered and enchanted, he succumbs. In an enchanted palace on the island, after consummating their union, Roland pledges to keep their troth a secret. He must leave to help his people fight the Saracens at Blois; pledging to be with him in spirit, Esclarmonde calls forth three maidens bearing the sword of St. George, which will protect him as long as he honors his vow of secrecy.

ACT III   Under siege, the citizens of Blois lament their plight as their king, Cléomer, tries to console them. When a Saracen envoy presents an ultimatum, Roland emerges from the crowd and sends back a challenge to meet the Saracen leader in single combat (*Reprends espoir, ô noble roi!*). As Roland leaves, the Bishop of Blois leads a prayer, which appears to be answered when Roland returns victorious—only to be offered the hand of Bathilde, Cléomer's daughter. Tactfully he declines the honor, saying he is sworn to silence as to why he cannot accept. The king pardons this offense, and the people hail Roland, who longs for nightfall to reunite him with his love.

§ At Cléomer's palace that night, Roland looks forward to being with Esclarmonde, who has promised to rejoin him in spirit, but the Bishop comes to threaten him with damnation if he does not confess his secret to God. Reluctantly, Roland admits his betrothal to a supernatural being, whom the Bishop calls an instrument of the devil. The Bishop withdraws, only to burst back on the scene with his cohorts after Esclarmonde has joined Roland. Exorcising her, the Bishop tears away Esclarmonde's veil, but she summons spirits of fire to protect her after cursing Roland for betraying his vows (*Roland! tu m'as trahie*). When Roland tries to drive off the priests, his sword breaks, and they repeat their exorcism as Esclarmonde disappears.

ACT IV   Forest of Ardennes. As wood spirits dance in a clearing, a Herald comes to announce the tournament in Byzantium to determine who will wed Esclarmonde. Parséis and Énéas enter in search of her. Énéas reminds his fiancée that her father, Phorcas, is now a hermit in these very woods. In fact, his cave is right here: Phorcas wanders out, reflecting fuzzily on the coming tournament *(Les temps vont s'accomplir)*. When Parséis and Énéas beg for his help, Phorcas instead fetches Esclarmonde by spirit powers so he can punish her for daring to choose her own husband. She appears, recalling her separation from Roland *(Je te retrouve, ô souvenir)*, but Phorcas insists Roland must die if she will not renounce him (ensemble: *Obéis, Esclarmonde, à l'inflexible loi*). She is left alone to face Roland, who has entered the forest. He pleads with her to flee with him *(Le bonheur que rien n'achève)*, and she nearly agrees, but spirit voices warn her, and Phorcas reappears, taking her inside the cave after forcing her to renounce Roland. The knight swoons, then revives as if from a dream and resolves to seek death in the tournament, not realizing that its prize is the same person as his beloved.

EPILOGUE As in the Prologue, Phorcas sits enthroned, ordering the iconostasis opened. The victor of the tournament is brought in with his visor lowered. Asked to identify himself, he refuses, having been disappointed in his wish for death. But Esclarmonde has recognized his voice as Roland's, and when she is unveiled, he is overjoyed to be reunited with his bride.

CHÉRUBIN

THREE ACTS
MUSIC: Jules Massenet
TEXT (French): Herni Cain and Francis de Croisset (Francis Wiener), based on the latter's play
WORLD PREMIERE: Monte Carlo, Salle Garnier, February 14, 1905
U.S. PREMIERE (concert performance): New York, Carnegie Hall, February 19, 1984
U.S. STAGE PREMIERE: New York, Manhattan School of Music, March 25, 1987

CHARACTERS

L'Ensoleillad, *prima ballerina of the Royal Opera in Madrid* . . Soprano
Nina, *the Duke's young ward* . . . . Soprano
The Countess . . . . Soprano
Chérubin, *a young officer* . . . . .Mezzo-Soprano
The Baroness . . . . .Mezzo-Soprano

The Duke	Tenor
Ricardo	Tenor
The Count	Baritone
The Baron	Baritone
The Innkeeper	Baritone
A Philosopher (Jacoppo), *Chérubin's tutor*	Bass

The story is a fanciful sequel to Mozart and Da Ponte's *Le Nozze di Figaro,* taking place not long after Cherubino's induction into Almaviva's regiment in Act I of that opera. Of the characters, only Chérubin (Cherubino) is recognizable, and the plot departs entirely from all three original Beaumarchais plays.

ACT I   At Chérubin's house, in or near Seville, the staff is preparing a celebration for his seventeenth birthday and his commissioning as an officer. Among those present are a Count (Almaviva), a Duke, and a Baron—all inclined to view Chérubin jealously as a bounder—plus a Philosopher (Jacoppo), the young man's tutor. Also present is the tutor's protégée Nina, the Duke's ward, who is in love with Chérubin and defends him *(Vous dites: c'est un polisson!).* The Duke reports that Chérubin has had the temerity to invite L'Ensoleillad, prima ballerina of the Royal Opera, to dance at the party. Chérubin appears, admitting he is smitten with the dancer *(Je suis gris! Je suis ivre!).* When the Countess (Almaviva), who is also Chérubin's godmother, arrives, he protests his love for her too, but she urges discretion. The Baroness, it appears, is yet another woman who has a crush on Chérubin. Villagers and farmhands dance a *fête pastorale.* When the Philosopher asks Chérubin why he seems sad, the youth confesses he cannot take his mind off pretty women *(Philosophe, dis-moi pourquoi)*—he wants to love them all at once. The Count, searching for Chérubin, wants to challenge him to a duel for writing a love poem to the Countess, but Nina declares that the verses—which she recites from memory *("Lorsque vous n'aurez rien à faire")*—were for her. Chérubin tells the Philosopher of his current love, L'Ensoleillad.

ACT II   In the courtyard of a nearby inn, the Innkeeper insists to prospective customers that all his rooms are taken. When the Countess and Baroness arrive, he welcomes them obsequiously, but they complain about the accommodations. Their husbands follow, trying to calm the women's complaints that they will have to share the inn with the likes of L'Ensoleillad, a mere adventuress. The Duke appears, confirming the dancer's reservations—evidently in the name of the king, whose mistress she is reputed to be. Some of Chérubin's fellow officers arrive, bent on celebrating. There is argument, even threat of a duel, over Chérubin's having kissed Pepa, Ricardo's sweetheart, on his way in; but the arrival of a carriage bearing a masked woman interrupts this. Chérubin kisses her too, apologizing when he discovers she is L'Ensoleillad. Now Chérubin and Ricardo start to duel, whereupon L'Ensoleillad faints and Ricardo is calmed by a reminder from the Philosopher *(Ah! comme l'on voit bien)* that Chérubin is only an impulsive lad of seventeen. Reviving, L'Ensoleillad assures everyone that no harm has resulted from the preceding fracas *(Vous parlez de péril)* and dances "La Manola" before retiring to her room. When the Philosopher urges Chérubin to take one woman at a time, the boy replies that he cannot *(Je ne peux me fixer),* and when L'Ensoleillad appears on her balcony, he sends the Philosopher away.

Intrigued by Chérubin, L'Ensoleillad comes back down to the courtyard, saying they will have this one night to themselves *(Qu'importe demain et tout l'avenir!).* As they wander off toward a nearby woods, the three noblemen converge, declaring they must protect the king's interests. Upon the couple's return, L'Ensoleillad is frightened to see the three, but Chérubin sends her off in another direction and diverts them. Once they are gone, hoping to catch him in the woods, he slips back to rejoin L'Ensoleillad on her balcony, climbing down a ladder when there is a disturbing noise. The Countess and Baroness, both thinking they hear Chérubin, toss him respectively a ribbon and a bouquet, while L'Ensoleillad tosses a garter. The three noblemen return, and Chérubin falls off the ladder, throwing it in their midst to avoid revealing which balcony it had been set against. Angered at the sight of Chérubin's love tokens, the three draw their swords, but the noise brings the Philosopher, guests, and hotel staff. The Mayor arrives and, unable to quell the disturbance, orders the three noblemen arrested.

ACT III   On the patio of the inn, Chérubin prepares his will, in case he should be killed in a duel *(Ah! je soupire un peu).* When the Philosopher tries to teach him some fencing tricks, the Innkeeper briefly fears another fight, but Chérubin's real danger comes from the Countess and Baroness, who advance on him, demanding to know for whom he meant his serenade the previous night. His reply is "L'Ensoleillad" when the women's husbands intrude. Now the women protest to their husbands that Chérubin's serenade to the dancer put each of them in a compromising light. Both couples mock the youth when he angrily tries to renew a duel with either of the husbands. L'Ensoleillad, hailed forth by a messenger from the king, prepares to leave, blithely praising "love that dies in one night" *(Vive l'amour qui rêve).* As she goes, Chérubin throws himself into the arms of the Philosopher, who assures him he will meet a girl he can love seriously.

A carriage draws near, carrying Nina, who plans to enter a convent *(Je ne pleure pas),* since her love is unrequited. Chérubin, touched by her dignified suffering, weeps and embraces her, declaring his love. The Duke, arriving to renew his duel with Chérubin, is greeted instead with a polite request for his ward's hand in marriage. Ricardo and the Philosopher quietly observe that "Donna Elvira" has finally domesticated "Don Giovanni."

DON QUICHOTTE

FIVE ACTS
MUSIC: Jules Massenet
TEXT (French): Henri Cain, after Jacques Le Lorrain's comedy *Le Chevalier de la Longue Figure,* based on Cervantes' novel
WORLD PREMIERE: Monte Carlo, Salle Garnier, February 19, 1910
U.S. PREMIERE: New Orleans, January 27, 1912
METROPOLITAN PREMIERE: April 3, 1926

CHARACTERS

Pedro	Soprano
Garcias	Soprano
Dulcinée	Mezzo-Soprano
Rodriguez	Tenor
Juan	Tenor
Sancho Pança, *Quichotte's retainer*	Baritone
Ténébrun, *bandit chief*	Baritone
Don Quichotte, *elderly knight*	Bass

ACT I   On a feast day in a town in sixteenth-century Spain, four suitors—Pedro, Garcias, Rodriguez, and Juan—serenade Dulcinée (Dulcinea) before her house *(Belle, dont le charme est l'empire).* She appears on her balcony, declaring that at twenty she wants more from life than just to be admired *(Alza! Quand la femme a vingt ans).* Cries herald the arrival of Don Quichotte (Quixote), whom three of the suitors describe as a deluded old eccentric; the fourth, Rodriguez, appreciates the knight's qualities of soul. Quichotte heaves into view aboard his old nag, Rosinante, accompanied by his stout and faithful esquire, Sancho Pança, who rides a donkey. The crowd greets them with affection, delighting Quichotte, who tells Sancho to distribute alms. Aside, Sancho grumbles that their supper is vanishing with this largesse. Quichotte thanks the crowd in courtly terms for its welcome *(Cette gaîté m'emparadise!),* whereupon he is pelted with flowers. As dusk approaches and the square starts to empty, Quichotte looks toward the balcony of Dulcinée, whom he idealizes. Sancho heads for a tavern while the old knight addresses his own serenade to the lady *(Quand apparaissent les étoiles)*—soon interrupted by Juan, with whom he gets into a quarrel and starts dueling, only to stop so he can finish his song. Dulcinée blocks the renewed duel between the two men, then sends Juan on an errand to fetch her mantilla. To Quichotte's protestations, she replies that he can show his sincerity by recovering the necklace taken from her the day before by the bandit Ténébrun. Juan returns and leads her to rejoin their friends. She throws a kiss to Quichotte, who believes she sincerely loves him (*Elle m'aime et va me revenir*).

ACT II   In the misty countryside at dawn, Quichotte wanders on horseback, led by Sancho, improvising another song in praise of Dulcinée (*C'est vers ton amour*). Sancho reproaches him for having attacked a herd of pigs and sheep the previous day, believing them to be bandits; and for letting Dulcinée make fools of both of them. Sancho believes no woman to be worth such effort (*Ce qui m'enchante en notre beau métier*). As the rising sun burns away the mist, Quichotte spies one windmill, then another and another. Taking them for giants, he draws his sword and defies them (*Géant, monstrueux cavalier*), then seizes his lance and rides to the attack, only to be caught by the seat of his pants and borne aloft by a sail of the closest windmill.

ACT III   At sunset, somewhere in the mountains, Quichotte examines the ground for bandit tracks. When a troupe of bandits really does appear, Sancho wakes with a start and runs away while his master, defying them, is quickly subdued. They plan to do away with Quichotte, but Ténébrun, the bandit chief, is moved by the knight's stoical, dignified air and questions him. Quichotte explains that he is a knight errant who redresses wrongs and helps the downtrodden (*Je suis le chevalier errant*), ending with a demand for the return of Dulcinée's necklace. Deeply impressed, Ténébrun hands it over. Ecstatically, Quichotte gives the bandits his benediction as they bow in awe of him, seeing him as a sort of holy fool.

ACT IV   An evening party is under way at Dulcinée's house. In the garden, she dismisses her four suitors, saying they bore her, and muses dreamily on what will happen when the joys of love are gone (*Lorsque le temps d'amour a fui*). To her guests in the garden she announces that she longs for a kind of love unlike any she has experienced so far (*Alza! Ne pensons qu'au plaisir d'aimer*). The guests dance, then reenter the house for dinner. Sancho appears and asks the footmen to announce Don Quichotte, who follows, reassuring Sancho they soon will have the castle of their dreams. First, Quichotte adds, he intends to wed Dulcinée. She reappears with the guests, who make fun of the eccentric knight, but when he gives her the recovered necklace, she embraces him. Mistaking her gratitude for love, he proposes to her in flowery language (*Marchez dans mon chemin*). She laughs off the idea of marriage (*Que j'abandonne ma maison?*), though she confesses admiration for Quichotte's character. She urges him to stay within her circle, but her rejection of his proposal makes him feel he must leave. She defends him to her friends, who nevertheless mock Quichotte until Sancho rounds on them, denouncing their callousness *(Ça, vous commettez tous un acte épouvantable)* before he leads Quichotte away.

ACT V   Nighttime on a mountain path. Tending his master, Sancho prays that the dozing Quichotte may be transported to a better world. Quichotte wakes and tells Sancho he feels death is near *(Sancho, mon bon Sancho, nous allons nous quitter)*. He offers Sancho the Island of Dreams, and in his final delirium imagines the voice of Dulcinée, who, transformed into a star, calls farewell to him from the heavens. Sancho collapses, sobbing, as his master dies.

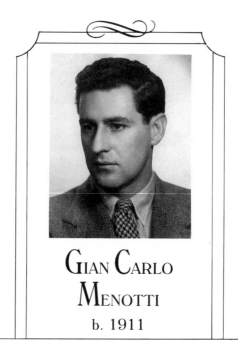

GIAN CARLO MENOTTI

b. 1911

*D*uring the nineteenth century, up to the time of Wagner's mature works, opera was viewed as popular entertainment. This strain continued through the declining years of Italian opera. Pietro Mascagni, the last survivor of the original verismo movement, stood up for the traditional aesthetic of his homeland until his death in 1945; his last opera, *Nerone* (1935), is recognizably the work of the composer who wrote *Cavalleria Rusticana* in the 1890s. Since World War II, however, European opera has followed Wagner's lead in being dominated by various schools of progressive intellectualism, having in common a return to the elitism of the Florentine Camerata, a group who in the early 1600s first developed opera as we know it. Contemporary views in Europe encourage opera by and for the informed specialist.

This is one of the reasons why Gian Carlo Menotti, an Italian composer trained first at the Milan Conservatory, made his career and residence largely in the United States, where opera appealing to a broad audience is still favored. Depending on one's point of view, Menotti's music is either refreshingly accessible and communicative or regressively conservative and derivative. It is possible to hold both views at once. What Menotti shares with the composers of viable operas in the past is a lack of concern with music for its own sake. His values are theatrical, and music is simply a means to a dramatic end.

Menotti's first performed opera, *Amelia al Ballo* (Amelia Goes to the Ball, 1937), sits squarely in the tradition of light, elegantly textured farce as spun out by Ermanno Wolf-Ferrari on the basis of Verdi's *Falstaff.* This and the radio opera *The Old Maid and the Thief* (1939) drew favorable attention, but Menotti came a cropper with *The Island God* (1942, briefly performed at the Met) and destroyed it. He had set a symbolic, legendary sort of subject; feeling it was wrong for him, he turned to veristic melodrama in *The Medium* (1946), one of his most popular works. Offered as a "musical drama" rather than an opera, *The Medium* ran for more than 200 performances in a Broadway theater. Its success may be counted one of the main factors that turned young American composers to thoughts of opera during subsequent decades.

The Consul won a Pulitzer Prize in America but stirred controversy in Europe, where leftists took offense at its apparent anti-Communist "propaganda." Menotti was careful, however, to avoid pointing a specific finger: totalitarianism, as he depicts it (the libretto began as an unproduced screenplay), can be of any political stripe. In *The Saint of Bleecker Street* he returned to the theme of *The Medium:* irreconcilability between a spiritual and a materialistic view of the world. Though he seems to urge that the two must accommodate each other, his ending offers no resolution.

While experiencing his share of failures, Menotti has never deviated from his aesthetic principles. Gifted with theatrical instinct, he also shows a facility for flowing, natural melodic word settings, and his character portrayals, if inclined toward exaggeration and cliché, are unfailingly strong in human interest. On balance, he has been by far the most successful opera composer in America in modern times, in terms of audiences reached and frequency of performance.

∾∾∾

THE CONSUL

THREE ACTS
MUSIC: Gian Carlo Menotti
TEXT (English): the composer
WORLD PREMIERE: Philadelphia, Shubert Theater, March 1, 1950

CHARACTERS

A Foreign Woman. . . . . Soprano
Magda Sorel . . . . Soprano
Anna Gomez, *a refugee and visa applicant* . . . . Soprano

The Secretary *to the Consul* . . . . .Mezzo-Soprano
The Mother, *John's mother* . . . . Alto
Vera Boronel, *a visa applicant.* . . . . Alto
A Magician (Nika Magadoff), *a visa applicant* . . . . Tenor
John Sorel, *Magda's husband* . . . . Baritone
Assan, *a glazier, friend of the Sorels* . . . . Baritone
Mr. Kofner, *a visa applicant* . . . . Bass-Baritone
Secret Police Agent . . . . Bass
Two Plainclothesmen . . . . Silent Roles

ACT I   Somewhere in a European police state, about 1950, John Sorel stumbles into his home, having been grazed by a shot from the secret police, who broke up an underground meeting from which he escaped. His wife, Magda, and his Mother help him hide on the roof when they see the police approaching. After two of his men search the place, the Secret Police Agent questions Magda, threatening her if she does not decide to name John's friends *(Mrs. Sorel, to be courageous is often a very selfish thing)*. He leaves her to think it over. Outside, the police can be heard arresting a neighbor. When John comes out of hiding, he says he must try to get to the border at once. He tells Magda to go to the Consulate the next day, tell their story, and try to get out of the country (trio: *Now, O lips, say good-bye*).

§ In the waiting room at the Consulate, the Secretary questions Mr. Kofner, an elderly applicant for a visa, who has been there many times but whose papers are never quite in order. He helps a Foreign Woman, who speaks only Italian, to apply for a visa to go to her sick daughter. When Magda asks the Secretary to see the Consul, she gets only an application form. One of the others waiting, the Magician, Nicholas (Nika) Magadoff, introduces himself to an apprehensive woman named Vera Boronel and shows one of his magic tricks to pass the time. The various applicants reflect on the toils of bureaucracy that hold them fast (quintet: *In endless waiting rooms*).

ACT II   A month has passed. Magda returns home from another endless day of waiting at the Consulate. Her baby has been sick, and John's Mother tries to keep the infant amused, then sings a lullaby *(I shall find for you shells and stars)*. This has the effect of putting the exhausted Magda to sleep too; she dreams that John has returned, accompanied by a ghoulish version of the Secretary, who he says is his sister. He asks to see his child, but another deathlike figure has taken the baby away. When Magda wakes in terror, a stone breaks the kitchen window. This is a prearranged signal for her to call Assan, the glazier, and get news of John. No sooner has she called Assan, however, than the Secret Police Agent walks in, still trying to get Magda to betray John's friends. He also has been extorting bribes from her. Enraged, she throws him out. Assan arrives as the Agent is leaving. When the coast is clear, he quickly tells Magda that John is hiding in the mountains and doesn't want to cross the frontier until he knows she can get out. Meanwhile, the Mother has discovered that the baby has died in his sleep. After Assan has left, Magda realizes this too. The Mother feels her own life ebbing away as she thinks of how she will never see John again, and John will never see his child again (*I'm not crying for him—not for us—but for John*).

§ A few days later, at the Consulate, a refugee named Anna Gomez renews her attempts to get a visa. Magda rushes in and begs once more to see the Consul. She is told to wait: it is now Nika Magadoff's turn in line. The Magician tries to disarm the Secretary with some of his sleight-of-hand tricks (*After all, I'm Nika Magadoff*), then hypnotizes the others in the waiting room (*Look into my eyes. You feel tired; you want to sleep. Breathe deeply*) and gets them to dance. When he cannot find his papers, he wakes the others and leaves. Magda tries again to present her case to the Secretary, who gives her the same mechanical answers. Magda bursts out in indignation at the lack of caring in the world around them (*To this we've come*), at the proliferation of meaningless papers. This has some effect on the Secretary, who says Magda may have a minute with the Consul after his important visitor has gone. The visitor, however, turns out to be the Secret Police Agent, and Magda faints at the sight as he leaves.

ACT III   Several days later, Magda is back at the Consulate, waiting, when Vera Boronel appears and learns that her visa is almost ready. The Secretary has her sign a sheaf of papers (duet: *All the documents must be signed*). Assan hurries in, looking for Magda: John, who has heard about the baby's and the Mother's death, wants desperately to come back across the border to see Magda, despite all warnings. Meanwhile, the Secretary and Boromel continue signing papers (quartet: *Here are some more*). To stop John, Madga writes a note for Assan to deliver; she will not tell its contents. All leave except the Secretary, who is getting ready to go, thinking of the people she has to deal with each day (*Oh, those faces!*), when a stranger appears: John Sorel, looking for his wife. The Secretary tells him he cannot stay there; the office is closed. The Secret Police Agent and two Plainclothesmen, who have trailed him, enter. It is against international law to arrest anyone at the Consulate, but they say— and he has to agree, having no other choice—that he will accompany them voluntarily. Personally involved for the first time in the case, the Secretary tells John she will call Magda.

§ Magda has resolved to end her life. Arriving home, she draws a chair before the stove and turns on the gas, covering her head with The Mother's shawl. As consciousness starts to fade, she sees apparitions of the people waiting at the Consulate, of John and his Mother, calling to her. She tries to follow them, but they leave without her. The last of the apparitions is Nika Magaloff (*Look into my eyes. You feel tired; you want to sleep. Breathe deeply).* The telephone rings, recalling her to reality, but as she reaches for it, her body falls slack in the chair.

THE SAINT OF BLEECKER STREET

THREE ACTS
MUSIC: Gian Carlo Menotti
TEXT (English): the composer
WORLD PREMIERE: New York, Broadway Theater, December 27, 1954

CHARACTERS

Carmela, *Annina's friend* . . . . Soprano
Maria Corona, *a newspaper vendor* . . . . Soprano
Annina, *a young orphan* . . . . Soprano
Assunta . . . . .Mezzo-Soprano
Desideria, *Michele's mistress* . . . . .Mezzo-Soprano
Michele, *Annina's brother* . . . . Tenor
Salvatore, *Carmela's fiancé* . . . . Baritone
Don Marco, *a priest* . . . . Bass

ACT I   New York City, Good Friday afternoon, 1954. In a cold-water flat on Bleecker Street, a young girl, Annina, is believed to be having holy visions in an adjoining room, while relatives and neighbors chant the Litany in the hall. A middle-aged woman, Maria Corona, has brought her retarded, speechless son in hopes of having him cured, but she is tired and skeptical. Others declare that Annina is a saint, who suffers the Passion of Christ every Holy Friday and has had authentic visions (chorus: *She soon will come*). While Maria Corona gets into an argument with a Young Woman, the others concentrate on Annina's room, from which the priest Don Marco soon appears, announcing that her vision has begun. Annina, in a trance, is carried out and proceeds to describe the Crucifixion as if she were an eyewitness *(Oh, sweet Jesus, spare me this agony).* When she comes to the nailing of Jesus to the Cross, stigmata appear on her palms. Don Marco, with help from Assunta and Carmela, struggles to keep the onlookers from touching her, but Maria Corona's son succeeds in doing so. Annina's brother, Michele, arrives from outside and orders the people away.

He carries Annina back to her room and confronts Don Marco, saying his sister needs medical attention, not ritual (*His saints? Enough of superstition!*). He declares he will protect and guide his sister with no outside help. Don Marco is forced to leave (*Ah, poor Michele, it is not I your rival, but God Himself*).

§ Late afternoon in an empty lot on Mulberry Street, with an Italian street fair, the Festival of San Gennaro, in progress in the background. Helping Carmela dress a little girl as an angel for the religious procession, Annina remarks that her brother won't let her attend it. Carmela confesses to Annina that she has changed her mind about becoming a nun with her, as she promised (*This coming May I'm going to be married*). Assunta joins them and asks Annina if she ever had a vision of heaven. The girl replies that she has seen only its gates (*But once, in the deep of night*). Maria Corona arrives to say that the Sons of San Gennaro, a street gang, want Annina in the procession and if necessary will take her there by force. Annina is worried for the safety of Michele, who soon appears, shooing the other women away. He tells Annina she is innocently gullible, a victim of simpleminded beliefs, and that he will never let her take the veil (*Sister, I shall hide you and take you away*). She replies that she will try to help him understand and share her faith. As the procession approaches, young men enter the lot and overpower Michele, leaving him manacled to the wire fence, and carry Annina off. After the procession and crowd have passed, Michele is set free by his lover, Desideria.

ACT II May has arrived. In an Italian basement restaurant on Bleecker Street, Carmela and her bridegroom, Salvatore, celebrate their wedding (chorus: *There never was such a pair*). Michele joins in toasting them, and Annina entrusts her friend to Salvatore (*Be good to her, be kind*). When the group has moved into the banquet room, Desideria appears, asking for Michele. Because of her liaison with him, she is considered a slut and has not been invited to the wedding. When he joins her, she confronts him with her ostracism (*Michele, try to understand*). He replies that he needs to lead his life freely, but he admits he is not ashamed to love her. She asks him to acknowledge this by taking her in to the party. He refuses on account of his sister, whose best friend is the bride. Desideria says he is preoccupied with Annina and is ruining the girl's life. Worn down by Desideria's pleas, Michele starts to take her into the banquet hall. When Don Marco emerges and suggests it would be a dangerous thing to do, given Michele's rather hostile relationship with the community, Michele comes close to fighting with him. This draws Annina and the other guests from the next room. Michele confronts them (*I know you all hate me*): seeing himself an outcast, unable to feel as Italian as they do, he throws his glassful of wine in their faces.

Some of the guests remain as Annina tries to calm Michele and get him to come home. At this, Desideria confronts him (*Yes, Michele, go home, go*), saying he is more in love with his sister than with her. A vehement argument follows, with Michele demanding that she take back what she said, while Desideria stands her ground. Finally, mad with rage, Michele seizes a knife from the bar and stabs Desideria in the back, then runs out. She falls and begs Annina for help. Annina prays with her as she dies.

ACT III   Late in the year, snow is falling. At Maria Corona's newsstand in the passageway of a subway station, Maria meets Annina and tries to cheer her up with chatter about the tabloids. After a while, Don Marco brings the fugitive Michele, who embraces the girl. He says he will not give himself up to the police; but when she tells him her health is deteriorating—her voices have told her she is going to die soon—he wishes he could take care of her. She replies that before dying, she wants to take the veil. He cries out against it *(No, no! I'll never consent to that)*, but she has made up her mind: "This is good-bye forever." Cursing Annina for abandoning her own brother, Michele runs out, and she collapses, comforted by Maria Corona.

§ In Annina's room not long afterward, she sits, accompanied by a nun, Don Marco, Maria Corona, Carmela, and Salvatore. They are awaiting authorization for Annina to take the veil. Carmela offers her own wedding dress for the ceremony. A Young Priest arrives with the message that permission has been given. Praying for her strength to last *(Oh, my Love, at last the hour has come)*, Annina goes into her room to dress. Neighbors arrive, remarking that Michele has been seen nearby, bent on stopping the ceremony. Annina returns, clad in bridal dress and veil, and is led through the brief ritual (Don Marco: *You are now dead unto the world)*: she is no longer Annina but Sister Angela. When Michele bursts in, Salvatore and another man restrain him. He calls out to his sister *(Listen, Annina! Listen to me!)*, but in her weakened, trancelike state she no longer hears him. He stands back, silent and incredulous, during what remains of the ceremony. The white veil is removed, Annina's hair is cut, and she is given a black veil. With her last strength she takes a few steps toward Don Marco and sinks to the floor. The priest takes her lifeless arm and puts the gold ring on her finger.

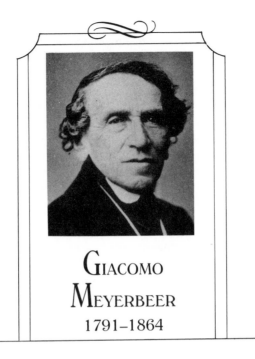

GIACOMO
MEYERBEER
1791–1864

orn the year of Mozart's death, to a prosperous, established Jewish family whose home was a gathering place for artists and intellectuals, Jakob Liebmann Meyer Beer showed early aptitude as a pianist and made his concert debut at eleven. His teachers included Muzio Clementi in piano and the Abbé Vogler in theory. Soon he was gaining recognition as a composer, but his early ventures onto the lyric stage made it apparent that he and the German musical theater were not compatible. Unlike Weber or Wagner, he was not to be a standard-bearer for emergent artistic nationalism. Instead, he would look abroad for his voice.

At twenty-three, he was about to give up hope of a career in music when in Vienna he met Antonio Salieri, a foremost composer / pedagogue of the day, who numbered Beethoven, Schubert, and Liszt among his pupils. Salieri sensed that the young man's talents would profit from a sojourn in Italy, where he could absorb practical knowledge about the voice and the stage.

The young man's chosen professional name, Giacomo Meyerbeer, shows his predilection for Italian-style opera. He did not leave for Italy at once but visited Paris, where his piano playing was well received. Impressed by Paris, he would return to make his home there, but it was in Italy—where he arrived in 1816—that the cornerstone of his art was laid. After living there for a year, he wrote, he felt himself transformed into a virtual Italian. Rossini, whom he idolized, provided the model for his operas written in Italy, his first successes in the genre. Italian audiences accepted the work of foreign-born composers, from Handel and Mozart on down, providing the Italian tradition of vocal writing was respected, and this Meyerbeer mastered readily.

An attempted comeback in Germany fizzled out, and Meyerbeer found himself again in Italy, where he reached international stature with *Margherita d'Anjou* (La Scala, 1820) and especially *Il Crociato in Egitto* (Teatro La Fenice, Venice, 1824). Now he was hailed for combining felicitous Italian vocal writing with the more serious, ambitious structural schemes of German instrumental music.

In Italy, Meyerbeer quit while he was ahead, moving back to Paris, the musical capital of Europe. His major works for the Parisian stage, *Robert le Diable* (1831), *Le Prophète* (1849), *Le Pardon de Ploërmel* (also known as *Dinorah,* 1859), and finally the posthumously produced *L'Africaine* (1865), showed a shrewd, systematic adaptation to the demand for spectacle that marked French grand opera. Meyerbeer never become a distinctive melodist; his materials were often commonplace, but he deployed them with an uncanny sense of theatrical appropriateness and timing. The weaknesses in his librettos—superficial shock, "effects without causes," as Wagner called them—were also the weaknesses of Meyerbeer's scores. On the plus side, he was a tireless craftsman who wrote musical directions more discerning and detailed than any composer before him, and who reworked material as much as necessary to get it right—the reason for *L'Africaine*'s long delay in reaching stage. As one of the chief architects of grand opera, he took the form epitomized in Rossini's *Guillaume Tell* (1829) and left it as legacy for the last and grandest of its descendants, Verdi's *Aida* (1871) and Wagner's *Götterdämmerung* (1876).

ROBERT LE DIABLE

(Robert the Devil)

FIVE ACTS
MUSIC: Giacomo Meyerbeer
TEXT (French): Eugène Scribe and Germain Delavigne
WORLD PREMIERE: Paris, Opéra, November 21, 1831
U.S. PREMIERE: New York, Park Theater, April 7, 1834 (in English)
METROPOLITAN PREMIERE: November 19, 1883 (in Italian)

CHARACTERS

Alice, *Robert's half sister* . . . . Soprano
Princess Isabelle *of Sicily* . . . . Soprano
Robert, *Duke of Normandy* . . . . Tenor
Raimbaut, *a Norman troubadour* . . . . Tenor
Bertram, *Robert's companion* . . . . Bass
Alberti, *a knight* . . . . Bass
Helena, *abbess of the monastery of St. Rosalie* . . . . Dancing Role

The historical Robert I, Duke of Normandy, a legendary hellion who later repented his ways, died in 1035 while returning from a pilgrimage to Jerusalem. His son William, born about eight years earlier, eventually ruled England as William I (William the Conqueror) from 1066 until 1087. The story of *Robert le Diable,* cut of whole cloth, would have taken place during the first quarter of the eleventh century.

ACT I   Eleventh-century Sicily, under Norman rule. On the shore at Palermo, knights are encamped for a tournament given by the Duke of Messina for the hand of Princess Isabelle. As they carouse *(Versez à tasses pleines),* Robert, a knight unknown to the others, toasts them and invites a vassal, the troubadour Raimbaut, to tell a story. Raimbaut relates how a Norman princess, Berthe, once fell in love with an unknown warrior who was suspected of being a demon *(Jadis régnait en Normandie);* from their marriage was born a son, Robert, who grew up to raise hell in the countryside. Hearing this reference to himself, Robert angrily orders the vassal arrested and hanged. Raimbaut begs for mercy, saying he is about to be married, at which Robert pardons him, thinking his fiancée might be an amusing present for the assemblage of knights. But when she is brought in, Robert recognizes her as Alice, his own half sister, and wants to talk to her alone.

After the others have withdrawn, she tells how their mother recently died *("Va! va!" dit-elle, "mon enfant"),* leaving her will to be read by Robert "when he is worthy." Alice offers the document to Robert, but he says he does not yet qualify to touch it. Then he explains that his passion for Isabelle, the Sicilian princess, led him rashly to challenge all the knights at court to combat, in which he was saved by his friend Bertram. At this, Bertram enters, and the sight of him terrifies Alice, who recognizes him as the devil portrayed in a painting in her village church. The girl leaves; Bertram urges Robert to gamble with the other knights and win some money. Robert calls on them to join him *(Ah! fortune, à ton caprice)* but loses everything, even his horses and armor. Bertram offers cold comfort, recalling that as Robert himself has said, gold is only an illusion.

ACT II   In a hall in the royal palace in Palermo, Robert wishes he had not lost sight of his mother's example *(Oh! ma mère, ombre si tendre).* In the distance he hears a ceremonial march for the tournament. Imagining he can still compete, even if armed only with a sword, he is brought back to reality by the arrival of Alice, who says his only hope is for her to intercede with Isabelle on his behalf. They leave together, and Isabelle enters, sad about the futility of her hopes of meeting Robert again *(En vain j'espère)*. Some girls present petitions to the princess, among them Alice, who gives her a letter from Robert. As the girls withdraw, Robert enters (duet: *Avec bonté voyez ma peine*), and she reveals that in response to his request, she has ordered weapons and armor for him.

Isabelle departs, and Bertram appears, pointing out Robert to a Herald, who presents him with a challenge to mortal combat from the Prince of Granada. Looking forward to this real test of his knighthood, Robert leaves with the Herald. The full court convenes to see a ballet in honor of six betrothed couples. It now appears that Bertram has used the phony challenge to lure Robert away from the tournament. The Prince of Granada asks Isabelle to present him with arms, inaugurating the event (chorus: *Sonnez, clairons, honorez la bannière*). While Isabelle proclaims the tournament open *(La trompette guerrière)*, she, Alice, and Raimbaut all privately note Robert's absence; Bertram stands enigmatically apart.

ACT III   The Rocks of St. Irene—a somber mountain landscape. Raimbaut comes for a rendezvous with Alice but instead meets Bertram, who gives him a purse full of money, noting aside how mankind mistakes wealth for happiness (duet: *Ah! l'honnête homme!*). Joshingly he dismisses Raimbaut with advice to take his wealth, delay marriage, and try some self-indulgence first.

It becomes apparent that Bertram is an infernal spirit, subject to orders from Satan, and that he is in fact Robert's father. As a chorus of demons is heard inside a nearby cavern, Bertram declares his love for Robert *(Ô mon fils, ô Robert)*, then enters the cavern, which belches flame.

Alice appears, searching for Raimbaut. She recalls her youth in Normandy and prays to the Virgin for protection *(Quand je quittai la Normandie)*. She hears Robert's name mentioned by the mysterious voices from the cavern, which she tries to investigate, but the supernatural phenomena terrify her, and she falls in a faint. Bertram emerges from the cavern, pale and shaken: he has been told that unless he can secure Robert's soul by midnight, he will lose him. Alice, reviving, overhears this. Bertram, who realizes she has overheard, threatens her and her loved ones with death if she does not keep quiet.

Robert is seen approaching (trio: *Fatal moment, cruel mystère!*). Alice starts to warn him, but Bertram's threats scare her off. Robert asks Bertram to make good his promise to save his fortunes. Bertram directs him to the ruins of an abbey, once condemned to hell's fire for the nuns' misdeeds. Robert is to bring from there an evergreen cypress branch that possesses mysterious powers. Robert swears he will not be daunted by the challenge (duet: *Des chevaliers de ma patrie*).

§ By moonlight, Bertram enters the ruined cloister of St. Rosalie and calls upon the spirits of nuns who in life were unfaithful to their vows, asking them to aid him in winning Robert's soul (*Jadis filles du ciel, aujourd'hui de l'enfer*). They resume the semblance of life and dance in re-creation of the worldly pleasures they once enjoyed (ballet). Robert arrives on his mission to retrieve the branch from the stone effigy of St. Rosalie, but her expression reminds him of his mother, disapproving of his action, and he is about to retire when the spirits of the condemned nuns surround him. Helena, who as Abbess is their leader, practices her charms on him and finally gets him to take the branch, whereupon the nuns return to their tombs and infernal voices are heard claiming Robert for their own (*Il est à nous!*).

ACT IV   Isabelle, Alice, and ladies of the court are gathered in the princess' bedroom to prepare her for her wedding. Alice tells Isabelle she is going to see Robert one more time, to give him a message from their mother, but that he is lost. Isabelle wants to learn more, but courtiers and the Prince of Granada, her bridegroom, interrupt. Robert comes with the cypress branch and puts them all in a trancelike sleep (*Du magique rameau qui s'abaisse sur eux*). Isabelle revives, shocked to see that he has renounced knightly honor in favor of infernal power (*Robert, toi que j'aime*). If she will not flee with him, he begs her to take his life, and in despair breaks the branch, at which the courtiers reawaken (chorus: *Quelle aventure?*); Robert is seized by guards as Isabelle swoons and Alice prays for her half brother.

ACT V   In the vestibule of Palermo Cathedral, Robert, rescued from his latest predicament by Bertram, pleads for the demon's help in saving Isabelle from marriage to the Prince of Granada. Bertram thinks he has persuaded the desperate man to sign over his soul, but chanting within the cathedral distracts Robert (duet with chorus: *O divine harmonie!*). Playing his last card, Bertram admits he is Robert's father (*Je t'ai trompé*). Out of filial loyalty, Robert is about to sign when Alice appears, pleading with him to join Isabelle, who is ready to marry him instead of her bridegroom. Meanwhile, Bertram, urging him to flee, produces the document he must sign to seal their bargain. Now Alice plays *her* trump card: Mother's last will and testament. Robert reads it (*"O mon fils, ma tendresse assidue*): she begs him not to be misled by the seducer who ruined her. With Alice reiterating their mother's words, and Bertram still playing on his fatherly authority, Robert is hopelessly torn (trio, Bertram: *Mon fils, jette sur moi la vue*). But when midnight strikes, he is saved by the bell. The earth opens to swallow Bertram. Alice revives the swooning Robert and leads him, amid the voices of worshippers, to join Isabelle in the main part of the cathedral (chorus: *Ah! chantez, troupe immortelle*).

L'AFRICAINE

(The African Woman)

FIVE ACTS
MUSIC: Giacomo Meyerbeer
TEXT (French): Eugène Scribe
WORLD PREMIERE: Paris, Opéra, April 28, 1865
U.S. PREMIERE: New York, Academy of Music, December 1, 1865
  (in Italian)
METROPOLITAN PREMIERE: December 7, 1888 (in German)

CHARACTERS

Sélika, *a slave* . . . . Soprano
Inès, *Don Diégo's daughter* . . . . Soprano
Anna, *Inès' confidante* . . . . Mezzo-Soprano
Vasco da Gama, *a naval officer* . . . . Tenor
Don Alvar, *council member* . . . . Tenor
Nélusko, *a slave* . . . . Baritone
High Priest of Brahma . . . . Bass-Baritone
Don Pédro, *president of the royal council* . . . . Bass
Don Diégo, *an admiral* . . . . Bass
Grand Inquisitor of Lisbon . . . . Bass

Vasco da Gama, the first European to make the sea voyage to India, did so in 1497–99, under the rule of King Manuel I of Portugal, whose queen (Isabel) was the daughter of Ferdinand and Isabella of Spain. The opera's title, *The African Woman,* is hard to explain in light of the heroine's origin on an island in the Indian Ocean, although Vasco had to pass around Africa to reach there. Her home might have been one of the Chagos, the Maldives, or the Seychelles; it might even have been Madagascar or Ceylon.

ACT I   In the King's council chamber in Lisbon, the lady Inès waits anxiously to find out why the council has called her. To her confidante, Anna, she recalls the song of farewell that her beloved Vasco da Gama sang before leaving as officer to the explorer Bernard Diaz (Bartolomeu Dias) *("Adieu, mon doux rivage").* Her father, Don Diégo, enters to say the king has chosen her a husband,

Don Pedro, admiral of the fleet. Pedro too appears, remarking that Diaz has been lost at sea after a storm. Fearing Vasco dead as well, Inès voices a private lament *(Loin de ta patrie).*

As president of the council, Pedro takes his place while the members file in, joined by the Grand Inquisitor and Bishops (chorus: *Dieu que le monde révère).* Pedro tells the council of Diaz's disaster, and a sole survivor is brought in: Vasco da Gama, who relates how the rest of the crew was lost. Audaciously he goes on to request a ship of his own, confident that he can succeed in navigating past the fatal reef, opening new trade routes for his country. He introduces two slaves he has brought back, Sélika and Nélusko, who appear to belong to an unknown race. Questioned as to the name of their country, Sélika—furtively warned by Nélusko not to reveal her identity as queen—replies that a slave has no country. Vasco is asked to leave, taking the slaves, so the council can deliberate his request. Fierce argument precedes the balloting, with many (led by Don Alvar) in favor of Vasco, many against. He is brought back and informed that the council denies his request. Defiantly he pleads his case, accusing the council of shortsightedness and greed, citing the success of Christopher Columbus *(C'est ainsi que naguère).* For this he is roundly condemned, and the prelates pronounce anathema on him *(Par nos voix, Dieu, lui-même).*

ACT II   In the dungeon of the Inquisition, Vasco lies dreaming fitfully and mentions the name of Inès. This upsets Sélika, who has become devoted to him and now fears a rival. She tries to console him with a song from her native land *(Sur mes genoux, fils du soleil).* Nélusko appears, meaning to kill this enemy of his country. Sélika tries to stop him, but his feeling runs high *(Quand l'amour m'entraîne, ou bien quand la haine),* and in desperation she wakes Vasco, causing Nélusko to hide his knife and withdraw. Vasco, seeing himself now enslaved too, burns with desire to realize his dream of reaching India. As he studies a chart of the voyage, Sélika points out how to avoid the reef. In his gratitude, he embraces the girl (duet: *Combien tu m'es chère),* but Inès enters the cell abruptly, accompanied by Anna, Don Pedro, and Don Alvar, to tell Vasco she has purchased his freedom—and now must part from him forever, as he is being sent into exile. Realizing she must suspect his feelings for Sélika, Vasco offers the two slaves to Inès; but when Pedro haughtily announces that the king has authorized *him* to make the exploratory voyage, Vasco sees his mistake, for Pedro will now have the conniving Nélusko to guide him. Inès confesses that to save Vasco from prison, she has promised her hand to Pedro. She and Vasco, pitied by Anna and Alvar, bemoan their separation, while Sélika sees her own hopes of Vasco's love vanishing; Nélusko and Pedro gloat over Vasco's banishment (septet, Inès: *Eh bien, sois libré par l'amour).*

ACT III   On board Pedro's ship, Inès, Anna, and the crew pray for St. Dominick's protection *(O céleste providence)* as they prepare to continue on their voyage. Don Alvar pays an unexpected visit to warn Pedro that the pilot, Nélusko, cannot be trusted and already has directed two other ships onto the rocks. Meanwhile, another strange, unidentified ship has appeared and is leading the way. Nélusko warns of an approaching typhoon and scares the crew with a description of Adamastor, a Neptune-like deity who will drown them all *(Adamastor, roi des vagues profondes)*. The strange ship, flying a Portuguese flag, draws near and dispatches a dory, from which Vasco comes aboard. Confronting him, Pedro orders the others away.

Vasco says they have reached the place where Diaz was shipwrecked: there is barely time to save the expedition. Pedro senses it is really Inès whom Vasco wants to rescue (duet: *Quel destin, ou plutôt quel aveugle délire*). They are about to duel when crewmen reappear and, at Pedro's orders, tie Vasco to the mast. Inès and Sélika emerge, drawn by the sound of Vasco's voice, and try to stop Pedro from ordering his death. Just then the storm strikes, driving the ship onto a reef, and natives swarm aboard, overpowering the Portuguese. Nélusko urges them on, but when they recognize Sélika, their queen, she prevents a massacre.

ACT IV A city in India, with a Hindu temple at one side and a palace at the other. Sélika enters with Nélusko, the High Priest, and "Indians of various castes," who welcome her as their returning queen (march, procession, ballet). Nélusko makes Sélika swear to uphold the laws of the land, adding that the men of the Portuguese expedition have been put to the sword. The High Priest intimates that one of them was spared; knowing this must be Vasco, Nélusko means to dispatch him too. The women of the expedition have been led to a grove.

As Sélika and the others leave, Vasco appears, hailing the enchanted land he has discovered *(Ô paradis, sorti de l'onde)*, but he is discovered by a crowd of natives, who cry for his death. As they are about to strike, Sélika stops them. When Nélusko and the High Priest challenge her to keep her vows, she declares that Vasco saved her on distant shores and won her hand as reward. Aside, she warns Nélusko that if he doesn't corroborate her story, she will die with Vasco. Unwillingly he does so, cursing himself for having delivered her to his rival *(Écrase-moi, tonnerre)*. After giving Sélika and Vasco a "holy potion" to sanctify their marriage, the High Priest leaves them alone.

Sélika tells Vasco that while the other ships and crewmen have been lost, his own ship remains offshore, and he is free to leave with his glory untarnished. Realizing at last that she loves him, and believing Inès dead, Vasco pleads with Sélika to be his wife (duet: *Ô transports, ô douce extase*).

ACT V Amid luxurious plants in the royal gardens, Inès revives, having seen her female companions die from the "fatal vapors of these seductive golden fruits." She prays for Vasco to rescue her *(Fleurs nouvelles, arbres nouveaux)*. He appears, but scarcely can he explain his dilemma, saying his destiny calls him to die far away, than Sélika surprises the pair. Though outraged at his betrayal, she realizes his love for Inès is genuine *(Hélas, il doit l'aimer toujours)* and that she herself must suffer for it. She summons Nélusko with orders to takes Vasco and Inès to the ship.

§ On a promontory overlooking the sea, Sélika forgives Vasco and inhales the perfume of the black manchineel tree, said to bring delirium and death *(D'ici je vois la mer)*. Gradually succumbing to the poisonous vapors, she hallucinates that Vasco has returned *(Un cygne au doux ramage),* but a distant cannon shot awakens her from her reverie to see the ship sailing away. Nélusko runs in but cannot persuade her to leave. Dying, she tells him she has achieved bliss. He too falls dying as the people arrive and gently bid farewell to their queen *(C'est ici le séjour de l'éternel amour!).*

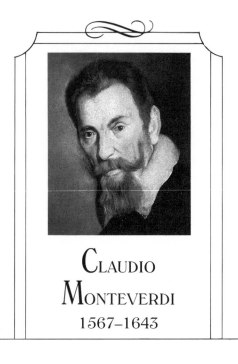

CLAUDIO
MONTEVERDI
1567–1643

W hen Monteverdi's *La Favola d'Orfeo,* one of the first surviving operas, was edited and orchestrated for the modern stage by Vincent d'Indy in 1904, the work had lain little disturbed for three centuries. After that, various other musicians tried their hand at fashioning performing versions, and today *L'Orfeo,* if not a standard repertory piece, is no longer unknown. It is disheartening, however, to realize how many early operas have been lost, and how close Monteverdi's few surviving operas came to being among them.

During the second half of the twentieth century, interest in older music began to spread beyond the province of a few scholars, and this resurgence gave rise to concern about the correct style of performance. In Monteverdi's day, and up through the time of Handel, it was customary to write recitative in a form of shorthand, with only a voice part and a figured bass indicating the harmonic accompaniment. Accompanying musicians would improvise accordingly. For the set instrumental pieces, Monteverdi indicated what instruments were to be used, and in fact *L'Orfeo* is probably the earliest instance of a full score being published. To adapt the work for modern performance, the old-style notation has to be translated to conform to current usage, with approximations or replacements for instruments that have become obsolete. It might have surprised Monteverdi that his works would be performed in centuries to come, but not that they would be arranged for prevailing instruments and conditions. Orchestrations of *L'Orfeo* by Giacomo Orefice, Ottorino

Respighi, and Gian Francesco Malipiero conform to the conventions of the Italian opera houses of the early twentieth century. With the development of an "authenticity" movement in the late decades of the twentieth century, the practice of using Renaissance instruments (restored, replicated, or adapted) has gained ground.

Once rediscovered, Monteverdi turned out to be surprisingly "modern." His idea of setting a text for voice antedated, and therefore circumvented, the baroque and romantic periods, with their glorification of singing for its own sake. The result is a directness of address and communication, together with a lucidity of texture that leaves open space for subtleties of nuance. These accents are left to the performer; only in later eras did it become customary to write detailed instructions for phrasing and dynamics. The performer therefore needs special skills to deal with early music, but it is the composer whose musical outline has made these subtleties of expression possible.

Monteverdi anticipated the development of the French opera-ballet, as well as Gluck's reforms of the latter eighteenth century and the studied simplicity of Erik Satie, Francis Poulenc, and Virgil Thomson in the twentieth. Monteverdi and the other initiators of the Florentine Camerata at the Palazzo Bardi, while considered the inventors of opera, drew upon sources already at hand—Greek drama as they imagined it, sacred mystery plays, dramatic or narrative madrigals, popular spectacles involving song and dance. Though writing for aristocratic audiences who would understand classical allusions, they did not neglect the need to entertain, and they took advantage of the new form to portray characters with individual quirks.

An interplay of such characters is especially evident in Monteverdi's two other major surviving operas, *Il Ritorno d'Ulisse in Patria* and *L'Incoronazione di Poppea.* These differ in that *Ulisse,* drawn from Homer's epic, makes a moral point: constancy is a virtue, and it pays. *Poppea,* on the other hand, holds a mirror up to licentious times: virtue is rewarded with exile or death, while immorality goes unpunished.

The recent discovery by musicologists that Monteverdi probably did not work alone but in the atelier system, as did painters of the period, has caused consternation amd disappointment. How could such a supreme artist have entrusted parts of his work to apprentices or collaborators? Two explanations suggest themselves. One, the artist then was not judged according to individualistic concepts that emerged later, during the Romantic era. Two, some of Monteverdi's colleagues, though forgotten today, were also highly accomplished. The work was what counted.

IL RITORNO D'ULISSE IN PATRIA

(Ulysses' Homecoming)

PROLOGUE AND THREE ACTS
MUSIC: Claudio Monteverdi
TEXT (Italian): Giacomo Badoaro, after Homer's *Odyssey*
WORLD PREMIERE: Venice, Teatro SS. Giovanni e Paolo, 1640
U.S. PREMIERE: Washington, D.C., Opera Society of Washington,
   January 18, 1974

CHARACTERS

Minerva, *goddess of wisdom* . . . . Soprano
Giunone, *Giove's wife* . . . . Soprano
Telemaco, *Ulisse's son* . . . . Mezzo-Soprano
Melanto, *Penelope's attendant* . . . . Mezzo-Soprano
Ericlea, *Penelope's nurse* . . . . Mezzo-Soprano
Penelope, *Ulisse's wife* . . . . Alto
Ulisse, *King of Ithaca* . . . . Tenor
Giove, *king of the gods* . . . . Tenor
Eurimaco, *Melanto's lover* . . . . Tenor
Pisandro ⎫   ⎫ Tenor
Anfinomo ⎬ *Penelope's suitors* . . . . ⎬ Tenor
Antinoo ⎭   ⎭ Bass
Eumente, *Ulisse's swineherd* . . . . Tenor
Iro, *the suitors' jester* . . . . Tenor
Mercurio, *messenger of the gods* . . . . Baritone
Nettuno, *god of the ocean* . . . . Bass

PROLOGUE   As allegorical figures of Human Frailty, Time, Fortune, and Love
hold discourse, Human Frailty admits that it is subject to the others. Time
confesses its voracity, Fortune its irrational whimsy, Love its deadly marksman-
ship. To be the victim of such forces, Human Frailty complains, is a wretched
lot indeed. Time, Fortune, and Love unite in agreeing with this (trio: *Per me
fragile quest'huom sarà*). Ulisse (Ulysses / Odysseus), hero of the following tale,
will be afflicted by all three of them.

ACT I   Penelope, supported by her old nurse, Ericlea, laments the fortunes of the Trojan War twenty years before, and the disappearance of her husband, Ulisse, for whose return she has never ceased to long (*Di misera regina*).

§ Elsewhere in the palace, Melanto, her maid, sings optimistically of the joys of love (*Duri e penosi son gli amorosi*), inspiring her suitor, Eurimaco, to shower her with compliments. They pledge fidelity (duet: *De' nostri amor concordi*). Melanto hopes to persuade Penelope to end her mourning and yield to the power of love.

§ Nettuno (Neptune / Poseidon), ruler of the sea, rises from the waves to ask Giove (Jupiter / Zeus), king of the gods, to punish the Phaeacians, who—in defiance of Nettuno's decree, but with the help of Minerva (Pallas Athene)— have led Ulisse back to Ithaca, his homeland (*Hanno i Feaci arditi*). Giove says he will let Nettuno punish them himself, since the offense took place in his realm (*Facciasi il tuo comando*). The Phaeacians are seen on their ship (chorus: *In questo basso mondo*), which Nettuno turns into a rock, petrifying them.

§ Delivered on the shore, Ulisse wakes, and not knowing where he is, suspects the Phaeacians of having betrayed him (*Dormo ancora o son desto?*). His patroness, Minerva, appears in the guise of a shepherd and tells him he is in Ithaca. After he has recounted his journey (*Io greco sono et hor di Creta io vengo*), she reveals her identity and instructs him to return to his castle disguised as an old beggar. Nymphs store his trophies in a cave. He is to go to the spring of Arethusa, where he will meet his faithful herdsman Eumete (Eumaeus), and where Minerva will bring Ulisse's son Telemaco (Telemachus) from Sparta to join him. Ulisse hails his good luck (*O fortunato Ulisse!*) as the goddess withdraws.

§ At the palace, Melanto praises Penelope's loyalty to the long-absent Ulisse but, believing him dead, counsels her to accept one of the suitors who have been besieging her (*Cara amata Regina!*). Penelope replies that Cupid is a fickle god, and that no one who has suffered so bitterly can love again.

§ Eumete, tending his herds and still sorrowing for his lost sovereign (*Pastor d'armenti può prati e boschi lodar*), has a brief visit from the comically gluttonous Iro (Irus), who is on his way to the palace to feast. Next, Eumete meets an old beggar (the disguised Ulisse), to whom he offers hospitality, and who assures him the king will return.

ACT II   Minerva brings Telemaco in a chariot to Eumete, who welcomes him as the king's son (*Oh gran figlio d'Ulisse!*). Telemaco asks the herdsman to go to the palace and tell Penelope her son has arrived. Alone with the old beggar, Telemaco sees him vanish (*Che veggio, ohimè, che miro?*), but Ulisse reappears, having shed his disguise. Telemaco is afraid to believe his eyes: perhaps this is an apparition, a trick. Ulisse reassures him that Minerva alone is responsible for his transformation, then urges the youth to go to Penelope; he himself will follow, but under his previous disguise.

§ At the palace, Melanto tells Eurimaco she has had no luck trying to persuade Penelope to accept one of her suitors. Eurimaco, having heard about the alleged fickleness of women, is impressed by the queen's steadfastness. The lovers agree not to let Penelope's mourning dampen their own happiness.

Antinoo, Anfinomo, and Pisandro (Antinous, Anfinomus, and Pisandrus), Penelope's suitors, urge her to love again, but she refuses *(Non voglio amar)*. They try to divert her with dancing (ballet). Eumete, the herdsman, arrives and tells her that her son is on his way, also that Ulisse is still alive and will soon return. After so much grief, she is hesitant to believe this, but the suitors react with alarm (Antinoo: *Compagni, udiste?*), and when she has left, they plot to do away with Telemaco as soon he gets there. An eagle passes overhead, and Eurimaco warns it is an omen from Zeus: they will be punished for their presumption. Shaken, the suitors decide to ply Penelope with extravagant gifts.

§ In the woods, Minerva appears to Ulisse and tells him she will have Penelope propose an archery contest: whoever can bend Ulisse's bow will win her hand. When the suitors have failed, Ulisse is to appear and use the bow to shoot them dead. Eumete, guiding Ulisse toward the palace, tells of the suitors' dread at news of his return.

§ Telemaco reports to Penelope the awesome beauty of Helen of Troy and how Paris paid with his life for loving her *(Del mio lungo viaggio)*. Penelope is repelled by the vanity of Helen's story, but Telemaco adds that it was Helen, an expert in reading omens, who predicted to him Ulisse's return and defeat of the suitors.

§ Eumete has brought the "beggar" to the palace, annoying Antinoo, who asks him to keep the old man out of the way during the festivities. The beggar enters nevertheless and answers Iro's haughty comments by wrestling with and defeating him. Penelope offers hospitality to the victor, sensing his nobility of spirit. Anfinomo brings her a gold crown, Pisandro robes and jewelry, Antinoo a hoard of gold treasure, all of which she accepts politely and noncommittally *(Non andran senza premio)* before asking Melanto to bring Ulisse's bow. This she presents as being also the bow of Cupid, which will vanquish her heart *(Ecco l'arco d'Ulisse)*. All three suitors try to bend the bow but cannot. Then the beggar asks to be allowed to try, saying he will not claim the prize if he succeeds. Readily bending the bow, he shoots the three suitors.

ACT III Bereft of the three suitors, whose hospitality kept his stomach full, Iro fears hunger more than death *(O dolor, o martir che l'alma attrista!)* and takes his own life.

At the palace, Penelope, though she had never intended to marry any of the suitors, interprets their death as but another sign of the fatality of love and sees only more grieving in store, despite Melanto's attempts to comfort her. When Eumete enters to tell her the beggar is actually Ulisse *(Forza d'occulto affetto),* she cannot believe it; when Telemaco too appears and explains Minerva's role, Penelope replies that the gods enjoy deceiving mortals.

§ At sea, Giunone (Juno / Hera) agrees to Minerva's request for help in restoring peace to Ulisse's life. She calls upon her husband, Giove, who asks Nettuno's agreement. As Nettuno grants it, a chorus from the waters and the heavens echoes his sentiments *(Giove amoroso fa il Ciel pietoso).* Giove sends Minerva to placate the Achaians, who want revenge on Ithaca for the suitors' death.

§ At the palace, Penelope's old nurse, Ericlea, wonders whether to keep silent or tell a secret that she knows about Ulisse *(Bel segreto taciuto).* As Telemaco and Eumete marvel at Penelope's stubborn skepticism, Ulisse appears in his real form *(O delle mie fatiche),* only to have Penelope still question his authenticity: perhaps he is a pretender to the throne, using magic or trickery to usurp it. Ericlea reveals her secret: she has recognized Ulisse in his bath by the scar inflicted on him by a wild boar. Even now Penelope hesitates to believe, but Ulisse convinces her by stating what no one else knows—that she covers her bed every night with a silken cloth she herself wove, depicting Diana, goddess of chastity. Now Penelope hails him as "my Phoenix risen from the Trojan ashes," and they are joyfully reunited (duet: *Sospirato mio sole!).*

WOLFGANG AMADEUS MOZART
1756–91

Though it was not until the 1930s and 1940s that Mozart began to be considered a standard opera composer, his works were never entirely out of the repertory. Performance style varied, however, from what lately has come to be considered a reasonable facsimile of eighteenth-century practice. Romanticism crept into the viewpoint of performers—inevitably, in the wake of such Mozart-loving romantics as Richard Wagner, Gustav Mahler, and Richard Strauss, all of whom conducted as well as composed.

Perhaps this was not altogether inappropriate, since Mozart himself contributed his share to the birth of romanticism. A creative experimenter, he was constantly expanding the harmonic vocabulary of his period and testing, stretching the forms everyone knew, such as the aria and ensemble, to serve more adventurous expressive purposes. Above all, he contributed to opera a humanization of its characters and a gift for musical portraiture that animates each personality. In ensembles, for example, he frequently managed to give each singer a different kind of musical line, blending them all into a logically organized whole.

In this respect, Mozart was subversive, and was so perceived by his contemporaries. His work was often criticized for its harmonic subtlety and structural complexity. He had mastered the accepted musical lingua franca, only to push its further development, overturning the status quo, inventing something that had not been found before. Because his operas have survived and those of his competitors have not, we are not obliged to note how safe and ordinary the latter seem by comparison. Performers and audiences alike balked at the difficulties he presented, but his enthusiasm was contagious and his genius persuasive.

The lesser-known, earlier operas of Mozart show him coming to terms with convention and making it his own. Because these operas are not the masterpieces he created later, they are often given short shrift. One of the most interesting of them, *La Finta Giardiniera,* shows the youthful prodigy of nineteen turning into a man. Reading the libretto alone, one would have to conclude the composer was biting off more than he could chew. On the printed page, his poet confronts him with a tangle of Italianate opera-buffa plot complications: mistaken identity, mad scenes, jealous fits, unrequited love. It is tiring to read and not especially convincing. Once Mozart gets hold of it, however, the characters start to take on a third dimension: they breathe and become real. Viewed in the light of modern psychology, the plights of these players show unexpected depth, of which Mozart was intuitively aware—a Freud before his time. There are even accents of real tragedy lurking just below the surface, as there would be in *Don Giovanni* twelve years later. In between, Mozart would write *Le Nozze di Figaro,* a distillation of the spirit he had discovered in *La Finta Giardiniera.*

Not all the early Mozart operas are readily stageworthy, but because they are by Mozart, effort is made to revive them occasionally. *La Finta Giardiniera* is long; the characters are numerous, the situations not always easy to make clear. Sometimes credible motivation takes second place to the librettist's need simply to make an effect. At such points one senses Mozart, a sort of musical Pirandello, saying, "But can't you see, these are people! They're real to *me!*" What on paper seems contrived becomes probable, even inevitable, through the emotional logic of music.

In its day, *La Finta Giardiniera* was not an unqualified success. Perhaps the mixture of opera-seria and opera-buffa elements confused a public used to lighter or heavier fare, but not both at once. The original was lost, giving way to German adaptations with spoken dialogue; only in 1978, during publication by Bärenreiter of the New Mozart Edition, did it reappear, in a restoration made possible by a copy of the manuscript unearthed in a library in Czechoslovakia. A production at Salzburg during International Mozart Week in 1980 was the first of the original version since 1775.

LA FINTA GIARDINIERA

(The Make-believe Gardener)

THREE ACTS
MUSIC: Wolfgang Amadeus Mozart
TEXT (Italian): Giuseppe Petrosellini, revision of a libretto for an
   opera by Pasquale Anfossi, 1774
WORLD PREMIERE: Munich, Court Theater, January 13, 1775
U.S. PREMIERE: New York, Mayfair Theater, January 18, 1927 (in
   English)

CHARACTERS

Ramiro, *a knight* . . . . Soprano
Marchesa Violante Onesti, *disguised as Sandrina,*
   working in the mayor's garden . . . . Soprano
Serpetta, *the mayor's housekeeper* . . . . Soprano
Arminda, *the mayor's niece* . . . . Soprano
Don Anchise, *Mayor of Lagonero* . . . . Tenor
Count Belfiore . . . . Tenor
Roberto, *the marchesa's servant, disguised as Nardo,*
   a gardener. . . . . Baritone

Posing beneath her station, Marchesa Violante Onesti has taken a job as Sandrina, a gardener, at the house of Don Anchise, a provincial *podestà* or mayor.
With her she has taken her servant Roberto, whom she introduces as her cousin
Nardo. She is looking for her former betrothed, Count Belfiore, who jealously
stabbed her in a quarrel and fled the scene, thinking her dead.

ACT I   In a garden outside the mayor's villa in rural Lagonero, Italy, during
the eighteenth century, five people state their diverse emotions. Sandrina and
the cavalier Ramiro, both jilted in love, are unhappy. Serpetta, the mayor's
maid, has designs on her boss and is annoyed by his attentions toward Sandrina; in turn, Nardo, attracted to Serpetta, cannot get anywhere with her.
The mayor tries to cheer Sandrina and then Ramiro, who scorns the idea of
finding a new sweetheart *(Se l'augellin sen fugge)*. Alone with Sandrina, the
mayor tells her of his affection, but she puts him off; he even proposes mar-

riage, with interruptions from the annoyed Serpetta. He imagines various instruments playing music of conflicting moods in his bosom *(Dentro il mio petto)*.

Sandrina feels impatient in her menial job, since there has been no sign of Count Belfiore, whom she hoped to find. She and Nardo recall the events that brought them here; he suggests she consider marrying the mayor, but she wants to leave. Ramiro wanders in, overhearing her remarks about the treachery of the male sex, and protests that some men—such as himself—are faithful and worthy of love. Sandrina feels he is laying all the blame on women, whose sad lot in life she deplores *(Noi donne poverine)*. Nardo, alone for a moment, compares the plight of these unhappy people with his own: unable to compel any response from Serpetta, he wishes he could ignore women entirely *(A forza di martelli)*.

§ In his villa, the mayor welcomes a new arrival, his niece Arminda. About to meet her arranged bridegroom for the first time, she behaves testily. When he arrives, he turns out to be Count Belfiore, the very man Sandrina has been trying to find. He greets Arminda with exaggerated courtliness *(Che beltà, che leggiadria)*. Unimpressed, she describes herself as stubborn and haughty but agrees to accept him—at the same time warning that he'd better behave *(Si promette facilmente)*. To impress the mayor, Belfiore claims a list of distinguished forbears all the way back to Ancient Rome *(Da Scirocco a Tramontana)*.

Serpetta feels like quitting rather than put up with Arminda's demands. To annoy Nardo, she sings about the man she would like to marry *(Un marito, oh Dio, vorrei)*—someone younger than Nardo. He keeps on trying to woo her, but she says she can find plenty of suitors *(Appena mi vedon chi cade)*.

Sandrina compares herself to a turtledove bereft of its mate *(Geme la tortorella)*. Arminda introduces herself and says she is going to marry—Count Belfiore. That name is too much for Sandrina, who faints. Arminda goes for help, leaving Sandrina in the care of Belfiore, who has just walked in. He thinks he recognizes her as Violante, his former fiancée, whom he had left for dead. As Sandrina revives, Arminda reappears with smelling salts—and suddenly sees Ramiro, her own cast-off fiancé. The mayor, walking in on this scene, cannot figure out what has happened, and the others are too stunned to explain (quartet/quintet: *Ah, che gran colpo è questo)*. They leave him scratching his head. He is assailed next by Serpetta, who says Sandrina and Belfiore are embracing in the garden, and Nardo, who says they are not; the three leave to find out.

§ Sandrina and Belfiore are indeed talking in the garden, trying to sort out their mixed reactions, when the others come upon them. Arminda is insulted, but Ramiro retorts that deception should feel natural to her. The mayor feels he too is being made a fool of (finale, Sandrina: *Ma voi, che pretendete)*. Serpetta is delighted to see Sandrina exposed as a flirt. Nardo wonders what will happen next.

ACT II   In an atrium of the villa, Ramiro tries to win back Arminda, who is
touched—but not enough to give up hope of marrying the handsome Belfiore.
She soon overhears the latter, however, muttering to himself that he must find
Sandrina. This arouses her indignation (*Vorrei punirti, indegno*), and she leaves
him wondering at her temper. Serpetta steps in and warns that he had better
make peace with such an explosive woman. Resenting her interference, he
departs. Seeing Nardo, Serpetta hints that she might like him better if he had
fancier manners. To humor her, he tries imitating upper-class Italian, French,
and English customs (*Con vezzo all'Italiana*).

Sandrina laments the irony of finding her beloved on the very day he is to
wed another. Belfiore enters, and she confronts him with his past misdeeds. In
his upset state he is still not sure she is Violante, though everything about her
seems to say she is (*Care pupille belle*). The mayor overhears his protestations
and, as Sandrina leaves, takes her place, further confusing Belfiore.

The mayor accuses Sandrina of trifling with his affection, which, he repeats,
is serious. She begs him to sympathize with her distress (*Una voce sento al core*).

A letter has arrived from Milan, informing Ramiro that Belfiore is wanted
for murder. The mayor learns this just as Arminda is urging him to get on
with the wedding. The mayor realizes that as justice of the peace, he will have
to deal with this matter, even if it means losing an advantageous marriage for
his niece (*Una damina, una nipote*). Arminda repulses Ramiro for his lying
accusations, but he dares to hope he can still win her back (*Dolce d'amor com-
pagna*).

The mayor tells Belfiore of the murder charge. Flustered, Belfiore gives
vague replies, but Sandrina comes in and offers to defend him, declaring it is
she who survived his jealous stabbing. Once alone with the grateful Belfiore,
she confounds him by saying she was only pretending—capitalizing on her
close resemblance to Violante. She leaves, and he feels his sanity shaken (*Già
divento freddo*).

Sandrina is nowhere to be found. As the others look for her, Nardo overhears
Serpetta say she has been abducted (at Arminda's behest) to a nearby forest.
As Nardo runs to tell Belfiore, Serpetta defends Arminda's (and her own) use
of guile: these days, a girl has to look out for herself (*Chi vuol godere il mondo*).

§ Sandrina is left by her abductors in a deserted, remote place near a ruined
aqueduct and a grotto. Terrified, she feels her spirits failing (*Ah, dal pianto*),
then hides in the grotto. From there she hears voices: Nardo and Belfiore are
groping their way into the wilderness (finale, Belfiore: *Fra quest'ombre, o questo
scuro*). From another direction, Arminda enters, hoping to catch Belfiore looking for Sandrina. The mayor and Serpetta too have each come separately to
search the woods. Hearing one another's noises, they start calling out, and
mistaken identities ensue. Ramiro arrives and joins in the general confusion.
Accusations of treachery and infidelity start to fly. The mayor wants to chal-

lenge Belfiore to a duel, but attention is polarized by Belfiore and Sandrina: out of their minds, they believe themselves transformed into the mythical Medusa and Hercules, urging everyone to calm down.

ACT III   In a courtyard, Serpetta tells Nardo not to give up hope: she may yet learn to like him. Belfiore, still demented, wanders in, thinking he is Mercury and Nardo is Venus. As Nardo tries to escape, he runs into Sandrina, also crazed, claiming to be Erminia. To divert them and get away, Nardo points to the sky, where he imagines the sun and moon in conflict *(Mirate che contrasto).*

§ In his villa, the mayor, still hoping to wed Sandrina, is needled by Serpetta, who reminds him he once encouraged her to think he might wed *her.* He is besieged next by Arminda, who hopes to catch Belfiore, and Ramiro, who wants to retrieve Arminda. In exasperation, the mayor tells them to do as they please *(Mio padrone, io dir volevo),* and leaves. Ramiro pleads with Arminda, but she tells him to forget her. Alone, he despairs of winning her back *(Va pure ad altri in braccio)* and expects to die.

§ In the garden, Sandrina and Belfiore lie sleeping. They wake, restored to their senses, and quarrel but gradually relent, finally admitting their love (duet: *Cosa fa? Alme belle innamorate).*

§ As Arminda persists in badgering the mayor, Nardo bursts in with news that the two who went mad have regained their sanity and gotten engaged. Arminda will now accept Ramiro, and Serpetta will take Nardo. The mayor gives each couple his blessing, saying he will remain single until he finds another Sandrina, and all hail the lady who pretended, out of faithful love, to be a gardener *(Viva pur la Giardiniera).*

MODEST MUSSORGSKY
1839–81

The image of Mussorgsky in his latter years as a disheveled alcoholic, disorganized in his work habits, pathetically unable to bring projects to completion, runs counter to his earlier life as the scion of a well-to-do family. Though his musical talent was encouraged, however, there was never any thought of his becoming a musician. He could entertain party guests by playing the piano, but his career was supposed to be in the military. He matriculated in officers' school and joined the czar's private regiment. Something of a dandy in those days, he also maintained a serious interest in music. He studied theory as much as he could—in his spare time, so to speak—with his friend Mily Balakirev, but never acquired a fully professional technique.

More and more obsessed with music, Mussorgsky decided in 1858 to resign his commission and devote himself to composing. His family inheritance was seriously impaired by the abolition of serfdom two years later, and though Mussorgsky did not mind ideologically—he was in sympathy with the peasantry—his personal travails increased. By 1863 he was obliged to find a civil service job as clerk at the Ministry of Transport, at which he toiled for seventeen years. Luckily he was supported in his musical aims by a group of cronies with similar interests. The influential critic Vladimir Stasov grouped these rather dissimilar nationalist composers as the Mighty Handful: Balakirev, Alexander Borodin, César Cui, Mussorgsky, and Nikolai Rimsky-Korsakov.

What this group shared was a desire to pursue unadulterated Russianness in music, as Glinka had done, rather than to incorporate Russian elements with cosmopolitan European style, as Tchaikovsky and Anton Rubinstein were doing. From the perspective of today, this schism seems greatly exaggerated, since Tchaikovsky's music strikes most foreigners as intensely Russian, while Balakirev's symphonies and concertos sound if anything more cosmopolitan than Tchaikovsky's. It was Mussorgsky who took the most chauvinistic position: Russianness for him was not a style or an aesthetic posture but a sort of musical religion. Nowhere is this dedication more apparent than in his songs and operas, which set a standard for natural, expressive Russian prosody, little influenced by European models. Native liturgical and folk music were his main sources.

Mussorgsky's first opera project, of which he completed only one act, was based on Gogol's *The Marriage.* This was superseded by *Boris Godunov,* an adaptation of Alexander Pushkin's verse drama. Together with another historical drama, *Khovanshchina,* to his own libretto, *Boris* was his main legacy. Meanwhile he had worked on other, abortive opera ideas, notably *Salammbô* (after Flaubert)—his only non-Russian subject—and *The Fair at Sorochintsy,* neither of which he managed to finish. All Mussorgsky's operas, including *Boris*—the only one he did complete—were subject to extensive revisions, some by the composer himself, later by colleagues anxious to keep his works alive by making them performable. The rescue of *The Fair at Sorochintsey* reveals a lesser-known side of Mussorgsky: his gusto for humorous folklore. Whether they embraced his work or not—many had reservations, or considered him a dilettante—Russian composers, from his own day to the present, have had to contend with him. There is something indelible and heartbreaking about his work. It possesses a genuineness that enabled him to plumb the Russian soul.

KHOVANSHCHINA

FIVE ACTS
MUSIC: Modest Mussorgsky
TEXT (Russian): the composer and Vladimir V. Stasov
WORLD PREMIERE: St. Petersburg, Kononov Theater, February 21, 1886
U.S. PREMIERE: Philadelphia, April 18, 1928
METROPOLITAN PREMIERE: February 16, 1950 (in English)

MODEST MUSSORGSKY

CHARACTERS

Emma, *a Lutheran girl* . . . . Soprano
Susanna, *an Old Believer* . . . . Soprano
Marfa, *a young widow, an Old Believer* . . . . .Mezzo-Soprano
Prince Andrei Khovansky, *Prince Ivan's son* . . . . Tenor
Prince Vassily Golitsin . . . . Tenor
A Scribe. . . . . Tenor
Shaklovity, *a boyar* . . . . Baritone
Kuzka, *a musketeer* . . . . Baritone
Prince Ivan Khovansky, *leader of the Streltsy* . . . . Bass
Dosifei, *head of the Old Believers* . . . . Bass

ACT I   Russia, latter seventeenth century (events conflated from period 1682–98). After a prelude depicting dawn over the Moscow River, several Streltsy (musketeers) on patrol enter Red Square in Moscow, boasting about the previous night's rioting, in which they killed a High Council member and a German. They rib the approaching Scribe, who sets up shop in his booth. After they have left, the boyar Shaklovity comes to dictate a letter for the Scribe to write: addressed to the rulers of Russia (Peter I, his brother Ivan, and sister Sophia), it denounces a plot by Prince Ivan Khovansky, the boyar who leads the Streltsy, and his son Andrei, to stir up rebellion and gain the throne for Andrei. Shaklovity leaves after ordering the letter delivered to the czarevna. A group of people wanders into the square (chorus: *Gospodi! Nastal vremiachko*), trying to scare the Scribe into reading them a proclamation posted on a column; he pretends it praises the exploits of the violent Streltsy. Distant trumpets herald the arrival of Ivan Khovansky, who tells his followers and the crowd *(Deti moi!)* that his Streltsy will maintain law and order. Buoyed by praise (chorus: *Slava lebediu*), he leaves with his entourage. A German Lutheran girl, Emma, runs in, pursued by the amorous Andrei, but his former beloved, Marfa, steps forward to defend the girl and defy Andrei, though he threatens her with a knife (trio: *Tak, kniazhe, ostalsia ty veren mne!*). A member of the Old Believers sect and a visionary, Marfa privately foresees immolation for herself and Andrei. Ivan returns and, taking a fancy to Emma himself, orders her kidnapped by the Streltsy. He and his son quarrel until the imposing Dosifei, leader of the Old Believers, upbraids them for their godless conduct, then urges a return to the traditional faith to save Russia *(Brat'ia, drugi, vremia za veru stat' pravoslavnuiu)*.

ACT II   In his palace, Prince Golitsin, a liberal who shares Czar Peter's view of a Westernized Russia, reads a letter from his former lover, Czarevna Sophia, whose continued advances he distrusts *("Svet moi bratets, Vasenka")*. He is visited by a Lutheran Pastor, who tells about the outrageous treatment of Emma and asks (unsuccessfully) for help in building another church in the German quarter. When the Pastor has gone, Marfa is announced: Golitsin has sent for her to read his future. Gazing into a bowl of water, she sees him exiled in disgrace *(Sily potainye, sily velikie)*. Shaken, he dismisses her and orders his servant to drown her in a marsh to prevent rumors, but she overhears and runs for her life. Golitsin regrets how quickly Russia will forget what he has done for her *(Mne grozit pozornaia opala)*.

Ivan Khovansky barges in unannounced, referring sarcastically to the humbled lot of the boyars—thanks to reforms supported by Golitsin. As they argue, Dosifei appears at the door listening, then steps between them, saying they must forget their quarrels for the good of the country. Himself a noble (Prince Miishetsky) before taking religious orders, he commands their grudging respect. Khovansky, a conservative, pays lip service to Dosifei's idea of upholding the old holy faith, but Golitsin, schooled in Europe and a believer in the Enlightenment, is distrustful. As Old Believers file outside, chanting, Marfa rushes in and tells how she narrowly escaped being murdered, thanks to some passing soldiers who rescued her. Shaklovity arrives with word that Peter the Great has found out about the plotted rebellion, which he dubbed "Khovanshchina"—the Khovansky business.

ACT III   The Old Believers, still chanting, pass through the Streltsy quarter, opposite the Kremlin. When Marfa reflects on her unrequited passion for Andrei *(Ishkodila mladeshen'ka)*, Susanna, an old woman from the group, berates her for sinful thoughts. Marfa tries unsuccessfully to calm her, as does Dosifei, to whom Marfa confides her vision of a holy, fiery death for herself and Andrei. Dosifei leads her away, leaving the square empty for Shaklovity to muse on his sleeping country's travails *(Spit streletskoe gnezdo)*. Hearing the garrison stir, he leaves.

The Streltsy stumble in, looking forward to more troublemaking *(Vali valom!)*. Their wives follow, cursing them as drunken good-for-nothings *(Akh, okainnie propoitsi!)*. Kuzka, one of the Streltsy, tries to mollify them with a song about how gossip turns wives against husbands *(Zavodilas v zakoul kakh)*. The Scribe appears, breathlessly relating that foreign mercenaries are on a rampage *(Otsy i brat'ia!)* and, joined by government troops, are heading for the Streltsy barracks. The Streltsy exhort Ivan Khovansky to lead them, but he refuses to fight the czar's forces.

ACT IV   Ivan Khovansky dines at his house while peasant girls intone a doleful song at their work. Annoyed, he orders them to sing something livelier. When Golitsin's servant comes to warn of imminent danger, he refuses to believe it and orders the man thrashed. After a dance by Persian slave girls, Shaklovity arrives, saying the czarevna wants Khovansky at a meeting of the High Council. Ordering his state robes, Khovansky dresses while the women compare him to a graceful swan *(Plyvët, lebëdushka)*. When he reaches the threshold, he is assassinated. Shaklovity mockingly repeats the women's refrain as they flee in panic.

§ In St. Basil's Square, amid a milling crowd, a carriage passes, bearing Golitsin into exile. Dosifei notes that both Khovansky and Golitsin have met a bad end, thanks to their machinations. Now the end is near for himself and his followers: Marfa has learned of the High Council's decision to have troops do away with them at their hermitage. Before leaving, Dosifei realizes the time has come for martyrdom and tells Marfa to bring Andrei along, so his soul can be saved. Andrei appears, still railing at Marfa for having taken Emma away, but his threats turn to entreaties when he sees the Streltsy led in for public execution. Offering to hide him, she leads him off as the Streltsy wives cry that their wicked men deserve death. At the last moment, however, Streshnev, a herald, tells the quaking victims that the czar has pardoned them.

ACT V That night, at the Old Believers' retreat in a forest outside Moscow, Dosifei declares they must fulfill God's will by saving their souls through martyrdom *(Zdes', na ètom meste sviate)*. Referring to Czar Peter as the Antichrist, sect members gather wood for their funeral pyre. Marfa assures the terrified Andrei that she still loves him and will be with him in death *(Spokoisia, kniazhe!)*. As approaching trumpets sound, Marfa lights the pyre. All die in the conflagration, and the arriving guardsmen recoil in horror.

THE FAIR AT SOROCHINTSY

(Sorochinskaya Yarmarka)

THREE ACTS

MUSIC: Modest Mussorgsky

TEXT (Russian): the composer, based on Nikolai Gogol's stories *Evenings on a Farm Near Dekanka*

WORLD PREMIERE: St. Petersburg, Comedy Theater, December 30, 1911

U.S. PREMIERE: New York, Metropolitan Opera, November 29, 1930 (in Italian)

CHARACTERS

Parasya, *Cherevik's daughter, Khivrya's stepdaughter* . . . . Soprano
Khivrya, *Cherevik's wife* . . . . .Mezzo-Soprano
Gritsko, *a peasant youth* . . . . Tenor
Afanasy Ivanovich, *the village priest's son*. . . . . Tenor

The Godfather (Kum), *Cherevik's old crony* . . . . Baritone
Cherevik, *an old countryman*. Bass
A Gypsy. . . . . Bass
Chernobog, *a devil* . . . . Bass

Of several attempts to create a performing version of *The Fair at Sorochintsy* from Mussorgsky's unfinished manuscript, the one by Vissarion Shebalin (1902–63), based on the complete scholarly edition of Mussorgsky's works by Pavel Lamm, has gained currency in Russia and is cited here.

ACT I Rural Ukraine, sometime during the nineteenth century. Peddlers and merchants are hawking their wares at the Sorochintsy Fair *(Kolësa! Vot gorshki!)*. A young girl, Parasya, tries to persuade her father, Cherevik, to buy her some ribbons; he says he cannot until he has sold the mare they brought to the fair. So she urges a group of young men not to be stingy with their girlfriends *(Sobiraitesia, podruzhki)*. A Gypsy warns the crowd that Red Shirt (the devil) may be lurking in a nearby hayloft. Gritsko, a young countryman, flirts with Parasya; she goes through the motions of discouraging him, but when he presents himself to her father as the son of Okhrim, an old chum, the two men hit it off and head for the pub. After the fair goes on for a while, the people disperse, and as darkness falls, Cherevik leaves the pub with his Godfather, another old crony, and they stumble around in the dark (duet: *Du-du, ru-du-du!*). Khivrya, Cherevik's wife, comes out of their house, and he tells her he has found a husband for their daughter. Khivrya objects, and as they argue, Gritsko overhears Cherevik giving in, saying there will be no wedding after all. Sadly, Gritsko wonders how to face this turn of events *(Zachem ty, serdtse)*. A Gypsy man appears and tries to cheer him by striking a deal for Gritsko's oxen if Parasya can be won with the Gypsy's help.

ACT II At the Godfather's house, Khivrya cooks while Cherevik sleeps off his hangover. When he wakes, she starts arguing with him as to whether he sold the mare (duet: *Tak ty menia ne slushalsia?*). She sends him away and fantasizes about her secret admirer, Afanasy Ivanovich, son of the village priest *(Ot-to chërtov syn!)*, who arrives to call on her, falling in a patch of nettles as he approaches the door. After eating his fill of the food she has been baking, he plies her with compliments and kisses her. Voices are heard approaching, so she hides him on the shelf above the stove, just as Cherevik, his Godfather, and friends arrive. They note that Khivrya seems nervous—perhaps she has been worrying about Red Shirt. After they have caroused for a while, the dishes fall from the shelf above the stove, and suspicion falls on the presence of an evil spirit. With bravado, Cherevik invites Red Shirt into the house, against the advice of his Godfather, who tells the story of Red Shirt *(Chto zhe delat', kum?)*: once the devil had to pawn his shirt with a pubkeeper, but when he came back a year later to redeem it, the old man, having sold it at a profit, pretended not to recognize him. After that, the pubkeeper was haunted by pigs' snouts—the devil's trademark—appearing in odd places. Now the devil returns every year at the time of the fair, still looking for his shirt. At this point a pig's snout appears. Afanasy falls off the shelf while the others mill around in a panic: the devil has arrived!

ACT III On a street in town, Cherevik, accidentally having put a pot instead of a hat on his head, runs with his Godfather from the house, pursued by the Gypsy and other locals, who cry that the two are thieves. Tied up, Cherevik and his Godfather commiserate: they never stole anything. One of their guards turns out to be Gritsko, who says he will gladly free them but in return asks Cherevik to promise marriage to his daughter. After the victims go home, it develops that the Gypsy planned their "arrest" as part of his bargain to help Gritsko win Parasya. Exhausted, Gritsko falls asleep there . . .

. . . and dreams about a devils' and witches' sabbath (ballet: Night on Bald Mountain). The chief deities of darkness—Chernobog, Kashchei, Topelets, Worm, Plague, and Death—appear, and Chernobog urges the spirits to enjoy themselves till dawn. Gritsko wakes afterward, thoroughly shaken.

The next morning, Parasya comes out of the Godfather's house in a happy mood, looking forward to dancing the gopak at the fair (*Ty ne grusti, moi milyi*). Cherevik, unnoticed, joins her in dancing about. The Godfather tells her she really is engaged to Gritsko, who arrives to embrace her (duet: *Gritsko! Lubyi moi*). Parasya's girlfriends congratulate her, and so does Cherevik, who wants to close the deal before his wife comes back from shopping and starts to object. When Khivrya does arrive, everyone ignores her protests and celebrates the betrothal (gopak: *Gopaka! Na berezhku ustavka*).

CARL AUGUST NIELSEN
1865–1931

arl August Nielsen, the best-known Danish composer of his generation, lived and worked under the northern shadow of Jean Sibelius in a world that was ready to recognize only one Scandinavian composer. Since the 1950s, however, largely as a result of recordings, Nielsen has taken his place as a major symphonist of the twentieth century. His two operas, *Saul and David* (1902) and *Maskarade* (1906), differ strongly in subject and tone—the former work stern and Biblical, the latter joyful and humane—but they share the composer's concern with fully delineating his characters by musical means. As a violinist, he played in the Royal Theater orchestra in Copenhagen and knew and respected the great repertory pieces, both light and serious, for their ability to bring a drama and its personalities to life.

Maskarade had its premiere on a Sunday, after a matinee performance of Heinrich Hertz's play *King René's Daughter,* on which Tchaikovsky's *Yolanta* (1892) is based. *Maskarade* also derives from a play, *Mascarade* (1724), by the Danish writer Ludvig Holberg (1684–1754), a work well known to all theater-going Danes. Because Nielsen and his librettist, Vilhelm Andersen, had to condense and simplify the dialogue, there was criticism of their presumption. Music, however, enhanced the warmth of Holberg's original while keeping much of its period flavor, and the opera version too soon became a classic.

The central theme of both play and opera is the charade of life itself: by appearing masked, people actually unmask themselves and reveal their true feelings. At the touching, sobering climax, Death appears and collects the masks. Though Holberg's characters stem from stock comic types, he imbues them with personal idiosyncrasies that give them individual life. The tradition of the masquerade is that of a great leveler, bringing aristocrats and commoners together without social barriers.

Nielsen's symphonies reveal his own character as highly profiled and distinctive. His music for *Maskarade,* like Wagner's for *Die Meistersinger,* partakes of a different feeling, that of mankind collectively. Melodies flow, and rhythms dance, as freely as in folk music. For sheer joie de vivre, *Maskarade* bears comparison with Berlioz's *Benvenuto Cellini* and *Béatrice et Bénédict,* Wolf-Ferrari's comedies and Verdi's *Falstaff.* Its relative lack of international currency may have to do with the fact that the text is in Danish, also with the composer's unassuming nature. "Sometimes I have the feeling that I am not myself," he wrote to his wife, "but only a kind of open pipe through which flows a stream of music moved by gentle but strong powers in blissful vibrations. At such times it is a happy thing to be a musician, believe me."

MASKARADE

THREE ACTS
MUSIC: Carl Nielsen
TEXT (Danish): Vilhelm Andersen, after the play by Ludvig Holberg
WORLD PREMIERE: Royal Theater, Copenhagen, November 11, 1906
U.S. PREMIERE: St. Paul, Minn., June 23, 1972

CHARACTERS

Leonora, *Leonard's daughter* . . . . Soprano
Pernille, *her maid.* . . . . Soprano
Magdelone, *Jeronimus' wife* . . . . .Mezzo-Soprano
Leander, *Jeronimus' son* . . . . Tenor
Arv, *Jeronimus' servant* . . . . Tenor
Jeronimus, *a burgher of Copenhagen* . . . . Bass-Baritone
Henrik, *Leander's valet.* . . . . Bass
Leonard, *Jeronimus' friend, a burgher of Slagelse* . . . . Bass
Master of the Masquerade . . . . Bass

ACT I   Copenhagen, 1723. In young Leander's room, he and his groom, Henrik, lie asleep in their respective beds, though it is already five in the afternoon:

they were out all night celebrating Carnival. Leander wakes and, realizing they have to get ready for another night of masquerading, wakens Henrik as well. Leander admits he fell in love the previous night and even exchanged rings with the girl *(Se denne Ring!)*. But Henrik reminds him that his stern father, Jeronimus, has arranged a match with the daughter of a crony, Leonard. Henrik describes what is likely to happen if Leander fails to honor the arrangement: parental disapproval on both sides, followed by a breach-of-promise case *(Vil Herren ej forsmaa)*. Magdelone, Leander's mother, stops in to ask about the masquerade, which she would like to attend herself, being fond of dancing *(Da jeg var ung)*. Jeronimus comes to ask for a little quiet, saying that at her age his wife's interest in partying is inappropriate. When he finds out that Leander has fallen in love with an unknown girl, he becomes even more upset and sends the others out, lamenting the loss of decorum since the good old days *(Det Satans Spind!)*.

Leonard arrives to call, embarrassed to explain that he has a similar problem: his daughter too has been smitten with a stranger at the masquerade (duet: *Min Datter er forrykt*). Jeronimus orders his servant, Arv, not to let anyone out of the house that evening without telling him. When Leander and Henrik reenter, Jeronimus asks his son to explain himself to Leonard. Seeing Leander at a loss for words, Henrik improvises an explanation of their appearance at the masquerade, calling such celebrations necessary in a country with so dour a winter climate *(I dette Land)*. Jeronimus, unimpressed, makes Leander and Henrik apologize to Leonard for their misconduct; as atonement, Leander must marry Leonard's daughter the following afternoon. He threatens to lock them in the house, but the two young men are determined to go masquerading again, and a quarrel ensues (quintet, Jeronimus: *Nu vel, vi faar at se, hvem der kan bedst!*).

ACT II   Arv stands guard in the dark street outside the house as the town clock strikes eight. The Night Watchman on his rounds warns that ghosts may be abroad, but Arv feels ready to handle any situation *(Jeg tar mig vel i Agt)*. He is jolted from thoughts of his sweetheart, the kitchen maid, when Henrik appears disguised as a ghost. The apparition scares Arv into confessing a number of minor misdeeds that Henrik, unmasking, uses as bargaining chips to make sure he and Leander can leave unnoticed. People begin to pass on their way to the nearby masquerade (students' chorus, *Af Sted!*; young girls' chorus, *Let paa Taa og Hus forbi!*). Leonard leaves the house, intending to go to the masquerade incognito; then Henrik and Leander slip out. Leander glances admiringly at his ancestral home but looks forward to a new life as the enlightened eighteenth century progresses *(Se, Henrik! se hvor Nat og Morke knuger)*.

The two young men greet the arrival of Leander's beloved, Leonora, as she arrives in a sedan chair, attended by her maid, Pernille. Leander exchanges romantic greetings with Leonora (duet: *Monsieur! Min Herre!*) before they enter the theater where the masquerade is taking place, leaving Pernille to flirt with Henrik *(Hør et Ord, Kavaller!)* before they too enter the theater. Jeronimus comes out of the house, ranting at Arv for letting the young men escape. He wants to pursue them but is stopped by a Doorman who says he cannot go inside without a mask. As Jeronimus enters the Mask Vendor's stall, Magdelone, making her way from the house, runs into Leonard. As both are masked, they do not recognize each other but enter the theater together. Jeronimus and Arv reappear, disguised as Bacchus and Cupid; Jeronimus is bent on teaching the young revelers a lesson *(Med dens egne Vaaben)*. After they go inside, the Mask Vendor closes his stall and the Night Watchman announces eight o'clock.

ACT III   In the main hall of the Grønnegade Theater, the masquerade is in full swing (chorus: *Gaa af Vejen!*) as Jeronimus enters with Arv, Magdelone with Leonard, not recognizing one another. Amid the dancing, Henrik exchanges flirtations with three girls he knows *(Himmel og Jord!)*; they sing him a madrigal about his faithless ways (trio: *At slig er Ungersvend i sin Tale)*. Leander and Leonora exchange more serious greetings (duet: *Ulignelige Pige)*, while Henrik takes up with Pernille. After dancing with Magdelone, Leonard asks her to lift her mask for a moment, but she discreetly declines; Jeronimus gives her a start by intruding, but he still doesn't recognize her and continues his search for Leander. Henrik has discovered Jeronimus' presence; to get him out of the way, Henrik appeals to an elderly Tutor for help, telling the story of Leander's romance *(Ak, Hr. Magister!)*. The Tutor hails Jeronimus in his Bacchus costume and suggests he live up to Bacchus' reputation. Meanwhile, rowdy students jostle Arv, who accidentally discovers Henrik and almost betrays him to Jeronimus—but Henrik quiets him by threatening to reveal his misdeeds. While ballet dancers perform a masque of Venus, Vulcan, and Mars, the Tutor continues to urge wine on Jeronimus. Joined by the Tutor, students sing of how Jupiter disguised himself as a bull, then as a cloud, to appear to women he loved (drinking song: *Naar Mars og Venus)*. Jeronimus, feeling giddy, tries to flirt with a ballerina *(Lille Strik, se jeg fik)*, then dances himself out of breath.

It is time to close the festivities with the traditional reminder of mortality. The Master of the Masquerade appears costumed as Corporal Mors, announcing that "An old general [Death] deputizes me to gather in recruits." He is followed by hussars in black, carrying a large funeral urn, before which the guests are to give up their earthly vanity—that is, to unmask. As they do so, the various members of Jeronimus' household recognize one another. Jeronimus' anger dissolves in consternation when he learns that Leonard's daughter is in fact the girl with whom Leander fell in love the night before. So all's well that ends well, and there is one more tradition to observe: a concluding Chain Dance, representing the Dance of Life (chorus: *Kehraus! Dans ud!)*.

JACQUES OFFENBACH
1819–80

Born in Cologne to a German Jewish family, Offenbach was sent to Paris to study while still in his teens. He was admitted to the Paris Conservatory as a cellist by the director, Luigi Cherubini, who made an exception to the rule that barred foreigners. Offenbach remained at the Conservatory only a year; later he studied composition with Fromental Halévy, but most of his musicianship seems to have been based on direct experience, performing in cafés, pit orchestras, and salons. From writing salon pieces he moved in the direction of vaudeville and comic opera, but success did not come overnight. Meanwhile, Offenbach continued a successful concert career as a solo cellist, even touring abroad.

Persistent in his attempts to get his comic operas staged, Offenbach finally resorted to staging some of them himself, starting the Bouffes Parisiens during the Paris Exposition of 1855. His programs of short works were a hit, and he was able to move his theater to larger, permanent quarters, where he expanded the repertory with comedies by other composers. At first, city regulations allowed him only a few performers, but gradually the law was relaxed to permit more ambitious productions. In due time the Bouffes Parisiens were invited to appear in London and Vienna.

During his career as a composer/impresario, Offenbach wrote a staggering number of comic operas in various genres, both short and full-length. The most enduring and well-known are *Orphée aux Enfers* (Orpheus in the Underworld, 1858), *La Belle Hélène* (1864), *La Grande-duchesse de Gérolstein* (1867),

257

and *La Périchole* (1868). Like the clown who longs to play Hamlet, he always wanted to write a grand opera, and in his last years he worked on *Les Contes d'Hoffmann,* which he left incomplete, but for which he wrote or sketched such a generous amount of music that several performing versions have been given in the latter twentieth century.

Offenbach, a superb craftsman and inspired mischiefmaker, excelled in a highly competitive, populous field that might be compared to that of Tin Pan Alley or the Broadway musical during its heyday. His buoyant satire and exuberant but sly humor left a permanent impression on colleagues and successors. Though foreign-born, he became the quintessential Parisian. Virtually every French composer has professed admiration and indebtedness toward him, and even Wagner found an occasional good word for him. His helpful influence is quite evident in the work of Arthur Sullivan, especially *Patience,* the most Offenbachian of the Gilbert and Sullivan operas. And it would be hard to imagine the raffish side of Francis Poulenc as anything but an offspring of the spirit of Offenbach.

LA PÉRICHOLE

THREE ACTS
MUSIC: Jacques Offenbach
TEXT (French): Henri Meilhac and Ludovic Halévy, after Prosper
 Mérimée's play *Le Carrosse du Saint-Sacrement*
WORLD PREMIERE: Paris, Variétés, October 6, 1868
U.S. PREMIERE: New York, Pike's Opera House, January 4, 1869
METROPOLITAN PREMIERE: December 21, 1956 (in English)

CHARACTERS

Périchole, *a street singer* . . . . Soprano
Piquillo, *another street singer, in love with her* . . . . Tenor
Comte Miguel de Panatellas, *lord-in-waiting to*
 the Viceroy of Peru . . . . Tenor
Don Andrès de Ribeira, *Viceroy of Peru* . . . . Baritone
Don Pedro de Hinoyosa, *Governor of Lima* . . . . Baritone
Marquis de Tarapote. . . . . Bass
Old Prisoner . . . . Speaking Role

ACT I Eighteenth-century Lima, Peru. In a public square, patrons of the Three Cousins tavern are celebrating the name day of the viceroy, Don Andrès de Ribeira. The local governor, Don Pedro de Hinoyosa, arrives disguised as a vegetable vendor, wanting to find out if people are enjoying themselves in accordance with his instructions. He is followed by the viceroy, disguised as a doctor; the crowd instantly recognizes him, but he believes he is incognito *(Sans en souffler mot à personne)*. Without recognizing Don Pedro or Count Panatellas, First Gentleman of the Chamber, he has a drink with them and leaves, to shouts of "Vive le vice-roi!," in which he joins, to make his disguise more convincing.

Into the square stroll the street singers Périchole and Piquillo, who are in love but cannot afford to marry. They deliver a ballad about a Spaniard who is an artful lover and his Indian girlfriend *(Le conquérant dit à la jeune Indienne);* when their collection yields nothing, they follow with a seguidilla duet about a muleteer and a young girl *(Vous a-t-on dit souvent)*. Before they can pass the hat again, a troupe arrives with performing dogs, diverting the public's attention. Looking for another way to make some money, Piquillo leaves Périchole to rest in the square, where she is surprised by the returning viceroy. Smitten with her, he offers the girl a position as lady-in-waiting at his court; warily she accepts, mainly out of hunger, on the condition that she can write a farewell note to Piquillo *(O mon cher amant, je te jure)*. Protocol requires that the viceroy's favorite lady-in-waiting be a married woman, so Panatellas is given the task of finding Périchole a husband. He happens upon Piquillo, who meanwhile has read the note and is on the point of hanging himself. Having no idea the bride is Périchole, he refuses; approached by the viceroy with a similar offer, she likewise refuses, so the officials ply them, separately, with drinks.

As a crowd gathers at news of a wedding, two drunken Notaries are enlisted to perform the ceremony (duet: *Tenez-nous bien par le bras*). Périchole, none too steady herself, is led in, veiled, extolling the dinner she has just been given *(Ah! quel dîner je viens de faire!)*. At first she still refuses the marriage, but then she recognizes Piquillo. He is too drunk to recognize her, declaring instead that he loves someone else and will be a faithless husband (duet: *Je dois vous prévenir, Madame*); she replies that she will repay him in kind. The ceremony proceeds (chorus: *Le beau mariage que nous voyons là!*), after which the bride and groom are whisked away in opposite directions in sedan chairs.

ACT II At the palace, court ladies use smelling salts to revive the chamberlain, the Marquis of Tarapote, who has fainted upon learning that a mere street singer is being installed as the viceroy's favorite. When Piquillo appears, beautifully dressed and wondering what has happened to him, court ladies assure him ironically that he is married to a lovely bride (ensemble: *On vante partout son sourire).* Some male courtiers arrive and scoff at Piquillo's opportunism in letting himself be married to the viceroy's intended mistress *(Quel marché de bassesse!).* Only when alone with Don Pedro and Panatellas does he manage to explain that in spite of having agreed to marry an unknown woman, he still hopes to find his true love again (trio: *Et là, maintenant que nous sommes seuls).* Free to ask for whatever he wants, he demands his freedom to leave. The ministers agree, but first he must present his bride at court: protocol demands it. Courtiers assemble. Midway through the ceremony, Piquillo recognizes Périchole's voice and starts to berate her. To calm him, she tells him to behave properly in these surroundings and trust her to manage the situation *(Que veulent dire ces colères. . . . Mon Dieu! que les hommes sont bêtes!).* But he throws her down before the viceroy as a faithless tart with whom he wants nothing more to do *(Écoute, O roi, je te présente).* At this, the furious Périchole says she wants nothing to do with *him,* either, as Piquillo is arrested and taken to a special dungeon for uncooperative husbands (ensemble: *Conduisez-le, bons courtisans).*

ACT III   In the cell, an Old Prisoner, who has been trying for twelve years to escape with the aid of a penknife, declares that in twelve more years he hopes to be free. He ducks out of sight as Piquillo is brought in. Don Pedro and Panatellas, who have escorted him there, credit Piquillo as the first man in Lima to stand up for a husband's rights (duet: *Les maris courbaient la tête),* then leave him alone to reflect on his plight *(On me proposait d'être infame).* As he dozes off, Périchole appears in the cell and wakes him up. He imagines she has come to make fun of him, but she confesses she really loves him, despite his obvious faults *(Tu n'es pas beau. . . . Je t'adore, brigand).* They reconcile, and she assures him she has resisted the viceroy's advances. But when she calls the jailer, meaning to bribe him to let them escape, he turns out to be the viceroy in disguise, unrecognized by them (trio: *Je suis le joli geôlier).* Périchole offers her diamonds in payment for Piquillo's freedom, adding that she too means to leave, but the viceroy angrily abandons his disguise and calls guards to chain the couple to the wall. They declare their scorn for him and their love for each other (trio: *Roi plus haut qu'une botte!),* while he makes a last-ditch attempt to cut a deal with Périchole: if she decides to "become reasonable," she should hum one of her songs, calling him back.

After the viceroy has left, the Old Prisoner reappears and sets the couple loose. Then the two men hide in the shadows as Périchole sings snatches of a song, drawing the viceroy so they can jump him, tie him up, and steal his keys.

§ Back in the public square, the three escaped prisoners beg the innkeepers of the Three Cousins not to give them away. As they run off, soldiers arrive, searching for them (chorus: *Les bandits sont partis).* The Three Cousins—Mastrilla, Berginella, and Guadalena—declare that Périchole missed her chance for advancement at court (trio: *Pauvres gens, où sont-ils?).* The viceroy appears, and to his surprise, Piquillo and Périchole enter as street singers, this time hymning his praises for showing mercy on two lovers (duet: *Écoutez, peup' d'Amérique*). Flattered, he lets Périchole keep her jewels. Only the Old Prisoner is sent back to jail, but he doesn't mind, because he still has his penknife. Preparing to leave, the minstrels reprise their song in praise of the Spaniard as a lover.

JOHN CHRISTOPHER PEPUSCH

1667–1752

*T*he term "parody" originally denoted simply a transfer of material for another purpose. Monteverdi's *Vespro della Beata Vergine,* for example, is in part a parody of his opera *L'Orfeo,* from which he borrowed some of the music. In more recent times, however, a parody is taken to mean an imitative satire. Almost any popular work, from Mozart's *Die Zauberflöte* to Wagner's *Ring* cycle, was fair game for a spoof in its day, and many such were produced. A classic example is Offenbach's *Orphée aux Enfers,* a takeoff on Gluck's *Orphée et Euridice.* Perhaps the grandfather of all opera parodies, and certainly the most durable, was *The Beggar's Opera,* which made fun of the popularity of Handel's Italian operas in London. The very title aims at the jugular, since Italian opera, then as (unfortunately) now, implied an elite audience, one capable of either understanding or ignoring the foreign language of the entertainment—to common listeners, an inscrutable barrier.

Much as one made fun of the antics of the outlandish divas and castratos of Italian opera, however, there was no avoiding the fact that Handel was an immensely popular composer. His tunes were sung and played in the street, and they were not excluded from *The Beggar's Opera,* which—appropriately for a beggar—solicited and gathered from everywhere. The original sixty-nine songs are said to have been scored by John Christopher Pepusch, who also wrote an overture on a tune called "Walpole, or The Happy Clown," a tipoff that the plot would satirize political events (the character of Macheath being Robert Walpole, Earl of Orford).

Pepusch, like Handel, was a naturalized English composer of German birth and training. A believer in the English-language lyric theater, he had written and arranged music for several masques. Knowledgeable about folk music, he is credited by history not only as the presumed arranger of *The Beggar's Opera* but as a founding father of ballad opera, which thrived during the eighteenth century and became the first form of opera performed in the United States, where it was a favorite with George Washington.

John Gay (1685–1732), author of the quick, witty text of *The Beggar's Opera,* with its keen characterizations and blunt home truths, was a theater manager as well as a playwright and poet. He knew Handel, having supplied text for the master's *Acis and Galatea* ten years before. Writing verses for *The Beggar's Opera,* he tailored them to fit popular tunes of his own choice, which Pepusch apparently arranged. Because the original words to these songs were known to the audience, there was irony or comedy implicit in their choice for given situations onstage. *The Beggar's Opera* was so overwhelmingly received that a sequel, *Polly,* was inevitable, but it was banned by the Lord Chamberlain and not produced until many years after Gay's death, by which time its topicality had become passé.

The Beggar's Opera eventually inspired a parody of its own, *Die Dreigroschenoper* (The Threepenny Opera, 1928)—like most parodies, a tribute to the original. Bertolt Brecht's text, updated to Victorian England, offered mordant commentary, matched by Kurt Weill's acid-etched score; the gallows humor had grown darker, as had the times. Outrageous allusion and mirthful caricature had become a social message, and Handel's generous frame was no longer in the mirror.

THE BEGGAR'S OPERA

THREE ACTS
MUSIC (arr.): Johann Christoph Pepusch
TEXT (English): John Gay
WORLD PREMIERE: London, Lincoln's Inn Fields Theatre, January 29, 1728
U.S. PREMIERE: New York, Nassau Street Theater, December 3, 1750

CHARACTERS

Polly Peachum . . . . Soprano
Lucy Lockit . . . . Soprano
Mrs. Peachum . . . . .Mezzo-Soprano
Diana Trapes . . . . .Mezzo-Soprano
Capt. Macheath, *a highwayman*. . . . . Tenor
Filch, *a pickpocket, employed by Peachum* . . . . Tenor
Lockit, *a jailor* . . . . Baritone
Peachum, *a dealer in stolen goods* . . . . Bass
Beggar. . . . . Speaking Role

ACT I London, early eighteenth century. Peachum, a businessman of the underworld, looks up from his account books to comment that all mankind is engaged in roguery (*Through all the employments of life*). Filch, a young pickpocket, comes to report the legal status of several of Peachum's clients, noting that women are particularly valuable allies for a criminal (*'Tis Woman that seduces all mankind*). When Filch has gone, Peacham goes through a list of other petty criminals, assessing their prospects. His wife joins him, remarking that women make poor judges of capital cases, because they are too soft-hearted toward handsome felons (*If any Wench Venus' Girdle wear*). The couple discusses Capt. Macheath, a talented highwayman who "keeps too good company ever to grow rich." Mrs. Peachum thinks Macheath might be serious about their daughter, Polly (*If Love the Virgin's Heart invade*), but Peachum draws the line at marriage and goes to find the girl so he can sound her out.

Alone, Mrs. Peachum sees no reason why marriage should hinder a woman (*A Maid is like the Golden Ore*). When Filch returns, she questions him about Polly's relationship with Macheath, but he protests he is bound to secrecy.

Meanwhile, Polly tells her father she is well aware of the danger of losing her virtue and knows how to encourage a man without giving in to him (*Virgins are like the fair Flower in its Lustre*). Needing her powers of persuasion for business purposes, he warns that he will cut her throat if he hears of her being married.

Mrs. Peachum, having coaxed from Filch the secret of Polly's marriage to Macheath, confronts father and daughter with the fact (trio: *Our Polly is a sad Slut!*). Pressed to confirm or deny it, Polly admits she did marry Macheath (*Can Love be control'd by Advice?*). Her mother faints; revived by a double cordial, she is more inclined to forgive (duet: *O Polly, you might have toy'd and kist*), and Peachum sees they must accept the situation. Polly is relieved (*I, like a Ship in Storms, was tost*). When she steps out to mind the shop, her father wonders whether Macheath may have other wives: if so, Polly's inheritance might vanish if her husband died (*A Fox may steal your Hens, Sir*).

Polly returns, and the discussion resumes: how does she propose to make her way as a married woman? To secure her inheritance, she should denounce

Macheath to the authorities and get him hanged. But Polly insists that because of her love for him, she could never do such a thing (*O ponder well! be not severe*); she could not survive without him (*The Turtle thus with plaintive Crying*). She steps out but overhears her parents' plan to denounce Macheath themselves. Alone, she resolves to save him—but how? She goes to Macheath, who has been hiding in her room (duet: *Pretty Polly, say*). Since meeting her, he declares, he has discovered constancy (*My Heart was so free*); now nothing could tear him from her side (duet: *Were I laid on Greenland's Coast*). She tells him they must indeed be parted, because her parents are planning to turn him in (*Oh what Pain it is to part!*). She hopes it will not be long before the way is clear for his return (duet: *The Miser thus a Shilling sees*).

ACT II   At a tavern near Newgate Prison, members of Macheath's band sit discussing their trade: is it any more dishonest than others? (*Fill ev'ry Glass, for Wine inspires us*). Macheath arrives and explains he has had a falling out with Peachum, which he hopes to resolve in a week or two. Meanwhile, since they cannot do business without Peachum, the others are to continue cooperating with him, while Macheath stays out of the way. The gang sets off about its affairs (*Let us take the Road*), and Macheath reflects on his fondness for women (*If the Heart of a Man is deprest with Cares*). He has sent for a group of whores, who enter and join him in a dance (chorus: *Youth's the Season made for Joys*). When Macheath asks one of them, Jenny Diver, if she is no longer fond of him, she replies that he is the one who will choose his company (*Before the Barn-Door crowing*). Amid banter as to what sort of men make the best clients, Jenny observes that gamblers and lawyers are especially treacherous (*The Gamesters and Lawyers are Jugglers alike*). The women shower attention on Macheath, but they have betrayed him: Peachum appears with Constables to take him to prison. At the thought of the gallows, Macheath affects bitter bravado (*At the Tree I shall suffer with Pleasure*).

§   At Newgate, the prisoner reflects ruefully that of all dangers, woman is the most treacherous (*Man may escape from Rope and Gun*). Lucy Lockit, the jailer's daughter, visits him, full of reproach (*Thus when a good Housewife sees a Rat*): Macheath had promised to marry her as well, and she accuses him of adding insult to injury (*How cruel are the Traitors*). He denies the rumor that he is married to Polly, saying it is vanity that makes her call herself his wife (*The first time at the Looking-glass*).

§   Lockit and Peachum agree to split the reward for Macheath, but the government is behind in its bounty payments (Lockit: *When you censure the Age*). When Peachum accuses Lockit of mishandling several recent cases, Lockit comes to blows with him, but the quarrel is quickly over.

§   The sobbing Lucy doesn't want to believe that Macheath really will be executed (*Is then his Fate decreed, Sir?*), but Lockit tells her to accept the inevitable *(You'll think ere many Days ensue)*. Macheath, visited again by Lucy, urges her to secure his release by offering her father a bribe *(If you at an Office solicit your Due)*. To his embarrassment, Polly arrives, declaring herself his wife and throwing herself upon his neck *(Thus when the Swallow, seeking Prey)*. Not wanting to spoil his chances of escape, Macheath disowns Polly, pretending she is out of her mind. Now both women accuse him of perfidy, and he sees he cannot deal with them in each other's presence *(How happy could I be with either)*. Lucy thinks he deserves hanging, and Polly is upset by his rejection (duet: *I am bubbled*). Macheath, still hoping to escape via Lucy, continues to disavow Polly, who will not give up her claim *(Cease your Funning)*. Lucy threatens to call her father and have Polly thrown out (duet: *Why how now, Madam Flirt?*). The dispute ends when Peachum arrives and hauls Polly away, over her fervent protests *(No Power on Earth can e'er divide)*.

Macheath renews his pleas to Lucy to get him out. She agrees to try, saying that after he goes into hiding, she will miss him sorely *(I like the Fox shall grieve)*.

ACT III Macheath has escaped, and Lockit, knowing Lucy responsible, demands his share of the bribe. She replies that she did it for love alone *(When young at the Bar you first taught me to score)*, though she suspects Polly is really married to Macheath and may be enjoying his company *(My Love is all Madness and Folly)*. Lockit resolves to stay on his guard toward Peachum, who doubtless will try to cheat him *(Thus Gamesters united in Friendship are found)*.

§ In a gambling house, Macheath rejoins some of his gang and gives them money, showing his friendship to be loyal *(The Modes of the Court so common are grown)*. They discuss the evening's pocket-picking plans and agree to meet later.

§ Going over stolen inventory at Peachum's warehouse, Lockit tells Peachum that their troublesome daughters hold the key to Macheath's whereabouts *(What Gudgeons are we Men!)*. Diana Trapes, a steady customer, drops by to see the two men, venturing the philosophy that lips should be used for kissing when young, for drinking when old *(In the Days of my Youth)*. She mentions recently seeing Macheath.

§ At Newgate, Lucy—like an opera-seria heroine—declares herself torn to pieces by jealousy, rage, love, and fear *(I'm like a Skiff on the Ocean tost)*. When Polly appears, Lucy turns hypocritical *(When a Wife's in her Pout)*, pretending to apologize. Polly refuses her offer of a (poisoned) cordial, and the women feign sympathy with each other's plight (duet: *A Curse attend that Woman's Love*). Polly recalls how harshly Macheath rejected her *(Among the Men, Coquets we find)*. Lucy persists in offering the drink *(Come, sweet Lass)*, Polly in refusing it.

Their conversation stops as Macheath, recaptured, is led back to prison. The two women turn toward him imploringly (duet: *Hither, dear Husband, turn your Eyes*). Macheath cannot say which of them is truly his wife *(Which way shall I turn me)*. Polly begs her father to save him *(When my Hero in Court appears)*; Lucy pleads with Lockit to do the same *(When he holds up his Hand)*. Lockit tells her there is no hope *(Ourselves, like the Great)*, and Macheath bids the girls a gallant farewell *(The Charge is prepar'd)* before he is led away for trial. Other prisoners dance about in their chains.

Awaiting the gallows, Macheath laments his lot *(O cruel Case!)*, then seeks solace in drink *(Of all the Friends in time of Grief)* and song *(Since I must swing. . . . But now again my Spirits sink. . . . But Valour the stronger grows. . . . If thus a Man can die. . . . So I drink off this Bumper. . . . But can I leave my pretty Hussies. . . . Their Eyes, their Lips. . . . Since Laws were made for ev'ry Degree)*. He is visited by members of his band, whom he advises to trust no one, and by Polly and Lucy, who wish they could die at his side (trio: *Would I might be hang'd!*). Four more women appear, all with children, claiming to be his wives as well. Seeing them, Macheath asks to be taken to the gallows.

The Beggar who planned the opera tells one of the actors that justice must be done and the moral stated, but since opera is an absurd art form, a happy end would suit public taste better. So Macheath is pardoned and chooses Polly, saying he was not really married to any of the others *(Thus I stand like the Turk, with his Doxies around)*. The company joins in his maxim: "The Wretch of To-day, may be happy To-morrow."

HANS PFITZNER
1869–1949

The composer of five operas, Pfitzner is remembered for the fourth, *Palestrina,* in which he set forth his ideas about the sources of inspiration. His stage career had begun in 1895 with *Der Arme Heinrich,* which derived to some extent from his admiration for the earlier operas of Wagner. Having drawn attention with *Der Arme Heinrich* while still in his twenties, Pfitzner was called to Berlin, where he taught for a decade at the Stern Conservatory. He went on to a career as conductor, taught further in Strasbourg, and took an interest in German romantic opera, arranging some scores of that period for performance. There is a story that once while conducting *Die Meistersinger,* Pfitzner handed over his baton to the concertmaster for Act III, put on Beckmesser's costume, and sang the role in place of the indisposed baritone.

Because of his conservative style and artistic beliefs, Pfitzner played into the hands of the emergent Nazis, whose nationalism he at first supported, though after their rise to power in the 1930s he no longer had much to say about them. Because of the relative intransigence of Richard Strauss, whose reputation was international, and from whom the Nazis got little more than lip service, it was evident that Pfitzner was being exploited as a foil. The ejection or silencing of modernists in all the arts, too, was an invitation to conservatives to take the stage.

Pfitzner seems to have been propelled in his work by the energy of his own contradictions. He venerated Wagner yet disapproved of the post-*Tristan* modernism that Wagner had set in motion. In *Palestrina,* he ends with what might be taken as a Catholic view of inspiration—that it comes directly from above, with the artist as intermediary—yet in Act II he presents a wry, jaundiced view of wrangling within the Church hierarchy. In this respect his work half-resembles Paul Hindemith's *Mathis der Maler*, which presents a more Protestant viewpoint: that the artist, in glorifying God, has only his own resources, faith, and hard work to sustain him, no mystical intervention. Though Pfitzner had little use for Hindemith's brand of musical modernism, the *Palestrina* score, particularly in Act II, is complex and thorny.

The effect of Nazi conservatism in the arts was to exalt so-called National Romanticism, a school that had flourished early in the century in the wake of *Tristan und Isolde*, with Jean Sibelius and Pfitzner as two of its leading exponents. Because Pfitzner was German, he became entangled with Nazi ideology, whereas Sibelius, a foreigner, remained untainted. Though Sibelius' music was smiled upon in Hitler's Germany, it remained popular abroad as well, which Pfitzner's never was. Having outlived his own prestige and aesthetics, Pfitzner survived World War II bitter and disillusioned. He died eighteen years after the unsuccessful premiere of the last of his operas, *Das Herz* (1931).

Palestrina, though seldom produced (largely because of its difficulty), remains one of the important operas of the twentieth century. Together with Berlioz's *Benvenuto Cellini* and Hindemith's *Mathis der Maler*, it stands as one of the few stage works to deal truthfully with the life and problems of the artist as an acolyte in a secular world. To this Pfitzner adds the theme of the tried-and-true versus the newly fashionable in art, naturally taking the side of the former. Berlioz and Pfitzner romanticized the artist, but such was their point of view: they romanticized themselves. All three composers affirm that while there is something otherworldly about art, it has be created in the real world, by real people.

PALESTRINA

THREE ACTS
MUSIC: Hans Pfitzner
TEXT (German): the composer
WORLD PREMIERE: Munich, Prinzregententheater, June 12, 1917
U.S. PREMIERE (concert performance): Berkeley, Calif., May 14, 1982

CHARACTERS

Ighino, *Palestrina's son* . . . . Soprano
Silla, *Palestrina's pupil* . . . . .Mezzo-Soprano

Giovanni Pierluigi Palestrina . . . . Tenor
Bernardo Novagerio, *papal legate*. . . . . Tenor
Abdisu, *Patriarch of Assyria*. . . . . Tenor
Giovanni Morone, *papal legate* . . . . Baritone
Carlo Borromeo, *cardinal from Rome* . . . . Baritone
Count Luna, *envoy from the King of Spain* . . . . Baritone
Avosmediano, *Bishop of Cadiz* . . . . Bass-Baritone
Bishop Ercole Severolus, *master of ceremonies at
    the Council of Trent* . . . . Bass-Baritone
Pope Pius IV . . . . Bass
Cardinal Christoph Madruscht. . . . . Bass
Cardinal of Lorraine . . . . Bass
Anton Brus von Müglitz, *Archbishop of Prague* . . . . Bass

Giovanni Pierluigi da Palestrina (1525 or 1526–94) began his musical life
as a choirboy and papal chapel singer. At the age of thirty or perhaps later (the
date is still under dispute), he wrote his *Missa Papae Marcelli* for the election
of, or in memory of, Pope Marcellus II (Cardinal Cervino), who died after only
three weeks in office. According to Wallace Brockway and Herbert Weinstock
in *Men of Music,* this mass is "as shrouded in legends and conflicting traditions
as the *Mona Lisa*" and represents "a peak in art comparable to the Sistine
frescoes." Though Palestrina wrote numerous other Masses and other liturgical
works, it was the Missa *Papae Marcelli* that qualified him as "the savior of
church music," because it met the papal criterion of setting the words poly-
phonically but intelligibly. Brockway and Weinstock assert, "Palestrina gave
music a new kind of beauty based on an understanding of integral structure."
The pope in Pfitzner's opera, Pius IV (Giovanni Angelo de' Medici), took office
in 1559.

ACT I   In the study of Palestrina's house in Rome, his pupil Silla feels ready
to leave his old master and move on to Florence, where a new kind of music,
no longer hidebound by polyphony, will come to flower *(Welch herrlich freier
Zug).* Palestrina's son Ighino enters, talking about his father's envious colleagues and professional hardships *(Ich wusste wohl, du würdest also reden).* In
hopes of diverting him, Silla sings a song he has composed *("Schönste, ungnäd'ge
Dame"),* but he stops when Palestrina enters with Cardinal Borromeo, who
frowns at such "cacophony." After Palestrina sends the two boys away, Borromeo lectures him about his obligation, as an artist and a Christian, to put his
talents back to work *(Nun setzt Euch zu mir her und hört).* The Pope has condemned the decadent state of music and ordered a return to unadorned Gre-
gorian chant in the Church. He has even ordered the destruction of many
existing masterpieces. But Germany's Emperor Ferdinand has shown concern
for saving these works. If a new Mass could be composed in pure polyphonic
style, it might induce His Holiness to change his mind. Palestrina feels too

old and worn for the task and tactfully refuses. Failing to persuade him, Borromeo leaves in a rage.

Alone, Palestrina regrets his inability to respond to the offer. If only his wife, Lucrezia, were still living, his love for her might inspire him. In his despair he is visited by ghosts of nine past composers from Spain, the Netherlands, Italy, Germany, and France, who tell him they still live through their work, and that he is chosen by God's will to carry it on. He replies that his only wish is to join them in death *(Wohl weiss ich, dass auch ihr einstmals in Nöten)*. Before fading from sight, they tell him he must fulfill his earthly mission *(In dir, Pierluigi, ist noch ein hellstes Licht)*. He raises his voice to heaven. An Angel appears and gives him the opening phrases of the Mass *(Kyrie eleison)*, which Palestrina, as if hypnotized, starts to write down. Other Angels appear and give him more music *(Gloria in excelsis Deo)*. Joined by the spirit of his wife, Lucrezia, he writes in a mood of growing exaltation *(Zu überschwenglichem Glück bin ich erhoben!)*. A vision of the heavens appears and dissolves gradually as he falls into exhausted sleep.

Silla and Ighino find him asleep when they come for their morning lesson. Seeing the sheets of music, they realize he has composed an entire Mass in one night. It is in the old polyphonic style, "but not so weighty." Silla wonders how a work dashed off in a single night could be worthy of the master.

Act II December 3, 1563, at Cardinal Madruscht's palace in Trent, Lombardy. By order of the Pope, the Council of Trent, after eighteen years and two interruptions, is about to come to an end. This is the last full session before the ceremonial conclusion. Bishop Severolus, the master of ceremonies, discusses details of procedure with other delegates. Borromeo sits with the papal legate Novagerio, talking about the difficulty of dealing with the emperor and the difficulty of uniting the Catholic world politically. Novagerio mentions Church music *(Was man leicht und sicher durchzusetzen dedenkt)*: surely the new Mass for the conclusion of the Council of Trent is ready? Borromeo says Palestrina was uncooperative and has been imprisoned.

Delegates fill the hall, discussing religious politics. Novagerio and Borromeo go to greet another papal legate, Morone, who will chair the conference. Spanish delegates make deprecating remarks about the Italians, who are always deferring to the Pope. Abdisu, the ancient Patriarch of Assyria, enters and draws a great deal of attention. Severolus calls the assembly to order and introduces Morone, who goes into a lengthy greeting *(Den Heil'gen Geist, der di Konzilien lenkt)*, mentioning the threat of heresies and the problem of conciliating Emperor Ferdinand. Morone has been to see Ferdinand and asks whether the forty-two points raised by him should be dealt with individually or left, as he recommends, to the Pope's discretion.

The Spanish delegation does not want to give these matters over to the Pope without discussing them. First is the question of a Mass to be written, upon the basis of which it will be decided whether to save polyphony—as

Ferdinand wishes—as the musical language of the Church. Borromeo and Novagerio say the Mass is being written and will be tried out in the papal palace. This satisfies the gathering, which goes on to argue over other points raised by the emperor, also over points of procedure. The Spaniards are at odds with the French and the Italians; after Count Luna, spokesman for the King of Spain, furiously declares he will see that Protestant factions are invited to the closing session, pandemonium breaks loose, quieted only by the sound of the noon bell.

Morone announces a break until two o'clock, exhorting the delegates to return in a more constructive frame of mind *(In der Verfassung des Gemüts)*. As the meeting breaks up, several delegates besiege Morone, pushing their respective agendas, even hoping to extend the Council for further sessions. Novagerio manages to restore peace between Morone and the angry Cardinal of Lorraine, but servants and hangers-on of the various nationalities fall to name-calling among themselves, and a free-for-all ensues, joined by rabble from the street. Order is restored only when Cardinal Madruscht brings soldiers and orders them to shoot, killing and wounding many. Others, attempting to flee, are arrested.

ACT III   Early evening at Palestrina's house, June 1565. He seems to have aged and at first fails to recognize five of his Choristers, who have come to be with him while his Mass is sung for the delegates at the papal palace. Ighino recalls the day his father was taken to prison and, to save him, Ighino had to surrender the manuscript of the Mass. Now the Mass has vindicated him and rescued polyphonic music for the Church. Voices of other Choristers are heard in the street, hailing Palestrina's achievement. They have come from the papal chapel, announcing that the Pope has approved the new work *(Ist Palestrina, der Meister hier?)* and is on his way over.

Pope Pius IV arrives, heralded by eight cardinals, including Borromeo, and borne in on a litter. He salutes Palestrina and asks him to take the leadership of the Sistine Choir *(Wie einst im himmlischen Zion Johannes der Heilige hörte)*. Palestrina kisses the feet of the Pope, who blesses him and all present, then leaves. Borromeo remains behind and, when he has sent away the lingering Choristers, kneels before Palestrina in deep emotion, begging forgiveness: "God speaks through you, and I could not perceive it!" After Palestrina embraces him, he rushes away, quite overcome.

Ighino, alone with his father, hugs him and wishes for him to be happy again. When Palestrina learns that Silla has left for Florence, he understands: "Youth is drawn to youth." Ighino runs out into the street to take part in the crowd singing his father's praises. Palestrina studies his dead wife's portrait for a few moments, then sits quietly at the organ after offering a prayer: "Now fashion me, the last stone on one of your thousand rings, oh God—and I will be of good heart and live in peace."

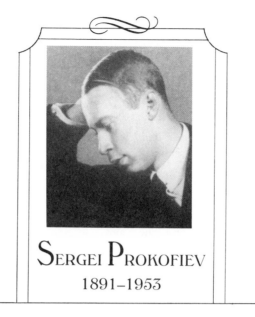

SERGEI PROKOFIEV
1891–1953

*P*rokofiev, like Tchaikovsky, longed for success in the opera house that was not to be his. Both kept trying, and both were rewarded with posthumous recognition beyond what they received in their lifetime. In the hierarchy of Russian opera, however, Mikhail Glinka remains the patron saint, Modest Mussorgsky the venerated disciple. Tchaikovsky and Prokofiev both wrote in a more international style with less specifically Russian aims.

Prokofiev, unlike his contemporary and rival Igor Stravinsky, did not study with Nikolai Rimsky-Korsakov and was little influenced by that prolific master. He worked instead from the principles set forth by Mussorgsky and Alexander Dargomyzhsky, both of whom placed primary importance on melodic shaping dictated by the Russian language. Though Prokofiev relied relatively little on Russian-sounding, folklike music, he nevertheless was guided by the words. This was not an unusual concern during the early decades of the twentieth century: one finds it in the operas of Claude Debussy and Leoš Janáček, both of them taken with Mussorgsky's ideas.

Prokofiev's preoccupation with the theater showed up early. When he was ten, his brief opera *The Giant,* to a libretto by the family cook, was performed at his home. He attempted four more projects, not all of them complete, before his first viable opera, *Maddalena,* emerged; unperformed during his lifetime, it has made occasional appearances since. *Maddalena* is stock verismo melodrama with cardboard characters, but the composer's aptitude for the lyric medium is apparent. His next opera, *The Gambler,* a more arresting work, proceeds with the dizzying whirl of a roulette wheel. Again he is standing outside his characters, but even as caricatures they are more interesting. *The Gambler* typifies Prokofiev's sardonic, mechanized side, reflecting the machine-age, anti-romantic values of modernists around the time of World War I.

The two works that followed, *The Love for Three Oranges* and *The Fiery Angel*, show Prokofiev's growing interest during the 1920s in the fantastic. *Oranges* purports to be a parody on traditional opera, but the object of its satire is closer to Glinka's *Ruslan and Ludmila* than to any European examples. *The Fiery Angel* deals with the confusion between wisdom and superstition that passed for spirituality in the Middle Ages. In every period, of course, there remains a dichotomy between knowledge and belief, but today, science and metaphysics, for better or worse, go their separate ways; Prokofiev captures the hysteria that results from compounding them. Between Renata and her demons, one is left wondering which possesses which. A shocking opera then as now, *The Fiery Angel* found no takers. Disheartened, Prokofiev moved back to Russia, by then the U.S.S.R., and entered a new phase.

Of the operas composed in Prokofiev's Soviet years, *Semyon Kotko*, though it did not fulfill the composer's hopes for a success in the genre of socialist realism, showed his determination to write more simply and lyrically. This trend reached fruition in *Betrothal in a Monastery*, which ranks with Prokofiev's ballets *Romeo and Juliet* and *Cinderella* as neoromantic escapism. If there is no socialist realism in *Betrothal*, there is warmer characterization and a flowing vocal line. The opera goes on rather long, presenting slowly what in Sheridan's play is fast-paced, but the music is so agreeable that one hardly cares. In the scene of the roistering monks there is a look backward toward *The Fiery Angel*.

Prokofiev's remaining operas, *War and Peace* and *The Story of a Real Man*, show different aspects of his coming to terms with Soviet dictates. Under pressure to make the former work into a patriotic epic, the composer revised and expanded it: no fewer than four versions exist, recalling the history of Mussorgsky's *Boris Godunov*. The work has continued in the repertory of the major Russian houses, but *The Story of a Real Man* was less fortunate, falling under condemnation by a Communist Party resolution on music in February 1948. The charge of "formalism," a catch-all buzzword, could have meant just about anything. What it meant for Prokofiev, a few years before his death, was that opera, the medium he loved, had slipped his grasp one last time.

THE GAMBLER
(Igrok)

FOUR ACTS
MUSIC: Sergei Prokofiev
TEXT (Russian): the composer, based on Fyodor Dostoyevsky's
   novella
WORLD PREMIERE: Brussels, Monnaie, April 29, 1929 (in French)
U.S. PREMIERE: New York, 85th Street Playhouse, April 4, 1957 (in
   English)

CHARACTERS

Pauline, *the General's ward* . . . . Soprano
Grandma, *the General's rich aunt* . . . . .Mezzo-Soprano
Blanche, *a demimondaine*. . . . . Alto
Alexei, *tutor to the General's children* . . . . Tenor
The Marquis . . . . Tenor
Prince Nilsky. . . . . Tenor
Mr. Astley, *a rich Englishman* . . . . Baritone
The General, *a retired army officer* . . . . Bass
Baron Würmerheim. . . . . Bass
Baroness Würmerheim . . . . Mute Role

ACT I At Roulettenberg, a fictitious spa somewhere in Central Europe,
1865. In the garden of the Grand Hotel, outside the casino, Alexei, age
twenty-five, a tutor to the General's family, encounters Pauline, the General's
ward, with whom he is love, and tells her he followed her instructions to pawn
her jewelry and gamble with the proceeds—but lost. The General, a middle-
aged man smitten with the much younger opportunist Blanche, enters with
her, the coldly shrewd Marquis, and an Englishman, Mr. Astley. Questioned
about his losses, Alexei claims the money was his own, from salary he had
saved. When the others suggest that a person in his modest position ought
not to gamble, Alexei irritably replies that life is too short to save money
gradually *(Da, eto tak)*. The General has just received a telegram from "Babu-
lenka," Pauline's Grandma in Moscow, and goes off with the others to send a
reply; they are all waiting for the old lady to die and leave them her money,

so they can gamble with it. Pauline returns, annoyed that she now cannot repay her debts to the insidious Marquis. Alexei insists on his infatuation with her *(Vy tak dumali!)*, but she senses cold greed behind his hysteria. Their conversation is interrupted by the General, who has just borrowed money from the Marquis and gives Alexei a large bill to get changed. Pauline capriciously dares Alexei—if he really loves her enough to do anything she asks—to go and flirt with a German Baroness sitting in the park, thereby annoying her husband. He does so, creating a stir and causing the Baron and Baroness to leave.

ACT II   In the lobby of the Grand Hotel, the General remonstrates with Alexei for his behavior. When the young man shows no sign of contrition, the General fires him. Alexei sticks to the view that he should be allowed to act as he wishes without interference. When Alexei leaves for a moment, the General tries unsuccessfully to enlist the Marquis' help in dealing with him to prevent scandal. As the two older men move off, Alexei returns, reflecting that everything is Pauline's fault: it was she who put him up to addressing the Baroness. Astley greets Alexei, and they discuss the cause of the General's apprehension: he is afraid any scandal might jeopardize his hopes of winning Blanche. At some point, it seems, Blanche had tried to borrow money from the Baron, causing a complaint from the Baroness. Since the Baron and Baroness are important people, the General wants to avoid further offending them. As the two men talk, Blanche passes through in search of the General. Astley goes on to explain that the General cannot propose to Blanche until he gets his inheritance from Grandma. Alexei takes the cynical view that since Pauline too will have an inheritance, she will then fall prey to the rapacious Marquis *(Tol'ko! Vy dumayete, tol'ko?)*.

Astley takes his leave as the Marquis appears, bent on controlling Alexei's behavior at the behest of the General. Finding the young man resistant, the Marquis wonders aloud how best to get around him *(Khorosho—prekrasno—yesli tak)*, then produces a note from Pauline telling Alexei to stop acting like a schoolboy. Alexei calls the Marquis a usurer and a parasite, accusing him of making Pauline write the note. As Alexei leaves angrily, Blanche and the General appear, asking whether the Marquis had any success in dealing with Alexei. The Marquis pretends he had, then turns to his chief topic of interest, Grandma's imminent demise: how soon do they expect news of her?

No sooner has the General predicted her death that very night than Grandma's voice is heard: she has arrived at the hotel, a picture of health. Though she greets Pauline with a certain affection, she quickly sees through the poses of the others. She announces she is over her illness and wants to recuperate at the spa, where she also looks forward to gambling. Blanche suspects the General of false promises, while the Marquis hopes his usual deceit and hypocrisy will suffice to deal with the old lady.

ACT III In an anteroom of the casino, the General is beside himself: Grandma has been gambling and losing large amounts, ignoring all entreaties to stop *(A starukha vszho igrayet)*. His hopes of success with Blanche are evaporating. When the Marquis steps in to announce that Grandma's losses are up to 40,000, the General decides it is time to call the police: surely they will see that she is senile and irresponsible, perhaps even send her to an asylum. No such luck, the Marquis assures him. Blanche makes another brief appearance, disillusioned with the General. When Alexei arrives, the General and the Marquis try to enlist his help in stopping Grandma from ruining them all. Prince Nilsky, who has been showing interest in Blanche, enters the salon and mentions that the old lady's losses have increased; this causes the General to collapse, momentarily stunned, before running into the casino. Blanche leaves with Nilsky. Alexei ponders the fate overtaking his erstwhile employer's family: his love for Pauline is the only thing that still connects him to them *(O da, razvyazka priblizhayetsya)*. Pauline appears, but his words to her are constrained, and the two are soon interrupted by Grandma, who is brought in looking tired. Having spent all the money she brought, she now wants to return to Moscow and has asked Astley to lend her enough for the train fare *(Zdravstvuite, batyushka Aleksei Ivanovich)*. When she invites Pauline to accompany her, the girl says she cannot leave just yet. As Grandma is carried off, the General comes back from the casino, fulminating that he has been disgraced by her losses and has lost Blanche to Nilsky.

ACT IV In Alexei's room at the hotel, he finds Pauline waiting to show him a letter from the Marquis. As Alexei reads it *(Neblagopriyatnye obstoyatel'stva zastavliayut)*, he realizes that the Marquis, pressured by loans he has made to the General, is trying to get Pauline to pay her debts to him by suggesting that if he were forced to sue, her own inheritance would be in jeopardy. Flattered that Pauline has turned to him for help, Alexei runs from the room like a madman.

§ In the gambling hall, Alexei joins a group of seasoned gamblers who discuss his every play as he wins repeatedly, finally quitting at 200,000. This breaks the bank, and the tables are closed for the evening. After an entr'acte, the other patrons are still discussing his phenomenal luck. Gathering his winnings, Alexei returns to his room, where in a daze he imagines the voices of croupiers and the comments of fellow gamblers. In due time he realizes Pauline is there, waiting for him, and he offers her the 50,000 she needs to repay the Marquis. She refuses and asks whether he really loves her *(Poslushay, ved'ty menya lyubish'?)*. For a moment it appears he is responding: they will go away together. Then, turning harsh again, Pauline demands the money, saying her love is just a commodity. When Alexei hands it to her, she throws it in his face and runs out. Alexei is left, dementedly recalling how he won twenty times in a row.

THE FIERY ANGEL
(Ognenniĭ Angel)

FIVE ACTS
MUSIC: Sergei Prokofiev
TEXT (Russian): the composer, based on Valery Bryusov's novel
WORLD PREMIERE (concert performance): Paris, Théâtre des Champs-
Elysées (French Radio), November 25, 1954 (in French)
STAGE PREMIERE: Venice, La Fenice, September 14, 1955 (in Italian)
U.S. PREMIERE: New York City Opera, September 22, 1965 (in
English)

CHARACTERS

Renata	Soprano
The Sorceress	Mezzo-Soprano
The Landlady of the inn	Contralto
Jakob Glock, *a bookseller*	Tenor
Agrippa von Nettesheim, *an alchemist*	Tenor
A Doctor	Tenor
Mephistopheles	Tenor
Ruprecht, *a knight*	Baritone
Mathias	Baritone
Faust	Baritone
Count Heinrich	Mute Role

The action takes place in the environs of Cologne, 1534.

ACT I   Ruprecht, a knight recently back in Europe from mercenary service
in the Americas, is shown to a dingy garret room in an inn. He tries to sleep
but is disturbed by cries from the adjacent room. Breaking down the door, he
finds a young woman, Renata, tormented by some sort of apparition, which
she keeps telling to leave. Ruprecht sees nothing but tries to comfort her. At
length she calms down and tells him that when she was eight, a white-clad
fiery angel named Madiel, with golden hair, appeared to her and became her
playmate *(Mne bylo vosem' let)*. When she turned sixteen and wanted him to
become her lover as well, he angrily left her. Later, after his voice had promised
he would return in human form, she thought she had found him in Count
Heinrich, with whom she spent a year at his castle; but he too abandoned her.

Meanwhile, the Landlady, drawn by the earlier commotion, comes to see what has been happening. To Ruprecht's inquiries, she replies that Renata is a loose woman whom she took in out of pity without realizing her troublesome nature. When the Landlady has left, Ruprecht begins to desire Renata, but she senses it and says she cannot give her love to anyone because of her devotion to Count Heinrich. She urges Ruprecht to accompany her to Cologne in search of him. The Landlady and her Servant reappear with a Fortuneteller, who recites spells to predict Renata's future but imagines she sees blood on the girl's clothes.

ACT II   In a room overlooking Cologne, Renata reads a book of sorcery. When Ruprecht appears, having tired of their futile search for Count Heinrich, she repeats that she is still determined to find him. Jakob Glock, a bookseller, delivers two more rare books on magic, then leaves. Ruprecht's desire for Renata has grown, but she still insists on her love for the incomparable Heinrich *(No my dolzhny naiti Ghenricha)*. She imagines that spirit rappings tell her she is about to see Heinrich, but her excitement leads nowhere. When Glock returns, he offers to take the couple to Agrippa of Nettesheim, a scholar of the occult.

§ In Agrippa's study, Ruprecht questions the learned doctor, who discourages him from meddling with magic. Agrippa disclaims any powers of alchemy or spiritualism, but three skeletons hanging in his laboratory mutter that he is lying. To further questions, Agrippa will reply only that true magic consists of scientific inquiry into all mysteries *(Istinnaia magiia est' nauka)*.

ACT III   Renata stands outside Heinrich's house, wondering why he has locked her out. Ruprecht, returning from Agrippa, sees her and learns she has located Heinrich, only to have him flee from her after declaring she came from the devil. She now realizes that Heinrich is only an ordinary man, not her angel Madiel, and asks Ruprecht to kill him, promising her love in return. Hesitant at first, Ruprecht is persuaded and knocks at the door. As he goes inside, Renata prays to Madiel to forgive her for thinking she had rediscovered him in the person of Heinrich *(Prosti menia, Madiel'!)*. But a window upstairs is thrown open, revealing Heinrich. Ruprecht challenges him; Renata now believes she has seen Madiel, her fiery angel, again. When Ruprecht comes out, saying he will duel with Heinrich the next day, she insists Heinrich must not be harmed *(Ego nelzia ubit')*.

§ On a precipice near the Rhine, Ruprecht lies wounded: obeying Renata, he had to spare Heinrich in the duel. Renata bends over Ruprecht solicitously, declaring she has discovered at last her love for him *(Da, tvoia liubov' posmela vzglianut')*. His friend Mathias brings a Doctor.

ACT IV   Convalescing from his wounds, Ruprecht is living with Renata in a house on a quiet square in Cologne, next door to a tavern. Renata now claims it would be sinful to give her love to him physically: she must enter a convent. He pleads with her, offering marriage, but she is adamant (duet: *Renata, moliu tebia*). When she says he has a devil within him, Faust and Mephistopheles appear and sit in the tavern garden. Renata cuts herself with a knife and threatens Ruprecht with it, then runs away. Mephistopheles orders wine and meat from the frightened Tavern Boy. When the Boy brings only wine, Mephistopheles eats him up. Faust upbraids the devil for his tiresome tricks, but the Innkeeper begs for return of the Boy, who is discovered in a nearby dustbin. Mephistopheles tries philosophizing *(Dorogoi Doktor)*, but Faust remains unimpressed by his sophistry. Spotting Ruprecht, who has just returned from unsuccessful pursuit of Renata, Mephistopheles invites the downhearted fellow to conduct him and Faust the following morning on a tour of Cologne.

ACT V   In a gloomy vault in a convent, Renata lies prostrate, in the dress of a novice, until the Mother Superior questions her about disturbing phenomena (wall knocking, invisible hands, visions and fits among the sisters) that have followed her arrival *(Sestra Renata, ia vizhu, chto ty ochen' neschastna)*. An Inquisitor, summoned to exorcise the demons, arrives and asks Renata how she can be sure her own visions do not come from the devil *(Vozlublennye brat'ia i sestri)*. As she replies that she has been called to a life of virtue, strange rappings are heard, and two young nuns are seized by convulsions. The Inquisitor pronounces an anathema, echoed by the nuns *(Ukhodi, temnyi dukh)*, but the two young nuns continue to act possessed. Hysteria mounts among the sisters, some of whom accuse Renata of bringing evil spirits, while others insist Renata is holy and implore her to save them. More of the nuns become possessed and start to dance wildly, stripping off their robes. Mephistopheles and Faust appear on an upper gallery with Ruprecht, whom Mephistopheles restrains from leaping down to help Renata. Many of the nuns turn on the Inquisitor. Protected by his retinue, he accuses Renata of carnal intercourse with the devil, condemning her to torture and burning at the stake, as all hell breaks loose in the convent.

BETROTHAL IN A MONASTERY/THE DUENNA

(Obrucheniye v Monastïrye/Duen'ya)

FOUR ACTS
MUSIC: Sergei Prokofiev
TEXT (Russian): the composer and Mira Mendelson, based on Richard Brinsley Sheridan's play *The Duenna*

BETROTHAL IN A MONASTERY/THE DUENNA

WORLD PREMIERE: Prague, National Theater, May 5, 1946
U.S. PREMIERE: New York, Greenwich Mews Playhouse, June 1, 1948 (in English, as *The Duenna*)

CHARACTERS

Luisa, *Don Jerome's daughter*	Soprano
Clara d'Almanza, *her friend*	Mezzo-Soprano
Rosina, *Clara's maid*	Alto
The Duenna (Margaret)	Alto
Don Jerome, *a rich man of Seville*	Tenor
Antonio d'Ercilla, *in love with Luisa*	Tenor
Lopez, *Ferdinand's servant*	Tenor
Ferdinand, *Don Jerome's son*	Baritone
Don Carlos, *an impoverished nobleman, Mendoza's friend*	Baritone
Father Augustine, *Father Superior of the monastery*	Baritone
Mendoza, *a rich fish merchant*	Bass

ACT I Seville, late eighteenth century. Toward evening, outside the house of the nobleman Don Jerome, he and a wealthy merchant, Mendoza, are discussing a scheme to buy up all the fishing boats and monopolize the local fish market (*Plavai, plavai rybka*). Although Mendoza has never met Luisa, Jerome's daughter, they agree that Mendoza should have her hand in marriage. As Mendoza withdraws, Jerome's son, Ferdinand, approaches with his servant, Lopez, and talks about his beloved Clara d'Almanza. He notices Antonio d'Ercilla coming near the house with a guitar to serenade his sister, Luisa, and decides to do the same thing before Clara's window. Antonio sings a love song (*K tebe v okno gliadit luna*) momentarily disturbed by three passing Masqueraders. Luisa appears at her window (duet: *Ty zhdësh' menia, liubimyi*), but their tender exchange is cut short by Don Jerome in his nightshirt, bent on catching the intruder. The Masqueraders, passing by again, jokingly seize Jerome instead. As a widowed father, he complains of the anxiety of bringing up a girl (*Esli est u vas doch'*): where did she learn to have such a mind of her own? He decides it would be best to marry her off quickly to Mendoza, before the young man with a guitar can steal her. He retires, and more Masqueraders appear in the street, dancing to soft offstage music.

ACT II In Jerome's house, Luisa discusses with her duenna, Margaret, the latter's plan: Luisa eventually should pretend to accept Mendoza as a husband; but the duenna, with an eye to his money, will marry him instead. After Margaret steps out and Jerome arrives with Ferdinand, Luisa refuses to consider Mendoza, and her father declares he will keep her under lock and key until she agrees. Ferdinand tries to reason with him, pleading for Antonio—and fearing that if Antonio loses Luisa, he may return to courting Clara. Jerome will not listen, but on his way out he encounters the duenna, who lets him catch her with a love letter that Antonio sent to Luisa. The duenna's scheme—to get herself fired—succeeds. Luisa, disguised in the duenna's clothes, escapes from the house, while the duenna takes her place in the locked room.

§ At the dockside, while vendors hawk fish, Mendoza greets and walks off with his friend Don Carlos, an impoverished nobleman. Clara and her maid, Rosina, enter, discussing Clara's plight: locked up by her stepmother, she has escaped. Luisa bumps into her, and they learn they are both in the same situation. Clara relates how Ferdinand surreptitiously entered her room, offending her sense of honor, though the key he used was soon to enable her to escape *(Ferdinand odin na svete vsekh dorozhe)*. Needing a place of refuge, the girls agree to meet at the Convent of St. Catherine. Clara leaves as Mendoza and Carlos wander back in, still conversing. Approaching them, Luisa identifies herself as "Clara" and asks Mendoza's help for a poor maiden in love. At first Mendoza thinks he is the object of her infatuation and protests he is already engaged, but she makes clear it is Antonio she is trying to find. Mendoza figures out that since Antonio evidently has played Luisa false with Clara, it is time to go to Luisa's house and press his own claim on her. Meanwhile, Carlos gallantly offers to protect Clara.

§ At Jerome's house, Mendoza reports to him that Clara has escaped her father's house detention. Jerome sends for Luisa but gets back word that she does not want her father to see her poorly dressed: she will come out if he leaves. When the coast is clear, the duenna presents herself to Mendoza, who finds her not up to her advance billing. Her flattery, however, disarms him: perhaps she is not so bad. She sings for him about a modest girl's response to courtship *(Kogda vokrug zelënoi devochki)*, then says she will be his only if he will steal her from the house in a romantic manner. She ducks back into her room as Jerome returns, bearing champagne.

ACT III   Carlos has taken Clara (the disguised Luisa) to Mendoza's house, where Mendoza brings Antonio, as per her request. She conceals herself as the men enter, Antonio expressing disbelief that Clara has asked for him. The matter is explained: she wants him to conduct her—no questions askedd, on his honor as a gentleman—to her lover. Antonio enters the room where the girl is waiting. Mendoza watches through the keyhole and sees them embracing, but Carlos, a man of principles, finds his spying objectionable. He also voices old-fashioned objections to Antonio's stealing another man's fiancée. Mendoza, burdened with no such scruples, brings out and congratulates the young couple, then boasts about his impending elopement with Jerome's daughter (quartet: *Solntse—èto ty!*).

§ At Jerome's house, he, a friend, and a servant noisily celebrate with home-made music: Jerome believes Luisa has run off with the very man he wanted her to marry. Carlos arrives with a note from Mendoza, requesting Jerome's approval for the marriage, which he grants. Soon afterward, an Urchin brings another note, this from Luisa, requesting the same; again he agrees, then orders a banquet prepared.

§ In the convent garden, Luisa arrives to find Clara dressed as a nun, intending to withdraw from the world because she was so compromised by Ferdinand's impetuosity. Antonio appears, followed by the Urchin with Jerome's note of approval. Realizing that Jerome has not properly understood the situation, Antonio insists they marry before going to him. They pledge their betrothal (duet: *Moia mechta, moia liubov'*) and leave Clara to muse about taking the veil *(Ushli, vesëlye).* She is startled to see Ferdinand, who has come in search, he believes, of Clara and Antonio. As he runs in pursuit of them, Clara inwardly forgives his offense against her honor *(Moi Ferdinand, ty tak menia revnuesh'?).*

ACT IV   As monks carouse over wine in a nearby monastery, Mendoza interrupts to ask them to perform a double marriage. Ferdinand, however, bursts in and challenges Antonio, who he believes has stolen his beloved Clara. Mendoza flees, fearing Ferdinand's revenge for his sister's elopement. Luisa faints as the two young men start to fight. Only the appearance of the real Clara, this time in men's clothes, starts to untangle the confusion. The monks marry the two young couples, drunkenly enjoining them to a life of virtue and temperance.

§ With the party under way at Jerome's house, Mendoza and his bride arrive. Jerome, too nonplussed to respond, is confronted next with Luisa and Antonio, who bear his note approving of their marriage. Ferdinand follows with a nun, who reveals herself to be Clara; they too have wed. The two young couples ask for Jerome's blessing. Mendoza runs off, trying to disown the duenna, who follows him, declaring her devotion. Jerome weighs the situation: Luisa has married a poor if respectable young man, while Ferdinand has married a wealthy girl, so it all comes out even. He toasts the newlyweds, and general rejoicing follows.

JEAN-PHILIPPE
RAMEAU
1683–1764

*B*orn three and a half years before the death of Lully, Rameau grew up in a music world dominated by the Italian-born Lully's French operas. Rameau himself studied in Italy, but only briefly. He soon built a reputation in church music, as a keyboard composer and performer, and as a theorist. He was already forty when he moved to Paris from the various provincial cities where he had been working, and fifty when he made his debut as an opera composer, with *Hippolyte et Aricie.*

Lully's operas still dominated the classic French repertory; his adherents considered Rameau an upstart and a threat. But by the time of the *Querelle des Bouffons* (1752–54)—the schism between traditionalists and pro-Italian reformers—Rameau found himself classified, along with Lully, among the reactionaries. Nevertheless, despite his loyalty to the established *tragédie lyrique,* he was an innovator, expanding the use of orchestrally accompanied *récitatif* and, as time went by, the vocal intricacy of *ariettes* (full-length, decorative da capo arias). He also made freer use of multi-voice ensembles than his precursors had done, and he introduced new instruments, venturing into rich orchestral coloration. His dramatic flair is evident in a wide range of emotional mood, often exploited for contrast.

In these respects Rameau was a sort of Hector Berlioz of his time—an adventurous, sanguine spirit who counted on classical form and restraint to harness and shape his imagination. Less bound by court tradition than Lully, he embodies the fluid blend of ballet, singing, and expressive, intelligible word-setting that stands as the particularly French contribution to opera. His theoretical writings typify the age of Enlightenment in establishing a scientific basis for the art of music; but significantly, he explains how best to use this art for purposes of emotional expression—the true call of the artist, as distinct from that of the inquiring mind.

HIPPOLYTE ET ARICIE

PROLOGUE AND FIVE ACTS
MUSIC: Jean-Philippe Rameau
TEXT (French): Simon Joseph Pellegrin
WORLD PREMIERE: Paris, Opéra, October 1, 1733
U.S. PREMIERE (concert performance): New York, Town Hall, April 11, 1954
U.S. STAGE PREMIERE: Boston, April 6, 1966

CHARACTERS

Aricie . . . . Soprano
Phèdre, *Thésée's wife, Hippolyte's stepmother* . . . . Soprano
Oenone, *Phèdre's confidante* . . . . Soprano
Diane, *the goddess Diana*. . . . . Soprano
L'Amour, *Cupid*. . . . . Soprano
Hippolyte, *Thésée's son by a previous marriage* . . . . . . .Countertenor
Arcas, *Thésée's confidant* . . . . .Countertenor
Tisiphone, *a fury*. . . . . .Countertenor
Mercure, *the god Mercury* . . . . Tenor
Jupiter, *ruler of the gods* . . . . Baritone
Thésée, *King of Athens*. . . . . Bass
Pluton, *ruler of the underworld*. . . . . Bass

This synopsis omits the Prologue, cut by the composer for the 1757 revival.

ACT I   In Troezen, in mythological times, Aricie—daughter of Pallas, former ruler of Athens, whom King Thésée (Theseus) has slain—is about to take her vows as a priestess of the goddess Diane (Diana). Hippolyte (Hippolytus), Thésée's son, with whom she is in love, comes to the temple to dissuade her, though it is by wish of Thésée himself that she means to renounce the world (*duet: Tu règnes sur nos coeurs*). A Priestess declares that love must be banished from this holy place *(Dieu d'amour, pour nos asiles),* seconded by the High Priestess, who affirms that only the chaste in heart can serve Diane *(Rendons un éternel hommage).*

Queen Phèdre (Phaedra), Hippolyte's stepmother, arrives to congratulate the girl on her vows, only to learn that Aricie, backed by Hippolyte, has decided not to go through with the ceremony. Phèdre, angry and fearful at this disobedience to the wishes of the absent Thésée, warns that the gods will punish it *(Eh bien! que la trompette sonne).* She is confounded, however, by the appearance of Diane herself, who reprimands the queen's severity and declares protection for the lovers. Phèdre, who secretly loves Hippolyte, bitterly faces the fact that he does not return her passion but loves Aricie *(Quoi! la terre et le ciel contre moi).* Her vows of vengeance are disturbed by a messenger, Arcas, who reports that he saw Thésée swallowed up by the underworld *(Ce qui vient de frapper mes yeux).*

Oenone, Phèdre's nurse and confidante, points out that Thésée's death would leave the queen free to pursue her love for Hippolyte. But Phèdre doubts that even the lure of the throne would induce the youth to give up Aricie.

ACT II Thésée, granted three wishes by his father, Neptune, has used the first to ask for entry to the underworld to join his friend Pirithoüs, who foolishly tried to abduct Proserpina, wife of Pluton (Pluto, ruler of the underworld). At the gates of hell, Tisiphone, one of the Furies, torments Thésée with terrible visions (duet: *Contente-toi d'une victime).* Pluton is revealed on his throne and reluctantly agrees to Thésée's plea for a fair trial before suffering eternal damnation. Pluton convenes his court (chorus: *Qu'ici l'on répande).* Thésée asks to see Pirithoüs, for whom he has braved the terrors of hell; only by undergoing death, Tisiphone tells him, can he be united with his friend. But the Three Fates declare that only Destiny, not they, can specify the time of Thésée's death. Making no progress in his plea to Pluton, Thésée uses Neptune's second wish, asking to be released from the underworld *(Ah! qu'on daigne du moins).* The powers of hell are unsympathetic, but Neptune has sent an envoy, Mercure (Mercury), to argue that cooperation among the gods is necessary for proper function of the universe: therefore, Pluton should release Thésée, enabling Neptune to keep his word. Pluton gives in, but the Three Fates warn Thésée that he will find another hell back on earth.

ACT III At Thésée's palace by the shore, Phèdre blames the goddess of love for her dilemma *(Cruelle mère des amours),* asking that Hippolyte's heart be softened toward her. Hippolyte enters with condolences for the reported death of Thésée. When Phèdre assures him of her goodwill, he misinterprets this to mean she no longer opposes his marriage to Aricie. Realizing why he has misunderstood, Phèdre flies into a rage (duet: *Ma fureur va tout entreprendre).* Hippolyte with horror sees at last that she is in love with him. When in desperation she asks him to kill her, he refuses, and she is about to do the deed herself when Thésée surprises them as they struggle over a sword. Neither will tell the cause of their strife, and both leave. Oenone, to protect her mistress, shifts the blame to Hippolyte by saying he was trying to make love to his stepmother.

As Thésée recognizes the truth of the Three Fates' prophecy that he would find hell at home, the people gather around him to celebrate his safe return, and he is forced to endure dances and songs offered in his honor (ballet). At length he is able to excuse himself. Alone, using the last of three wishes granted him by Neptune, he calls upon the sea god for vengeance against his son (*Puissant maître des flots*). The ocean boils angrily, signifying that Neptune has heard his plea.

ACT IV   In a wood of Diana near the sea, Hippolyte laments his banishment by his father and the loss of Aricie (*Ah! faut-il, en un jour*). Aricie finds him, and in view of the queen's hatred toward them, the two decide their only choice is to flee together. Hunters appear, and a Huntress urges the lovers to emulate the boldness of the hunt (*Amants, quelle est votre faiblesse!*). There is dancing, but soon a storm blows up and a horrible monster appears from the sea, sent by the reluctant Neptune in response to Thésée's third and last wish. Hippolyte, followed anxiously by Aricie, goes forth to meet it and disappears from sight. Phèdre arrives. As soon as she learns of Hippolyte's apparent death, she blames herself: it was her incestuous love for the youth that caused Thésée to call on Neptune for vengeance (*Non, sa mort est mon seul ouvrage*).

ACT V   At the same spot in the woods, Thésée struggles with his own remorse. Dying, Phèdre has confessed her guilty love for Hippolyte. Thésée sees his own death and return to the underworld as the only way out (*Grands Dieux! de quels remords*). As he is about to throw himself into the sea, Neptune emerges and stops him, saying Hippolyte is not dead but has been saved by Diane's intervention (*Diane a pris soin de son sort*). When Neptune adds that Thésée's punishment is never to see his son again, the king sadly wishes the youth a happier life is some far-off place (*Je ne te verrai plus!*). Aricie, having lost all trace of Hippolyte, finds herself is a magical garden. As she mourns the loss of her lover (*Où suis-je?*), Diane appears with shepherds and shepherd-esses, whom she tells that she has chosen a hero to be their new king (*Peuple toujours soumis*). Aricie is unwilling to be consoled by Diane's offer of a bride-groom, but when she hears his voice, she realizes it is Hippolyte (duet: *Dieux! Qu'entends-je!*). Diane unites the lovers and invites them to a celebration (chorus and ballet: *Chantons sur la musette*): this shall be their kingdom.

LES INDES GALANTES

(The Noble Indies)

OPERA-BALLET IN PROLOGUE AND FOUR ENTRÉES
MUSIC: Jean-Philippe Rameau
TEXT (French): Louis Fuzelier
WORLD PREMIERE: Paris, Opéra, August 23, 1735
U.S. PREMIERE (concert performance): New York, Town Hall,
    March 1, 1961

CHARACTERS

PROLOGUE
Hébé, *goddess of youth* . . . . Soprano
L'Amour, *Cupid.* . . . . Soprano
Bellone, *god of war.* . . . . Baritone

ENTRÉE I
Émilie . . . . Soprano
Valère, *her husband.* . . . . Tenor
Pasha Osman . . . . Bass

ENTRÉE II
Phani, *a Peruvian girl* . . . . Soprano
Don Carlos, *a Spanish officer.* . . . . Tenor
Huascar, *an Inca priest* . . . . Bass

ENTRÉE III
Zaïre, Fatime, *slave girls.* . . . . Sopranos
Tacmas, *a Persian prince* . . . . Tenor
Ali, *his friend.* . . . . Baritone

ENTRÉE IV
Zima, *an American Indian girl* . . . . Soprano
Damon, *a French officer.* . . . . Tenor
Adario, *an Indian brave* . . . . Baritone
Don Alvar, *a Spanish officer* . . . . Bass

The action takes place around the time of composition (1735) but also introduces figures from mythology in the Prologue.

PROLOGUE In the background, the palace of Hébé; to either side, gardens. Hébé, Greek goddess of youth, introduces the performance with a call to love *(Amants, surs de plaire),* summoning young people from four nations (France, Spain, Italy, Poland), who dance. Bellone (Mars), god of war, enters with warriors and martial sounds, drawing the young men to follow him in pursuit of glory *(La Gloire vous appelle),* so that they abandon their sweethearts. Then L'Amour (Cupid) descends from the sky; displeased that war has lured the lovers away *(Pourquoi Mars à l'Amour declara-t-il la Guerre?),* he sends his minions to follow them in foreign lands and restore love to their hearts.

ENTREE I *The Magnanimous Turk.* In the gardens of Pasha Osman, Émilie, a foreigner, to discourage Osman's advances, tells him how she was kidnapped from her wedding by brigands and brought here as a captive *(Apprenez mon destin rigoureux!).* Osman still hopes to win her over by treating her with consideration. Alone, she watches a storm come up. Among prisoners from a shipwreck is Valère, her husband. Their joyful reunion is tempered by the appearance of Osman. Though he speaks of wrath and punishment, however, Osman unites the lovers. He himself was once a slave of Valère, who set him free; now he returns the favor. Émilie and Valère praise their benefactor and welcome their happiness before embarking for home.

ENTREE II *The Incas of Peru.* In a desert setting, Carlos, a Spanish officer, urges Phani, a native girl, to accept his love. She explains that she willingly would marry him but fears what her people might do: only if he brings help to abduct her can she feel safe. When he leaves, Huascar, an Inca priest, comes to tell Phani of his own love for her *(Obéissons sans balancer).* When she fails to respond, he accuses her of loving one of the Spanish conquerors. Other Incas arrive to celebrate the Festival of the Sun, with Huascar leading the ceremony *(Brillant soleil).* As the natives sing and dance, an earthquake alarms them, and a distant volcano starts to erupt, darkening the sky with its smoke. Huascar tells Phani this is an omen: the gods want her to marry him. He is trying to frighten her into fleeing with him when Carlos appears. After explaining that Huascar caused the eruption himself by throwing a rock into the crater, Carlos takes Phani to safety while Huascar invites the rage of the gods on his own head *(La flamme se ralume).* He dies in an avalanche of flaming rocks.

ENTREE III *The Flowers—Persian Festival.* In the gardens of Ali's palace, Tacmas, a Persian prince, enters in disguise as a merchant woman, greeted by his friend Ali. Tacmas confesses his love for Zaïre, Ali's slave *(L'objet a qui je rends les armes),* while Ali feels similarly drawn to Fatime, Tacmas' slave. As the disguised Tacmas listens, Zaïre sings of her own (unidentified) love; to find out who that might be, Tacmas steps forward and questions the girl solicitously. He even shows her a portrait of himself (sans disguise) but cannot make out her strong reaction to it. As Zaïre leaves, Fatime enters, disguised as a Polish slave, so he questions her too. She likewise speaks of an unnamed love *(Dans ces jar-*

dins). When Ali leads Zaïre back into the garden, she confesses her love for Tacmas, who has removed his disguise *(Deviez-vous vous méprendre),* adding that she is of royal blood. Tacmas gives his slave Fatime to Ali (quartet: *Tendre amour).* The Festival of Flowers is announced, leading into a ballet that shows the life and fate of various flowers in a garden, ending with a general gavotte.

ENTRÉE IV *The Savages.* In an American forest bordering on the French and Spanish colonies, a warrior commander, Adario, welcomes peace with the invaders but worries that his beloved Zima might respond to the courtship of two rivals, Damon (a French officer) and Don Alvar (a Spanish officer). Concealing himself, he listens to their conversation as they prepare to meet Zima. She arrives, telling them nature encourages love in these unspoiled surroundings *(Nous suivons sur les bords);* but nature also urges lovers to be truthful, and in truth she does not love either of them. Damon presses his case *(La terre, les cieux et les mers),* adding that inconstancy is no crime. Zima replies that lovers are free in her society—but not after marriage. Damon and Alvar accuse each other of being bad prospective husbands: the Frenchman too philandering, the Spaniard too jealous and possessive. Zima explains that Alvar loves too much, Damon not enough. When Adario springs from hiding, Zima praises him as the man of her choice, in preference to these too civilized Europeans, who leave the scene, distraught. Adario thanks Zima for her constancy *(Je ne vous peindrai point),* and they pledge their troth as the peace celebration is prepared. Tribesmen join them in praising the joys and values of the "noble savage," with dancing that depicts a peacepipe ceremony and a joining of warrior men and women, culminating in a final chaconne.

CASTOR ET POLLUX

PROLOGUE AND FIVE ACTS
MUSIC: Jean-Philippe Rameau
TEXT (French): Pierre-Joseph Justin Bernard
WORLD PREMIERE: Paris, Opéra, October 24, 1737
U.S. PREMIERE (concert performance): Poughkeepsie, N.Y., Vassar
  College, March 6, 1937

CHARACTERS

Minerve, *the goddess Minerva (Athena)* . . . . .Soprano
Vénus, *goddess of love* . . . . .Soprano

Phébé, *a Spartan princess*. Soprano
Télaïre, *daughter of the Sun* . . . . Soprano
L'Amour, *Cupid, son of Venus* . . . . Countertenor or Soprano
Castor, *son of Tyndarus and Leda* . . . . .Countertenor
High Priest of Jupiter. . . . . Tenor
Jupiter, *chief of the gods* . . . . Baritone
Mars, *god of war* . . . . Baritone
Pollux, *son of Jupiter and Leda* . . . . Bass
Hébé, *Jupiter's daughter, goddess of youth* . . . . Dancer

As in Richard Strauss' *Ariadne auf Naxos,* this mythological tale explains the origin of a heavenly constellation—in the present case, Gemini (The Twins) or Dioscuri. Castor and Pollux, though eventually twin stars, were not actually twins but half brothers, sons of Leda. Castor's father was Tyndarus. Of the two, only Pollux, fathered by Jupiter (Zeus) in the form of a swan, was born with divine status.

PROLOGUE   In an allegory on the Peace of Vienna, which in 1736 concluded the War of the Polish Succession, Mars, the god of war, is subdued by Vénus, Minerve, and L'Amour (Cupid, Venus' son). Mars, having accomplished his purpose, pays tribute to Vénus *(Je vous revois, belle Déesse)* amid scenes of dancing.

ACT I   Sparta, mythical antiquity. A monument has been set up for the funeral of Castor, King of Sparta. In a dialogue between Castor's beloved, Télaïre, and the Spartan princess Phébé, who loves Pollux, it appears that Pollux wants to avenge his brother's death, but Télaïre feels he should not risk his own life. Left alone, she renounces the light represented by her father, the sun (Apollo), and wishes to join Castor in the realm of death *(Tristes apprêts).* Pollux arrives with athletes and warriors bearing the body of Castor's slayer, Lincée (Linceus), a rival suitor, whom they have killed in revenge. Presenting the body to Télaïre, Pollux reveals his own love for her. Having been so close to his late brother, he feels he has inherited Castor's emotions. Tactfully, she deflects his attentions by asking him to intercede with his father, Jupiter, to restore Castor to life *(Allez, Prince, à ses pieds osez vous faire entendre).* Pollux, torn by the conflict of his devotion to both Castor and Télaïre, realizes he can be true to both only by doing as she asks.

ACT II   At the temple of Jupiter, preparations have been made for a sacrifice. Pollux, praying, places his destiny in Jupiter's hands *(Nature, Amour, qui partagez mon coeur).* Télaïre joins him, saying her own destiny is to love Castor. Pollux wonders why he could not have died instead of his brother, since each is now condemned to separation from the woman he loves. The High Priest announces that Jupiter will make his will known *(Le souverain des Dieux),* whereupon the god appears, seated on his throne. Pollux begs him to restore

Castor to the world of the living. Jupiter, though sympathetic, says he must respect the laws of the underworld, ruled by his brother Pluto. Pollux offers to face Pluto himself, but Jupiter reveals that in entering the underworld Pollux would be required to take Castor's place in order to free him. Pollux resolves to make this sacrifice. Jupiter, hoping to dissuade him, calls forth Celestial Pleasures—led by his daughter Hébé, goddess of youth—to show instead the allure of Olympian eternal life in heaven. Resolutely, Pollux rejects their entreaties.

ACT III   At the entrance to the underworld, Phébé urges a group of Spartans to prevent their new king, Pollux, from entering. When Pollux appears, she pleads with him to be moved by her own love; but when he remains adamant, she decides to follow him. They are joined by Télaïre, who on the advice of her father's Oracle urges Pollux to persevere *(Aux pieds de ses autels)*. He confesses to the distressed Phébé that it is Télaïre he loves (trio: *Je ne verrai plus ce que j'aime)*. Phébé now places her trust in the underworld's demons to prevent Pollux's passage (chorus: *Brisons tous nos fers*), but he fights them off, and Mercure (Mercury) appears, conducting him into the abyss. Télaïre retreats, leaving Phébé to bemoan her inability to follow Pollux *(Tout cède à ce héros vainqueur!)*.

ACT IV   In the Elysian Fields, Castor takes no joy in the peaceful beauty surrounding him: his thoughts are only of Télaïre *(Séjour de l'eternelle paix)*. Happy Spirits dance for him in vain. His first pleasure comes from seeing Pollux arrive (duet: *Mais, qui s'offre à mes yeux?)* with news that Castor's death has been avenged and he has been elevated to divinity, sparing his life. His happiness is spoiled, however, when he learns that Pollux will remain in the Elysian Fields in his place. Pollux further confesses his own love for Télaïre but assures Castor he has renounced it to come there. Castor, unwilling to see his return to life bought at such a price, decides to go back for only a single day, see Télaïre once more, and then yield his earthly place to Pollux. Mercure reappears to lead Castor away.

ACT V   In the environs of Sparta, Phébé seethes with jealousy at the sight of Télaïre and Castor reunited *(Castor revoit le jour)*. The lovers themselves, however, are not happy for long, as Castor tells Télaïre they now must bid each other farewell forever. He sends away a group of Spartans who come to celebrate the couple's wedding. Castor's noble motives are mistaken by Télaïre for lack of love (duet: *Eh quoi! tous ces objets ne peuvent t'attendrir?)*. Castor fears that the gods will punish him if he is irresolute, and for a moment, rumblings of thunder seem to bear him out. But when Jupiter descends, borne by an eagle, it is to announce that the gods have decided to release Castor from his vow: he need not return to the nether world, and Pollux too will be set free. In fact, the brothers will share immortality. Pollux appears, saying he has conquered his love for Télaïre *(Pour vaincre mon amour)*; he has seen Phébé, however, lost to the underworld. The gods are revealed on Olympus, and Jupiter calls upon Apollo to light the universe and shine with glory on the newly inducted immortals *(Tant de vertus doivent prétendre)*. Télaïre too is invited to remain among the gods. Heavenly spheres descend and dance, while Castor and Pollux are assigned their place in the heavens as the Gemini constellation, protectors of seafarers.

Nikolai Rimsky-Korsakov
1844–1908

Though born in the area of Novgorod, Rimsky-Korsakov spent most of his life in St. Petersburg and is closely associated with the musical life of that cosmopolitan city. Of his more than a dozen operas, few have been performed outside Russia with any frequency, but three factors have lowered the barriers to their unfamiliarity: visits abroad by the Bolshoi and Kirov companies, the great expansion of recorded repertory during the CD era, and the fall of the Iron Curtain.

During Rimsky-Korsakov's formative years, nationalism was taking hold in Russian music, spurred by the example of Glinka. The more chauvinistic the declared ideals of the nationalists, the greater their conflict with the standards of the academic community, allied to foreign, European models. Since Rimsky himself, from 1871 onward, was a professor at the St. Petersburg Conservatory, he became the victim of a cultural split personality; but its very tensions sparked his creative imagination. He was able to put his theoretical skills and technical professionalism to the service of his fondness for folkloric and fantastic subjects. As a master of orchestration, Rimsky has had few peers, and the textbook he wrote on the subject is still widely used.

The three operas dealt with here demonstrate different facets of his artistic personality. In *Sadko,* as in his perennially popular tone poem *Sheherazade,* he indulges a fondness for yarn spinning. By writing different kinds of music for the "real" people and for the fantastic characters, he was able to create separate worlds for them and, when necessary, to bring the two worlds into contact.

The Czar's Bride represents Rimsky's flirtation with the more traditional, European sort of opera, its score divided into conventional set pieces, though subject and coloration remain highly Russian, notably in the striking unaccompanied solo for mezzo-soprano. Oddly enough, this opera's cosmopolitan format acted as a barrier to its acceptance in the West, where Rimsky was expected to maintain a more folkloristic façade. Finally, in *The Legend of the Invisible City of Kitezh,* the composer shows his inclination toward pantheistic mysticism.

Rimsky was not a religious believer, but he allowed himself to be carried away by the Kitezh legend. Where in many a romantic opera of the mid-nineteenth century the unlucky hero and heroine promise to meet again in heaven, Rimsky goes one step farther by actually placing them there: this work ends in the "better world" so often seen only in the imagination of the principals. Like most of his other operas, *Kitezh* displays his gift for pageantry, but it also shows uncommon delicacy in portraying its heroine, the Maiden Fevronia.

The most famous of Rimsky's pupils, Igor Stravinsky, sometimes spoke patronizingly of his teacher (as he did of most other composers), meanwhile borrowing copiously from Rimsky's armament of instrumental effects and colors. In his own way, Stravinsky carried forward Rimsky's legacy, though he did so primarily in ballet, which superseded opera in popularity during the years when Stravinsky wrote most of his work.

In the latter twentieth century, with international recognition widening at last, Rimsky's operas have begun to open a large, varied new area of the world repertory.

SADKO

SEVEN SCENES
MUSIC: Nikolai Rimsky-Korsakov
TEXT (Russian): the composer and Vladimir Ivanovich Belsky
WORLD PREMIERE: Moscow, Solodovnikov Theater, January 7, 1898
U.S. PREMIERE: New York, Metropolitan Opera, January 25, 1930
    (in French)

CHARACTERS

Volkhova, *daughter of the Sea King* . . . . Soprano
Lyubava, *Sadko's wife.* . . . . .Mezzo-Soprano

Nezhata, *a minstrel from Kiev* . . . . .Mezzo-Soprano
Sadko, *a minstrel of Novgorod* . . . . Tenor
A Hindu Merchant . . . . Tenor
A Venetian Merchant . . . . Baritone
The Sea King. . . . . Bass
A Viking Merchant . . . . Bass

Though its name means "New City," Novgorod is actually one of the oldest Russian cities. Rurik, father of the first Russian ruling dynasty, is said to have founded the Russian state there in the year 862. *Sadko* takes place in a time of fanciful tales—which, judging from the emphasis on ships and trade, would seem to have been the Middle Ages. The prosperous Novgorod depicted by Rimsky-Korsakov, with its thriving guilds, is not unlike the mid-sixteenth-century Nuremberg of *Die Meistersinger* and might be roughly contemporaneous with it.

TABLEAU I   At a banquet, merchants of Novgorod sing the praises of their guild and their city (*Sobralis'a my, gosti torgovye*). At their behest, the minstrel Nezhata renders a ballad about the heroic Volkh Vseslavevich from Kiev, who made himself czar of India (*Prosvet'a svetel mesiats na nebe*). The merchants want to hear something about Novgorod, so another minstrel, Sadko, presents himself and sings of expanding Novgorod's overseas trade to bring great wealth (*Kaby byla u menia kazna*). Reaction is mixed, but most dismiss Sadko as a braggart. Unfazed by their threats, he leaves them to their old ways, vowing to sing instead to the waters of Lake Ilmen. After he has left, two other minstrels, Duda and Sopel, take over the entertainment, making fun of Sadko, suggesting he should make his fortune by angling for golden fish.

TABLEAU II   On a bright summer night by the shore of Lake Ilmen, as Sadko salutes the beauty of the solitary spot (*Oy ty, tëmnaia dubravushka!*), white swans swim up and turn into maidens: the Sea Princess Volkhova, with her sisters and playmates. Taken with Sadko and his serenade, Volkhova sits down with him on the bank (duet: *Svetiat rosoiu medv'ianaiu kosy tvoi*). She says she is the daughter of the Sea King but will marry a mortal—Sadko. Though already married, Sadko is prepared to leave terrestrial life behind and follow Volkhova, who has enchanted him. She tells him they cannot be united yet, but she eventually will be able to join him (*Prosti, moi milyi, skoro utro*) and meanwhile will provide gold-finned fishes in the lake, from which he can become rich. At the approach of dawn, the Sea King rises from the waters and calls his daughters back into the depths.

TABLEAU III   At Sadko's house, his wife Lyubava waits sadly for his return, afraid that his wanderlust has conquered the love he once had for her (*Vsiu noch' zhdala ego ia ponaprasnu*). When he comes home, Sadko is still filled with wonder at the memory of his adventure with the sea princess. Paying scant attention to his wife, he declares he will go the merchants' pier and lay a wager that there are gold-finned fishes in Lake Ilmen. Though she worries for his sanity and safety, he takes off.

TABLEAU IV   At the pier by Lake Ilmen on Holy Cross Day, merchants and foreign tradesmen mill about, admiring the display of merchandise and calling for entertainment from the minstrels Duda and Sopel, who lead a chorus of praise for the hops from which ale is made *(Oi, Dunai!)*. At length Sadko joins the crowd and declares that he knows of a marvel: there are gold-finned fish in Lake Ilmen *(Poklon vam, gosti imenitye!)*. Greeted with general disbelief, he bets his head against all the merchants' goods. Some of the men, Sadko among them, take to boats to test his claim. Sadko hears the voice of the sea princess promising him three gold-finned fish, which appear in the net. Sadko has won his bet and become the richest merchant in Novgorod. Nezhata improvises a song about this amazing achievement *(Kak na ozere na Ilmene)*. Sadko, rich enough from the golden fish, tells the merchants to keep their wares and calls on the foreign traders to sing of their lands.

The Viking Merchant sings of the stern fjords and courageous warriors of his homeland *(A skaly groznie drobiatsia s rëvom volny)*, the Indian Merchant of his country's gems and the Phoenix, a bird with a maiden's face and exquisite voice *(Ni shest' almazof)*. Then the Venetian Merchant sings the praises of the Queen of the Sea, glorious Venice *(Gorod kammenyi, gorod vsem mat')*. Moved to do some exploring of foreign lands, Sadko prepares to set out on a voyage of discovery, asking the people to look after his neglected wife *(Den' ko vecheru vecheriaetsia)*. At this she appears, bewailing his departure, but he sails off into the setting sun.

TABLEAU V   At sea, Sadko's ship alone is becalmed as others of the fleet keep on sailing. He declares that tribute must be paid to the Sea King *(Goi, vy korabel'shiki)*, whereupon his Bodyguard and sailors throw some treasure overboard. Then he tells them they must each write his name on a piece of wood and throw it in the sea. But he knows what is really required: his own appearance before the Sea King. So he bids his crew put him on a raft and sail back to Novgorod without him *(Goi, druzhina vernaia)*. As soon as this is done, the sails fill with wind and the ship leaves Sadko to be welcomed by Volkhova, the sea princess, who has waited to be reunited with him. He sinks into the waters.

TABLEAU VI   In the depths, Sadko is welcomed to the palace of the Sea King and Queen. He sings in their honor *(Sinee more grozno)*, praising their power and the beauty of their kingdom. Giving Sadko his daughter, the Sea King orders a wedding prepared *(Goi, vy somy usachi)*, with all sea creatures in attendance. Gold and silver fish dance; then Sadko plays his lyre to accompany a general dance, which, as it grows more frenzied, stirs up a sea storm, causing ships to sink. Suddenly an Apparition—an ancient warrior, disguised as a pilgrim—breaks Sadko's lyre and stops the dance, declaring that the Sea King has overstepped his power and must relinquish it *(Ay, ne v poru raspliasalsia)*.

His kingdom will sink, while Sadko must return to Novgorod and his new bride become a river to serve the city. The newlyweds rise toward the surface.

TABLEAU VII   Back on the shore of Lake Ilmen, Volkhova sings a lullaby to the sleeping Sadko *(Son po bereshku khodil)*. She is to be transformed into a river and, in that form, will stay near him forever. As she vanishes in a mist, the voice of Sadko's earthly wife, Lyubava, is heard, still mourning his loss. He wakes to the sound and calls her; they are happily reunited (duet: *A i zdravastvui zhe ty*). The newly formed River Volkhov appears from the mist, flowing into Lake Ilmen and lighted by the rising sun. Ships sail along the river, including Sadko's flagship: the sacrifice of the Sea King's daughter has given Novgorod new access to the ocean. Merchants and townspeople gather to welcome Sadko and the river. Amid general celebration, he tells the story of his travels (omitting mention of his bigamous marriage) and how the River Volkhov came to be given to Novgorod (finale, Sadko: *V staranakh gulial ia dal'nikh*). Bells of the city ring out as the people praise the mighty waters (chorus: *Moriu sinemu slava!*).

THE CZAR'S BRIDE

(Tsarskaya Nyevyesta)

FOUR ACTS
MUSIC: Nikolai Rimsky-Korsakov
TEXT (Russian): Ilya Fyodorovich Tyumenev, based on a scenario by the composer, after Lev Alexandrovich Mey's play
WORLD PREMIERE: Moscow, Solodovnikov Theater, November 3, 1899
U.S. PREMIERE: Seattle, January 6, 1922

CHARACTERS

Marfa, *Sobakin's daughter* . . . . Soprano
Domna Ivanovna Saburova, *a merchant's wife* . . . . Soprano
Lyubasha . . . . .Mezzo-Soprano
Dunyasha, *Domna Ivanovna's daughter, Marfa's friend* . . . . Alto
Ivan Sergeievich Lykov, *nobleman* . . . . Tenor
Yelisei Bomelius, *the czar's physician* . . . . Tenor
Grigori Grigorievich Gryaznoi, *a nobleman* . . . . Baritone

Vasily Stepanovich Sobakin, *Novgorod merchant* . . . . Bass
Grigory Lukianovich Malyuta Skuratov, *an old soldier* . . . . . . Bass

The story is based on events in the fall of 1571, when Ivan the Terrible, for two years a widower, chose as his new bride Marfa, daughter of the merchant Sobakin from Novgorod. Though the wedding took place on October 28, Marfa, evidently poisoned, died two weeks later. The principal characters of Lev Mey's drama were actual persons, but the playwright fictionalized their story.

ACT I   Waiting for dinner guests at his mansion, the nobleman Grigori Gryaznoi broods on his infatuation with Marfa, who is engaged to her child-hood sweetheart, Ivan Lykov. Gryaznoi, now that his libertine days as an Oprichnik (member of the czar's personal guard) are over, feels true love and is determined to marry the girl himself *(S uma ne idët krasavitsa!)*. His fellow Oprichniks arrive, headed by Malyuta Skuratov, an old soldier in favor with the czar, along with Lykov and a Dutch alchemist, Yelisei Bomelius, the czar's physician. The Oprichniks welcome Gryaznoi's hospitality *(My laskoi budem sity)*, and Lykov describes his recent travels abroad *(Inoe vsë, i liudi, i zemlia)*. Singers and dancers come in to entertain the guests, starting with a hymn of praise to the czar *(Slava na nebe solntsu vysokomu)*, moving on to a song in praise of wine and beer *(Kak za rechen'koi iar xmel)*. Gryaznoi's mistress, Lyubasha, enters and sings a sad unaccompanied ballad about a girl who will die rather than go through with a forced marriage to an old man *(Snariazhai skorei, matushka rodimoya)*. As the guests leave, Lyubasha overhears Gryaznoi speaking in confidence to Bomelius, asking for a love potion (trio: *Akh, ne veritsia*). After Bomelius leaves, she asks Gryaznoi whether he is tired of her (duet: *Znat'ne liubish' bol'she*), then accuses him of loving someone else. Looking for an excuse to leave, he hears a bell calling him to morning prayers. Alone, Lyubasha swears to find out who has stolen his heart *(Postoi! Kuda ty?)*.

ACT II   Autumn on a street in Alexandrovskaya village, near the houses of Bomelius and the Sobakin family. A crowd, enjoying the mild weather *(Vot Bog privël vecherenku otslushat')*, turns quiet when a troop of Oprichniks approaches the house of a supposed traitor, Prince Gvozdev-Rostovsky, and goes inside. Resuming their gossip, the townspeople discuss the czar's search for a new bride, then tell two young men who have visited Bomelius not to trust his devilish potions.

Marfa enters from the convent with her friend Dunyasha and her family's housekeeper, Petrovna. Marfa tells of her happiness with Lykov, her fiancé *(V Novgorode ne riadam)*, but her reverie is interrupted by the appearance of two mysterious horsemen—one of them the czar, whom she doesn't recognize, who looks at her intently before riding away. Lykov and Marfa's father appear, looking forward to the wedding (quartet: *Pogodi, moia milaia*). They go into the house. After an interlude, Lyubasha, disguised under a veil, arrives and looks in the window: she has discovered her rival *(Razvedala! Tak vot gnezdo golubki?)*. She knocks on Bomelius' door and asks him if can give her a potion to cause a woman's beauty to wither. He says yes; it is dangerous and expensive, but in exchange for Lyubasha's favors, he would part with it. Her disgusted reaction causes him to try blackmail: tomorrow he will tell Gryaznoi of her request. Only the sound of a girl's laughter from the Sobakin house persuades her to give in to the loathsome bargain. While Bomelius is in his house brewing the potion, she assesses her rival *(Vot do chevo ia dozhila)*, then hears Lybov and Sobakin talk about Gryaznoi's coming to visit the next day. Bomelius returns and takes Lyubasha inside. The Oprichniks leave next door, their brutal mission accomplished.

ACT III   The next day at Sobakin's house, Gryaznoi has arrived and is talking with Lykov and the host. Lykov expresses his impatience to marry Marfa, but Sobakin says the wedding has to be delayed until Czar Ivan has conducted his inspection of eligible girls. Aside, Gryaznoi hopes the potion he ordered from Bomelius will work on Marfa (trio: *Mne bez neë prozhit' nedolgo*). While Sobakin steps out to fetch drinks, Gryaznoi admits to Lykov that he too felt attracted to Marfa, but he pretends to be content to serve as best man at their wedding *(Chto sdelal by?)*. Sobakin returns, followed shortly by Domna Saburova, another merchant's wife, the mother of Marfa's friend Dunyasha. She relates how the girls fared at their audience with the czar, who seemed to like them; then she leaves. Lykov sits apart, hoping Dunyasha will be the czar's choice *(Neuzheli Duniasha?)*. He proposes a drink, at which Gryaznoi slips powder into one of the glasses, preparing it for Marfa, who arrives with Dunyasha, Domna, and some servant girls. A traditional toast is drunk to Marfa and Lykov's engagement (ensemble: *Nu, detki, dai vam Bog i doli*). Malyuta Skuratov enters with some boyars and announces that the czar has chosen Marfa *(Vasilii! Nash velikii gosudar')*. As Sobakin kneels and bows to the ground, the others react in stunned silence.

ACT IV   At the czar's palace, Sobakin reflects that while honor and good fortune have come to him, he cannot enjoy them, because of his daughter's unhappiness. Domna comes from an adjoining room, where Marfa is resting, suddenly strangely ill. When Gryaznoi arrives with news, Marfa, looking pale, rushes in to hear it: Lykov supposedly confessed to having drugged her, for which he was condemned, and Gryaznoi himself executed him. Marfa faints, and the others voice concern for her (ensemble: *Zagublena stradalitsa tsarevna!*). Sobakin cannot believe Lykov was guilty—he must have confessed under torture—but who is the real culprit? When Marfa revives, she hallucinates that Lykov is with her. Gryaznoi, consumed by guilt, blurts out that he accused Lykov falsely, adding that he himself loved Marfa to the point of madness and gave her a potion *(Da, bezumny)*. The others are horrified, not only by this but by Marfa's illusions of being reunited with Lykov *(Ivan Sergeich, khochesh' v sad poidëm?)*. Lyubasha pushes her way in and confronts Gryaznoi, telling him she too got a powder from Bomelius—a death potion—and substituted it for the love potion that Gryaznoi meant for Marfa. She goads him into stabbing her and falls dead. Gryaznoi, before being led away, implores forgiveness from Marfa, but she is in her own world, succumbing to the slow poison and calling out for Lykov to "Come back tomorrow, Vanya!"

THE LEGEND OF THE INVISIBLE CITY OF KITEZH AND THE MAIDEN FEVRONIA

(Skazaniye o Nevidimom Grade Kitezhe i Dyevye Fevronii)

THREE ACTS

MUSIC: Nikolai Rimsky-Korsakov

TEXT (Russian): Vladimir Ivanovich Belsky

WORLD PREMIERE: St. Petersburg, Maryinsky Theater, February 20, 1907

U.S. PREMIERE (concert performance): Ann Arbor, University of Michigan, May 21, 1932

U.S. STAGE PREMIERE: Philadelphia, Academy of Music, February 4, 1936

CHARACTERS

The Maiden Fevronia . . . . Soprano
Alkanost, Sirin, *birds of Paradise* . . . . Sopranos
A Boy, *Prince Yuri's page*. . . . . .Mezzo-Soprano
Prince Vsevolod Yuryevich, *son of Prince Yuri* . . . . Tenor
Grishka Kuterma, *a peasant drunkard* . . . . Tenor
Fyodor Poyarok, *Vsevolod's best man* . . . . Baritone
Prince Yuri Vsevolodovich, *ruler of Kitezh* . . . . Bass
Burundai, Bedyai, *Tatar warriors* . . . . Basses

ACT I   Legendary medieval Russia, around the time of the Mongol invasion, A.D. 1223. In the "forests beyond the Volga," the Maiden Fevronia—a child of nature, who lives there with her younger brother— gathers herbs and grasses to hang in the sun. Thankfully she praises the woods for having brought her up and sustained her in a loving environment *(Akh, ty les, moi les)*. She is able to communicate with the birds and animals, but they flee at the approach of a stranger, a young man who gazes admiringly at Fevronia. After a moment of shyness she offers him refreshment and tends a wound he has sustained in an encounter with a bear. When he asks if she goes to church, she replies that the church is too far away, but that nature itself is a place of worship. Enchanted by the girl, he declares his love and gives her a ring; she admits to similar feelings (duet: *Nenagliadnyi moi, bogom suzhenyi!*). When a hunting party is heard approaching, he realizes he must rejoin his companions. Promising to come back, he bids her adieu. Shortly after, his friend Fyodor Poyarok appears, looking for him, and reveals to Fevronia that the young man is Prince Vsevolod, son of Prince Yuri, ruler of the city of Kitezh.

§ In Little Kitezh, a town on the left bank of the Volga, merchants' stalls are set up in the main square. A bear trainer and an old minstrel entertain the crowd. A shabby, drunken peasant, Grishka Kuterma, is thrown out of the tavern and begs some money from a group of nobles *(Nam-to chto? My ved' liudi guliashchie)*. Carriages appear, bringing the wedding party of Vsevolod and Fevronia. Grishka insolently greets Fevronia as a commoner like himself. When others try to lead him away, Fevronia stops them and shows kindness to him, but he repays her with further sarcasm, warning that the future may bring her sorrow *(Vsemu miru nizko klaniaius')*. Suddenly more peasants run in, reporting that Tatar invaders have fallen upon the town and are laying it waste, setting fires and committing atrocities (chorus: *Oi, beda idët, liudi*). Tatar soldiers enter the square; their leaders, Bedyai and Burundai, decide to hold Fevronia prisoner. When Grishka is seized, they promise to spare him if he will show the way to the citadel of Great Kitezh, which they want to plunder. Threatened with torture, he agrees. Fevronia prays intently for Great Kitezh to be made invisible.

ACT II Before the cathedral in Great Kitezh, Prince Yuri and Vsevolod are greeted by Fyodor Poyarok, who has been blinded by the invaders. Prince Yuri bemoans the fate that seems about to befall their city. To the top of the bell tower he sends a Youth, who reports seeing clouds of dust and galloping horses on every side. Yuri leads the people in prayer (chorus: *Chudnaia nebesnaia tasritsa*). Vsevolod prepares to lead the young men of the city to battle the enemy (soldiers: *Podnialasia s polunochi*). As they march away, a golden mist descends to shroud the city from sight, and the bells of all the churches start ringing spontaneously. (Orchestral interlude: Battle of Kerzhenets.)

§ In a forest bordering Lake Svetly Yar, Bedyai and Burundai make their way to the shore, following Grishka's directions, but they can see only fog on the opposite bank, where Great Kitezh is supposed to stand. The Tatars pitch camp for the night, abusing Grishka because he misled them. After drinking wine (chorus: *Ne vorony*), the soldiers leave or settle down to sleep. When Bedyai and Burundai fall to arguing as to which will get Fevronia as his share of the booty, Burundai kills Bedyai with an ax. Then he drowsily, drunkenly tries to console the girl, but she draws away, lamenting the loss of Vsevolod, who has been mortally wounded (*Akh, ty milyi zhenikh moi*). She hears Grishka calling softly, begging her not to forsake him, in spite of his unforgivable sin in betraying Kitezh to the Tatars. She takes a knife from the sleeping Burundai and sets Grishka free. He heads recklessly toward the lake, where, by dawn's first light, he sees not the city of Kitezh but only its reflection on the water. His cries rouse the Tatars, who at first are jubilant but then, suspecting the apparition to be a result of sorcery by evil demons, take fright and flee.

ACT III   At night, Fevronia wanders through a deep forest, followed by Grishka. Once more he taunts her for having the presumption to marry a prince (*Vozgordilas' ty*), but soon he breaks down in guilty sobbing and begs her to help him pray. After attempting this, he starts to hallucinate about being pursued by devils and runs wildly away.

Unable to call him back, she lies down to rest and gradually becomes aware of flowers opening around her (*Posmotriu ia: chto zdes' tsvetikov*): spring appears to have returned. Sirin and Alkonost, Birds of Paradise, announce her death and afterlife. The spirit of Vsevolod approaches, and they greet each other in solemn happiness (duet: *My s toboiu ne rasstanemsia*). It is time at last to go to their wedding ceremony.

§ As the clouds disperse, Kitezh appears, miraculously transformed into a heavenly city. Among the white-clad crowd that gathers, Poyarok is seen, then Prince Yuri. Fevronia entreats the people to accept her, despite her humble origins, as Vsevolod's bride (*Klanaius' vam, pravednye liudi*). When she asks how Grishka can be brought there, Yuri tells her Grishka is not yet spiritually ready, so she sends him a reassuring letter, written down by Poyarok: "Do not count us with the dead: we still live . . . in a golden place" (*V mërtvykh ne vmenia ty nas*). As the Youth departs to find Grishka on earth and give him the letter, Fevronia and Vsevolod enter the cathedral (chorus: *Zdes' ni placha, ni bolezni*).

GIOACHINO ROSSINI
1792–1868

For the first half of his life, Rossini was the most famous opera composer in the world. He then stopped writing operas and became a
sort of musical elder statesman. Among his reasons, he had worked
himself to exhaustion meeting public demand during his youth and
felt he had earned a rest. Further, he developed health problems, including a
terrible ringing in his ears. Last but not least, he saw fashions changing and
felt neither the need, the desire, nor the ability to keep up with them.

The age of so-called grand opera had begun, and Rossini himself had helped
inaugurate it with three of his large-scale works for the Paris stage. Two of
these—*Le Siège de Corinthe* and *Moïse et Pharaon*—were reworkings of scores he
originally had composed to Italian texts for Naples, *Maometto II* and *Mosè in
Egitto.* The third, *Guillaume Tell,* became the prototypical French grand
opera—broad and expansive, with highly developed choral episodes and awesome stage pictures. In keeping with the new fashion, there was less ornate
vocal writing and more opportunity for bigger-sounding voices. The Paris
Opéra was a large theater, and its orchestra far exceeded the pit bands of
Rossini's youth. He handled all these resources in masterly fashion, but he did
not particularly like them. He devoted the rest of his life to enjoying good
food, encouraging younger musicians, and presiding over musicales at his
home. In artistic circles, he remained one of the most popular characters and
sought-after hosts of his time.

"Mozart was the inspiration of my youth, the despair of my maturity and
the consolation of my old age," Rossini declared. His training and his models
were classical. As a student he wrote an opera seria, *Demetrio e Polibio,* and

several times later he returned to this chaste form, with its obligatory happy ending. What really made his fame was his incomparably light, witty touch with comic subjects. But after his death, with virtuoso bel canto singing of the old school in eclipse (Rossini himself had been trained as a singer in boyhood), his only regularly performed work was *Il Barbiere di Siviglia.* For the better part of a century it was mostly forgotten that he had written other comedies, and his serious operas disappeared altogether.

In fact, however, Rossini was a highly accomplished composer of serious dramas. In Naples in 1815 he met the prima donna Isabella Colbran, whom he married, and whose art influenced a number of ambitious serious works written during his remaining years in Italy. These included *Mosè in Egitto, La Donna del Lago, Maometto II,* and *Semiramide,* the *Aida* of its day. Rossini's generous use of the chorus in these operas prepared him for the transition to France, where such treatment was expected. He continued to write an occasional comedy, such as the "semi-serious" *La Gazza Ladra,* and after arriving on the Parisian scene he wrote two more, *Il Viaggio a Reims* (to an Italian text, for the Théâtre Italien, where that language was still sung) and *Le Comte Ory,* for which he pirated music from *Il Viaggio a Reims.* His remaining efforts went into building up the grand-opera form that put him out of business.

The Rossini revival since the 1950s owes much of its impetus to scholarship: his scores are now studied with the same care as those of Verdi and Wagner, and there is a Rossini Foundation in his native town of Pesaro. But musicology alone cannot bring scores to life, and for this there have been such technically accomplished singers as Maria Callas, Joan Sutherland, Renata Scotto, and Marilyn Horne. Male singers have caught up in their mastery of bel canto, and Rossini's name also has been associated with those of Samuel Ramey, Rockwell Blake, Chris Merritt, Ernesto Palacio, and Raúl Giménez. He would have felt at home with them, and might even have taken up his pen once more.

TANCREDI

TWO ACTS
MUSIC: Gioachino Rossini
TEXT (Italian): Gaetano Rossi and Luigi Lechi, based on Voltaire's
 Tancrède and Tasso's *Gerusalemme Liberata*

WORLD PREMIERE: Venice, La Fenice, February 6, 1813
U.S. PREMIERE: New York, Park Theater, December 31, 1825

CHARACTERS

Amenaide, *Argirio's daughter* . . . . Soprano
Isaura, *a noblewoman, Amenaide's confidante* . . . . Soprano
Tancredi, *an exiled Syracusan knight* . . . . .Mezzo-Soprano
Roggiero, *Tancredi's squire.* . . . . .Mezzo-Soprano
Argirio, *ruler of Syracuse* . . . . Tenor
Orbazzano, *a Syracusan nobleman* . . . . Bass

Though originally composed with a happy ending appropriate to an opera seria, *Tancredi* is customarily performed with the tragic ending Rossini originally intended, which he substituted in a Ferrara production several months after the premiere.

ACT I Syracuse, Sicily, A.D. 1005. A feud between Argirio and Orbazzano has been resolved. In Argirio's castle, he leads the knights and populace in hailing the return of peace (ensemble: *Se amistà verace*). It is now possible to present a united front against the invading Moors; Argirio announces that Orbazzano will lead the defenders. Orbazzano, warning against treasonous dealings with the foe, also fears that the exiled knight Tancredi may bear a grudge against his home city.

Accompanied by a female entourage, Argirio's daughter Amenaide appears, thanking them for their greetings and privately worrying about her love for Tancredi, which she dares not reveal *(Come dolce all'alma mia)*. Orbazzano joins her, saying her father has given him her hand in marriage. Though she cannot openly disobey, Amenaide tries to delay the ceremony at least until the next day. Alone, her friend Isaura bemoans Amenaide's plight: secretly betrothed to Tancredi, how can she marry someone else? *(Amenaide sventurata!)*.

§ A boat docks alongside the gardens of Argirio's palace, and Tancredi arrives from Messina, greeting his "ungrateful fatherland" and hoping for a reunion with his beloved Amenaide *(Di tanti palpiti)*. Intending to surprise the girl, he sends his companion Roggiero to find and bring her. Then he dispatches knights to serve notice that an "unknown warrior" has arrived to offer his services in defense of Syracuse. He sees Amenaide approaching, but since she is not alone, he withdraws and overhears her conversation with her father. It develops that Solamir, the Moorish leader, has asked for Amenaide's hand and is surrounding the city with troops; also, word is out that the "rebel" Tancredi has returned, perhaps seeking revenge for his exile. If found in Syracuse, Tancredi would be subject to the death penalty. And because of Solamir's imminent attack, Amenaide's marriage to Orbazzano must take place at once (Argirio: *Pensa che sei mia figlia*). Aside, Amenaide dreads the result if a letter she secretly sent to Tancredi were intercepted. After Argirio leaves her, she is confronted by Tancredi himself, compounding her fears for his life. To save him, she pretends to love him no longer and urges him to flee (duet: *L'aura che intorno spiri*). She dares not tell him of her forced engagement to another man, but he is stung by her rejection.

§ In a public square near the city walls, nobles and warriors gather before a Gothic cathedral for the wedding. Tancredi rashly presents himself as an "unknown warrior" and offers Argirio his services. Not recognizing him, Argirio accepts. Amenaide tells her father she cannot love or marry Orbazzano. Overhearing this, Orbazzano furiously confronts her with her letter to Tancredi, which was intercepted; since Tancredi's name was not mentioned in the letter, Orbazzano assumes it was meant for Solamir, her would-be Moorish suitor. As a traitor, he declares, she deserves death. Hearing this, Tancredi believes the accusation, but Amenaide can neither acknowledge him in public nor tell for whom the letter was really meant (ensemble: *Ciel! che feci! fier cimento!*). Orbazzano and the crowd cry for her punishment.

ACT II   In Argirio's castle, Orbazzano, still furious, brings the Senate's death warrant against Amenaide and challenges Argirio to sign it. Torn between love and outrage toward his daughter, Argirio reluctantly does so *(Ah! segnar invano io tento)*. When the others have left, Isaura prays for Amenaide to be comforted and spared *(Tu che i miseri conforti)*.

§ In prison, Amenaide ponders the irony of being reviled by both lover and country, neither of which she has betrayed. Perhaps someday Tancredi will learn the truth and forgive her memory *(No, che il morir non è sì barbaro per me)*. Orbazzano, Argirio, guards and knights arrive to take her to execution. She still cannot exculpate herself without revealing for whom her letter was intended. But Tancredi, unexpectedly offering to fight in her defense, steps forward and challenges Orbazzano. Amenaide is led away by the guards, leaving Argirio briefly alone with Tancredi; though both men feel betrayed by Amenaide, both want to save her (duet: *Ah! se de' mali miei*).

Isaura enters in search of Amenaide, wanting to be with her at the last. Amenaide prays for Tancredi *(Giusto Dio che umile adoro)*, then learns he has killed Orbazzano in the duel. Though the crowd now considers Amenaide vindicated and hails her champion, Tancredi takes little comfort in his victory, since he still feels betrayed. He is about to leave when Amenaide stops him, but he will not hear her explain (duet: *Lasciami: non t'ascolto*). Heartbroken, he takes his leave, gesturing to Roggiero not to accompany him. Isaura takes Roggiero aside and reveals the truth about the letter. For the sake of his friend's happiness, Roggiero wants to believe her *(Torni alfin ridente e bella)*.

§ In a mountain pass, with cascades forming the Fountain of Arethusa, and Mt. Aetna in the distance, Tancredi pauses in his restless wandering to think of his lost love *(Ah! che scordar non so)*. Knights are heard searching for him to help in the city's defense. Amenaide and Argirio appear, together with the knights, but Tancredi still will not listen to her, preferring to die in battle *(Perchè turbar la calma di questo cor?)*. He accompanies the soldiers to the fray, leaving Amenaide and Isaura to their anxiety. Tancredi is carried in, victorious but gravely wounded. Amenaide pleads with him one more time, and Argirio tells him the disputed letter was really meant for him. At last Tancredi believes Amenaide's vow of fidelity. Taking her hand, he asks Argirio to pronounce them married, so he can die with his every wish fulfilled *(Quel pianto mi scende al cor)*.

IL TURCO IN ITALIA

(The Turk in Italy)

TWO ACTS
MUSIC: Gioachino Rossini
TEXT (Italian): Felice Romani
WORLD PREMIERE: Milan, La Scala, August 14, 1814
U.S. PREMIERE: New York, Park Theater, March 14, 1826

CHARACTERS

Fiorilla, *Geronio's wife* . . . . Soprano
Zaida, *Selim's Turkish fiancée*. . . . . .Mezzo-Soprano
Narciso, *in love with Fiorilla* . . . . Tenor
Albazar, *Selim's confidant*. . . . . Tenor
Prosdocimo, *a poet* . . . . Baritone
Selim, *a Turkish prince*. . . . . Bass
Don Geronio, *Fiorilla's husband* . . . . Bass

ACT I   Italy, early nineteenth century. On a solitary beach near Naples, a group of Gypsies, led by Zaida and Albazar, hail their nomadic existence. Observing them, the poet Prosdocimo thinks they would be good characters for the opera libretto he has to write. To invent a plot, he seizes upon the arrival of Geronio, a doting husband who wants his fortune told: will he ever be able to understand his flighty wife? *(Vado in traccia d'una Zingara).* Zaida, reading Geronio's palm, says he is henpecked. He leaves, pursued by the Gypsies, but Zaida and Albazar stay behind to tell the poet their story. Zaida used to be a slave to Pasha Selim, who wanted to marry her; but rivals accused her of infidelity, so she was condemned to death. Albazar, appointed to execute her, saved her instead, and the two escaped *(Udite: egli mi amava).* The poet decides to garnish his plot with a Turkish sultan, who will arrive in Italy, hear her story, and take her back to Selim, whom she still loves (Poet: *Il caso è molto raro in verità).* The three leave.

Fiorilla, Geronio's wife, arrives, declaring her whim of loving someone different each day *(Non si dà follia maggiore).* Some Turks arrive by boat, and their leader, Selim, salutes Italy *(Bella Italia, alfin ti miro).* She greets him, and they are immediately drawn to each other (duet: *Con un poco di modestia).* He and his entourage escort her away.

The poet returns, and as he contemplates how to use Zaida in his story, he is approached by Narciso, a cast-off admirer of Fiorilla's—another likely candidate for the cast of characters. Geronio joins them, complaining that he just saw his wife with a Turk, whom she invited to their house for coffee. The poet is delighted to discover that the Turk is Selim, Zaida's beloved, and imagines all sorts of imbroglios developing (trio: *Un marito—scimunito!),* but the other men want no take part of his libretto.

§ At Geronio's house, Fiorilla entertains Selim, who is annoyed by the arrival of Geronio and Narciso; they in turn are beside themselves to see him there (quartet, Selim: *Io stupisco, mi sorprende).* Finding that four's a crowd, all depart except Geronio. He tells his troubles to the poet, who advises him not to be such a complaisant husband. Geronio decides to stand up to Fiorilla when she returns, but she deflects criticism by accusing him of being cold toward her (duet, Geronio: *Per piacere alla Signora).* Arguing, they leave. The poet, satisfied with events so far, determines to fetch Zaida and have her meet Selim, so a regular opera plot can be developed *(Ho quasi del mio Dramma).*

§ Back by the shore, as the Gypsies vaunt their fortune-telling skills, Selim arrives as if to sail back to Turkey, but Zaida approaches, reads Selim's palm, and they recognize each other happily. This stalls the poet's hopes for plot complications, but he is gratified by the arrival of Narciso, who sings a forlorn serenade while searching for Fiorilla *(Perchè mai se son tradito).* Next comes the disguised Fiorilla herself, surrounded by friends and stalked by the angry Geronio. Zaida and Fiorilla fight over Selim, who tries to calm them. The poet likes this lively development, and the bystanders compare the rivals' confrontation to a volcanic eruption (ensemble: *Quando il vento improvviso).*

ACT II   At an inn, the poet fortifies Geronio with wine and encouraging words as they await Fiorilla's arrival. Selim appears and, as the poet eavesdrops, tries to convince Geronio to sell Fiorilla, as is the custom in Turkey (duet: *D'un bell'uso di Turchia*). When Geronio refuses, Selim threatens to abduct her. They challenge each other to a duel—an outcome unforeseen by the poet, who worries how to save the plot with a new twist. Fiorilla arrives with companions, still happy in her inconstancy (*Se il zefiro si posa*). Annoyed by Zaida's defiance, she has invited the girl for a showdown—not because Fiorilla wants Selim for herself, which she doesn't, but to cut Zaida's pride down to size. As soon as Zaida appears, Fiorilla confronts Selim with the girl, insisting he choose. He stalls, causing Zaida to leave in a huff. Fiorilla too challenges his indecision: if he prefers Zaida, he should follow her. Selim concludes that Italian women don't understand Turkish ways (duet: *Credete alle femmine*). Both soon relent, however, and pledge their affection.

The poet tells Geronio his latest plan: Zaida, disguised as Fiorilla, is to appear at the masquerade that evening to lure Selim into taking her back to Turkey, while Geronio, disguised as Selim, is to deceive Fiorilla. Narciso, overhearing this, vows to intercept Fiorilla for himself *(Tutto io vo' tentar)*.

The poet briefs Albazar for his role in the masquerade. Albazar, caring only for Zaida's happiness, regrets on her behalf that Selim has proved fickle (*Ah! sarebbe troppo dolce*).

§ At the masquerade, Narciso, having put on a Selim disguise himself, courts Fiorilla while the real Selim courts Zaida, whom he takes to be Fiorilla. Geronio, seeing two Selim–Fiorilla couples, doesn't know which is the real one (quintet: *Quale di lor la moglie mia sarà?*). Perplexity is still unresolved when the two couples exit on opposite sides, leaving Geronio frustrated.

§ Back at a room in the inn, Albazar prepares for Selim's return to Turkey with the supposed Fiorilla (actually Zaida). The poet tells Geronio that the "extra" Selim was Narciso; when Fiorilla discovered this, she set out in search of the real one. He now tells Geronio to serve Fiorilla with a writ of separation, Geronio fears that if he tries this he really will lose her, but Albazar enters, saying that Selim and Zaida, reunited, are off for Turkey.

To provoke Fiorilla into livening his final scene with an aria, the poet hands her Geronio's letter of separation. Reading it, she casts aside her finery, dresses as if in mourning, and prepares to return, humbled, to her parents (*"I vostri cenci vi mando"*). The poet counsels Geronio to follow her discreetly and forgive her after she has suffered enough.

§ At the shore, Fiorilla prepares to sail back to her parents in Sorrento; seeing Selim's ship, she rues the day it arrived. Geronio approaches, and they are tenderly reconciled, to the poet's satisfaction (trio, Fiorilla: *Son la vite sul campo appassita*). Selim and Zaida pass en route to their ship, apologizing to Geronio and Fiorilla. The poet is delighted with his ending. Only Narciso is unhappy and resolves to learn his lesson. Everyone expresses relief that all's well that ends well (*Restate contenti*).

LA GAZZA LADRA

(The Thieving Magpie)

TWO ACTS
MUSIC: Gioachino Rossini
TEXT (Italian): Giovanni Gherardini, after J. M. T. Baudoin d'Aubi-
   gny and Louis-Charles Caigniez's play *La Pie Voleuse*
WORLD PREMIERE: Milan, La Scala, May 31, 1817
U.S. PREMIERE: New Orleans, Théâtre d'Orléans, December 20, 1828
   (in French)

CHARACTERS

Ninetta, *a servant* . . . . Soprano
Lucia, *Fabrizio's wife* . . . . .Mezzo-Soprano
Pippo, *a young peasant in Fabrizio's service* . . . . .Mezzo-Soprano
Giannetto, *Fabrizio's son, a soldier* . . . . Tenor
Isacco, *a wandering peddler* . . . . Tenor
Antonio, *the town jailor* . . . . Tenor
Fernando Villabella, *Ninetta's father, a soldier* . . . . Baritone
Fabrizio Vingradito, *a rich farmer* . . . . Bass
Gottardo, *the village mayor* . . . . Bass
Ernesto, *Fernando's friend, a soldier* . . . . Bass

ACT I   In the Italian countryside, early nineteenth century. At the home of
Fabrizio Vingradito, a well-to-do tenant farmer, the household prepares to
welcome Fabrizio's son, Giannetto, newly discharged from the army. As villagers gather in the courtyard, a magpie in an open cage calls the name of Pippo,
one of the youths, and there is joking about the bird's skill at mimickry.
Lucia, mistress of the house, gets after the servants to busy themselves with
preparations. When Fabrizio enters, he and Lucia discuss the desirability of
their son's getting married. Who would be a suitable girl? The magpie chirps
the name "Ninetta," one of the servant girls, with whom Giannetto has been in
love, but the parents disagree about her—father in favor, mother disapproving
(ensemble: *Là seduto l'amato Giannetto*). When the villagers have left, Lucia
sends the servants off as well and confides to her husband that she finds Ninetta
lazy and careless: she has lost a silver fork. Fabrizio reminds Lucia that the girl
has lost her mother, and that her poor father is a career soldier (*Rispetta in lei*

le sue sventure). When the couple steps into the garden to look for Giannetto, who is expected momentarily, Ninetta arrives, happy because both her boy-friend and her father will be returning from the army *(Tutto sorridere mi veggo intorno).* Fabrizio greets her, indicating that he approves his son's interest in her, but when Lucia comes back, she treats the girl critically and reminds her of the lost fork.

A peddler, Isacco, wanders in, hawking his wares: combs, knives, matches, and the like *(Stringhe e ferri da calzette).* When Pippo sends him away, saying no one has any money to spend today, the old man reminds him that he buys as well as sells. Ninetta and Pippo are both excited to hear a commotion in the background, announcing Giannetto's arrival. The young man hurries to find Ninetta and greet her *(Vieni fra queste braccia).* Pippo proposes a toast *(Tocchiamo, beviamo);* after joining in, and dancing around the table, the villag-ers leave the courtyard. Giannetto inquires about his uncle, who is bothered by gout, and Fabrizio proposes they go to the uncle's house nearby for a visit. Pippo and Ninetta are left in charge. When Pippo goes into the kitchen, Ninetta sees an old man approaching warily and soon realizes it is her father, Fernando, wearing ragged clothes to escape detection: her tells how he got into a quarrel with his captain and was condemned to death for it, but was helped by friends to escape *(Ieri, sul tramonar del sole).* As the two discuss his plight, the Mayor is seen approaching. There is no time for Fernando to escape, so he sits at the table, wrapped in a cloak, hoping not to be noticed. The Mayor enters, preoccupied with how to press his attentions on Ninetta *(Sì, sì, Ninetta, sola, soletta).* He sees the girl, who tells him the other man is a vagrant who stopped for refreshment and a rest. While Fernando pretends to be asleep, the Mayor insists on trying to interest Ninetta in his romantic intentions.

Giorgio, the town clerk, brings a message from a police officer. While the Mayor tries to read it, Ninetta urges her father, sotto voce, to escape; but he has no money, and she has none either. He gives her a place setting of silver-ware from his pocket, the last of his valuable possessions, and tells her to sell it, then put the money in a hollow chestnut tree on the hillside, where he can pick it up later. The Mayor asks Ninetta to help him read the document, a description of an army deserter named Fernando. Thinking fast, the girl falsi-fies the description so it does not apply to her father. Satisfied that the old man is not a suspect, the Mayor orders him to leave, but Fernando remains hidden to overhear what transpires. When the Mayor once again declares his love for Ninetta (trio: *Oh Nume benefico),* Fernando is outraged and reenters to protect his daughter. At length he does flee, at Ninetta's urging. As she reaches out her arms toward the departing man, the Magpie is seen to leave its cage and steal a spoon from the table.

Later, as Isacco passes in the street, Ninetta calls him and sells the place setting her father gave her. As he leaves, Pippo comes in with the Magpie's cage, looking for the escaped bird, which sits on the windowsill calling Pippo's name, then flies into its cage. Ninetta wants to hide the money in the tree for her father, but the return of her employers, with the Mayor and Giorgio, prevents her from leaving. As Giannetto is introduced to the local officials, who compliment him on his military record, Lucia counts out the silverware in a basket and finds a spoon missing. Having lost a fork not long before, she is suspicious and, despite Fabrizio's protectiveness toward Ninetta, wants an investigation. The Mayor remarks that the penalty for domestic theft is death. When Giannetto asks who the thief could be, the Magpie calls out Ninetta's name, causing her to burst into tears. The Mayor dictates a report to the town clerk (ensemble: *"In casa di Messere Fabrizio Vingradito"*), and in the course of answering the Mayor's questions, Ninetta gives away her father's name—that of the deserter who is wanted for a crime. She drops the money she got from the peddler, arousing further suspicion from Lucia (who thinks she stole the silverware and sold it) and the Mayor (who wants to punish her for rejecting his advances).

Pippo brings back Isacco, who says he bought a fork and spoon from the girl a short while ago. Isacco already has resold the items, and to make matters worse, he recalls that the monogram on them read "F.V."—her father's initials, but also her employer's. The town clerk returns with militiamen, and all the farm employees appear. The Mayor orders Ninetta arrested (ensemble: *In prigione costei sia condotta*), but the others, even Lucia, denounce his harshness as the girl is led away.

ACT II   In the jail at the town hall, Antonio, the custodian, tries to console Ninetta and admits Giannetto, who begs Ninetta to clear herself; but since she has no evidence in her defense, she cannot (duet: *Forsè un dì conoscerete*). Giannetto has to leave when the Mayor arrives, offering in a conciliatory tone to get her free—in exchange for her affections (*Sì per voi, pupille amate*). When she refuses, saying she doesn't fear the death sentence, he turns vengeful and threatening (*Udrai la sentenza*), as voices outside call for the court session to begin. When he has gone, Pippo pays Ninetta a quick visit; she asks him to lend her three scudi and put the money in the hollow chestnut tree. As pledge—and also as a memento, in case she dies—she gives him her cross (duet: *Deh pensa che domani*). She also asks him to give her ring to Giannetto.

§ Back at the farm, Lucia realizes that Ninetta's guilt has not been proved. When Fernando comes in search of his daughter, Lucia tearfully admits the girl has been arrested. Though he is a wanted man, Fernando resolves to risk everything to help her (*Ah lungi il timore!*) and rushes away.

§ In the village square, Lucia comes out of church, having prayed for Ninetta's innocence (*A questo seno*).

§ In the courtroom, the presiding Judge announces that a unanimous verdict of guilty has been reached (*Tremate, o popoli*). Giannetto tells the Judge that Ninetta is keeping a secret that would save her; but she cannot divulge it. Suddenly Fernando enters the court, offering his own life to save his daughter.

Because sentence already has been pronounced, however, the law must be obeyed. All present feel sympathy for Ninetta and Fernando (chorus: *Sino il pianto è negato al mio ciglio*), who are led off.

§ In the village square, Ernesto brings news that Fernando has been pardoned by the king. When Ernesto goes in search of the Mayor, Pippo sits down to count the money he has left after putting Ninetta's coins in the hollow tree. As he converses with Giorgio, the Magpie flies down, steals a coin, and flies to the bell tower.

Ninetta pauses before the church to utter a prayer *(Deh tu reggi in tal momento)* on her way to execution.

When Pippo and Antonio climb the bell tower to get back Pippo's coin, they find the missing silverware as well, hidden there by the Magpie. Hoping to save Ninetta in time, they ring the church bell. This attracts villagers, to whom they announce their discovery—but a volley of shots in the distance gives the impression that the execution already has taken place. This turns out to be a false alarm: the shots were for joy. Giannetto hands the Mayor a reprieve from the Judge, freeing the girl, who greets her friends once more *(Queste grida di letizia)* but is still worried about her father; he appears, and she learns of his pardon. Lucia asks Ninetta's forgiveness and blesses her marriage to Giannetto. The Mayor stands apart, seized with remorse, as everyone else celebrates.

Mosè in Egitto

(Moses in Egypt)

THREE ACTS

MUSIC: Gioachino Rossini

TEXT (Italian): Andrea Leone Tottola, based on Francesco Ringhieri's play *L'Osiride,* and the Old Testament

WORLD PREMIERE: Naples, San Carlo, March 5, 1818

U.S. PREMIERE (concert performance): New York, Masonic Hall, December 22, 1832

U.S. STAGE PREMIERE: New York, Italian Opera House, March 2, 1835

CHARACTERS

Elcia, *a young Hebrew woman* . . . . Soprano
Amaltea, *Faraone's wife* . . . . .Mezzo-Soprano

Amenosi, *Elcia's confidante*. . . . . .Mezzo-Soprano
Aronne, *Mosè's brother* . . . . Tenor
Osiride, *Faraone's son* . . . . Tenor
Mambre, *an Egyptian priest* . . . . Tenor
Faraone (Pharaoh), *King of Egypt* . . . . Bass
Mosè, *leader of the Israelites* . . . . Bass

The story presented here follows the second (1819) version of the score as originally written for Naples.

ACT I Egypt, Biblical antiquity. Because Faraone (the Pharaoh) has gone back on his promise to release the captive Israelites, the land has been plunged in darkness. His people reproach him, and he sends for Mosè (Moses), then promises to obey the wishes of the Hebrew God. Mosè arrives and, though counseled by his brother Aronne (Aaron) not to trust the Pharaoh, raises his voice in prayer to Jehovah *(Eterno! immenso! incomprensibil Dio!)*, whereupon daylight is restored. The Egyptians are dumbfounded and the Hebrews delighted (quintet: *Celeste man placata!*).

Osiride (Osiris), son of the Pharaoh, is upset by the thought of losing Elcia, a young Israelite woman with whom he is secretly in love. He confides his anxiety to Mambre, an Egyptian priest, who resents the "charlatan" Mosè and promises to find a way to stop the Hebrews' departure. Elcia comes to bid farewell to Osiride (duet: *Ah! se puoi così lasciarmi*); though loath to leave him, she means to follow Mosè and her people into the desert.

Amaltea, wife of the Pharaoh, privately persuaded by the Israelites' faith, urges her husband not to go back on his word; she is afraid he may be swayed by Osiride's pleas. Her fears are justified: the Pharaoh again revokes his promise, threatening death to any who try to leave Egypt.

§ The Hebrews, innocent of this development, are preparing joyfully to set forth (prayer: *Alto stupor sarà nel cor*). Elcia's friend Amenosi tries to comfort her at the loss of Osiride (duet: *Tutto mi ride intorno*). Mambre and Osiride arrive to tell the Hebrews that their permission to leave has been revoked. While the Egyptian priest and prince accuse Mosè of fakery, he threatens God's punishment against the Pharaoh's treachery (ensemble: *All'idea di tanto eccesso*). The Pharaoh himself appears, confirming his verdict that the Hebrews cannot go. Mosè with a wave of his staff calls down a rain of fire and hailstones from the heavens.

ACT II At the Pharaoh's palace, with crops now suffering from a blight called down by Mosè, the Pharaoh again changes his mind, decides to be rid of the troublesome Israelites, and tells Aronne they must leave that very day. He also promises Osiride marriage to the princess of Armenia and cannot understand why the youth receives the idea unhappily (duet: *Parlar, spiegar non posso*).

Mosè seeks out Amaltea, knowing her to be sympathetic, but she warns him of the Pharaoh's uncontrollable fickleness and prays that her hopes will not be in vain *(La pace mia smarrita)*.

When Aronne tells Mosè he has seen Osiride abduct Elcia, Mosè sends his brother to tell Amaltea what has happened.

§ In a cavern where he has brought her, Osiride tells Elcia he has been betrothed against his will and wants to escape with her to a simple life in the woods (duet, Elcia: *E in così mesta tenebrosa caverna*). They are surprised by Amaltea and Aronne with guards, but Osiride stands up to his mother and refuses to give up his "unworthy" love; likewise, Elcia tells Aronne she cannot deny her unfortunate love for the Egyptian prince (quartet, Amaltea: *Involto in fiamma rea*). When Osiride goes so far as to say he will renounce the throne, however, Elcia tells him to think of his future and renounce her instead.

The Pharaoh, again going back on his word, tells Mosè the Hebrews cannot leave after all, because of military threats from the Midianites and Philistines. Mosè denounces this, saying God speaks through him *(Non è Mosè. Raggiona sul suo labbro quel Dio),* adding that firstborn children throughout the land, including Osiride, will be smitten by God's thunderbolts. Enraged by Mosè's arrogance, the Pharaoh orders him arrested. Before he is led off, Mosè warns the ruler one more time that he may lament his rashness too late *(Tu di ceppi m'aggravi la mano)*.

To Mambre, the Pharaoh declares that he will prove the vanity of Mosè's threats by enthroning Osiride next to himself and having Osiride pronounce the death sentence on Mosè. Mambre summons the nobles to hear this latest decree (chorus: *Se a mitigar tue cure*). Osiride takes the throne and orders Mosè to bow before him; Mosè retorts that while he has to bow to temporal authority, it is foolish for Osiride to brave the wrath of God. Elcia intervenes, asking Osiride to desist and openly admitting her love for him. She urges him to accept the royal marriage and let the Israelites go *(Porgi la destra amata)*. He says he is unwilling to give her up, but he also insists Mosè must die for his effrontery. At this, Osiride is struck dead by lightning, to the grief of his father and Elcia and the consternation of all the others.

ACT III   The Israelites are on their way at last, approaching the shore of the Red Sea. Mosè leads his people in prayer for a safe avenue of escape *(Dal tuo stellato soglio)*. Egyptian soldiers are seen approaching in pursuit from the hills, but when Mosè touches the sea with his staff, the waters part to let the Hebrews through. The Egyptians, including the Pharaoh and Mambre, are drowned when they try to follow.

LA DONNA DEL LAGO

(The Lady of the Lake)

TWO ACTS
MUSIC: Gioachino Rossini
TEXT (Italian): Andrea Leone Tottola, based on Walter Scott's poem
WORLD PREMIERE: Naples, San Carlo, September 24, 1819
U.S. PREMIERE: New York, Park Theater, August 26, 1829 (in French)

CHARACTERS

Elena, *daughter of Douglas* . . . . Soprano
Albina, *her confidante* .Mezzo-Soprano
Malcolm Groem, *a rebel leader* . . . . .Mezzo-Soprano
Uberto (*James V of Scotland incognito*) . . . . Tenor
Rodrigo, *a rebel leader* . . . . Tenor
Serano, *a retainer of Douglas* . . . . Tenor
Douglas of Angus, *a rebel leader* . . . . Bass

James V (1512–42) reigned as King of Scotland from 1513 to 1542. In a power struggle he was held captive in 1526 by his stepfather, Archibald Douglas, sixth Earl of Angus, from whom he broke free in 1528, causing Angus to flee to England. Eventually in 1542 the king, also opposed by some of his Protestant nobles, was defeated by Henry VIII's forces at Solway Moss. He died soon after and was succeeded by his ill-fated daughter Mary, Queen of Scots. Sir Walter Scott's highly fictional narrative poem *The Lady of the Lake* (1810) inspired this most romantic of Rossini's Italian operas.

ACT I   In a sylvan setting by Loch Katrine, at the foot of the Rock of Benledi in the Scottish Highlands, shepherds and hunters pass on their way to nearby fields and woods. Elena (Ellen), in a boat on the lake, muses on her love for Malcolm, a Highland rebel *(O, mattutini albori!)*. As she steps ashore, she is greeted by Uberto (Hubert—the king in disguise), who introduces himself as a hunter. Struck by the girl's beauty, he accepts her offer of hospitality at her home across the lake; they embark (duet: *Ah! sgombra omai l'affanno*). When his fellow hunters return, looking for him, they pray for his safety and hope to find him (*Tu che ne leggi nel cor fedel*).

§ At Elena's home, Uberto, startled to see a familiar coat of arms, asks who his host may be and learns that Elena is the daughter of Douglas of Angus, an exile from court. The king, who regrets the loss of Douglas, realizes he must not give away his identity. Friends come to welcome Elena, but she is shocked to learn from them that the rebel leader, Rodrigo (Roderick Dhu), apparently with her father's blessing, wants to marry her. Uberto dares to hope that his own affection for her is returned (ensemble: *D'Inibaca Donzella*). Elena, however, loves Malcolm and fears having to accept an unwanted marriage. Uberto tears himself away, since prudence dictates return to his companions. Elena's confidante, Albina, will accompany him back across the lake.

Malcolm enters alone, fearing that after months of absence he may have lost Elena (*Elena! o tu, che chiamo!*). He steps out of sight when Douglas appears with the girl. Though Malcolm is delighted to overhear Elena's attempted refusal, he also hears her father insist on the marriage of his choice as a patriotic and familial duty (*Taci, lo voglio, e basti!*). When Douglas has left, Malcolm greets Elena, and the two renew their pledge of love (*O sposi, o al tenebroso regno*)

§ On a plain not far from the lake, the clansmen hail Rodrigo (*Qual rapido torrente*). He pledges to lead them to victory (*Eccomi a voi, miei prodi*). When Douglas appears, shortly followed by Elena, Rodrigo proudly welcomes her as his fiancée but cannot help noticing her dejected mood (ensemble: *D'opposti affetti un vortice*). Malcolm arrives with his men and presents himself to Rodrigo as a military ally, but when he learns that Rodrigo considers himself engaged to Elena, Malcolm can scarcely conceal his shock. Douglas and Rodrigo likewise sense that something is afoot between Elena and Malcolm. Confrontation is averted when Serano enters with news that the enemy is advancing. Rodrigo calls upon the Bards for an inspirational hymn (Bards: *Già un raggio forier d'immenso splendor*). A meteor streaking across the sky appears to be a good omen, and the troops swarm up the hill.

ACT II Uberto, dressed as a shepherd, standing in a thick woods near a cavern, cannot put Elena from his mind (*O fiamma soave*). As he disappears among the trees, Serano finds Elena, who reassures him that she is with Albina and is waiting to meet her father. Uberto sees her and steps forward, declaring his love (*Arcani si funesti perchè tacermi, ingrata!*). When she says she cannot return his love, he gives her a jeweled ring, claiming he once got it from the King of Scotland; if ever she needs help, she should present it to the king. As they converse, their duet is turned into a trio by Rodrigo, who discovers them and jealously challenges Uberto to identify himself. Uberto proudly declares he is loyal to the king and disdains the rebels. Rodrigo calls his soldiers from hiding in the woods. Unintimidated, Uberto continues to defy him, so

Rodrigo gives him one of the soldiers' swords (ensemble: *Vendetta accendimi di rabbia il seno!*), and the two men go off to fight.

§ At the cavern, Malcolm finds Albina waiting for Elena and tells her the king's forces are winning. Serano arrives to add that Duncan has gone to give himself up to the king, in hopes of saving his daughter and restoring peace. Learning of this, Elena has gone to the King as well. Malcolm again fears he has lost her *(Ah! Si pera: ormai la morte)*. Rebel warriors stumble in with the report that Rodrigo has been killed.

§ At Stirling Castle, Elena waits anxiously for an audience with the king. She hears Uberto's voice in the next room *(Aurora! Ah sorgerai)* and greets him with great relief. When he leads her to the throne room, filled with courtiers, she is astonished to learn that Uberto is actually Giacomo (James V), the king himself. He grants her request to pardon her father. After some hesitation he forgives Malcolm as well, giving the couple his blessing. Elena thanks him *(Tanti affetti in tal momento),* and all express relief at the happy outcome.

IL VIAGGIO A REIMS

(The Journey to Reims)

ONE ACT
MUSIC: Gioachino Rossini
TEXT (Italian): Luigi Balocchi, based on Mme. de Staël's novel
    Corinne, ou l'Italie
WORLD PREMIERE: Paris, Théâtre Italien, June 19, 1825
U.S. PREMIERE: St. Louis Opera, June 12, 1986

CHARACTERS

Corinna, *a Roman poetess* . . . . Soprano
Countess di Folleville, *a young widow* . . . . Soprano
Mme. Cortese, *owner of a spa hotel* . . . . Soprano
Marchesa Melibea, *a Polish widow* . . . . Mezzo-Soprano
Chevalier Belfiore, *a young French officer* . . . . Tenor
Count di Libenskof, *a Russian general* . . . . Tenor
Don Alvaro, *a Spanish grandee* . . . . Baritone
Lord Sidney, *an English colonel* . . . . Bass
Don Profondo, *a man of letters* . . . . Bass
Barone di Trombonok, *a German major* . . . . Bass

This opera was written in Italian for the Théâtre Italien in Paris in honor of the coronation of the Bourbon King Charles X, using all the major stars available at the time (there are ten leading roles in a cast of eighteen), with an ensemble for fourteen individual voices. After several performances it was withdrawn by Rossini, who reused some of the music in *Le Comte Ory* (1828). The score was not reconstructed until the 1970s.

PART I   In the lobby of the Golden Lily spa hotel at Polombières in May 1825, Maddalena, the hotel housekeeper, fussily oversees preparations for the hotel guests' proposed journey to Reims for the coronation. Don Prudenzio, the spa doctor, declares a day off from taking the mineral baths, so that everyone can get ready for the trip. Mme. Cortese, the proprietor, hails the good weather *(Di vaghi raggi adorno)*: she herself will stay behind to mind the hotel. The Countess di Folleville, an attractive young lady of fashion, faints when she learns from her cousin, Don Luigino, that a carriage bringing her wardrobe has met with an accident. When she revives, she laments that now she cannot go to Reims *(Partir, o ciel! desio),* but her maid, Modestina, produces a Parisian bonnet that survived the wreck. Baron Trombonok, a music-loving German officer, announces he will serve as treasurer for the voyage. Among the other guests, Don Alvaro (a Spanish admiral) and Count Libenskof (a Russian general) turn out to be rivals for the love of Marchese Melibea, a Polish widow (sextet: *Non pavento alcun periglio)*, but their anger is calmed by the Roman poetess Corinna, who sings the praises of joy and love *(Arpa gentil)*.

All leave the lobby except Mme. Cortese, who wonders at the inability of yet another guest, Lord Sidney, to confess his love for the poetess. He enters, having flowers delivered to Corinna's door *(Invan strappar dal core)*. Questioned unsuccessfully by Don Profondo about how to acquire some rare English antiquities, he takes his leave. Profondo gives Corinna a letter from Rome and departs. No sooner has she gathered up Sidney's flowers than she is accosted by Chevalier Belfiore, an unwelcome but persistent suitor (duet: *Nel suo divin sembiante)*. Before going their separate ways, they are overheard by Profondo; though amused by the duplicity of Belfiore, who also pays court to Folleville, he remains interested mainly in antiquities, singing their praises in detail *(Medaglie incomparabili)*. When the countess herself appears, he admits to her that he saw Belfiore with Corinna. Travel arrangements now dominate the thoughts of the guests as they reconvene—only to learn that no more horses can be found in Polombières to draw their carriages (ensemble: *A tal colpo inaspettato)*. Their distress is somewhat mollified, however, when word arrives that the newly crowned king will return shortly to Paris, where Folleville offers her hospitality to all. Melibea and the jealous Libenskof are left alone with Trombonok, who tries to mediate between them, then bows out while they reconcile (duet: *D'alma celeste, o Dio!)*.

PART II   In the hotel garden, dinner is being arranged. A traveling company of singers and dancers arrives to entertain the guests (chorus: *L'allegria è un sommo bene*), who then individually deliver toasts from their own homelands: a German anthem (Trombonok), polonaise (Melibea), Russian hymn (Libenskof), Spanish song (Alvaro), English anthem (Sidney), French song (Belfiore, Folleville), and tyrolienne (Cortese). Finally the guests draw lots as to the subject of an improvisation by Corinna, which turns out to be in honor of the new king himself—represented by the inn's trademark, the royal gold fleur de lys. A chorus with dancing *(Con sacro zelo)* caps the festivities.

LE SIÈGE DE CORINTHE

(The Siege of Corinth)

THREE ACTS
MUSIC: Gioachino Rossini
TEXT (French): Luigi Balocchi and Alexandre Soumet, based on Cesare della Valle's libretto for Rossini's *Maometto II*
WORLD PREMIERE: Paris, Opéra, October 9, 1826
U.S. PREMIERE: New York, Italian Opera House, February 6, 1835 (in Italian as *L'Assedio di Corinto*)
METROPOLITAN PREMIERE: April 7, 1975 (in Italian as *L'Assedio di Corinto*)

CHARACTERS

Pamira, *Cléomène's daughter* . . . . Soprano
Ismène, *her confidante* . . . . .Mezzo-Soprano
Néoclès, *a young Greek officer* . . . . Tenor*
Cléomène, *Governor of Corinth* . . . . Tenor
Omar, *Cléomène's confidant* . . . . Tenor
Adraste, *a Greek warrior*. . . . . Tenor
Mahomet II, *Emperor of the Turks*. . . . . Bass
Hiéros, *guardian of the catacombs* . . . . Bass

*Mezzo-Soprano in the Italian version

ACT I   Corinth, 1458. Five years after the fall of Constantinople, Mahomet (Mohammed) II, determined to extend the Ottoman Empire still further, has laid siege to the Greek city of Corinth. In the vestibule of the Senate, Cléomène, governor of the city, agonizes over whether to surrender, saving more bloodshed and destruction, now that so many defenders have been killed.

The people are disheartened, but a young officer, Néoclès, rallies them to fight on (ensemble: *Le glaive homicide sera notre égide*). As the Greeks go to mount a new counterattack, Néoclès reminds Cléomène that he has promised the hand of his daughter, Pamira, to Néoclès in marriage. When the young woman enters, however, she admits she secretly pledged her faith to a certain Almanzor, whom she met in Athens. Despite her father's threats, she will not renounce her vow (trio: *Ciel, sois propice à ma prière!*). Reentering Greeks cry that the battle is going badly. Cléomène gives his daughter a sword with which to take her own life if the Turks are victorious, rather than become a slave in the victor's harem (Pamira: *Rassurez-vous, mon père!*). Cléomène and Néoclès leave to join the fray.

§ Having won the city, the Turks march into the main square (chorus: *La flamme rapide*). Mahomet assures his troops they will conquer everywhere they go *(Chef d'un peuple indomptable)*. Aside, he explains to his confidant, Omar, that having visited Greece earlier under the alias of Almanzor, he longs to find the young woman with whom he fell in love *(Une jeune beauté se montra dans Athènes)*. When Cléomène is brought in and refuses to surrender, Mahomet orders an assault on the Greeks' last bastion, but Pamira enters with other Greek women and throws herself at his feet, begging for mercy for her countrymen. She and Mahomet recognize each other; her beloved is the enemy of her people (ensemble, Pamira: *Ah, l'amant qui m'enchaîne mérite ma haine!*). Mahomet asks to marry her, only to have Cléomène indignantly refuse, cursing his daughter. Pamira is unnerved by her father's hostility, but Mahomet is determined to have things his way *(Viens, suis-moi, mon amour)*.

ACT II   In Mahomet's tent, Pamira bemoans her situation, caught between the conqueror's love and her loyalty to her father; death seems the only way out, and she prays to her deceased mother for solace *(Jours de deuil et d'horreur!)*. Mahomet arrives and tries to comfort her with reassurances: they will be married, and her father will accept the situation (duet: *Pourquoi ces alarmes?*). But as they prepare to go to the altar, a commotion heralds Néoclès, who recklessly has broken through to challenge Mahomet, saying the Greeks, too proud to give up, see Pamira as a traitor *(Toi qui les vis combattre)*. To save Néoclès from Mahomet's threats, she declares he is her brother. If so, Mahomet retorts, her brother will serve as witness to their wedding (trio: *Pamire, sois à moi!*). Omar bursts in to report that the Greeks have resumed fighting. When she hears her father calling to her, while her people express their willingness to die, Pamira renounces Mahomet to return to the Greeks; furiously, Mahomet condemns them all to perish by the sword (ensemble: *Funeste délire!*).

ACT III   Among the catacombs of Corinth, illuminated by torches, Néoclès arrives with a fellow soldier, Adraste, whom he dispatches to tell Cléomène of Pamira's return. Alone, Néoclès hears Pamira and Ismène, with other Greek women, praying in the background. He himself prays that with the Greek cause lost, Pamira may somehow be spared *(Grand Dieu, faut-il qu'un peuple qui t'adore*).* When Cléomène appears, still cursing his daughter *(Je ne vois qu'un objet dont l'impure faiblesse),* she herself follows, imploring his pardon, saying she has come to die with him. She pledges her faith to Néoclès, and Cléomène, won over, blesses the pair (trio: *Céleste providence*). As the men prepare to leave to rejoin the hopeless Greek cause, all three fear they will meet again only in heaven.

Hiéros, guardian of the catacombs, stops Cléomène and Néoclès: the Turks have driven the Greeks back, and there is nothing left but to die with with a dignity that future generations will remember. Greek soldiers who have arrived, together with women of Corinth, bow down while Hiéros pronounces a benediction of the military banners *(Au nom du Dieu qui vous inspire).* Clairvoyantly he foretells the eventual liberation of the Greeks from Turkish domination. Thus inspired, all imagine their collective tomb turned into an altar *(Répondons à ce cri de victoire).* Pamira steps forward and prepares the group for a noble death, leading them in prayer *(Juste Ciel! De ta clémence).*

Mahomet and his men storm in, only to see Pamira stab herself after leading the women in a final hymn *(Chantons l'hymne au courage).* Corinth is seen engulfed in flames: the city has committed suicide rather than submit to the slavery of defeat.

[*In the adaptation performed by the Metropolitan Opera in 1974—reverting to an Italian text, with extensive musical modifications by Thomas Schippers and Randolph Mickelson—Neocle (Néoclès), known in *Maometto II* as Calbo, sings a different aria here, *Non temer d'un basso affetto,* in which he renews his pledge of love to Pamira, who he believes could never betray her people. After he has left, Maometto (Mahomet) storms in and makes one last futile attempt to bring Cleomene around to his wishes. Neocle returns, and a furious trio ensues: Maometto, learning that Neocle is not Pamira's brother but her betrothed, swears to kill him in single combat. He leaves to await his rival, who stays to reconcile Cleomene with Pamira. Iero (Hiéros) appears, accompanied by Greek women and soldiers, and the finale proceeds as in the French version.]

LE COMTE ORY

(Count Ory)

TWO ACTS
MUSIC: Gioachino Rossini

TEXT (French): Eugène Scribe and Charles Gaspard Delestre-Poirson,
after a medieval ballad
WORLD PREMIERE: Paris, Opéra, August 20, 1828
U.S. PREMIERE: New Orleans, Théâtre d'Orléans, December 16, 1830

CHARACTERS

Alice, *a peasant girl* . . . . Soprano
Countess Adèle. . . . . Soprano
Isolier, *Ory's page* . . . . .Mezzo-Soprano
Ragonde, *Adèle's companion* . . . . .Mezzo-Soprano
Count Ory, *a young, profligate nobleman* . . . . Tenor
Raimbaud, *Ory's friend*. Baritone
The Tutor, *charged with Ory's education*. . . . . Baritone

The action takes place around the year 1200, at the castle of the Count of
Formoutiers, in the French countryside of the Touraine.

ACT I   The men of the castle are away on a Crusade, and the women have
vowed to shun men. Outside the castle, Count Ory and his friend Raimbaud
scheme to gain access to Countess Adèle (sister of the Count of Formoutiers),
with whom Ory is infatuated. Raimbaud announces to the ladies of the castle
that a wise hermit (the disguised Ory) is available for consultation (*Jouvencelles,
venez vite*). The ladies, in jovial spirits, bring food and wine. Dame Ragonde,
the castle stewardess, says Adèle is anxious about the safety of her menfolk
and would like to consult the hermit (*Quand Madame la Comtesse*). Ory appears,
in hermit garb, urging the ladies to talk with him freely (*Que les destins pro-
spères*). A couple of villagers tell him their wishes—for a gentle wife, for marriage to a sweetheart—and Ragonde expresses her desire for her husband's safe
return from the Crusade. She also asks if Adèle can speak with the friar (*De
grâce, encore un mot*); he says he will gladly await her.
   Ory's Tutor arrives with Isolier, page boy to Ory's father, the Duke. Isolier,
a cousin of Adèle's, has a crush on her and hopes for a chance to see her. The
Tutor, for his part, hopes to find Ory, for whose welfare he is responsible, and
who is rumored to be in the vicinity (*Veiller sans cesse*). When attractive women
appear, the Tutor surmises that Ory cannot be far away; he learns that the
hermit has been there for about a week—the same time that Ory has been
missing (*Cette aventure fort singulière*). The Tutor withdraws to get help in
bringing Ory home if he should find him. Isolier stays to confer with the
hermit, whom he doesn't recognize as Ory. The youth confides his love for
Adèle and his plan for gaining entry to the castle by dressing as a female
pilgrim. Ory, though angry at the page for being his rival, thinks the plan
might work for himself (duet: *Noble page du Comte Ory*).

A march heralds the arrival of Adèle, who tells the hermit of her lingering melancholy *(En proie à la tristesse)*. He advises her to fall in love, saying heaven releases her from her vows of celibacy (duet: *Si dans mon assistance*). His plan backfires when she begins to show affection for Isolier, so he warns her to beware of "the page of that dreadful Count Ory." Meanwhile, the Tutor reenters with his entourage from Ory's court, hoping to find their master and take him home. The Tutor, seeing Raimbaud, has little difficulty recognizing Ory, who is forced to admit his identity. Ragonde shows Adèle a letter indicating that the castle's menfolk are on their way home—more bad news for Ory. He decides to act quickly, calling on his companions to retreat with him and plan a new strategy (ensemble: *Aux chants de la victoire*).

ACT II   Inside the castle, Adèle and Ragonde remark that they feel safe there from the profligate Ory. As a storm breaks, voices are heard outside—fourteen female pilgrims asking for shelter *(Noble châtelaine, voyez notre peine)*. To protect them from Ory, they are brought inside. One of them (Ory in woman's dress) begs to speak with Adèle and tells her how much he admires her (duet: *Ah! quel respect, Madame*). At mention of Ory's name, however, she makes plain her aversion to his advances. When she leaves to arrange refreshments, Ory explains to his Tutor, who is among his companions, that the idea for their escapade was Isolier's; the Tutor is uneasy, fearing loss of his job if Ory's father finds out. When fruit and milk are brought, the men are distressed with such austere fare; but Raimbaud, who has discovered the wine cellar, comes to their rescue *(Dans ce lieu solitaire)*. Gradually a raucous party develops (chorus: *Buvons soudain!*), but the visitors quiet down when Adèle returns, saying it is bedtime. Ory and his confederates withdraw.

Adèle is disconcerted by the arrival of Isolier, since no man is allowed inside the castle during the Crusaders' absence; he announces their surprise return that very night. When the page learns there are female pilgrims in the castle, he realizes his own idea for infiltrating the place has been plagiarized by Ory. Adèle hears Ory approaching. Isolier puts on female disguise and has Adèle stand concealed behind him. Ory, believing in the darkness that he is addressing Adèle directly, tells her he is "Sister Colette" and cannot sleep (trio: *À la faveur de cette nuit obscure*); he makes advances to Isolier, who keeps Adèle posted on what is happening. At length, Ory is rash enough to reveal his identity and declare his love—still holding Isolier's hand without realizing the trick. But sounds of the Crusaders' return are heard. Isolier removes his disguise; Ory confesses that his companions are all men in disguise. Adèle tells them to leave at once: Isolier will lead them via a secret passage. On his way out, Ory gallantly concedes victory to the powers of wedlock (finale, Adèle: *Écoutez ces chants de victoire*).

GUILLAUME TELL
(William Tell)

FOUR ACTS
MUSIC: Gioachino Rossini
TEXT (French): Étienne de Jouy and Hippolyte-Louis-Florent Bis
   (additions by Armand Marrast and Adolph Crémieux), based on
   Johann Christoph Friedrich von Schiller's play
WORLD PREMIERE: Paris, Opéra, August 3, 1829
U.S. PREMIERE: New York, Park Theater, September 19, 1831
METROPOLITAN PREMIERE: November 28, 1884 (in German)

CHARACTERS

Mathilde, *princess of the house of Hapsburg* . . . . Soprano
Jemmy, *Tell's son* . . . . Soprano
Hedwige, *Tell's wife* . . . . .Mezzo-Soprano
Arnold Melcthal, *a young soldier* . . . . Tenor
Rodolphe, *commander of Gesler's archers* . . . . Tenor
Ruodi, *a fisherman* . . . . Tenor
Guillaume Tell, *a Swiss farmer and patriot* . . . . Baritone
Leuthold, *a herdsman*. . . . . Baritone
Walter Furst, *a Swiss conspirator* . . . . Bass
Melcthal, *Arnold's father*. . . . . Bass
Gesler, *governor of the cantons of Schwyz and Uri*. . . . . Bass

Wilhelm (William) Tell appears to have been a legendary rather than historical figure. The league of three cantons was formed in 1291, and the uprising that freed them of the Austrian bailiffs took place on January 1, 1308.

ACT I   At Bürglen in the canton of Uri, on the lower reaches of the Schachtental torrent, villagers are decorating cottages for three couples whose wedding is about to be celebrated. The people and Ruodi, a fisherman, sing happily, but Guillaume Tell, who has been working in his field, cannot share their mood: he is concerned about the plight of his country, oppressed by Austrian rule (*Il chante en son ivresse*). Melcthal, a local patriarch, arrives with his son Arnold, and they join the others in celebrating work, marriage, and love (ensemble and chorus: *Célébrons tous en ce beau jour*). As most leave for the festival, Melcthal remarks that he wishes his son would marry too, then goes into the nearby house with Tell, his wife, Hedwige, and their son, Jemmy.

Alone, Arnold, who has been serving as a soldier with the Austrian garrison, reflects on the conflict between his patriotism and his love for Mathilde, a princess of the Austrian royal family, whom he once saved from an avalanche (*O Mathilde, je t'aime!*). Tell soon joins him; sensing the young man's inner struggle, he nevertheless feels that Arnold will support the independence movement. As villagers return to complete the marriage ceremony, Arnold envies the happiness of the newlyweds. Melcthal addresses the people, urging them to preserve the spirit of independence so their children will be ready to defend it.

When sounds of a hunting party are heard nearby, Tell recognizes the presence of the Austrian bailiff, Gesler, who has forbidden nationalistic Swiss ceremonies like the wedding that just took place. Tell calls upon the people to resist tyranny (*Gesler proscrit ces voeux*), then follows Arnold, who has tried to slip away. Arnold, despite his love for Mathilde, is soon persuaded that rebellion is necessary. Once again the Austrian hunting horns are heard. Arnold is willing to challenge the tyrant, but Tell cautions him to think of his father's safety. Then Tell urges the villagers to go ahead and make merry: it is a form of defiance (chorus: *Hymenée, ta journée fortunée*). The six newlyweds dance (Pas de Six), followed by a dance for archers (chorus: *Enfants de la nature*).

Leuthold, a herdsman, stumbles in, asking for help. He has killed an Austrian soldier who tried to abduct his daughter, and other soldiers are in pursuit. He has tried to get Ruodi, the fisherman, to ferry him across the torrent, but Ruodi is afraid to take the risk. Tell commandeers the boat and shoves off with Leuthold just as the soldiers arrive. Rodolphe, commander of Gesler's archers, curses in frustration and orders Melchtal seized when the old man refuses to say who helped Leuthold get away (ensemble: *Si du rivage*).

ACT II   On the heights of Rütli, overlooking Lake Lucerne, an Austrian hunting party passes to one side; on the other, Swiss farmers and herdsmen end their day's work as evening approaches. Mathilde, in hopes of seeing Arnold, has lingered behind the hunting party (*Sombre forêt*). He has seen her and approaches, half-expecting her to send him away because of the differences in their rank and nationality. But she asks him to stay (duet: *Oui, vous l'arrachez à mon âme*), saying she returns his love. She agrees to meet him the next day, but approaching steps cause her to leave. Tell and Walter Fürst, another Swiss patriot, appear and confront Arnold with his divided loyalties (trio: *Quand l'Helvétie est un champ de supplices*), then tell him the Austrians have killed old Melchtal. This clinches Arnold's resolve to join the insurgents.

Through the woods, men of the adjoining cantons of Unterwalden, Schwyz, and Uri arrive and declare their determination to join Tell in the fight for freedom (*Jurons par nos dangers*).

ACT III   In a ruined chapel on the grounds of the bailiff's castle at Altdorf, Arnold meets Mathilde and tells her he must renounce her love in order to avenge his father's murder (duet: *Pour notre amour plus d'espérance*).

§ In the main square of Altdorf, in view of the castle, preparations are under way for a festival to celebrate 100 years of Austrian rule in Switzerland. Gesler has placed on a pike a "trophy" of his coat of arms, topped by his hat, and declares that everyone must bow in submission to it *(Vainement dans son insolence)*. To humiliate the local population, he has some young Swiss brought in and compelled to dance (Pas de Trois, a cappella chorus and dance: *Toi que l'oiseau ne suivrait pas)*. Then some of his soldiers force Swiss women to dance with them (Pas de Soldats), and everyone bows before the bailiff's hat—except Tell and Jemmy. Gesler warns them to comply, but Tell is defiant. Meanwhile, Rodolphe recognizes him as the man who saved Leuthold from the soldiers. Gesler orders him seized. When Tell tries to send Jemmy to safety (and to light signal fires for the uprising), Gesler stops the boy. He orders Tell to save his son's life by shooting an apple from his head with a single arrow. Tell quietly instructs Jemmy to kneel and hold as still as he can *(Sois immobile)*, then takes aim and shoots the apple. Amid general relief, Gesler notices a second arrow, which Tell says was for the tyrant himself, if the first shot failed. The infuriated Gesler now orders both Tell and Jemmy put in irons, but Mathilde arrives and takes the boy under her imperial protection. Gesler orders Tell taken to an island castle in the lake, where nameless reptiles will devour him (ensemble: *Quand l'orgueil les égare)*. The Swiss are indignant, but Gesler and his soldiers keep them at bay while Tell, echoed by his people, pronounces a curse on the bailiff *(Anathème sur Gesler!)*.

ACT IV Arnold has returned to his father's house and looks at it with sadness *(Asile héréditaire)*. His recollections are dispelled by the cries of Swiss Confederates: Tell has been taken prisoner, and they want to save him, but they have no arms. Arnold directs them behind the house, where his father and Tell kept a cache of weapons. Then he rallies them to go with him to Altdorf and rescue Tell *(Amis, secondez ma vengeance)*.

§ On a rocky shore at the foot of the Achsenberg, on the edge of Lake Lucerne, with Tell's cottage in view on a high eminence, a storm is brewing. Hedwige, believing her husband and son lost, is determined to confront Gesler, even if it means her own death. But Jemmy appears with Mathilde and reassures his mother that Tell will be able to escape (trio, Mathilde: *Je rends à votre amour un fils)*. Mathilde declares she will stay as a hostage, in defiance of Gesler, to ensure Tell's return. Even now, however, Gesler's men are ferrying Tell across the lake to prison. Jemmy, recalling that his father wanted him to start a signal fire for the uprising, hurries off. Hedwige, Mathilde, and the gathered people pray for Tell *(Toi, qui du faible es l'espérance)*.

Leuthold runs in to relate that Tell's boat is being driven ashore by the tempest; since Tell is the only one aboard able to land the vessel, his hands have been freed to steer it. Tell jumps ashore and pushes the boat, containing Gesler and his men, back out. On the mountainside he sees a fire: unable to find anything else to burn, Jemmy has ignited their own house, first saving Tell's weapons. Gesler and the soldiers follow in pursuit, but Tell shoots Gesler with an arrow, felling him into the water. Frightened by the legendary marksman, the soldiers flee. When Walter and his forces arrive, alerted by the fire, Tell says the tyrant lies dead in the lake. Arnold arrives with his own men to report that Altdorf has been taken: he hands Tell the banner that flew over the castle in Act III. As the storm clears, the Swiss landscape appears, and all give thanks for their victory (Tell: *Tout change et grandit en ces lieux!*).

Aulis Sallinen
b. 1935

The premiere of Aulis Sallinen's opera *Ratsumies* (The Horseman) at Olavinlinna castle during the Savonlinna Festival in 1975 signaled a new era for Finnish opera. Prior to that time, the original Savonlinna Festival and National Opera in Helsinki had introduced a series of native works, none of which had attracted attention beyond the country's borders. Since Savonlinna now attracts an international audience, this situation changed with *The Horseman*. Four years later in Helsinki, Sallinen produced *Punainen Viiva* (The Red Line), another work depicting frontier life during an earlier period in Finnish history. The new opera later had guest performances at the Royal Opera House, Covent Garden, in London, and during a visit by Finnish National Opera to the Metropolitan Opera House in April 1983.

The Red Line, written in what the composer calls a "more friendly" idiom than that of *The Horseman,* is more realistic than poetic, embodying principles of verismo. It was not well received during guest performances in the U.S.S.R., because it depicts socialist reform as a mixed blessing. Set during unrest a decade before Finnish independence, it presents an agitator who promises benefits to the frontier folk if they will vote to the left. Though they respond and make their point, their lot is little changed: the real adversary is a hostile climate, in which the odds are against mere survival. In the opera, a marauding bear represents both the threat of nature and of the ominous power of Russia, whose empire at that time still included Finland. Sallinen has explained that his aim was to show sympathy for the poor settlers while making clear there could be no easy answers to their predicament.

Sallinen, who studied with the distinguished Finnish composers Aare Meri-kanto and Joonas Kokkonen, was interested primarily in orchestral and chamber music before taking the operatic plunge with *The Horseman.* Though reluctant to commit a couple of years' work to composing another opera, he was persuaded by the success of *The Red Line* to devote himself more to the stage: *The King Goes Forth to France, Kullervo,* and *The Palace* were the result. Of these, only *Kullervo* is on a Finnish historical (in this case mythological) subject.

The composer's stylistic vocabulary, variable in its degree of "modernism" (dissonance, atonality, and serialism), has always been communicative. His works have been likened to landscapes in which natural growth takes place. Discovery of his aptitude for opera came as a surprise to Sallinen himself, since he had never been especially attracted to operas in the standard repertory, except for Mozart's; but once involved with the stage, he has kept moving in new directions. Audiences have not always followed him into whimsy and poetic abstruseness as willingly as they did into the keen portraiture and gripping relationships of *The Red Line*—a straightforward drama whose only real problem is its ending. Since the death of the central figure is not seen onstage and is only reported quickly, it has no time to sink in: unlike the death of Turiddu in *Cavalleria Rusticana,* it has not been prepared. One feels the composer would like to have countered with some message or symbol of hope, but the thought comes too late.

THE RED LINE

(Punainen Viiva)

TWO ACTS AND EPILOGUE

MUSIC: Aulis Sallinen

TEXT (Finnish): the composer, based on Ilmari Kianto's novel

WORLD PREMIERE: Helsinki, Finnish National Opera, November 30, 1978

U.S. PREMIERE: New York, Metropolitan Opera House (Finnish National Opera), April 27, 1983

CHARACTERS

Riika, *Topi's wife* . . . . Soprano
Kaisa, *a neighbor* . . . . Alto

Puntarpää, *a political agitator* . . . . Tenor
The Vicar . . . . Tenor
Topi, *a homesteader* . . . . Baritone
A Young Priest. . . . . Bass-Baritone
Simana Arhippaini, *a peddler* . . . . Bass

The story, though fictional, deals with a real period in Finnish history: the era of "Russification," when the Russian government, thereto benign under the relatively enlightened rule of Czar Alexander I, decided that Finland should be more closely incorporated, legally and culturally, into the Russian Empire. The Finnish people, who for decades had been loyal subjects of the czar, began to resist, sowing the seeds of their eventual independence. The author of *The Red Line* uses a bear to represent not only the threat of Russia but the hostile forces of nature in a demanding, unyielding frontier environment.

ACT I   Shortly before Christmas 1906, in a northern region of Finland (perhaps the province of Kainuu, home of Ilmari Kianto, who wrote the original story), the homesteader Topi finds evidence that a marauding bear has killed another of his sheep. His wife, Riika, compares their meager subsistence to the more comfortable life she knew as a girl working on a farm *(Ja siinä on sitten mies kokonaisen karhun tappajaksi)*. She fears that poverty will turn their hearts to stone: there is barely enough bread for the rest of the week, and the children have no shoes.

In sleep, Topi dreams that he visits the vicarage to ask for poor relief. The Vicar chides him for not being a regular churchgoer, but Topi says their cottage is too far out in the woods. He shows a coffin he has brought, containing the bodies of his three children, dead from starvation and cold. For the burial he will be charged one mark, according to law. Topi wakes and heads for the settlement with some game birds he has shot, hoping to trade them for flour. Alone, Riika reflects that she cannot blame Topi for their lot: he does his best. What would she do if he died? *(Pahasti tein, kun sanoin Topia tolloksi)*.

The next day, with Topi still gone, the traveling peddler Simana stops by on his way home from trading in Sweden. The children besiege him with questions about the world outside. He answers them with a cheerful ballad of riddles *(Vestmanviiki tietä ratsasti)*. Topi arrives with flour, coffee, and news of a meeting he attended, where political ideas were discussed *(No, annahan kun kerron)*: things will be better after the upcoming election, when poor people can vote for Socialist candidates by marking the ballot with a red line. As he speaks, the Cobbler and his wife are seen giving parts of their talk. There will be a larger meeting for everyone on New Year's Day at the citizens' assembly.

§ At the meeting, Puntarpää, a professional agitator, delivers an impassioned speech about the march of socialism, skillfully playing upon his audience's fundamentalist religious beliefs *(Aateveljet! Aatesisaret!)*. A Young Priest tries to question the wisdom of stirring up class hatred, but the agitator puts him down as a "lackey of the rich" and appeals to everyone's sense of freedom and brotherhood *(Kuulitteko nyt? Näittekö nyt?)*. Vividly characterizing the misery with which they are all familiar, he easily sways them to "Help the Party, and it will help you."

ACT II   Neighbors from a nearby homestead visit with Topi and Riika on Twelfth Night. Riika reads aloud from a Socialist pamphlet, interrupted by questions and comments. One of the neighbors, Kaisa, cautions that these new doctrines may be temptations from the devil *(Helvetin veräjiä kohti ollaan menossa oikein kruunun kyydillä!)*. When Topi asks how to mark the ballot, another neighbor, Epra, tells him to prick his thumb with a knife and draw the red line with blood; but Riika says there will be pencils—an implement Topi admits he has never used *(Piiretään! Hyvähän se on sanoa)*. Another neighbor, Tiina, hears dogs barking in the distance: they have heard what people cannot—the hibernating bear turning in his sleep.

§   In the village, the Young Priest and the agitator take turns leading the choir on election day, March 15, 1907, hailing the return of spring (chorus: *Onko Suomessa kevät?*). Riika and Topi sign up to vote and join the others waiting at the polling place.

§   As snow falls outside the cabin, Riika waits for news of the election results *(Tuiskuaa lunta)*. Kaisa returns, having heard the children are sick—a result, she fears, of the Devil's handiwork in these new liberal ideas. Seeing the little girl Linta Maria already dead, she sings a lullaby for the child *(Tuuti lasta Tuonelahan)*. Topi, who has been away logging, trudges home through the snow to find his daughter dead. He reports despairingly that he could find no help in the village, and now he will have to buy boards for a coffin, just as in his dream.

EPILOGUE   Kunilla, the cobbler's wife, arrives with news from Helsinki that the Socialist Party is ahead in the election, promising a better life for the poor *(Uutisia Helsingistä)*. When Kaisa reprimands her, saying God's punishment already has struck this household, Kunilla retorts that the rich are the ones responsible for such misfortune. Topi notices the barking of dogs in the distance: the bear must have returned from its winter sleep. He rushes out to investigate. Watching from the door, Riika sees him try to kill the bear, but it grapples with him and slashes his throat with its paw. As he lies dying, his blood draws a red line in the snow.

ARNOLD
SCHOENBERG
1874–1951

*D*uring Schoenberg's World War I army service, another soldier asked him, "You aren't the Schoenberg who writes that awful music, are you?" He replied, "Somebody had to be it." Those who had to deal with him in later life would have welcomed some of that ready humor in place of the bitter diatribes he regularly delivered against critics and the musical establishment.

Schoenberg's embitterment was caused by the fact that in order to advance music to its next stage of historical development, as he saw it, he had to fly in the face of what most people believed. His own efforts on behalf of traditional music were considerable: his early compositions derived from the tradition of Brahms, Wagner, and Mahler, and he went on to write one of the standard textbooks on harmony. Schoenberg knew that the accepted rules of music had been developed over centuries of trial and error, with great effort, by innumerable musicians of talent or genius. He had no intention of negating or ignoring this system but wanted to create a further one, based on different principles. Working his way through a period of atonality, to which his monodrama *Erwartung* belongs, he arrived step by step at serialism or dodecaphony, a theory postulating the equal importance of all twelve tones in the chromatic scale. To ensure this principle, he proposed that no tone should be repeated until all eleven others had been sounded.

There was a self-serving element in the development of this theory. Schoenberg intended to become the leader of a new school of composition that would succeeed—as, say, the Bauhaus did in the field of design—in making German culture intellectually preeminent in the world. He could not foresee that Hitler's adherents would take a wholly different view of "modern art," declaring most of it degenerate and driving out most of the artists, including Schoenberg, who would end his days a U.S. citizen.

Listeners are little concerned with theory, whether of a composer or of a political movement. Alban Berg, a convert to Schoenberg's teachings, insisted the listener need not and *should* not be made aware of the ordering of structural materials: these are the concern only of the composer and, perhaps, of a few qualified critics. A work of music, like a building or a painting, does not exist to show how it is made.

Thanks to Schoenberg's fine ear for instrumental colors and blends, his music has its own distinctive appeal. It may sound strange, but it does not sound theoretical. What once seemed iconoclastic and revolutionary now seems part of a familiar, even dated, sonic pallette. As he predicted, Schoenberg the composer has become a modern classic. The hope of Schoenberg the didactic theoretician, however—that his system would take over the future of music—has not been fulfilled. Serialism has become just another extension of the composer's range of technical choices.

The listener to *Erwartung* will find it steeped in the spirit of its time, a mixture of fin-de-siècle nostalgia and worldweariness with modern angst. What was the world coming to? Sigmund Freud and his colleagues were probing the recesses of the human psyche; the expressionists, Fauves, and Blue Rider school were standing the arts on their head. These advances were exciting, but they were unsettling. The malaise is implicit in Schoenberg's restless music. In his writing for the soprano, he combines *Sprechstimme* (rhythmically annotated speech) with *Sprechgesang* (halfway between speech and song) and conventional singing, expanding the expressive horizons of the voice, throwing the listener off balance with the unexpected. The avant-garde, like the Woman in *Erwartung,* was groping obsessively through a dark forest of metaphor and possibility. Never again could music return to an illusion of security.

ERWARTUNG

(Expectation)

ONE ACT
MUSIC: Arnold Schoenberg

TEXT (German): Marie Pappenheim
WORLD PREMIERE: Prague, Neues Deutsches Theater, June 6, 1924
(ISCM Festival)
U.S. PREMIERE (concert performance): New York, Carnegie Hall,
November 15, 1951
U.S. STAGE PREMIERE: Washington, D.C., Opera Society of Washing-
ton, December 28, 1960
METROPOLITAN PREMIERE: January 16, 1989

CHARACTER

The Woman . . . . Soprano

As in Bartók's *Bluebeard's Castle,* the setting for *Erwartung* can be taken both
literally and figuratively—either way, or both ways at once. The landscape
depicted has literal details, but it also sets forth, as in an expressionist painting, an image of the inner psyche. The symbols used are those often encountered in dreams and in psychoanalysis. The central dramatic question—did
the Woman kill her lover?—is inescapable but remains unanswered. Is this the
Woman's dream, is it her deranged recollection, or is it actually happening? In
any of these cases, it reflects her state of mind rather than an external reality.

SCENE I   A lone Woman approaches the edge of a dark forest, of which only
the nearest trees and the beginning of a path are revealed by moonlight.
Assessing the ominous atmosphere, she hesitates to enter *(Feig bist du, willst
ihn nicht suchen?);* but she is determined to look for her lover. She hopes to
raise her courage by singing, which also will enable him to hear her approach.

SCENE II   Having followed the path into the forest, the Woman is frightened
by unseen branches that brush against her like hands. To steady herself, she
recollects how peaceful the town looked as she left it *(Und die Stadt im hellen
Nebel).* She had been waiting for her lover to come to her by the usual path,
but he had not appeared. She thinks she hears crying sounds *(Wer weint da?)*
and is startled by a nightbird's call. When she tries to run, she trips and falls
over what she at first takes to be a body—no, it is just a tree trunk.

SCENE III   She emerges into a clearing, where the moonlight reveals tall
grasses and ferns *(Da kommt ein Licht!)*—and her own shadow, whose movement frightens her, as does a sound from the grass.

SCENE IV   The Woman emerges where the path leads out of the forest. A
connected path is seen leading to a shuttered house in the background. Her
search for her lover has been futile *(Er ist auch nicht da).* Seeing the house, she
says she cannot enter there: an unknown woman will drive her away. Looking

for a place to sit and rest, she stumbles against something near the dark edge of the woods—and discovers the body of her lover.

At first she goes into denial, thinking she only imagined what she has seen *(Das Mondlicht . . . nein, dort)*. But when she decides to go back and look for him in the forest, she sees the body again and has to accept the fact that she has found him. She hopes vainly that she can revive him *(Was soll ich tun)*, then starts to recall the past three days, when she has not seen him. She was so convinced he would come to her this night . . . she felt his presence as she passed through the woods. . . .

But her recollections gradually take on a tone of accusation. She had suspected him of an affair with the woman in the house—"the woman with the white arms" *(Du siehst wieder dort hin?)*. She kicks the body and accuses him of making love to this other woman. As her anger subsides into lamentation, she recalls how utterly she devoted herself to him during the past year *(Oh! nicht einmal die Gnade)*. Now day is approaching: she will be left alone, aimless in her life, lost without him *(Liebster, der Morgen kommt)*. Where can he be? Oh . . . he is here. . . .

FRANZ SCHREKER
1878–1934

*S*chreker and Alexander Zemlinsky, influential in their time, were largely forgotten for about thirty years—roughly from the mid-1930s until the mid-1960s, when curiosity gradually led to a revival of interest in their work. Their eclipse is attributable mainly to the Nazi campaign against "degenerate" art in general, and Jewish artists in particular. But there was another factor at work: changing tastes. Late romanticism in music at the turn of the century tended to take the form of verismo (in Italy), so-called impressionism (chiefly in France), or expressionism (in Germany and Austria). A more drastic and controversial step was modernism, embodied in Arnold Schoenberg's break with traditional tonality. Of German-speaking composers who continued along established paths, only Richard Strauss managed to avoid eclipse.

The fact that modernists such as Schoenberg and his disciple Alban Berg admired Schreker and Zemlinsky did not help the latter two, who remained late romantics and suffered the consequences. Viewed from the perspective of today, both are interesting for having tempered the extremes of expressionism with the subtler musical language of impressionism, also sampling the avant-garde departures from conventional tonality.

Franz Schreker, born in Monaco, studied in Vienna with a conservative teacher, Robert Fuchs, and in his mid-thirties became a teacher himself, in which capacity he remained influential for the rest of his life. Schreker's compositions began to appear in the late 1890s, and by 1903 he had essayed a one-act opera, *Flammen.* Around that time he began work on a full-length opera, *Der Ferne Klang,* but did not complete it until 1910, after friends and advisers had discouraged him with their comments. Meanwhile, in Vienna he had founded the Philharmonic Chorus, with which he conducted premieres by contemporary composers. The premiere of *Der Ferne Klang* in Frankfurt in 1912 caught the public ear, much as Erich Wolfgang Korngold's *Die Tote Stadt* would do later (1920).

The hero of *Der Ferne Klang,* like that of Charpentier's *Louise* (1900), is a "Bohemian," a fashionably unconventional artist. This one fails in his romantic quest to fulfill a vision. Schreker makes full use of the orchestra, and there are experimental touches—notably the café scene, with two conversations going on at once at nearby tables—that left a mark on later composers, such as Berg in *Wozzeck* and Bernd Alois Zimmermann in *Die Soldaten.* As an allegory of the unreachable goal toward which every artist directs his life, *Der Ferne Klang* remains telling. In his later operas, Schreker explored more perverse and shocking subjects; though the music is often suitably lurid, one feels the composer overreaching, leaving himself open to the charge of "degeneracy."

In 1920, Schreker had taken the prestigious directorship of the Berlin High School for Music. While there he composed his last four operas, but in 1932, the year of the premiere of *Der Schmied von Gent,* he was forced to resign under pressure from the Nazis. He retreated to the Prussian Academy of Art, where he conducted a master class until the following year, when he suffered a fatal stroke. Reduced in so short a time to status as a nonperson, he might have remained so, if not for the restless tides of taste and curiosity that have brought revivals of his works in recent years.

Der Ferne Klang

(The Distant Sound)

THREE ACTS
MUSIC: Franz Schreker
TEXT (German): the composer
WORLD PREMIERE: Frankfurt, Alte Oper, August 18, 1912

CHARACTERS

Grete Graumann. . . . . .Soprano
Graumann's Wife, *Grete's mother* . . . . .Mezzo-Soprano

An Old Woman	Mezzo-Soprano
Fritz, *a young artist*	Tenor
A Chevalier	Tenor
A Suspicious Individual	Tenor
A Count	Baritone
A Ham Actor, *crony of Graumann*	Baritone
Rudolf, *Fritz's friend and doctor*	Bass-Baritone
Dr. Vigelius, *a shady lawyer, crony of Graumann*	Bass
Old Graumann, *a retired minor official*	Bass
Landlord of the Swan tavern	Bass

Schreker's libretto and score identify Fritz only as an "artist" and his work performed in Act III, Scene 1, only as a "piece," which could mean either a play (possibly with incidental music) or an opera.

ACT I A small town in Germany, about 1885. In the sparsely furnished lower-middle-class home of old Graumann and his Wife, their daughter, Grete, anxiously questions her sweetheart, Fritz, about his intention of setting out to make his way in the world. If she were to come with him, as she wants, he is afraid their love would be smothered by the harsh realities of trying to make a living. His plan is to work hard to express his own individual voice—to capture the "distant sound" of harps, caressed by the wind, that he thinks he can hear—and to become "an artist by the grace of God," returning to Grete prosperous and famous (*Ich muss, Liebste, ich muss!*). She is not convinced: Fritz has brought the only ray of hope into her otherwise dreary life. He tries to reassure her (duet: *Doch wollt' ich mich neigen*). Hearing rowdy sounds outside from her father and his cronies, who have been gambling, Grete realizes that Fritz must escape this depressing atmosphere even if she cannot, so she bids him a quick farewell.

An Old Woman appears, looking for Grete's mother. She remarks that Grete's boyfriend shouldn't be going off at a time when her father and his gang might be up to something (*Gar nicht schön von dem jungen Herrn!*). As the Old Woman leaves, Grete wonders whether she has seen her somewhere before.

Grete's mother comes in, shaking her head about the way her husband carries on at the Swan, the tavern across the street. When Grete offers to go into domestic service to earn extra money for the family, however, the mother will not hear of it. Boisterous cries are raised outside about an engagement and a wedding. Graumann stumbles in with his cronies: the Innkeeper, the shady lawyer Dr. Vigelius, a Ham Actor, and others from the tavern. The Actor addresses Grete and her mother with the news that Graumann bet his daughter at gambling and lost her to the Innkeeper (*Verehrte Frau! Schönes Fräulein!*). Grete, dumbfounded, hears Vigelius' account of the "jolly game" in which she was bartered (*Das war ein lustiges Spiel!*). She stammers that she is engaged to someone else, but her father threatens her, while the Innkeeper assures her of his good intentions (*Fräulein, sollten sich's überlegen*), and even her mother seems inclined to encourage the advantageous match. Grete puts up no more objections, but as soon as she is left alone, she jumps out the window into the street, determined to find Fritz and escape with him.

§ In woods near a lake, Grete at nightfall realizes she cannot find her beloved (*Fritz find' ich nicht mehr*). She is about to throw herself into the water when moonlight transfigures the scene, turning her thoughts to life and love. As she falls asleep, the Old Woman appears to her as if in a dream, offering to lead her to a comfortable house with nice clothes and pleasant pastimes, where she will be surrounded by love and happiness (*Liegt ein schönes Kindchen im Moos*). When the Old Woman adds she will find Grete a sweetheart, the girl thinks she means Fritz and follows her.

ACT II   Ten years have passed. In the Casa di Maschere, a Venetian house of pleasure, courtesans and their clients prepare for an evening of partying (ensemble: *Kommt geschwind, Mizi, Mary, die Gondel des Grafen!*). Grete has become the star attraction and is courted by a Count, among others (men: *Greta! Endlich! Zu lange entziehst Du Dich unserer Sehnsucht*). In the years since she gave up her search for Fritz, she has become jaded and tired of so much admiration (*Seit vielen Jahren dünkt mich*). To escape her painful lost memories, however, she sees no choice but to continue taking refuge in idle pleasure. She promises herself to the one who will sing the most winning song. The Count offers a ballad about a king cursed with a glowing crown, which he finally throws into the ocean—only to have a mermaid appear and haul him underwater (*In einem Lande ein bleicher König*). A Chevalier counters with more cheerful verses about the Flowermaidens of Sorrento (*Wer kennt sie nicht, die reizenden kleinen Blumenmädchen von Sorrent?*). Pressed to make a choice, Grete seems sad and indifferent, prompting the Count to ask her what is wrong (*Ich glaube Dir nicht*). She confesses that something about him stirs sad memories for her.

Meanwhile, a new guest has arrived by boat: Fritz, now sporting a beard. He recognizes Grete at once, but she has trouble believing it is he. He tells how, embittered by the emptiness of success, he has lost his sense of direction and purpose and hoped to regain it by finding her (*Schuldbeladen und reuig steh' ich vor Dir*). So fervent is his narrative that she announces he has won her in the song contest. Coming to his senses, he realizes that his idealized beloved, whom he had hoped to marry, has sunk into a life of shame. When the Count challenges him to take back his insulting words, Fritz boards his boat, declaring he will not fight over a whore. Defeated, Grete turns herself over to the Count. The orchestra strikes up a Csárdás, setting off a wild celebration.

ACT III   Five years later, in a large German city, Vigelius and the Actor are seated in the café garden of a theater where Fritz's work is having its premiere. Both have worked their way out of the small town where they started; but now the Actor has refused bit parts from the big-city theater because he found them demeaning. He reminds Vigelius about the dirty trick they played on Graumann's daughter at the Swan tavern in the old days. A member of the ensemble from the theater arrives: it is intermission, and he has time to kill before his next appearance. He asks to join the two men at their table and relates how the new piece is a great success. The Actor, skeptical of modern writers, is surprised.

A Policeman leads Grete, now known as "Tini," to a nearby table. The theater player continues to tell about *The Harp,* as the piece is called. Meanwhile, Grete tells the Waitress she was in the theater but felt unwell and had to leave. A suspicious-looking Individual approaches Grete, sits down, and makes overtures. The theater player has to leave but says he will be back after the show. Grete tells the Individual she doesn't recognize him, but he persists in his attentions. As she continues to discourage him, the theater player comes back to report an abrupt change of fortune: the last act has displeased the audience. When Grete turns to the other table for help in dealing with her unwanted admirer, Vigelius recognizes her and comes to her aid.

Theater patrons arrive, chattering about the depressing, negative effect of the autobiographical last act and expressing sympathy for the author, who they have heard is seriously ill. Grete knows she must go to him *(Was sagen die Leute?).* When she falls from weakness, Vigelius declares he will take her where she wants to go.

§ The next day, in Fritz's study, he sits at his desk, realizing too late how he pursued fame at the cost of his youthful dream *(Wie seltsam das ist!).* His friend Rudolf arrives and urges him to rework the last act of his play, thereby completing "an immortal work," but Fritz says he lacks the strength and must accept failure. When he asks about the woman who fell ill during the performance, Rudolf says she turned out to be just a streetwalker. This reminds Fritz of how he rejected Grete at their last meeting *(Dirne! Ja, das war es).* In doing so, he renounced love, inspiration, and the ability to write about happiness. Feeling sympathy for the woman, he asks Rudolf to find her and bring her to him.

When Rudolf has gone, Fritz, prompted by distant bells, sadly recalls the elusive "distant sound" of his youth. Vigelius arrives and, feeling guilty about his part in the trick played on Grete fifteen years before *(Eine schwere Schuld),* speaks of a poor woman who has fallen on hard times. Fritz offers cash, but Vigelius says it is not a question of money. Meanwhile, Fritz seems to hear the sound of a thousand harps. When Vigelius reminds him of the episode in Venice, Fritz realizes he is referring to Grete, and wants desperately to see her. She has been waiting in the garden and comes in. The excitement of their reunion taxes his feverish health to the limit, but he declares he has experienced happiness at last (duet: *Deine Wangen, mein Liebster).* He asks if she too can hear the "distant sound," like music of the spheres: its secret is that of enduring love. Now, he declares, I have found my last act—I can rewrite it. But he collapses, dying, in Grete's arms.

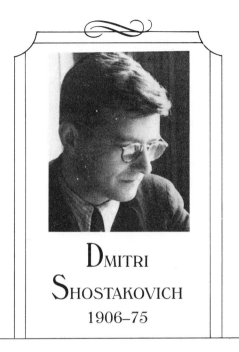

Dmitri Shostakovich
1906–75

*S*hostakovich shared with Sergei Prokofiev the distinction of being one of the two best-known Soviet composers of their generation. The symphonic works of both were widely performed abroad, but their operas scarcely seemed to exist, in large part because of political interference at home. Prokofiev persevered in writing operas, but Shostakovich gave up, depriving the twentieth-century lyric stage of one of its major natural talents.

It was as a pianist for silent films that the young Shostakovich developed his flair for musical parody and for "Mickey Mousing"—matching music to action. *The Nose,* produced when he was twenty-four, displays the comedic side of this aptitude. The story, after a satirical play by Gogol, is patently absurd, like a Keystone Kops farce or an animated cartoon. The Keystone Kops element returns in his only full-length opera, *Lady Macbeth of the Mtsensk District,* but here the composer, now twenty-eight, also reveals his serious side. There are Grand Guignol elements, seemingly borrowed from horror movies, alongside social commentary that mocks and condemns the greed and ignorance of most of the characters. The music is graphic and energetic, sometimes underscoring the action, sometimes going its own way to express the composer's anger or amusement.

Shostakovich was depicting elements of Soviet life, a fact he took care to disguise by choosing a story from the previous century. Beneath his caricature of the buffoonish gendarmes, for example, lies his disgust with the mechanics of a police state. Though his heroine is a murderess, his sympathies lie with her: he sees her as the victim of a repressive society, driven to a point where she has no choice. In her hopelessness, she makes her own destruction inevitable.

The title *Lady Macbeth of the Mtsensk District* seems far-fetched, as parallels between Katerina Ismailova and Shakespeare's Lady are slight. Nikolai Leskov, author of the original story (1866), shared a fondness for Shakespearean parallels with Ivan Turgenev, who wrote stories entitled *A Hamlet of the Shchigrovsky District* (1849) and *A Lear of the Steppe* (1870). Shostakovich's *Lady Macbeth* appeared at a time when avant-garde experimentation was still approved in the Soviet theater. At first the work was warmly received, playing eighty-three performances in Leningrad alone, but after it reached Moscow, Stalin was persuaded to attended a performance, early in 1936. He left in a fury; one is reminded of Hitler's outrage at seeing a nude woman in a bathtub in Hindemith's *Neues vom Tage.* Almost overnight, modernism in the Soviet theater was officially dead. In an editorial (not an ordinary music review) in *Pravda,* entitled "Chaos Instead of Music," Shostakovich was roundly condemned; Stalin is believed to have dictated all or parts of the article himself. In shortorder, Shostakovich's name became infamous even to Soviet citizens who had not yet heard of him. The young composer packed his suitcase, expecting to be taken off to a prison camp. Instead, he was pilloried and ostracized culturally, his opera branded as "un-Soviet, unwholesome, cheap, eccentric and leftist."

Shostakovich survived this traumatic episode, as well as later denunciations, but in his work he went partially underground. Outwardly he paid lip service to the new ideals of "socialist realism," but even the symphonies, his more "public" compositions, appear to be filled with double meanings and disguised assaults on the system. Naturally loathing his country's enemies, he did his patriotic duty as a fire warden during World War II, yet it was evident that he saw little difference between the evils of fascism and those of Stalin's regime.

There always had been duality in Shostakovich's work. Even the youthful First Symphony is divided between two playfully sardonic movements and two of threnody, perhaps for victims of the Russian Revolution. This ambivalence remains a disturbing factor in *Lady Macbeth,* tempting some stage directors to treat it as fantastic farce, others as Russian verismo, when in fact it is more than either, an amalgam of both. Starting as satire, it ends as tragedy.

Shostakovich never stopped believing in his opera, and to make it performable again he revised it under the title *Katerina Ismailova,* toning down or replacing some of the sex and violence. In this form it returned to the stage in Moscow in 1963 and was recorded. While it is easy to say that Shostakovich had to bowdlerize his work to make it eligible for political rehabilitation, it is also true that with maturity he had second thoughts and undertook at least some of the changes willingly. In either form, *Lady Macbeth* makes its point and remains a strong, personally felt statement by this complex composer.

THE NOSE

(Nos)

PRELUDE, THREE ACTS, AND EPILOGUE
MUSIC: Dmitri Shostakovich
TEXT (Russian): the composer, Yevgeny Zamyatin, Georgy Ionin, and
    Alexander Preiss, based on Nikolai Gogol's story
WORLD PREMIERE: Leningrad, Maly Theater, January 18, 1930
U.S. PREMIERE: Santa Fe Opera, August 11, 1965 (in English)

CHARACTERS

Praskovya Osipovna, *the barber's wife* . . . . Soprano
Daughter of Pelageya Grigoryevna Podtochina . . . . Soprano
Pelageya Grigoryevna Podtochina . . . . .Mezzo-Soprano
District Police Inspector . . . . Tenor
The Nose . . . . Tenor
Yaryzhkin, *acquaintance of Kovalyov* . . . . Tenor
Pyotr Fyodorovich, *friend of Kovalyov* . . . . Tenor
Ivan, *Kovalyov's servant* . . . . Tenor
Maj. Platon Kuzmich Kovalyov, *collegiate assessor* . . . . . . Baritone
Ivan Yakovlevich, *a barber* . . . . Bass

The action takes place in St. Petersburg, Russia, in the mid-nineteenth century.

PRELUDE   After the overture, Major Kovalyov is seen getting a shave from the barber Ivan Yakovlevich.

ACT I   In his apartment behind the barbershop, Ivan Yakovlevich wakes to the smell of bread being baked by his wife, Praskovya. He asks for bread instead of his usual morning coffee; but as he cuts into the loaf, he finds a nose baked into the bread. His wife berates him for shaving his customers so carelessly that he cut the nose off one of them. She demands that it—and Ivan Yakovlevich himself—leave the house at once *(I slyshat' ne khochu)*. The barber cannot imagine where the nose came from.

§ Hurrying along an embankment, Ivan Yakovlevich drops the nose, wrapped in paper, but is noticed by a Police Inspector, who tells him he dropped something and makes him pick it up. Further attempts to get rid of the parcel are futile, as Ivan Yakovlevich keeps running into people of his acquaintance who wonder at his odd behavior. Then the Police Inspector questions him suspiciously about his presence by the river.

§ Major Kovalyov wakes up in his bedroom, looks in a mirror, and realizes he has lost his nose. Upset, he hurries off to find the Police Commissioner.

§ In Kazan Cathedral, Kovalyov joins other worshippers, covering his noseless face with a handkerchief. To his surprise, he sees his nose in the uniform of a State Councilor and tries to broach the subject of getting it back *(Kak mne obiasnit' emu?)*. The Nose, however, takes on airs in its new identity and says there can be no relationship between the two of them. When Kovalyov's attention is distracted momentarily by a woman entering the cathedral, the Nose makes its exit.

ACT II   Kovalyov, sitting in a cab, calls out to the Doorman that he wants to see the Police Commissioner—who has just left. So he tells the driver to take him to the newspaper office.

§ Kovalyov makes his way into the newspaper office and has to compete for the attention of a Clerk, who is taking a classified ad from a talkative Footman. Kovalyov starts to explain that he has lost his nose but doesn't want his name used, to avoid embarrassment. To make matters worse, the Nose is now going about town presenting itself as a State Councilor *(Ia ne mogu vam skazat')*. The office staff takes this as a great joke. Kovalyov grows upset as he describes how the loss of his nose will interfere with his courtship of a certain young lady. The Clerk decides to refuse the ad, because it might turn out to be scandalous or libelous *(Èto vam kazhetsia)*. To prove he is telling the truth, Kovalyov removes the handkerchief from his face; when the Clerk still demurs and jokingly offers him snuff, which of course he cannot sniff without a nose, Kovalyov angrily runs out, leaving the staff to read with amusement through a fresh batch of classified ads (octet: *Otpuskaetsia v usluzhenie kucher trezvovo povedeniia)*.

§ In Kovalyov's apartment, his servant, Ivan, is singing about his girlfriend *(Nepobedimoi siloi priverzhen ia k miloi)*, to his own balalaika accompaniment, when Kovalyov enters, still upset, and carries on about the many possible bad consequences of being without a nose *(Bozhe moi, za chto takoe neschast'e?)*.

ACT III   At a coach station on the outskirts of the city, the Police Inspector is assigning some Policemen to ambush a suspect. As they wait, they begin a song *(Podzhav khvost, kak sobaka)*, but they quiet down when various citizens start to arrive, preparing to board the stagecoach. A Woman Street Vendor attracts the Policemen's lecherous attention as the departing passengers exchange remarks (ensemble: *Sudarynia! Zdes' prebudet prianost' vremeni*). As the coach starts to leave, the Nose rushes in to catch it, frightening the horse and causing the Coachman to fire his gun. Panic ensues as the Nose starts to flee but stumbles over the Police Inspector, who alerts his squad to seize the culprit. The Policemen beat up the Nose, reducing it to its original size. The Police Inspector wraps it in paper and takes it away.

§ The Police Inspector calls at Kovalyov's apartment to inform him that his nose has been found, adding that the barber Ivan Yakovlevich is being held as an accomplice. After returning the nose to Kovalyov, the Inspector hints that he could use money for his children's education, so Kovalyov pays him a reward. After the Inspector has left, Kovalyov greets his nose with delight (*On, tochno! On!*) but discovers it will not stick to his face, so he sends his servant to fetch a Doctor. A cursory look convinces the Doctor that it would be better not to try to attach the nose: Kovalyov should keep it, unless he should get a good offer to sell it (*Verite li, chto ia nikogda iz korysti ne lechil*). After the Doctor takes his leave, Kovalyov's friend Yaryzhkin next appears, but his suggestions are no help either. Kovalyov speculates that the widow Podtochina, who wants him to marry her Daughter, must have set in motion the events that cost him his nose (*Vinoiu ètovo do zhen byt' ne kto drugoi*). He starts to write her a letter . . .

§ . . . and the scene fades to show her fortune-telling for her Daughter with playing cards. Just as she predicts a marriage proposal from Kovalyov, the servant arrives with his letter. As the Daughter reads it, she sees it is no proposal but an accusation of witchcraft and a threat of legal action ("*Milostivaia gosudarinia, Pelageia Grigorevna!*")

§ The scene returns to Kovalyov and Yaryzhkin, reading the widow's reply ("*Milostivyi gosudar', Platon Kuzmich!*"), in which she denies any harmful intentions toward him and, on the contrary, suggests he should be satisfied with her Daughter's hand. Kovalyov believes she must be innocent after all.

§ A group of Gentlemen comment on the newspaper report that Kovalyov's nose has taken leave of his face and is walking about on its own. They see a man approaching who they think is Kovalyov, but it turns out to be someone else. A new arrival on the scene informs them that the Nose is in Junker's store.

§ Outside the store, bleachers have been set up and bystanders are buying tickets, jostling to catch a glimpse of the Nose inside the store, until another newcomer says the Nose is walking in the Summer Garden. The crowd excitedly leaves to go there.

§ Though rumors are flying, the Nose doesn't appear in the Summer Garden either, and the Police have to spray the crowd with water to disperse it.

§ At Kovalyov's apartment, he dances with joy: his nose is back on his face at last. The barber Ivan Yakovlevich arrives to shave him, just as in the first scene.

§ Kovalyov strolls along the Nevsky Prospekt, greeting acquaintances, until he encounters the widow Podtochina and her Daughter. He greets the older lady effusively, telling her a pointless joke, but when she invites him to dinner the next day—adding that a proposal to her Daughter would not be amiss— he politely takes his leave, safeguarding his bachelor freedom.

EPILOGUE A chorus of citizens skeptically reviews the story of the Nose, finding it full of improbabilities *(Vot kakaia istoriia)*. But life is peppered with absurdities, after all, and the public is gullible. If it makes a good story, what's the harm? Kovalyov, back in form, flirts with a girl selling false shirt fronts and walks off, smiling with self-satisfaction.

LADY MACBETH OF THE MTSENSK DISTRICT
(Ledi Makbet Mtsenskogo Vyezda)

FOUR ACTS
MUSIC: Dmitri Shostakovich
TEXT (Russian): the composer and Alexander Preis, based on Nikolai Leskov's story
WORLD PREMIERE: Leningrad, Maly Theater, January 22, 1934
U.S. PREMIERE (semi-staged): Cleveland, Severance Hall, January 31, 1935
REVISED VERSION, *Katerina Ismailova*
WORLD PREMIERE: Moscow, Stanislavsky / Nemirovich-Dachenko Theater, December 26, 1962
U.S. PREMIERE: San Francisco Opera, October 23, 1964

CHARACTERS

Katerina Lvovna Ismailova, *Zinovy's wife* . . . . Soprano
Aksinya, *cook in the Ismailov household* . . . . Soprano
Sonyetka, *a convict* .Mezzo-Soprano
Zinovy Borisovich Ismailov, *a merchant* . . . . Tenor
Sergei, *a farm worker*. . . . . Tenor
A Shabby Peasant . . . . Tenor

Chief of Police . . . . Baritone
Boris Timofeyevich Ismailov, *Zinovy's father, a merchant* . . . . . Bass
A Priest . . . . Bass
Old Convict . . . . Bass

ACT I   Provincial Russia, mid-nineteenth century. Katerina Lvovna Ismailova, trapped in a loveless marriage to a landowner, lies on her bed, yawning with boredom but unable to sleep *(Net, ne spitsia)*. Her overbearing father-in-law, Boris, looks in to ask if she will prepare his favorite sautéed mushrooms; at the same time, he reproves her for laziness and for not having produced a child in four years of marriage. When she says her husband has been unable to make her pregnant, Boris blames her coldness as a wife and warns her against taking a lover *(Vsë ot baby zavisit)*. Telling her to fix poison for the rats, which have been getting into the flour again, he leaves. She does so, muttering that he too is a rat and deserves poison. Her ineffectual husband, Zinovy, appears with other men of the farm and learns he must go to oversee repairs to a broken dam at the mill, some distance away. Boris questions a new farmhand, Sergei, as to why he left his old job, but is distracted when horses are brought for Zinovy's departure. Boris now insists that Katerina observe the old custom of kneeling to swear fidelity during her husband's absence. As the men leave, the cook, Aksinya, gossips to Katerina that the new worker, Sergei, was fired from his last job for carrying on with the mistress.

§ In the yard, serfs torment, pinch, and caress Aksinya, whom they have trapped in a barrel. Katerina arrives and berates the men for abusing a woman *(Mnogo vy, muzhiki)*. If women are as strong as she claims, Sergei says, can he test her strength? He squeezes her hand, and when she pushes him, they start to wrestle. Boris intrudes, ordering the men back to work and demanding his mushrooms.

§ Back in her bedroom that evening, Katerina tells Boris she is going to sleep. When he leaves, she gives voice to her loneliness and restlessness *(Zherebënok k kobylke toropitsia)*. Sergei knocks, under pretext of borrowing something to read. Reminding her of their wrestling match, he seizes and embraces her. His advances are delayed briefly when Boris, locking up for the night, calls from the hallway to see if she is safely in bed. Assured that he is gone, the two make love passionately.

ACT II   A week later, Boris wanders in the yard in the early morning hours, noticing that Katerina's light is on *(Svet v okne)*. Naturally she cannot sleep, he surmises, since she is young and frustrated: he ought to satisfy her himself. His fantasies come to a halt when Sergei climbs out the window and down the drainpipe. Boris grabs him and calls the other farmhands, then thrashes him with a whip. From her window, Katerina cannot get Boris to stop; since she is locked in, she slides down the drainpipe herself. The serfs hold her back from attacking Boris, who eventually runs out of strength and orders Sergei locked in the storeroom. When Boris asks if there is anything to eat, Katerina goes to fetch the leftover mushrooms, this time lacing them with rat poison. Boris, after having the Porter send word to Zinovy of trouble at home, eats the mushrooms and immediately is stricken, yelling for a priest. Katerina takes his keys to the storeroom and leaves him to the mercies of the farmhands, who fetch the local Priest. With his dying words, Boris says he has been poisoned *(Batia, ispovedatsia)* and points accusingly at the returning Katerina, but her convincing lamentations make it seem likely the old man was delirious.

In Katerina's bedroom some time later, she wakens Sergei and kisses him ardently, but he says that because Zinovy will soon be back, the affair will have to end *(Katia, prikhodit konets liubvi nashei)*. She pledges to make Sergei her husband, but as he dozes, she sees and hears the ghost of Boris cursing her. She is shaken further by sounds of Zinovy's return. Sergei hides before Katerina lets Zinovy in, but Sergei in his haste has left his belt, which the husband discovers on the bed. This gives him courage to confront Katerina about her rumored infidelity *(Kak zhivëte, mozhete?)*. When she defies him, he starts striking her with the belt. She calls Sergei, who helps her strangle Zinovy, then finishes him off with a blow from a heavy candlestick. Sergei carries the body to the cellar, puts it in a dry well, and covers it with stones.

ACT III   On the day of their wedding, Sergei and Katerina leave for church. A Shabby Peasant who frequents the farm wanders in drunk, singing about the glories of booze *(U menia byla kuma)*. Finding no one around, he ventures into the cellar to find wine but is repelled by the stench, then discovers Zinovy's corpse and runs out.

§   At the police station, a Sergeant and his men complain about their poor pay and lack of opportunities to collect bribes (ensemble: *No za vsë svoi staraniia*). It also galls them not to be invited to Katerina's wedding celebration. A policeman brings in a Nihilist Teacher he has arrested, but questioning of the innocuous man is interrupted by the Shabby Peasant, blurting out his discovery. This gives the police an excuse to invade the party (ensemble: *Skoro, skoro*).

§   In the garden at the farm, drunken guests and the local Priest hail the newlyweds *(Slava suprugam)*, but Katerina notices the cellar lock has been broken. Quietly she tells Sergei they will have to escape as soon as they can *(Sergei, nado bezhat')*. As he goes into the house to get money, the police arrive. Seeing it is too late, Katerina lets herself be arrested. Sergei tries to run but is caught. The police congratulate themselves.

ACT IV   On their way to Siberia, a band of shackled convicts pause to rest near a bridge. Led by an Old Convict, they lament the hopelessness and hardship of their fate *(Ekh, ty put', tsepiami vskopanny)*. Katerina bribes a sentry for some vodka and finds Sergei, who sulks and accuses her of ruining his life. She reflects sadly that being a prisoner has left her no strength to deal with Sergei's rejection *(Ne legko posle pochëta)*. Meanwhile, Sergei makes up to a pretty convict, Sonyetka, who asks him to get her some stockings from his rich wife. Sergei returns to Katerina and tells her the shackles have bruised his legs so badly that he will be unable to continue the march. Katerina gives him her stockings, only to see him take them to Sonyetka, whom he carries off. The other women make fun of Katerina, who escapes their jeers to contemplate the bleak landscape, which mirrors her emotions *(V lesu, v samoi chashche)*. Sonyetka, returning from the tryst with Sergei, mockingly thanks her for the stockings, then goes to stand on the bridge while an Officer orders the prisoners to resume their journey. Roused by the Old Prisoner, Katerina goes to Sonyetka and pushes her off the bridge, then jumps after her. Seeing both women drown in the icy current, the Officer moves the other convicts on their way.

BEDŘICH SMETANA
1824–84

*D*espite discouragement from his father, a brewmaster in the town of
Litomyšl, Bedřich Smetana as a young man harbored ambitions as a
piano virtuoso. After the financial failure of his first concert tour, he
sought the advice of Franz Liszt, who helped him establish a piano
school, and this project fared better. In 1856, Smetana accepted an offer to go
to Sweden as music director of the Göteborg Philharmonic, a post he held for
five years, meanwhile starting on a parallel career in composition. By the time
he returned home for good in the early 1860s, Bohemia had been granted
some autonomy within the Austro–Hungarian Empire, stimulating artists to
deal with nationalistic and folkloric subjects. This Smetana did in his tone
poems and eventually in a series of operas, starting with *The Brandenburgers in
Bohemia* (1863).

In those days, German was the language of most educated Bohemians, and
Smetana had to make a conscious effort to master Czech prosody in his musical
settings. After his second opera, *The Bartered Bride* (1866), which remains his
most famous, he returned from comedy to another historical subject with *Dalibor*. The text was the work of Josef Wenzig, a school administrator and member
of the Czech Diet. Though a patriotic Czech, Wenzig was German-speaking
and wrote his poem in German, subsequently transforming it into a libretto.
For an idiomatic Czech translation he turned to a pupil of his, Ervin Spindler.
Smetana at first tried to set the two languages simultaneously, hoping for
performances abroad in the German version, but soon he abandoned this idea
and concentrated on the Czech, leaving the German to be adapted later.

During his work on *Dalibor*, Smetana was appointed conductor at the Czech

Opera in Prague. The duties of this post delayed his progress on the score, but when it was finished, it served to dedicate the laying of the cornerstone for the new National Theater. At first *Dalibor* was received with enthusiasm, but Smetana soon found himself under fire for the imagined sin of "Wagnerism." True, he had used recurring motifs in the music, but this device was hardly an invention of Wagner's. A closer source of inspiration was Beethoven's *Fidelio*, with the major difference that in *Dalibor* there is a tragic (though heroic) ending. "The work was, at the time," writes Jiří Berkovec, "of symbolic significance for the situation in which the whole Czech nation found itself."

Dalibor had only fifteen performances during Smetana's lifetime. After his death, the work gradually was redeemed, in large measure thanks to the enthusiasm of Gustav Mahler, who introduced it (albeit with the *Retuschen*, or retouchings, for which he was famous) during his first season of directorship at the Vienna Court Opera in 1897. By 1924, according to Alfred Loewenberg's *Annals of Opera*, the work had reached its 300th performance in Prague alone. In its homeland it stands in the regular repertory alongside *The Bartered Bride*, the national folk opera, and Smetana's later *Libuše*, the national festival epic.

DALIBOR

THREE ACTS
MUSIC: Bedřich Smetana
TEXT (Czech): Joseph Wenzig (written in German, translated by Ervin Špindler)
WORLD PREMIERE: Prague, New Town Theater, May 16, 1868
U.S. PREMIERE: Chicago, Sokol Hall, April 13, 1924

CHARACTERS

Milada, *sister of the dead burgrave* . . . . Soprano
Jitka, *a village girl on Dalibor's estate* . . . . Soprano
Dalibor, *a knight* . . . . Tenor
Vítek, *Dalibor's squire* . . . . Tenor
Vladislav, *King of Bohemia* . . . . Baritone
Budivoj, *captain of the castle guard* . . . . Baritone
Beneš, *a jailor* . . . . Bass

The legend of Dalibor grew up around a real person: Dalibor of Kozojedy, who was tried and condemned to death on March 13, 1498, for having taken under his protection the rebellious serfs of Adam of Ploskovice—thereby, according to the charge, usurping Adam's rightful estate.

ACT I In a courtyard of the Royal Castle in Prague, a curious crowd awaits the trial of Dalibor. A young woman, Jitka, recalls how Dalibor once rescued her as an orphan and gave her fatherly care *(Opuštěného sirotka malého);* now that she is about to be married, she wants to rally her protector's friends to rescue him. King Vladislav arrives with the Judges and announces that Dalibor is accused of leading an assault on Ploskovice Castle and murdering the burgrave. Milada, the burgrave's sister, tells her story of the raid *(Volám! Ó mějte smilování!).* Dalibor is brought forward and testifies that he acted to avenge the death of his friend Zdeněk, a musician, who was beheaded after a quarrel with the local authorities, backed by the lord of Ploskovice *(Zapírat nechci, nejsemť zvyklý lháti).* Proudly he admits that if he goes free, he will seek further vengeance and would even defy the king's authority if necessary. Such is his courageous eloquence that the people and even Milada are swayed, but the king and Judges realize they are dealing with an unrepentant troublemaker. Dalibor is condemned to life imprisonment. Though Milada declares she has forgiven him and begs for his freedom, the king tells her the law must be upheld. As the tribunal disperses, Jitka approaches Milada and pledges to help Dalibor escape.

ACT II In a street outside an inn in the Lower Town, Jitka finds her fiancé, Vítek, who has been drinking with Dalibor's mercenaries, and tells him that Milada, disguised as a minstrel youth, has worked her way into the prison (duet: *Ta duše, ta touha*). At a sign from Milada, they can attack the castle and rescue Dalibor. Vítek tells the soldiers to be ready and swears them to secrecy (chorus: *Sláva tobě!*).

§ Inside the castle, the captain of the guard, Budivoj, instructs the warden Beneš to be careful: Dalibor has many friends, and they may attempt a rescue. When Milada, in boy's clothing, passes with a basket of food, Beneš identifies him as an orphan beggar who now serves as a prison assistant *(Bez strachu buďte, pane, vše povím!).* Budivoj leaves Beneš, who reflects briefly on the grimness of a jailer's life *(Ach, jak těžký žalářníka)* before Milada cheers him by saying his dinner is ready (duet: *Hotovo všechno, sedněte sem!).* Before eating, Beneš wants to take care of Dalibor's request for a fiddle to play while in prison. He goes to look for his old fiddle while Milada prays for success in saving Dalibor *(Ó nebe! Dej, ať tak se stane!).* Beneš brings the violin and sends the "youth" to the lower dungeon.

§ In his cell, Dalibor imagines hearing the sounds of his friend Zdenek's violin *(Nebyl to on zas?).* Milada brings him the fiddle, which he seizes eagerly.

She identifies herself, begs his forgiveness, and explains how she gained access to the prison. Dalibor welcomes her joyfully (duet: *Jsem Milada!*), and the two declare their love.

ACT III   In a royal chamber, Budivoj tells the king there is an insurgency afoot in favor of Dalibor. He presents Beneš, who reports indignantly how the youth he trusted has vanished from the prison, leaving behind a purse in hopes of ensuring Beneš' silence *(Čtyřicet let již tomu bude)*. The king calls on the Judges for a decision; while they deliberate, he muses on the heavy burden of ruling justly *(Krásný to cíl jež panovníku kyne)*. To stave off further intrigue, the Judges decree that Dalibor should be executed that same day—nobly, by the sword. The king hesitates to condemn so worthy a man, but he has to bow to the law.

§ On the night when Dalibor is supposed to be saved, having broken some of the bars from his cell window, he can almost taste freedom *(Ha, kým to kouzlem)*. But when he steps to the window to play a signal to his rescuers on the violin, a string snaps—an unlucky sign. Budivoj bursts in with his retainers, cursing the fact that he let the supposed "youth" get away. Dalibor is happy to learn that Milada has reached safety *(Již vím, to byl ten mládec)*, but Budivoj tells him he has been condemned to die at once. Dalibor pronounces himself ready to join his friend Zdeněk in death, where he hopes Milada eventually will join him too *(Nuž buď si tak!)*.

§ Meanwhile, outside the prison tower, Milada, Jitka, Vítek, and Dalibor's mercenaries wait in vain for the expected signal on the violin. Instead, they see the castle suddenly illuminated with torches, while funeral bells start to ring. Milada decides they must attack *(Nuž vzhůru! Pojď'me!)*. Their forces surge forward, but soon Dalibor appears, bearing the mortally wounded Milada, who dies in his arms. When Budivoj catches up with him, calling on him to surrender, Dalibor fights his captor and lets himself be killed.

GASPARE SPONTINI
1774–1851

$\mathcal{S}$pontini, one of the founding fathers of French grand opera, began his career as a disciple of Cimarosa in Naples, where he wrote about a dozen successful works in the opera-buffa form. The takeover of Naples by Napoleon's forces had something to do with Spontini's move in 1802 to Paris, where one of his Italian comedies was produced at the Théâtre Italien, but at first he found it difficult to adjust to the musical expectations of the French public. His first French opera, *La Petite Maison* (1804), was not well received, but his second, *Milton* (dealing with the English poet's years of blindness), made him famous in France and the German-speaking countries.

Étienne de Jouy, who wrote the libretto for *Milton,* guided Spontini toward grand opera with *La Vestale,* a classical tale redolent of Italian opera seria but with a prominent role for the chorus, which was a feature of French style. Napoleon and Empress Josephine stood behind Spontini, though he encountered opposition from critics and the public as a foreign interloper, and his next opera, *Fernand Cortez,* was even more grand, celebrating conquest and imperial glory. Here he made notable use of the ballet as a dramatic element. Like Gluck, he had succeeded in adapting to the requirements of *tragédie lyrique*—the legacy of Lully and Rameau—blending classical elements and a certain severity with the Empire taste for grandiosity and spectacle.

Though he was appointed artistic director and chief conductor of the Théâtre Italien, Spontini's days in Paris were numbered. Disliked as a martinet and an irascible tyrant, he insisted on orchestral discipline to a degree theretofore unknown in the opera house. (Spontini is credited as one of the first conductors to use a baton.) His next major opera, *Olympie,* succeeded only after he had revised it considerably. It did, however, lead to his appointment as music director at Kaiser Friedrich Wilhelm III's Berlin Court Opera. Again he was resented as a foreigner, though he achieved a certain grudging fame for his practice of rehearsing the various sections of the orchestra separately—a routine that appealed to the drillmaster side of the Prussian mentality.

Spontini had not been in Germany long when he found himself in rivalry with the rising national spirit of romanticism, embodied in Weber's new opera *Der Freischütz.* As he had done in France, he tried to adapt to the local taste. His operas written for Berlin—*Lalla Rûkh, Nurmahal,* and *Alcidor*—reflect this attempt, but the public was not won over. His final work, *Agnes von Hohenstaufen,* though presented as a German historical drama, harked back in many ways to French grand opera. This work and *Olympie* have been revived during the latter twentieth century, but it is on the more familiar *La Vestale* that Spontini's historical reputation rests. Admired by Wagner and Berlioz, he remains, like Cherubini, a conductor's composer and a composer's composer— a classicist swept up, but never borne away, in the swirling currents of a rising tide of romanticism.

LA VESTALE

(The Vestal Virgin)

THREE ACTS
MUSIC: Gaspare Spontini
TEXT (French): Étienne de Jouy
WORLD PREMIERE: Paris, Opéra, December 15, 1807
U.S. PREMIERE: New Orleans, Théâtre d'Orléans, February 17, 1828
METROPOLITAN PREMIERE: November 12, 1925 (in Italian)

CHARACTERS

Julia, *a young Vestal Virgin* . . . . Soprano
The Chief Priestess . . . . .Mezzo-Soprano
Licinio, *a Roman general* . . . . Tenor
Cinna, *a centurion.* .Tenor/Baritone
The Pontifex Maximus (High Priest) . . . . Bass

ACT I   Ancient Rome, during the reign of Numa Pompilius, successor to Romulus. On the steps of the Temple of Vesta, Licinio, a Roman general, stands alone at daybreak. He is greeted by his friend Cinna, a captain, who asks what seems to be troubling him *(Dans le sein d'un ami fidèle)*. Though Licinio is about to receive public honors for his victory, he has lost his beloved Julia (duet: *Quand l'amitié seconde mon courage)*. Five years earlier, in obedience to her dying father's wish, she took vows as a Vestal Virgin after he had refused to let her marry Licinio. As day dawns, the men leave.

Vestal Virgins file into the temple, singing a hymn to the goddess *(Fille du ciel, éternelle Vesta)*. Julia is among them, ashamed of her secret longing to break her vows. The Grand Vestal, head of the group, announces that today the conquering hero is to be crowned with laurel in the Capitol. She assigns Julia to guard the sacred flame in the temple, which must never be allowed to go out; she warns the girl of dire consequences if she fails *(L'Amour est un monstre barbare)*. Julia asks to be excused from this awesome duty, but the Grand Vestal is adamant, adding that Julia must crown the victor. Left alone, the girl bemoans her fate, knowing how the sight of Licinio will affect her *(Licinio, je vais donc te revoir)*. As his chariot draws near, the other Vestals summon her to take her place in the temple.

The procession enters the piazza (chorus: *De lauriers couvrons les chemins)*, led by the High Priest (Pontifex Maximus), senators, and various dignitaries. Julia and the other Vestals emerge from the temple and stand on the steps. Licinio announces that with the aid of Mars, god of war, his legions have achieved victory; now they have come to give thanks to the gods. The Grand Vestal hands Julia the laurel wreath *(Sur le dépôt de la flamme immortelle)*. As the populace chants the glory of Vesta, the chaste goddess, Julia crowns him with the wreath. Licinio speaks to her softly, saying he will abduct her from the temple that night, but the Grand Vestal keeps her eye on the girl. Julia stays beside the sacred flame, which burns on a tripod, while Licinio joins the two Consuls to watch games and dances (ballet) until the High Priest declares the ceremony at an end, and the people repeat their hymn of glory.

ACT II   That evening, inside the temple, the Vestals hail the eternal flame on the altar, and the Grand Vestal gives Julia a rod of gold with which to stir and maintain it. After the others have left, Julia prays to the goddess *(Toi che j'implore avec effroi)*; because of her love for Licinio, she feels unworthy of the holy office. Licinio finds her *(Les dieux prendront pitié)*; as he declares his love; the flame grows dim, and Julia tends it, then responds to him (duet: *Quel trouble, quels transports)*. Cinna comes to warn Licinio that his presence in the sanctuary has been discovered (trio: Julia: *Ah! si je te suis chère)*. At Julia's insistence, the men flee, leaving her to be confronted by the High Priest, some of the populace, and the Vestals. The fire on the altar has gone out, showing the goddess' anger at the intrusion of profane love in her temple.

Julia confesses her offense and is prepared to die, praying to Latona (Leto, patroness of the unfortunate) that Licinio be spared (*Ô des infortunés, déesse tutélaire!*). When the High Priest demands her lover's name, she refuses to reveal it. She is stripped of her Vestal insignia and white veil, which is replaced with a black one.

ACT III At the Scelleratus Ager (Field of Infamy), where Vestals guilty of violating their vows are entombed alive, a sepulcher has been prepared for Julia. Licinio, entering alone, sees it and reacts with angry horror (*Qu'ai-je vu! quels apprêts!*). Cinna reports that while his troops are afraid to defy the goddess Vesta, a group of friends has gathered nearby to help abduct Julia. Before trying so rash a move, he says, Licinio should try to persuade the High Priest to pardon her. As soon as the prelate arrives, Licinio does try, but without success. When Licinio admits he himself is the cause of Julia's downfall, the High Priest retorts that Licinio too should face a traitor's fate. As a last resort, Licinio threatens to rally forces to rescue the girl (duet: *C'est à toi de trembler*), but the High Priest is implacable. Julia is led in, bids her sisters farewell, and kneels before the Grand Vestal (duet: *Adieu, mes tendres soeurs*), asking and receiving her mercy. The girl also bids farewell to her nameless lover (*Toi qui je laisse sur la terre*).

The High Priest orders Julia's veil placed on the altar, where, if Vesta chooses to pardon the offense, she will cause the veil to catch fire. Women pray for this to happen and wait. When it does not, the High Priest hands Julia a lamp and orders her to descend into her tomb. Licinio arrives with followers, determined to rescue her, but she enters the tomb, hoping to prevent bloodshed. A melee is averted when sudden darkness, thunder, and lightning spread consternation (chorus: *Ô terreur! ô disgrâce!*). The High Priest notes a miracle: Julia's veil has taken fire, reigniting the sacred flame. He turns to Licinio, saying Julia has been pardoned and freed from her vows.

§ At the Temple of Venus, the Vestals wish happiness to the lovers, who are united amid general rejoicing.

JOHANN STRAUSS II
1825–99

*T*he son of a well-known Viennese violinist, composer, and dance-band leader, Johann Strauss II, together with his brothers Josef and Eduard, carried on the family tradition. All three produced dance music—waltzes, polkas, mazurkas, and so forth, as well as marches—with Johann II, the eldest, having the longest and most prolific career. During the 1850s and 1860s the Strauss orchestra enjoyed international renown, but Johann, on the threshold of middle age, now found touring strenuous and turned the leadership of the group over to Eduard. From 1870 onward, Johann devoted himself more and more to writing for the theater instead.

It is often claimed that Strauss had little theatrical sense and was indifferent to the quality of a libretto, but his dance rhythms translated readily to the stage, and his gift for graceful melody lent itself to the singing voice. In fact, it was a singer—his first wife, Jetty Treffz—who encouraged him to turn his hand to operetta. He was also urged to do so by his most illustrious competitor, Jacques Offenbach. After several moderately successful attempts, in 1874 he scored the greatest hit in the history of nineteenth-century Viennese operetta with *Die Fledermaus,* which remains the classic of its genre.

The fact that Strauss was a master of light music has tended to obscure the fact that he also was a serious musician. Of a frequently morose and withdrawn temperament, he was accustomed to hard work, as his enormous output attests. Johannes Brahms was a personal friend of long standing. Hans Fantel, a biographer of the Strauss family, reports that Wagner entrusted to Strauss' baton the Viennese premiere of orchestral excerpts from *Tristan und Isolde:* "Wagner characterized Strauss as 'the most musical mind in Europe.' Apparently he meant it." Not surprisingly, Strauss, like Offenbach, harbored the ambition to write a serious opera.

This ambition remained unfulfilled, but some of the Viennese composer's stage works, notably *Der Zigeunerbaron* and *Ritter Pázmán,* hint at what he might have achieved. *Der Zigeunerbaron,* his most enduring operetta after *Die Fledermaus,* was produced a decade later. By that time, Strauss was nearly sixty. With help from his second wife, Adele, he made this score more operatic, tying the musical forms closely to the text and dramatic flow. It is clear from the score of *Der Zigeunerbaron* that Strauss knew the Hungarian style of popular "Gypsy" music thoroughly and identified with the romantic myth of vagabond freedom that the Gypsies represented. With *Ritter Pázmán,* he attempted a *komische Oper*—that is, a German-language opéra comique—but achieved little more than a succès d'estime, and he returned to operetta for his remaining four stage works.

In the age of the compact disc, many of Strauss' less familiar dance pieces (and those of his brothers) have been brought back—enough to convince even the casual listener that here was more than just the composer of a waltz called *On the Beautiful Blue Danube.* Several of his operettas, notably *Eine Nacht in Venedig* (1883), enjoy occasional revival. Strauss did not live to see the twentieth century; as Fantel notes, "He would not have been at home in it at all." His music has carried on undaunted, however, exemplifying the social graces and cultural elegance of the Viennese Belle Époque.

DER ZIGEUNERBARON

(The Gypsy Baron)

THREE ACTS
MUSIC: Johann Strauss Jr.
TEXT (German): Ignaz Schnitzer, based on Marius Jókai's story *Saffi*
WORLD PREMIERE: Vienna, Theater an der Wien, October 24, 1885
U.S. PREMIERE: New York, Casino Theater, February 15, 1886
METROPOLITAN PREMIERE: February 15, 1906

CHARACTERS

Saffi, *Czipra's daughter* . . . . Soprano
Arsena, *Zsupán's daughter* . . . . Soprano

Czipra, *a Gypsy matriarch* . . . . .Mezzo-Soprano
Mirabella, *her governess*. . . . . .Mezzo-Soprano
Sándor Barinkay . . . . Tenor
Ottokar . . . . Tenor
Count Peter Homonay . . . . Baritone
Count Carnero . . . . Baritone
Kálmán Zsupán, *a well-to-do pig farmer* . . . . Baritone

This story is based on the most complete available version. In most stage productions, certain numbers (though not always the same ones) are omitted, and the order of numbers may be altered.

The action takes place in the Banat District of Temesvár Province, Hungary, and in Vienna, at the start of the reign of Empress Maria Theresa, in 1740. The War of the Austrian Succession—the military conflict referred to in *Der Zigeunerbaron*—also figures in Verdi's *La Forza del Destino*.

ACT I   A general amnesty has permitted Sándor Barinkay to return to his native province after twenty years' exile, which resulted from his father's association with the late Pasha during the Turkish occupation. As boatmen woo their girlfriends *(Das wär kein rechter Schifferknecht)*, two locals, Ottokar and the well-to-do pig farmer Kálmán Zsupán, pass by in their weekly occupation of digging for a treasure they believe is buried nearby *(Jeden Tag Müh und Plag)*, mocked by the old Gypsy woman Czipra. Zsupán has been working a tract of land that belonged to Barinkay's father, who died in exile twenty-five years before, and whose heirs are not expected to reappear.

They *have* reappeared, however, in the person of Barinkay, who presently enters to look over the land and tell how he tamed wild animals for a traveling circus during his years of exile *(Als flotter Geist)*. His escort, the local official Ludovico Carnero, summons Czipra to recognize Barinkay and authenticate his claim to the land. She reads his palm and predicts that after he marries, a dream will reveal to his bride the location of the treasure buried somewhere around the Gypsy castle *(Bald wird man dich viel umweben)*. Zsupán, summoned as the next witness, expatiates on the joys of pig farming *(Ja, das Schreiben und das Lesen)*. Barinkay, seeing much of his property turned into a swamp for Zsupán's pigs, suggests marriage with Zsupán's daughter to consolidate their holdings and avoid disputes. Meanwhile, Carnero recognizes in the girl's nurse, Mirabella, the wife he lost twenty-two years earlier during a battle with the Turks over the city of Belgrade. She reveals that Ottokar is their son. Then she tells how she tried to stay near her husband during the battle *(Just sind es zweiundzwanzig Jahre)* but could not, later falling under the amorous protection of the Pasha.

Zsupán's daughter, Arsena, arrives. Though Barinkay finds her attractive, her heart belongs to Ottokar (ensemble: *Dem Freier naht die Braut*). To stall for time, she declares she wouldn't consider marrying Barinkay unless he were at least a baron. With this, the party disperses, leaving Czipra to reflect on the Gypsies' fearsome reputation *(So elend und so treu ist keiner)*. Her daughter Saffi joins her and repeats the song with more optimistic words *(Doch treu und wahr)*. Barinkay approaches, charmed by Saffi, and asks her to show him his new home; but before they can leave, Ottokar appears in search of Arsena *(Wie traut die Frösche quaken)*. In anger, Barinkay overhears the young couple make fun of his courtship of Arsena and pledge their love. Czipra and Saffi restrain him with assurances that he is now lord of the local Gypsies, who draw near and pledge their support.

§ Barinkay goes to Zsupán's house to announce that the Gypsies have made him their baron *(Komm her und schau dir die Leute an)*. Arsena still rejects him, on the grounds that a Gypsy title has no validity, so he declares he wants none of her: he will marry Saffi instead. This catches Saffi by surprise, but the Gypsies voice approval, while Arsena and her father take it as an insult. Zsupán and his people heap indignant threats on Barinkay and the Gypsies, who retort in kind.

ACT II   Czipra, Saffi, and Barinkay have spent the night in the ruins of the old castle (trio: *Mein Aug' bewacht*). Barinkay reassures the girl that he wants her for his wife. She relates a dream in which Barinkay's father told of treasure buried in the castle (trio: *Ein Greis ist mir im Traum erschienen*). Following her instructions, Barinkay taps on various marble slabs until he finds the right one, and the treasure is revealed. Pali, one of the Gypsies, calls his henchmen to wake up and get to work at their trade as metalsmiths, forging tools and, if necessary, weapons (chorus: *Ha, das Eisen wird gefüge*).

Zsupán arrives with his crew, and Carnero, in his capacity as deputy chairman of Empress Maria Theresa's morals commission, charges Barinkay with an illicit relationship for which he must answer to the law. Barinkay replies that he and Saffi are married. By whom?—by the stork, cardinal, and nightingale (duet: *Wer uns getraut?*). Carnero snorts at this and, with backing from Mirabella and Zsupán, extols the watchful eye of the morals commission (trio: *Nur keusch und rein*). Ottokar bursts in, having found a gold coin, but the discovery of the army's long-lost war treasury is interrupted by the appearance of Count Homonay at the head of a recruiting party. Seeing Ottokar and Zsupán try to slink away, he seizes them by the hand and pronounces them signed up for the army. Zsupán insists in vain that he is too frail to serve *(Mir helfen die Doktoren nicht mehr)*. When Carnero accuses Barinkay of trying to appropriate the treasure, Barinkay donates it to the army; when Carnero accuses Barinkay of "marrying" Saffi under false pretenses, Homonay congratulates the couple. Carnero insists, however, that a hearing on the case be held in Vienna. Homonay says he will lead the way there; meanwhile, the recruiting should go on *(Bruder, komm zum Militär)*, as Spanish forces are threatening the homeland.

Arguments resume between Barinkay's Gypsy forces and Zsupán's crowd, provoking Czipra to reveal a secret: Saffi is not her daughter but that of the last Pasha of Temesvár, entrusted to her care, and therefore is a princess, outranking them all (ensemble: *Ein Fürstenkind*): a document proves it. Barinkay believes he is unworthy of her and must give her up *(Ach, von Euch muss ich gehn!)*. Over her protests, he signs up with the army, as do many others, looking forward to a quick victory and triumphant return to Vienna, which everyone wants to visit (ensemble: *O voll Fröhlichkeit gibt es weit und breit*).

ACT III Outside the gates of Vienna, the populace awaits the return of the victorious Austrian troops, which have not only repelled the Spanish invasion but made possible a peace with Bavaria and Prussia. Arsena, pining for Ottokar, confesses to Mirabella and Carnero that love can be an upsetting as well as an enlightening experience for a young girl *(Ein Mädchen hat es gar nicht gut)*. Homonay appears and hands Carnero a document disbanding the morals commission; Carnero, annoyed and frustrated, is pensioned off and now can spend all his time with Mirabella.

The troops start to arrive, first among them Zsupán, who brags of his supposed exploits *(Von des Tajo Strand)*. Attention is readily diverted by Barinkay and his Gypsy battalion (soldiers' chorus: *Hurrah, die Schlacht mitgemacht*). Homonay greets him as a hero and gives him two documents—one returning to him all the treasure found in his castle, the other making him a baron of the empire. Zsupán now is more than willing to have Barinkay as son-in-law, but Barinkay asks Arsena's hand for Ottokar, not for himself. As a third reward for his bravery, Homonay offers official blessings on Barinkay's marriage to Saffi (duet, Saffi-Barinkay: *So Blick in Blick und Mund an Mund*). Barinkay happily recalls his adventurous early life, embraces Saffi, and hails the other couple, Arsena and Ottokar (choral reprise: *Ja, das alles, auf Ehr'*).

RICHARD STRAUSS
1864–1949

The most successful German opera composer after Wagner, Strauss came from a bourgeois background and started out conservatively, writing romantic music in the vein of Mendelssohn. He had been sheltered from Wagnerian influence by his father, the principal horn player of the Munich opera orchestra. The elder Strauss considered Wagner a fraud, but the younger, like most of his generation, soon welcomed Wagner's ideas about the Music of the Future and started looking ahead.

The earliest Strauss compositions to attract widespread attention, and eventually to enter the world orchestra repertory, were tone poems in the Liszt format—compact symphonic works attached to a literary program, such as *Don Juan, Till Eulenspiegel,* and *Don Quixote.* The step from there to opera was natural enough, and Strauss' first successful operas, the short, punchy *Salome* (1905) and *Elektra* (1909), are still sometimes called tone poems with voices added. *Elektra* in particular was considered a shockingly modern work, flirting with atonality, but Strauss later noted that after *Elektra* he had chosen to return to "the path of Melos." The prodigal result of his homecoming was *Der Rosenkavalier* (1911), one of the longest, most extravagantly orchestrated of all opera comedies, but also one of the most persistently popular.

Strauss kept on writing operas up to the 1940s. It is generally agreed that except for *Salome,* adapted from Oscar Wilde's French play, Strauss' best stage works were written with Hugo von Hofmannsthal. The two men came from different backgrounds, Hofmannsthal being an aristocrat; their friendship was limited to their work, but they brought out the best in each other. They did not always tame each other's excesses: their two next-to-last collaborations,

Die Frau ohne Schatten (1919) and *Die ägyptische Helena* (1928), show abundant evidence of rampant fantasy. But their final one, *Arabella* (1933), returns to real situations and people, capturing a conversational intimacy and spontaneity that would stand Strauss in good stead in his valedictory *Capriccio,* written after death had deprived him of Hofmannsthal's help.

For *Die Schweigsame Frau* (perhaps the noisiest of his operas), *Daphne,* and his other remaining stage works, Strauss had to turn to new collaborators. The choice of a distinguished Jewish writer, Stefan Zweig, for the text of *Die Schweigsame Frau* drew fire from the Nazis. Strauss switched to the pedestrian Joseph Gregor for *Daphne* and *Die Liebe der Danae*—both retreats into the world of classicism.

His later operas, though revived far less often than his triumphs of middle life, have their adherents. Like wine, Strauss' music mellowed, acquiring a pale elegance that suits the palate of connoisseurs. And he never lost his touch for sending voices (particularly soprano voices) arching into orbit, or for conjuring up whatever orchestral color the stage situation might require.

INTERMEZZO

TWO ACTS
MUSIC: Richard Strauss
TEXT (German): the composer
WORLD PREMIERE: Dresden, Staatsoper, November 4, 1924
U.S. PREMIERE (concert performance): New York (Philharmonic Hall), February 11, 1963
U.S. STAGE PREMIERE: Philadelphia, Curtis Institute, February 24, 1977

CHARACTERS

Christine Storch, *Robert's wife.*	Soprano
Anna, *the Storchs' chambermaid*	Soprano
Baron Lummer, *a down-at-the-heels minor aristocrat.*	Tenor
Robert Stroh, *conductor*	Tenor
Robert Storch, *conductor, Christine's husband.*	Baritone
A Legal Counselor ⎫	⎧ Baritone
A Business Counselor ⎬ *cronies of Storch*	⎨ Baritone
A Singer ⎭	⎩ Bass

For *Intermezzo,* Strauss broke with his usual practice by writing his own libretto and choosing a modern subject. The story, drawn from an episode early in his married life, is treated in conversational style, foreshadowing that of the composer's final opera, *Capriccio.*

ACT I At a rented house in Grundlsee, a winter resort, early twentieth century. In the dressing room, composer-conductor Robert Storch and his wife pack his suitcase for a two-month conducting engagement, bickering about the servants and household chores. Christine deplores the life of a musician, which she considers degrading *(Das nicht . . . aber mir passt das ganze Milieu nicht).* When the sleigh arrives to take Robert to the station, she annoys him by seeming indifferent to his departure. After he has left, the maid Anna fixes her mistress' hair and asks why Christine doesn't accompany her husband on his trips; she retorts that the household could never function without her *(Sie sehn doch, was ich zu tun habe!).* She also reveals that she resents Robert's imperturbable good nature. A phone call comes from an acquaintance, who invites Christine to go skating.

§ At the toboggan run, Christine's sled knocks down a skier who is trying to cross her path. Her annoyance dissipates when she learns he is Baron Lummer, whose family her parents knew in Linz. She identifies herself as the wife of the famous Robert Storch and invites the baron to call on her.

§ At the Grundlsee Inn, Christine, having just waltzed (badly, she thinks) with Lummer, chats with him about the spa. They dance again before the waltz ends.

§ The next day, Christine checks out a rented room for Lummer at the home of acquaintances, the local Notary and his wife.

§ In her dining room, Christine is finishing a letter to her husband, describing Lummer; she suggests that Robert might be able to help him out, since the youth's family is not interested in his intellectual pursuits *("Es ist wirklich ein sehr netter, ungeheuer bescheidener Mensch").* Lummer is announced and says he is pleased with his lodgings but declines an invitation to supper. She asks why Lummer is not getting on with his work, to which he replies that since his family refuses financial help, he cannot continue his nature studies at the university. Christine brings up the idea of help from Robert, whom she describes in extravagant terms *(O sicher, mein Mann!).* Lummer seems impatient for more immediate assistance but hesitates to ask.

§ In Lummer's room at the Notary's house, he reflects on his real feelings toward Christine: she rather bores him, but he hopes to get her help. When his girlfriend, Resi, stops by to pick him up, he asks her to wait a few minutes, then sets about writing a letter of request to Christine *("Verehrte, Gnädige Frau! So freundlich Sie heute zu mir waren").*

§ At the Storch house, Christine fumes over his letter, in which he has had the temerity to ask for a loan of 1,000 marks. Arriving in the midst of a snowstorm, Lummer follows up his request with a personal visit, but she scuttles his hopes *(Also das ich ihnen nur gleich heraussage)*. At this point, however, the maid brings another letter that obviously shocks Christine: addressed to Robert, it sets a date for the following evening after the opera and is signed "Your Mieze Maier"—evidently a woman of easy morals. Seeing Christine upset, Lummer leaves, and she composes a telegram to Robert: "You know Mieze Maier! I have proof that you've betrayed me! So we are parted forever" *(Ich telegraphiere. Du kennst Mieze Maier!)*. She rings for Anna, orders the telegram sent and the bags packed.

In the bedroom of the Storchs' child, Franzl, Christine tearfully tells him they will be leaving. When she speaks badly of Robert, the boy objects, but Christine pays no heed, kneeling melodramatically beside the bed to pray.

ACT II   At the home of the Business Counselor in Vienna, he and three friends are playing the card game *Skat* and discussing the wife of their friend Robert Storch, who they agree is difficult, rude, and temperamental. Robert himself enters and joins the game. Between plays, the men continue their banter about Christine; Robert defends her *(Nur nicht übertreiben!)*, saying he needs a spirited wife. But suddenly her telegram is delivered. Stunned, he insists he doesn't know any Mieze Maier, though the others seem doubtful. He excuses himself and leaves.

§ In the Notary's office in Grundlsee, Christine says she wants a divorce. Thinking that Lummer might be the cause, he starts to tell her the baron has a girlfriend, but she cuts him short, showing Mieze Maier's note and brushing aside the recommendation that she needs more evidence. When the Notary says he must see Robert too, she leaves, declaring she will find another lawyer.

§ In the Prater, the park in central Vienna, Robert walks about in despair: he has tried repeatedly to reach Christine, but she hasn't responded *(Es ist einfach zum Rasendwerden!)*. The conductor Robert Stroh, one of the members of the recent card party, finds him and explains with embarrassment that he has figured out what happened: Mieze Maier mistook him, Stroh, for the "great composer" Storch, and misaddressed her note. Storch, while relieved, blames Stroh for his part in the confusion *(Nun, da bin ich ihnen aber schon ausserordentlich dankbar)* and insists he help resolve the resulting problems.

§ In Christine's dressing room, she still has not managed to leave Grundlsee but has sent Lummer to Vienna to check on Mieze Maier. Her maid Anna suggests that it might have helped for Lummer to take along a photo of Robert, to make sure he is the right man. A telegram arrives from Robert, explaining that Stroh was mistaken for him. Then Stroh himself is announced.

§ In the dining room some time later, Christine, having heard Stroh's explanation, prepares for Robert's return; but when he arrives, she is quarrelsome and distrustful. Despite his attempts to calm her, she goes back to wanting a divorce. Robert, out of patience, leaves the room. Shortly after, Lummer arrives from Vienna, having found Mieze Maier and learned only that she knows a man she believes to be Robert Storch. Now Christine says the misunderstanding with her husband already has been resolved. Lummer leaves. When Robert reenters, she explains her relationship with Lummer, and the couple finally reconciles.

DIE ÄGYPTISCHE HELENA

(The Egyptian Helen)

TWO ACTS
MUSIC: Richard Strauss
TEXT (German): Hugo von Hofmannsthal
WORLD PREMIERE: Dresden, Staatsoper, June 6, 1928
U.S. PREMIERE: New York, Metropolitan Opera, November 6, 1928

CHARACTERS

Helena, *formerly Helen of Troy* . . . . Soprano
Hermione, *daughter of Helen and Menelas* . . . . Soprano
Aithra, *daughter of an Egyptian king* . . . . Soprano
Omniscient Mussel . . . . Contralto
Menelas, *Helena's husband* . . . . Tenor
Da-ud, *Altair's son* . . . . Tenor
Altair, *Prince of the Mountains* . . . . Baritone

ACT I Mythological past (1200 B.C., after the Trojan War). In her island palace, the sorceress Aithra waits in vain for Poseidon's return. The oracle-like Omniscient Mussel tells her that Poseidon is far away at the moment but faithful in his love for her. The Mussel then tells of a ship on which the most beautiful woman in the world, Helena (Helen of Troy), is about to be murdered in her sleep by her husband, Menelas (Menelaus). To save the victim, Aithra conjures up a flash storm to shipwreck the passengers, who soon make their way ashore and appear at the palace. Helena has been trying to restore her marriage *(Bei jener Nacht),* but Menelas cannot forgive her betrayal with Paris at the start of the Trojan War. He has kept their daughter, Hermione, safe from knowing her own mother. Menelas starts once again to stab his wife, but the sight of her beauty by moonlight makes him hesitate. To ensure that he doesn't kill her, Aithra invokes elves to torment him; they make him believe that his rival, Paris, is there, and he rushes outside to confront the specter. Aithra's magic then helps Helena regain her original youthful beauty, and a lotus drink banishes her anxiety. Servant girls take her to another room.

When Menelas stumbles back in, raving about having surprised the wraithlike couple, Helena and Paris, and killed them both, Aithra gives him the soothing drink as well. Hearing of his still-conflicting emotions toward his wife *(Zerspalten das Herz!)*, the sorceress tries to tell him that when he lost Helena to Paris, nine years before, the gods actually substituted a wraith to fool Paris into thinking he possessed her, while the real woman was hidden away in the castle of Aithra's father on the slopes of the Atlas Mountains (in northwest Africa). There Helena still lies, waiting for her husband to wake her *(Schuldlos schlummernd)*; the woman in the next room is the wraith. Now Aithra will transport him by magic to the castle. He remains bewildered and hesitant but gradually yields to the illusion that the original Helena will be restored to him. In a pavilion at the foot of the mountain, the two can be reunited. Aithra advises the use of the lotus potion to keep disruptive recollections at bay.

ACT II   In the pavilion, Helena awakens and hails the couple's second wedding night *(Zweite Brautnacht!)*. Menelas, also awakening, still distrusts his senses. She tries to soothe him with more lotus juice, but the sight of his sword revives jarring memories, and he seems about to reject the woman as illusory. Desert horsemen appear, and Altair, prince of the mountains, bows before Helena, offering gifts; his son, Da-ud, joins in praising her beauty. This recalls to Menelas how Helena was fêted at Troy, but he tries to conceal his jealousy as Altair and Da-ud invite him on a hunting party. Bidding farewell to Helena, still uncertain as to who she really is, he leaves for the hunt. Aithra appears as one of the serving girls, wanting to help Helena by warning that one of the vials she packed contains a potion of forgetfulness but the other a potion of recollection. Against Aithra's strong advice, Helena declares that recollection will be necessary to restore her marriage: the illusions of returning to an untouched past have not been real, have not worked.

At a sign from Helena, the maidservants withdraw when Altair returns, paying bold court to her and inviting her to a banquet in her honor *(Bald dir der vertraute!)*. Even when word arrives that Menelas has killed Da-ud during the hunt, Altair is not dissuaded, but he steps away when the youth's body is brought in, followed by Menelas, who remains confused, thinking it was Paris he killed. Again defying Aithra's counsel, Helena orders the potion of recollection prepared as time for the feast draws near. Menelas now imagines that the real Helena has died, and he means to join her in death: the Helena before him is the illusory one *(Helena, oder wie ich sonst dich nenne)*. When he takes what he thinks is the potion of death, however, he sees the dead Helena as the living one: both are united *(Ewig erwählt von diesem Blick!)*. Altair and his cohorts seize and separate the couple, but Aithra opens the tent to reveal a phalanx of Poseidon's soldiers escorting the child Hermione. Recognizing Aithra the sorceress, Altair bows to her power. Hermione, reunited at last with her parents, will go home with them to begin their life together.

DIE SCHWEIGSAME FRAU

(The Silent Woman)

THREE ACTS

MUSIC: Richard Strauss

TEXT (German): Stefan Zweig, after Ben Jonson's *Epicoene, or The Silent Woman*

WORLD PREMIERE: Dresden, Staatsoper, June 24, 1935

U.S. PREMIERE: New York City Opera, October 7, 1958 (in English)

CHARACTERS

Aminta, *Henry's wife* . . . . Soprano
Isotta ⎱ *actresses* . . . . ⎰ Soprano
Carlotta ⎰ . . . . ⎱ Mezzo-Soprano
Housekeeper . . . . Alto
Henry Morosus. *Sir Morosus' nephew* . . . . Tenor
The Barber . . . . Baritone
Sir Morosus, *a retired sea captain* . . . . Bass
Cesare Vanuzzi, *impresario of traveling players* . . . . Bass

ACT I   In his house in eighteenth-century England, cluttered with nautical memorabilia, the retired mariner Sir Morosus is still asleep when his Barber makes a daily call, welcomed by the chatty Housekeeper, who wants the Barber to suggest her as a wife for her employer. When he loses patience with her, their bickering rouses Morosus, who hates noise and rails against the old woman as the Barber tries to calm him, then lathers him for a shave. Morosus rants further about all the different noises of the world that bother him *(Still? Um Mitternacht still?)*. When the Barber suggests marriage to a quiet, docile young woman, Morosus expresses reservations, especially regarding his age, but the Barber assures him that such a paragon can be found (*Mädchen nur, die nichts erfahren*).

A sudden bang at the door heralds an unexpected visitor: Henry, Morosus' long-lost nephew. At first Morosus is delighted and insists the young man stay at his house, but he soon discovers that the "troops" who came along are actually a "troupe," the traveling opera company of one Cesare Vanuzzi, which will be playing at the Haymarket Theatre. Not only are singers noisy, but theirs is a disreputable profession; and to make matters worse, Henry is married to one of them, Aminta. A dispute ensues, leading to Morosus' disinheriting Henry. The old man orders the Barber to find him a quiet wife after all, then storms out. To the disgruntled visitors the Barber explains that Morosus' ears were sensitized by a shipboard explosion, years before. Then he details the treasure stored in the basement (*Da unten im Keller*)—sixty or seventy thousand pounds' worth—that could be Henry's to inherit.

Aminta sadly offers to give up the marriage for Henry's sake (duet: *Nicht an mich, Geliebte, denke*), but he will not hear of it. The Barber points out that if they lose this opportunity, the money will go to someone else (*Sehr rechtschaffen gedacht, junger Herr*); wouldn't one of the troupe's young ingenues like to play the silent wife that Morosus has requested? Isotta says she would tease him with jokes and laughter (*Ich würde lachen*); Carlotta says she would sing all day (*Ich würde singen*); obviously neither will do. The Barber hatches a better idea: suppose someone would play-act the role, pretend to marry the old man, make him glad to be rid of her, and return Henry to his good graces? Aminta strikes him as right for the job. A detailed plan of action is laid out, the Barber instructing everyone in what role to play (*Nun kostumiert euch*).

ACT II   In Morosus' house the next day, despite the Housekeeper's forebodings, he dresses for his wedding. The Barber arrives with the three disguised girls from the troupe, begging Morosus to interview them gently (*Nur das Eine lasst Euch bitten*). Carlotta, as a country wench, has little to say for herself, but Isotta launches into a mock-serious palm reading of Morosus' hand, annoying him. Aminta, as "Timidia," pleads that she cannot make conversation but prefers quiet domestic occupations. Morosus is enchanted with her, to the feigned disgust of the other two, who leave in a huff. When Morosus explains his joy at finding a wife (*Kind, gib dich keiner Täuschung hin*), Aminta is touched and almost loses her composure. The Barber brings Vanuzzi, disguised as a priest, with another trouper, Morbio, dressed as a notary, who prattles of legal formalities but is cut short to perform the "ceremony" (ensemble: *Wunderbar, sie anzuschauen*). No sooner is it done than a ragged bunch of "seamen" (members of Vanuzzi's company) burst in, professing to remember Morosus from his sailing days and raising a racket. Horrified and enraged, Morosus has to be restrained, but eventually the intruders repair to a tavern, leaving him and his bride. With difficulty (since she really finds him sympathetic), Aminta starts her performance as a demanding shrew: she will start by redecorating the house. Henry appears, pretending to remonstrate with the girl, who defies him as well, though she does withdraw to her room. Morosus is relieved to hear that Henry will bring a lawyer next day to dissolve the union; if this succeeds, Morosus promises to make Henry his heir. The old man retires, reassured that Timidia will be kept quiet. Aminta joins Henry, regretting the role she has played *(Ach Gott, der arme alte Mann)* but knowing it will soon be over, as she and her real husband embrace.

ACT III   The next morning, "workmen" (again members of the troupe) redecorate under Timidia's direction. When the work stops, it is only so she can have her singing lesson, with Henry and Farfallo, a member of the troupe (both disguised), as teacher and accompanist. She starts a duet from Monteverdi's *L'Incoronazione di Poppea (Sento un certo non so che)*, joined by Henry. Morosus comes to beg for quiet, but the singers continue until the Barber steps in to announce the Chief Justice of England's imminent arrival. Meanwhile, the Barber tries to negotiate grounds for a settlement between Morosus and Timidia, who refuses all offers. When the "judge" (Vanuzzi, disguised) draws near, Morosus leaves to dress formally, and the conspirators joke briefly before he returns for the hearing. A legal discussion follows, in which Timidia is accused of having a prior relationship with another man (played, with conviction, by the disguised Henry). The judge finds her guilty and annuls the marriage, but his decision is overthrown because no prior contract was made requiring the bride to be a virgin. Though told he can appeal, Morosus is in suicidal despair, the more so because the hearing caused such a racket. Henry and Aminta, deciding it is time to end the charade, unmask and beg his pardon. At first confused, then angry, Morosus finally bursts out laughing and congratulates all the players on their convincing performance *(Aber grossartig habt ihr das gemacht)*. Vanuzzi and company toast and serenade him *(Die Ihr feindlich aufgenommen)*, hoping they have brought joy to a house once ruled by gloom. Then they leave Morosus alone with Henry and Aminta, whom he assures of his relief, happiness, and affection *(Wie schön ist doch die Musik)*.

DAPHNE

ONE ACT
MUSIC: Richard Strauss
TEXT (German): Joseph Gregor

WORLD PREMIERE: Dresden, Staatsoper, October 15, 1938
U.S. PREMIERE (concert performance): New York, Brooklyn College, October 7, 1960
U.S. STAGE PREMIERE: Sante Fe Opera, July 29, 1964

CHARACTERS

Daphne, *Peneios and Gaea's daughter* . . . . Soprano
Gaea, *Peneios' wife* . . . . Contralto
Leukippos, *a shepherd* . . . . Tenor
Apollo, *god of the sun*. Tenor
Peneios, *a fisherman* . . . . Bass

Mythological Greece, in a rural landscape at the foot of Mt. Olympus, with the River Peneios flowing across the background. As evening approaches, four Shepherds discuss the coming festivities of Dionysus (Bacchus), marking the start of spring. Daphne, daughter of the fisherman Peneios (named for the river god) and Gaea (named for the earth goddess), listen as the Shepherds go off in the distance. The girl feels at one with nature and wishes the day would not end so soon, especially as it brings the frightening darkness, with its festivities whose wildness she mistrusts (*O bleib, geliebter Tag!*). When she embraces a tree, which she regards with kinship, her childhood friend Leukippos jumps from behind it, alarming her. Now a young shepherd, he is beginning to feel the Dionysian spirit and wants to court his former playmate. In annoyance at her lack of response, he breaks his flute, whose playing she always liked, and leaves abruptly.

Daphne's mother, a practical sort who does not grasp her child's oneness with nature, comes to call her to the house. For Gaea, Daphne's rapture is something that should be changing soon into thoughts of love and domesticity (*Dein Zagen kenn ich*). She offers the girl fine clothes and ornaments for the feast, but Daphne begs to remain dressed as she is.

As she and Gaia leave for the house, the two Maids who brought the new clothes cannot understand her refusal to dress up (*Und dies edle Kleid*). When Leukippos returns, dampened by Daphne's rejection, the Maids lure him with the clothes (*Hör uns, Schäfer!*): if he will disguise himself as a girl, he can be close to Daphne again. The three dance off.

Peneios enters with Gaea and some Shepherds. Hinting at his own relationship to the gods, he says he recognizes the setting sun as Phoebus Apollo and looks forward to the bacchanal (*Wisset, ich sah ihn*). Gaea and the Shepherds are afraid the gods might take his words badly. As if in reply, echoing laughter and red flashes of lightning appear, followed by Apollo—unrecognized, in the guise of a herdsman.

Politely greeting Peneios and Gaea, the herdsman says he was brought here by sounds and scents of the approaching feast *(Ein Rinderhirt bin ich)*. Briefly left alone, he wonders why he has allowed himself to stoop to this deception, but when Daphne is brought from the house to welcome him, he is smitten with her. Performing the rites of hospitality, she washes the stranger's hands and offers him a blue cloak. When she asks where he has come from, he frankly states that he saw her from the sun chariot circling the sky *(Was können an Weite)*, but she does not understand. Sensing nevertheless that he is in sympathy with her inmost thoughts, she trusts him as a brother and sinks innocently in his embrace. Speaking of the power of sunlight, he offers her the love of all nature *(Alles Lebendige, Tier und Gewässer)*, but when he kisses her in more than brotherly fashion, she recoils, frightened.

Sounds of the feast are heard, and Peneios leads a procession of celebrants, who spread over the hillside. Young men in rams' masks perform a wild dance, and girls—including Leukippos in disguise—bring wine. Daphne, while not recognizing him, feels this unknown "girl" to be a kindred spirit. They dance together, arousing the jealousy of Apollo, who suddenly calls the feast a blasphemous mockery. The Shepherds confront him, but he cows them by swinging his bow, conjuring up a rumble of thunder. This turns into a storm, which panics the sheep and cattle, calling the Shepherds away from the festivities.

Apollo accuses Leukippos of deceiving Daphne and trying to take her away from him. Leukippos responds by removing his disguise and urging Daphne to join him in the Dionysian revels *(Ja, ich bekenne!)*. When he dares Apollo to unmask as well, the god admits his identity *(Jeden heiligen Morgen)*, only to be cursed as a liar by Leukippos. Enraged at the youth, Apollo shoots him dead with an arrow.

Daphne mourns Leukippos, understanding at last that he truly loved her *(Unheilvolle Daphne!)*. Apollo, chastened and confused by this collision between godly and human passions, calls on the other gods to forgive him for the harm he has done *(Götter! Brüder im hohen Olympos!)*. To keep Daphne forever alive amid the nature she loves, he ordains that she be changed into a laurel tree *(Priesterlich diene, verwandelte Daphne)*: her leaves shall form the crown of heroes, and he will shine on her every morning.

He disappears. As darkness falls, Daphne, left alone, rushes forward and suddenly stops, fixed in one spot. She realizes she is becoming one with the trees that she loves. As her human form vanishes, a laurel appears in her place, with her voice still emerging from its branches: she will be a symbol of unending love *(Apollo! Bruder! Nimm mein Gezweige)*.

IGOR STRAVINSKY
1882–1971

*M*ore so than any other major composer, Igor Stravinsky experimented with and changed his style during the course of his career. Even admirers had trouble keeping up with what seemed at the time an about-face, notably his abrupt conversion to neoclassicism after World War I and his embrace of serialism toward the end of his life. Darius Milhaud stated the case simply: "One never knew what Igor would think of next, but it was always a surprise, always something interesting."

Le Rossignol, Stravinsky's first opera, belongs to two different periods in his creative life. Begun in Russia while he was still a pupil of Rimsky-Korsakov, it was completed only after Stravinsky had written his epoch-making ballets for the impresario Serge Diaghilev, *L'Oiseau de Feu* (The Firebird), *Petrouchka,* and *Le Sacre du Printemps* (The Rite of Spring). So *Le Rossignol* starts in the vein of Rimsky-Korsakov's own operas and concludes as a postscript to three "modern" ballets, the last of which was considered extremely avant-garde in 1913.

Though his teacher had been a dedicated opera composer, Stravinsky during his Paris years shared the thinking of most young composers during the first third of the twentieth century, who regarded opera as a vulgar, passé art form—"something barbers went to," as Aaron Copland put it—and ballet was embraced instead. Stravinsky in fact remained ambivalent: his curiosity was too great for him to leave such a large stone unturned. Rather than address himself to it directly, he explored its outskirts. The latter parts of *Le Rossignol* suggest the opera-ballet amalgam that had been pioneered by Lully, Rameau, and Gluck and carried into French grand opera by Spontini. The neoclassical *Pulcinella* adopts the form of a commedia dell'arte entertainment, with both singing and dancing. *L'Histoire du Soldat,* with narration and dance, suggests a medieval morality play. Stravinsky returned to an idea of this kind in his last decade, when he set part of the old York miracle play as *The Flood,* using his serial idiom; the work was introduced on television.

Stravinsky returned to *Le Rossignol,* after having laid it aside in 1909, and completed it in response to an offer from the Moscow Free Theater to present it during the 1913–14 season. It was not until the late 1940s, however, that he gave in and wrote a full-length conventional opera, *The Rake's Progress,* a major contribution to the twentieth-century repertory. In the meantime, he continued to experiment, writing the chamber operas *Renard* and *Mavra,* performed in Paris in 1922. Otherwise, the closest he came to the lyric stage was with the opera-oratorio *Oedipus Rex* (1927) and the "melodrama" *Perséphone* (1934). Both were performed in opera houses but not conventionally staged. *Oedipus Rex* was meant to be performed ceremonially, with the soloists stylized and dehumanized; *Perséphone* employed a narrator and involved some dancing, but only one singing soloist.

Oedipus Rex is one of Stravinsky's most eclectic scores. Nominally neoclassical, as befits its severe subject, it is less chaste than its kindred work, the *Symphony of Psalms* (1930), reaching as far afield as Debussy and Puccini in stylistic allusion. The chorus-based oratorio format, with monolithically simple narration by a speaker, keeps dramatic realism at a stiff arm's length. There are, to be sure, touching moments—Jocasta's brave front against rising odds, the people's sympathy for the defeated Oedipus—but they are like watching a tear run down the cheek of a statue.

In 1983–84, the Metropolitan Opera presented *Le Rossignol, Le Sacre du Printemps,* and *Oedipus Rex* on a triple bill, juxtaposing the before-and-after periods of Stravinsky's stylistically most adventurous work *(Le Sacre)* with that work itself.

LE ROSSIGNOL

(Solovey/The Nightingale)

THREE ACTS
MUSIC: Igor Stravinsky
TEXT (Russian): the composer and Stepan Mitousoff, based on Hans
  Christian Andersen's story *The Emperor's Nightingale*

378

IGOR STRAVINSKY

WORLD PREMIERE: Paris, Opéra, May 26, 1914 (in French)
U.S. PREMIERE: New York, Metropolitan Opera, March 6, 1926 (in French)

CHARACTERS

The Nightingale . . . . Soprano
The Cook . . . . .Mezzo-Soprano
Death . . . . Alto
The Fisherman . . . . Tenor
The Emperor of China . . . . Baritone
The Chamberlain . . . . Bass
The Bonze . . . . Bass

In many folkloric traditions, including the Russian, birds hold a place of spiritual significance, standing between the worlds of the living and the dead. In Rimsky-Korsakov's *Legend of the Invisible City of Kitezh,* for example, Alkonost and Sirin are birds of paradise, whose task it is to announce death to the Maiden Fevronia and lead her to eternal life.

ACT I   China, legendary antiquity. On the shore of the ocean, a Fisherman appears by moonlight to cast his nets *(Nevod brosal nebesnyi dukh).* As he does so, a Nightingale perches on a tree in the nearby forest and begins a song of enchanting beauty about the nocturnal scene *(Akh! S neba vysoty blesnuv zvezda upala).* The imperial Cook leads the Chamberlain, Bonze (priest), and courtiers into the forest in search of the Nightingale, whose song has earned fame. At first they mistake other sounds for the song they want to hear, but at length the Nightingale appears and is invited by the Chamberlain to sing for the Emperor at his palace. Though the Nightingale says its song is best heard in the forest, it agrees to go if that is the Emperor's wish. It lights on the Cook's hand, and the group starts its journey back to court.

ACT II   A procession is formed to bear the Nightingale to the palace. The courtiers and servants speak excitedly about the bird, which no one has yet seen. When the Cook arrives, she tells them the Nightingale is an inconspicuous little gray bird, unremarkable except for its voice, which brings tears to one's eyes. The bird and its escorts arrive and proceed into the palace (Chinese March). There the Emperor signals the Nightingale to sing, which it does *(Akh, serdtse dobroe)*—"Ah, joyous heart, fragrant garden, blossoming flowers." The Emperor, deeply moved, offers to reward the bird with the order of the golden slipper, but the Nightingale refuses, saying the tears in the Emperor's eyes are reward enough.

Three Japanese Ambassadors are shown in, bearing a brightly jeweled mechanical nightingale as a gift for the Emperor. As it performs, the real Nightingale slips away. When the Emperor discovers this, he is annoyed and pronounces the real Nightingale banished from his empire: from now on, the mechanical one is the official court singer.

ACT III   Years later, the Emperor lies on his deathbed. Death, accompanied by Specters, has taken away the royal crown, scepter, and banner (Specters: *My vse pred toboi*). Not wanting to hear these lugubrious voices, the Emperor calls for musicians, whereupon the Nightingale flies in the window and starts to sing for him *(Noch siniaia uzh blizitsia k kontsu)*, describing the end of night. Even Death is charmed and urges the Nightingale to sing more, which the bird agrees to do only if Death will return the Emperor's crown, scepter, and banner. Death does so, eventually disappearing when the Nightingale has finished its song about the melancholy garden of the dead *(Pechalnyi svetit mesiats)*. The Emperor thanks the bird and offers it a position of honor at court, but once again the Nightingale says it is reward enough to see tears in the Emperor's eyes. Promising to return each night from the forest and sing for the Emperor, the bird flies off.

The Chamberlain enters to the strains of a funeral march and, believing the Emperor dead, draws the curtains on the bed. The court assembles to pay respects to the departed. Suddenly the bedcurtains open, revealing the Emperor in full regalia, restored to health and greeting his subjects.

By the shore, the Fisherman gives a brief epilogue, saying the birds of the forest speak for the spirit of heaven *(Solntse vzoshlo, konchilas' noch')*.

OEDIPUS REX

(Oedipus the King)

TWO ACTS
MUSIC: Igor Stravinsky
TEXT (Latin): Jean Cocteau (written in French, translated by Jean Daniélou), based on Sophocles' tragedy
WORLD PREMIERE (concert performance): Paris, Théâtre Sarah Bernhardt, May 30, 1927
STAGE PREMIERE: Vienna, Staatsoper, February 23, 1928
U.S. PREMIERE (concert performance): Boston, Symphony Hall, February 24, 1928

IGOR STRAVINSKY

U.S. STAGE PREMIERE: Philadelphia, Metropolitan Opera House, April 10, 1931
METROPOLITAN PREMIERE: December 3, 1981

CHARACTERS

Jocasta, *Oedipus' wife*	Mezzo-Soprano
Oedipus, *King of Thebes*	Tenor
A Shepherd	Tenor
Creon, *Jocasta's brother*	Bass-Baritone
A Messenger	Bass-Baritone
Tiresias, *a soothsayer*	Bass
Narrator	Speaking Role

ACT I   Thebes, principal city of Boeotia in ancient Greece, is beset by the plague. The people call upon their king, Oedipus, to save them *(Caedit nos pestis)*. He promises to do so and has sent his brother-in-law, Creon, to consult the Oracle at Delphi. When Creon returns, he reports the Oracle's verdict *(Respondit deus)*: the death of King Laius, Oedipus' predecessor on the throne, must be avenged. Only when the slayer is driven out will the gods lift the plague. Oedipus pledges to root out the criminal, and the people turn to the blind seer Tiresias for further help. But Tiresias refuses to interpret the Oracle, knowing that Oedipus is a pawn of the cruel gods. Only when Oedipus accuses him of wanting the throne for himself does he reveal that "The slayer of the king is a king." Oedipus accuses him again of treasonous scheming with Creon to take over the throne *(Invidia fortunam odit)*. The people sing the praises of Queen Jocasta.

ACT II   Appearing before the people, Jocasta tries to quiet the dispute between Oedipus and Tiresias by reminding them that oracles are not truthful *(Nonn' erubescite, reges)*: did not the Oracle foretell that Laius would be slain by Jocasta's own son? But Laius was killed at a crossroads by an unknown assassin. Privately, Oedipus confides to Jocasta his fear: at mention of the crossroads, he recalled that on his way to Thebes from Corinth he had killed an old man at a crossroads (duet: *Pavesco subito, Jocasta*). Oedipus wants to consult the Oracle again, and to question a Shepherd who had witnessed his crime. The Shepherd appears; so does a Messenger, bearing news that Polybus, King of Corinth and supposed father of Oedipus, is dead *(Senex mortuus Polybus)*. The Messenger further relates that Polybus was not Oedipus' true father—that Oedipus was an abandoned child, found by the Messenger on a mountain and taken to the Shepherd for help. The crowd believes that this shows Oedipus to be of divine and miraculous birth *(Resciturus sum monstrum)*, but the Shepherd confirms that the child had been abandoned by mortal parents *(Oportebat tacere)*. Seeing

Jocasta hasten away, Oedipus at first wants to believe she is ashamed of his humble birth, about which he asks for more information. Together, the Messenger and Shepherd break the news to him that he was the child of Laius and Jocasta, that he slew his father and unwittingly married his mother *(In monte reppertus est)*. Oedipus is stunned to realize the truth at last *(Natus sum quo nefastum est)*.

The Messenger and Chorus relate how Jocasta has hanged herself, and how Oedipus, finding her dead, blinded himself with her brooch and showed himself before the people *(Divum Jocastae caput mortuum!)*. He must be driven from the city, in accordance with the Oracle. The people bid farewell to him sadly, saying they loved him *(Ecce! Regem Oedipoda)*.

KAROL
SZYMANOWSKI
1882–1937

orn in Ukraine to a cultured Polish family, Szymanowski moved to Warsaw at nineteen and formed a new-music group with other young musicians. At first influenced by German composers, notably Richard Strauss, he composed an opera, *Hagith,* at thirty, using a German libretto on a quasi-Biblical subject that showed his interest in the Near East. It was not performed until a decade later. Meanwhile, he began a series of travels—to Italy in 1908 and 1910, to Sicily in 1911 and 1914— that deepened his curiosity and knowledge about ancient societies and the classical world. "In Sicily," he wrote, "the cultures of East and West overlapped with each other and created a specific ambience that still exists to this day." These historical sources, with which he identified in an autobiographical way, nourished his most important work, *King Roger,* which he began composing during a visit to the United States.

The isolation and alienation that Szymanowski must have felt, as a privileged intellectual and a homosexual, emerge in *King Roger,* a subjectively free treatment of the myth of King Pentheus confronted by the god Dionysus. In his original version, Szymanowski had King Roger (the Pentheus figure, transplanted to ancient Sicily) follow Dionysus, but in his revision he has the king resist the allure of the Dionysian cult, striving instead to absorb it within his own convictions. (On a related theme, that of Pentheus' mother, who unwittingly killed her son during Dionysian revels, Szymanowski composed the cantata *Agave* in 1917.)

King Roger has an admirably simple libretto, but the score is elaborate in mood painting and orchestral coloration. A lack of real drama is problematic, but the composer's sense of archaic flavor is almost as seductive as the blandishments of Dionysus himself, who comes disguised as a shepherd. In both subject and treatment, *King Roger* bears a family resemblance to three later works: Ottorino Respighi's *La Fiamma,* Hans Werner Henze's *The Bassarids,* and Benjamin Britten's *Death in Venice.* Despite Szymanowski's sensitivity to other composers (notably Alexander Scriabin and the so-called French impressionists), he ends up standing as a lone individualist in twentieth-century music. In this respect he recalls the American composer Charles Tomlinson Griffes, who was intoxicated by some of the same influences and evinced a similar aesthetic viewpoint.

Szymanowski today is usually overlooked in favor of bolder composers of his generation who came to dominate the twentieth-century musical scene, such as Debussy, Stravinsky, Schoenberg, Berg, and Bartók. *King Roger,* because it is not particularly stageworthy, has been presented only occasionally, but it has been recorded and keeps returning to the attention of connoisseurs whose interests extend to the byways of the period. Szymanowski, fifty-four when he died of tuberculosis in a Lausanne sanatorium, connects the ancient past with the refined sensibilities of our own time in a distinctly personal way.

KING ROGER

(Król Roger)

THREE ACTS
MUSIC: Karol Szymanowski
TEXT (Polish): the composer and Jaroslaw Iwaszkiewcz, after Euripides' *The Bacchae*
WORLD PREMIERE: Warsaw, Wielki Theater, June 19, 1926
U.S. PREMIERE: Long Beach, Cal., Terrace Theater, January 24, 1988

CHARACTERS

Roksana, *the King's wife* . . . . Soprano
An Abbess . . . . .Mezzo-Soprano
Edrisi, *an Arab scholar* . . . . Tenor
The Shepherd (Dionysus) . . . . Tenor

Roger II, *King of Sicily* . . . . Baritone
The Archbishop . . . . Bass

Though the characters of the Christian King Roger II, who ruled Sicily 1130–54, and his adviser Abu Abdullah Mohammed esch sherif al-Edrisi (1099–1164), are historical, the story line of the opera is fictional. It was suggested by an episode in Euripides' *Bacchae,* on which Hans Werner Henze's *The Bassarids* also is based; but beyond showing the power of Dionysus (disguised as a Shepherd), Szymanowski seems to have wished, in his rewrite of the final scene, to represent King Roger as somehow becoming able to reconcile the Dionysian and Apollonian principles—by embracing both the bacchanalian revels and the sun (Apollo).

ACT I   In the Byzantine cathedral of Palermo, mid-twelfth century, a service is in progress when King Roger arrives with his court. The Archbishop informs the king that a mysterious Shepherd has been circulating among the Sicilians, preaching a pagan doctrine that has begun to seduce many. Edrisi, the king's adviser, confirms this report. The ecclesiastical authorities call on the king to sentence the interloper to prison, but Queen Roksana urges that he be given a fair hearing. The Shepherd is led in and calmly answers questions as to his teaching *(Mòj Bóg jest piękny, jako ja),* then waxes eloquent in addressing the crowd. Roger grows angry with Roksana's insistent pleas on the Shepherd's behalf and sentences the young man to death. Just as quickly, however, he withdraws his decision and says the Shepherd should be let go, subject to an interview at the royal palace that same evening. The worshippers and ecclesiastics are afraid of the stranger and unhappy with the king's leniency.

ACT II   In the inner courtyard of his royal palace that night, Roger confides his uneasy feelings to Edrisi *(Niepokój bladych gwiazd w zielonem morzu nieba płonie!)* as he awaits the charismatic Shepherd. Roksana, he is well aware, has been swayed by the youth; her voice is heard offstage, hoping for Roger to be swayed as well *(Uśnijcie krwawe sny króla Rogera).* Finally the Shepherd is admitted, and Roger questions him again: where has he come from? In poetically evasive terms, the Shepherd explains that he comes from everywhere, from all nature, representing love and freedom. As he speaks, the courtyard gradually fills with people, many of them young, responding to him with rapt attention. Roger's reaction remains skeptical and hostile, but the Shepherd is unfazed *(Tajemnych głębiin życia żar wszechmochna)* and calls upon musicians to play, so his followers can dance. Roksana, transfixed, joins them. In growing anxiety, Roger orders the man seized by guards, but the Shepherd challenges him *(Kto śmie mój czar tań cuchem pętać bów?),* then starts to leave, followed by many of the others, including Roksana. He invites—dares—Roger to meet him by the shore. Edrisi attends anxiously to the king, who is in despair.

ACT III   In the ruins of an ancient amphitheater near the sea, Edrisi and Roger find broken statues and, in the center, an altar on which offerings apparently have just been made. Roksana's voice is heard calling Roger's name. As the moon appears, the Shepherd is heard in the distance, calling on Roger to overcome fear. Roger is relieved and delighted to see her *(Tyżeśto, Roksano!)*; after at first claiming the Shepherd has left, she then admits he is everywhere, in all things *(Jest wgwiazd uśmiechu)*. As if hypnotized, Roger joins her in building a sacrificial fire. The Shepherd appears, summoning his followers *(Bije płomień ku niebiosom, blask nadziemski)*. As dawn approaches, figures in increasing numbers enter the amphitheater and gather around him. Roksana throws off her cloak and is seen dressed as a Maenad as she disappears among the crowd, which melts away into the distance. Feeling a sense of great liberation at last, Roger climbs to the upper reaches of the amphitheater and spreads wide his arms, as if offering himself to the day *(Słonce!)*.

Piotr Ilyich Tchaikovsky
1840–93

*T*chaikovsky is a classic example of a late bloomer in music. Though he was impressed by *Don Giovanni* at the age of ten and dreamed of composing an opera at fourteen, after his mother's death from cholera, he became serious about composition only after reaching the age of twenty. Then, in about six years, he crammed enough knowledge into his head to become a teacher of harmony. He was thirty before he began to write music that is still performed today.

Tchaikovsky loved the stage, but though his ballets enjoy familiarity in the West, his operas are generally regarded as footnotes to his career as a symphonist. This is not the case in Russia, where Tchaikovsky, a die-hard czarist, was given quick if artificial political rehabilitation by the Soviet cultural authorities and became a staple of the opera repertory. Meanwhile, in the West, he was represented by an occasional *Eugene Onegin* or *Queen of Spades*. Visits by the Bolshoi and Kirov companies helped to boost the image of these works. During the 1980s, and especially with the influx of Eastern Bloc singers that followed the demise of their Communist governments, it became commonplace for Russian operas to be heard abroad in the original language. The belated discovery of this repertory has even led to the study of Russian as an operatic language by the younger generation of singers.

Tchaikovsky's operas, though based predominantly on Russian subjects, are more eclectic and international in style than those of Mussorgsky or Rimsky-Korsakov. Oddly, this has militated against acceptance abroad, where deep-dyed local color seems to ease the path for works perceived as exotic or ethnic. French and Italian examples attracted this composer, who went to Florence to compose *Queen of Spades;* he admired Wagner, without becoming a Wagnerian, but his heart belonged to *Carmen,* which he heard in Paris in 1876, soon after its premiere. Two Tchaikovsky operas are on French subjects: *The Maid of Orléans,* after Friedrich Schiller's drama about Joan of Arc; and *Yolanta.* The first is somewhat reminiscent of *Lohengrin* in its adaptation of French grand-opera style. *Yolanta,* the last of Tchaikovsky's operas, relies far less on the chorus and is a more progressive score in its sensitive instrumentation and formal plasticity. Belonging to the period of the *Pathétique* Symphony, it represents the composer's most developed and final style.

A lack of dramatic event is certainly a problem with *Yolanta,* whose story furthermore seems naive and potentially saccharine. It attracted the composer with its medieval French locale and stylized symbolism, akin to that of the Pre-Raphaelite movement. It is hardly a novel idea to equate light with love, or sight with aesthetic awareness, but the story has the virtue of directness. It helps to know that *Yolanta* was commissioned to accompany Tchaikovsky's ballet *The Nutcracker* on a double bill. Like the story of Cinderella, it was intended for the young in heart; the mellowness of its mature score comes as an unexpected dividend.

YOLANTA

(Iolanta)

ONE ACT
MUSIC: Piotr Ilyich Tchaikovsky
TEXT (Russian): Modest Tchaikovsky, based on Henrik Hertz's play
   King René's Daughter, after Hans Christian Andersen's story
WORLD PREMIERE: St. Petersberg, Maryinsky Theater, December 18,
   1892
U.S. PREMIERE: Scarborough-on-Hudson, N.Y., Garden Theater, Sep-
   tember 10, 1933

CHARACTERS

Yolanta, *the King's daughter* . . . . Soprano
Brigitte, *her friend* . . . . Soprano

Laura, *another friend* . . . . .Mezzo-Soprano
Marthe, *Yolanta's nurse and Bertrand's wife* . . . . . . .Mezzo-Soprano
Count Vaudémont, *a Burgundian knight* . . . . Tenor
Alméric, *the king's armor bearer* . . . . Tenor
Ibn Hakia, *a Moorish doctor* . . . . Baritone
Bertrand, *the gatekeeper*. Baritone
Robert, *Duke of Burgundy*. . . . . Bass-Baritone
René, *King of Provence* . . . . Bass

The historical daughter of King René of Provence (1409–80), Margaret of Anjou, married Henry VI of England in 1445. The story of Yolanta is fictitious, but her father, known as "Good King René," one of the last of the Angevin dynasty, also remains one of the last exemplars of medieval culture and chivalry. His legend served as inspiration for Darius Milhaud's suite for woodwind quintet *La Chéminée du Roi René* (1939).

A royal garden in southern France, mid-fifteenth century. Princess Yolanta (Yolande) has been brought up ignorant of the fact that she is blind. The court provides a carefully sheltered environment in which no one ever mentions this fact, but the girl as she matures has come to sense there is something her companions are not telling her: do people have eyes only so they can weep? *(Otchego èto prezhde ne znala ni toski ia . . . ?)*. A group of girls runs in, having gathered baskets of flowers (chorus: *Vot tebe liutiki*). Yolanta feels tired and asks her nurse, Marthe, to sing her a childhood song. As she falls asleep, her friends Brigitte and Laura join in the lullaby *(Spi, pust' Angely krylami navevaiut sny)*, then carry her to rest nearby.

A hunting party is heard in the distance. The king's new messenger, a soldier named Alméric, presents himself at the gate to herald René's arrival. Bertrand, an old retainer, explains that the place is kept secluded because of Yolanta's blindness. The king appears, accompanied by a wise Moorish doctor, Ibn Hakia, in whom he places his last hope for restoration of Yolanta's sight. When the doctor goes to examine the sleeping girl, René offers a prayer for her to be cured *(Gospod' moi, esli greshen ia . . . ?)*. Ibn Hakia returns to say that there is hope, but first Yolanta must be made aware of her condition: to cure the body, the spirit must awaken its will *(Dva mira: plotskii i dukhovnyi)*. Without the certainty of a successful outcome, however, René cannot bring himself to agree to this. He and Ibn Hakia withdraw.

Two knights—Robert, Duke of Burgundy, and his friend Count Godefroy de Vaudémont—arrive at the garden, looking for the castle of King René. Robert, betrothed to Yolanta since birth, has never met the girl but wants to ask her father to break the engagement, as he is in love with Countess Mathilde of Lorraine *(Kto mozhet sravnitsia s Matildoi moei . . . ?)*. Vaudémont replies that an earthly love, such as Robert describes, is not for him: he would prefer a pure, spiritual type of girl, a chivalric ideal *(O, pridi, svetlyi prizrak)*. Though a sign is posted threatening death to trespassers, the knights are unafraid and start to look around, soon discovering Yolanta asleep. Vaudémont is immediately smitten by her ethereal beauty. Robert suspects she is an enchantress and tries to lead his friend away, but Vaudémont stays, fascinated, as Yolanta wakes. Robert, fearing a trap, dashes off to fetch soldiers while Yolanta brings wine. When Vaudémont praises her beauty, she is puzzled, never having heard mention of sight. He asks her for a red rose, but she picks a white one. Soon Vaudémont realizes she is blind. With enthusiasm he describes the wonders of light *(Chudnyi pervenets tvoren'ia)*. Though she professes to be happy as she is, she would like to share the experience of light with him *(Ty govorish' tak sladko)*.

King René and Yolanta's attendants suddenly appear, and the king is terribly upset to learn that the stranger has told Yolanta of her blindness. Ibn Hakia, however, says it is a good thing: "Now her consciousness has been awakened." René is willing to go along with this idea—if it works. If not, Vaudémont shall suffer the death penalty for his brash intrusion. Yolanta, appalled by the severity of her father's sentence, is motivated to see in order to save Vaudémont, and this is exactly what Ibn Hakia wants. Her attendants escort her toward the castle with the doctor.

René tells Vaudémont that he can go free: the death sentence was pronounced only for its shock value, to help Yolanta. Vaudémont identifies himself, with his titles of nobility, and asks for her hand in marriage. The king regrets that his daughter is already engaged to another, but at this moment Robert's return is announced. Robert says he will honor his commitment to marry Yolanta if the king wishes, but he would like to be released from it. Complimenting his chivalry, the king frees him and pledges Yolanta's hand to Vaudémont instead.

Bertrand enters to report on the girl's treatment: he left her praying intently for the knight to be spared. Now her attendants follow, proclaiming that she can see. When she returns to the garden, she is frightened at first by the strange gift of sight, but her fear gives way to joy when she learns to recognize the people around her, especially her father and Vaudémont, who revealed light and love to her. All join in a prayer of thanks to God *(Primi khvalu rabov smirennykh, Bozhe moi!)*.

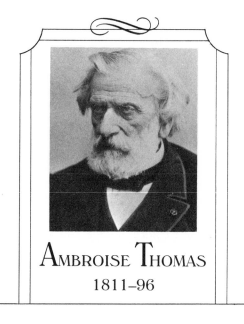

AMBROISE THOMAS
1811–96

*A*lthough the eighteenth of Ambroise Thomas' twenty operas, *Mignon,* was once a repertory staple—Verdi considered it a better example of French opera than *Carmen*—it had fallen out of fashion by the mid-twentieth century. An expert craftsman, Thomas had a piquant, dance-related sense of rhythm, as well as the charm and fluency of melody required of an opera composer. Like his colleague Charles Gounod, he knew how to please audiences without asking too much of them. Conservative and academic in taste, he drew his stylistic examples from masters of the recent past, notably Daniel-François Auber, Gioachino Rossini, and Gaetano Donizetti, and specialized in the genre of opéra comique, with ballet episodes and spoken dialogue.

Thomas is credited with twenty operas, most of which scored only a passing success, and several of which were outright failures. A master of adapting his style and reworking his material, he was not easily discouraged. Diligence eventually repaid him in 1866, when *Mignon* became overnight one of the most popular of all French operas. Thomas lived to see its 1,000th performance celebrated in 1894.

Responding to the public taste, Thomas had written *Mignon* to a story by Goethe, emulating Gounod's *Faust.* When Gounod came up with another winner in *Romeéo et Juliette,* Thomas was close behind with a version of Shakespeare's *Hamlet.* The work was well received, but later generations have vilified it as a superficial gloss on one of the great tragedies in English literature. Thomas had acquiesced in a relatively happy ending: Hamlet, though broken-hearted, lives on and is obliged to take the throne. Similarly, he had accepted the convention of a happy ending for *Mignon*. Writing *Mignon* for the Opéra Comique, a Paris theater where a tragic outcome was rarely tolerated, he had little choice; but *Hamlet*, written as a grand opera with sung dialogue, could have followed the play more closely.

In view of the mutilations visited upon Shakespeare by those who bowdlerized and revised his plays, the opera *Hamlet* seems less gross a departure, and when the work was produced in London, Thomas made amends with an alternative, Shakespearean finale. Somewhat more troubling is the sentimentalization of Hamlet's attitude, as a conventional romantic lover, toward Ophélie. In the opera, it is nobility of duty and mission, rather than a perverse quirk of character, that motivates his rejection of the girl. Thomas comes closest to the spirit of Shakespeare in the first appearance of the ghost, Hamlet's wrenching confrontation with his mother, and the play-within-the-play.

Heavy with honors, Thomas quit while he was ahead. Though he lived more than a quarter century after *Hamlet*, he wrote only one more opera, *Françoise de Rimini*, drawn from Dante. Back in 1851, the composer had taken over chairmanship of the Académie des Beaux-Arts upon the death of Spontini. Twenty years later, in 1871, he became director of the Paris Conservatory, succeeding his colleague Auber. He remained in this post until his death, overseeing the traditional training of a new generation of musicians, whom he tried to protect from what he saw as the threat of Wagnerism. Like Camille Saint-Saëns after him, he had become almost a living fossil. Only from the perspective of another century would his music start to seem young again.

HAMLET

FIVE ACTS
MUSIC: Ambroise Thomas
TEXT (French): Jules Barbier and Michel Carré, based on William
  Shakespeare's play
WORLD PREMIERE: Paris, Opéra, March 9, 1868
U.S. PREMIERE: New York, Academy of Music, March 22, 1872
METROPOLITAN PREMIERE: March 10, 1884 (in Italian)

CHARACTERS

Ophélie, *Laërte's sister* . . . . Soprano
Queen Gertrude, *Hamlet's mother* . . . . .Mezzo-Soprano

Laërte, *friend of Hamlet* . . . . Tenor
Hamlet, *Prince of Denmark* . . . . Baritone
King Claudius, *Gertrude's second husband* . . . . Bass
Polonius, *father of Ophélie and Laërte* . . . . Bass
Ghost of Hamlet's Father . . . . Bass

The earliest transcript of the Hamlet legend dates from about 1200, indicating a time of action prior to the thirteenth century.

ACT I   At the castle of Elsinore in Denmark, courtiers hail King Claudius and his bride, Gertrude, widow of his brother and predecessor, King Hamlet. Polonius, the court chamberlain, places the crown on Gertrude's head, and Claudius salutes her (*Ô toi qui fus la femme de mon frère*). When all have left the hall, Gertrude's son Hamlet wanders in, lamenting the fact that she has remarried scarcely two months after his father's death (*Vains regrets!*). Polonius' daughter Ophélie approaches, concerned by his distracted manner and by reports that he may be leaving the court. He denies any loss of love for her (duet: *Doute de la lumière*), saying it is "human inconstancy" that has caused his withdrawal into himself. The girl's brother, Laërte, comes to bid them both good-bye, as he is about to leave on a diplomatic mission to Norway (*Pour mon pays, en serviteur fidèle*), and entrusts Ophélie to Hamlet's care. Hamlet, not wishing to attend the wedding banquet, leaves. Horatio and Marcellus come looking for him, reporting to younger officers that that they saw the late king's Ghost upon the castle ramparts the night before. Not finding Hamlet, they proceed to the banquet.

§ On the ramparts later that night, Hamlet joins Horatio and Marcellus on their watch. They tell him of the apparition, which reappears at the stroke of midnight. Hamlet addresses the Ghost (*Spectre infernal! Image vénerée!*), which confides that Claudius murdered his own brother to gain the throne. Calling for vengeance (*Venge-moi, mon fils!*), the spirit cautions Hamlet against passing judgment on his mother: "Leave her to heaven." As dawn approaches, the Ghost departs. Hamlet swears to remember and obey its commands.

ACT II   Ophélie, reading a romance in the garden (*"Adieu, dit-il, ayez foi!"*), wonders again why Hamlet is so indifferent. When he passes by but shuns her, she realizes she is right about his change of attitude. Gertrude finds her there and, when Ophélie asks permission to leave the court for a nunnery, urges her instead to stay. Hamlet, the queen says, truly loves the girl but is going through a period of seeming madness, in which she can be of help (*Dans son regard plus sombre*). When Claudius appears, Gertrude excuses Ophélie and starts to discuss Hamlet, who wanders in again, rebuffing Claudius' attempts to befriend him. He does suggest entertainment from a group of players he has brought (*Par ma foi, vous serez témoins*). The actors arrive, offering their services to the king *(Princes sans apanages)*. Hamlet asks them to prepare to perform *The Murder of Gonzago*, but first he proposes a round of drinks to lighten the atmosphere *(O vin, dissipe la tristesse!)*.

§ In the great hall of Elsinore, a stage has been set up. The guests file in (Danish March) and take their places. As the play progresses in pantomime, Hamlet delivers a narration: as a king lies asleep in his garden *(C'est le vieux Roi Gonzague)*, he is poisoned by a villain, who takes the crown for himself. Claudius guiltily orders the actors away, confirming Hamlet's suspicions. Hamlet pretends to slip into madness, demanding that the usurper be punished, even grabbing the crown from Claudius' head (ensemble, Claudius: *O mortelle offense! Aveugle démence!*). With the court in disorder, Claudius rushes out, followed by the others.

ACT III   In a chamber in the queen's apartments, Hamlet wonders why he did not avenge his father's murder when he had the chance. He wonders at the mystery of death, where he might join his father *(Être ou ne pas être! Ô mystère!)*, then hides behind a curtain as the king enters. But Claudius' prayer to his brother's soul for forgiveness *(Je t'implore, ô mon frère!)* shows such contrition that Hamlet once again postpones his revenge: the man should die unshriven, amid the dissolute pleasures of court. When Polonius arrives, Claudius insists he has seen the late king's Ghost. Polonius' reassurances tell Hamlet that Polonius was an accomplice to the murder. Stepping out from hiding, he meets Gertrude and Ophélie and, denying his love for the girl, tells her to "Get thee to a nunnery" (trio: *Allez dans un cloître, allez, Ophélie!*). After Ophélie has left in tears, Hamlet charges his mother with the offense against his father, driving Gertrude to beg for mercy *(Pardonne, hélas! ta voix m'accable!)*. When she momentarily faints, the Ghost reappears to Hamlet, reminding him not to seek vengeance against his mother. She revives, convinced Hamlet has gone mad.

ACT IV   By a lakeside, peasants celebrate the joys of springtime *(Voici la riante saison)*. They are perplexed by the sight of a strange girl, Ophélie, who asks to join their revels. She imagines she is Hamlet's wife (mad scene: *À vos jeux, mes amis*), distributing wildflowers among the girls, but her song turns more somber with the tale of a Wili—a forsaken, drowned fiancée *(Pâle et blonde)*. Frightened by her unhinged state, the peasants back off as she slides into the water.

ACT V   In the churchyard near Elsinore, two Gravediggers reflect on death as the great leveler of mankind's pomp and aspirations (duet: *Dame ou prince, homme ou femme*). Hamlet appears from the wilderness and, as they trudge off, muses on Ophélie, asking her forgiveness for his desertion *(Comme une pâle fleur)*. Laërte approaches, challenging him for the same thing. As Hamlet reluctantly draws his sword, a funeral procession is heard, and Hamlet learns of

Ophélie's death. The girl's body is carried in (chorus: *Comme la fleur nouvelle*), followed by the court, to whom Hamlet's strange behavior seems only further proof of madness. Meanwhile, the Ghost appears again, and this time Gertrude sees it too, as do the others. It orders Hamlet to delay no longer in his vengeance. At this, Hamlet throws himself upon Claudius and runs him through. The queen is destined for a nunnery, while Hamlet, though he cries "My spirit is in the tomb," must live to rule in his father's place.

[In an alternative version of the final scene, fashioned by Thomas for the London stage, the Ghost does not appear. Hamlet kneels by Ophélie's body, finally makes good his pledge to kill Claudius, then joins the girl in death. In yet another version, arranged by Richard Bonynge for a production in Sydney in 1982, Hamlet dies as a result of a wound inflicted by Laërte during their duel, as in Shakespeare.]

VIRGIL THOMSON
1896–1989

*B*orn in Kansas City, Virgil Thomson served as a church organist in his youth and took up composition while studying at Harvard. After studies with Nadia Boulanger in Paris in 1920–21, he returned there in 1925 to live until World War II. French music, with its emphasis on the intelligible, metrically regular (to the point of monotony) setting of words, exerted a major influence on Thomson's style. Equally important, however, was his familiarity with American folk songs and hymns.

It was natural that Thomson would collaborate with Gertrude Stein, another American expatriate living in France. Although Stein was not especially musical, her poetry has its own kind of musicality, and her aesthetic ideals were compatible with his. Together they worked on *Four Saints in Three Acts,* Thomson's first opera. The composer had to trim some of the poet's flights of fancy and wordplay, shaping the text according to the needs of a musical structure. Fitted out with a scenario by Thomson's painter friend Maurice Grosser and sets by Florine Stettheimer, largely made of cellophane, *Four Saints* created an avant-garde happening at its premiere. Thomson had chosen an all-black cast—unusual at the time, except for a show specifically about blacks. Thomson had not planned this in advance but found himself drawn to the richness of the singers' voices, based on a culture of spirituals akin to the hymns with which he was familiar. This kinship stressed the spirituality of theme that Stein had chosen.

Four Saints in Three Acts, to which the librettist playfully adds a fourth act, drew a cult following, which has materialized for each of its infrequent revivals. Though the text makes no conventional sense, it could be argued that many other librettos make none either. Opera being an irrational art form, Stein and Thomson took every advantage of its irrationality. What opera can do uniquely well is to evoke moods, stir emotions, connect worldly reality to the reality of imagination and spirit. *Four Saints* has an aura of wonder, tenderness, and nostalgia that only words and music together can create. The whole of Stein–Thomson surpassed either of its parts.

The two artists worked together again on *The Mother of Us All,* produced in 1947, the year after Stein's death. A fanciful evocation of the suffragette leader Susan B. Anthony, *The Mother of Us All* is more literal than *Four Saints,* but there is still no attempt at realism or continuous dramatic narration. Thomson's final opera, *Lord Byron* (1972), with libretto by Jack Larson, is more conventionally designed, but Thomson's purpose remains, as it always was, the pursuit of poetic theater—a genre to which he found music peculiarly suited.

FOUR SAINTS IN THREE ACTS

PROLOGUE AND FOUR ACTS
MUSIC: Virgil Thomson
TEXT (English): Gertrude Stein
WORLD PREMIERE (concert performance): Ann Arbor, Michigan, May 20, 1933
STAGE PREMIERE: Hartford, Conn., Avery Memorial Theater, February 8, 1934
METROPOLITAN PREMIERE (Mini-Met, Forum Theater): February 20, 1973

CHARACTERS

St. Teresa I	Soprano
St. Settlement	Soprano
Commère	Mezzo-Soprano
St. Teresa II	Alto
St. Chavez	Tenor
St. Ignatius Loyola	Baritone
Compère	Bass

The following text is adapted from the scenario written by Maurice Grosser for the original production, adding references to the libretto.

Four Saints in Three Acts is both an opera and a choreographic spectacle. Imaginary but characteristic incidents from the lives of the saints constitute its action. Its scene is laid in sixteenth-century Spain. Its principal characters are St. Teresa of Avila, St. Ignatius Loyola, and their respective confidants, St. Settlement and St. Chavez—both of these last without historical prototypes. These are the Four Saints referred to in the title.

Other characters are a Compère and Commère, a small chorus of named saints—St. Pilar, St. Ferdinand, and others—and a larger chorus of unnamed saints. St. Teresa, for reasons of musical convenience, is represented by two singers dressed exactly alike. This device of the composer has no hidden significance and is not anywhere reflected in the poet's text, though Miss Stein found it thoroughly acceptable. The Compère and Commère, who speak to the audience and to each other about the progress of the opera, have also, as characters, been introduced by the composer.

The present scenario [by Maurice Grosser] was written after both the text and the music had been completed, although it was done with the help of both the poet and the composer. Without doubt, other solutions to the problems of staging could be found that would serve equally well. Gertrude Stein, however, did intend St. Ignatius' "Pigeons on the grass alas" to represent a vision of the Holy Ghost, and the passage at the end of Act III, "Letting pin in letting let," to represent a religious procession. The ballets were also suggested by her.

One should not try to interpret too literally the words of this opera, nor should one fall into the opposite error of thinking they mean nothing at all. On the contrary, they mean many things at once.

PROLOGUE A pageant, or Sunday-school entertainment, on the steps of the cathedral at Avila. For the instruction of saints and visitors, St. Teresa enacts scenes from her own saintly life. The portal of the cathedral, in which the tableaux will be performed, is closed off by a small curtain. The Compère and Commère, downstage at left and right, and Chorus I, grouped on the steps, sing a choral prologue *(To know to know to love her so)*. The entrance of St. Teresa I is announced by the Compère. At the end of the prologue, other saints, who form Chorus II, are introduced.

ACT I Seven tableaux are posed in the portal, chiefly by St. Teresa II. Between the tableaux there is commentary, mostly by the Compère, Commère, and Chorus. Tableau I shows a garden in early spring. St. Teresa II is seated under a tree, painting flowers on giant Easter eggs. She receives visitors and converses with St. Teresa I. St. Ignatius joins the guests, greets St. Teresa, and watches the entertainment *(St. Teresa seated but not surrounded)*.

In Tableau II, St. Teresa II, holding a dove, is being photographed by St. Settlement (Chorus I: *St. Teresa could be photographed having been dressed dressed like a lady*). In Tableau III, St. Teresa II is seated while St. Ignatius, kneeling, serenades her (Teresa I and II: *Leave later gaily the troubadour plays his guitar*).

At the end of the tableau, she rises and asks, "Can women have wishes?"

In Tableau IV, St. Ignatius offers her flowers (Teresa I: *St. Teresa can never change herbs for pansies and dry them*). At the end of the tableau, she asks, "How many saints can remember a house which was built before they can remember." This image is carried over into Tableau V, where St. Ignatius shows St. Teresa II a model of a large house, a Heavenly Mansion. In Tableau VI, St. Teresa II, an angel hovering over her, is shown in an attitude of ecstasy *(There can be no peace on earth with calm)*. In Tableau VII, she rocks in her arms an unseen child (Chorus I: *Those used to winter like winter and summer*). The act ends with comments, congratulations, and general sociability (trio: *They never knew about it*).

ACT II   A garden party in the country near Barcelona. The Compère and Commère observe the scene without taking part in it. Both St. Teresas and St. Ignatius join them, and there is performed for them a Dance of the Angels (Teresa I: *How many saints are there in it*). St. Chavez enters, introduces himself, and organizes a party game (Chorus I: *All Saints at all Saints*), at the end of which everybody goes out (Ignatius: *Settled passing this in having giv'n in*), leaving the Compère and Commère alone. There takes place between them a tender scene *(Scene eight / To wait);* and the two Teresas, coming in, are pleased to observe it (Teresa I: *To be asked how much of it is finished*). The other saints, returning for refreshments, toast the happy couple. Everyone prepares to go home. The saints play one more game. St. Plan, having gone to get his mantle, returns with a telescope. As the two St. Teresas look through it, there appears in the sky the vision of a Heavenly Mansion. The saints kneel, wonder, and rejoice (ensemble: *How many windows are there in it*). The vision ends, and the saints again prepare to leave. St. Teresa I desires the telescope. St. Ignatius refuses it to her. St. Chavez consoles her; and all leave slowly except St. Chavez, who remains alone on the stage.

ACT III   The garden of a monastery on a seacoast, with low trees and a garden wall. The men saints are seated on the ground in a circle, mending a fish net. St. Settlement and the two St. Teresas, passing by behind the garden wall, converse with St. Ignatius about monastic life *(With withdrawn. How do you do)*. The men put up their work, and St. Ignatius describes to them his vision of the Holy Ghost *(Pigeons on the grass alas)*. The men are only half convinced that the vision is true, until they hear miraculously the voices of a heavenly chorus *(Let Lucy Lily Lily Lucy)*. They crowd around St. Ignatius, who calls them to order *(In line and in line please say it first in line)*. After a military drill, St. Chavez lectures to them *(St. Ignatius might be admired for himself alone)*.

Now a group of sailors and young girls crosses the stage, executing a dance in the Spanish style. St. Ignatius again calls his men to order *(Left to left left to left)*. The women saints enter; they have heard of his vision and do not believe it. There is a storm in miniature, without rain, as St. Ignatius reproves them and predicts the Last Judgment *(Once in a while and where and where around)*.

Everyone is a little frightened. Men and women together form a devotional and expiatory procession, singing hymns as they cross the stage *(One two three as one one and one one one)*. St. Settlement and St. Stephen are the last to leave.

ACT IV   After a short intermezzo, the Compère and Commère, in front of the house curtain, discuss whether there is to be a fourth act *(How many acts are there in it)*. When they finally agree, the curtain rises, revealing all the saints reassembled in heaven. They sing their happy memories of life on earth *(One at a time regularly)* and join at the last in a hymn of communion *(When this you see remember me)*.

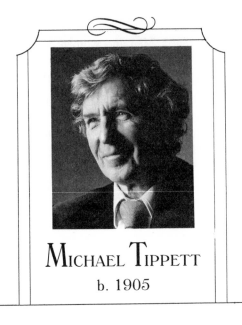

MICHAEL TIPPETT
b. 1905

fter the operas of Benjamin Britten, those of Michael Tippett (eight years Britten's elder) have been the most important to emerge from England during the second half of the twentieth century. The work of the two composers has been markedly different. Britten's operas demonstrate variety, technical control, and an emotional containment verging on stoicism. Those of Tippett are ebullient, rhapsodic, disorderly, and emotionally forthcoming. Tippett's bursts of musical enthusiasm, his capacity for optimism as well as sober compassion, have endeared him to those listeners who are unfazed by his prolixity of ideas and the often impenetrable language of the librettos he writes for himself.

Tippett's rejection of establishment values is one of the keys to his development. Seeing totalitarianism of both the right and the left as a threat to artistic individualism, he became a Trotskyite pacifist during World War II and served two months in prison for refusing to aid the war effort except through music. A knockabout professional life—odd jobs and teaching—preceded his settling into composition during the postwar decades. Having tried his hand at a folksong opera, *Robin Hood* (1934), he turned to the opera stage with *The Midsummer Marriage,* produced in 1955. In it, amid allusions to mythology and psychiatry, he showed his concern with the Jungian notion that each person must recognize and reconcile the light and dark sides of his own nature; failure to do so causes breakdown of communication and relationships, eventually conflict and self-destruction.

His next opera, *King Priam,* reflects a determination to write a more disciplined work. Like Walton's *Troilus and Cressida,* it treats a classical Trojan War theme in modern-day terms, recognizing that human dilemmas do not change over time. There is a return to Tippett's love of complexity, however, in *The Knot Garden,* another essay on the conundrums of human relationships, but one with a basically positive message: in the maze of experience, people can find themselves if they try. Similar concerns pervade his subsequent operas, *The Ice Break* and *New Year.*

Though genuinely fearful of man's capacity to destroy the world, Tippett has remained a dedicated humanist, a believer in the power of imagination and vision to lift man's spirit above the clouds that blanket the world of everyday reality. The reconciliation of divergent elements has been a persistent aim in his musical style and dramatic imagery. He does not make it easy to follow him, but his music urges the listener on, and the reward may be no less than insight, even self-discovery.

KING PRIAM

THREE ACTS
MUSIC: Michael Tippett
TEXT (English): the composer, after Homer's *Iliad*
WORLD PREMIERE: Coventry, England, Coventry Theater, May 29, 1962

CHARACTERS

Hecuba, *Priam's wife* . . . . Soprano
Andromache, *Hector's wife* . . . . Soprano
Helen, *Menelaus' wife, Paris' lover* . . . . Mezzo-Soprano
Nurse . . . . Mezzo-Soprano
Paris, *Priam's second son* . . . . Tenor
Achilles, *a Greek hero* . . . . Tenor
A Young Guard . . . . Tenor
Hector, *Priam's eldest son* . . . . Baritone
Patroclus, *Achilles' friend* . . . . Baritone
Priam, *King of Troy* . . . . Bass-Baritone
An Old Man . . . . Bass

The Trojan War of legend lasted ten years and took place in the environs of the Phrygian city of Troy (in Latin, Ilium), a site now known as Hissarlik in

Anatolia (Turkey). The legend is believed to have been based on an actual conflict about 1200 B.C., in which the Greeks invaders sought control of trade through the strait of the Dardanelles (Hellespont), whose mouth was close to Troy.

ACT I: *Prelude.* As the infant Paris lies in his cradle, his parents, King Priam and Queen Hecuba of Troy, learn from a seer, the Old Man, that Hecuba's disturbing dreams mean the child is fated to cause his father's death. Reluctantly the parents decide the child must be killed (Priam: *A father and a King*).

First Interlude. The Chorus reflects that man at the start of his life is born without choice: his parents make choices for him, even that of life or death. The Young Guard, whose job it was to remove the infant Paris, argues that it is wrong to decide against life for one's child (ensemble: *Time alone will tell*).

§ Some years later, Priam and his elder son, Hector, are on a hunt. As Hector is about to capture a raging bull, an unknown young boy jumps on the bull's back and rides it away. Huntsmen catch the animal and bring back the boy, who tells Hector he is a shepherd's son and wants to become a warrior. Priam and Hector agree to take him back to Troy if his father will agree. The boy says his name is Paris. Priam muses that he had hoped his second son might not have been killed after all. Yet he sees too that if he chooses life for the youth, he may be choosing death for himself *(So I hoped it might be)*. He takes Paris back to Troy.

Second Interlude. The Chorus reflects on the inexorable forces that drive and shape human existence *(Ah, but life is a bitter charade)*. Guests appear for the wedding of Hector, now grown to young manhood, and Andromache, "every inch a princess." Paris, never at ease with his older brother, has left for Greece.

§ Some time later, at Menelaus' house in Sparta, Paris has been having an affair with Helen, Menelaus' wife, and is about to be sent away. Seeing that he will cause a war by eloping with Helen, Paris pleads for guidance from Zeus *(If I fetch her, she will come)*. Hermes (Mercury), messenger of the gods, appears, telling Paris to award an apple to the most beautiful of three goddesses— Athene (Minerva), Hera (Juno), and Aphrodite (Venus)—who appear before him. Faced with an impossible choice, Paris bases his decision on what each goddess will offer in return. Athene promises distinction in battle; she reminds him of his mother, Hecuba. Hera offers domestic harmony, reminding him of Andromache, his brother's wife. Aphrodite simply pronounces his name in a way that embodies Helen for him, so he awards her the prize, despite curses from the other two.

ACT II On the walls of Troy, Hector, in armor to fight the Greeks, taunts Paris as a playboy *(So you've given up fighting!)*. Priam enters and orders them to unite against the Greeks, who are themselves divided: Achilles cannot forgive King Agamemnon for stealing from him a girl he won after his victory at Thebes. Since Achilles sulks in his tent and refuses to fight, it is the right time for a Trojan attack. When Paris leaves to arm himself, Hector continues to criticize his brother resentfully, sympathizing with Menelaus (*I tell you, father, but I'm filled with shame*). Hector leaves for battle, followed by Paris.

First Interlude. The Old Man calls on Hermes to lead him for a glimpse of the legendary Greek hero. They cross the plain to the tent of Achilles, who sings a sad song to his friend Patroclus, remembering their homeland (*O rich-soiled land*). Since Patroclus cannot persuade him to return to the battle, and since the Trojans are about to set fire to the Greeks' ships, Patroclus offers to borrow Achilles' armor and let the Greeks think he is Achilles. This plan delights Achilles (*Hector has fired the ships*), so long as he himself still gets the glory.

Second Interlude. The Old Man, fearing that the tide of war is turning against Troy, asks Hermes to warn Priam. Scarcely has Hermes done so than Paris brings news that Hector has killed Patroclus in single combat and taken Achilles' armor. Hector appears, wearing the armor, and pompously asks his father and brother to join him in giving thanks (trio: *O Zeus, King of all gods and goddesses*). But Achilles, roused to fury by his friend's death, appears and delivers his awesome war cry. The Trojans stand transfixed.

ACT III   Filled with foreboding, Andromache awaits her husband's return (*Yes, Prince Hector will want his bath*). Hecuba arrives and asks her to go to the city walls and plead with Hector to come back rather than face Achilles alone: otherwise Troy will lose him and its other heroes. Andromache refuses and, when Helen comes, denounces her as a whore, saying she should return to the Greeks (*"My husband Paris"—Listen to that!*). Helen replies that as the daughter of Zeus and Leda, she is singular in comparison with ordinary women (*Let her rave. I, Helen, am untouched*). Hecuba angrily wishes she had smothered Paris at birth to prevent Helen's coming to Troy. Sensing the nearness of death for their men, Hecuba prays to Athene, Andromache to Hera, Helen to Aphrodite (trio: *Woman to Goddess, I to you*).

First Interlude. Serving women comment on news of Hector's death and wonder how Priam will take it.

In Priam's chambers, Paris alone has the courage to tell him of Hector's death. Priam, in his rage and grief, calls Paris a coward who should have died instead of Hector. Paris leaves, swearing to avenge his brother. Priam imagines the Young Guard, Old Man, and Nurse from the Prelude; they say that as Hector killed Patroclus and Achilles killed Hector, Paris now will kill Achilles, and Achilles' son Neoptolemus in revenge will kill Paris. Priam proudly refuses to accept anyone's judgment of him as a father and a king (*These things are tricks*).

Second Interlude. In his tent, Achilles sits contemplating the shrouded body of Hector and mourning Patroclus. Priam, led by Hermes, comes to ransom Hector's body. At first Achilles responds roughly *(Then you are mad, old man?)*, but when he has heard Priam's plea *(I clasp your knees, Achilles),* he says he may take the body. Achilles declares he will seek death in battle. Priam says Paris is destined to kill him; Achilles says his own son Neoptolemus is destined to kill Priam.

Third Interlude. Hermes addresses the audience *(Do not imagine all the secrets of life),* asking them to feel pity and terror at Priam's death.

Before an altar, Paris tells Priam he has killed Achilles, avenging Hector. Priam tells Paris to guard him while he prays. When Hecuba comes to say all is lost, Priam, withdrawn into a world of his own, can no longer see her. When Andromache comes, she grudgingly acknowledges Paris' slaying of Achilles— "Too late!"—but adds that Neoptolemus has killed her own son and is raging for vengeance. Priam cannot see her either; she leaves, silently passing Helen, who embraces Paris for the last time. Recognizing Helen as the embodiment of some eternal principle, Priam knows she will go back to Greece and gently bids her farewell. Hermes returns to Hades, preparing the way for Priam, who is killed by Neoptolemus when the Greeks burst in.

The Knot Garden

THREE ACTS AND EPILOGUE
MUSIC: Michael Tippett
TEXT (English): the composer
WORLD PREMIERE: London, Covent Garden, December 2, 1970
U.S. PREMIERE: Evanston, Ill., Northwestern University, February
22, 1974

CHARACTERS

Flora, *Faber and Thea's ward* . . . . Soprano
Denise, *Thea's sister* . . . . Soprano
Thea, *Faber's wife.* . . . . Mezzo-Soprano
Dov, *Mel's lover.* . . . . Tenor
Mangus, *a psychoanalyst* . . . . Baritone
Faber, *a civil engineer.* . . . . Baritone
Mel, *a writer* . . . . Bass-Baritone

ACT I: CONFRONTATION   In a labyrinthine garden in England, c. 1970, a whirling storm has as its center Mangus, a psychoanalyst, lying on a couch, emerging from a dream represented by the storm. Equating himself with Prospero in *The Tempest,* he declares he has come to put the other characters to rights. Thea, a matron in her thirties, appears and turns down Magnus' offer of help with her gardening: she keeps the garden as a private preserve. Flora, adolescent ward of Thea and her husband, runs in crying and is led toward the inner garden by Mangus. Thea's husband, Faber, immediately follows and is accused by Thea of trying to molest the girl, whom he should be protecting. As Thea steps out, Faber laments that their marriage has degenerated into daily arguments, adding that Flora seems to be imagining his advances. Suddenly he realizes it is time for work and leaves. Mangus returns and notes the defenses the two use to keep up their estrangement. His task is nominally to help Flora, whom he compares to Miranda in *The Tempest;* but Thea and Faber are really the ones who need help.

Picking flowers, Flora tells Thea that Denise, Thea's sister, is due to arrive. Thea leaves Flora alone, soon to be interrupted by the arrival of Dov, a musician, and his black male lover, Mel, a writer; they are costumed as Ariel and Caliban in *The Tempest* and clown around with Flora (Dov, Mel: *Ca-ca-Caliban was a bad man*) until Thea reappears and dampens their spirits. Magnus says the others will have to act out a play-within-the-play, with him as Prospero *(Adults too play later).* He takes Flora to fetch more costumes.

Thea leads Mel into the maze of the garden, implying a sexual attraction between them; something similar happens when Faber returns and appears tentatively attracted to Dov. Flora defuses the momentary tension by bringing Mangus with costumes and announcing that Denise has arrived. Denise, lamed by torture, is a political activist who has escaped from captivity in a foreign country *(O, you may stare in horror).* Not knowing how to put her at ease, the others improvise a blues ensemble, led by Mel *(Do, do not, "Do not torment me").*

ACT II: LABYRINTH   In the maze at the center of the garden, characters are drawn in from one side and ejected from the other, meeting briefly in the middle but then being separated as if by centrifugal force. Thea faces Denise in this manner, but their guardedness prevents them from communicating. Denise next encounters Faber, who would like to discover more about her sister's motivation, but Denise feels no need to get involved with him. Faber meets Flora and shows his desire for her *(This is absurd. Flora, come here),* but she is fearful and quickly replaced by Thea, who hits Faber with a whip, saying he needs a woman's discipline *(Take that, you cur).* When Dov takes her place, and Faber renews his tentative overtures, Faber is replaced by Mel, who joins Dov in a song-and-dance exchange (duet: *One day we meet together, brother).* Denise, taking Dov's place, calls on Mel to respond to her passion for social justice.

The maze suddenly goes into reverse and is accelerated. Dov is swept back in and thrown onto the forestage. Mel is whirled away after Denise; Flora returns, still fleeing Faber; he follows and briefly, wordlessly confronts Thea. Dov finds Flora lying nearby and comforts her with a pop song, seemingly autobiographical *(I was born in a big town)*, but Mel reappears and says, "I taught you that."

ACT III: CHARADE   Thea and Denise do not take part in the charade, an allegory of *The Tempest;* the other five variously step in and out of their roles. Mangus puts on his robe as Prospero but assures the skeptical Thea that the play, not he, holds the power to change and resolve.

On an imaginary island, Mel (Caliban) crawls about as Flora (Miranda) and Mangus explore. Mangus tries to teach Mel to get up from all fours—to become civilized. Meanwhile, Dov (Ariel) sings of freedom, air, and light from a nearby tree in which he is imprisoned, and from which Mangus releases him. When Dov, carried away by his new freedom, tries to vent his resentment against the earthbound, untamed nature personified by Mel, Mangus stops him from going beyond the script.

Thea comments on how the script changes as soon as real people start to play the parts *(Two unruly spirits born!)*. Denise, still preoccupied with the discipline and sense of purpose she knew as a freedom fighter *(I do not understand confusion),* resists Thea's suggestion that Mel, a warmer, less disciplined personality, could give her something she needs.

As Dov guards the sleeping Flora, Mel creeps up and tries to rape her. Though Mangus has warned Dov of the attack, it is Denise who comes to the girl's rescue. As Flora makes her escape, Denise is alarmed by her own reaction to Mel's natural sensuality. She too leaves, but Mel follows her.

Thea accuses Mangus of pandering, but he invites her to watch a scene of reconciliation between Flora and Faber, who are playing chess. The game is soon ended: throwing the chessboard over, Flora declares her freedom from the limits of the game. She runs off, followed by Dov. Mangus tells Thea and Faber to pick up the pieces. As the two men leave, Thea sees the point: the ordered game of marriage can be resumed according to its rules *(I am no more afraid)*. Nature—formerly her escape, as represented by her garden—she now sees embodied in herself and Faber.

Flora seems glad to be leaving the island, but Mangus takes a more active role in resolving the dilemmas of the remaining characters. Faber, acting as jailer, charges his "prisoner" Dov with sulking; Dov, as Ariel, replies that he longs for freedom. Mangus orders him set free. Mel, as Caliban, also wants to be liberated and to rule the island, which he sees as rightfully his. Mangus cautions him not to overreach, and Dov teases him *(Ca-ca-Caliban)*.

Mangus abruptly halts the charade *(Enough! We look in the abyss)*. Neither the Caliban side of our nature nor the intervention of a magician can save us, but each character has found hope in accepting oneself entire, as one is. Freed from the prison of individual isolation, each can now reach out to others. Denise starts to leave with Mel, followed somewhat expectantly by Dov, who has not found his resolution yet. Flora, independent and alone, dances off; Mangus disappears.

EPILOGUE   Thea and Mangus are left in the garden. They put aside the symbols of their estrangement—she her seed packets, he his business papers. As darkness surrounds them, each feels restored to a sense of self, thereby to a renewal of their relationship (*Our enmity's transcended in desire. . . . Memory recedes in the moment. . . . The curtain rises*).

RALPH VAUGHAN WILLIAMS
1872–1958

Vaughan Williams is considered, along with Gustav Holst and Rutland Boughton, among the few composers who strove valiantly to give life to English opera during a period when almost no one cared anything about it. In Vaughan Williams' case, it was doubtless his teacher Charles Villiers Stanford (1852–1924), himself the composer of ten operas (including the moderately successful *Shamus O'Brien,* 1896), who provided inspiration and impetus. A trip to Germany when Vaughan Williams was seventeen also helped, inspiring an admiration for Wagner, which he shared with George Bernard Shaw.

When the young man started composing his own first opera, it was not a Wagnerian work but a quintessentially English folk tale, *Hugh the Drover,* written alongside *A London Symphony,* his first major orchestral score. Begun in 1910, *Hugh the Drover* lay unperformed until 1924, by which time it had lost its innocence to the experience of World War I, in which the composer also served. *Hugh the Drover* preserves an image of idyllic English country life that could not be revived, comparable to that of Czech life in Smetana's *The Bartered Bride.* Together with folk songs, Vaughan Williams used original material written in a folklike idiom. This he was well prepared to do, having devoted roughly a decade of his life (1903–13) to collecting and editing English folk music, in much the same way that Béla Bartók and Zoltán Kodály gathered Hungarian and Romanian folk music. During that same formative period, Vaughan Williams had written incidental music for plays and studied briefly in Paris with Maurice Ravel, emerging with an enhanced technique and focused sense of his own musical identity.

Although none of his operas was given a thoroughly satisfactory production in England or aroused much popularity, Vaughan Williams continued to write them—five in all. His second, *Sir John in Love,* based on Shakespeare's Falstaff, continued in a folk-based idiom, evoking the Elizabethan period. His third, *Riders to the Sea,* often called his masterpiece in the form, is a one-act setting of J. M. Synge's tragedy about Irish fishermen and their families. This was followed by a lighthearted work in mixed genre, *The Poisoned Kiss,* and the serious, cantata-like "morality" *The Pilgrim's Progress,* actually begun in 1909 but not completed until 1949 and performed in 1951.

It has been claimed, with justification, that only on the basis of such works as these was Benjamin Britten able to resurrect English opera after the war with *Peter Grimes* (1945). All composers work with reference to their artistic forebears, and in the case of opera—a particularly traditional form—precedent is as important to the musician as it is to the lawyer. Britten in a personal sense had little use for Vaughan Williams, but the antecedents of Britten's "parables for church performance" *(Curlew River, The Burning Fiery Furnace, The Prodigal Son)* are inescapably those of *The Pilgrim's Progress,* and there is more than a passing family resemblance between *Albert Herring* and *Hugh the Drover.* To Britten belongs the credit for taking what his brave predecessors had done and making it stick. To Vaughan Williams, Gustav Holst, and Rutland Boughton belongs credit for having jolted the mired coach of English opera into motion at last.

⌘

Hugh the Drover, or Love in the Stocks

TWO ACTS
MUSIC: Ralph Vaughan Williams
TEXT (English): Harold Child
WORLD PREMIERE: London, His Majesty's Theater, July 14, 1924
U.S. PREMIERE: Washington, D.C., Poli's Theater, February 21, 1928

CHARACTERS

Mary, *the Constable's daughter* . . . . Soprano
Susan ⎱ *village girls* . . . . ⎰ Soprano
Nancy ⎰ . . . . ⎱ Alto

Aunt Jane, *the Constable's sister*	Alto
Hugh the Drover	Tenor
William	Tenor
John the Butcher	Bass-Baritone
The Constable	Bass
Robert	Bass

ACT I   A small town in the Cotswolds on a Monday, the last day of April, about 1812. On the outskirts, a fair is in progress. Vendors offer their wares, but the crowd is cautious about spending. A Showman brings an effigy of Napoleon ("Old Boney"), to be burned that night, and warns that if any spies for the French are near, they should beware the heroism of the local men *(Cold blows the wind on Cotsall)*. To the tune of the Trumpeter, the Showman leads a procession off, but some of the bystanders stay when they hear a Ballad-Seller approach. At their request he sings a love song *(As I was a-walking one morning in spring)*, which reminds the Constable's daughter, Mary, of her impending marriage to John, a butcher. She bursts into tears and is comforted by her Aunt Jane, but her father, who arranged the match, shows no sympathy *(Mary in tears? 'Tis rank ingratitude)*. John himself appears and offers to take on anyone who thinks he can beat him *(Show me a richer man in all this town)*. He wants to take Mary around the fair, but she refuses to go with him, saying they aren't married yet. The crowd and Aunt Jane take Mary's side, while John and the Constable are defiant (ensemble, Aunt Jane: *You dare to touch her*). The argument is quelled by the arrival of the Fool and Hobby Horse, followed by Morris Men (dancers), who lead a march that takes the crowd away (chorus: *Way for the Morris Men*).

Alone with Aunt Jane, Mary confesses she doesn't love John, who frightens her. Aunt Jane says motherhood will bring fulfillment *(Sweet heart, life must be full of care)*. Mary prefers the idea of roaming free but says she will obey her father. This is overheard by Hugh, a young man who has wandered in, mending his whip. He compares Mary to a bird that longs for freedom but would be safer in its cage *(Sweet little linnet)*. Sensing a kindred spirit, Mary shows immediate interest in Hugh, despite Aunt Jane's disapproval. He explains he is a drover—he rounds up ponies for the army *(Horse-hoofs thunder down the valleys)*. His romantic description of his life draws Mary to his side. As they embrace, Aunt Jane runs off, but the two continue to declare their love (duet, Mary: *In the night-time I have seen you riding*) until Aunt Jane returns with the Constable, who curses Hugh as a seducer.

As the crowd returns, looking forward to a boxing match, Hugh decides to accept an open challenge to fight John, the local champion. He steps forward and declares the prize shall be Mary's hand. The local men are divided as to which man they favor, while Mary is afraid for Hugh's safety (ensemble, Mary:

Ah no! you shall not fight him). After three rounds, Hugh succeeds in felling John for the count.

Scarcely has Hugh been fêted as the victor, however, than the recovering John and the Constable, after a brief conference, accuse him of being a wanted man—a spy for the French. Their flimsy "evidence" is the fifty pounds in gold, carried in his knapsack, that he offered as security before the fight. The fickle crowd is swayed (chorus: *O! the devil and Bonyparty*), and on the Constable's orders, Hugh is arrested.

Act II   In the marketplace at four the next morning, John and his cronies are still carousing at the inn while Hugh sits in the stocks, trying to face death in the same carefree way he did life *(Gaily I go to die).* John emerges from the inn and taunts Hugh. When the square is deserted again, Mary steals in, having got hold of the keys to set Hugh free *(Turn, stubborn key).* Mary wants him to escape and save his life, but since she is resigned to staying behind and marrying John, Hugh refuses to go without her. Dawn approaches, and with it a group of villagers who have been celebrating the First of May. Hatching a scheme, Mary joins Hugh in the stocks, and they draw his cloak over them as the townspeople approach, headed by John with a flowering branch to put outside Mary's door. Aunt Jane and the Constable join the group and discover that Mary is missing from her room. Eventually she is discovered in the stocks and released. Facing public disgrace, she sticks by Hugh (ensemble: *The girl's gone mad).* Her father disowns her and refuses to put up any dowry if John still wants her, but John doesn't *(A trollop from the stocks is no fit wife).*

The crowd falls to fighting: one faction wants to throw John in the pond, while his friends defend him. A riot is avoided only by a bugle in the distance: soldiers are approaching. When the squad arrives, John tells the Sergeant that the "spy" is awaiting punishment, but the Sergeant recognizes Hugh as the man who saved him from a snowdrift one night. He declares that "His Majesty has no better friend in England than Hugh the Drover," then decides to impress the unwilling John into the army. As John is marched off, Mary and Hugh find themselves alone. She is suddenly afraid to face the life of a wanderer; he soon restores her courage (duet: *Oh, the sky shall be our roof).* The townspeople return, urging the two to stay, but they head together for the open road.

GIUSEPPE VERDI
1813–1901

Verdi, born three years before Rossini's *Il Barbiere di Siviglia,* died one year before Debussy's *Pelléas et Mélisande* and five years before Strauss' *Salome.* In nearly nine decades of life, he had made the voyage from the heyday of bel canto to the threshold of the twentieth century. The bulk of the standard repertory being made up of nineteenth-century operas, Verdi was around for the birth of most, and indeed he wrote many of them.

Verdi rose to the top of a crowded, competitive profession not by outlasting his colleagues but by going them one better. Although his qualities took time to be fully appreciated, they had the virtue of continuing to improve, as he himself did, with the passage of time. Verdi today is generally considered the most skillful and versatile musical dramatist among Italian opera composers.

A late starter, he was already twenty-nine at the time of his first major success, *Nabucco* (1842). Like Rossini, he retired at the height of his fame from systematically turning out operas; unlike Rossini, he did continue to write them, but at his own pace. Of Verdi's twenty-six operas, all but four were composed during the first half of a fifty-four-year period of activity. Of that first half, the "galley years" 1842–53 contained the most concentrated period of work, with every year seeing one or two new operas produced. This period culminated with *La Traviata* in 1853. After that, Verdi turned in new directions, composing for Paris and St. Petersburg, absorbing the influence of French grand opera. His late works came few and far between: he had retired to his country estate at Sant' Agata, managing his property and business affairs. When he did write them—*Aida* (1871), *Otello* (1887), and finally *Fals-*

taff (1893)—it became apparent that this Old Master was no fossil but still moving forward in his art.

In the decades after World War II, interest turned back to operas of the bel canto period, which had declined under the impact of Wagner and a change toward louder, less agile singing. When singers like Maria Callas, Leyla Gencer, Renata Scotto, Joan Sutherland, and Marilyn Horne appeared, cultivating the neglected bel canto technique, producers and public rediscovered Rossini, Donizetti, and Bellini. (In due time they began to rediscover Handel as well.) This change of focus cast new light on the earlier operas of Verdi, which had grown from the ethos of bel canto. His own later works had cast a shadow over them.

Of the group considered here, *I Lombardi,* the earliest (1843), is an expansion of the formula that had produced *Nabucco* the year before. The Biblical story serves as a background for Verdi's specialty, the portrayal of characters in the toils of emotional conflict—love versus loyalty, public obligations versus personal. The year after *I Lombardi,* Verdi wrote an even darker work, *I Due Foscari,* probing another favorite theme, that of parent-child relationships. Here too are the moral questions of justice, retribution, and forgiveness—taken up in full in *Stiffelio.* Meanwhile, with *Attila* (1846), Verdi addressed a hero who is also a villain, depending on one's point of view. The plot of *Attila* would do for a Victor Mature movie, but Verdi saw beyond its creaky mechanics to look into the hearts of a warrior maiden (borrowed from *Nabucco*), an ambivalent patriot (Foresto), and a "noble savage" (Attila).

Stiffelio marks an advance in dramatic sophistication: having savored success, Verdi was ready to take risks. The subject of a Protestant minister and an errant wife was daring for Catholic Italy in 1850; viewed with hindsight, it seems to point toward *Otello,* thirty-seven years later. After the work was poorly received, Verdi reconstructed it into the more conventional *Aroldo.* For over a century, the original *Stiffelio* score was believed lost, but scholarship finally restored it. Today, with its blunt confrontations and somber colors, it grapples again with the moral and emotional dilemmas that fueled Verdi's fires—and made him a perennially timely musical dramatist.

I LOMBARDI ALLA PRIMA CROCIATA

(The Lombards on the First Crusade)

FOUR ACTS
MUSIC: Giuseppe Verdi
TEXT (Italian): Temistocle Solera, after Tomasso Grossi's poem
WORLD PREMIERE: Milan, La Scala, February 11, 1843
U.S. PREMIERE: New York, Palmo's Opera House, March 3, 1847
METROPOLITAN PREMIERE: December 2, 1993

CHARACTERS

Viclinda, *Arvino's wife* . . . . Soprano
Giselda, *her daughter* . . . . Soprano
Sofia, *Acciano's wife* . . . . Soprano
Arvino, *Folco's son* . . . . Tenor
Oronte, *Acciano's son* . . . . Tenor
Pagano, *Folco's son*/A Hermit . . . . Bass
Pirro, *Pagano's henchman* . . . . Bass
Acciano, *tyrant of Antioch* . . . . Bass

ACT I   *The Revenge.* Milan, 1095, at the start of the First Crusade. The powerful family of Folco, Lord of Rò, has been torn by a feud between two brothers, Pagano and Arvino, over the love of Viclinda. Though now she has been married to Arvino for two decades and borne him a daughter, Giselda, Pagano still nurses his grudge. In the square before the Basilica of St. Ambrose, the public remarks on Pagano's return, supposedly repentant, after long exile in the Holy Land. Pagano and Arvino emerge from the church and exchange a kiss of peace, but Pagano turns aside to plot with his squire Pirro to kidnap Viclinda that very night. When Arvino is named by acclamation to lead the Crusade, the two brothers make a show of joining in the enterprise (ensemble: *All'empio che infrange la santa promessa*). Everyone leaves except Pagano and Pirro, who resume their scheming as voices in a nearby cloister mark the approach of darkness (chorus: *A te nell'ora infausta*). Declaring he never could forget Viclinda *(Sciaguarata! hai tu creduto)*, Pagano rallies his followers.

§ In a hall in Folco's palace shortly afterward, Viclinda, Giselda, and Arvino all feel uneasy. Giselda offers a prayer *(Salve Maria!)*, but no sooner have they retired than Pagano steals into Arvino's room, emerges with a bloody dagger, and tries to abduct the protesting Viclinda while the palace burns with fires set by his minions. Arvino's unexpected appearance stuns Pagano, who learns that by mistake he has killed his father, not his brother. When Arvino draws his sword against Pagano, Viclinda steps between them, preventing further bloodshed, but Pagano tries to take his own life, only to be restrained by onlookers. Far worse, they declare, that he should live, bear the mark of Cain, and wander the earth suffering for his crime *(Mostro d'averno orribile).*

Act II *The Man of the Cave.* In the palace of Acciano, ruler of Antioch, ambassadors join him in denouncing the infidel Crusaders *(Or che d'Europa il fulmine).* His wife, Sofia, secretly a Christian, enters with their son Oronte, who has fallen in love with Giselda, now their prisoner *(La mia letizia infondere);* both feel that the girl's faith must reveal the true love of God.

§ On a desert mountaintop, a Hermit appears from the mouth of a cave, longing for the arrival of the liberating Crusaders *(Ma quando un suon terribile).* Pirro arrives in Muslim garb, searching for the holy man: having renounced Christianity to survive as a fugitive, Pirro is consumed by remorse for this and for his past crimes. The Hermit tells him to take heart: in the distance the Crusaders' march can be heard. Pirro jumps at the chance to betray the defenses of Antioch so the Crusaders can take the city. The Hermit conceals Pirro in his cave as the Lombards arrive, also searching for the holy man, who arms himself to join them, promising Arvino to help free Giselda from captivity. The soldiers vow to prevail *(Stolto Allhà! sovra il capo ti piomba).*

§ In the harem at Antioch, serving women wonder what is troubling Giselda. Deciding she wants to pray, they leave her alone. Addressing the memory of Viclinda, who has died in the interim, she prays for guidance *(Se vano è il pregare),* but cries within the palace soon intrude: through Pirro's treachery, Crusaders are routing the unsuspecting Turks. Arvino, expecting Giselda to be overjoyed at her rescue, is greeted instead by her revulsion at the violence and plunder: surely this is not God's will *(No! giusta causa non è).* She even foretells the revenge the Turks will exact later in Europe. The Hermit, seeing the girl nearly beside herself, stops Arvino from striking her down.

Act III *The Conversion.* In the Valley of Jehoshaphat, with Jerusalem in the distance, the Crusaders halt at the sight of their goal *(Gerusalem! la grande, la promessa città!).* As they move on, Giselda, leaving her father's tent for a breath of fresh air, meets her beloved Oronte, disguised in Lombard clothing. Having believed him dead, she is overjoyed to see him, and though he warns of his outcast state (duet: *Per dirupi e per foreste),* she insists on fleeing with him and bids farewell to the camp *(O belle, a questa misera, tende lombarde, addio!).* As voices are heard approaching, the couple escapes. When Arvino finds her missing, he again curses his daughter, this time for her disappearance. His family troubles are aggravated further by news that his erring brother, Pagano, has been sighted near the camp. He vows to settle this old score once and for all (*Sì! del ciel che non punisce*).

§ Inside a cave, Giselda seeks shelter with Oronte, wounded during their flight. The Hermit discovers them, condemning their love but offering to save Oronte's soul by baptizing him with water from the nearby River Jordan. Oronte, feeling himself already converted by Giselda's love, welcomes the opportunity. As Giselda weeps, he dies believing they will be reunited in heaven, while the Hermit reassures him of salvation (trio: *Qual voluttà trascorrere*).

ACT IV *The Holy Sepulcher.* At the Hermit's cave, Giselda, sick with fever, has been kept safe from her father's wrath. Now the holy man brings Arvino, successfully urging him to forgive her. When the men have left to find water to revive the girl, she dreams of blessed spirits, among them Oronte, who tells her he is in heaven (*In cielo benedetto*) and that the spring of Siloam will provide water for the Crusaders. She awakens, convinced of having experienced a true vision (*Non fu sogno!*).

§ At the Lombard camp, the weary Crusaders long for their homeland (*O Signore, dal tetto natio*). Giselda, the Hermit, and Arvino arrive to tell them they can find water at Siloam. After the spring is revealed, they regain their enthusiasm to take up the campaign for Jerusalem.

§ To Arvino's tent, with the assault under way, Arvino and Giselda bring the severely wounded Hermit, who in semi-delirium confesses he is in fact Pagano, black sheep of the Folco family (*Un breve istante solo resta a me di vita*). Since he has earned forgiveness from both God and man, the reconciliation this time is sincere all around. As the Lombards thank God for their victory, the tent is opened, so the dying man can see the Holy City with the Crusaders' banners flying over it.

I DUE FOSCARI

(The Two Foscari)

THREE ACTS
MUSIC: Giuseppe Verdi
TEXT (Italian): Francesco Maria Piave, after Lord Byron's tragedy

I DUE FOSCARI

WORLD PREMIERE: Rome, Teatro Argentina, November 3, 1844
U.S. PREMIERE: Boston, Howard Athenaeum, May 10, 1847

CHARACTERS

Lucrezia Contarini, *Jacopo's wife* . . . . Soprano
Pisana, *Lucrezia's confidante* . . . . Soprano
Jacopo Foscari, *Francesco's son* . . . . Tenor
Barbarigo, *senator, member of the Council of Ten* . . . . Tenor
Francesco Foscari, *Doge of Venice* . . . . Baritone
Jacopo Loredano, *member of the Council of Ten* . . . . Bass

In April 1423, Francesco Foscari was elected Doge of Venice, defeating Pietro Loredano, for whose subsequent death the new doge was blamed by Loredano's heirs. In 1450, the doge's son Jacopo was similarly blamed for the murder of Ermolao Donato, head of the Council of Ten, which had sentenced Jacopo Foscari to exile for allegedly accepting bribes from foreign rulers.

ACT I   Venice, 1457. Francesco Foscari, doge for the past thirty-four years, is now in his eighties. In the Doge's Palace, the Council of Ten and the Junta assemble, singing the praises of their mysterious city (*Silenzio, misterio*). The doge's son Jacopo has returned unlawfully to Venice after being exiled in Crete for a crime he did not commit; the Council now must decide his fate. Led in to await their decision, he recalls how he longed for home while he was away (*Dal più remoto esilio*), then goes in for his hearing before the Council, whose hostility he fears.

§ In the Foscari Palace, the doge's daughter-in-law, Lucrezia, insists on seeing him but is detained by attendants. She prays (*Tu al cui sguardo onnipossente*). Her companion, Pisana, tearfully brings word that Jacopo, Lucrezia's husband, has been "granted the clemency of new exile," whereupon Lucrezia curses the heartlessness of his judges (*O patrizi, tremate*).

§ In an anteroom of the Council Chamber, the members recess from the trial, saying that Jacopo offered nothing in his defense, and the evidence—a letter he wrote to Francesco Sforza, Duke of Milan, asking for help—brands him as a traitor. He will be sent back to Crete alone (*Imparziale tal sentenza*).

§ Alone in his apartments, the doge reflects that in the impotence of age he can do little for his son except weep (*O vecchio cor, che batti*). Lucrezia is shown in and accuses him of doing nothing to save Jacopo (duet: *Son leggi ai Dieci*). Admitting that the fateful letter did break Venetian law, Francesco only wishes he had the power to pardon his son. Seeing his tears, Lucrezia dares hope he is moved enough to do something about Jacopo's plight.

Act II   Imprisoned, Jacopo deliriously imagines specters rising from the ground, among them Carmagnola, a victim of the Ten for whose death Jacopo was not responsible *(Non maledirmi, o prode)*. Lucrezia arrives to find him in a state of collapse. After not recognizing her at first, he feels his joy tempered by apprehension about his fate (duet: *Non, non morrai*). Hearing a gondolier's voice on the lagoon, he expresses a forlorn hope of someday, somehow rejoining his wife and children *(Là si ride)*. Both rejoice upon seeing Francesco appear, only to learn that he can offer Jacopo nothing but a father's farewell (trio: *Nel tuo paterno amplesso*). Before the doge can leave, Jacopo Loredano, who harbors a longstanding grudge against the Foscari family, enters with others of the Council to inform Jacopo coldly that a boat is waiting to take him back to Crete. Lucrezia, who wants to go with him, is told she cannot. As Jacopo and Lucrezia curse Loredano's villainy, Francesco tells them their anger is useless (ensemble: *Ah sì, il tempo che mai non s'arresta*). Jacopo is led away.

§ In the Council Chamber, the Council and Junta repeat their call for exile of the traitor *(Non fia che di Venezia)*. The doge appears and says he must bow to the law. Jacopo is brought in to hear Loredano read the sentence. Though he appeals to his father for clemency, the judgment cannot be challenged. Lucrezia bursts in with her two children, desperately hoping to soften the hearts of the judges, but her pleas fall on deaf ears (finale: *Queste innocenti lagrime*).

Act III   The Piazzetta of San Marco, late in the day, before the traditional regatta. As crowds make merry, even the dour Loredano invites them to sing a barcarole for the competing boatmen (chorus: *Tace il vento*). From a galley that draws up, guards escort Jacopo, who laments to Lucrezia that he wishes the sea would swallow him *(Da voi lontano è morte il viver mio)*. The masked Loredano, after urging Jacopo's hasty departure, removes his disguise so as to identify his vengeance against the Foscaris (ensemble: *Oh ciel, che veggio mai!*).

§ In the doge's apartments, Francesco laments that the last of his four sons—the first three having died—is now taken from him *(Oh morto fossi allora)*. Barbarigo, a senator (and member of the Junta) sympathetic toward him, enters with news that a dying man, Erizzo, has confessed to the murder of Ermolao Donato, for which Jacopo was falsely exiled. No sooner does Francesco imagine his son restored to him, however, than Lucrezia comes to say Jacopo himself has died of grief *(Più non vive!)*. The Council and Junta next arrive, Loredano announcing their decision that Francesco should retire as doge. At first he refuses, reminding the Council that in the past, when he twice tried to abdicate, they made him swear to serve till death. But realizing he must relent, he gives up his official ring. Unwilling to let the "unworthy" Loredano take his crown, he gives that to another official. As Loredano triumphantly announces the new doge, Malipiero, Lucrezia starts to lead Francesco away;

but at the sound of the bells of San Marco, he too falters and falls dead of grief (finale: *Quel bronzo ferale*).

ATTILA

PROLOGUE AND THREE ACTS
MUSIC: Giuseppe Verdi
TEXT (Italian): Temistocle Solera, based on Zacharias Werner's play
  Attila, König der Hunnen
WORLD PREMIERE: Venice, La Fenice, March 17, 1846
U.S. PREMIERE: New York, Niblo's Garden Theater, April 15, 1850

CHARACTERS

Odabella, *warrior daughter of the Lord of Aquileia*. . . . . . . .Soprano
Uldino, *Attila's Breton slave*. . . . . Tenor
Foresto, *a knight of Aquileia* . . . . Tenor
Ezio, *a Roman general* . . . . Baritone
Attila, *King of the Huns* . . . . Bass
Pope Leo I . . . . Bass

PROLOGUE Aquileia (present-day Friuli, in the Veneto of Italy), A.D. 452. Conquering soldiers—Huns, Heruls, and Ostrogoths—are feasting in honor of their victory and their leader, Attila, who arrives in a chariot. He asks about some female prisoners, who are reported to be fierce warriors; one of them, Odabella, tells him the women of Italy will fight to defend their land (duet: *Allor che i forti corrono*). Impressed, he offers to reward her bravery with what-ever she asks. When she requests a sword, he gives her his own, and she declares her intention of using it on him as soon as she gets the chance. After she and the other women are led away, Attila receives Ezio, the Roman envoy, whom he already knows as a worthy foe. Ezio suggests they form an alliance: Attila can have "the universe," so long as Italy remains in Ezio's own hands *(Tardo per gli anni, e tremulo)*. Attila contemptuously refuses: he intends to conquer Italy (duet: *Vanitosi! Che abbietti a dormenti*).

§ On the island of Rivus Altus (later the Venetian Rialto), a band of Hermits huddles in the wake of a storm. Refugees from Aquileia approach, led by Foresto, deeply concerned over the fate of his fiancée, Odabella, who he knows is Attila's prisoner *(Ella in poter del barbaro!)*. He resolves to beat back the barbarian horde.

ACT I   At night in a forest near Attila's camp, Odabella encounters Foresto, disguised as one of the barbarians; she had believed him dead in battle. He rages jealously at her apparent capitulation to the foe (duet: *Per te d'amore, furente, insano*). She protests that her sole wish is to emulate the feat of the Biblical heroine Judith, who infiltrated the camp of the enemy general Holofernes and decapitated him. Reconciled, they embrace.

§ In his tent, Attila tells his servant Uldino of a vision he has had: on the verge of conquering Rome, he was stopped by an old man who told him he could conquer only mortals, not territory sacred to God *(Mentre gonfiarsi l'anima)*. Realizing it was just a dream, he determines to attack Rome as soon as possible. Druids and other counselors, summoned to his side, receive his orders to march at once, but unfamiliar voices are heard. They belong to an approaching peace delegation of Roman women and children in white, led by Pope Leo and six other old men. Attila is shaken to see the man of whom he dreamt, and to hear him utter the same words (ensemble: *No! non è sogno ch'or l'alma invade!*).

ACT II   In Ezio's camp outside Rome, the general reads a dispatch from Emperor Valentinian, recalling him to the city because of an armistice with the Huns. Angrily he realizes he must go, setting aside his plans for a noble victory *(Dagli immortali vertici)*. A delegation arrives from Attila, inviting him to the enemy leader's tent. His guide is to be Foresto, whom he does not recognize, still disguised as a barbarian. Foresto tells him that when a signal fire is set, the Roman troops can ambush the unwary Huns. Ezio agrees, seeing a chance for glory, though it means disobeying the emperor.

§ Attila welcomes Ezio to his tent, though the Druids warn that in the sky they see omens of betrayal. As a storm bursts upon the festivities, Foresto seeks out Odabella to assure her that vengeance is near, while Ezio reminds Attila of his proposed alliance, which Attila still indignantly refuses (ensemble: *Lo spirto de' monti*). Attempting to resume the feast, Attila is offered a wine cup, only to have Odabella declare it poisoned. When Attila learns that the poisoner is Foresto, he wants to kill him, but Odabella, to ensure Foresto's escape, pretends she wants to dispatch the "traitor" by her own hand. Attila agrees, adding that he will reward the girl by making her his wife the next day. Foresto leaves, again convinced that Odabella has played him false, while Ezio plans to lead the attack against Attila on his wedding day (ensemble, Attila: *Ezio, in Roma annuncia intanto*).

ACT III   In the woods between Attila's and Ezio's camps, Foresto learns from Uldino that the wedding procession has begun. Angrily he wonders how Odabella could have betrayed him *(Che non avrebbe il misero)*. Ezio joins him, and as they catch strains of the wedding hymn, they plan to strike. Odabella appears, having fled Attila's camp, but she cannot convince Foresto of her good faith (trio: *Te sol quest'anima*). Attila himself arrives and reproaches all of them for plotting against him, though Odabella justifies herself by saying he murdered her father (quartet: *Nella tenda, al tuo letto d'appresso*). As the approaching Roman army is heard calling for revenge, Odabella prevents Foresto from killing Attila—so she can do so herself. His dying words are, "And you too, Odabella?"

STIFFELIO

THREE ACTS

MUSIC: Giuseppe Verdi

TEXT (Italian): Francesco Maria Piave, based on Émile Souvestre and Eugène Bourgeois' play *Le Pasteur, ou L'Évangile et le Foyer*

WORLD PREMIERE: Trieste, Teatro Grande, November 16, 1850

U.S. PREMIERE: Brooklyn, Academy of Music (New York Grand Opera), June 4, 1976

METROPOLITAN PREMIERE: October 21, 1993

CHARACTERS

Lina, *Stiffelio's wife* . . . . Soprano
Stiffelio, *an Assasverian preacher* . . . . Tenor
Raffaele di Leuthold, *a nobleman* . . . . Tenor
Stankar, *Lina's father, an old colonel* . . . . Baritone
Jorg, *an old preacher* . . . . Bass

ACT I Austrian Tyrol near Salzburg, early nineteenth century. Rodolfo Müller, known as Stiffelio, is a Protestant minister of the Assasverian sect. During his absence on a preaching tour, his wife, Lina, succumbed to the advances of Raffaele di Leuthold, a young nobleman staying at the home of her father, Count Stankar, a retired military officer. Unaware of this, Stiffelio returns home to Stankar's castle, where his stern old mentor, Jorg, has been praying for the success of Stiffelio's preaching. Others of the household come to greet Stiffelio (ensemble: *Come felici tutti*), who relates an incident told him on his way home by the boatman Walter: a young man jumped into the lake from a window early in the morning eight days before, leaving behind a distraught young woman. Having retrieved a wallet of papers dropped by the man, Walter gave this to Stiffelio, who now throws it in the fire to prevent its incriminating anyone. Lina and Raffaele breathe private sighs of relief, but Stankar, who suspects their affair, finds his suspicions bolstered and resolves to punish the seducer (ensemble: *Colla cenere disperso sia quel nome*). Parishioners gather outside to welcome Stiffelio, who remains briefly alone with Lina as the others withdraw. He describes the world of sin and misery he saw on his travels *(Vidi dovunque gemere)*, then remarks that she is no longer wearing his mother's ring. Her guilty reaction prompts him to suspect she has betrayed him *(Ah! v'appare in fronte scritto)*. Stankar, stepping in to remind Stiffelio that his parishioners are waiting, sees how angry the pastor seems.

As the two men leave, Lina offers a desperate plea to God for forgiveness *(A te ascenda, o Dio clemente)* before Stankar comes back to question her, finding a note she has just started writing to Stiffelio, confessing her unworthiness. She asks Stankar to spare Raffaele, prompting an accusation that she lacks the courage to be truly remorseful *(Dite che il fallo a tergere)*. She has dishonored her father too, he adds, while she can reply only that she sinned unwillingly (duet: *Ed io pure in faccio agl'uomini)*. To save the family reputation, he orders her not to confess to her husband, then leads her out. When Jorg and Raffaele reenter individually, Jorg notices the young man concealing a note to Lina in a volume of Klopstock's *Messiah* with a lock on its binding. No sooner has this happened than Federico, Lina's cousin, comes to fetch the book at Stiffelio's request.

§ In a reception hall of the castle, a crowd has gathered to celebrate the pastor's return (chorus: *Plaudiam!*). Aside, Jorg tells Stiffelio he saw "a gentleman" slip a note into a locked book. Questioned about the subject of his upcoming sermon, Stiffelio pointedly says it will be about Judas—and the subject of betrayal in general *(Non solo all'iniquo)*. Asking for the book, he finds it locked and tells Lina, who has a key, to open it; when she hesitates, he breaks the lock and takes out the note, but Stankar seizes it and tears it up. Stiffelio turns his anger on Stankar, whom Lina defends, saying his age and authority deserve respect. Aside, Stankar orders Raffaele to meet him in the cemetery for a duel (finale: *Oh qual m'invade ed agita terribile pensiero!)*.

ACT II   In the cemetery at nighttime, Lina, deeply upset, comes for a rendezvous requested by Raffaele. She prays at her mother's tomb for strength and guidance *(Ah dagli scanni eterei)*, then warns the arriving Raffaele that her father knows of their affair. She disclaims Raffaele's love and asks the return of her letters and ring, but he protests that his love is genuine (duet: *Lina! Parlate sommesso per pietade)*. When she begs him to leave, he insists on staying to protect her. Stankar intrudes, carrying two swords and ordering Lina away.

Raffaele refuses to fight an old man, but Stankar goads him by calling him an adventurer and an upstart—actually a foundling, not of noble birth *(S'ora invano t'ha gridato vile, infame)*.

The noise of their ensuing duel brings Stiffelio out of the church to insist they stop, in the name of God. Now the outraged Stankar blurts out that in Raffaele, Stiffelio is pardoning his own betrayer. Thunderstruck, Stiffelio demands of Lina—brought back by the commotion—that she answer the charge, but she cannot respond (quartet: *Un accento proferite*). When Stankar points out that Raffaele, not Lina, is the seducer, Stiffelio grabs Stankar's sword and challenges the young man, who refuses to fight him. A hymn is heard from the church; Jorg comes out, telling Stiffelio the congregation is waiting for him. Torn by conflicting passions, Stiffelio remembers he is a minister, but he still cannot forgive Lina. As he curses her, Jorg reminds him that Christ on the Cross forgave all mankind.

ACT III   In his castle, Stankar has found a letter appearing to indicate that Raffaele means to flee, taking Lina. Deeply upset and dishonored, the old man briefly contemplates suicide, starting a farewell note to his daughter *(Lina, pensai che un angelo)*. But when Jorg appears, announcing that Raffaele is on his way there, Stankar's thoughts turn again to vengeance. He leaves the room, whereupon Jorg brings Stiffelio for a confrontation with Raffaele. Stiffelio unexpectedly asks what Raffaele would do if Lina were free, but the young man is too dumbfounded to reply. Stiffelio shows him to an adjacent room, where he will be able to hear what transpires with Lina, who arrives next.

Saying he plans to go away (duet: *Opposto è il calle)*, Stiffelio offers her an annulment, based on his having had a different name (Rodolfo Müller) when they married. She signs the proferred document so that she can talk to him not as his wife but as a woman seeking confession from her minister. As God is her witness, she declares, she loves only Stiffelio and was dishonored by a seducer. Stiffelio replies that Raffaele is in the next room and will have to die for his transgression. At this point Stankar reappears, announcing that he already has killed Raffaele. As Jorg leads Stiffelio off to address his congregation, Lina laments that she is unforgiven.

§ In the church, Lina joins the congregation in a prayer *(Non punirmi, Signor)*. Taking the pulpit, Stiffelio sees her and is unnerved, but Jorg urges him to open the Bible at random and let the Lord inspire his sermon. He reads the account of Christ with the woman taken in adultery *(Allor Gesù rivolta al popolo assembrato)*—"And the woman arose, pardoned"—adding: "God has pronounced it." As the congregation repeats his words, Lina cries out her thanks to God.

RICHARD WAGNER
1813–83

"*R*ossini, how I love him!" Wagner is said to have remarked while watching a rehearsal of *Il Barbiere di Siviglia.* "But don't tell my Wagnerians—they'd never forgive me." Apochryphal or not, this anecdote sums up four of Wagner's salient characteristics: his chauvinism and ego, his penetrating musical judgment, his sense of humor. By "Wagnerians" he may have meant musicians who strove to write like him; these he discouraged, exhorting them, "Something new, children, always something new!" When he encountered Bizet's *Carmen,* his comment allegedly was "At last someone with ideas in his head."

What we mean by "Wagnerians" today is an army of devotees of his music dramas. Many latter-day Wagnerians dismiss the Master's early works. Wagner himself, however, was not ashamed of his reverence for Mozart and Weber, or his interest in the works of Heinrich Marschner—even of Meyerbeer, whom he later turned against and ridiculed. *Rienzi,* Wagner's first resounding success, is a German grand opera in the French mold. It hardly could have come into being without Meyerbeer's example.

Wagner's two earlier operas, *Die Feen* (after Carlo Gozzi's fable play *La Donna Serpente*) and *Das Liebesverbot* (loosely patterned after Shakespeare's *Measure for Measure*), are occasionally revived, only because they are by Wagner. In these scores one sees the composer's stage sense and hears pre-echoes of musical ideas to be developed later. Also of note are the non-German subjects: Wagner had yet to immerse himself in nationalism.

Rienzi differs from these earlier efforts in that some aspects of Wagner's later style already appear full-blown. Anyone who doubts this need only listen to the scene in *Die Walküre* where Siegmund pulls the sword from the tree, to jubilant fanfares straight out of *Rienzi*. Similarly, the ensembles of *Tannhäuser* and *Lohengrin* are prefigured in *Rienzi*. Wagner had learned to think big and write large. The subject still lies far afield—an English novel about Rome—but otherwise the composer seems to be finding his way home.

There are plenty of inherited ideas and conventions in *Rienzi* too, notably its turns of vocal bravura and the trouser role of Adriano, inspired by Wilhelmine Schröder-Devrient, a sovereign singing actress of the day. It was for her Leonore in Beethoven's *Fidelio,* however—not for Italian or French roles—that Wagner revered this artist. It was Schröder-Devrient, he vowed, who had awakened him to his calling as a theater composer.

An extroverted, bombastic work with moments of introspection, such as Rienzi's prayer, this opera made Wagner's name in Germany and abroad. For some time it outperformed in public appeal his subsequent, more adventurous scores, starting with *Der Fliegende Holländer,* written a year later. *Holländer* marks a further stride into Wagner's familiar mature style, but this work too is often discounted by the Wagnerian faithful.

Rienzi suffered a fate comparable to that of Mozart's final opera, *La Clemenza di Tito,* which it somewhat resembles in subject matter. Initial popularity having died down, both works simply faded from the stage. During three seasons at the Metropolitan Opera (1885–86, 1886–87, 1889–90), *Rienzi,* buoyed by the high tide of Wagner's reputation, surfaced for a total of twenty-one heavily cut performances. The score is so long that from the first it sometimes was split into two evenings: Wagner had not yet mastered his unique way of stretching the time scale so that length does not pall. Revivals in recent years have been cut as well.

The youthful energy of *Rienzi* was a wellspring from which Wagner continued to draw after the opera itself, largely as a result of his own reforms, had become a period piece. It remains a grand spectacle and a challenge for major singers.

RIENZI

FIVE ACTS
MUSIC: Richard Wagner
TEXT (German): the composer, based on Edward Bulwer-Lytton's novel
WORLD PREMIERE: Dresden, Court Opera, October 20, 1842

U.S. PREMIERE: New York, Academy of Music, March 4, 1878
METROPOLITAN PREMIERE: February 5, 1886

CHARACTERS

Irene, *Rienzi's sister*		Soprano
Adriano, *Colonna's son*		.Mezzo-Soprano
Cola Rienzi, *Roman Tribune and papal notary*		Tenor
Baroncelli	⎱	Tenor
Stefano Colonna	*Roman citizens* . . . . ⎰	Bass
Paolo Orsini	⎰	Bass
Cecco del Vecchio		Bass
Raimondo, *papal legate*		Bass

Wagner's opera and Bulwer-Lytton's novel are based loosely on the life of Cola di Rienzi (1313?–54), who was given "wide dictatorial powers" to govern Rome in 1347 but was forced out by the barons. Imprisoned for a time by the Holy Roman Emperor Charles IV, who wanted him tried by the Inquisition, he was freed by Pope Innocent VI and returned in triumph to Rome as an autocratic ruler, only to be murdered soon afterward during a popular uprising. Subsequent generations idealized him as a forefather of the idea of a united Italy.

ACT I Nighttime in a street in Rome near the basilica of St. John Lateran, mid-fourteenth century. Paolo Osini, leader of a noble faction, means to kidnap Irene, sister of the papal notary Cola Rienzi, and has set a ladder against the window of Rienzi's house. His followers are about to succeed when Stefano Colonna, head of a rival faction, arrives and challenges them, aided by his son Adriano, who loves Irene and fights to defend her. The general public tries to break up the melee that follows. Raimondo, the papal legate, appears and calls for peace, but the nobles order him aside. Only with the appearance of Rienzi does the fighting stop. He denounces the nobles' lawless behavior, which has driven the Pope to Avignon and filled the people of Rome with fear *(Dies ist eu'r Handwerk)*. The nobles scorn him as a plebeian. Deciding to continue their fight outside the city gates, free of interference by the rabble, they move away. Rienzi plans to lock the city gates behind them, forcing them to negotiate before they can return. He asks the people to be ready for a trumpet call that will summon them to fight for freedom from the tyranny of the nobles (ensemble, Rienzi: *Wohlan, so mag es sein!*).

Rienzi comforts Irene and asks Adriano why he has not gone off with his relatives. Adriano fears Rienzi's republican ambitions but admires his courage and principles; he feels guilty as well about the past murder of Rienzi's and

Irene's younger brother by a member of the Colonna tribe. When Rienzi urges Adriano to join him and "Be a Roman!," Irene sees nobility in Adriano's motives (trio: *Noch schlägt in seiner Brust*), and Rienzi entrusts her to his care as he returns toward the Lateran church. Alone with the young man who saved her from kidnapping, Irene pledges herself to him, and he assures her of his love (duet: *Ja, eine Welt voll Leiden*).

At daybreak, a trumpeter blows a long note to summon the citizens. From within the church a hymn can be heard *(Erwacht, ihr Schläfer nah und fern)*. Accompanied by religious dignitaries, Rienzi emerges in armor, pledging that Roman citizens shall be free to live without fear *(Die Freiheit Roms sei das Gesetz)*. When the people want to acclaim him as king, he refuses, saying the Senate should still be the ruling body: he will accept only the title of tribune. In this capacity the people hail him *(Rienzi, Heil dir, Volkstribun!)*.

ACT II   The nobles, with the city gates locked against them, have had to accept Rienzi's terms, pledging to obey the law. Temporarily subdued, they have taken their resistance underground.

§ In a great hall at the Capitol, youthful envoys from noble families appear, declaring that the countryside around Rome is now at peace. Rienzi, in full regalia as tribune, enters and asks for their report (Peace Envoy: *Ich sah die Städte*), whereupon Rienzi falls to his knees and leads the Church dignitaries and Senators in a prayer of thanks. Colonna, Orsini, and their retinues file in, pretending to make peace with Rienzi, who thanks them, with a reminder of their pledge to stay within the law *(Des Friedens, des Gesetzes Grösse nur)*. As soon as he is gone, they plot to assassinate him. Adriano, overhearing, steps forward and confronts them, but Colonna harshly dares him to betray his own father to Rienzi (ensemble, Adriano: *Entsetzlich! Ha, mein Schreckenslos!*). Adriano is left with his conflict of loyalties.

A procession of citizens, headed by the Senate and nobles, enters the hall. Rienzi greets them, together with a group of foreign ambassadors *(In Namen Roms seid mir gegrüsst!)*. To the nobles' annoyance, he pledges Rome's allegiance to the Holy Roman Emperor, who is about to be elected. As an elaborate entertainment is prepared, Adriano warns Rienzi of danger. Dancers appear and enact a pantomime (Procession of Warriors—Fight of the Gladiators—Entrance of the Virgins—Festal Dance). Toward the conclusion, Colonna tries to stab him; Rienzi is saved only by armor under his robes. The Senators decree death for the nobles, who are led away.

Adriano, having warned Rienzi of the assassination attempt, feels he has betrayed his father. When he and Irene beg for the death sentence to be lifted, he goes so far as to threaten Rienzi. Monks' voices are heard intoning a *Miserere* for the prisoners. When Rienzi asks the people to forgive his would-be assassins, they resist. He prevails and exacts another pledge of allegiance from the condemned nobles. But while Rienzi prays that forgiveness will soften their hearts *(O lasst der Gnade Himmelslicht)*, the nobles assuage their humiliation with further hopes of revenge.

ACT III   Amid the ruins of the ancient Forum, word spreads that the nobles have fled the city and raised an army, with which they are preparing to attack. Angry at this betrayal, Rienzi has to admit to the prominent citizens Cecco and Baroncelli that they were right to question his amnesty for the nobles. He calls upon the people to rise in defense of Rome *(Ihr Römer, auf!)*. All rush off to arms.

Adriano enters, beside himself because he has no choice but to turn either against his father or against the brother of his beloved Irene *(Gerechter Gott, so ist's entschieden schon!)*. His only hope lies in somehow reconciling the opposed factions.

The people reassemble, exhorted again by Rienzi, and raise their voices in a battle hymn *(Auf, Römer, auf, für Herd und für Altäre!)*. Adriano pleads with Rienzi to be sent on a peacemaking mission, but Rienzi reminds him that the nobles have proved themselves untrustworthy. As the armed men march forth, Adriano bids farewell to Irene, saying he must seek death by his father's side, but she clings to him as sounds of battle are heard, and he realizes the conflict is already taking place. He, Irene, and Roman women pray for mercy for the fallen *(O Heil'ge Jungfrau, hab Erbarmen!)*. Rienzi and his troops return, bearing the bodies of Colonna and Orsini. At the sight of his slain father, Adriano swears vengeance on Rienzi *(Weh dem, der mir verwandtes Blut vergossen hat!)*, who leads a triumphal procession toward the Capitol.

ACT IV   In the square before the Lateran church, Baroncelli tells the people that the German ambassadors have been recalled by the emperor: "For this we have to thank the arrogance with which Rienzi disputed the election of the Roman Emperor with the German princes." Baroncelli suggests that when Rienzi first pardoned the nobles, he was trying to form a secret alliance with them, because of Irene's link with Adriano. Appearing from the crowd, Adriano verifies what Baroncelli says, urging the people to distrust Rienzi *(Colonna! Ach, darf ich ihn nennen)*. As a procession of religious dignitaries approaches, the onlookers feel they cannot rebel, because Rienzi is still supported by the Church. Adriano resolves to strike him down on the steps of the Lateran.

As Rienzi draws near, accompanied by Irene and a retinue, Adriano feels unable to go through with his assassination attempt. Rienzi cows the would-be conspirators by urging them to join in paying respects to those who died for Rome's dignity and freedom. When he reaches the church door, however, he is met not with the expected *Te Deum* but with a curse of excommunication (Priests and Monks: *Vae, tibi maledicto!*). Raimondo, the papal legate, turns him away. The Pope in Avignon has been persuaded by renegade nobles and by the German Emperor to disavow Rienzi. Adriano urges Irene to flee to safety with him, but she will not leave her brother.

ACT V   Alone in the Capitol, Rienzi, forsaken by the Church and his fellow Romans, prays to God for support *(Allmächt'ger Vater, blick herab!)*. When Irene enters, he praises her loyalty and pours out his pain at being rejected by the city he loved, likening it to a faithless bride *(Wohl lieb' auch ich!)*. He urges her to save herself, but she refuses (duet: *In unserem treuen Bunde*).

As evening descends, Rienzi leaves to arm himself for his last ordeal. Irene encounters Adriano, who makes one more attempt to persuade her *(Ha, meine Liebe, ja, ich fühl's)*. When she pushes him off, he tries to save her by force from the approaching mob. She gets away, and he dashes out.

§ Outside the Capitol, the people, strengthened by the support of the Church, gather to stone Rienzi and burn the Capitol. Rienzi, in armor but with his head bare, appears on a balcony and calls on them to remember what he has done for them *(Bedenkt, wer macht' euch gross und frei?)*. Unmindful, they set firebrands in the building. Rienzi and Irene stand engulfed in flames on the balcony. Adriano appears with a group of nobles, who start driving the people away. Adriano rushes inside to rescue Irene but loses his loses his life with her and Rienzi when the building collapses.

WILLIAM WALTON
1902–83

$\mathcal{U}$nlike Benjamin Britten and Michael Tippett, the most noteworthy English opera composers after World War II, Walton came not from a middle-class or working-class background but from the intelligentsia. A protégé of the literary Sitwell family, he possessed an uproarious sense of humor, apparent in his early success *Façade,* to recited poems of Edith Sitwell. In this respect he bears comparison with Francis Poulenc, whom he also resembles in the seriousness of his "other" side, shown by his first major orchestral work, a Symphony (No. 1), over which he labored for several years in the early 1930s. Reflecting his admiration for Sibelius, the Symphony proved a major contribution to a literature previously enriched by Edward Elgar and Ralph Vaughan Williams. Meanwhile, Walton had written a Viola Concerto, one of the few such major works in the violist's repertory; and in 1939 he produced a Violin Concerto, which has enjoyed comparable favor.

Two aspects of Walton's musical personality had become clear: on the one hand, the playful and satirical; on the other, a sincere romanticism whose lushness seemed out of date in the mid-twentieth century. He loved opera and was interested in writing one, but for such a major project, the librettist and subject had to be right. With the help of a dear friend, Lady Alice Wimborne, and the BBC's Stanford Robinson, he found these in the poet Christopher Hassall and, through him, in Chaucer's version of the *Troilus and Cressida* story. Shakespeare's play on the same tale, being more centered on the Trojan War and less sympathetic to the heroine, provided relatively little source material.

Walton worked on the score on the island of Ischia, in the Bay of Naples, where he had moved with his new wife, the former Susana Gil, his junior by a quarter century; the opera is dedicated to her. In this atmosphere, the Italianate side of Walton's lyricism came to the fore. He said he wanted to write a bel canto opera, and there are florid lines for the singers. When *Troilus* was first performed, in 1954, critics noted that Hassall had chosen poetic twentieth-century language for a classical subject, which then was garbed in unashamedly romantic, Puccinian music. Comparison with Tippett's *King Priam* (1962), likewise in a Trojan War setting, is instructive: Tippett's work is spare and modern, setting forth political realities, whereas Walton is interested chiefly in telling a love story.

Cressida was written with Elisabeth Schwarzkopf in mind; she did not play the role onstage but recorded highlights the year after the premiere. It is indicative of cautious times that EMI did not venture the expense of recording the complete opera. Though produced abroad and given respectful notice, *Troilus* was a succès d'estime. Even after a brief revival in London in 1963, Walton feared for the work's future, so when another revival was proposed for 1976, with the eminent British singer Janet Baker, Walton agreed to adapt Cressida for mezzo-soprano. Besides the transpositions needed for her, he made some cuts and changes. This time, a complete recording was made, but once more the opera came to rest.

Rethinking the score yet again, Walton decided the brighter soprano keys suited Cressida better. Prior to his death in 1983, he reinstated some earlier cuts and reworked a few passages. In this final form, closer to the original, *Troilus and Cressida* was recorded by Opera North, Leeds, in 1995. The composer had never written another full-length opera, but his big cantata *Belshazzar's Feast* (1931) has a distinctly dramatic flavor, and his one-act comedy *The Bear* (1967), after Chekhov, has enjoyed a lively career of its own, attesting to the durability of Walton's wit.

TROILUS AND CRESSIDA

THREE ACTS
MUSIC: William Walton
TEXT (English): Christopher Hassall, after Geoffrey Chaucer's poem
WORLD PREMIERE: London, Covent Garden, December 3, 1954
U.S. PREMIERE: San Francisco, San Francisco Opera, October 7, 1955
REVISED VERSION
WORLD PREMIERE: London, Covent Garden, November 12, 1976

WILLIAM WALTON

CHARACTERS

Cressida, *Calkas' daughter* . . . . Soprano
Evadne, *her servant* .Mezzo-Soprano
Troilus, *Prince of Troy* . . . . Tenor
Pandarus, *Calkas' brother* . . . . Tenor
Antenor, *Captain of Trojan spears* . . . . Baritone
Horaste, *Pandarus' friend* . . . . Baritone
Diomede, *Prince of Argos* . . . . Baritone
Calkas, *High Priest of Pallas* . . . . Bass

The historical origins of the legendary Trojan War place it about 1200 B.C. The tale of Troilus and Cressida, based on figures of the Greek myth, first appears in the Middle Ages, in the writing of Benoît de Sainte-Maure, from whom it was picked up by Boccaccio for his *Filostrato,* thence by Chaucer and Shakespeare.

ACT I   After ten years of siege by the Greeks, Trojan clergy and worshippers pray at the temple of Pallas for the goddess to aid their cause, but skeptical onlookers carp that it will do no good. The high priest, Calkas, claiming to cite the Oracle at Delphi, urges the people to negotiate a peace with the Greeks. Antenor, an army captain, accuses Calkas of being in the pay of the enemy. Prince Troilus, a son of King Hector and Queen Hecuba, pushes his way through the crowd and saves Calkas from being seized. Antenor, withdrawing with the others, suspects Troilus' motives in defending Calkas: could the priest's lovely widowed daughter, Cressida, have turned his friend's head?

Alone near the altar, Troilus chafes at Cressida's duties as a novice in the temple, declaring that his love burns far more brightly than the candles she must tend *(Is Cressida a slave. . . ?).* When she appears, he tries to convince her, but she has been badly hurt by her husband's death and wants the protection of a cloistered life (duet, Cressida: *Morning and evening I have felt your glance).* Before she leaves, the conversation is overheard by her Uncle Pandarus, carried in on a litter, who offers to plead with Cressida on Troilus' behalf. Troilus accepts his offer and leaves *(I haunt her beauty like a naked soul).* Pandarus withdraws at the approach of Calkas with Cressida and her servant, Evadne, who try to stop the priest from leaving Troy. Sensing that Calkas will defect to the Greeks, Pandarus follows in hopes of preventing this. Cressida, alone, recalls from childhood how her father always vacillated *(Slowly it all comes back):* Troilus now seems the only dependable man in her life, but the gods are against her loving him. Pandarus, returning, confirms her father's desertion but hints that "The House of Priam is a shield to cover you." Before he can carry the subject further, Troilus appears with a group of soldiers and learns the Greeks have captured Antenor. Determined to get his friend back by whatever means, he goes in search of the high priest to bless the swords of a rescue party. Pandarus seizes the moment to invite Cressida for supper the following day. Because Cressida is beginning to yield to her love for Troilus (*Troilus and Cressida—the sound of our names together*), she gives Pandarus her red scarf to offer as a token to Troilus. When she is gone, Troilus returns, shocked that the father of his beloved has turned traitor. Pandarus diverts his thoughts by giving him the scarf (Troilus: *Goddess of mortal love, tall Aphrodite*).

ACT II   At Pandarus' house the following evening, Cressida and Evadne play chess with two other guests as the host notes a squall approaching. Aside, he sends a servant to fetch Troilus. Cressida is persuaded to stay rather than risk going home in the storm. Preparing for bed, she cannot put thoughts of Troilus out of her mind (*At the haunted end of the day*). Pandarus reappears, saying that "by marvellous accident" Troilus happens to have come to his house. Confronted with his conniving, Pandarus cheerfully admits having planned the rendezvous. He steps out, leaving Troilus to kneel and plead his love (*If one last doubt*). This time, Cressida is persuaded (duet: *New life, new love! I am reborn*). The lovers embrace as the storm rages outside.

The next morning, a delegation of Greek soldiers appears at Pandarus' house, led by Diomede, Prince of Calydon and Argos. Calkas has requested that his daughter Cressida be brought to him in the Greek camp; in return, the Greeks will send back their prisoner Antenor, whom Troilus was unable to rescue the day before. Pandarus refuses the deal, but Diomede produces royal seals to show that higher authorities already have agreed to it. He then opens the alcove, finds Cressida there alone, and announces he will wait for her outside. When he has left, Troilus reappears from hiding and tells Cressida they dare not disobey a royal decision; he will come to her by bribing the night sentries at the Greek camp (duet: *We were alone, and then we were together*). Troilus gives her back the red scarf as a token of their pledged fidelity. Greek soldiers escort her away.

ACT III   Ten weeks later, at the Greek encampment, early evening. Cressida waits in vain for word from Troilus. She bids Evadne go to the palisade for one more hour in hopes of receiving a message. When Evadne says the case is hopeless, adding that Cressida would do better to accept the attentions of Diomede, Cressida lets fly at her, then subsides into despair (*Troilus! No answering sign on the walls*). Calkas emerges from his tent and chides her for her aloofness from him and from Diomede, who could save both their fortunes if she would show him favor (*Cressid, daughter, why so heavy-hearted. . . ?*).

When her father has left, Cressida muses on her dilemma (*You gods, O deathless gods*): though she still longs for Troilus, she hears nothing from him, and meanwhile she is not insensible to the attractions of Diomede, who obviously desires her. He arrives in hopes of hearing her answer and asks for her red scarf to attach to his helmet (*No, my belov'd. Nothing but this!*). When Evadne passes by, signaling "no news," Cressida gives Diomede the scarf and tells him to take her as well. Overjoyed, he embraces her and leaves. After Cressida has returned to her tent, Evadne throws into the brazier a scroll, "burn'd like the rest": in connivance with Calkas, she has been destroying messages from Troilus. Scarcely has she done so than Troilus and Pandarus appear: during a brief truce, they have come for Cressida.

When Cressida emerges from her tent and realizes Troilus is there, he tells her he has sent message after message, none of which reached her (*Time and again have I bribed the sentries*); now his father will arrange her ransom. She replies that she is beyond ransom: "I am bought and sold." Trumpets are heard, with Greeks hailing Cressida as "Bride of Calydon and Argos." Troilus and Pandarus retreat into the shadows as Diomede, wearing the red scarf on his helmet, appears with Calkas. Troilus accosts Diomede and claims Cressida as his own betrothed. Cressida hesitates, then goes to Troilus and embraces him. He wonders at her betrayal; Diomede scorns her; Calkas and Evadne see Troilus' death as their only salvation (sextet, Diomede: *Troy, false heart, yet fair!*).

Troilus challenges and then throws himself on Diomede, who does not want to fight him, but Troilus is stabbed in the back by Calkas and led away, dying. Diomede orders Calkas returned to Troy in chains. As for Cressida, "That whore . . . shall remain with us. She has her uses." The crowd disperses. Retrieving her red scarf and Troilus' sword from the ground (*At last a message! A token out of Troy*), Cressida calls on Troilus to look back "from the silent stream of sleep and long forgetting" and see her join him in death: "I am still your Cressida." With that she stabs herself.

ROBERT WARD
b. 1917

obert Ward belongs to a conservative cadre of American composers whose work has suffered from the more newsworthy achievements of the serialists and the avant-garde, but nevertheless appeals persistently to audiences. During undergraduate years at the Eastman School and graduate work at Juilliard, he studied with such noted figures as Howard Hanson, Bernard Rogers, and Frederick Jacobi. After a decade of teaching at Juilliard, he spent the period 1956–67 as an executive in the music-publishing business, then went south to resume his academic career until 1987, when he retired.

Remarkably for a first opera, his *Pantaloon* made a successful debut at Juilliard in 1956 and went on, under the new title *He Who Gets Slapped,* to New York City Opera. It is still regarded with honor by many who remember it. The success of this work prompted New York City Opera to commission *The Crucible,* which unfortunately eclipsed it. Based on Arthur Miller's well-known play, an allegory of the McCarthy era, *The Crucible* uses solid, conservative musical language, akin to that of Menotti, to support and further a gripping narrative. The characters are varied and interesting; the historical period of the Salem witch trials is still vivid and capable of producing "pity and terror," the responses elicited by classical Greek drama.

For the coloration of this score, Ward relied on the idiom of Protestant hymn tunes for some of his inspiration, deploying long melodic lines and singable phrases that give sweep as well as individual character to his characters' utterances. His reward was a popularity and durability for *The Crucible* comparable to that achieved by Carlisle Floyd's *Susannah,* the other prototypical opera of Americana.

Ward's subsequent stage works, including *The Lady from Colorado* (1964, to his third libretto by Bernard Stambler); *Claudia Legare* (1978, based on Ibsen's *Hedda Gabler*); *Abelard and Hélise* (1982); *Minutes Till Midnight* (1982); and the one-act *Roman Fever* (1993, after an Edith Wharton story), were introduced by regional American companies, in each case with considerable success. But none has rivaled the enviable track record set by *The Crucible,* a classic of its genre.

THE CRUCIBLE

FOUR ACTS
MUSIC: Robert Ward
TEXT (English): Bernard Stambler, based on Arthur Miller's play
WORLD PREMIERE: New York City Opera, October 26, 1961

CHARACTERS

Abigail Williams	Soprano
Ann Putnam, *Thomas' wife*	Soprano
Mary Warren	Soprano
Sarah Good	Soprano
Rebecca Nurse, *Francis' wife*	Mezzo-Soprano
Elizabeth Proctor, *John's wife*	Mezzo-Soprano
Betty Parris	Mezzo-Soprano
Tituba, *a slave woman from Barbados*	Alto
Rev. Samuel Parris	Tenor
Giles Corey	Tenor
Judge Danforth	Tenor
John Proctor	Baritone
Thomas Putnam	Baritone
Francis Nurse	Bass
Rev. John Hale	Bass

ACT I   Colonial Massachusetts, spring 1692. In Rev. Parris' house, as his daughter Betty lies motionless on her sickbed, the worried father questions his niece, Abigail Williams, about the night he found her and Betty performing some sort of rite in the woods, but she replies evasively. Downstairs, the Putnams arrive to report that their daughter Ruth also has succumbed to a strange, trancelike illness: they suspect witchcraft. When another couple, Rebecca and Francis Nurse, joins the group with Giles Corey, the latter hints that Putnam's real interest lies in taking over the property of those condemned for witchcraft. Yet another member of the community, John Proctor, appears. Arguments and accusations start to fly, sparked by the high-handed way in which Putnam, without consulting the parish, has sent for Rev. Hale to come from another town to consult on witchcraft. Parris tries to calm everyone by leading a hymn *(Jesus, my consolation),* but the sound arouses a scream from the "possessed" Betty, drawing the adults to her bedroom. The newly arrived Rev. Hale speaks authoritatively about witchcraft but can get no replies to his questions directed toward Betty. Tituba, a slave woman from Barbados, is sent for, and Abigail tries to implicate her in sorcery (quintet: *That slave's a witch),* which Tituba denies. Under pressure, however, she admits she has refused the devil's urging to kill various people, including the "mean" Rev. Parris, and she accepts the suggestion that a witchlike old woman she saw might have been Sarah Good. Betty sits up in bed and appears to return to normal as Hale declares the Satanic spell broken. The group repeats its hymn, except for Abigail, who privately laments that she once sinned and committed herself to the devil but now wants to be saved.

ACT II   In Proctor's farmhouse, a week later, as he and his wife, Elizabeth, discuss the witch trials at Salem, it emerges that Abigail, who once lived with the Proctors as a servant, had an affair with John. He fears that if he speaks out against her for giving false witness concerning supposed witches, she will retaliate by implicating him. Mary Warren, the Proctors' present servant, returns from Salem to report that only those who confess are spared hanging. Rev. Hale knocks at the door with a group of men: Abigail has charged Elizabeth with harming her through witchcraft, using a "poppet" (doll). One of the men, Cheever, spies such a poppet in the kitchen. Under questioning from Proctor, Mary admits she made the doll, and stuck a pin into it, when Abigail was with her. Uncertain whether to believe this, Hale and his posse take Elizabeth away to appear in court. Proctor, furious, tells Mary she must give the court her own story. Mary, however, is terrified that Abigail will hex her and also ruin Proctor by charging him with lechery. So be it, John declares *(Good! We will slide together into our own pit of hell);* but he cannot let his wife die for his own sins.

ACT III   Two days later, at evening in woods near the village, Abigail and Proctor meet briefly. She is still amorous, but he tells her she must free those she has accused. Believing she is now doing God's work by exposing hypocrisy and witchcraft, she refuses, adding that if Elizabeth dies, it will be John's fault for his stubborn resistance to Abigail's advances.

§ At the town meetinghouse the following morning, Judge Danforth starts the trial with an invocation *(Open Thou my lips, O Lord)*, then hears Corey accuse Putnam of trying to get his land by prompting a charge of witchcraft against his wife. Danforth orders Corey arrested and interrogated. Proctor next testifies that the girls charging witchcraft against various defendants have lied: his reluctant witness, Mary, starts to corroborate this, but her testimony is denied by Abigail, who leads the other girl witnesses in feigned seizures as she accuses Mary of casting a spell on her. Trying to shock the truth out of Abigail, Proctor admits his affair with her. Danforth calls Elizabeth as a witness to confirm this, but not knowing of her husband's confession, she fails to do so. Hale, with growing doubts about the whole procedure, declares, "There is private vengeance working in these trials," but Abigail feigns another seizure, imagining that Mary has taken the form of an attacking bird to claw her face. Frightened by the "fits" of Abigail and the other accusing girls, Mary turns against Proctor, saying he forced her to serve the devil. The crowd cries out against Proctor while Mary joins Abigail and the girls in their chanting.

ACT IV   Before dawn in a hall of the jailhouse, Tituba nostalgically recalls the warmth of Barbados *(The Devil say he's coming)*. Abigail appears from outside and bribes the jailer, Cheever, to see the condemned Proctor: she has come to help him escape, but he turns her away. Danforth and Hale appear next, the latter urging postponement of the hanging, the former adamant. Elizabeth is brought in: Hale hopes she can get Proctor to save himself by a false confession. Seeing his wife, Proctor for a moment is almost swayed, but a fellow prisoner, Rebecca Nurse, reminds him that he would damn himself by signing a falsehood. Tearing up the confession, he joins the other condemned prisoners on the path to the gallows.

CARL MARIA
VON WEBER
1786–1826

*A*t the time of Weber's birth, Mozart was shortly to write *Die Zauber-flöte,* a testament in the German singspiel style (with spoken dialogue) and a forerunner of the nature-oriented romanticism that soon would nationalize German music. Weber, a cousin of Mozart's wife, Constanze, was to become the father of German romantic opera with *Der Freischütz* (1821), still widely performed today. He was less fortunate with his other operas, though the overtures to the two major ones, *Euryanthe* and *Oberon,* remain concert favorites, alongside that to *Der Freischütz.*

Weber's calling as an opera composer may be said to have begun in childhood, when he tried his hand at *Das Waldmädchen* and *Peter Schmoll und seine Nachbarn.* It was not until 1813, however, with his appointment as director of the German opera theater in Prague, that he began to leave his mark. Too busy with this job to compose, he built a repertory of works that had a formative influence on German opera; these were largely in the opéra-comique genre, with music by Cherubini, Spontini, Grétry, Boieldieu, and others. Written in the French style, they were closer to the German singspiel than were the Italian works then being performed in Dresden, where Weber moved in 1816 as director of a competitive theater. In both cities he was considered a reformer of theater practice, organizing a rehearsal schedule and drilling his performers as an ensemble.

Der Freischütz impressed both the operagoing public and the intellectuals of the day as a truly German statement. Weber, however, did not want to write another singspiel and moved on to grand opera with *Euryanthe,* which proved less successful, mainly because of an awkward libretto. By now, Weber's fame abroad had led to a commission from London, but contrary to the composer's preference, *Oberon* was to be written to the English taste, with spoken dialogue. By now seriously ill with tuberculosis, he had little choice but to comply, intending to rewrite the work afterward in a German version with sung recitatives. This he was never able to do, as death overtook him at the age of thirtynine while he was still in London.

Weber's importance in his day extended beyond his own compositions to a creative approach to opera performance. He also wrote influential critical articles, in which he set forth the precepts of a new school of German opera. Both his writings and his music greatly influenced a later crusader and polemicist, Richard Wagner. Mendelssohn and Berlioz also profited by his example. Weber's individuality as a composer, however, enabled him to be remembered not only for his influence but for his standards. In an era when opera was often written simply to please the public, without taxing its taste or imagination, Weber dared lead the way to a higher level of artistic vision for an emerging national awareness.

OBERON

THREE ACTS
MUSIC: Carl Maria von Weber
TEXT (English): James Robertson Planché, after Christopher Martin Wieland's poem
WORLD PREMIERE: London, Covent Garden, April 12, 1826
U.S. PREMIERE: New York, Park Theater, September 20, 1826
METROPOLITAN PREMIERE: December 28, 1918

CHARACTERS

Reiza, *daughter of Haroun al Rachid* . . . . Soprano
Fatima, *Reiza's attendant.* . . . . .Mezzo-Soprano
Puck, *an elf, Oberon's attendant* . . . . .Mezzo-Soprano
Oberon, *King of the Elves* . . . . Tenor
Sir Huon of Bordeaux, *Duke of Guyenne.* . . . . Tenor
Sherasmin, *Huon's squire.* . . . . Baritone

Haroun al Rachid, *Caliph of Baghdad*
Almanzor, *Emir of Tunis*
Roshana, *wife of Almanzor* ⎬ . . . . .Speaking Roles
Abdallah, *a pirate*
Babekan, *a Saracen prince*

The original text of *Oberon* is generally considered dramatically weak and confusing. Planché, the librettist, made changes when the opera was revived in London in 1860 in an Italian version, with sung recitatives arranged by Julius Benedict. German versions have incorporated more extensive changes. For the Metropolitan Opera production of 1918–20, sung in English, *Oberon* was cut and adapted by its conductor, Artur Bodanzky. The story below essentially follows Planché's plot as outlined in *The New Grove Dictionary of Opera*.

ACT I   In his fairy kingdom, A.D. 806, Oberon lies sleeping while elves sing a soft serenade *(Light as fairy foot can fall)*. Puck, an attendant spirit, arrives and dismisses them, explaining that Oberon and his wife, Titania, have quarreled and refuse to be reconciled until a mortal couple can be found to show true constancy. Oberon wakes and voices his sorrow *(Fatal vow! Not even slumber)*. Puck reports that he may have found a couple to put to the test. The knight he has in mind is Huon of Bordeaux, Duke of Guyenne, who—in a vision conjured up by Puck—is seen resting with his squire Sherasmin in an enchanted forest.

§ Puck beguiles Huon with a dream of Reiza, daughter of the Caliph of Baghdad, who calls on him to rescue her *(0, why art thou sleeping. . . ?)*. Oberon wakes Huon and offers to help him find his beloved. He offers the knight a magic horn that will bring help in need, also a goblet that will fill itself magically with wine but burn the lips of any infidel. Oberon's cohorts convey Huon and Sherasmin to Baghdad (ensemble, Huon: *Deign, fair spirit, my steps to guide!*).

§ By the banks of the Tigris, Huon and Sherasmin save Prince Babekan from a lion. Babekan tries to drink from the goblet, but it burns his lips. He repays his rescuers by attacking them, but they drive him away. Huon learns that Babekan is to wed Reiza, whom he resolves to rescue *(Ah! 'tis a glorious sight to see)*.

ACT II   In the palace of Haroun al Rachid, Caliph of Baghdad, Reiza is led in for her wedding ceremony. Huon and Sherasmin come to her rescue. When Babekan defies them, Huon kills him, then sounds his magic horn, freezing the palace guards in their tracks. After the two men escape with Reiza and Fatima to the palace garden, where Huon fends off more guards, Oberon appears and conjures up a ship to take them to Greece. Sherasmin tarries to listen to Fatima's blandishments *(A lonely Arab maid);* when Huon comes to fetch him, the two couples look forward to their voyage (quartet: *Over the dark blue waters).*

§ At night on a rocky landscape, Puck—ordered by Oberon to test Huon further—summons supernatural beings *(Spirits of air and earth and sea)* and assigns them "To wreck a bark upon the coast." They conjure up a storm. When it has subsided, Huon is washed ashore and prays for the unconscious Reiza, whom he has carried to safety *(Ruler of this awful hour!).* When Reiza regains consciousness, he tells her the magic horn has been lost, then goes to look for food and water. As the sea gradually calms and sunlight returns, Reiza exclaims in awe at the power of the waters *(Ocean! thou mighty monster!)* and waves her scarf at a ship that appears. But it turns out to be a pirate ship, whose captain, Abdallah, means to sell her into slavery. Dragging her away, the pirates attack Huon, who has tried to save her, and leave him unconscious.

Oberon arrives to find Huon and decides that "For seven days he shall lie in a dream; then I will bring him to Tunis [for his] final test." Oberon reflects on Huon's knightly character *(From boyhood trained).* Mermaids appear from the depths and sway to and fro *(Oh! 'tis pleasure to float on the sea).* Puck and Oberon invite the elves and nature spirits to dance and enjoy themselves, now that their toil is done (chorus: *Who would stay in lone coral cave. . . ?*)

ACT III Separated from Huon and Reiza during the shipwreck, Fatima and Sherasmin have been sold as slaves by their pirate captors. In Tunis, Fatima longs for her homeland *(O Araby!).* Sherasmin joins her in nostalgic recollection of childhood *(On the banks of sweet Garonne).* When Puck causes Huon to appear, Fatima reveals that Reiza, captured by a different pirate ship, is now held in the emir's palace. Huon's only hope of finding her is to join Sherasmin in posing as a gardener (trio: *And must I then dissemble?).*

§ Inside the palace, the emir, Almanzor, welcomes Reiza to his harem. She has assumed that Huon is dead *(Mourn thou, poor heart),* but when she realizes he is there, disguised as a gardener, she sends him a bouquet as a message, to his boundless relief *(I revel in hope and joy).* Almanzor, however, is determined to win her over. His wife, Roshana, jealous of his attentions to Reiza, has spied Huon working in the garden and taken a fancy to him. When he receives a message that a lady in the palace has sent for him, he thinks it must be Reiza and hurries inside, only to find Roshana waiting to lure him with dancing girls and slaves (chorus: *For thee hath beauty decked her bower!).* He refuses her advances, but when Almanzor finds him there, he is seized and condemned.

§ In a public square, Almanzor is preparing to have Huon burned at the stake when Abdallah interrupts, arguing about his share of some booty washed ashore. Almanzor wants to keep all the jewels but offers Abdallah the magic horn, thinking it worthless. When Abdallah objects, Almanzor threatens him, so he leaves, tossing the horn to Sherasmin.

Huon is led in, whereupon Reiza begs Almanzor to spare him. Almanzor offers Huon freedom if he will leave Reiza behind; Huon refuses, so the furious Almanzor condemns both to the stake. But Sherasmin passes the magic horn to Huon, who sounds it. Suddenly everyone starts dancing (chorus: *Hark! What notes are swelling!*). A further blast brings forth Oberon; reunited at last with his fairy queen, Titania, he tells Huon and Reiza that their trials are over and bids them farewell. He will return them to France, where they are to appear before the emperor.

§ At Charlemagne's throne, a march ushers in the royal procession. Huon bows and introduces Reiza as the bride he has won from the Saracens *(Behold! Obedient to the oath he swore)*. The courtiers hail "Reiza the lovely and Huon the bold."

KURT WEILL
1900–50

*B*orn into a musical background—his father was a cantor in Dessau—
Kurt Weill early developed a fascination with the theater that was
to permeate his life's work. His years of schooling were interspersed
with periods of practical experience as a coach, apprentice conductor,
and teacher, all of which inclined him toward the concept that Paul Hindemith called *Gebrauchmusik*—practical music, useful and accessible to a broad
public. In Europe, however, then as now, artists were classified as intellectuals,
and it was as a "serious" composer that Weill wrote his first works, in the
accepted astringent, modern style of the 1920s. These included his first surviving opera, *Der Protagonist* (1925), to an expressionist text by Georg Kaiser; the
"free atonality" of Weill's score is tempered with "neoclassical angularity . . .
indebted to Stravinsky rather than Schoenberg," according to Stephen Hinton
in *The New Grove Dictionary of Opera.*

Weill, who admired Schoenberg and would have liked to study with him
but could not, for financial reasons, found himself increasingly drawn to cabaret dance and song forms in his next few theater pieces. In 1926 he married
the singing actress Lotte Lenja ("Lenya" in the United States), and with the
Mahagonny-Songspiel in 1927 he began his collaboration with the playwright
Bertolt Brecht. Their most famous work, *Die Dreigroschenoper* (The Threepenny
Opera), appeared the following year in Berlin. Capturing the brittle mood of
the Weimar Republic, it drew a great deal of attention to Weill, annoying
Brecht, who considered his dramatic ideas the important element. Still, the
two wanted to write a real, full-length opera, which they did by expanding
the *Mahagonny-Songspiel,* a cabaret revue, into *Aufstieg und Fall der Stadt Maha-*

gonny (Rise and Fall of the City of Mahagonny, 1930). Shortly thereafter, their last collaboration, the "school opera" *Der Jasager,* appeared.

Weill, by now famous in Germany and Austria, was soon to become notorious as well, a textbook example of what the Nazis termed a "degenerate" artist. He saw two more stage works produced, *Die Bürgschaft* and *Der Silbersee,* the latter in several cities, before emigrating to Paris in 1933. As a Jew, and as a collaborator of the "cultural Bolshevik" Brecht, he was blacklisted in Hitler's Germany. After two difficult years of trying to start anew, he came to New York with Lenya in the fall of 1935 for *The Eternal Road,* Franz Werfel's Biblical drama, which opened at the old Manhattan Opera House in 1937; though a critical success, it lost money.

During his remaining years, Weill had a second career in the United States as a composer for the Broadway musical stage, a medium less alien to his earlier aspirations than might be imagined. Given his talent as a songwriter, desire to reach a general audience, curiosity, and keen intellect, Weill set out to explore the possibilities of the American musical theater. Besides a series of innovative commercial shows, he wrote *Down in the Valley* (1948), a modestly scaled, folk-song–based opera that appealed to workshops, and *Street Scene* (1946), a full-scale musical setting of Elmer Rice's play.

In *Street Scene,* which Weill considered his most successful achievement, he brought together, as Gian Carlo Menotti did in *The Medium* that same year, elements of Puccinian verismo with accepted Broadway techniques, which he expanded in a quasi-operatic way. Rice's sorely dated libretto suffers from an arbitrary denouement, as unrealistic as those of *Porgy and Bess* or *The Tender Land:* is this young woman really going to abandon the responsibilities she has just inherited—her younger brother, their parents' apartment—and renounce her sweetheart, to escape to a new life alone in the middle of nowhere? But the characters, drawn from stock, take on life from Langston Hughes' fresh lyrics and Weill's smoothly crafted score. The composer brings together various genres to achieve a blend of sentiment and tough-minded satire, social commentary, and believable human interest. This is both the old and the new Kurt Weill, a virtuoso with the theater in his bones.

STREET SCENE

TWO ACTS
MUSIC: Kurt Weill

TEXT (English): Elmer Rice, based on his play, lyrics by Langston Hughes

WORLD PREMIERE: Philadelphia, Shubert Theater, December 16, 1946

CHARACTERS

Anna Maurrant. . . . . Soprano
Rose Maurrant, *her daughter* . . . . Soprano
Willie Maurrant, *her son*. . . . . Boy Soprano
Sam Kaplan, *a poet*. . . . . Tenor
Abraham Kaplan, *his father*. . . . . Tenor
Lippo Fiorentino, *a neighbor* . . . . Tenor
Henry Davis, *the janitor*. Baritone
Harry Easter, *a real-estate salesman* . . . . Baritone
Frank Maurrant, *Anna's husband* . . . . Bass-Baritone

Elmer Rice's play *Street Scene* dates from 1929, at the threshold of the Great Depression, and reflects New York City life at that time. (Harry Easter's mention of nylon hose in Act I appears to be an inadvertent anachronism.)

ACT I   On the sidewalk outside a drab apartment building, the tenants are outside or at their windows, coping with the heat of a June evening. They exchange small talk. Henry, the janitor, sings the blues as he brings out a garbage can *(I got a marble and a star)*. One of the tenants, Anna Maurrant, gives her son Willie a dime to get an ice-cream cone, sparking gossip among Mmes. Jones, Olsen, and Fiorentino about Mrs. Maurrant's apparent affair with the milk-company collector, Steve Sankey (trio: *You wouldn't think a married woman*). But they stop when Mrs. Maurrant rejoins them, wishing for her daughter Rose to get home from work. Sam Kaplan, Rose's sweetheart, stops on the way to the library to talk to her mother. Anxious Daniel Buchanan passes by to get his expectant wife an orange *(When a woman has a baby)*. Frank Maurrant, Anna's gruff, authoritarian husband, arrives home and goes inside, leaving his wife to wonder why happiness is so elusive in a world of everyday reality *(Somehow I never could believe)*.

Sankey passes en route—he says—to get ginger ale for his wife, but when Mrs. Maurrant goes out too, ostensibly to look for her son, the gossips assume she is meeting Sankey (quartet: *Get a load of that!*). They wonder if Maurrant suspects anything. Mrs. Fiorentino's husband, Lippo, arrives; joined by Henry, the janitor, all sing the praises of that great American institution the ice-cream parlor (sextet: *Hats off to the ice-cream cone!*). When Mrs. Maurrant returns, an argument develops between her husband and Sam Kaplan's father, Abraham, a radical-minded tenant who declares Maurrant's domineering attitude typical of an exploitive society. Maurrant's anger subsides, but he sticks to his hidebound beliefs (*Let things be like they always was*).

High school children enter, celebrating Jenny Hildebrand's art prize and scholarship, though her family, deserted by the father, is about to be evicted for not paying the rent (Jenny: *Dearest friends and neighbors*). There is celebration and dancing, but Maurrant resents his wife's having a good time. Their boy Willie returns, escorted by Sam, who extricated him from a fight with another boy. As Mrs. Maurrant takes Willie upstairs, Maurrant heads for a bar and the gossips resume their backbiting. Sam deplores their attitude and wonders to himself how he can feel so lonely in a place so full of people (*At night when everything is quiet*).

Rose Maurrant finally arrives home, escorted by Harry Easter, a married colleague from the real-estate office who is trying to set her up as his mistress (*Wouldn't you like to be on Broadway?*). She visualizes a different life of sincere love (*I've looked in the windows. . . . What good would the moon be?*). She finally gets rid of Easter when her father approaches, angry at her for staying out late and associating with a married man. Buchanan's wife has started in labor; Rose offers help. Mrs. Jones' coarse daughter Mae appears with her equally crass boyfriend, Dick McGann, followed by her brother Vincent, who makes a pass at the preoccupied Rose. Sam interferes but is knocked down by Vincent, who leaves. Briefly alone with Sam, Rose reassures him of her regard for his intelligence and sensitivity. She suspects the rumors about her mother's affair are true. Sam is discouraged by the atmosphere of the place, and the two wish they could escape to something better (duet, Sam: *Pain! Nothing but pain!*). Called by her father from the window, Rose kisses Sam good-night and goes upstairs.

ACT II The next morning. Comings and goings of various tenants. Children play a game of forfeits (*If we catch you*); when they turn rowdy, Sam and Rose (separately) intervene. Mrs. Maurrant has been up all night helping Buchanan's wife deliver her baby. Maurrant, carrying a satchel for a day's trip to New Haven on business, reacts irritably to Rose's attempts to persuade him to treat his wife more considerately. When Mrs. Maurrant returns, he criticizes her for helping a neighbor and neglecting her own family (trio: *You've got no right to talk to her / me like that*). After he leaves, Willie appears, bound for school, and Mrs. Maurrant shows affectionate tact toward him (*Somebody's gonna be so handsome*). On her way to work as a teacher, Shirley Kaplan tries to discourage Rose's interest in her brother Sam, who shortly joins Rose. She tells him about Harry Easter's proposition the night before, and Sam is shocked. Again they wish they could escape to a better life (duet: *When birds get old enough*). Easter comes to pick up Rose for their boss' funeral. From her window, Mrs. Maurrant sees Sankey and asks him to come up: she has to talk to him. A Marshal brings a warrant to dispossess the Hildebrand family. Then Maurrant reappears, alarming Sam, who tries to stop him and is pushed aside.

Shots ring out from the Maurrant apartment. Maurrant returns downstairs, holds the onlookers at bay with his pistol, and escapes into the basement amid cries for an ambulance. The Marshal tries to control the crowd: general confusion. Rose returns to the building in time to see her mother borne out to the ambulance (chorus: *The summer's bright. . . . But love and death have gone away together*).

That afternoon, two Nursemaids wheel their charges past; having read the story in the newspaper, they are curious to see the murder house (duet: *Sleep, baby dear, the picture is right here*). Rose returns from the hospital, where her mother died. Shots are heard, and Maurrant is brought in by two Policemen. To Rose, he claims he must have been driven out of his mind by jealousy. He insists he loved his wife, though he was never able to show it *(I'd been drinkin', Rose)*.

After the police take him away, Rose tells Sam she has decided to go away— by herself. He protests passionately *(I'll go where you go)*, but she insists. The neighbors revert to complaining about the heat.

HUGO WEISGALL
b. 1912

*B*orn in Czechoslovakia, the son of a former opera singer turned cantor and composer of synagogue music, Hugo Weisgall moved with his family to the United States in 1920 and became a citizen in 1926. He studied at the Peabody Conservatory in Baltimore, later with Roger Sessions, and earned diplomas from the Curtis Institute in Philadelphia in composition and conducting. In 1941 he joined the military, serving in diplomatic capacities because of his language fluency. Returning to the United States in 1947, he pursued parallel careers in teaching, performance, and composition, serving on the faculty first at Johns Hopkins University, then at the Juilliard School.

Though unequivocally an American composer, Weisgall frequently looked abroad for subjects when writing operas. *Night* and *Lilith,* written in the early 1930s, drew upon classics of Jewish literature, while *The Tenor* (1952) and *The Stronger,* chamber-scale works, used material by the German dramatist Frank Wedekind (source of Alban Berg's *Lulu*) and the Swedish August Strindberg, respectively. Midway in his production of operas, which went on to several more works, some of them large-scale, came *Six Characters in Search of an Author,* after the disturbing play by Luigi Pirandello.

The text of *Six Characters* is deliberately enigmatic and poses dramatic riddles. It is never specified, for example, whether the Child is a boy or a girl; the Child's death and the Boy's suicide at the end seem more coup de théâtre than dramatic outcome; and it is unclear how the Father could have become involved in a possible affair with his own Stepdaughter without realizing who she was. The audience's mystification, however, is part of Pirandello's plan, and by his peculiar alchemy the play works grippingly in the theater. Much the same is true of Weisgall's setting, introduced by New York City Opera in the spring of 1959 as part of a second American spring season sponsored by a Ford Foundation grant. In Virgil Thomson's opinion, noted in an *Opera News* interview in 1966, "The best [new] opera I've seen in the last ten years is Hugo Weisgall's *Six Characters in Search of an Author,* based on Pirandello. That's a serious subject, treated by a serious composer. The whole thing appeals to the higher faculties and is interesting."

Six Characters in Search of an Author

THREE ACTS
MUSIC: Hugo Weisgall
TEXT (English): Denis Johnston, based on Luigi Pirandello's play
WORLD PREMIERE: New York City Opera, April 26, 1959

CHARACTERS

THE COMPANY
The Coloratura . . . . Soprano
The Prompter . . . . Soprano
The Mezzo . . . . Mezzo-Soprano
The Wardrobe Mistress . . . . Alto
The Director . . . . Tenor
The Tenore Buffo . . . . Tenor
The Accompanist . . . . Baritone
The Stage Manager . . . . Baritone
The Basso Cantante . . . . Bass

THE CHARACTERS
The Stepdaughter . . . . Soprano
The Mother . . . . Mezzo-Soprano
The Father . . . . Baritone
The Son . . . . Baritone
The Child ⎫
The Baby ⎬ . . . . Silent Roles

Mme. Pace . . . . Alto

Pirandello's drama takes place in the modern theater at the time the play was written (1921). For the opera, which followed in the mid-1950s, the idea of a contemporary action still holds; but with the passage of time Pirandello inevitably has come to be regarded as a writer of a certain period, and *Six Characters* reflects not only a universal situation but a specific mood of tension and mystery identified with Italy in the unsettled period just before fascism.

ACT I   On the stage of a provincial opera house, a rehearsal is about to begin. One by one the singers arrive, discussing their various problems with the Accompanist, Prompter, and Stage Manager. The Director tries to start the rehearsal *(Today we shall rehearse our Novelty again)*, though no one has much enthusiasm for adding a modern work to the repertory. The arrival of the small chorus and Wardrobe Mistress further delays matters, but eventually, after the Coloratura has made her late entrance, the rehearsal begins with her aria in the role of the Queen of Sheba *("Here is balm of Gennesareth")*. As she sings, Six Characters—apparently a family—file onto the stage and stand listening. No one knows who they are or why they are there, so the Director orders them off the stage, but the Father explains that they have come in search of an author *(Do not laugh, ladies and gentlemen)*. Though they are just ordinary people, as characters in a drama they feel entitled to a certain immortality; but their author, having created them, refused to complete the work he was supposed to write. The Stepdaughter persuades the Director to let her sing *(A quiet room through which the shadows creep)*, enumerating the Six Characters (Mother, Son, Baby, a Boy, the Father, and herself), whose dysfunctional relationship suggests an unrealized drama. She and the two youngest children are illegitimate, the Mother's children by another man; she, the Stepdaughter, is somehow embroiled with the Father and feels she must get away.

The Father insists on telling his own version *(Please, she is only trying to upset me)*: his wife had an affair with his clerk, and seeing that she was miserable, he allowed the two to go off together. Left alone, he sought solace. . . . The Stepdaughter interrupts to say she had gone to work as a prostitute for Mme. Pace, a dressmaker, where the Father came as a client. The Father says the Mother arrived in time to put a stop to the inevitable, but the Stepdaughter claims, *"almost* in time." The Son, who is legitimate, resents the other children and hates the Mother for having produced them *(They always try to put me in the wrong)*.

The singers from the opera company disagree as to whether this has promise as an opera story. The chorus is more enthusiastic *(I'm sure it's worth attempting)*, suggesting a librettist be brought in, but the Mother tells the Director, "You can write it down as we perform it." He takes the Six Characters into his office for a story conference.

ACT II   With the stage in semi-darkness, one of the Six Characters, the Boy, steals out of the conference in the Director's office and disappears into the wings, where the Stage Manager catches him meddling with the lights. Among the others, as they emerge, there are differences of opinion: the Stepdaughter refuses to have anyone else provide her motivation, while the Son denounces the baring of his parents' problems as indecent. The Stage Manager disarms the Son of a prop gun he has found; the Boy watches to see where it will be put. The Director calls on the Stage Manager (*Good Pampanickli*) to provide some scenery for the dressmaker's shop. As it is being put together, discussion about casting gets under way; the Six Characters want to play themselves, but the company protests strenuously (ensemble: *Are they members of the union?*). To the Father, who says, "Alas, sir, we are merely characters—all that we do is live," the Director explains the facts of opera life (*Then let me tell you, sir, what singers are*). By adding hats to complete the picture of the dressmaker's shop, the Stepdaughter calls Mme. Pace into being—as the Father explains, "formed and invoked by the magic of the stage itself." Amid comments from the ensemble, who find Mme. Pace amusing, she and the Stepdaughter rehearse their dialogue, but the Mother intrudes angrily. At this, Mme. Pace refuses to continue and leaves.

The Father and Stepdaughter resume the scene where he visits the shop as a client, but the Director substitutes his singers. They in turn try to act the scene, with critical comments from Father and Stepdaughter. Finding the singers a parody of the real-life situation, the Stepdaughter laughs, angering them (ensemble, Coloratura: *Really! I will not stay here and be made a fool of*). When the Director manages to get back to the scene, the Stepdaughter insists that at this point her character has to disrobe. The Director finds this unacceptable in his theater, but the Mother assures him such things are part of real life. Then the Father declares the final scene must show him, the Mother, and Son left alone together, locked in a tragic relationship they can neither escape nor change (*Our future is as real as our past*). The Director insists on returning to the scene at hand. The Stepdaughter agrees to a compromise: instead of undressing, she can have at least one arm bare as she embraces the Father (*You can't get away from it*). At the key moment, the Mother bursts in with a wild cry (ensemble: *The climax is coming*).

ACT III   With everyone onstage for more rehearsal, a fountain is positioned to create a garden scene. The Stage Manager notices the gun missing from the prop room. The Stepdaughter says the next scene shows how the illegitimate children were brought to the Mother and Father's house over the Son's objections. Illusion, the Father tells the Director, must be taken seriously (*Your business, sir—but our reality*). For ordinary people, reality changes from day to day; but for characters in a drama, seeking immortality through art, reality becomes fixed and inevitable. Furthermore, a character, once created, takes on a life of its own, which the author may not have foreseen. The Stepdaughter agrees: she has tried in vain to persuade the author to finish their story (*Yes, how many times*).

Finally it is agreed that the closing scene will take place in the garden rather than the house, so the Child can be in the sunshine. The Stepdaughter leaves the Child with the Boy in the background by the fountain, playing, while the Mother starts an emotional confrontation with the Son (*You would not answer me in the bedroom*). He resists, not wanting to go on with it, but finally strikes her and vents his anger about the other children. Meanwhile, the singers are commenting on the roles they will have to copy. Approaching the fountain, the Son discovers to his horror that the Boy has drowned the Child. As he takes the Child's body, he sees the Boy snatch the revolver from among the trees. With a scream, the Stepdaughter tears the Child's body from the Son's arms and bears it offstage. The Son demands the gun from the Boy, who retreats behind a scenery tree; the tree falls, revealing him standing on a box with the gun pointed at his head. As the gun goes off, the lights black out, and the company stumbles about in confusion.

When light is restored, the Six Characters are nowhere to be seen. The Director declares the rehearsal over and sends everyone home, including the audience. But as the choristers are heard intoning some lines of a Requiem—begun in a joking manner—a greenish light discloses the Father, Mother, and Son, followed by the Stepdaughter, wending their way back toward where they first appeared. Abruptly, the Stepdaughter laughs, throws her arms up, and runs off in the opposite direction, leaving the stage empty.

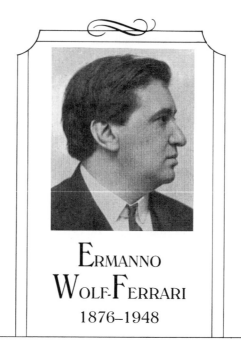

ERMANNO WOLF-FERRARI
1876–1948

$\mathcal{L}$ike Ferruccio Busoni, Wolf-Ferrari inherited a mixed nationality. Venetian by birth, he added his Italian mother's maiden name, Ferrari, to his surname. His father, a Bavarian-born painter, encouraged his talents as a visual artist, but after a visit to Bayreuth, the young man decided to concentrate on music and switched his field of study. In Munich, his teacher was Joseph Rheinberger; he left the Academy of Musical Art before graduation and returned to Venice. For the rest of his life he resided alternately in Venice and Munich, with sojourns in Zurich during World War I and after World War II. Again like Busoni, he was torn apart by the conflict between his motherland and fatherland in World War I.

Wolf-Ferrari's music, considering that he was a contemporary of Richard Strauss and Franz Schreker, remained conservative, though in later years he pursued a penchant, evident even in his earlier works, toward adventurous harmony. He is generally considered to have excelled in his five Venetian comedies based on plays by Carlo Goldoni; in those, he carried forward the fleet-footed style of Verdi's *Falstaff,* which he applied to a revival of the spirit of commedia dell'arte, meanwhile using techniques of harmonic chromaticism and subtlety that were more characteristic of German music. The spur to his creation of these works, starting with *Le Donne Curiose* in 1903, appears to have been Mascagni's *Le Maschere* (1901), a vapid, sentimental approach to similar material. Wolf-Ferrari certainly influenced Strauss in the depiction of a commedia dell'arte troupe in *Ariadne auf Naxos* (1911): the premieres of both *Le Donne Curiose* (1903) and *I Quatro Rusteghi* (1906) took place in Strauss' home city of Munich.

The reason for these dislocated premieres was that early in the century, Wolf-Ferrari was appreciated more in Germany than in Italy. To win Italian audiences, he had to resort to an essay in the popular verismo style—*I Gioielli della Madonna* (The Jewels of the Madonna, 1911), and even that was tried out first in Berlin. The remaining Goldoni comedies, however—*Gli Amanti Sposi* (1925), *La Vedova Scaltra* (1931), and *Il Campiello* (1936)—had their premieres in Italian theaters. Meanwhile, he had tried his hand at other genres: *Das Himmelskleid,* after a Perrault fairy tale, introduced in Munich in 1927; and *Sly,* suggested by a passage in Shakespeare's *The Taming of the Shrew,* a serious opera given at La Scala in 1927.

Il Segreto di Susanna, first performed at Munich in 1909 as *Susannens Geheimnis,* is a relative trifle based on the fad for smoking, specifically as a symbol of the nascent movement toward women's independence. Both tobacco and women's lib are treated as a joke, but the humor is of the parlor variety, unlike that of commedia dell'arte. The work enjoyed a vogue as a curtain raiser, and its overture became a concert favorite. Today, this type of period drawing-room comedy pales beside the glowing wit and masterly pacing of such a score as *I Quatro Rusteghi,* with its trenchant characterizations and crackling ensembles.

I Quatro Rusteghi is written in Venetian dialect—virtually a language of its own, accounting for the spelling of "Quatro" with only one t. In earlier Italian operas, it was not unusual to introduce a single character who sings in Neapolitan or Venetian, as a comic type; the fact that *all* Wolf-Ferrari's characters sing in dialect makes the work a distinctly Venetian comedy. The 1951 New York City Opera production sidestepped the language barrier by adapting Edward J. Dent's translation for Sadler's Wells, London.

Wolf-Ferrari's comic style, with its flowing melody and deft dialogue, remains a model of the genre. No other latter-day composer has handled commedia dell'arte more deftly, but the best examples influenced by him—Gian Carlo Menotti's *Amelia Goes to the Ball,* for example, or Vittorio Giannini's *The Taming of the Shrew*—are worthy successors to this particular tradition.

I QUATRO RUSTEGHI

(The Four Ruffians)

THREE ACTS
MUSIC: Ermanno Wolf-Ferrari

ERMANNO WOLF-FERRARI

TEXT (Venetian dialect): Giuseppe Pizzolato, based on Goldoni's play *I Rusteghi*

WORLD PREMIERE: Munich, Hoftheater, March 19, 1906 (in German)

U.S. PREMIERE: New York City Opera, October 18, 1951 (in English)

CHARACTERS

Lucieta, *Lunardo's daughter by his first wife.* . . . . Soprano
Marina, *Filipeto's aunt* . . . . Soprano
Felice, *Canciano's wife* . . . . Soprano
Margarita, *Lunardo's second wife.* . . . . .Mezzo-Soprano
Filipeto, *Lunardo's son* . . . . Tenor
Count Riccardo Arcolai, *a visitor to Venice* . . . . Tenor
Simon, *Marina's husband* . . . . Baritone
Lunardo, *a merchant* . . . . Bass
Maurizio, *a merchant* . . . . Bass
Cancian, *a wealthy merchant* . . . . Bass

ACT I Venice, Carnival time, mid-eighteenth century. In the home of Lunardo, a businessman, his daughter Lucieta sits working with her stepmother, Margarita. The girl had hoped that with remarriage, her father would relax his strictness; but the women are still confined to the house, even during Carnival. Lucieta wonders if she will be married. Margarita dares not tell her that her father is already arranging a match for her (duet: *La fa che me bisega*). Lunardo arrives, inveighing against idle merrymaking but hoping he may soon cheer Lucieta with news of her engagement (trio: *Mo via, sior pure*). First he announces he has invited three cronies for dinner; then he complains that his womenfolk don't appreciate the company of such good solid citizens *(Eh! Al dì d'ancuo parona)*. Sending Lucieta from the room, he confides to Margarita that he is betrothing the girl to Filipeto, son of one of his cronies, Maurizio. According to his rigid standards, the couple must not meet before their wedding. When Margarita balks at his intransigence, he ushers her out and welcomes Maurizio, with whom he discusses the terms of the engagement. No extravagances: family heirlooms will do for the bride's jewelry (duet: *Oh! a proposito*).

§ On the roof terrace of Marina's house, she is arranging flowers *(Che ghe somegio a una rosa bianca)* and hanging up the laundry when her nephew Filipeto rushes in, agitated by news that his father has found him a bride: what will he do if he doesn't like her? *(Che el cor pol stuzzegar)*. Marina promises to find a way for him to meet the girl first (duet: *Ah! Magari, ah! Benedeta*). Simon, Marina's husband, appears and rudely dismisses Filipeto, then tells Marina they are dining out, though he refuses to say where. After he leaves,

Marina fumes at his bullheadedness *(Gh la fazzo, cospetina!)* until unexpected guests arrive—Felice, her merchant husband, Cancian, and Riccardo, a Florentine admirer of Felice's whom her husband has to tolerate. Felice tells Marina it is to Lunardo's house they are going for dinner; Marina reveals that a marriage is being arranged. As the women discuss how to get around the men's plans, Cancian expresses his boredom, Riccardo his foppish adulation of Felice (quartet: *Che i casca i orsi in trapola*). With the return of Marina's husband, Simon, Marina protests his rudeness toward the guests *(Vado e taso malagrazia)* and stalks out. The others take their leave as well.

ACT II   In a reception room at Lunardo's house, Lucieta, having figured out that she is the object of marriage arrangements, complains of having gotten short shrift from her stepmother. As if in reply, Margarita brings in some of her own old finery to dress the girl for dinner. Lunardo, finding the women so dressed up, disapproves. The first couple to arrive, Marina and Simon, join in taking sides—the women dismissing the men as grouches, the men complaining of the women's frivolity (quintet: *Mo marameo!*). In the old days, Simon and Lunardo insist, women were modest and obedient *(O care memorie del tempo passà);* today, they are insolent hussies. Felice and Cancian are next to arrive, leaving Margarita to lament Marina's having taken Lucieta aside and told her about the marriage plans. When Lucieta and Margarita rejoin them, Marina and Felice congratulate the girl *(Novizza! I nostri rispetti!),* who wonders when she can see her fiancé, hoping they will like each other *(Mi no, ma gnanca l'orco).* Felice says the youth will soon be there, disguised as a woman wearing a domino, who she will pretend is her sister. Soon the masked Filipeto and Riccardo appear at the door; Filipeto takes an instant liking to Lucieta, but in order to see him she has to rely on Marina's subterfuge of offering him snuff, for which he must remove his mask.

The others delight in seeing how quickly the young people are drawn to each other (ensemble: *Ghe con cussì darente*), but the Carnival maskers have to hide as Lunardo and his two cronies reenter. Lunardo announces the engagement and welcomes Filipeto's widower father, Maurizio, but the latter says he couldn't find the young man to bring him along. Riccardo, hearing himself slighted, bursts out of hiding to protest and, in doing so, gives away Filipeto's presence. The air is filled with recriminations (ensemble: *Sconto in camera?*). Maurizio drags his son away, and Lucieta faints, as the other men and women leave in separate factions.

ACT III   In Lunardo's house, Lunardo, Simon, and Cancian—three of the "four curmudgeons" or "ruffians" of the opera's title—commiserate again about the perfidy of women. Lunardo proposes breaking the engagement and sending his daughter to a convent. Simon suggests a more realistic approach: accept women for what they are, and make the best of it. Felice dares to intrude, upbraiding the men for their callous treatment and urging them to come to their senses *(Oe, paron, anca mi)*. Cancian, in spite of himself, is impressed by his wife's performance. She brings the other wives and Lucieta to beg for a reasonable solution (ensemble: *Grazia domandemo*); despite renewed recriminations, they persuade the men not to stalk out. The fourth "'curmudgeon," Maurizio, appears with Filipeto and Riccardo. The two fathers, still bossing their children, gruffly order them—to marry. Finally reconciled, all go to dinner.

IL SEGRETO DI SUSANNA

(Susanna's Secret)

ONE ACT
MUSIC: Ermanno Wolf-Farrari
TEXT (Italian): Enrico Golisciani
WORLD PREMIERE: Munich, Hoftheater, December 4, 1909 (in German)
U.S. PREMIERE: New York, Metropolitan Opera House (Chicago Opera Company), March 14, 1911
METROPOLITAN PREMIERE: December 13, 1912

CHARACTERS

Countess Susanna . . . . Soprano
Count Gil, *her husband* . . . . Baritone
Sante, *their servant* . . . . Silent Role

The action takes place somewhere in the Piedmont section of Italy, around 1909 (the date of the premiere). In "an elegant parlor" of Count Gil's home, the young man (age thirty) is perplexed and annoyed to smell tobacco smoke, since neither he nor his recently wedded wife, Susanna, is a smoker. He inveighs against the habit *(Sì . . . ben lo conosco, l'odor moleste),* even suspecting that Susanna has been visited by a secret lover, and questions the mute servant, Sante, who registers ignorance of the source of the smell. Susanna, who has been heard playing the piano in the next room, enters, and Gil mentions that he had seen her outside the building a while back. Though his suspicion is correct, she denies it, and they exchange endearments. Sante brings hot chocolate, and the two recall their early courtship (duet: *Parmi rivivere tutti i momenti*), but soon Gil notices the tobacco scent again on her clothing. He asks her to confess her secret, meaning that she has been dallying with a lover. Her secret actually, of course, is that she has taken up smoking, but she hesitates to reveal it, fanning his jealousy into a fury. Soon he is breaking things. She withdraws to her room in tears.

During an intermezzo, Sante straightens up the furnishings while Gil fitfully tries to calm down. After a while, Susanna reappears, offering him his gloves, hat, and umbrella: isn't he expected tonight at his club? Immediately he suspects her reasons for wanting him out of the house, so he plans to leave, then return unexpectedly. She begs for some words of reconciliation *(Se v'offesi non volendo)*. Partly won over but still suspicious, he leaves her to lament his anger and reaffirm her love for him. Then she lights up a cigarette, while Sante takes a pinch of snuff. Both are startled by Gil's unexpected reappearance. Sante hides behind the curtains, and Susanna, putting away her cigarettes, opens the door for her husband, whose doubts are fully awakened by the fresh smell of tobacco smoke. He rushes about, looking for the hidden "lover," while Sante ducks out, returning at Gil's command to join in the search. Susanna, totally perplexed, believes Gil has misplaced his umbrella and is looking for it. In his frustration he breaks the umbrella, then storms out, crying that he will be back. Susanna tries to calm down by lighting up again *(Oh gioia, la nube leggera)*, enjoying the dreamy halo of smoke, but after a while Gil appears at the window, brandishing his broken umbrella. This time he discovers her secret and begs her forgiveness. She offers to stop smoking, but instead he decides to join her in the habit, and together they contemplate the joys of their fashionable vice (duet: *Tutto è fumo a questo mondo*): everything in the world goes up in smoke except true love, which glows forever.

ALEXANDER ZEMLINSKY
1871–1942

Zemlinsky, rescued from obscurity in recent times, wrote or worked on thirteen operas between 1893 and 1939, of which seven were performed during his lifetime. He also earned a high reputation as opera conductor for many years in Berlin and Prague. Though a friend and mentor to the composers of the New Viennese School (Arnold Schoenberg, Anton Webern, and Alban Berg), he never embraced dodecaphonism as a system. His music remains aesthetically closer to Mahler, Strauss, Schreker, and such early Schoenberg as *Gurrelieder.*

In the years 1915–21, Zemlinsky wrote, alongside other works, two short operas based on stories by Oscar Wilde: *Eine Florentinische Tragödie* (A Florentine Tragedy), a veristic melodrama; and *Der Zwerg* (from Wilde's *The Birthday of the Infanta*), a bitter allegorical fairy tale. Franz Werfel noted that the composer was moving away from music drama toward opera; Berg noted the "endless sweet and overflowing melodic element." In *Der Zwerg,* the tale of an ugly dwarf with a beautiful, unspoiled soul struck a resounding autobiographical chord in Zemlinsky, a homely man, who was always aware of his status as something of an outsider. This opera also taps a theme found again in Hans Werner Henze's *Der Junge Lord,* that of the callousness and hypocrisy of so-called polite society, which will tolerate the occasional outsider for amusement but will not accept who he really is.

Der Zwerg, introduced under Otto Klemperer's baton at Cologne, became the most frequently performed of Zemlinsky's operas up through the 1920s, before they were banished by Nazi cultural policy against "decadent" art and Jewish artists. After Hitler's takeover of Austria, Zemlinsky escaped to the United States, where he lived, forgotten by most of the musical world, as an exile in Larchmont, north of New York City. Interest in his operas did not begin to stir again until the 1970s. *Der Zwerg* owes its rebirth to a notable 1981 Hamburg State Opera production, for which, with permission from the composer's widow, the libretto was revised closer to Wilde's story and the title changed to *Der Geburtstag der Infantin.*

This production had a salutary effect on the gradual revival of interest in Zemlinsky's operas, several of which have been produced onstage and recorded. Schoenberg, who admired Zemlinsky's meticulous professionalism and craftsmanship, claimed, "I know of no post-Wagnerian composer who could fulfill the theater's needs with such noble musical substance as he."

Risë Stevens, who had sung *Carmen* (in German) under Zemlinsky at the German Theater in Prague during her early career, spoke highly of him as a conductor. Recommendations of this sort did him no good during his years of exile, when neither his podium skills nor his compositions were in demand. In Europe he also had been noted for his operetta performances, and early in the century he had written some cabaret songs in Vienna. Now, well-meaning New York friends tried to set him up as another Kurt Weill, assigning him a pseudonym under which to write popular songs, but nothing came of this.

During the high tide of dodecaphonism, Zemlinsky was considered an anachronism, a holdout against what seemed to be the inevitable tides of twentieth-century music. The rebirth of Gustav Mahler's symphonies after World War II served as both cause and effect of a change in the climate of opinion. Seen in that light, Zemlinsky was to opera what Mahler had been to the symphony. Schoenberg further remarked that "His ideas, his form, his sound and every turn of phrase sprang straight from the plot, from the scene and from the singer's voice with a clarity and precision of the very highest quality."

DER GEBURTSTAG DER INFANTIN/DER ZWERG

(The Birthday of the Infanta / The Dwarf)

ONE ACT

MUSIC: Alexander Zemlinsky

TEXT (German): Georg C. Claren, revised 1981 by Adolf Dresen, from Oscar Wilde's tale *The Birthday of the Infanta*

WORLD PREMIERE: Cologne, New Theater, May 29, 1922
U.S. PREMIERE: Charleston, South Carolina, Festival of Two Worlds,
June 4, 1993

CHARACTERS

Donna Clara, *young Infanta (Princess) of Spain* . . . . Soprano
Ghita, *her favorite maid* . . . . Soprano
Three Maids . . . . Sopranos
The Dwarf . . . . Tenor
Don Estoban, *the court major-domo* . . . . Bass

The plot as given here follows revisions made by Adolf Dresen, with the
approval of the composer's widow, for the Hamburg State Opera production
of 1981, bringing the libretto closer to Oscar Wilde's original story.

Sometime during the fairy-tale past, in the royal Spanish court in Madrid. In
a hall of the palace, Don Estoban, the major-domo, barks instructions to a
crew of Maids—headed by Ghita, the Infanta's favorite—who are setting up
for the Infanta's birthday party. As they work, the Maids admire the various
birthday presents. Outside on the lawn, the Infanta and her friends play ring-
around-the-rosie and tag. Donna Clara, the Infanta, wants to come inside and
see her gifts, but Estoban insists it is not time yet: protocol must be observed.
The girls stage a boisterous scuffle with the staff, who try to keep them outside. The servants lose, but when Estoban pleads with her, the Infanta goes
back outdoors with her friends. Given a respite, the Maids inquire about the
presents, which Estoban describes briefly until he comes to a cage, covered
with a cloth, which contains a Dwarf captured by huntsmen the day before
(*Sie fingen gestern einen Zwerg*). The Dwarf, he says, is tame and well-spoken but
repulsive and utterly naive.

   The Infanta returns and is dressed by her Maids for the celebration, which
starts with her standing on a platform and greeting numerous guests, who
arrive and are served cake. At length the princess moves on to the birthday
table, and Estoban presents the Dwarf, which he mockingly describes as a
handsome knight (*Der Herrscher macht der Infantin ein Geschenk von seltner Schön-
heit*). The court ladies are put off by his ugliness and unkempt clothes, but the
Infanta greets him with curiosity. The Dwarf says his father is a charcoal
burner in the forest; he produces a piece of charcoal and shows how it can be
used to draw pictures. Invited to sing, he offers a ballad about an orange that
bleeds its juice after being stabbed with a pin by a maiden (*Mädchen, nimm die
leuchtende Orange*). When the Infanta asks him to choose one of the Maids as
his wife, Estoban is outraged, but the Dwarf pronounces the Infanta the most

beautiful of all and chooses her *(Und wärn es die herrlichsten Engel des Paradieses)*.

The Infanta clears the room so she can play with the Dwarf alone. She shows him the puppets and other toys she has received, then asks him to tell a story. He makes one up, aided by the use of puppets, to describe how he, as a gallant knight, rescues her from a dragon *(In diesem Loch wirst du bewacht von einem Drachen)*. She goes along with the fantasy, imagining a rousing reception when they return to Madrid. The Dwarf declares he would bring peace and happiness into the world for everyone, but her idea of his attendance upon her is quite different: she equates him with her pet parrot, dog, and ponies. When he asks if she won't run away with him to his home in the woods, she laughs. When he leaps forward to embrace and kiss her, she disengages herself and welcomes the intrusion of Ghita, her maid, who says it is time for the dancing to begin. Aside to Ghita, the Infanta says the Dwarf has no idea what he looks like, and that he claims to love her. Ghita sympathizes with the Dwarf, but the Maids and the Infanta find his grotesqueness merely amusing. After he dances with the Infanta, Ghita draws him aside and breaks it to him gently that he is an object of amusement—that he cannot see himself as he is, as others see him *(Zwerg, o Zwerg! Dir hat Gott etwas Furchtbares gegeben)*. She leaves him alone with the puppets, wondering what she meant; but when he decides to go and look for the Infanta, he passes a mirror for the first time in his life. At first he thinks the creature he sees is some kind of monster *(He du, was willst du von mir?)*, but as it duplicates his every move, he realizes it is a reflection of himself.

When the Infanta returns, he tries to deny what he has seen and begs her desperately to play with him so he can regain his happy mood, but she is interested only in being amused. Now he thinks of hiding in the woods, of burying himself in a hole and never being seen again. The Infanta points out that he is a monster, not a human being, but he replies that he loves her. With a strangled cry, he falls to the floor. Alarmed by his wild behavior, the Infanta approaches cautiously. "Tell me it isn't true," he gasps. "Tell me I'm handsome." Ghita enters and realizes that as she feared, the Dwarf has died of a broken heart. Before hurrying back to the ballroom, the Infanta remarks childishly that next time she wants a toy without a heart.

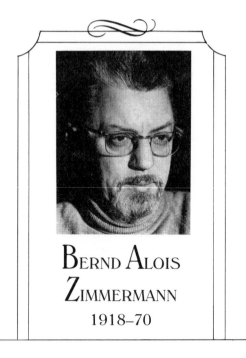

BERND ALOIS
ZIMMERMANN
1918–70

ie Soldaten created a considerable furor when it was first produced, five years before the composer's suicide. Of extreme musical and theatrical complexity, the score was considered impossible, but its real novelty lay in its presentation of simultaneous scenes: at one point, for example, three different events are acted and sung at the same time on different parts of the stage. The composer, an intellectual of wide-ranging background, offered philosophical reasoning behind his concept of the "sphericality of time," which he traced to readings in St. Augustine. In practice, however, the result is a theatrical technique for which precedents exist in Mozart's *Don Giovanni,* Schreker's *Der Ferne Klang,* and Charles Ives' *Three Places in New England.*

Zimmermann, born in the environs of Cologne, described himself as "a very Rhineland mixture of monk and Bacchus." His use of a "collage" that includes musical quotations and allusions, many of them so fleeting as to be casually undetectable, depended on his concept of history and time, whereby past, present, and future are seen to be continually intersecting and making reference to one another. Jakob Lenz's play *Die Soldaten,* which dates back to 1776, the year of the American Revolution, was avant-garde theater for its day—an unflinching look not only at man's inhumanity but at the possibilities of the stage. It lent itself to Zimmermann's equally serious, probing musical method. (Lenz himself appears as a character in two other musical stage works, Franz Lehár's fancifully romanticized *Friederike* [1928] and Wolfgang Rihm's *Jakob*

Lenz [1979], which realistically portrays the poet's decline into mental illness.)

The play *Die Soldaten* reflects the prominent role of the military in eighteenth-century life. By setting his drama in Lille (near the Belgian border, restored to France by the Peace of Utrecht in 1713), Lenz may have hoped to avoid censure for an attack on Prussian militarism, which evidently was his target. Mercilessly depicting the dehumanizing effects of regimentation, discipline, and superimposed order, together with the false aura of glory and nobility conferred by an officer's uniform, *Die Soldaten* has come to represent antimilitarism in general.

Zimmermann, a student of musical history as well as of present-day experimental techniques, wrote in an eclectic, comprehensive modernism that did not qualify him for any of the schools of advanced music that were ascendant during the period in which he wrote *Die Soldaten*, 1957–64. Construction principles of serialism are much in evidence in the score, but it is not wholly serial. As with Berg's *Wozzeck,* to which it is often compared, *Die Soldaten* makes its effect primarily as a theater experience, during which the listener need not necessarily pay much attention to the music as such. Zimmermann, who had done radio and film work, understood the function of his score as one of background as well as structural support. This is perhaps the truly "modern" aspect of *Die Soldaten,* as distinct from the concerted, musicocentric principle on which most traditional opera is based.

Difficulties of production rested at first not only on the density and unfamiliarity of the musical idiom but on the size of the orchestra, whose many large instruments could not be accommodated in a standard theater pit. In Germany it was said at first that *Die Soldaten* could not be produced at all; then that only in Germany could it be produced. In fact it has been staged elsewhere, though unlike *Wozzeck*—which enjoyed a certain vogue between its 1925 premiere and the Nazi ban on "decadent" art—*Die Soldaten* has shown no signs of attaching itself to the fringe repertory. It is likely to remain a special event, on view only occasionally; and its scarcity is likely to feed the myth of *Die Soldaten* as an inscrutably important work, a landmark of twentieth-century opera, the most significant achievement of a German-speaking composer since *Wozzeck.*

DIE SOLDATEN

(The Soldiers)

FOUR ACTS
MUSIC: Bernd Alois Zimmermann

TEXT (German): the composer, based on Jakob Lenz's play
WORLD PREMIERE: Cologne, Opera House, February 15, 1965
U.S. PREMIERE: Opera Company of Boston, January 22, 1982

CHARACTERS

Marie, *Wesener's daughter* . . . . Soprano
Charlotte, *her sister* .Mezzo-Soprano
Countess de la Roche . . . . .Mezzo-Soprano
Wesener's Old Mother . . . . Alto
Stolzius' Mother . . . . Alto
Desportes, *a young nobleman in the French army* . . . . Tenor
Capt. Pirzel . . . . Tenor
The Young Count, *the Countess' son* . . . . Tenor
Stolzius, *a draper* . . . . Baritone
Eisenhardt, *an army chaplain* . . . . Baritone
Capt. Haudy . . . . Baritone
Capt. Mary . . . . Baritone
Wesener, *a merchant* . . . . Bass
Obrist, *Count of Spannheim* . . . . Bass

ACT I *Strophe.* Lille, mid-eighteenth century. In the home of Wesener, a dealer in fashion accessories, his daughter Marie, not proficient in spelling, is struggling to write a thank-you note to Mme Stolzius, whose family she recently visited in Armentières. Helping her, her sister Charlotte notices the girl's dreamy asides, and remarks, to Marie's annoyance, that she must be in love with the Stolzius son *(Ich weiss ja doch, dass du verliebt in ihn bist)*.

Chaconne I. At their house in Armentières, young Stolzius, a draper, complains of a headache to his Mother, who believes the problem is infatuation with the recently departed Marie. When she shows him Marie's thank-you note, he wants to write an answer, but she reminds him to attend to the cloth ordered by the Colonel of the local garrison.

Ricercare I. Desportes—a baron serving as officer in the French army—enters the Wesener house and greets Marie with compliments. When she questions his sincerity, he protests that the very sight of her gives him painful pleasure *(Ist das falsch, wenn ich mich vom Regiment wegstehle)*. After Wesener himself appears, Desportes asks if he may take Marie to the theater, but Wesener, fearing gossip about his daughter, firmly refuses *(Um Vergebung! Nein!)*. Desportes curtly takes his leave. When Marie, disappointed, asks why she could not go, Wesener lectures her on the easy morals of the soldiery *(Weil er dir ein paar Schmeicheleien)*. She protests that she is no longer a child.

Toccata I. By the city moat, three Young Officers, Chaplain Eisenhardt, and three captains—Haudy, Mary, and Pirzel—engage in an animated argument about whether the theater is a good influence. Haudy maintains that because it is amusing, the theater can teach more effectively than a dull sermon *(Herr! Ich behaupte ihnen hier)*. To the idea that respectable girls may stray because of easy morals onstage, he retorts that "A whore will always become a whore." The chaplain, however, insists that whores are made, not born—he has seen too many middle-class girls seduced.

Nocturne I. In her room, Marie is visited by her widowed father, who expresses concern for her: has Desportes mentioned love? She shows him a poem that Desportes has sent her, and he reads it aloud *("Du höchster Gegenstand von meinen reinen Trieben")*. Though he doubts the man's intentions, the idea of his daughter as a baroness is hard to resist. Meanwhile, he advises her not to turn her back on Stolzius: he will help her compose a letter to him. After Wesener leaves, Marie feels a sense of foreboding as a storm approaches. She still loves Stolzius, but can she improve her lot in life? *(Das Herz ist mir so schwer)*.

ACT II *Toccata II.* In a café, groups of soldiers are engaged in various conversations, of which boisterous, drunken fragments emerge. The chaplain complains that "poor Stolzius," who is not present, has been alienated from Marie by some of the soldiers. A dance starts up, glorifying army life (Rondo à la Marche) (chorus: *Atmet in Lust! Kürzer die Brust!*). An Andalusian Waitress dances and is surrounded by stamping officers (Sentimental Variations). Capt. Haudy says he has located Stolzius, who may be expected to make an honest woman of Marie.

Stolzius arrives, apologizes for intruding, and is treated with exaggerated courtesy by the officers. Their remarks about his supposed fiancée, however, quickly give him the idea that Desportes has been courting her. Extremely upset, he begs his leave. Haudy curses his fellow officers for their drunken tactlessness.

Capriccio, Chorale, Chaconne II. Desportes enters Wesener's house to find Marie in tears, holding a letter from Stolzius. When Desportes asks why she bothers with such an "impertinent ass," Marie says she is practically engaged to him. Desportes says he will compose a reply; she is not meant to marry a bourgeois. But Marie, sensing that Desportes' background will prevent him from marrying her either, wants to write the letter herself. Desportes interferes, adding words of his own to the paper, and a playful tussle ensues. As the couple retreats to a room in the background, Wesener's Old Mother overhears them and prays for the girl.

Meanwhile, a room in Stolzius' house also appears in the background, off to the other side. Stolzius' Mother is taking him to task for his interest in Marie, "a soldier's whore." Stolzius lamely defends Marie, saying the officer has turned her head; finally he declares he will find a way to avenge himself on Desportes *(Oh, du sollst mir's bezahlen)*.

ACT III   *Rondino.* At the filled-in moat of Armentières, Chaplain Eisenhardt tries to get Pirzel to stop his vague philosophizing and discuss Capt. Mary's reasons for wanting to stay in Lille. Eisenhardt fears there may be an involvement with a woman. Pirzel notes that soldiering and lovemaking alike are "all mechanical."

Stage Play. Stolzius has joined the army and become orderly to Capt. Mary. At first, he seems changed almost beyond recognition; Stolzius tells Mary that this is because he has grown a moustache *(Das macht der Schnurrbart, gnädiger Herr)*.

Ricercare II. At Wesener's house, Charlotte scolds her sister for treating Capt. Mary with the same familiarity as she showed Desportes. Marie protests that since Desportes has left Lille, the only way to get news of him is through his fellow officer. She urges Charlotte to come with her when the carriage arrives to pick her up; Charlotte, unconvinced, calls her a camp follower. Capt. Mary arrives, shadowed by Stolzius, whom he refers to as "Kaspar." Both girls note the orderly's resemblance to Stolzius—the man who, Marie says, let her down. The sisters accompany Mary to his carriage. (Romanza).

Nocturne II. At her home in Lille, Countess de la Roche worries about her son, the Young Count: usually like a friend with her, he has taken to keeping his love life secret *(Muss denn ein Kind seiner Mutter bis ins Grab Schmerzen schaffen?)*. When he arrives home, he explains that Miss Wesener is just a nice girl of his acquaintance *(Gnädige Mutter, ich schwöre Ihnen)*. On the subject of Marie's doubtful reputation, he says it is a shame she fell into the wrong hands. His mother tells him to leave town for a while: she personally will look after Marie.

Tropes. At the Wesener house, Charlotte says Capt. Mary is reported to have a new girlfriend, but Marie is preoccupied with her new interest in the Young Count. They are interrupted by the arrival of the Countess, who puts Marie at ease by offering friendship, then asks if the girl realizes to what extent she is the subject of town gossip *(Nicht lauter böse, auch gute sprechen von Ihnen)*. Rather than aspiring to marry above her class, she should be content to make a good burgher happy. When Marie says the young man loves her, the Countess tells her to forget marriage to her son: he is already engaged. To restore the girl's reputation, she offers her a position as companion in her household. The three women lament the fate of girlish ideals in a world of hard reality (trio: *Ach, ihr Wünsche junger Jahre*). Marie asks for time to think the offer over.

ACT IV   *Toccata III.* Marie has accepted the post in the Countess' household, only to flee after being caught by the Countess in a meeting with Capt. Mary in the garden. In a dreamlike atmosphere, fragments of her recent life form a hallucinatory collage, witnessed by all the other characters. Guests in a ballroom wonder if only wrongdoers can be happy, while their victims have to suffer (chorus: *Und müssen denn die zittern, die Unrecht leiden*). Charlotte and the older characters are searching in vain for Marie, who has collapsed by the wayside en route to Armentières. Meanwhile, Desportes has dispatched his Gamekeeper to prevent her from getting there; considering her fair game, the man rapes her. Stolzius buys poison at a pharmacy to kill Desportes. Each character reacts in his own way to Marie's disappearance, according to his own guilt or concern (ensemble: *Marie fortgelaufen!*).

Chaconne III. In Capt. Mary's quarters, Desportes justifies his abandonment of Marie by saying she was a whore from the start *(Wie ich dir sage, es ist eine Hure vom Anfang an gewesen)*. Stolzius serves the soup, in which he has put poison, and cries out Marie's name as Desportes collapses in agony. When Capt. Mary draws his sword, Stolzius seizes it and says not to go to the trouble of killing him: he will do it himself. With his dying breath he curses Desportes for the ruin he has caused *(Und ich bin Stolzius).*

Nocturne III. Chaplain Eisenhardt's voice is heard in the background, reciting the Lord's Prayer in Latin, while ghostly ranks of soldiers file into the distance. Wesener walks beside the Lys River, absorbed in thought. When a ragged woman tugs at his sleeve, he takes her to be a streetwalker, but she begs for alms, saying she has nothing to eat. Recalling that his own daughter might be begging somewhere, he gives the woman a coin and moves in the direction of the soldiers—not having recognized her as Marie. She sinks weeping to the ground.

BIBLIOGRAPHY

L'Avant-Scène Opéra No. 81 (Paris: Éditions Premières Loges, 1985).

Brockway, Wallace, and Herbert Weinstock. *The World of Opera.* New York: Modern Library, 1966; *Men of Music.* New York: Simon & Schuster, 1939.

The Columbia Encyclopedia. New York: Columbia University Press, 1975.

Davidson, Gladys. *The Barnes Book of the Opera.* Barnes, 1962.

Ewen, David. *The Milton Cross New Encyclopedia of the Great Composers and Their Music.* New York: Doubleday, 1969.

Fantel, Hans. *The Waltz Kings.* New York: William Morrow, 1971.

Graves, Robert. *The Greek Myths.* New York: Penguin, 1977.

Hamilton, David, ed. *The Metropolitan Opera Encyclopedia.* New York: Simon & Schuster, 1987.

Holden, Amanda, Nicholas Kenyon, and Stephen Walsh, eds. *The Viking Opera Guide.* New York: Penguin, 1993.

Jellinek, George. *History Through the Opera Glass.* White Plains, N.Y.: Pro/Am Music Resources, 1994.

Mysteries of the Unknown: Hauntings. New York: Time-Life Books, 1989.

The New Grove Dictionary of Opera. New York: Macmillan, 1992.

Phillips-Matz, Mary Jane. *Verdi.* New York: Oxford University Press, 1993.

Sachs, Harvey. *Toscanini.* Philadelphia: J. B. Lippincott, 1978.

Siepmann, Katherine Baker, ed. *Benét's Reader's Encyclopedia.* New York: HarperCollins, 1987.

Warrack, John, and West Ewan. *The Oxford Dictionary of Opera.* New York: Oxford University Press, 1992.

Wells, John. *Candide* synopsis for Deutsche Grammophon (1991).

Recording liner notes by Patric Schmid, Susana Walton, Gillian Widdicombe, and others